THE BOOK ®

Peugeot 106
Service and Repair Manual

Mark Coombs and Steve Rendle

Models covered
Peugeot 106 models with petrol and diesel engines, including Rallye and special/limited editions;
3- & 5-door Hatchback

954 cc, 1124 cc, 1294 cc, 1360 cc & 1587 cc petrol engines
1360 cc & 1527 cc diesel engines

(1882 - 368 - 5AF4)

© Haynes Publishing 2002

ABCD

A book in the **Haynes Service and Repair Manual Series**

All rights reserved. No part of this book may be reproduced or transmitted in any form or by any means, electronic or mechanical, including photocopying, recording or by any information storage or retrieval system, without permission in writing from the copyright holder.

ISBN 1 85960 934 1

British Library Cataloguing in Publication Data
A catalogue record for this book is available from the British Library.

Printed in the USA

Haynes Publishing
Sparkford, Yeovil, Somerset BA22 7JJ, England

Haynes North America, Inc
861 Lawrence Drive, Newbury Park, California 91320, USA

Editions Haynes
4, Rue de l'Abreuvoir
92415 COURBEVOIE CEDEX, France

Haynes Publishing Nordiska AB
Box 1504, 751 45 UPPSALA, Sweden

Contents

LIVING WITH YOUR PEUGEOT 106

Roadside repairs

Weekly checks

Lubricants, fluids and tyre pressures

MAINTENANCE

Routine maintenance and servicing

Contents

REPAIRS AND OVERHAUL

REFERENCE

The Peugeot 106 range was introduced in the UK in the Autumn of 1991. Originally, the 106 was available with a choice of 1.0 litre (954 cc), 1.1 litre (1124 cc) and 1.4 litre (1360 cc) petrol engines. At first, models were only available in a three-door Hatchback form.

All engines are derived from the well-proven TU series engines which have appeared in many Peugeot and Citroën vehicles. The engine is of four-cylinder overhead camshaft design, mounted transversely and inclined to the rear, with the transmission mounted on the left-hand side. All models have a four- or five-speed manual transmission.

In late 1992, a 1.4 litre (1360 cc) diesel engine was added to the range, and in early 1993, five-door versions of all models were introduced. In early 1994, a new 1.3 litre (1294 cc) petrol-engined Rallye model was introduced, and in mid-1994, a 1.6 litre (1587 cc) petrol engine was added to the range. The 1.4 litre diesel engine was superseded by a 1.5 litre (1527 cc) version in July 1994. All the new engines are again derived from the TU series engine. Finally, in July 1996, a major facelift was undertaken which included revisions to the exterior styling and interior trim as well as numerous safety related changes. This facelift also saw the introduction of the 1587 cc 16-valve petrol engine for the top of the range models.

All models have fully-independent front suspension. The rear suspension is semi-independent, with torsion bars and trailing arms.

A wide range of standard and optional equipment is available within the 106 range to suit most tastes, including central locking, electric windows, electric sunroof, anti-lock braking system and air bag. An anti-lock braking system and air conditioning system are available as options on certain models.

Provided that regular servicing is carried out in accordance with the manufacturer's recommendations, the Peugeot 106 should prove reliable and very economical. The engine compartment is well-designed, and most of the items requiring frequent attention are easily accessible.

Peugeot 106 XL/XLD 3-door Hatchback

Peugeot 106 Rallye 3-door Hatchback

The Peugeot 106 Team

Haynes manuals are produced by dedicated and enthusiastic people working in close co-operation. The team responsible for the creation of this book included:

Authors	**Steve Rendle** **Marc Coombs**
Sub-editor	**Sophie Yar**
Editor & Page Make-up	**Steve Churchill**
Workshop manager	**Paul Buckland**
Photo Scans	**John Martin**
Cover illustration & Line Art	**Roger Healing**
Wiring diagrams	**Matthew Marke** **Carole Turk** **Steve Tanswell**

We hope the book will help you to get the maximum enjoyment from your car. By carrying out routine maintenance as described you will ensure your car's reliability and preserve its resale value.

Your Peugeot 106 Manual

The aim of this manual is to help you get the best value from your vehicle. It can do so in several ways. It can help you decide what work must be done (even should you choose to get it done by a garage), provide information on routine maintenance and servicing, and give a logical course of action and diagnosis when random faults occur. However, it is hoped that you will use the manual by tackling the work yourself. On simpler jobs it may even be quicker than booking the car into a garage and going there twice, to leave and collect it. Perhaps most important, a lot of money can be saved by avoiding the costs a garage must charge to cover its labour and overheads.

The manual has drawings and descriptions to show the function of the various components so that their layout can be understood. Tasks are described and photographed in a clear step-by-step sequence.

References to the 'left' or 'right' are in the sense of a person in the driver's seat, facing forward.

Acknowledgements

Thanks are due to Duckhams Oils who provided the lubrication data. Certain illustrations are the copyright of the Peugeot Talbot Motor Company Limited, and are used with their permission. Thanks are also due to Draper Tools Limited, who provided some of the workshop tools, and to all those people at Sparkford who helped in the production of this manual.

We take great pride in the accuracy of information given in this manual, but vehicle manufacturers make alterations and design changes during the production run of a particular vehicle of which they do not inform us. No liability can be accepted by the authors or publishers for loss, damage or injury caused by any errors in, or omissions from, the information given.

Working on your car can be dangerous. This page shows just some of the potential risks and hazards, with the aim of creating a safety-conscious attitude.

General hazards

Scalding

• Don't remove the radiator or expansion tank cap while the engine is hot.
• Engine oil, automatic transmission fluid or power steering fluid may also be dangerously hot if the engine has recently been running.

Burning

• Beware of burns from the exhaust system and from any part of the engine. Brake discs and drums can also be extremely hot immediately after use.

Crushing

• When working under or near a raised vehicle, always supplement the jack with axle stands, or use drive-on ramps. *Never venture under a car which is only supported by a jack.*
• Take care if loosening or tightening high-torque nuts when the vehicle is on stands. Initial loosening and final tightening should be done with the wheels on the ground.

Fire

• Fuel is highly flammable; fuel vapour is explosive.
• Don't let fuel spill onto a hot engine.
• Do not smoke or allow naked lights (including pilot lights) anywhere near a vehicle being worked on. Also beware of creating sparks (electrically or by use of tools).
• Fuel vapour is heavier than air, so don't work on the fuel system with the vehicle over an inspection pit.
• Another cause of fire is an electrical overload or short-circuit. Take care when repairing or modifying the vehicle wiring.
• Keep a fire extinguisher handy, of a type suitable for use on fuel and electrical fires.

Electric shock

• Ignition HT voltage can be dangerous, especially to people with heart problems or a pacemaker. Don't work on or near the ignition system with the engine running or the ignition switched on.

• Mains voltage is also dangerous. Make sure that any mains-operated equipment is correctly earthed. Mains power points should be protected by a residual current device (RCD) circuit breaker.

Fume or gas intoxication

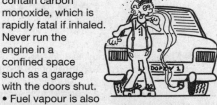

• Exhaust fumes are poisonous; they often contain carbon monoxide, which is rapidly fatal if inhaled. Never run the engine in a confined space such as a garage with the doors shut.
• Fuel vapour is also poisonous, as are the vapours from some cleaning solvents and paint thinners.

Poisonous or irritant substances

• Avoid skin contact with battery acid and with any fuel, fluid or lubricant, especially antifreeze, brake hydraulic fluid and Diesel fuel. Don't syphon them by mouth. If such a substance is swallowed or gets into the eyes, seek medical advice.
• Prolonged contact with used engine oil can cause skin cancer. Wear gloves or use a barrier cream if necessary. Change out of oil-soaked clothes and do not keep oily rags in your pocket.
• Air conditioning refrigerant forms a poisonous gas if exposed to a naked flame (including a cigarette). It can also cause skin burns on contact.

Asbestos

• Asbestos dust can cause cancer if inhaled or swallowed. Asbestos may be found in gaskets and in brake and clutch linings. When dealing with such components it is safest to assume that they contain asbestos.

Special hazards

Hydrofluoric acid

• This extremely corrosive acid is formed when certain types of synthetic rubber, found in some O-rings, oil seals, fuel hoses etc, are exposed to temperatures above 400°C. The rubber changes into a charred or sticky substance containing the acid. *Once formed, the acid remains dangerous for years. If it gets onto the skin, it may be necessary to amputate the limb concerned.*
• When dealing with a vehicle which has suffered a fire, or with components salvaged from such a vehicle, wear protective gloves and discard them after use.

The battery

• Batteries contain sulphuric acid, which attacks clothing, eyes and skin. Take care when topping-up or carrying the battery.
• The hydrogen gas given off by the battery is highly explosive. Never cause a spark or allow a naked light nearby. Be careful when connecting and disconnecting battery chargers or jump leads.

Air bags

• Air bags can cause injury if they go off accidentally. Take care when removing the steering wheel and/or facia. Special storage instructions may apply.

Diesel injection equipment

• Diesel injection pumps supply fuel at very high pressure. Take care when working on the fuel injectors and fuel pipes.

⚠️ *Warning: Never expose the hands, face or any other part of the body to injector spray; the fuel can penetrate the skin with potentially fatal results.*

Remember...

DO

• Do use eye protection when using power tools, and when working under the vehicle.

• Do wear gloves or use barrier cream to protect your hands when necessary.

• Do get someone to check periodically that all is well when working alone on the vehicle.

• Do keep loose clothing and long hair well out of the way of moving mechanical parts.

• Do remove rings, wristwatch etc, before working on the vehicle – especially the electrical system.

• Do ensure that any lifting or jacking equipment has a safe working load rating adequate for the job.

DON'T

• Don't attempt to lift a heavy component which may be beyond your capability – get assistance.

• Don't rush to finish a job, or take unverified short cuts.

• Don't use ill-fitting tools which may slip and cause injury.

• Don't leave tools or parts lying around where someone can trip over them. Mop up oil and fuel spills at once.

• Don't allow children or pets to play in or near a vehicle being worked on.

The following pages are intended to help in dealing with common roadside emergencies and breakdowns. You will find more detailed fault finding information at the back of the manual, and repair information in the main chapters.

If your car won't start and the starter motor doesn't turn

☐ If it's a model with automatic transmission, make sure the selector is in 'P' or 'N'.
☐ Open the bonnet and make sure that the battery terminals are clean and tight.
☐ Switch on the headlights and try to start the engine. If the headlights go very dim when you're trying to start, the battery is probably flat. Get out of trouble by jump starting (see next page) using a friend's car.

If your car won't start even though the starter motor turns as normal

☐ Is there fuel in the tank?
☐ Is there moisture on electrical components under the bonnet? Switch off the ignition, then wipe off any obvious dampness with a dry cloth. Spray a water-repellent aerosol product (WD-40 or equivalent) on ignition and fuel system electrical connectors like those shown in the photos. Pay special attention to the ignition coil wiring connector and HT leads. (Note that Diesel engines don't normally suffer from damp.)

A Check the security and condition of the battery terminals.

B Check that the HT leads are securely connected to the spark plugs (petrol engine models).

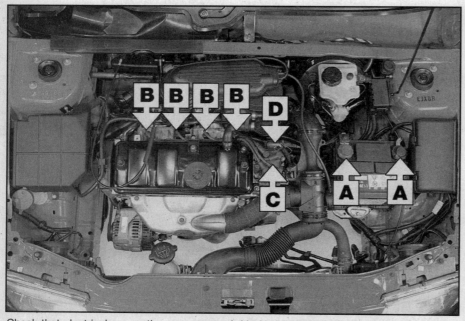

Check that electrical connections are secure (with the ignition switched off) and spray them with a water dispersant spray like WD40 if you suspect a problem due to damp

C Also check the four HT lead connections to the ignition coil (petrol engine models).

D Check that the ignition coil LT wiring is securely connected (petrol engine models).

HAYNES HiNT

Jump starting will get you out of trouble, but you must correct whatever made the battery go flat in the first place. There are three possibilities:

1 *The battery has been drained by repeated attempts to start, or by leaving the lights on.*

2 *The charging system is not working properly (alternator drivebelt slack or broken, alternator wiring fault or alternator itself faulty).*

3 *The battery itself is at fault (electrolyte low, or battery worn out).*

When jump-starting a car using a booster battery, observe the following precautions:

✔ Before connecting the booster battery, make sure that the ignition is switched off.

✔ Ensure that all electrical equipment (lights, heater, wipers, etc) is switched off.

✔ Take note of any special precautions printed on the battery case.

Jump starting

✔ Make sure that the booster battery is the same voltage as the discharged one in the vehicle.

✔ If the battery is being jump-started from the battery in another vehicle, the two vehicles MUST NOT TOUCH each other.

✔ Make sure that the transmission is in neutral (or PARK, in the case of automatic transmission).

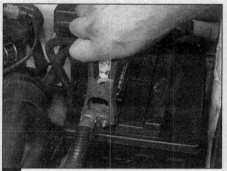

1 Connect one end of the red jump lead to the positive (+) terminal of the flat battery

2 Connect the other end of the red lead to the positive (+) terminal of the booster battery.

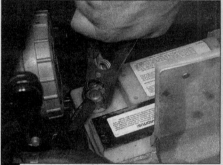

3 Connect one end of the black jump lead to the negative (-) terminal of the booster battery

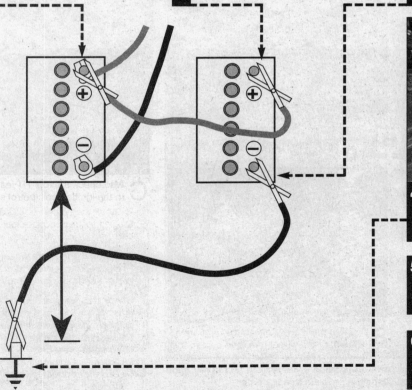

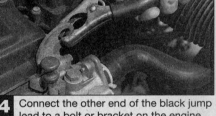

4 Connect the other end of the black jump lead to a bolt or bracket on the engine block, well away from the battery, on the vehicle to be started.

5 Make sure that the jump leads will not come into contact with the fan, drive-belts or other moving parts of the engine.

6 Start the engine using the booster battery and run it at idle speed. Switch on the lights, rear window demister and heater blower motor, then disconnect the jump leads in the reverse order of connection. Turn off the lights etc.

Wheel changing

Warning: Do not change a wheel in a situation where you risk being hit by another vehicle. On busy roads, try to stop in a lay-by or a gateway. Be wary of passing traffic while changing the wheel - it is easy to become distracted by the job in hand.

Preparation

☐ When a puncture occurs, stop as soon as it is safe to do so.

☐ Park on firm level ground, if possible, and well out of the way of other traffic.

☐ Use hazard warning lights if necessary.

☐ If you have one, use a warning triangle to alert other drivers of your presence.

☐ Apply the handbrake and engage first or reverse gear (or Park on models with automatic transmission.

☐ Chock the wheel diagonally opposite the one being removed – a couple of large stones will do for this.

☐ If the ground is soft, use a flat piece of wood to spread the load under the jack.

Changing the wheel

1 Unclip the wheel brace located at the left-hand side of the luggage compartment.

2 From inside the luggage compartment, use the wheel brace to lower the spare wheel cradle.

3 Unhook the cradle, lower it to the ground and slide the spare wheel out from the underside of the car.

4 Remove the jack from its location in the centre of the spare wheel.

5 Remove the wheel trim (where fitted) then slacken each wheel bolt by a half turn.

6 Locate the jack below the reinforced jacking point and on firm ground (don't jack the car at any other point on the sill).

Finally...

☐ Remove the wheel chocks and stow the tools in the appropriate locations in the car.

☐ Don't leave the spare wheel cradle empty and unsecured – it could drop onto the ground while the car is moving.

☐ Check the tyre pressure on the wheel just fitted. If it is low, or if you don't have a pressure gauge with you, drive slowly to the nearest garage and inflate the tyre to the correct pressure.

☐ Have the damaged tyre or wheel repaired, or renew it, as soon as possible.

7 Turn the jack handle clockwise until the wheel is raised clear of the ground, remove the bolts and lift the wheel clear. Position the spare wheel and fit the bolts. Tighten moderately with the wheel brace, then lower the car to the ground.

8 Tighten the wheel bolts in the sequence shown, fit the wheel trim, and secure the punctured wheel and jack in the spare wheel cradle.

Identifying leaks

Puddles on the garage floor or drive, or obvious wetness under the bonnet or underneath the car, suggest a leak that needs investigating. It can sometimes be difficult to decide where the leak is coming from, especially if the engine bay is very dirty already. Leaking oil or fluid can also be blown rearwards by the passage of air under the car, giving a false impression of where the problem lies.

 Warning: Most automotive oils and fluids are poisonous. Wash them off skin, and change out of contaminated clothing, without delay.

HAYNES HiNT The smell of a fluid leaking from the car may provide a clue to what's leaking. Some fluids are distictively coloured. It may help to clean the car carefully and to park it over some clean paper overnight as an aid to locating the source of the leak.
Remember that some leaks may only occur while the engine is running.

Sump oil

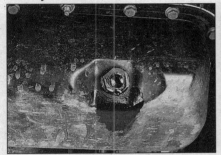

Engine oil may leak from the drain plug...

Oil from filter

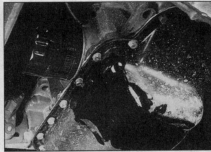

...or from the base of the oil filter.

Gearbox oil

Gearbox oil can leak from the seals at the inboard ends of the driveshafts.

Antifreeze

Leaking antifreeze often leaves a crystalline deposit like this.

Brake fluid

A leak occurring at a wheel is almost certainly brake fluid.

Power steering fluid

Power steering fluid may leak from the pipe connectors on the steering rack.

Towing

When all else fails, you may find yourself having to get a tow home – or of course you may be helping somebody else. Long-distance recovery should only be done by a garage or breakdown service. For shorter distances, DIY towing using another car is easy enough, but observe the following points:

☐ Use a proper tow-rope – they are not expensive. The vehicle being towed must display an 'ON TOW' sign in its rear window.
☐ Always turn the ignition key to the 'on' position when the vehicle is being towed, so that the steering lock is released, and that the direction indicator and brake lights will work.
☐ Only attach the tow-rope to the towing eyes provided **(see illustration)**.
☐ Before being towed, release the handbrake and select neutral on the transmission.

☐ Note that greater-than-usual pedal pressure will be required to operate the brakes, since the vacuum servo unit is only operational with the engine running.
☐ On models with power steering, greater-than-usual steering effort will also be required.
☐ The driver of the car being towed must keep the tow-rope taut at all times to avoid snatching.
☐ Make sure that both drivers know the route before setting off.
☐ Only drive at moderate speeds and keep the distance towed to a minimum. Drive smoothly and allow plenty of time for slowing down at junctions.
☐ On models with automatic transmission, special precautions apply. If in doubt, do not tow, or transmission damage may result.

 Warning: To prevent damage to the catalytic converter, a vehicle must not be push-started, or started by towing, when the engine is at operating temperature. Use jump leads (see "Jump starting").

Rear towing eye located behind the access cover in the rear bumper

Introduction

There are some very simple checks which need only take a few minutes to carry out, but which could save you a lot of inconvenience and expense.

These "Weekly checks" require no great skill or special tools, and the small amount of time they take to perform could prove to be very well spent, for example;

☐ Keeping an eye on tyre condition and pressures, will not only help to stop them wearing out prematurely, but could also save your life.

☐ Many breakdowns are caused by electrical problems. Battery-related faults are particularly common, and a quick check on a regular basis will often prevent the majority of these.

☐ If your car develops a brake fluid leak, the first time you might know about it is when your brakes don't work properly. Checking the level regularly will give advance warning of this kind of problem.

☐ If the oil or coolant levels run low, the cost of repairing any engine damage will be far greater than fixing the leak, for example.

Underbonnet check points

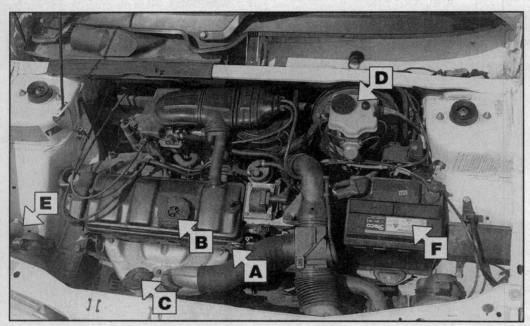

◀ **Petrol model (1.1 litre shown)**

A *Engine oil level dipstick*

B *Engine oil filler cap*

C *Radiator filler cap*

D *Brake fluid reservoir*

E *Screen washer fluid reservoir*

F *Battery*

◀ **Diesel model (1.4 litre shown)**

A *Engine oil level dipstick*

B *Engine oil filler cap*

C *Coolant expansion tank*

D *Brake fluid reservoir*

E *Screen washer fluid reservoir*

F *Battery*

Engine oil level

Before you start
✔ Make sure that your car is on level ground.
✔ Check the oil level before the car is driven, or at least 5 minutes after the engine has been switched off.

 HAYNES HINT *If the oil is checked immediately after driving the vehicle, some of the oil will remain in the upper engine components, resulting in an inaccurate reading on the dipstick!*

The correct oil
Modern engines place great demands on their oil. It is very important that the correct oil for your car is used (See "Lubricants, fluids and tyre pressures").

Car Care
● If you have to add oil frequently, you should check whether you have any oil leaks. Place some clean paper under the car overnight, and check for stains in the morning. If there are no leaks, the engine may be burning oil.

● Always maintain the level between the upper and lower dipstick marks (see photo 3). If the level is too low severe engine damage may occur. Oil seal failure may result if the engine is overfilled by adding too much oil.

1 The dipstick is located in a tube at the front of the engine on all models.

2 Withdraw the dipstick. Using a clean rag or paper towel, wipe all the oil from the dipstick. Insert the clean dipstick into the tube as far as it will go, then withdraw it again.

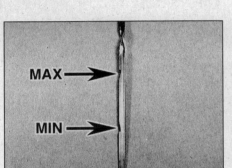

3 Note the oil level on the end of the dipstick, which should be between the upper (MAX) mark and lower (MIN) mark. Approximately 1.5 litres of oil will raise the level from the lower mark to the upper mark.

4 Oil is added through the filler cap. Unscrew the cap and top-up the level; a funnel may help to reduce spillage. Add the oil slowly, checking the level on the dipstick often. Don't overfill (see "Car Care" left).

Coolant level

⚠ **Warning: DO NOT attempt to remove the expansion tank pressure cap when the engine is hot, as there is a very great risk of scalding. Do not leave open containers of coolant about, as it is poisonous.**

Car Care
● Adding coolant should not be necessary on a regular basis. If frequent topping-up is required, it is likely there is a leak. Check the radiator, all hoses and joint faces for signs of staining or wetness, and rectify as necessary.

● It is important that antifreeze is used in the cooling system all year round, not just during the winter months. Don't top-up with water alone, as the antifreeze will become too diluted.

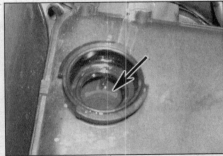

1 The coolant level is checked in the expansion tank, which is built into the side of the radiator on petrol models or located at the right-hand side of the engine compartment on diesel models. When the engine is cold, the coolant level should be between the "MAX" and "MIN" marks. On diesel models (shown) the maximum coolant level is indicated by a red marker visible inside the expansion tank.

2 If topping-up is necessary, wait until the engine is cold then turn the pressure cap on the expansion tank slowly anti-clockwise, and pause until any pressure remaining in the system is released. Unscrew the cap and lift off.

3 Add a mixture of water and antifreeze to the expansion tank, until the coolant level is up to the "MAX" level mark. Refit the cap, turning it clockwise as far as it will go until it is secure. Re-check that the cap is securely tightened once the engine is warm.

Power steering fluid level

Before you start:
✔ Park the vehicle on level ground.
✔ Set the steering wheel straight-ahead.
✔ The engine should be turned off.

 For the check to be accurate, the steering must not be turned once the engine has been stopped.

Safety First!
● The need for frequent topping-up indicates a leak, which should be investigated immediately.

1 The power steering fluid reservoir is located on the left-hand side of the engine compartment. The fluid level should be checked with the engine stopped. A translucent reservoir is fitted, with "MAX" and "MIN" markings on the side of the reservoir.

2 The fluid level should be between the "MAX" and "MIN" marks. If topping-up is necessary, and before removing the cap, wipe the surrounding area so that dirt does not enter the reservoir.

3 When topping-up, use the specified type of fluid, and do not overfill the reservoir. When the level is correct, securely refit the cap.

Brake fluid level

⚠ *Warning:*
● *Brake fluid can harm your eyes and damage painted surfaces, so use extreme caution when handling and pouring it.*
● *Do not use fluid that has been standing open for some time, as it absorbs moisture from the air, which can cause a dangerous loss of braking effectiveness.*

 ● *Make sure that your car is on level ground.*
● *The fluid level in the reservoir will drop slightly as the brake pads wear down, but the fluid level must never be allowed to drop below the "MIN" mark.*

Safety First!
● If the reservoir requires repeated topping-up this is an indication of a fluid leak somewhere in the system, which should be investigated immediately.

● If a leak is suspected, the car should not be driven until the braking system has been checked. Never take any risks where brakes are concerned.

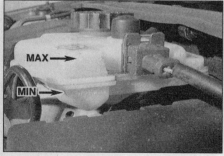

1 The "MAX" and "MIN" marks are indicated on the side of the reservoir, which is located on the front of the vacuum servo unit in the engine compartment. The fluid level must be kept between these two marks.

2 If topping-up is necessary, first wipe the area around the filler cap with a clean rag before removing the cap. When adding fluid, it's a good idea to inspect the reservoir. The system should be drained and refilled if dirt is seen in the fluid (see Chapter 9).

3 Carefully add fluid, avoiding spilling it on surrounding paintwork. Use only the specified hydraulic fluid; mixing different types of fluid can cause damage to the system and/or a loss of braking effectiveness. After filling to the correct level, refit the cap securely and wipe off any spilt fluid.

Battery

Caution: Before carrying out any work on the vehicle battery, read the precautions given in "Safety first" at the start of this manual.

✔ Make sure that the battery tray is in good condition, and that the clamp is tight. Corrosion on the tray, retaining clamp and the battery itself can be removed with a solution of water and baking soda. Thoroughly rinse all cleaned areas with water. Any metal parts damaged by corrosion should be covered with a zinc-based primer, then painted.

✔ Periodically (approximately every three months), check the charge condition of the battery as described in Chapter 5A.

✔ If the battery is flat, and you need to jump start your vehicle, see *Roadside Repairs*.

1 The battery is located on the left-hand side of the engine compartment. Lift off the cover, then inspect the exterior of the battery for damage such as a cracked case.

2 Check the tightness of the battery cable clamps to ensure good electrical connections. You should not be able to move them. Also check each cable for cracks and frayed conductors.

HAYNES HiNT

Battery corrosion can be kept to a minimum by applying a layer of petroleum jelly to the clamps and terminals after they are reconnected.

3 If corrosion (white, fluffy deposits) is evident, remove the cables from the battery terminals, clean them with a small wire brush, then refit them. Automotive stores sell a tool for cleaning the battery post . . .

4 . . . as well as the battery cable clamps

Electrical systems

✔ Check all external lights and the horn. Refer to the appropriate Sections of Chapter 12 for details if any of the circuits are found to be inoperative.

✔ Visually check all accessible wiring connectors, harnesses and retaining clips for security, and for signs of chafing or damage.

HAYNES HiNT

If you need to check your brake lights and indicators unaided, back up to a wall or garage door and operate the lights. The reflected light should show if they are working properly.

1 If a single indicator light, brake light or headlight has failed, it is likely that a bulb has blown and will need to be replaced. Refer to Chapter 12 for details. If both brake lights have failed, it is possible that the brake light switch operated by the brake pedal has failed. Refer to Chapter 9 for details.

2 If more than one indicator light or tail light has failed it is likely that either a fuse has blown or that there is a fault in the circuit (see Chapter 12). The main fuses are located in the fuseboxes situated in the facia in the passenger compartment and in the engine compartment (refer to Chapter 12).

3 To replace a blown fuse, remove it, where applicable, using the plastic tool provided. Fit a new fuse of the same rating, available from car accessory shops. It is important that you find the reason that the fuse blew (see *"Electrical fault finding"* in Chapter 12).

Tyre condition and pressure

It is very important that tyres are in good condition, and at the correct pressure - having a tyre failure at any speed is highly dangerous. Tyre wear is influenced by driving style - harsh braking and acceleration, or fast cornering, will all produce more rapid tyre wear. As a general rule, the front tyres wear out faster than the rears. Interchanging the tyres from front to rear ("rotating" the tyres) may result in more even wear. However, if this is completely effective, you may have the expense of replacing all four tyres at once! Remove any nails or stones embedded in the tread before they penetrate the tyre to cause deflation. If removal of a nail does reveal that the tyre has been punctured, refit the nail so that its point of penetration is marked. Then immediately change the wheel, and have the tyre repaired by a tyre dealer.

Regularly check the tyres for damage in the form of cuts or bulges, especially in the sidewalls. Periodically remove the wheels, and clean any dirt or mud from the inside and outside surfaces. Examine the wheel rims for signs of rusting, corrosion or other damage. Light alloy wheels are easily damaged by "kerbing" whilst parking; steel wheels may also become dented or buckled. A new wheel is very often the only way to overcome severe damage.

New tyres should be balanced when they are fitted, but it may become necessary to re-balance them as they wear, or if the balance weights fitted to the wheel rim should fall off. Unbalanced tyres will wear more quickly, as will the steering and suspension components. Wheel imbalance is normally signified by vibration, particularly at a certain speed (typically around 50 mph). If this vibration is felt only through the steering, then it is likely that just the front wheels need balancing. If, however, the vibration is felt through the whole car, the rear wheels could be out of balance. Wheel balancing should be carried out by a tyre dealer or garage.

1 Tread Depth - visual check

The original tyres have tread wear safety bands (B), which will appear when the tread depth reaches approximately 1.6 mm. The band positions are indicated by a triangular mark on the tyre sidewall (A).

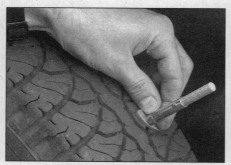

2 Tread Depth - manual check

Alternatively, tread wear can be monitored with a simple, inexpensive device known as a tread depth indicator gauge.

3 Tyre Pressure Check

Check the tyre pressures regularly with the tyres cold. Do not adjust the tyre pressures immediately after the vehicle has been used, or an inaccurate setting will result. Tyre pressures are shown on Page 0•16.

Tyre tread wear patterns

Shoulder Wear

Underinflation (wear on both sides)
Under-inflation will cause overheating of the tyre, because the tyre will flex too much, and the tread will not sit correctly on the road surface. This will cause a loss of grip and excessive wear, not to mention the danger of sudden tyre failure due to heat build-up.
Check and adjust pressures
Incorrect wheel camber (wear on one side)
Repair or renew suspension parts
Hard cornering
Reduce speed!

Centre Wear

Overinflation
Over-inflation will cause rapid wear of the centre part of the tyre tread, coupled with reduced grip, harsher ride, and the danger of shock damage occurring in the tyre casing.
Check and adjust pressures

If you sometimes have to inflate your car's tyres to the higher pressures specified for maximum load or sustained high speed, don't forget to reduce the pressures to normal afterwards.

Uneven Wear

Front tyres may wear unevenly as a result of wheel misalignment. Most tyre dealers and garages can check and adjust the wheel alignment (or "tracking") for a modest charge.
Incorrect camber or castor
Repair or renew suspension parts
Malfunctioning suspension
Repair or renew suspension parts
Unbalanced wheel
Balance tyres
Incorrect toe setting
Adjust front wheel alignment
Note: *The feathered edge of the tread which typifies toe wear is best checked by feel.*

Washer fluid level

Screenwash additives not only keep the winscreen clean during foul weather, they also prevent the washer system freezing in cold weather - which is when you are likely to need it most. Don't top up using plain water as the screenwash will become too diluted, and will freeze during cold weather.

The windscreen/tailgate washer fluid reservoir is located at the front right-hand side of the engine compartment. If topping-up is necessary, open the cap.

When topping-up the reservoir, a screen-wash additive should be added in the quantities recommended on the bottle. *On no account use coolant antifreeze in the washer system - this could discolour or damage paintwork.*

Wiper blades

Check the condition of the wiper blades; if they are cracked or show any signs of deterioration, or if the glass swept area is smeared, renew them. Wiper blades should be renewed annually.

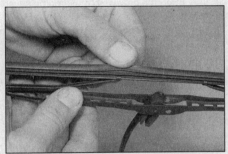 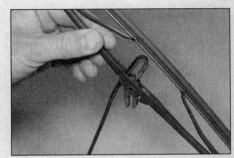

To remove a windscreen wiper blade, pull the arm fully away from the screen until it locks. Swivel the blade through 90°, then depress the locking clip at the base of the mounting block and slide the blade from the arm.

Advanced driving

Many people see the words 'advanced driving' and believe that it won't interest them or that it is a style of driving beyond their own abilities. Nothing could be further from the truth. Advanced driving is straightforward safe, sensible driving - the sort of driving we should all do every time we get behind the wheel.

An average of 10 people are killed every day on UK roads and 870 more are injured, some seriously. Lives are ruined daily, usually because somebody did something stupid. Something like 95% of all accidents are due to human error, mostly driver failure. Sometimes we make genuine mistakes - everyone does. Sometimes we have lapses of concentration. Sometimes we deliberately take risks.

For many people, the process of 'learning to drive' doesn't go much further than learning how to pass the driving test because of a common belief that good drivers are made by 'experience'.

Learning to drive by 'experience' teaches three driving skills:

- ☐ Quick reactions. (Whoops, that was close!)
- ☐ Good handling skills. (Horn, swerve, brake, horn).
- ☐ Reliance on vehicle technology. (Great stuff this ABS, stop in no distance even in the wet...)

Drivers whose skills are 'experience based' generally have a lot of near misses and the odd accident. The results can be seen every day in our courts and our hospital casualty departments.

Advanced drivers have learnt to control the risks by controlling the position and speed of their vehicle. They avoid accidents and near misses, even if the drivers around them make mistakes.

The key skills of advanced driving are **concentration,** effective all-round **observation, anticipation** and **planning.** When **good vehicle handling** is added to these skills, all driving situations can be approached and negotiated in a safe, methodical way, leaving nothing to chance.

Concentration means applying your mind to safe driving, completely excluding anything that's not relevant. Driving is usually the most dangerous activity that most of us undertake in our daily routines. It deserves our full attention.

Observation means not just looking, but seeing and seeking out the information found in the driving environment.

Anticipation means asking yourself what is happening, what you can reasonably expect to happen and what could happen unexpectedly. (One of the commonest words used in compiling accident reports is 'suddenly'.)

Planning is the link between seeing something and taking the appropriate action. For many drivers, planning is the missing link.

If you want to become a safer and more skilful driver and you want to enjoy your driving more, contact the Institute of Advanced Motorists on 0208 994 4403 or write to IAM House, Chiswick High Road, London W4 4HS for an information pack.

Lubricants and fluids

Engine (petrol)	Multigrade engine oil, viscosity SAE 10W/30 to 15W/50, to API SH/SJ and/or ACEA A3-96 *(Duckhams QXR Premium Petrol Engine Oil, or Duckhams Hypergrade Petrol Engine Oil)*
Engine (diesel)	Multigrade engine oil, viscosity SAE 15W/40, to API CF/CD and/or ACEA B3-96 *(Duckhams QXR Premium Diesel Engine Oil, or Duckhams Hypergrade Diesel Engine Oil)*
Cooling system	Ethylene-glycol based antifreeze *(Duckhams Antifreeze and Summer Coolant)*
Manual gearbox	Esso gear oil 75W/80W *(Duckhams Hypoid Gear Oil 75W-80W GL-5)*
Automatic transmission	Esso automatic transmission fluid ATF D *(Duckhams ATF Autotrans III)*
Power steering reservoir	Esso automatic transmission fluid ATF D *(Duckhams ATF Autotrans III)*
Brake fluid reservoir	Hydraulic fluid to SAE J1703, DOT 4 *(Duckhams Universal Brake & Clutch Fluid)*

Choosing your engine oil

Engines need oil, not only to lubricate moving parts and minimise wear, but also to maximise power output and to improve fuel economy. By introducing a simplified and improved range of engine oils, Duckhams has taken away the confusion and made it easier for you to choose the right oil for your engine.

HOW ENGINE OIL WORKS

• Beating friction

Without oil, the moving surfaces inside your engine will rub together, heat up and melt, quickly causing the engine to seize. Engine oil creates a film which separates these moving parts, preventing wear and heat build-up.

• Cooling hot-spots

Temperatures inside the engine can exceed 1000° C. The engine oil circulates and acts as a coolant, transferring heat from the hot-spots to the sump.

• Cleaning the engine internally

Good quality engine oils clean the inside of your engine, collecting and dispersing combustion deposits and controlling them until they are trapped by the oil filter or flushed out at oil change.

OIL CARE - FOLLOW THE CODE

To handle and dispose of used engine oil safely, always:

0800 66 33 66
www.oilbankline.org.uk

• **Avoid skin contact with used engine oil.** Repeated or prolonged contact can be harmful.
• **Dispose of used oil and empty packs in a responsible manner in an authorised disposal site.** Call 0800 663366 to find the one nearest to you. Never tip oil down drains or onto the ground.

DUCKHAMS ENGINE OILS

For the driver who demands a premium quality oil for complete reassurance, we recommend synthetic formula **Duckhams QXR Premium Engine Oils**.
For the driver who requires a straightforward quality engine oil, we recommend **Duckhams Hypergrade Engine Oils**.

For further information and advice, call the Duckhams UK Helpline on 0800 212988.

Tyre pressures (tyres cold)

Note: *Refer to the tyre pressure data plate on the rear edge of the driver's door (visible when the door is open) for the correct tyre pressures for your particular vehicle. Pressures apply only to original-equipment tyres, and may vary if any other make or type is fitted; check with the tyre manufacturer or supplier for correct pressures if necessary.*

	Front	Rear
Petrol models		
All except 145/70 R 13 T and 155/70 R 13 T	2.2 bars (32 psi)	2.2 bars (32 psi)
145/70 R 13 T and 155/70 R 13 T	2.3 bars (33 psi)	2.3 bars (33 psi)
Diesel models		
With power steering	2.2 bars (32 psi)	2.2 bars (32 psi)
Without power steering	2.3 bars (33 psi)	2.3 bars (33 psi)

Chapter 1 Part A:
Routine maintenance and servicing - petrol models

Contents

Degrees of difficulty

 Easy, suitable for novice with little experience

 Fairly easy, suitable for beginner with some experience

 Fairly difficult, suitable for competent DIY mechanic

 Difficult, suitable for experienced DIY mechanic

Very difficult, suitable for expert DIY or professional

1A

Lubricants and fluids

Refer to *"Weekly checks"*

Capacities

Engine oil

Models up to 1997 (approximately):
Excluding filter .... 3.2 litres
Including filter .... 3.5 litres
Models from 1997 (approximately):
Excluding filter .... 2.9 litres
Including filter .... 3.2 litres

Cooling system

All models (except engine type TU5J4, code NFX) .... 5.5 litres
Engine type TU5J4, code NFX .... 4.8 litres

Transmission

Manual .... 2.0 litres
Automatic
From dry .... 4.5 litres
Drain and refill .... 2.5 litres

Power-assisted steering .... 1.7 litres (approximately)

Fuel tank .... 45.0 litres

Washer reservoirs

Windscreen washers only .... 1.5 litres
Windscreen and tailgate washers .... 2.8 litres
Headlight washer reservoir .... 5.6 litres

Cooling system

Antifreeze mixture:
28% antifreeze .... Protection down to -15°C
50% antifreeze .... Protection down to -30°C
Note: *Refer to antifreeze manufacturer for latest recommendations.*

Fuel system

Idle speed:
Carburettor models:
954 and 1124 cc models .... 700 ± 50 rpm
1360 cc models .... 750 ± 50 rpm
Fuel-injected models*:
Single-point injection models .... 850 ± 50 rpm (not adjustable - controlled by ECU)
Multi-point injection models .... 900 ± 50 rpm (not adjustable - controlled by ECU)
Idle mixture CO content:
Carburettor models:
954 and 1124 cc models .... 1.3 ± 0.5 %
1360 cc models .... 1.5 ± 0.5 %
Fuel-injected models*:
1360 cc (K6B engine) models .... 1.0 to 2.0 % (adjustable via mixture potentiometer)
All other models .... Less than 1.0 % (not adjustable - controlled by ECU)
*See the relevant Part of Chapter 4 for further information

Ignition system

Spark plugs:	Type	Electrode gap
954 cc:		
TU9M 1993-2001	Eyquem RFC42LS or	0.9 mm
	Bosch FR8LDC	0.9 mm
1124 cc:		
TU1M:		
1993-1996	Eyquem RFC42LS	0.8 mm
1996-2001	Eyquem RFC52LS or	0.9 mm
	Bosch FR7LDC	0.9 mm
1294 cc:		
TU2J2 1993-1996	NGK BKR6EK	0.9 mm
1360 cc:		
TU3FJ2 1991-1995	Eyquem RFC58LS3	1.2 mm
TU3MC 1993-1996	Eyquem RFC52LS	0.8 mm
TU3JP 1996-2001	Eyquem RFC52LZ2E or	0.9 mm
	Bosch FR7KDC	0.9 mm
1587 cc:		
TU5JP:		
1994-1996	Bosch RC7BMC	1.0 mm
1996-1998	Eyquem RFC58LZ2E or	1.0 mm
	Bosch FR6KDC	1.0 mm
TU5J2:		
1994-1996	Bosch RC8DMC	1.0 mm
1997-1998	Bosch RC9YC4	1.0 mm
TU5JP4 1996-2001	Eyquem RFC58LZ2E or	1.0 mm
	Bosch FR6KDC	1.0 mm

Brakes

Brake pad friction material minimum thickness	2.0 mm
Brake shoe friction material minimum thickness	1.5 mm

Tyre pressures

See end of *"Weekly checks"*

Torque wrench settings

	Nm	lbf ft
Roadwheel bolts	85	63
Spark plugs	25	18
Transmission filler/level and drain plugs	25	18

1A

The maintenance intervals in this manual are provided with the assumption that you, not the dealer, will be carrying out the work. These are the minimum maintenance intervals based on the schedule recommended by us for vehicles driven daily. If you wish to keep your vehicle in peak condition at all times, you may wish to perform some of these procedures more often. We encourage frequent maintenance, because it enhances the efficiency, performance and resale value of your vehicle.

If the vehicle is driven in dusty areas, used to tow a trailer, or driven frequently at slow speeds (idling in traffic) or on short journeys, more frequent maintenance intervals are recommended. Peugeot actually recommend that the service intervals are halved for vehicles which are used under these conditions.

When the vehicle is new, it should be serviced by a factory-authorised dealer service department, in order to preserve the factory warranty.

During 1994, Peugeot introduced extended maintenance intervals on their petrol models. 'Normal servicing' (as described below for 6000 miles/10 000 km or 12 months), for these models has been extended to 9000 miles (15 000 km) or 12 months. However, our own recommendations would be as shown below, due to the benefits as described in paragraph 1.

In addition to the items shown below, where applicable, the ECU should be checked for any fault codes (refer to Chapter 4C for details).

Every 250 miles (400 km) or weekly
☐ Refer to "Weekly checks".

Every 6000 miles (10 000 km) or 12 months - whichever comes first
☐ Renew the engine oil and filter (Section 3).
☐ Check all underbonnet components for fluid leaks (Section 4).
☐ Check the steering and suspension components (Section 5).
☐ Check the condition of the driveshaft rubber gaiters (Section 6).
☐ Check the automatic transmission fluid level (Section 7).

Every 12 000 miles (20 000 km)
In addition to all the items listed above, carry out the following:
☐ Check the air conditioning system refrigerant - where applicable (Section 8).
☐ Renew the spark plugs - at 18,000 miles for 1994-on models (Section 9).
☐ Renew the fuel filter - carburettor models (Section 10).
☐ Clean the fuel pick-up filter - fuel-injected models (Section 11).
☐ Renew the automatic transmission fluid - at 18,000 miles for 1994-on models (Section 12).
☐ Check the ignition system and ignition timing (Section 13).
☐ Check the idle speed and mixture adjustment (Section 14).
☐ Check the emission control system hoses and components (Section 15).
☐ Check the auxiliary drivebelt, and renew if necessary (Section 16).
☐ Check the clutch adjustment (Section 17).
☐ Lubricate the clutch control mechanism (Section 17).
☐ Check the front brake pads, and renew if necessary (Section 18).
☐ Check the operation of the handbrake (Section 19).
☐ Lubricate all hinges and locks (Section 20).
☐ Carry out a road test (Section 21).

Every 24 000 miles (40 000 km)
In addition to all the items listed above, carry out the following:
☐ Renew the air filter – at 36,000 miles for 1994-on models (Section 22).

Every 36 000 miles (60 000 km) or 4 years - whichever comes first
In addition to all the items listed above, carry out the following:
☐ Check the condition of the rear drum brake shoes (Section 23).
☐ Check the condition of the rear disc brake pads (Section 24).
☐ Check the manual transmission oil level (Section 25).
☐ Renew the fuel filter - fuel injection models (Section 26).
☐ Renew the timing belt (Section 27).*

*Note: Although the normal interval for timing belt renewal is 72 000 miles (120 000 km), it is strongly recommended that the interval is halved to 36 000 miles (60 000 km) on vehicles which are subjected to intensive use, ie. mainly short journeys or a lot of stop-start driving. The actual belt renewal interval is therefore very much up to the individual owner, but bear in mind that severe engine damage will result if the belt breaks.

Every 72 000 miles (120 000 km)
In addition to all the items listed above, carry out the following:
☐ Renew the timing belt (Section 27).*

*This is the interval recommended by Peugeot, but we recommend that the belt is changed more frequently, at 36 000 miles - see above.

Every 2 years (regardless of mileage)
☐ Renew the coolant (Section 28).
☐ Renew the brake fluid (Section 29).

Underbonnet view of an 1124 cc (TU1 engine) carburettor model

1   Engine oil filler cap
2   Engine oil dipstick
3   Battery earth (negative)
    terminal
4   Master cylinder/brake fluid
    reservoir
5   Auxiliary fusebox
6   Engine oil filter
7   Radiator filler cap
8   Alternator
9   Fuel pump
10 Braking system vacuum
    servo unit
11 Ignition HT coil
12 Relay box
13 Suspension strut upper
    mounting
14 Air cleaner air temperature
    control valve
15 Carburettor
16 Air cleaner housing

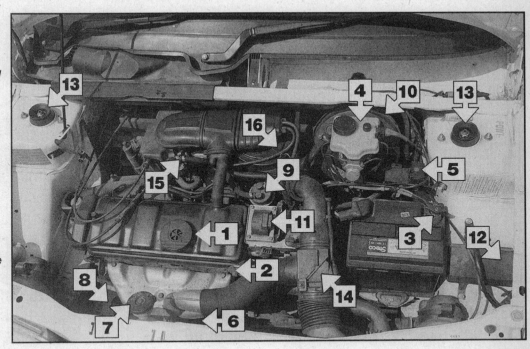

Underbonnet view of a 1360 cc (TU3 engine) fuel-injected model

1   Engine oil filler cap
2   Engine oil dipstick
3   Battery earth (negative)
    terminal
4   Master cylinder/brake fluid
    reservoir
5   Auxiliary fusebox
6   Engine oil filter
7   Radiator filler cap
8   Alternator
9   Washer fluid reservoir filler
    cap
10 Braking system vacuum
    servo unit
11 Ignition HT coil
12 Plastic box containing the
    fuel injection ECU, relay
    unit and injector resistor
13 Suspension strut upper
    mounting
14 Air cleaner air temperature
    control valve
15 Throttle body assembly
16 Air cleaner housing

Rear underbody view

1   Spare wheel
2   Fuel tank
3   Handbrake cable
4   Fuel filter
5   Tailpipe
6   Rear shock absorber
7   Rear suspension tubular crossmember
8   Torsion bar
9   Rear axle mounting bracket
10 Torsion bar
11 Trailing arm
12 Fuel tank filler hose

Front underbody view - diesel model shown (petrol models similar)

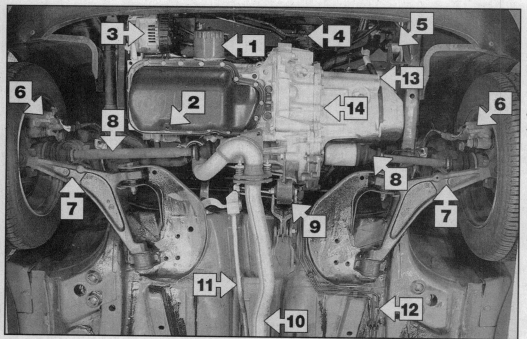

1   Oil filter
2   Sump drain plug
3   Alternator
4   Radiator cooling fan
5   Horn
6   Brake caliper
7   Lower arm
8   Driveshaft
9   Engine/transmission rear mounting
10 Exhaust system
11 Gearchange linkage selector rod
12 Brake pipes
13 Transmission filler/level plug
14 Transmission drain plug

1 General information

This Chapter is designed to help the home mechanic maintain his/her vehicle for safety, economy, long life and peak performance.

The Chapter contains a master maintenance schedule, followed by Sections dealing specifically with each task in the schedule. Visual checks, adjustments, component renewal and other helpful items are included. Refer to the accompanying illustrations of the engine compartment and the underside of the vehicle for the locations of the various components.

Servicing your vehicle in accordance with the mileage/time maintenance schedule and the following Sections will provide a planned maintenance programme, which should result in a long and reliable service life. This is a comprehensive plan, so maintaining some items but not others at the specified service intervals, will not produce the same results.

As you service your vehicle, you will discover that many of the procedures can - and should - be grouped together, because of the particular procedure being performed, or because of the close proximity of two otherwise-unrelated components to one another. For example, if the vehicle is raised for any reason, the exhaust can be inspected at the same time as the suspension and steering components.

The first step in this maintenance programme is to prepare yourself before the actual work begins. Read through all the Sections relevant to the work to be carried out, then make a list and gather together all the parts and tools required. If a problem is encountered, seek advice from a parts specialist, or a dealer service department.

2 Regular maintenance

1 If, from the time the vehicle is new, the routine maintenance schedule is followed closely, and frequent checks are made of fluid levels and high-wear items, as suggested throughout this manual, the engine will be kept in relatively good running condition, and the need for additional work will be minimised.

2 It is possible that there will be times when the engine is running poorly due to the lack of regular maintenance. This is even more likely if a used vehicle, which has not received regular and frequent maintenance checks, is purchased. In such cases, additional work may need to be carried out, outside of the regular maintenance intervals.

3 If engine wear is suspected, a compression test (refer to the relevant Part of Chapter 2) will provide valuable information regarding the overall performance of the main internal components. Such a test can be used as a basis to decide on the extent of the work to be carried out. If, for example, a compression test indicates serious internal engine wear, conventional maintenance as described in this Chapter will not greatly improve the performance of the engine, and may prove a waste of time and money, unless extensive overhaul work (Chapter 2C) is carried out first.

4 The following series of operations are those most often required to improve the performance of a generally poor-running engine:

Primary operations

a) Clean, inspect and test the battery (See "Weekly checks").
b) Check all the engine-related fluids (See "Weekly checks").
c) Check the condition and tension of the auxiliary drivebelt (Section 16).
d) Renew the spark plugs (Section 9).
e) Inspect the distributor cap, rotor arm and HT leads - as applicable (Section 13).
f) Check the condition of the air filter, and renew if necessary (Section 22).
g) Renew the fuel filter (Section 10 or 26 as applicable).
h) Clean the fuel pick-up filter, where fitted (Section 11).
i) Check the condition of all hoses, and check for fluid leaks (Section 4).
j) Check the idle speed and mixture settings (Section 14).

5 If the above operations do not prove fully effective, carry out the following secondary operations:

Secondary operations

All items listed under "Primary operations", plus the following:

a) Check the charging system (Chapter 5A).
b) Check the ignition system (Chapter 5B).
c) Check the fuel system (relevant Part of Chapter 4).
d) Renew the distributor cap and rotor arm - as applicable (Section 13).
e) Renew the ignition HT leads (Section 13).

1A

Every 6000 miles (10 000 km) or 12 months

3 Engine oil and filter renewal

Note: *A suitable square-section wrench may be required to undo the sump drain plug on some models. These wrenches can be obtained from most motor factors or your Peugeot dealer.*

1 Frequent oil and filter changes are the most important preventative maintenance procedures which can be undertaken by the DIY owner. As engine oil ages, it becomes diluted and contaminated, which leads to premature engine wear.

2 Before starting this procedure, gather together all the necessary tools and materials. Also make sure that you have plenty of clean rags and newspapers handy, to mop up any spills. Ideally, the engine oil should be warm, as it will drain better, and more built-up sludge will be removed with it. Take care, however, not to touch the exhaust or any other hot parts of the engine when working under the vehicle. To avoid any possibility of scalding, and to protect yourself from possible skin irritants and other harmful contaminants in used engine oils, it is advisable to wear gloves when carrying out this work. Access to the underside of the vehicle will be greatly improved if it can be raised on a lift, driven onto ramps, or jacked up and supported on axle stands (see

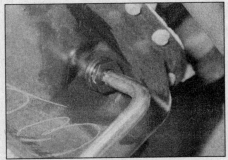

3.3 Slackening the sump drain plug with a square-section wrench

"Jacking and vehicle support"). Whichever method is chosen, make sure that the vehicle remains level, or if it is at an angle, that the drain plug is at the lowest point.

3 Slacken the drain plug about half a turn; on some models, a square-section wrench may be needed to slacken the plug **(see illustration)**. Position the draining container under the drain plug, then remove the plug completely. If possible, try to keep the plug pressed into the sump while unscrewing it by hand the last couple of turns. As the plug releases from the threads, move it away sharply so the stream of oil issuing from the sump runs into the container, not up your sleeve! Recover the sealing ring from the drain plug.

4 Allow some time for the old oil to drain, noting that it may be necessary to reposition the container as the oil flow slows to a trickle.

5 After all the oil has drained, wipe off the drain plug with a clean rag, and fit a new sealing washer. Clean the area around the drain plug opening, and refit the plug. Tighten the plug securely.

6 If the filter is also to be renewed, move the container into position under the oil filter, which is located on the front side of the cylinder block, below the inlet manifold.

7 Using an oil filter removal tool if necessary, slacken the filter initially, then unscrew it by hand the rest of the way **(see illustration)**. Empty the oil in the old filter into the container.

8 Use a clean rag to remove all oil, dirt and sludge from the filter sealing area on the engine. Check the old filter to make sure that the rubber sealing ring hasn't stuck to the engine. If it has, carefully remove it.

9 Apply a light coating of clean engine oil to the sealing ring on the new filter, then screw it into position on the engine. Tighten the filter firmly by hand only - **do not** use any tools.

10 Remove the old oil and all tools from under the car then lower the car to the ground (if applicable).

11 Remove the dipstick, then unscrew the oil filler cap from the cylinder head cover. Fill the engine, using the correct grade and type of oil (see *"Weekly checks"*). An oil can spout or funnel may help to reduce spillage. Pour in half the specified quantity of oil first, then wait a few minutes for the oil to fall to the sump. Continue adding oil a small quantity at a time until the level is up to the lower mark on the dipstick. Adding a further 1.5 litres will bring the level up to the upper mark on the dipstick. Refit the filler cap.

12 Start the engine and run it for a few minutes; check for leaks around the oil filter seal and the sump drain plug. Note that there may be a delay of a few seconds before the oil pressure warning light goes out when the engine is first started, as the oil circulates through the engine oil galleries and the new oil filter (where fitted) before the pressure builds up.

13 Switch off the engine, and wait a few minutes for the oil to settle in the sump once more. With the new oil circulated and the filter completely full, recheck the level on the dipstick, and add more oil as necessary.

14 Dispose of the used engine oil safely, with reference to *"General repair procedures"*.

4 Hose and fluid leak check

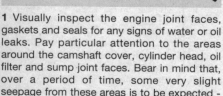

1 Visually inspect the engine joint faces, gaskets and seals for any signs of water or oil leaks. Pay particular attention to the areas around the camshaft cover, cylinder head, oil filter and sump joint faces. Bear in mind that, over a period of time, some very slight seepage from these areas is to be expected - what you are really looking for is any indication of a serious leak. Should a leak be found, renew the offending gasket or oil seal by referring to the appropriate Chapters in this manual.

2 Also check the security and condition of all

3.7 Using an oil filter removal tool to slacken the oil filter

the engine-related pipes and hoses. Ensure that all cable ties or securing clips are in place and in good condition. Clips which are broken or missing can lead to chafing of the hoses, pipes or wiring, which could cause more serious problems in the future.

3 Carefully check the radiator hoses and heater hoses along their entire length. Renew any hose which is cracked, swollen or deteriorated. Cracks will show up better if the hose is squeezed. Pay close attention to the hose clips that secure the hoses to the cooling system components. Hose clips can pinch and puncture hoses, resulting in cooling system leaks. If the original Peugeot crimped-type hose clips are used, it may be a good idea to replace them with standard worm-drive clips.

4 Inspect all the cooling system components (hoses, joint faces etc.) for leaks.

5 Where any problems are found on system components, renew the component or gasket with reference to Chapter 3.

 HAYNES HINT *A leak in the cooling system will usually show up as white- or rust-coloured, crusty deposits around the area of the leak*

6 Where applicable, inspect the automatic transmission fluid cooler hoses for leaks or deterioration.

7 With the vehicle raised, inspect the petrol tank and filler neck for punctures, cracks and other damage. The connection between the filler neck and tank is especially critical. Sometimes a rubber filler neck or connecting hose will leak due to loose retaining clamps or deteriorated rubber.

8 Carefully check all rubber hoses and metal fuel lines leading away from the petrol tank. Check for loose connections, deteriorated hoses, crimped lines, and other damage. Pay particular attention to the vent pipes and hoses, which often loop up around the filler neck and can become blocked or crimped. Follow the lines to the front of the vehicle, carefully inspecting them all the way. Renew damaged sections as necessary.

9 From within the engine compartment, check the security of all fuel hose attachments and pipe unions, and inspect the fuel hoses

and vacuum hoses for kinks, chafing and deterioration.

10 Where applicable, check the condition of the power steering fluid hoses and pipes.

5 Steering and suspension check

Front suspension and steering check

1 Raise the front of the vehicle, and securely support it on axle stands (see *"Jacking and vehicle support"*).

2 Visually inspect the balljoint dust covers and the steering rack-and-pinion gaiters for splits, chafing or deterioration. Any wear of these components will cause loss of lubricant, together with dirt and water entry, resulting in rapid deterioration of the balljoints or steering gear.

3 On vehicles with power steering, check the fluid hoses for chafing or deterioration, and the pipe and hose unions for fluid leaks. Also check for signs of fluid leakage under pressure from the steering gear rubber gaiters, which would indicate failed fluid seals within the steering gear.

4 Grasp the roadwheel at the 12 o'clock and 6 o'clock positions, and try to rock it. Very slight free play may be felt, but if the movement is appreciable, further investigation is necessary to determine the source. Continue rocking the wheel while an assistant depresses the footbrake. If the movement is now eliminated or significantly reduced, it is likely that the hub bearings are at fault. If the free play is still evident with the footbrake depressed, then there is wear in the suspension joints or mountings.

5 Now grasp the wheel at the 9 o'clock and 3 o'clock positions, and try to rock it as before. Any movement felt now may again be caused by wear in the hub bearings or the steering track-rod balljoints. If the inner or outer balljoint is worn, the visual movement will be obvious.

6 Using a large screwdriver or flat bar, check for wear in the suspension mounting bushes by levering between the relevant suspension component and its attachment point. Some movement is to be expected as the mountings are made of rubber, but excessive wear should be obvious. Also check the condition of any visible rubber bushes, looking for splits, cracks or contamination of the rubber.

7 With the car standing on its wheels, have an assistant turn the steering wheel back and forth about an eighth of a turn each way. There should be very little, if any, lost movement between the steering wheel and roadwheels. If this is not the case, closely observe the joints and mountings previously described, but in addition, check the steering column universal joints for wear, and the rack-and-pinion steering gear itself.

Suspension strut/shock absorber check

8 Check for any signs of fluid leakage around the suspension strut/shock absorber body, or from the rubber gaiter around the piston rod. Should any fluid be noticed, the suspension strut/shock absorber is defective internally, and should be renewed.

Note: *Suspension struts/shock absorbers should always be renewed in pairs on the same axle.*

9 The efficiency of the suspension strut/shock absorber may be checked by bouncing the vehicle at each corner. Generally speaking, the body will return to its normal position and stop after being depressed. If it rises and returns on a rebound, the suspension strut/shock absorber is probably suspect. Examine also the suspension strut/shock absorber upper and lower mountings for any signs of wear.

6 Driveshaft gaiter check

1 With the vehicle raised and securely supported on stands (see *"Jacking and vehicle support"*), turn the steering onto full lock, then slowly rotate the roadwheel. Inspect the condition of the outer constant velocity (CV) joint rubber gaiters, squeezing the gaiters to open out the folds. Check for signs of cracking, splits or deterioration of the rubber, which may allow the grease to escape, and lead to water and grit entry into the joint. Also check the security and condition of the retaining clips. Repeat these checks on the inner CV joints. If any damage or deterioration is found, the gaiters should be renewed as described in Chapter 8.

2 At the same time, check the general condition of the CV joints themselves by first holding the driveshaft and attempting to rotate the wheel. Repeat this check by holding the inner joint and attempting to rotate the driveshaft. Any appreciable movement indicates wear in the joints, wear in the driveshaft splines, or a loose driveshaft retaining nut.

7 Automatic transmission fluid level check

1 Take the vehicle on a moderate journey, to warm the transmission up to normal operating temperature, then park the vehicle on level ground. Leave the engine idling and move the selector lever to the "P" (PARK) position. The fluid level is checked using the dipstick located at the front of the engine compartment, directly in front of the transmission. The dipstick top is brightly-coloured for easy identification.

2 With the engine idling and the handbrake and footbrake firmly applied, move the selector lever through all the gear positions, then back to the "P" position. With the selector lever returned to the "P" position and the engine still idling, withdraw the dipstick from the tube, and wipe all the fluid from its end with a clean rag or paper towel. Insert the clean dipstick back into the tube as far as it

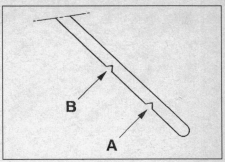

7.2 Automatic transmission dipstick lower mark (A) and upper mark (B)

will go, then withdraw it once more. Note the fluid level on the end of the dipstick which should be between the upper and lower marks **(see illustration)**.

3 If topping-up is necessary, add the required quantity of the specified fluid to the transmission via the dipstick tube. Use a funnel with a fine-mesh gauze, to avoid spillage, and to ensure that no foreign matter enters the transmission.

Caution: Never overfill the transmission so that the fluid level is above the upper mark.

4 After topping-up, take the vehicle on a short run to distribute the fresh fluid, then recheck the level again, topping-up if necessary.

5 Always maintain the level between the two dipstick marks. If the level is allowed to fall below the lower mark, fluid starvation may result, which could lead to severe transmission damage.

6 Frequent need for topping-up indicates that there is a leak, which should be found and corrected before it becomes serious.

1A

Every 12 000 miles (20 000 km)

8 Air conditioning system refrigerant check

⚠️ *Warning: The system should be drained and recharged only by a Peugeot dealer or air conditioning specialist. Do not attempt to carry out the work yourself, as the refrigerant is a highly-dangerous substance (refer to Chapter 3).*

1 In order to check the condition of the refrigerant, a humidity indicator and a sight glass are provided on top of the drier bottle, located in the engine compartment **(see illustration)**.

Refrigerant humidity check

2 Check the colour of the humidity indicator. Blue indicates that the condition of the refrigerant is satisfactory. Red indicates that the refrigerant is saturated with humidity. If the indicator shows red, the system should be drained and recharged, and a new drier bottle should be fitted.

⚠️ *Warning: Do not attempt to open the refrigerant circuit. Refer to the precautions in Chapter 3.*

Refrigerant flow check

3 Run the engine, and switch on the air conditioning.

8.1 Air conditioning drier bottle sight glass (1) and humidity indicator (2)

4 After a few minutes, inspect the sight glass, and check the fluid flow. Clear fluid should be visible - if not, the following will help to diagnose the problem:

a) *Clear fluid flow - the system is functioning correctly.*

b) *No fluid flow - have the system checked for leaks by a Peugeot dealer or air conditioning specialist.*

c) *Continuous stream of clear air bubbles in fluid - refrigerant level low - have the system recharged by a Peugeot dealer or air conditioning specialist.*

d) *Milky air bubbles visible - high humidity (see paragraph 2).*

9 Spark plug renewal

1 The correct functioning of the spark plugs is vital for the correct running and efficiency of the engine. It is essential that the plugs fitted are appropriate for the engine (a suitable type is specified at the beginning of this Chapter).

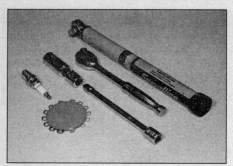

9.6 Tools required for spark plug removal, gap adjustment and refitting

9.11 Measuring the spark plug gap with a feeler blade

9.12 Adjusting the spark plug electrode gap using a special adjusting tool

If this type is used and the engine is in good condition, the spark plugs should not need attention between scheduled replacement intervals. Spark plug cleaning is rarely necessary, and should not be attempted unless specialised equipment is available, as damage can easily be caused to the firing ends.

2 On 1587 cc (16-valve) models, to gain access to the spark plugs, the ignition coil unit fitted in the centre of the cylinder head cover must first be removed. Disconnect the wiring connector at the left-hand end of the coil unit, then undo the retaining bolts and lift the coil unit upwards, off the spark plugs and from its location in the cylinder head cover.

3 On certain models, to improve access to some of the plugs, it may be necessary to remove the air inlet ducting (refer to the relevant Part of Chapter 4 for further information).

4 On 8-valve models, if the marks on the original-equipment spark plug (HT) leads cannot be seen, mark the leads "1" to "4", to correspond to the cylinder the lead serves (No 1 cylinder is at the transmission end of the engine). Pull the leads from the plugs by gripping the end fitting, not the lead, otherwise the lead connection may be fractured.

5 It is advisable to remove the dirt from the spark plug recesses using a clean brush, vacuum cleaner or compressed air before removing the plugs, to prevent dirt dropping into the cylinders.

6 Unscrew the plugs using a spark plug spanner, suitable box spanner or a deep socket and extension bar **(see illustration)**. Keep the socket aligned with the spark plug - if it is forcibly moved to one side, the ceramic insulator may be broken off. As each plug is removed, examine it as follows.

7 Examination of the spark plugs will give a good indication of the condition of the engine. If the insulator nose of the spark plug is clean and white, with no deposits, this is indicative of a weak mixture or too hot a plug (a hot plug transfers heat away from the electrode slowly, a cold plug transfers heat away quickly).

8 If the tip and insulator nose are covered with hard black-looking deposits, then this is indicative that the mixture is too rich. Should

the plug be black and oily, then it is likely that the engine is fairly worn, as well as the mixture being too rich.

9 If the insulator nose is covered with light tan to greyish-brown deposits, then the mixture is correct and it is likely that the engine is in good condition.

10 The spark plug electrode gap is of considerable importance as, if it is too large or too small, the size of the spark and its efficiency will be seriously impaired. The gap should be set to the value given in the Specifications at the beginning of this Chapter.

11 To set the gap, measure it with a feeler blade and then bend open, or closed, the outer plug electrode until the correct gap is achieved **(see illustration)**. The centre electrode should never be bent, as this may crack the insulator and cause plug failure, if nothing worse. If using feeler blades, the gap is correct when the appropriate-size blade is a firm sliding fit.

HAYNES HiNT

It is very often difficult to insert spark plugs into their holes without cross-threading them. To avoid this possibility, fit a short length of 5/16 inch internal diameter rubber hose over the end of the spark plug. The flexible hose acts as a universal joint to help align the plug with the plug hole. Should the plug begin to cross-thread, the hose will slip on the spark plug, preventing thread damage to the aluminium cylinder head. Remove the rubber hose, and tighten the plug to the specified torque using the spark plug socket and a torque wrench.

12 Special spark plug electrode gap adjusting tools are available from most motor accessory shops, or from some spark plug manufacturers **(see illustration)**. Read the manufacturer's information before gapping a new set of plugs; some types of plugs have specially shaped electrodes which cannot be adjusted.

13 Before fitting the spark plugs, check that the threaded connector sleeves are tight, and that the plug exterior surfaces and threads are clean **(see Haynes Hint)**.

14 Remove the rubber hose (if used), and tighten the plug to the specified torque using the spark plug socket and a torque wrench. Refit the remaining spark plugs in the same manner.

15 On 16-valve models, refit the ignition coil unit to the cylinder head cover and secure with the retaining bolts tightened securely. Reconnect the coil unit wiring connectors.

16 On 8-valve models, connect the HT leads in the correct order, and refit any components removed for access.

10 Fuel filter renewal - carburettor models

⚠ *Warning: Before carrying out the following operation, refer to the precautions given in "Safety first!" at the beginning of this manual, and follow them implicitly. Petrol is a highly-dangerous and volatile liquid, and the precautions necessary when handling it cannot be overstressed.*

1 The fuel filter is situated underneath the rear of the vehicle, adjacent to the fuel tank. To gain access to the filter, chock the front wheels, then jack up the rear of the vehicle and support it on axle stands (see *"Jacking and vehicle support"*).

2 Seal off the fuel hoses leading to and from the filter, using proprietary hose clamps, with rounded jaws - do not use G-clamps, Mole Grips or similar with flat or square jaws as these could damage the hose internally, causing leakage later.

3 Unclip the filter retaining strap from the left-hand side of the fuel tank **(see illustration)**.

4 Noting the direction of the arrow marked on the filter body, release the retaining clips or quick-release fittings and disconnect the fuel hoses from the filter (see illustration). Where the original Peugeot crimped-type clips are still fitted, cut and discard them; replace them with standard worm-drive hose clips on installation.

5 Remove the filter from the vehicle. Dispose safely of the old filter; it will be highly inflammable, and may explode if thrown on a fire.

6 Slide the new filter into position, ensuring that the arrow on the filter body is pointing in the direction of the fuel flow, as noted when removing the old filter. The flow direction can otherwise be determined by tracing the fuel hoses back along their length.

7 Connect the fuel hoses to the filter, securing them in position with their retaining clips (where applicable). Where quick-release hose unions are fitted, press each hose onto its respective filter port until it 'snaps' into position.

8 Clip the filter strap back onto the fuel tank then lower the vehicle to the ground.

9 Start the engine and check the filter hose connections for leaks.

11 Fuel pick-up filter cleaning - fuel-injected models

1 Refer to Chapter 4B, and remove the fuel pump from the tank. Remove the pick-up filter from the base of the pump (see illustration).

2 Wash the pick-up filter in fresh fuel to remove any debris from it. Inspect the filter for signs of clogging or splitting, and renew if necessary.

3 Fit the filter securely to the base of the pump, then refit the pump to the fuel tank as described in Chapter 4B.

12 Automatic transmission fluid renewal

1 Take the vehicle on a short run, to warm the transmission up to operating temperature.

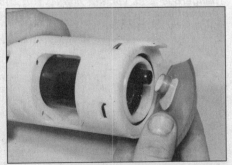

11.1 On fuel-injected models, the pick-up filter is a push fit onto the base of the pump

10.3 Release the fuel filter strap from the tank . . .

2 Park the car on level ground, then switch off the ignition and apply the handbrake firmly. Chock the rear wheels then jack up the front of the car and support it on axle stands (see "*Jacking and vehicle support*"). Note that, when refilling and checking the fluid level, the car must be lowered to the ground, and level, to ensure accuracy.

3 Remove the dipstick, then position a suitable container under the transmission. The transmission has two drain plugs: one on the sump, and another on the bottom of the differential housing (see illustration).

> ⚠ **Warning: If the fluid is hot, take precautions against scalding.**

4 Unscrew both drain plugs, and allow the fluid to drain completely into the container. Clean the drain plugs, being especially careful to wipe any metallic particles off the magnetic insert. Discard the original sealing washers; these should be renewed whenever they are disturbed.

5 When the fluid has finished draining, clean the drain plug threads and those of the transmission casing. Fit a new sealing washer to each drain plug, and refit the plugs to the transmission, tightening each securely. If the car was raised for the draining operation, now lower it to the ground. Make sure that the car is level (front-to-rear and side-to-side).

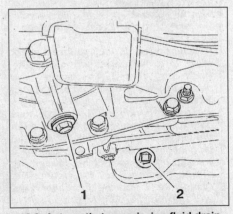

12.3 Automatic transmission fluid drain plugs (1 and 2)

10.4 . . . then detach the hoses and remove the filter. Note the direction of the arrow on the filter body (arrowed)

6 Refilling the transmission is an awkward operation, adding the specified type of fluid to the transmission a little at a time via the dipstick tube. Use a funnel with a fine-mesh gauze, to avoid spillage, and to ensure that no foreign matter enters the transmission. Allow plenty of time for the fluid level to settle properly. Fill the transmission until the level reaches the upper mark on the dipstick.

7 Once the level is up to the upper mark on the dipstick, refit the dipstick. Start the engine, and allow it to idle for a few minutes. Switch the engine off, then recheck the level, topping-up if necessary. Take the car on a moderate journey to fully distribute the new fluid around the transmission, then recheck the fluid level as described in Section 7.

13 Ignition system check

> ⚠ **Warning: Voltages produced by an electronic ignition system are considerably higher than those produced by conventional ignition systems. Extreme care must be taken when working on the system with the ignition switched on. Persons with surgically-implanted cardiac pacemaker devices should keep well clear of the ignition circuits, components and test equipment.**

1 The ignition system components should be checked for damage or deterioration as described under the relevant sub-heading.

Ignition systems incorporating a distributor

General component check

2 The spark plug (HT) leads should be checked whenever new spark plugs are fitted.

3 Ensure that the leads are numbered before removing them, to avoid confusion when refitting. Pull the leads from the plugs by gripping the end fitting, not the lead, otherwise the lead connection may be fractured.

4 Check inside the end fitting for signs of corrosion, which will look like a white crusty

1A

13.9 The rotor arm is a push fit on the distributor shaft (1360 cc model shown)

powder. Push the end fitting back onto the spark plug, ensuring that it is a tight fit on the plug. If not, remove the lead again and use pliers to carefully crimp the metal connector inside the end fitting until it fits securely on the end of the spark plug.

5 Using a clean rag, wipe the entire length of the lead to remove any built-up dirt and grease. Once the lead is clean, check for burns, cracks and other damage. Do not bend the lead excessively, nor pull the lead lengthwise - the conductor inside might break.

6 Disconnect the other end of the lead from the distributor cap. Again, pull only on the end fitting. Check for corrosion and a tight fit in the same manner as the spark plug end. If an ohmmeter is available, check the resistance of the lead by connecting the meter between the spark plug end of the lead and the segment inside the distributor cap. Refit the lead securely on completion.

7 Check the remaining leads one at a time, in the same way.

8 If new spark plug (HT) leads are required, purchase a set for your specific car and engine.

9 Unscrew its retaining screws and remove the distributor cap. Wipe it clean, and carefully inspect it inside and out for signs of cracks, black carbon tracks (tracking) and worn, burned or loose contacts; check that the cap's carbon brush is unworn, free to move against spring pressure, and making good contact with the rotor arm. Also inspect the cap seal for signs of wear or damage, and renew if necessary. Remove the rotor arm from the distributor shaft and inspect the rotor arm **(see illustration)**. It is common practice to renew the cap and rotor arm whenever new spark plug (HT) leads are fitted. When refitting, ensure that the arm is securely pressed onto the shaft, and tighten the cap retaining screws securely.

> **HAYNES HINT**
> When fitting a new distributor cap, remove the leads from the old cap one at a time, and fit them to the new cap in the exact same location - do not simultaneously remove all the leads from the old cap, or firing order confusion may occur.

10 Even with the ignition system in first-class condition, some engines may still occasionally experience poor starting attributable to damp ignition components. To disperse moisture, a water-dispersant aerosol can be very effective.

Ignition timing - check and adjustment

11 Check the ignition timing as described in Chapter 5B.

Static (distributorless) ignition systems

General component check

12 Check the condition of the HT leads as described above in paragraphs 3 to 8.

Ignition timing - check and adjustment

13 Refer to Chapter 5B.

---

14 Idle speed and mixture check and adjustment

1 Before checking the idle speed and mixture setting, always check the following first:
 a) Check the ignition timing (Chapter 5B).
 b) Check that the spark plugs are in good condition and correctly gapped (Section 9).
 c) Check that the accelerator cable and, on carburettor models, the choke cable is correctly adjusted (see relevant Part of Chapter 4).
 d) Check that the crankcase breather hoses are secure, with no leaks or kinks (Section 15).
 e) Check that the air cleaner filter element is clean (Section 22).
 f) Check that the exhaust system is in good condition (see relevant Part of Chapter 4).
 g) If the engine is running very roughly, check the compression pressures and valve clearances as described in Chapter 2A.
 h) On fuel-injected models, check that the fuel injection/ignition system warning light is not illuminated (see relevant Part of Chapter 4).

2 Take the car on a journey of sufficient length to warm it up to normal operating temperature. Proceed as described under the relevant sub-heading.

14.4a Adjusting the idle speed (screw arrowed) - 954 cc and 1124 cc carburettor models

Note: *Adjustment should be completed within two minutes of return, without stopping the engine. If this cannot be achieved, or if the radiator electric cooling fan operates, first wait for the cooling fan to stop. Clear any excess fuel from the inlet manifold by racing the engine two or three times to between 2000 and 3000 rpm, then allow it to idle again.*

Carburettor models

3 Ensure all electrical loads are switched off and the choke lever is pushed fully in; if the car does not have a tachometer (rev counter), connect one to the engine following its manufacturer's instructions. Note the idle speed, and compare it with that specified.

4 The idle speed adjusting screw is on the throttle linkage on the right-hand side of the carburettor. It may be necessary to remove a retaining clip and plastic cover to gain access to the carburettor. On 954 and 1124 cc models, the screw is easily accessible from above; on 1360 cc models, the screw is adjusted from behind the carburettor, and access is a little awkward. Using a suitable flat-bladed screwdriver, turn the idle screw in or out as necessary to obtain the specified speed **(see illustrations)**.

5 The idle mixture (exhaust gas CO level) is set at the factory, and should require no further adjustment. If, due to a change in engine characteristics (carbon build-up, bore wear etc.) or after a major carburettor overhaul, the mixture setting is lost, it can be reset. Note, however, that an exhaust gas analyser (CO meter) will be required to check the mixture, in order to set it with the necessary standard of accuracy; if this is not available, the car must be taken to a Peugeot dealer for the work to be carried out.

6 If an exhaust gas analyser is available, follow its manufacturer's instructions to check the exhaust gas CO level. If adjustment is required, it is made via the mixture adjustment screw. On 954 and 1124 cc models, the screw is located on the left hand side of the carburettor base; on 1360 cc models, it is located at the right-hand rear corner of the carburettor base. The screw is covered with a tamperproof plug to prevent unnecessary adjustment. To gain access to the screw, use a sharp instrument to hook out the plug.

14.4b Adjusting the idle speed - 1360 cc carburettor models

7 Using a suitable flat-bladed screwdriver, turn the mixture adjustment screw (in very small increments) until the CO level is correct. Turning the screw in (clockwise) weakens the mixture and reduces the CO level, turning it out will richen the mixture and increase the CO level **(see illustrations)**.

8 When adjustments are complete, disconnect any test equipment and fit a new tamperproof plug to the mixture adjustment screw. Recheck the idle speed and, if necessary, readjust.

Fuel-injected models

1360 cc (K6B engine) models without a catalytic converter

9 The idle speed is under full control of the engine management (fuel injection/ignition) ECU, and is not adjustable (see paragraph 13). However, the idle speed mixture content can be adjusted as follows.

10 The idle mixture is set at the factory, and should require no further adjustment. If, due to a change in engine characteristics (carbon build-up, bore wear etc.) the mixture setting is lost, it can be reset. Note, however, that an exhaust gas analyser (CO meter) will be required to check the mixture, in order to set it with the necessary standard of accuracy; if this is not available, the car must be taken to a Peugeot dealer for the work to be carried out.

11 If an exhaust gas analyser is available, follow its manufacturer's instructions to check the exhaust gas CO level. Adjustment is made using the screw on the mixture adjustment potentiometer, which is situated on the right-hand side of the engine compartment, on the underside of the ECU bracket. Using a suitable flat-bladed screwdriver, turn the screw (in very small increments) until the level is correct.

12 When adjustments are complete, disconnect any test equipment.

All other models

13 Experienced home mechanics with a considerable amount of skill and equipment (including a good-quality tachometer and a good-quality, carefully-calibrated exhaust gas analyser) may be able to *check* the exhaust CO level and the idle speed. However, if these are found to be in need of *adjustment*, the car **must** be taken to a suitably-equipped Peugeot dealer.

14 On later (July 1992 onwards) 1124 cc models, fitted with a Magneti Marelli G6 engine management (fuel injection/ignition) system, adjustment of the mixture setting (exhaust gas CO level) is possible, but adjustments can only be made by reprogramming the engine management ECU using special electronic test equipment which is connected to the diagnostic wiring connector (see Chapter 4B).

15 On all other vehicles, adjustments are not possible. If the idle speed and/or exhaust gas CO level is incorrect, there must be a fault in the engine management system, and the vehicle should be taken to a Peugeot dealer for testing (see relevant Part of Chapter 4).

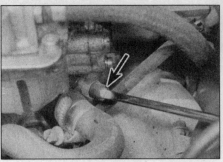

14.7a Adjusting the idle mixture/CO level (screw arrowed) - 954 cc and 1124 cc carburettor models

15 Emission control systems check

1 Details of the emission control system components are given in Chapter 4E.

2 Checking consists simply of a visual check for obvious signs of damaged or leaking hoses and joints.

3 Detailed checking and testing of the evaporative and/or exhaust emission systems (as applicable) should be entrusted to a Peugeot dealer.

16 Auxiliary drivebelt check and renewal

1 On all models, only one auxiliary drivebelt is fitted. The belt drives the alternator and (where fitted) the power steering pump or air conditioning compressor.

Checking the drivebelt condition

2 Apply the handbrake, then jack up the front of the car and support it on axle stands (see *"Jacking and vehicle support"*). Remove the right-hand front roadwheel and wheel arch liner. Where necessary, undo the retaining nut, and free the coolant hoses from the retaining clip to improve access to the crankshaft sprocket bolt.

3 Using a suitable socket and extension bar

16.8a Loosen the alternator mounting bolts, then slacken the adjuster bolt (arrowed) . . .

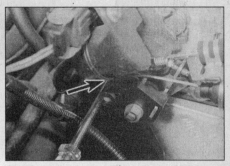

14.7b Adjusting the idle mixture/CO level (screw arrowed) - 1360 cc carburettor models

fitted to the crankshaft sprocket bolt, rotate the crankshaft so that the entire length of the drivebelt can be examined. Examine the drivebelt for cracks, splitting, fraying, or other damage. Check also for signs of glazing (shiny patches) and for separation of the belt plies. Renew the belt if worn or damaged.

4 If the condition of the belt is satisfactory, check the drivebelt tension as described below under the relevant sub-heading.

Drivebelt (models without air conditioning) - removal, refitting and tensioning

Note: *On 16-valve engines, the procedures are the same with and without air conditioning and are as described for models with air conditioning in paragraphs 17 to 29.*

Removal

5 If not already done, carry out the operations described in paragraph 2.

6 Disconnect the battery negative terminal (refer to *"Disconnecting the battery"* in the Reference Section of this manual).

7 Slacken both the alternator upper and lower mounting bolts, and the bolt securing the adjuster strap to the mounting bracket.

8 Back off the adjuster bolt to relieve the tension in the drivebelt, then slip the drivebelt from the pulleys **(see illustrations)**.

Refitting

9 Fit the belt around the pulleys, ensuring that the belt is of the correct type if it is being renewed, and take up the slack in the belt by tightening the adjuster bolt.

16.8b . . . and slip the drivebelt off its pulleys

1A

10 Tension the drivebelt as described in the following paragraphs.

Tensioning

11 If not already done, carry out the operations described in paragraph 2.

12 Correct tensioning of the drivebelt will ensure that it has a long life. Beware, however, of overtightening, as this can cause wear in the alternator bearings.

13 The belt should be tensioned so that, under firm thumb pressure, there is approximately 5.0 mm of free movement at the mid-point between the pulleys, on the longest belt run.

14 To adjust, with the upper mounting bolt just holding the alternator firm, and the lower mounting bolt loosened, turn the adjuster bolt until the correct tension is achieved. Rotate the crankshaft through two complete turns, then recheck the tension. When the tension is correct, securely tighten both the alternator mounting bolts and, where necessary, the bolt securing the adjuster strap to its mounting bracket.

15 Reconnect the battery negative terminal.

16 Clip the coolant hoses in position and secure them with the retaining nut (where removed). Refit the wheel arch liner and roadwheel, and lower the vehicle to the ground.

Drivebelt (models with air conditioning) - removal, refitting and tensioning

Removal

17 If not already done, carry out the operations described in paragraph 2.

18 Disconnect the battery negative terminal (refer to "Disconnecting the battery" in the Reference Section of this manual).

19 Slacken the two bolts securing the tensioner pulley assembly to the engine, and the lower alternator mounting bolt.

20 Rotate the adjuster bolt to move the tensioner pulley away from the drivebelt, until there is sufficient slack for the drivebelt to be removed from the pulleys.

Refitting

21 Fit the belt around the pulleys, ensuring that the belt is of the correct type if it is being renewed, and take up the slack in the belt by tightening the adjuster bolt.

22 Tension the drivebelt as described in the following paragraphs.

Tensioning

23 If not already done, carry out the operations described in paragraph 2.

24 Correct tensioning of the drivebelt will ensure that it has a long life. Beware, however, of overtightening, as this can cause wear in the alternator bearings.

25 The belt should be tensioned so that, under firm thumb pressure, there is approximately 5.0 mm of free movement at the mid-point between the pulleys, on the longest belt run.

18.2 Brake pad friction material thickness can be checked with the pads in place - ATE type caliper shown

26 To adjust the tension, with the two tensioner pulley assembly retaining bolts and the lower alternator mounting bolt slackened, rotate the adjuster bolt until the correct tension is achieved. Once the belt is correctly tensioned, rotate the crankshaft through two complete turns, and recheck the tension.

27 When the belt is correctly tensioned, securely tighten the tensioner pulley assembly retaining bolts, and the lower alternator mounting bolt.

28 Reconnect the battery negative terminal.

29 Clip the coolant hoses back in position, and secure with the retaining nut (where removed). Refit the wheel arch liner and roadwheel, and lower the vehicle to the ground.

17 Clutch adjustment check and control mechanism lubrication

1 Check that the clutch pedal moves smoothly and easily through its full travel, and that the clutch itself functions correctly, with no trace of slip or drag.

2 Adjust the clutch cable as described in Chapter 6 (where necessary).

3 If excessive effort is required to operate the clutch, check first that the cable is correctly routed and undamaged, then remove the pedal and check that its pivot is properly greased. Refer to Chapter 6 for further information.

19.6 Handbrake cable adjuster nut (arrowed)

18 Front brake pad check

1 Firmly apply the handbrake, then jack up the front of the car and support it securely on axle stands (see "Jacking and vehicle support"). Remove the front roadwheels.

2 For a quick check, the thickness of friction material remaining on each brake pad can be measured through the aperture in the caliper body (see illustration). If any pad's friction material is worn to the specified thickness or less, all four pads must be renewed as a set.

3 For a comprehensive check, the brake pads should be removed and cleaned. The operation of the caliper can then also be checked, and the condition of the brake disc itself can be fully examined on both sides. Refer to Chapter 9 for further information.

19 Handbrake check and adjustment

1 Chock the front wheels, then jack up the rear of the vehicle, and support securely on axle stands (see "Jacking and vehicle support").

2 Apply the footbrake firmly several times to establish correct shoe-to-drum clearance, then apply and release the handbrake several times to ensure that the self-adjust mechanism has compensated fully for any wear in the linings.

3 Fully release the handbrake, and check that the rear wheels rotate freely, without binding. If not, check that all cables are routed correctly, and check that the cable components and levers move freely.

> **HAYNES HiNT**
> *If the handbrake mechanism fails to operate, or appears to be seized on one side of the vehicle only, remove the relevant brake drum (see Chapter 9) and check the handbrake lever pivot on the trailing brake shoe - it is possible for the lever to seize due to corrosion. If necessary, remove the lever, and clean the contact faces of the lever, brake shoe, and pivot.*

4 If all components are free to move, but the wheels still bind when rotated, adjustment is required as follows.

5 Again, apply the footbrake several times to settle the shoes.

6 Ensure that the handbrake is fully released, then working under the vehicle, slacken the adjuster nut on the cable equaliser assembly until the drums are free to rotate (see illustration).

7 Inside the vehicle, apply the handbrake so that the lever is on its 4th notch up from the "off" position.

8 Tighten the adjuster nut until the brake shoes just rub on the drums (slight resistance as the wheels are rotated).

9 Check that there is a total handbrake lever travel of between 4 and 7 notches (the wheels should lock fully after a maximum 7 notches of handbrake lever movement).

10 Check that both the left- and right-hand rear cables move together when the handbrake is operated.

11 Fully release the handbrake, and check that both rear wheels turn freely by hand.

12 Check that the handbrake warning light illuminates from the 4th notch of handbrake lever travel.

13 On completion, lower the vehicle to the ground.

20 Hinge and lock lubrication

1 Work around the vehicle, and lubricate the hinges of the bonnet, doors and tailgate with a light machine oil.

2 Lightly lubricate the bonnet release mechanism and exposed section of inner cable with a smear of grease.

3 Check carefully the security and operation of all hinges, latches and locks, adjusting them where required. Check the operation of the central locking system (if fitted).

4 Check the condition and operation of the tailgate struts, renewing them if either is leaking or no longer able to support the tailgate securely when raised.

21 Road test

Instruments and electrical equipment

1 Check the operation of all instruments and electrical equipment.

2 Make sure that all instruments read correctly, and switch on all electrical equipment in turn to check that it functions properly.

Steering and suspension

3 Check for any abnormalities in the steering, suspension, handling or road "feel".

4 Drive the vehicle, and check that there are no unusual vibrations or noises.

5 Check that the steering feels positive, with no excessive "sloppiness" or roughness, and check for any suspension noises when cornering, or when driving over bumps.

Drivetrain

6 Check the performance of the engine, clutch, transmission and driveshafts.

7 Listen for any unusual noises from the engine, clutch and transmission.

8 Make sure that the engine runs smoothly when idling, and that there is no hesitation when accelerating.

9 Check that the clutch action is smooth and progressive, that the drive is taken up smoothly, and that the pedal travel is not excessive. Also listen for any noises when the clutch pedal is depressed.

10 Check that all gears can be engaged smoothly, without noise, and that the gear lever action is not abnormally vague or "notchy".

11 Listen for a metallic clicking sound from the front of the vehicle, as the vehicle is driven slowly in a circle with the steering on full lock. Carry out this check in both directions. If a clicking noise is heard, this indicates wear in a driveshaft joint, in which case, the complete driveshaft must be renewed (see Chapter 8).

Check the operation and performance of the braking system

12 Make sure that the vehicle does not pull to one side when braking, and that the wheels do not lock prematurely when braking hard.

13 Check that there is no vibration through the steering when braking.

14 Check that the handbrake operates correctly, without excessive movement of the lever, and that it holds the vehicle stationary on a slope.

15 Test the operation of the brake servo unit as follows. With the engine off, depress the footbrake four or five times to exhaust the vacuum. Start the engine, holding the brake pedal depressed. As the engine starts, there should be a noticeable "give" in the brake pedal as vacuum builds up. Allow the engine to run for at least two minutes, and then switch it off. If the brake pedal is depressed now, it should be possible to detect a hiss from the servo as the pedal is depressed. After about four or five applications, no further hissing should be heard, and the pedal should feel considerably firmer.

Every 24 000 miles (40 000 km)

22 Air filter renewal

954 and 1124 cc models

1 Slacken the retaining clips (where fitted) and disconnect the vacuum and breather hoses from the front of the air cleaner housing-to-carburettor/throttle body duct. Where crimped-type hose clips or ties are fitted, cut and discard them; replace them with standard worm-drive hose clips or new cable ties on refitting.

2 Slacken the retaining clips, then lift the duct off the top of the carburettor/throttle body and air cleaner housing. Disconnect the air temperature control valve hose from the end of the duct, and remove the duct from the engine compartment. Recover the rubber sealing ring(s) from the top of the carburettor /throttle body and/or air cleaner housing (as applicable).

3 Release the retaining clips securing the lid to the top of the air cleaner housing. Lift the lid away from the housing, and recover the sealing ring (see illustration). On some models, it will be necessary to twist the lid to release it. Inspect the sealing ring for signs of damage or deterioration, and renew if necessary.

4 Where the air filter element is not an integral part of the lid, lift the element out of the housing (see illustration). Fit the new element, making sure it is correctly positioned in the housing.

5 Fit the sealing ring to the housing, then refit the lid and secure it in position with the retaining clips.

6 Refit the air cleaner-to-carburettor/throttle body duct. Ensure that the duct is correctly seated on its sealing rings, and securely tighten its retaining clips.

7 Reconnect the vacuum and breather hoses to the duct, and secure them in position with the retaining clips (where fitted).

22.3 Release the air cleaner lid retaining clips and lift off the lid

22.4 On some models, the air cleaner element is available separately from the air cleaner lid

1A

1294 cc models

8 Slacken the retaining clip, and disconnect the intake duct from the side of the air cleaner housing.
9 Release the retaining clips, then remove the cover from the housing. Withdraw the filter element, noting which way around it is fitted.
10 Fit the new element, ensuring that it is fitted the correct way around and is correctly seated in the housing. Install the cover, and secure it in position with the retaining clips.
11 Reconnect the intake duct, and securely tighten its retaining clip.

1360 cc carburettor and single-point injection petrol models

12 Refer to the information given in paragraphs 1 to 7.

1360 cc multi-point injection petrol models, and all 1587 cc models

13 Slacken the retaining clip, and disconnect the intake duct from the air cleaner housing lid.
14 Release the retaining clips (where fitted), then unclip the lid and position it clear of the housing.

15 Recover the sealing ring from the top of the filter housing, and lift the element out of the housing. Inspect the sealing ring for signs of damage or deterioration, and renew if necessary.
16 Fit the new element, making sure it is correctly seated in the housing.
17 Refit the sealing ring to the top of the housing, and securely refit the housing lid. Where necessary, secure the lid in position with its retaining clips.
18 Reconnect the intake duct, and securely tighten its retaining clip.

Every 36 000 miles (60 000 km) or 4 years

23 Rear brake shoe condition check - models with rear drum brakes

1 Remove the rear brake drums, and check the brake shoes for signs of wear or contamination. At the same time, also inspect the wheel cylinders for signs of leakage, and the brake drum for signs of wear. Refer to the relevant Sections of Chapter 9 for further information.

24 Rear brake pad condition check - models with rear disc brakes

1 Chock the front wheels then jack up the rear of the vehicle and support it on axle stands (see "Jacking and vehicle support"). Remove the rear roadwheels.
2 For a quick check, the thickness of friction material remaining on each brake pad can be measured through the top of the caliper body. If any pad's friction material is worn to the specified thickness or less, all four pads must be renewed as a set.
3 For a comprehensive check, the brake pads should be removed and cleaned. This will permit the operation of the caliper to be checked, and the condition of the brake disc itself to be fully examined on both sides. Refer to Chapter 9 for further information.

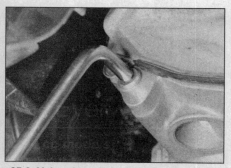

25.2 Using the square-section wrench to unscrew the transmission filler/level plug

25 Manual transmission oil level check

Note: *A suitable square-section wrench may be required to undo the transmission filler/level plug on some models. These wrenches can be obtained from most motor factors or your Peugeot dealer.*

1 Park the car on a level surface. The oil level must be checked before the car is driven, or at least 5 minutes after the engine has been switched off.

> **HAYNES HiNT** *If the oil is checked immediately after driving the car, some of the oil will remain distributed around the transmission components, resulting in an inaccurate level reading.*

2 Wipe clean the area around the filler/level plug, which is situated on the left-hand end of the transmission **(see illustration)**. Unscrew the plug and clean it; discard the sealing washer.
3 The oil level should reach the lower edge of the filler/level hole. A certain amount of oil will have gathered behind the filler/level plug, and will trickle out when it is removed; this does **not** necessarily indicate that the level is correct. To ensure that a true level is established, wait until the initial trickle has

25.3 Topping-up the transmission oil level

stopped, then add oil as necessary until a trickle of new oil can be seen emerging **(see illustration)**. The level will be correct when the flow ceases; use only good-quality oil of the specified type.
4 Filling the transmission with oil is an extremely awkward operation; above all, allow plenty of time for the oil level to settle properly before checking it. If a large amount is added to the transmission, and a large amount flows out on checking the level, refit the filler/level plug and take the vehicle on a short journey so that the new oil is distributed fully around the transmission components, then recheck the level when it has settled again.
5 If the transmission has been overfilled so that oil flows out as soon as the filler/level plug is removed, check that the car is completely level (front-to-rear and side-to-side), and allow the surplus to drain off into a suitable container.
6 When the level is correct, fit a new sealing washer to the filler/level plug. Refit the plug, tightening it to the specified torque wrench setting. Wash off any spilt oil.

26 Fuel filter renewal - fuel-injected models

⚠ **Warning: Before carrying out the following operation, refer to the precautions given in "Safety first!" at the beginning of this manual, and follow them implicitly. Petrol is a highly-dangerous and volatile liquid, and the precautions necessary when handling it cannot be overstressed.**

1 Refer to the information given for carburettor models in Section 10, noting that it will be necessary to depressurise the fuel system before the fuel hoses are disconnected from the filter (see relevant Part of Chapter 4).

27 Timing belt renewal

Refer to Chapter 2A.

Every 2 years (regardless of mileage)

28 Coolant renewal

Cooling system draining

⚠️ **Warning: Wait until the engine is cold before starting this procedure. Do not allow antifreeze to come in contact with your skin, or with the painted surfaces of the vehicle. Rinse off spills immediately with plenty of water. Never leave antifreeze lying around in an open container, or in a puddle in the driveway or on the garage floor. Children and pets are attracted by its sweet smell, but antifreeze can be fatal if ingested.**

1 With the engine completely cold, remove the expansion tank filler cap. Turn the cap anti-clockwise until it reaches the first stop. Wait until any pressure remaining in the system is released, then push the cap down, turn it anti-clockwise to the second stop, and lift it off.

2 Position a suitable container beneath the coolant drain outlet at the lower left-hand side of the radiator.

3 Loosen the drain plug (there is no need to remove it completely) and allow the coolant to drain into the container. If desired, a length of tubing can be fitted to the drain outlet to direct the flow of coolant during draining.

4 To assist draining, open the cooling system bleed screws. These are located in the coolant gallery or hose (as applicable) at the right-hand side of the engine compartment, in the thermostat housing, and in the top left-hand side of the radiator.

5 When the flow of coolant stops, reposition the container below the cylinder block drain plug, located at the front left-hand corner of the cylinder block.

6 Remove the drain plug, and allow the coolant to drain into the container.

7 If the coolant has been drained for a reason other than renewal, then provided it is clean and less than two years old, it can be re-used, though this is not recommended.

8 Refit the radiator and cylinder block drain plugs on completion of draining.

Cooling system flushing

9 If coolant renewal has been neglected, or if the antifreeze mixture has become diluted, then in time, the cooling system may gradually lose efficiency, as the coolant passages become restricted due to rust, scale deposits, and other sediment. The cooling system efficiency can be restored by flushing the system clean.

10 The radiator should be flushed independently of the engine, to avoid unnecessary contamination.

Radiator flushing

11 To flush the radiator, first tighten the radiator drain plug, and the radiator bleed screw, where applicable.

12 Disconnect the top and bottom hoses from the radiator with reference to Chapter 3.

13 Insert a garden hose into the radiator top inlet. Direct a flow of clean water through the radiator, and continue flushing until clean water emerges from the radiator bottom outlet.

14 If after a reasonable period, the water still does not run clear, the radiator can be flushed with a good proprietary cleaning agent. It is important that their manufacturer's instructions are followed carefully. If the contamination is particularly bad, insert the hose in the radiator bottom outlet, and reverse-flush the radiator.

Engine flushing

15 To flush the engine, first refit the cylinder block drain plug, and tighten the cooling system bleed screws.

16 Remove the thermostat as described in Chapter 3, then temporarily refit the thermostat cover.

17 With the top and bottom hoses disconnected from the radiator, insert a garden hose into the radiator top hose. Direct a clean flow of water through the engine, and continue flushing until clean water emerges from the radiator bottom hose.

18 On completion of flushing, refit the thermostat and reconnect the hoses with reference to Chapter 3.

Cooling system filling

19 Before attempting to fill the cooling system, make sure that all hoses and clips are in good condition, and that the clips are tight. Note that an antifreeze mixture must be used all year round, to prevent corrosion of the engine components (see following sub-Section). Also check that the radiator and cylinder block drain plugs are in place and tight.

20 Remove the expansion tank filler cap.

21 Open all the cooling system bleed screws (see paragraph 4).

22 Some of the cooling system hoses are positioned at a higher level than the top of the radiator expansion tank. It is therefore necessary to use a "header tank" when refilling the cooling system, to reduce the possibility of air being trapped in the system. Although Peugeot dealers use a special header tank, the same effect can be achieved by using a suitable bottle, with a seal between the bottle and the expansion tank.

23 Fit the "header tank" to the expansion tank and slowly fill the system. Coolant will emerge from each of the bleed screws in turn, starting with the lowest screw. As soon as coolant free from air bubbles emerges from the lowest screw, tighten that screw, and watch the next bleed screw in the system. Repeat the procedure until the coolant is emerging from the highest bleed screw in the cooling system and all bleed screws are securely tightened. Note that the bleed screws should be tightened in the following order:

a) Radiator bleed screw (petrol models only).
b) Thermostat housing bleed screw.
c) Coolant gallery or hose (as applicable) bleed screw.

24 Ensure that the "header tank" is full (at least 0.5 litres of coolant). Start the engine, and run it at a fast idle speed (do not exceed 2000 rpm) until the cooling fan cuts in, and then cuts out. Stop the engine.

25 Allow the engine to cool, then remove the "header tank".

⚠️ **Warning: Take great care not to scald yourself with the hot coolant.**

26 When the engine has cooled, check the coolant level as described in "Weekly checks". Top-up the level if necessary, and refit the expansion tank cap.

Antifreeze mixture

27 The antifreeze should always be renewed at the specified intervals. This is necessary not only to maintain the antifreeze properties, but also to prevent corrosion which would otherwise occur as the corrosion inhibitors become progressively less effective.

28 Always use an ethylene-glycol based antifreeze which is suitable for use in mixed-metal cooling systems. The quantity of antifreeze and levels of protection are indicated in the Specifications.

29 Before adding antifreeze, the cooling system should be completely drained, preferably flushed, and all hoses checked for condition and security.

30 After filling with antifreeze, a label should be attached to the expansion tank, stating the type and concentration of antifreeze used, and the date installed. Any subsequent topping-up should be made with the same type and concentration of antifreeze.

31 Do not use engine antifreeze in the windscreen/tailgate washer system, as it will cause damage to the vehicle paintwork. A screenwash additive should be added to the washer system in the quantities stated on the bottle..

29 Brake fluid renewal

⚠️ **Warning: Brake hydraulic fluid can harm your eyes and damage painted surfaces, so use extreme caution when handling and pouring it. Do not use fluid that has been standing open for some time, as it absorbs moisture from the air. Excess moisture can cause a dangerous loss of braking effectiveness.**

1A

1 The procedure is similar to that for the bleeding of the hydraulic system as described in Chapter 9, except that the brake fluid reservoir should be emptied by siphoning, using a clean poultry baster or similar before starting, and allowance should be made for the old fluid to be expelled when bleeding a section of the circuit.

2 Working as described in Chapter 9, open the first bleed screw in the sequence, and pump the brake pedal gently until nearly all the old fluid has been emptied from the master cylinder reservoir.

 Old hydraulic fluid is invariably much darker in colour than the new, making it easy to distinguish the two.

3 Top-up to the "MAX" level with new fluid, and continue pumping until only the new fluid remains in the reservoir, and new fluid can be seen emerging from the bleed screw. Tighten the screw, and top the reservoir level up to the "MAX" level line.

4 Work through all the remaining bleed screws in the sequence until new fluid can be seen at all of them. Be careful to keep the master cylinder reservoir topped-up to above the "MIN" level at all times, or air may enter the system and greatly increase the length of the task.

5 When the operation is complete, check that all bleed screws are securely tightened, and that their dust caps are refitted. Wash off all traces of spilt fluid, and recheck the master cylinder reservoir fluid level.

6 Check the operation of the brakes before taking the car on the road.

Chapter 1 Part B:
Routine maintenance and servicing - diesel models

Contents

Degrees of difficulty

Easy, suitable for novice with little experience		**Fairly easy,** suitable for beginner with some experience		**Fairly difficult,** suitable for competent DIY mechanic		**Difficult,** suitable for experienced DIY mechanic		**Very difficult,** suitable for expert DIY or professional

Lubricants and fluids

Refer to *"Weekly checks"*

Capacities

Engine oil

TUD3 engines:
Excluding filter	3.2 litres
Including filter	3.5 litres

TUD5 engines:
Excluding filter	4.25 litres
Including filter	4.55 litres

Cooling system	6.0 litres (approximately)
Transmission	2.0 litres
Power-assisted steering	1.7 litres (approximately)
Fuel tank	45.0 litres

Washer reservoirs

Windscreen washers only	1.5 litres
Windscreen and tailgate washers	2.8 litres
Headlight washer reservoir	5.6 litres

Cooling system

Antifreeze mixture:
28% antifreeze	Protection down to -15°C
50% antifreeze	Protection down to -30°C

Note: *Refer to antifreeze manufacturer for latest recommendations.*

Fuel system

Idle speed:
TUD 3 engines	780 ± 20 rpm
TUD 5 engines before July 1996 - Lucas pump	775 ± 25 rpm
TUD 5 engines from July 1996, without air conditioning	775 ± 100 rpm
TUD 5 engines from July 1996, with air conditioning	850 ± 25 rpm

Anti-stall speed:
TUD 3 (with 1.0 mm shim/feeler blade inserted)	1600 rpm

TUD 5:
Lucas pump (with 1.5 mm shim/feeler blade inserted)	1600 ± 100 rpm
Bosch pump (with 1.0 mm shim/feeler blade inserted)	825 ± 100 rpm

Brakes

Brake pad friction material minimum thickness	2.0 mm
Brake shoe friction material minimum thickness	1.5 mm

Tyre pressures

See end of *"Weekly checks"*

Torque wrench settings

	Nm	lbf ft
Roadwheel bolts	85	63
Transmission filler/level and drain plugs	25	18

The maintenance intervals in this manual are provided with the assumption that you, not the dealer, will be carrying out the work. These are the minimum maintenance intervals based on the schedule recommended by us for vehicles driven daily. If you wish to keep your vehicle in peak condition at all times, you may wish to perform some of these procedures more often. We encourage frequent maintenance, because it enhances the efficiency, performance and resale value of your vehicle.

If the vehicle is driven in dusty areas, used to tow a trailer, or driven frequently at slow speeds (idling in traffic) or on short journeys, more frequent maintenance intervals are recommended. Peugeot actually recommend that the service intervals are halved for vehicles which are used under these conditions.

When the vehicle is new, it should be serviced by a factory-authorised dealer service department, in order to preserve the factory warranty.

Every 250 miles (400 km) or weekly

☐ Refer to "Weekly checks"

Every 6000 miles (10 000 km) or 12 months - whichever comes first

☐ Renew the engine oil and filter (Section 3).
☐ Drain any water from the fuel filter (Section 4).
☐ Check all underbonnet components for fluid leaks (Section 5).
☐ Check the steering and suspension components (Section 6).
☐ Check the condition of the driveshaft rubber gaiters (Section 7).

Every 12 000 miles (20 000 km)

In addition to all the items listed above, carry out the following:
☐ Check the air conditioning system refrigerant - where applicable (Section 8).
☐ Clean the fuel pick-up filter (Section 9).
☐ Check the idle speed and anti-stall speed (Section 10).
☐ Check the emission control system hoses and components (Section 11).
☐ Check the auxiliary drivebelt, and renew if necessary (Section 12).
☐ Check the clutch adjustment (Section 13).
☐ Lubricate the clutch control mechanism (Section 13).
☐ Check the front brake pads, and renew if necessary (Section 14).
☐ Check the operation of the handbrake (Section 15).
☐ Renew the fuel filter (Section 16).
☐ Lubricate all hinges and locks (Section 17).
☐ Carry out a road test (Section 18).

Every 24 000 miles (40 000 km)

In addition to all the items listed above, carry out the following:
☐ Renew the air filter – at 36,000 miles for 1994-on models (Section 19).

Every 36 000 miles (60 000 km) or 4 years - whichever comes first

In addition to all the items listed above, carry out the following:
☐ Check the condition of the rear drum brake shoes (Section 20).
☐ Check the manual transmission oil level (Section 21).
☐ Renew the timing belt (Section 22).*

*Note: Although the normal interval for timing belt renewal is 72 000 miles (120 000 km), it is strongly recommended that the interval is halved to 36 000 miles (60 000 km) on vehicles which are subjected to intensive use, ie. mainly short journeys or a lot of stop-start driving. The actual belt renewal interval is therefore very much up to the individual owner, but bear in mind that severe engine damage will result if the belt breaks.

Every 72 000 miles (120 000 km)

In addition to all the items listed above, carry out the following:
☐ Renew the timing belt (Section 22).*

*This is the interval recommended by Peugeot, but we recommend that the belt is changed more frequently, at 36 000 miles - see above.

Every 2 years (regardless of mileage)

☐ Renew the coolant (Section 23).
☐ Renew the brake fluid (Section 24).

1B

Underbonnet view of a 1360 cc (TUD3 engine) model

1 Engine oil filler cap
2 Engine oil dipstick
3 Battery earth (negative) terminal
4 Master cylinder/brake fluid reservoir
5 Auxiliary fusebox
6 Fuel injection pump
7 Expansion tank filler cap
8 Braking system vacuum pump
9 Washer fluid reservoir filler cap
10 Braking system vacuum servo unit
11 Preheating control unit
12 Relay box
13 Suspension strut upper mounting
14 Air cleaner housing
15 Fuel system priming bulb

Front underbody view - 1360 cc model

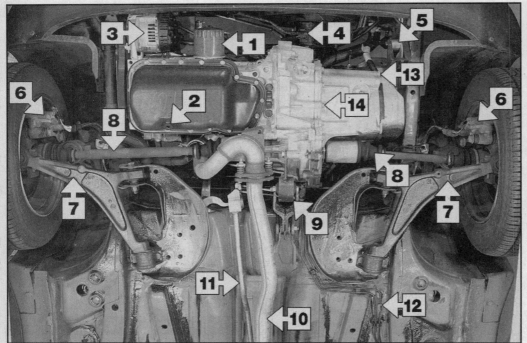

1 Oil filter
2 Sump drain plug
3 Alternator
4 Radiator cooling fan
5 Horn
6 Brake caliper
7 Lower arm
8 Driveshaft
9 Engine/transmission rear mounting
10 Exhaust system
11 Gearchange linkage selector rod
12 Brake pipes
13 Transmission filler/level plug
14 Transmission drain plug

Rear underbody view - petrol model shown (diesel model similar)

1 Spare wheel
2 Fuel tank
3 Handbrake cable
4 Fuel filter
5 Tailpipe
6 Rear shock absorber
7 Rear suspension tubular crossmember
8 Torsion bar
9 Rear axle mounting bracket
10 Torsion bar
11 Trailing arm
12 Fuel tank filler hose

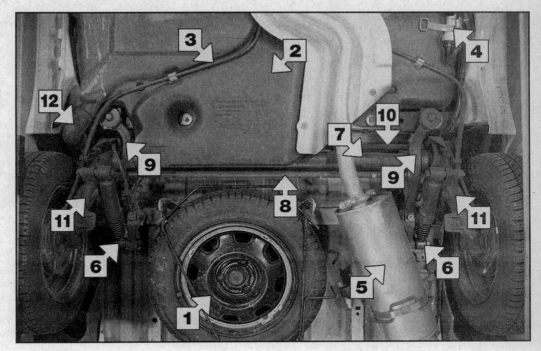

Maintenance procedures

1 General information

This Chapter is designed to help the home mechanic maintain his/her vehicle for safety, economy, long life and peak performance.

The Chapter contains a master maintenance schedule, followed by Sections dealing specifically with each task in the schedule. Visual checks, adjustments, component renewal and other helpful items are included. Refer to the accompanying illustrations of the engine compartment and the underside of the vehicle for the locations of the various components.

Servicing your vehicle in accordance with the mileage/time maintenance schedule and the following Sections will provide a planned maintenance programme, which should result in a long and reliable service life. This is a comprehensive plan, so maintaining some items but not others at the specified service intervals, will not produce the same results.

As you service your vehicle, you will discover that many of the procedures can - and should - be grouped together, because of the particular procedure being performed, or because of the proximity of two otherwise-unrelated components to one another. For example, if the vehicle is raised for any reason, the exhaust can be inspected at the same time as the suspension and steering components.

The first step in this maintenance programme is to prepare yourself before the actual work begins. Read through all the Sections relevant to the work to be carried out, then make a list and gather all the parts and tools required. If a problem is encountered, seek advice from a parts specialist, or a dealer service department.

2 Regular maintenance

1 If, from the time the vehicle is new, the routine maintenance schedule is followed closely, and frequent checks are made of fluid levels and high-wear items, as suggested throughout this manual, the engine will be kept in relatively good running condition, and the need for additional work will be minimised.
2 It is possible that there will be times when the engine is running poorly due to the lack of regular maintenance. This is even more likely if a used vehicle, which has not received regular and frequent maintenance checks, is purchased. In such cases, additional work may need to be carried out, outside of the regular maintenance intervals.
3 If engine wear is suspected, a compression test or leakdown test (refer to the relevant Part of Chapter 2) will provide valuable information regarding the overall performance of the main internal components. Such a test can be used as a basis to decide on the extent of the work to be carried out. If, for example, a compression or

leakdown test indicates serious internal engine wear, conventional maintenance as described in this Chapter will not greatly improve the performance of the engine, and may prove a waste of time and money, unless extensive overhaul work (Chapter 2C) is carried out first.
4 The following series of operations are those most often required to improve the performance of a generally poor-running engine:

Primary operations

a) Clean, inspect and test the battery (See "Weekly checks").
b) Check all the engine-related fluids (see "Weekly checks").
c) Check the condition and tension of the auxiliary drivebelt (Section 12).
d) Check the condition of the air filter, and renew if necessary (Section 19).
e) Check the fuel filter (Sections 4 and 16).
f) Clean the fuel pick-up filter (Section 9).
g) Check the condition of all hoses, and check for fluid leaks (Section 5).
h) Check the idle speed and anti-stall speed (Section 10).

5 If the above operations do not prove fully effective, carry out the following secondary operations:

Secondary operations

All items listed under "Primary operations", plus the following:

a) Check the charging system (Chapter 5A).
b) Check the preheating system (Chapter 5C).
c) Check the fuel system (Chapter 4D).

1B

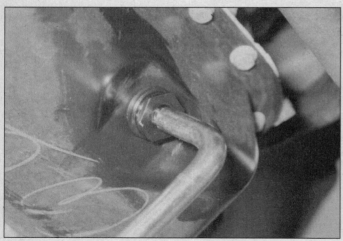

3.3 Slackening the sump drain plug with a square-section wrench

3.7 Using an oil filter removal tool to slacken the oil filter

Every 6000 miles (10 000 km) or 12 months

3 Engine oil and filter renewal

Note: *A suitable square-section wrench may be required on some models to undo the sump drain plug. These wrenches can be obtained from most motor factors or your Peugeot dealer.*

1 Frequent oil and filter changes are among the most important preventative maintenance procedures for the DIY owner. As engine oil ages, it becomes diluted and contaminated, which leads to premature engine wear.

2 Before starting this procedure, gather together all the necessary tools and materials. Also make sure that you have plenty of clean rags and newspapers handy, to mop up any spills. Ideally, the engine oil should be warm, as it will drain better, and more built-up sludge will be removed with it. Take care, however, not to touch the exhaust or any other hot parts of the engine when working under the vehicle. To avoid any possibility of scalding, and to protect yourself from possible skin irritants and other harmful contaminants in used engine oils, it is advisable to wear gloves when carrying out this work. Access to the underside of the vehicle will be greatly improved if it can be raised on a lift, driven onto ramps, or jacked up and supported on axle stands (see *"Jacking and Vehicle Support"*). Whichever method is chosen, make sure that the vehicle remains level, or if it is at an angle, that the drain plug is at the lowest point.

3 Slacken the drain plug about half a turn; on some models, a square-section wrench may be needed to slacken the plug **(see illustration)**. Position the draining container under the drain plug, then remove the plug completely. If possible, try to keep the plug pressed into the

sump while unscrewing it by hand the last couple of turns. As the plug releases from the threads, move it away sharply so the stream of oil issuing from the sump runs into the container, not up your sleeve! Recover the sealing ring from the drain plug.

4 Allow some time for the old oil to drain, noting that it may be necessary to reposition the container as the oil flow slows to a trickle.

5 After all the oil has drained, wipe off the drain plug with a clean rag, and fit a new sealing washer. Clean the area around the drain plug opening, and refit the plug. Tighten the plug securely.

6 If the filter is also to be renewed, move the container into position under the oil filter, which is located on the front side of the cylinder block, below the inlet manifold.

7 Using an oil filter removal tool if necessary, slacken the filter initially, then unscrew it by hand the rest of the way **(see illustration)**. Empty the oil in the old filter into the container.

8 Use a clean rag to remove all oil, dirt and sludge from the filter sealing area on the engine. Check the old filter to make sure that the rubber sealing ring hasn't stuck to the engine. If it has, carefully remove it.

9 Apply a light coating of clean engine oil to the sealing ring on the new filter, then screw it into position on the engine. Tighten the filter firmly by hand only - **do not** use any tools.

10 Remove the old oil and all tools from under the car, then lower the car to the ground (if applicable).

11 Remove the dipstick, then unscrew the oil filler cap from the cylinder head cover. Fill the engine, using the correct grade and type of oil (see *"Weekly checks"*). An oil can spout or funnel may help to reduce spillage. Pour in half the specified quantity of oil first, then wait a few minutes for the oil to fall to the sump. Continue adding oil a small quantity at a time

until the level is up to the lower mark on the dipstick. Adding approximately 1.5 litres will bring the level up to the upper mark on the dipstick. Refit the filler cap.

12 Start the engine and run it for a few minutes; check for leaks around the oil filter seal and the sump drain plug. Note that there may be a brief delay before the oil pressure warning light goes out when the engine is first started, as the oil circulates through the engine oil galleries and the new oil filter (where fitted) before the pressure builds up.

13 Switch off the engine, and wait a few minutes for the oil to settle in the sump once more. With the new oil circulated and the filter completely full, recheck the level on the dipstick, and add more oil as necessary.

14 Dispose of the used engine oil safely, with reference to *"General repair procedures"*.

4 Fuel filter water draining

1 A water drain screw and tube are provided at the base of the fuel filter **(see illustration)**.

4.1 Fuel filter drain screw (battery removed for clarity)

2 Place a suitable container beneath the drain tube, and cover the clutch bellhousing.

3 Open the drain screw by turning it anticlockwise, and allow fuel and water to drain until fuel, free from water, emerges from the end of the tube. Close the drain screw, and tighten it securely.

4 Dispose of the drained fuel safely.

5 Start the engine. If difficulty is experienced, bleed the fuel system (see Chapter 4D).

5 Hose and fluid leak check

1 Visually inspect the engine joint faces, gaskets and seals for any signs of water or oil leaks. Pay particular attention to the areas around the camshaft cover, cylinder head, oil filter and sump joint faces. Bear in mind that, over a period of time, some very slight seepage from these areas is to be expected - what you are really looking for is any indication of a serious leak. Should a leak be found, renew the gasket or oil seal by referring to the appropriate Chapters in this manual.

2 Also check the security and condition of all the engine-related pipes and hoses. Ensure that all cable ties or securing clips are in place, and in good condition. Clips which are broken or missing can lead to chafing of the hoses, pipes or wiring, which could cause more serious problems in the future.

3 Carefully check the radiator hoses and heater hoses along their entire length. Renew any hose which is cracked, swollen or deteriorated. Cracks will show up better if the hose is squeezed. Pay close attention to the hose clips that secure the hoses to the cooling system components. Hose clips can pinch and puncture hoses, resulting in cooling system leaks. If the original Peugeot crimped-type hose clips are used, it may be a good idea to replace them with standard worm-drive clips.

4 Inspect all the cooling system components (hoses, joint faces etc.) for leaks.

HAYNES HINT *A leak in the cooling system will usually show up as white- or rust-coloured, crusty deposits around the area of the leak*

5 Where any problems are found on system components, renew the component or gasket with reference to Chapter 3.

6 With the vehicle raised, inspect the fuel tank and filler neck for punctures, cracks and other damage. The connection between the filler neck and tank is especially critical. Sometimes a rubber filler neck or connecting hose will leak due to loose retaining clamps or deteriorated rubber.

7 Carefully check all rubber hoses and metal fuel lines leading away from the fuel tank. Check for loose connections, deteriorated hoses, crimped lines, and other damage. Pay particular attention to the vent pipes and hoses, which often loop up around the filler neck and can become blocked or crimped. Follow the lines to the front of the vehicle, carefully inspecting them all the way. Renew damaged sections as necessary.

8 From within the engine compartment, check the security of all fuel hose attachments and pipe unions, and inspect the fuel hoses and vacuum hoses for kinks, chafing and deterioration.

9 Where applicable, check the condition of the power steering fluid hoses and pipes.

6 Steering and suspension check

Front suspension and steering check

1 Raise the front of the vehicle, and securely support it on axle stands (see *"Jacking and vehicle support"*).

2 Inspect the balljoint dust covers and the steering rack-and-pinion gaiters for splits, chafing or damage. Any wear of these parts will cause loss of lubricant, together with dirt and water entry, resulting in rapid deterioration of the balljoints or steering gear.

3 On models with power steering, check the fluid hoses for chafing or damage, and the pipe and hose unions for leaks. Also check for signs of leakage under pressure from the steering gear rubber gaiters, which would indicate failed fluid seals within the steering gear.

4 Grasp the roadwheel at the 12 o'clock and 6 o'clock positions, and try to rock it. Very slight free play may be felt, but if the movement is appreciable, further investigation is necessary to determine the source. Continue rocking the wheel while an assistant depresses the footbrake. If the movement is now eliminated or significantly reduced, it is likely that the hub bearings are at fault. If the free play is still evident with the footbrake depressed, then there is wear in the suspension joints or mountings.

5 Now grasp the wheel at the 9 o'clock and 3 o'clock positions, and try to rock it as before. Any movement felt now may again be caused by wear in the hub bearings or the steering track-rod balljoints. If the inner or outer balljoint is worn, the movement will be obvious.

6 Using a large screwdriver or flat bar, check for wear in the suspension mounting bushes by levering between the relevant suspension component and its attachment point. Some movement is to be expected as the mountings

are made of rubber, but excessive wear should be obvious. Also check the condition of any visible rubber bushes, looking for splits, cracks or contamination of the rubber.

7 With the car standing on its wheels, have an assistant turn the steering wheel back and forth about an eighth of a turn each way. There should be very little, if any, lost movement between the steering wheel and roadwheels. If this is not the case, closely observe the joints and mountings previously described, but in addition, check the steering column universal joints for wear, and the steering gear itself.

Suspension strut/shock absorber check

8 Check for any signs of fluid leakage around the suspension strut/shock absorber body, or from the rubber gaiter around the piston rod. Should any fluid be noticed, the suspension strut/shock absorber is defective internally, and should be renewed.

Note: *Suspension struts/shock absorbers should always be renewed in pairs on the same axle.*

9 The efficiency of the suspension strut/shock absorber may be checked by bouncing the vehicle at each corner. Generally speaking, the body will return to its normal position and stop after being depressed. If it rises and returns on a rebound, the suspension strut/shock absorber is probably suspect. Examine also the suspension strut/shock absorber upper and lower mountings for any signs of wear.

7 Driveshaft gaiter check

1 With the vehicle raised and securely supported on stands (see *"Jacking and vehicle support"*), turn the steering onto full lock, then slowly rotate the roadwheel. Inspect the condition of the outer constant velocity (CV) joint rubber gaiters, squeezing the gaiters to open out the folds. Check for signs of cracking, splits or deterioration of the rubber, which may allow the grease to escape, and lead to water and grit entry into the joint. Also check the security and condition of the retaining clips. Repeat these checks on the inner CV joints. If any damage or deterioration is found, the gaiters should be renewed (see Chapter 8).

2 At the same time, check the general condition of the CV joints themselves by first holding the driveshaft and attempting to rotate the wheel. Repeat this check by holding the inner joint and attempting to rotate the driveshaft. Any appreciable movement indicates wear in the joints, wear in the driveshaft splines, or a loose driveshaft retaining nut.

1B

Every 12 000 miles (20 000 km)

8 Air conditioning system refrigerant check

 Warning: The system should be drained and recharged only by a Peugeot dealer or air conditioning specialist. Do not attempt to carry out the work yourself, as the refrigerant is a highly-dangerous substance (refer to Chapter 3).

1 In order to check the condition of the refrigerant, a humidity indicator and a sight glass are provided on top of the drier bottle, located in the front, right-hand corner of the engine compartment **(see illustration)**.

Refrigerant humidity check

2 Check the colour of the humidity indicator. Blue indicates that the condition of the refrigerant is satisfactory. Red indicates that the refrigerant is saturated with humidity. If the indicator shows red, the system should be drained and recharged, and a new drier bottle should be fitted.

 Warning: Do not attempt to open the refrigerant circuit. Refer to the precautions in Chapter 3.

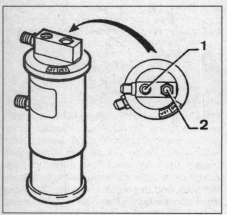

8.1 Air conditioning drier bottle sight glass (1) and humidity indicator (2)

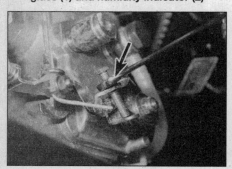

10.5a Slacken the locknut (location arrowed) . . .

Refrigerant flow check

3 Run the engine, and switch on the air conditioning.

4 After a few minutes, inspect the sight glass, and check the fluid flow. Clear fluid should be visible - if not, the following will help to diagnose the problem:

a) Clear fluid flow - the system is functioning correctly.

b) No fluid flow - have the system checked for leaks by a Peugeot dealer or air conditioning specialist.

c) Continuous stream of clear air bubbles in fluid - refrigerant level low - have the system recharged by a Peugeot dealer or air conditioning specialist.

d) Milky air bubbles visible - high humidity (see paragraph 2).

9 Fuel pick-up filter cleaning

1 Remove the fuel pick-up unit from the tank as described in Chapter 4D. Remove the filter from the base of the pick-up unit **(see illustration)**.

2 Wash the pick-up filter in fresh fuel to remove any debris from it. Inspect the filter for signs of clogging or splitting, and renew if necessary.

3 Fit the filter securely to the base of the pickup unit, then refit the unit to the fuel tank as described in Chapter 4B.

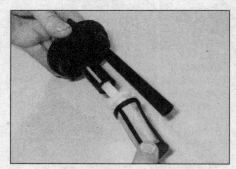

9.1 The filter is clipped onto the base of the fuel pick-up unit

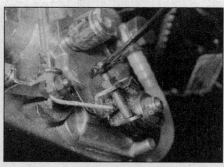

10.5b . . . then turn the idle speed screw as necessary

10 Idle speed and anti-stall speed check and adjustment

1 The usual type of tachometer (rev counter), which works from ignition system pulses, cannot be used on diesel engines. A diagnostic socket is provided for the use of Peugeot test equipment, but this will not normally be available to the home mechanic. If it is not felt that adjusting the idle speed "by ear" is satisfactory, it will be necessary to purchase or hire an appropriate tachometer, or else leave the task to a Peugeot dealer or other suitably equipped specialist.

2 Before making adjustments, warm up the engine to normal operating temperature. Make sure that the accelerator cable and fast idle cables are correctly adjusted as described in Chapter 4D.

Idle speed - check and adjustment

3 Start the engine and check that the engine idles at the specified speed. If necessary, adjustments can be made using the idle speed adjustment screw on the top of the pump.

4 On versions equipped with a Bosch pump, loosen the anti-stall adjustment screw until it just loses contact with the pump accelerator lever.

5 Loosen the locknut, then adjust the screw (as necessary) until the position is found where the engine is idling at the specified speed **(see illustrations)**. Once the screw is correctly positioned, securely tighten the locknut.

6 Check the anti-stall adjustment as described below.

Anti-stall - check and adjustment

7 Adjust the idle speed as described above, then switch off the engine.

8 Insert a shim or feeler blade of the correct thickness (see Specifications), between the pump accelerator lever and the anti-stall adjustment screw **(see illustration)**.

10.8 Insert a shim or feeler blade (arrowed) between the anti-stall adjustment screw and the accelerator lever . . .

9 Start the engine and allow it to idle. The engine should now run at the specified anti-stall speed (see Specifications).

10 If adjustment is necessary, loosen the locknut, and turn the anti-stall adjustment screw as required, until the anti-stall speed is correct **(see illustration)**. Hold the screw in this position, and securely tighten the locknut.

11 Remove the shim or feeler blade, then recheck the idle speed.

12 Move the accelerator lever to increase the engine speed to approximately 3000 rpm, then quickly release the lever. The deceleration period should be between 2.5 and 3.5 seconds, and the engine speed should drop to approximately 50 rpm below idle.

13 If the deceleration is too fast and the engine stalls, screw the anti-stall adjustment screw in a quarter of a turn towards the accelerator lever. If the deceleration is too slow, resulting in poor engine braking, unscrew it a quarter of a turn away from the lever. Adjust as necessary, then securely retighten the locknut.

14 Recheck the idle speed and, if necessary, adjust as described above.

15 With the engine idling, check the operation of the manual stop control by turning the stop lever anti-clockwise **(see illustrations 1.1a and 1.1b in Chapter 4D)**. The engine must stop instantly.

16 Where applicable, disconnect the tachometer on completion.

10.10 . . . then slacken the locknut and turn the screw (arrowed) to set the anti-stall speed

3 Using a suitable socket and extension bar fitted to the crankshaft sprocket bolt, rotate the crankshaft so that the entire length of the drivebelt can be examined. Examine the drivebelt for cracks, splitting, fraying, or other damage. Check also for signs of glazing (shiny patches) and for separation of the belt plies. Renew the belt if worn or damaged.

4 If the condition of the belt is satisfactory, check the drivebelt tension as described below under the relevant sub-heading.

Removal

5 If not already done, carry out the operations described in paragraph 2.

6 Disconnect the battery negative terminal (refer to *"Disconnecting the battery"* in the Reference Section of this manual).

7 Slacken the two bolts securing the tensioner pulley assembly to the engine, and the lower alternator mounting bolt.

8 Rotate the adjuster bolt to move the tensioner pulley away from the drivebelt, until there is sufficient slack for the drivebelt to be removed from the pulleys.

Refitting

9 Fit the belt around the pulleys, ensuring that the belt is of the correct type if it is being renewed, and take up the slack in the belt by tightening the adjuster bolt.

10 Tension the drivebelt as described in the following paragraphs.

Tensioning

11 If not already done, carry out the operations described in paragraph 2.

12 Correct tensioning of the drivebelt will ensure that it has a long life. Beware, however, of overtightening, as this can cause wear in the alternator bearings.

13 The belt should be tensioned so that, under firm thumb pressure, there is approximately 5.0 mm of free movement at the mid-point between the pulleys, on the longest belt run.

14 To adjust the tension, with the two tensioner pulley assembly retaining bolts and the lower alternator mounting bolt slackened, rotate the adjuster bolt until the correct tension is achieved. Once the belt is correctly tensioned, rotate the crankshaft through two

complete turns, and recheck the tension.

15 When the belt is correctly tensioned, securely tighten the tensioner pulley assembly retaining bolts, and the lower alternator mounting bolt.

16 Reconnect the battery negative terminal.

17 Clip the coolant hoses back in position, and secure with the retaining nut (where removed). Refit the wheel arch liner and the roadwheel, and lower the vehicle to the ground.

13 Clutch adjustment check and control mechanism lubrication

1 Check that the clutch pedal moves smoothly and easily through its full travel, and that the clutch itself functions correctly, with no trace of slip or drag.

2 Adjust the clutch as described in Chapter 6 (where necessary).

3 If excessive effort is required to operate the clutch, check first that the cable is correctly routed and undamaged, then remove the pedal and check that its pivot is properly greased. Refer to Chapter 6 for further information.

14 Front brake pad check

1 Firmly apply the handbrake, then jack up the front of the car and support it securely on axle stands (see *"Jacking and Vehicle Support"*). Remove the front roadwheels.

2 For a quick check, the thickness of friction material remaining on each brake pad can be measured through the aperture in the caliper body **(see illustration)**. If any pad's friction material is worn to the specified thickness or less, *all four pads must be renewed as a set*.

3 For a comprehensive check, the brake pads should be removed and cleaned. The operation of the caliper can then also be checked, and the condition of the brake disc itself can be fully examined on both sides. Refer to Chapter 9 for further information.

11 Emission control systems check

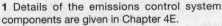

1 Details of the emissions control system components are given in Chapter 4E.

2 Checking consists simply of a visual check for obvious signs of damaged or leaking hoses and joints.

3 Detailed checking and testing of the evaporative and/or exhaust emissions systems (as applicable) should be entrusted to a Peugeot dealer.

12 Auxiliary drivebelt check and renewal

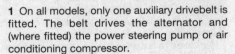

1 On all models, only one auxiliary drivebelt is fitted. The belt drives the alternator and (where fitted) the power steering pump or air conditioning compressor.

Checking the drivebelt condition

2 Apply the handbrake, then jack up the front of the car and support it on axle stands (see *"Jacking and vehicle support"*). Remove the right-hand front roadwheel and the wheel arch liner. Where necessary, undo the retaining nut, and free the coolant hoses from the retaining clip to improve access to the crankshaft sprocket bolt.

14.2 Brake pad friction material thickness can be checked with the pads in place - ATE type caliper shown

1B

15.6 Handbrake cable adjuster nut (arrowed)

15 Handbrake check and adjustment

1 Chock the front wheels, then jack up the rear of the vehicle, and support securely on axle stands (see *"Jacking and vehicle support"*).

2 Apply the footbrake firmly several times to establish correct shoe-to-drum clearance, then apply and release the handbrake several times to ensure that the self-adjust mechanism has compensated fully for any wear in the linings.

3 Fully release the handbrake, and check that the rear wheels rotate freely, without binding. If not, check that all cables are routed correctly and that the cable components and levers move freely.

> **HAYNES HINT** *If the handbrake mechanism fails to operate, or appears to be seized on one side of the vehicle only, remove the relevant brake drum (see Chapter 9) and check the handbrake lever pivot on the trailing brake shoe - it is possible for the lever to seize due to corrosion. If necessary, remove the lever and clean the contact faces of the lever, brake shoe, and pivot.*

4 If all components are free to move, but the wheels still bind when rotated, adjustment is required as follows.

16.4 If necessary, a chain wrench can be used to unscrew the fuel filter

5 Again, apply the footbrake several times to settle the shoes.

6 Ensure that the handbrake is fully released, then working under the vehicle, slacken the adjuster nut on the cable equaliser assembly until the drums are free to rotate **(see illustration)**.

7 Inside the vehicle, apply the handbrake so that the lever is on its 4th notch up from the "off" position.

8 Tighten the adjuster nut until the brake shoes just rub on the drums (slight resistance as the wheels are rotated).

9 Check that there is a total handbrake lever travel of between 4 and 7 notches (the wheels should lock fully after a maximum 7 notches of handbrake lever movement).

10 Check that both the left- and right-hand rear cables move together when the handbrake is operated.

11 Fully release the handbrake, and check that both rear wheels turn freely by hand.

12 Check that the handbrake warning light illuminates from the 4th notch of handbrake lever travel.

13 On completion, lower the vehicle to the ground.

16 Fuel filter renewal

1 The fuel filter is screwed onto the underside of the filter/thermostat housing on the left-hand end of the cylinder head. To improve access to the filter, remove the battery as described in Chapter 5A.

2 Cover the clutch bellhousing with a piece of plastic sheeting, to protect the clutch from fuel spillage.

3 Position a suitable container under the end of the fuel filter drain hose. Open the drain screw on the base of the filter, and allow the fuel to drain completely.

4 When the filter has drained, close the bleed screw and unscrew the filter. In the absence of the special fuel filter socket (Purflux no. F76, a shaped socket that fits the base of the filter), the filter can be unscrewed using a suitable strap or chain wrench **(see illustration)**.

5 Remove the filter, and dispose of it safely. Ensure that the sealing ring comes away with the filter, and does not stick to the filter/thermostat housing mating surface.

6 Apply a smear of clean diesel to the filter sealing ring, and wipe clean the housing mating surface. Screw the filter on until its sealing ring lightly contacts the housing mating surface, then tighten it through a further three-quarters of a turn.

7 Prime the fuel system as described in Chapter 4D.

8 Open the drain screw until clean fuel flows from the hose, then close the drain screw and withdraw the container from under the hose.

9 Refit the battery, and start the engine. If difficulty is encountered, bleed the fuel system as described in Chapter 4D.

17 Hinge and lock lubrication

1 Work around the vehicle, and lubricate the hinges of the bonnet, doors and tailgate with a general-purpose light oil.

2 Lightly lubricate the bonnet release mechanism and exposed section of inner cable with a smear of grease.

3 Check carefully the security and operation of all hinges, latches and locks, adjusting them where required. Check the operation of the central locking system (if fitted).

4 Check the condition and operation of the tailgate struts, renewing them if either is leaking or no longer able to support the tailgate securely when raised.

18 Road test

Instruments and electrical equipment

1 Check the operation of all instruments and electrical equipment.

2 Make sure that all instruments read correctly, and switch on all electrical equipment in turn to check that it works properly.

Steering and suspension

3 Check for any abnormalities in the steering, suspension, handling or road "feel".

4 Drive the vehicle, and check that there are no unusual vibrations or noises.

5 Check that the steering feels positive, with no excessive "sloppiness" or roughness, and check for any suspension noises when cornering, or when driving over bumps.

Drivetrain

6 Check the performance of the engine, clutch, transmission and driveshafts.

7 Listen for any unusual noises from the engine, clutch and transmission.

8 Make sure that the engine runs smoothly when idling, and that there is no hesitation when accelerating.

9 Check that the clutch action is smooth and progressive, that the drive is taken up smoothly, and that the pedal travel is not excessive. Also listen for any noises when the clutch pedal is depressed.

10 Check that all gears can be engaged smoothly, without noise, and that the gear lever action is not abnormally vague or "notchy".

11 Listen for a metallic clicking sound from the front of the vehicle, as the vehicle is driven slowly in a circle with the steering on full lock. Carry out this check in both directions. If a clicking noise is heard, this indicates wear in a driveshaft joint, in which case, the complete driveshaft must be renewed (see Chapter 8).

Check the operation and performance of the braking system

12 Make sure that the vehicle does not pull to one side when braking, and that the wheels do not lock prematurely when braking hard.

13 Check that there is no vibration through the steering when braking.

14 Check that the handbrake operates correctly, without excessive movement of the lever, and that it holds the vehicle stationary on a slope.

15 Test the operation of the brake servo unit as follows. With the engine off, depress the footbrake four or five times to exhaust the vacuum. Start the engine, holding the brake pedal depressed. As the engine starts, there should be a noticeable "give" in the brake pedal as vacuum builds up. Allow the engine to run for at least two minutes, and then switch it off. If the brake pedal is depressed now, it should be possible to detect a hiss from the servo as the pedal is depressed. After about four or five applications, no further hissing should be heard, and the pedal should feel considerably firmer.

Every 24 000 miles (40 000 km)

19 Air filter renewal

1.4 litre models

1 Slacken the retaining clip and disconnect the breather hose from the left-hand end of the air cleaner cover **(see illustration)**.

2 Slacken and remove the three retaining screws from the front of the air cleaner housing cover. Work around the cover, undoing all its quick-release fasteners, then lift off the cover, noting the four sealing rings **(see illustrations)**.

3 Lift out the filter element, noting which way around it is fitted. Inspect the cover sealing rings for signs of damage or deterioration, and renew as necessary **(see illustrations)**.

4 Fit the new filter element, ensuring that it is correctly seated in the inlet manifold.

5 Ensure each sealing ring is correctly seated in its recess in the cover, then refit the cover to the manifold.

6 Secure the cover in position with its quick-release fasteners, then refit the three retaining screws and tighten them securely.

1.5 litre models

7 Slacken the clips and detach the connecting tube and air intake duct from the air cleaner housing cover.

8 Slacken and withdraw the retaining screws, then remove the cover from the air cleaner housing and withdraw the filter element, noting its orientation.

9 Remove all traces of dirt and debris from the inside of the air cleaner housing, using a cloth.

10 Fit the new element, ensuring that it is fitted the correct way round and is correctly seated in the housing.

11 Install the cover and secure it in position with the retaining screws. Refit the connecting tube and air intake ducts and tighten the retaining clips securely.

19.1 Slacken the retaining clip and disconnect the breather hose from the air cleaner cover

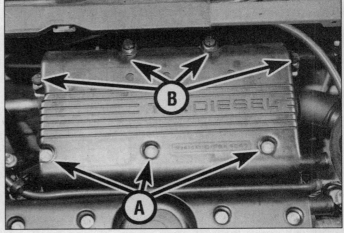

19.2a Air cleaner cover retaining screws (A) and quick-release fasteners (B)

19.2b Lift off the cover . . .

19.3a . . . and withdraw the element

19.3b Check the air cleaner cover O-rings for signs of damage, and renew if necessary

1B

Every 36 000 miles (60 000 km) or 4 years

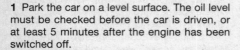

20 Rear brake shoe check

1 Remove the rear brake drums, and check the brake shoes for wear or contamination. At the same time, also inspect the wheel cylinders for signs of leakage, and the brake drum for signs of wear. Refer to the relevant Sections of Chapter 9 for further information.

21 Manual transmission oil level check

1 Park the car on a level surface. The oil level must be checked before the car is driven, or at least 5 minutes after the engine has been switched off.

HAYNES HiNT *If the oil is checked immediately after driving the car, some of the oil will remain distributed around the transmission, resulting in an inaccurate level reading.*

2 Prise out the clips and remove the access cover from the left-hand wheelarch liner.
3 Wipe clean the area around the filler/level plug, which is on the left-hand end of transmission **(see illustration)**. Unscrew the plug and clean it; discard the sealing washer.
4 The oil level should reach the lower edge of

21.3 Using the square-section wrench to unscrew the transmission filler/level plug

the filler/level hole. A certain amount of oil will have gathered behind the filler/level plug, and will trickle out when it is removed; this does **not** necessarily indicate that the level is correct. To ensure that a true level is established, wait until the initial trickle has stopped, then add oil as necessary until a trickle of new oil can be seen emerging **(see illustration)**. The level will be correct when the flow ceases; use only good-quality oil of the specified type (refer to "*Lubricants and fluids*").
5 Filling the transmission with oil is an extremely awkward operation; above all, allow plenty of time for the oil level to settle properly before checking it. If a large amount is added to the transmission, and a large amount flows out on checking the level, refit the filler/level plug and take the vehicle on a short journey so that the new oil is distributed fully around the transmission components, then recheck

21.4 Topping-up the transmission oil

the level when it has settled again.
6 If the transmission has been overfilled so that oil flows out as soon as the filler/level plug is removed, check that the car is completely level (front-to-rear and side-to-side), and allow the surplus to drain off into a suitable container.
7 When the level is correct, fit a new sealing washer to the filler/level plug. Refit the plug, tightening it to the specified torque wrench setting. Wash off any spilt oil then refit the access cover securing it in position with the retaining clips.

22 Timing belt renewal

Refer to Chapter 2B.

Every 2 years (regardless of mileage)

23 Coolant renewal

Cooling system draining

⚠ **Warning: Wait until the engine is cold before starting this procedure. Do not allow antifreeze to come in contact with your skin, or with the painted surfaces of the vehicle. Rinse off spills immediately with plenty of water. Never leave antifreeze lying around in an open container, or in a puddle in the driveway or on the garage floor. Children and pets are attracted by its sweet smell, but antifreeze can be fatal if ingested.**
1 With the engine completely cold, remove the expansion tank filler cap. Turn the cap anti-clockwise until it reaches the first stop. Wait until any pressure remaining in the system is released, then push the cap down, turn it anti-clockwise to the second stop, and lift it off.

2 Position a suitable container beneath the coolant drain outlet at the lower left-hand side of the radiator.
3 Loosen the drain plug (there is no need to remove it completely) and allow the coolant to drain into the container. If desired, a length of tubing can be fitted to the drain outlet to direct the flow of coolant during draining.
4 To assist draining, open the cooling system bleed screws. These are located in the heater matrix outlet hose union (to improve access, it may be located in an extension hose), on the engine compartment bulkhead, and on the top of the thermostat housing. On some models, there may also be a bleed screw in the top left-hand end of the radiator.
5 When the flow of coolant stops, reposition the container below the cylinder block drain plug. The drain plug is located at the rear of the cylinder block.
6 Remove the drain plug, and allow the coolant to drain into the container.
7 If the coolant has been drained for a reason other than renewal, then provided it is clean and less than two years old, it can be re-used,

though this is not recommended.
8 Refit the radiator and cylinder block drain plugs on completion of draining.

Cooling system flushing

9 If coolant renewal has been neglected, or if the antifreeze mixture has become diluted, then in time, the cooling system may gradually lose efficiency, as the coolant passages become restricted due to rust, scale deposits, and other sediment. The cooling system efficiency can be restored by flushing the system clean.
10 The radiator should be flushed independently of the engine, to avoid unnecessary contamination.

Radiator flushing

11 To flush the radiator, first tighten the radiator drain plug, and the radiator bleed screw, where applicable.
12 Disconnect the top and bottom hoses and any other relevant hoses from the radiator, with reference to Chapter 3.
13 Insert a garden hose into the radiator top inlet. Direct a flow of clean water through the

radiator, and keep flushing until clean water emerges from the radiator bottom outlet.

14 If after a reasonable period, the water still does not run clear, the radiator can be flushed with a good proprietary cleaning agent. It is important that their manufacturer's instructions are followed carefully. If the contamination is particularly bad, insert the hose in the radiator bottom outlet, and reverse-flush the radiator.

Engine flushing

15 To flush the engine, first refit the cylinder block drain plug, and tighten the cooling system bleed screws.

16 Remove the thermostat as described in Chapter 3, then temporarily refit the thermostat cover.

17 With the top and bottom hoses disconnected from the radiator, insert a garden hose into the radiator top hose. Direct a clean flow of water through the engine, and continue flushing until clean water emerges from the radiator bottom hose.

18 On completion of flushing, refit the thermostat and reconnect the hoses with reference to Chapter 3.

Cooling system filling

19 Before attempting to fill the cooling system, make sure that all hoses and clips are in good condition, and that the clips are tight. An antifreeze mixture must be used all year round, to prevent corrosion of the engine components (see following sub-Section). Also check that the radiator and cylinder block drain plugs are in place and tight.

20 Remove the expansion tank filler cap.

21 Open all the cooling system bleed screws (see paragraph 4).

22 Some of the cooling system hoses are positioned at a higher level than the top of the radiator expansion tank. It is therefore necessary to use a "header tank" when refilling the cooling system, to reduce the possibility of air being trapped in the system. Although Peugeot dealers use a special header tank, the same effect can be achieved by using a suitable bottle, with a seal between the bottle and the expansion tank.

23 Fit the "header tank" to the expansion tank; the expansion tank breather hose should be clamped. Slowly fill the system. Coolant will emerge from each of the bleed screws in turn, starting with the lowest screw. As soon as coolant free from air bubbles emerges from the lowest screw, tighten that screw, and watch the next bleed screw in the system. Repeat the procedure until the coolant is emerging from the highest bleed screw in the cooling system and all bleed screws are securely tightened.

24 Ensure that the "header tank" is full (at least 0.5 litres of coolant). Start the engine, and run it at a fast idle speed (do not exceed 2000 rpm) until the cooling fan cuts in, and then cuts out. Stop the engine.

25 Allow the engine to cool, then remove the "header tank". Remove the clamp from the expansion tank breather hose.

 Warning: Take great care not to scald yourself with the hot coolant during this operation.

26 When the engine has cooled, check the coolant level as described in "*Weekly checks*". Top-up the level if necessary, and refit the expansion tank cap.

Antifreeze mixture

27 The antifreeze should always be renewed at the specified intervals. This is necessary not only to maintain the antifreeze properties, but also to prevent corrosion which would otherwise occur as the corrosion inhibitors become progressively less effective.

28 Always use an ethylene-glycol based antifreeze which is suitable for use in mixed-metal cooling systems. The quantity of antifreeze and levels of protection are indicated in the Specifications.

29 Before adding antifreeze, the cooling system should be completely drained, preferably flushed, and all hoses checked for condition and security.

30 After filling with antifreeze, a label should be attached to the expansion tank, stating the type and concentration of antifreeze used, and the date installed. Any subsequent topping-up should be made with the same type and concentration of antifreeze.

31 Do not use engine antifreeze in the windscreen/tailgate washer system, as it will cause damage to the vehicle paintwork. A screenwash additive should be added to the washer system in the quantities stated on the bottle.

24 Brake fluid renewal

 Warning: Brake hydraulic fluid can harm your eyes and damage painted surfaces, so use extreme caution when handling and pouring it. Do not use fluid that has been standing open for some time, as it absorbs moisture from the air. Excess moisture can cause a dangerous loss of braking effectiveness.

1 The procedure is similar to that for the bleeding of the hydraulic system as described in Chapter 9, except that the brake fluid reservoir should be emptied by siphoning, using a clean poultry baster or similar before starting, and allowance should be made for the old fluid to be expelled when bleeding a section of the circuit.

2 Working as described in Chapter 9, open the first bleed screw in the sequence, and pump the brake pedal gently until nearly all the old fluid has been emptied from the master cylinder reservoir.

HAYNES HiNT *Old hydraulic fluid is invariably much darker in colour than the new, making it easy to distinguish the two.*

1B

3 Top-up to the "MAX" level with new fluid, and continue pumping until only the new fluid remains in the reservoir, and new fluid can be seen emerging from the bleed screw. Tighten the screw, and top the reservoir level up to the "MAX" level line.

4 Work through all the remaining bleed screws in the sequence until new fluid can be seen at all of them. Be careful to keep the master cylinder reservoir topped-up to above the "MIN" level at all times, or air may enter the system and greatly increase the length of the task.

5 When the operation is complete, check that all bleed screws are securely tightened, and that their dust caps are refitted. Wash off all traces of spilt fluid, and recheck the master cylinder reservoir fluid level.

6 Check the operation of the brakes before taking the car on the road.

Chapter 2 Part A:
Petrol engine in-car repair procedures

Contents

Degrees of difficulty

Easy, suitable for novice with little experience	**Fairly easy,** suitable for beginner with some experience	**Fairly difficult,** suitable for competent DIY mechanic	**Difficult,** suitable for experienced DIY mechanic	**Very difficult,** suitable for expert DIY or professional

Specifications

2A

Engine (general)

Designation:
954 cc engine	TU9
1124 cc engine	TU1
1294 cc engine	TU2
1360 cc engine	TU3
1587 cc engine	TU5

Engine codes*:
954 cc carburettor petrol engine	C1A (TU9K)
954 cc fuel-injected petrol engine	CDZ and CDY (TU9M)
1124 cc carburettor petrol engine:	
Up to mid-1996	H1A (TU1K)
Mid-1996 onward	H3A (TU1)
1124 cc fuel-injected petrol engine:	
Up to mid-1996	HDZ and HDY (TU1M)
Mid-1996 onward	HDZ and HDY (TU1M+)
1294 cc fuel-injected engine	MFZ (TU2J2)
1360 cc carburettor engine:	
Up to mid-1996	K2D (TU3F)
Mid-1996 onward	K5A (TU3.2TR)
1360 cc single point fuel-injected engine	KDX and KDY (TU3M or TU3MC)
1360 cc multi-point fuel-injected engine:	
Up to mid-1996	K6B (TU3FJ2) and KFZ (TU3FJ2)
Mid-1996 onward	KFX (TU3JP)
1587 cc (8-valve) fuel-injected engine:	
Up to mid 1996	NFY (TU5J2) and NFZ (TU5JP)
Mid-1996 onward	NFW (TU5J2) and NFZ (TU5JP)
1587 cc (16-valve) fuel-injected engine	NFX (TU5J4)

*The engine code is situated on the front left-hand end of the cylinder block. It is either stamped on a plate which is riveted to the block (aluminium block engines) or stamped directly on the cylinder block (cast-iron block engines). The code given in brackets is the factory identification number.

Engine (general) - continued

Bore:
954 cc engine .... 70.00 mm
1124 cc engine .... 72.00 mm
1294 cc engine .... 75.00 mm
1360 cc engine .... 75.00 mm
1587 cc engine .... 78.50 mm
Stroke:
954 cc engine .... 62.00 mm
1124 cc engine .... 69.00 mm
1294 cc engine .... 73.20 mm
1360 cc engine .... 77.00 mm
1587 cc engine .... 82.00 mm
Direction of crankshaft rotation .... Clockwise (viewed from right-hand side of vehicle)
No 1 cylinder location .... At transmission end of block
Compression ratio (typical):
954 cc engine .... 9.4 : 1
1124 cc engine .... 9.4 : 1
1294 cc engine .... 10.2 : 1
1360 cc engine .... 9.3 : 1
1587 cc (8-valve) engine .... 9.6 : 1
1587 cc (16-valve) engine .... 10.8 : 1

Camshaft

Drive .... Toothed belt
Number of bearings 5
Camshaft bearing journal diameter (outside diameter):
All except 1587 cc (16-valve) engines:
No 1 .... 36.950 to 36.925 mm
No 2 .... 40.650 to 40.625 mm
No 3 .... 41.250 to 41.225 mm
No 4 .... 41.850 to 41.825 mm
No 5 .... 42.450 to 42.425 mm
1587 cc (16-valve) engines .... Not available
Cylinder head bearing journal diameter (inside diameter):
All except 1587 cc (16-valve) engines:
No 1 .... 37.000 to 37.039 mm
No 2 .... 40.700 to 47.739 mm
No 3 .... 41.300 to 41.339 mm
No 4 .... 41.900 to 41.939 mm
No 5 .... 42.500 to 42.539 mm
1587 cc (16-valve) engines .... Not available

Valve clearances (8-valve engines only)

Inlet .... 0.20 mm
Exhaust .... 0.40 mm

Lubrication system

Oil pump type .... Gear-type, chain-driven off the crankshaft
Minimum oil pressure at 90°C .... 4 bars at 4000 rpm
Oil pressure warning switch operating pressure .... 0.8 bars

Torque wrench settings

	Nm	lbf ft
All except 1587 cc (16-valve) engines		
Cylinder head cover nuts	16	12
Timing belt cover bolts	8	6
Crankshaft pulley retaining bolts	8	6
Timing belt tensioner pulley nut	23	17
Camshaft sprocket retaining bolt	80	59
Crankshaft sprocket retaining bolt	110	81
Camshaft thrust fork retaining bolt	16	12
Cylinder head bolts (aluminium block engine):		
Stage 1	20	15
Stage 2	Angle-tighten a further 240°	
Cylinder head bolts (cast-iron block engine):		
Stage 1	20	15
Stage 2	Angle-tighten a further 120°	
Stage 3	Angle-tighten a further 120°	

Torque wrench settings (continued)

	Nm	lbf ft
All except 1587 cc (16-valve) engines (continued)		
Sump drain plug	30	22
Sump retaining nuts and bolts	8	6
Oil pump retaining bolts	8	6
Flywheel retaining nuts and bolts	65	48
Piston oil jet spray tube bolts - 1587 cc models	10	7
Big-end bearing cap nuts	40	30
Main bearing ladder casting (aluminium block engine):		
11 mm bolts:		
Stage 1	20	15
Stage 2	Angle-tighten a further 45°	
6 mm bolts	8	6
Main bearing cap bolts (cast-iron block engine):		
Stage 1	20	15
Stage 2	Angle-tighten a further 45°	
Engine/transmission right-hand mounting:		
Pre-July 1996 models:		
Mounting bracket-to-engine nuts	50	37
Mounting bracket-to-body 8 mm nut(s)	20	15
Mounting bracket-to-body 10 mm nut(s)	50	37
July 1996 models onward:		
Mounting bracket-to-engine nuts	45	33
Flexible mounting-to-mounting bracket bolt	28	21
Flexible mounting-to-body bolts	30	22
Left-hand engine/transmission mounting:		
Mounting bracket-to-body bolts	30	22
Centre nut	85	63
Engine/transmission rear mounting:		
Mounting link bolts	55	40
Mounting-to-transmission bolts	85	63
Engine-to-transmission fixing bolts	35	26
1587 cc (16-valve) engines		
Cylinder head cover nuts	10	7
Camshaft bearing housings:		
Stage 1	5	4
Stage 2	10	7
Timing belt cover bolts	8	6
Crankshaft pulley retaining bolts	25	18
Timing belt tensioner pulley nut	23	17
Camshaft sprocket-to-hub retaining bolts	10	7
Camshaft sprocket hub-to-camshaft retaining bolts	80	59
Crankshaft sprocket retaining bolt	110	81
Cylinder head bolts:		
Stage 1	20	15
Stage 2	Angle-tighten a further 260°	
Sump drain plug	30	22
Sump retaining nuts and bolts	8	6
Oil pump retaining bolts	10	7
Flywheel retaining nuts and bolts	65	48
Big-end bearing cap nuts	37.5	28
Main bearing cap bolts:		
Stage 1	20	15
Stage 2	Angle-tighten a further 50°	
Engine/transmission right-hand mounting:		
Mounting bracket-to-engine nuts	45	33
Flexible mounting-to-mounting bracket bolt	28	21
Flexible mounting-to-body bolts	25	18
Left-hand engine/transmission mounting:		
Mounting bracket-to-body bolts	30	22
Centre nut	85	63
Engine/transmission rear mounting:		
Mounting link bolts	55	40
Mounting-to-transmission bolts	85	63
Engine-to-transmission fixing bolts	35	26

1 General information

Using this Chapter

Chapter 2 is divided into three Parts; A, B and C. Repair operations that can be carried out with the engine in the vehicle are described in Parts A (TU series petrol engines) and B (TUD series diesel engines). Part C covers the removal of the engine/transmission as a unit, and describes the engine dismantling and overhaul procedures.

In Parts A and B, the assumption is made that the engine is installed in the vehicle, with all ancillaries connected. If the engine has been removed for overhaul, the preliminary dismantling information which precedes each operation may be ignored.

TU series engine description

All petrol engines in the Peugeot 106 model range come from the TU series engines. The TU engine is a well-proven unit which has been fitted to several other Peugeot and Citroën vehicles. The engine is of the in-line four-cylinder, overhead camshaft (OHC) type, mounted transversely at the front of the car **(see illustration)**. The clutch and transmission are attached to its left-hand end.

1.3 Cutaway view of the TU series petrol engine

The 106 range is fitted with 954 cc, 1124 cc, 1294 cc, 1360 cc and 1587 cc versions of the engine; carburettor and fuel-injected versions are available. The engine is available in both aluminium and cast-iron cylinder block versions.

The crankshaft runs in five main bearings. Thrustwashers are fitted to No 2 main bearing (upper half) to control crankshaft endfloat.

The connecting rods rotate on horizontally-split bearing shells at their big-ends. The pistons are attached to the connecting rods by gudgeon pins, which are an interference fit in the connecting rod small-end eyes. The aluminium-alloy pistons are fitted with three piston rings - two compression rings and an oil control ring.

On aluminium block engines, the cylinder bores have replaceable wet liners. Sealing O-rings are fitted at the base of each liner, to prevent the escape of coolant into the sump.

On cast-iron block engines, the cylinder bores are an integral part of the cylinder block. On this type of engine, the cylinder bores are sometimes referred to as having dry liners.

The inlet and exhaust valves are each closed by coil springs, and operate in guides pressed into the cylinder head; the valve seat inserts are also pressed into the cylinder head, and can be renewed separately if worn.

On 8-valve engines, the camshaft, which rotates directly in the cylinder head, is driven by a toothed timing belt, and operates the eight valves via rocker arms. Valve clearances are adjusted by a screw-and-locknut arrangement. The timing belt also drives the coolant pump.

On 16-valve engines, the cylinder head forms the camshaft lower bearings and a bearing housing bolted over each camshaft forms the upper bearings. The camshafts, driven by a toothed timing belt, operate the sixteen valves via followers located beneath each cam lobe. Valve clearances are self-adjusting by means of hydraulic tappets fitted to the cam followers.

Lubrication is by means of an oil pump, which is driven (via a chain and sprocket) off the right-hand end of the crankshaft. It draws oil through a strainer located in the sump, and then forces it through an externally-mounted filter into galleries in the cylinder block/crankcase. From there, the oil is distributed to the crankshaft (main bearings) and camshaft(s). The big-end bearings are supplied with oil via internal drillings in the crankshaft, while the camshaft bearings also receive a pressurised supply. The camshaft lobes and valves are lubricated by splash, as are all other engine components. On 1294 cc models and some 1360 cc and 1587 cc models, an oil cooler is fitted to control the oil temperature under arduous operating conditions.

Throughout this manual, it is often necessary to identify the engines not only by their capacity, but also by their engine code,

which can be found on the front face of the cylinder block, at the transmission end. On models with an aluminium cylinder block, the code is stamped on a plate which is riveted to the block; on models with a cast-iron cylinder block, the number is stamped on a machined surface on the cylinder block itself. The first part of the engine number gives the engine code - eg **KDX** (see illustration).

Repair operations possible with the engine in the car

The following work can be carried out with the engine in the car:
a) *Compression pressure - testing.*
b) *Cylinder head cover - removal and refitting.*
c) *Timing belt covers - removal and refitting.*
d) *Timing belt - removal, refitting and adjustment.*
e) *Timing belt tensioner and sprockets - removal and refitting.*
f) *Camshaft oil seal - renewal.*
g) *Camshaft and rocker arms (8-valve engines) - removal, inspection and refitting.**
h) *Camshaft and followers (16-valve engines) - removal, inspection and refitting.*
i) *Cylinder head - removal and refitting.*
j) *Cylinder head and pistons - decarbonising (refer to Part C of this Chapter).*
k) *Sump - removal and refitting.*
l) *Oil pump - removal, overhaul and refitting.*
m) *Oil cooler (where fitted) - removal and refitting.*
n) *Crankshaft oil seals - renewal.*
o) *Engine/transmission mountings - inspection and renewal.*
p) *Flywheel/driveplate - removal, inspection and refitting.*

The cylinder head must be removed for the successful completion of this work. Refer to Section 12 for details.

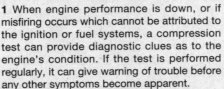

2 Compression test - description and interpretation

1 When engine performance is down, or if misfiring occurs which cannot be attributed to the ignition or fuel systems, a compression test can provide diagnostic clues as to the engine's condition. If the test is performed regularly, it can give warning of trouble before any other symptoms become apparent.
2 The engine must be fully warmed-up to normal operating temperature, the battery must be fully charged, and all the spark plugs must be removed (Chapter 1A). The aid of an assistant will also be required.
3 On models with an ignition system incorporating a distributor, disable the ignition system by disconnecting the ignition HT coil lead from the distributor cap and earthing it on the cylinder block. Use a jumper lead or similar wire to make a good connection.

1.12 On aluminium block engines, the engine code is stamped on a plate (arrowed) attached to the front of the cylinder block - viewed from above

4 On models with a static (distributorless) ignition system, disable the ignition system by disconnecting the LT wiring connector from the ignition HT coil(s), referring to Chapter 5B for further information.
5 Fit a compression tester to the No 1 cylinder spark plug hole - the type of tester which screws into the plug thread is to be preferred.
6 Have the assistant hold the throttle wide open, and crank the engine on the starter motor; after one or two revolutions, the compression pressure should build up to a maximum figure, and then stabilise. Record the highest reading obtained.
7 Repeat the test on the remaining cylinders, recording the pressure in each.
8 All cylinders should produce very similar pressures; a difference of more than 2 bars between any two cylinders indicates a fault. Note that the compression should build up quickly in a healthy engine; low compression on the first stroke, followed by gradually-increasing pressure on successive strokes, indicates worn piston rings. A low compression reading on the first stroke, which does not build up during successive strokes, indicates leaking valves or a blown head gasket (a cracked head could also be the cause). Deposits on the undersides of the valve heads can also cause low compression.
9 Although Peugeot do not specify exact compression pressures, as a guide, any cylinder pressure of below 10 bars can be considered as less than healthy. Refer to a Peugeot dealer or other specialist if in doubt as to whether a particular pressure reading is acceptable.
10 If the pressure in any cylinder is low, carry out the following test to isolate the cause. Introduce a teaspoonful of clean oil into that cylinder through its spark plug hole, and repeat the test.
11 If the addition of oil temporarily improves the compression pressure, this indicates that bore or piston wear is responsible for the pressure loss. No improvement suggests that leaking or burnt valves, or a blown head gasket, may be to blame.

2A

3.4 Insert a 6 mm bolt (arrowed) through hole in cylinder block flange and into timing hole in the flywheel . . .

3.5 . . . then insert a 10 mm bolt through the cam sprocket timing hole, and locate it in the cylinder head - 8-valve engines

12 A low reading from two adjacent cylinders is almost certainly due to the head gasket having blown between them; the presence of coolant in the engine oil will confirm this.

13 If one cylinder is about 20 percent lower than the others and the engine has a slightly rough idle, a worn camshaft lobe could be the cause.

14 If the compression reading is unusually high, the combustion chambers are probably coated with carbon deposits. If this is the case, the cylinder head should be removed and decarbonised.

15 On completion of the test, refit the spark plugs and reconnect the ignition system.

3 Engine assembly/ valve timing holes - general information and usage

Note: *Do not attempt to rotate the engine whilst the crankshaft/camshaft are locked in position. If the engine is to be left in this state for a long period of time, it is a good idea to place warning notices inside the vehicle, and*

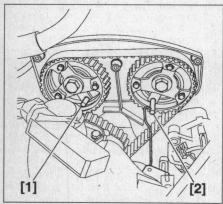

3.15 Camshaft sprockets locked in position with suitable dowels (1 and 2) - 16-valve engines

in the engine compartment. This will reduce the possibility of the engine being accidentally cranked on the starter motor, which is likely to cause damage with the locking tools in place.

1 On all models, timing holes are drilled in the camshaft sprocket and in the flywheel. The holes are used to ensure that the crankshaft and camshaft are correctly positioned when assembling the engine (to prevent the possibility of the valves contacting the pistons when refitting the cylinder head), or refitting the timing belt. When the timing holes are aligned with access holes in the cylinder head and the front of the cylinder block, suitable-diameter pins or bolts can be inserted to lock both the camshaft and crankshaft in position, preventing them from rotating. Proceed as follows. **Note:** *With the timing holes aligned, No 1 cylinder is at TDC.*

8-valve engines

2 Remove the timing belt upper cover as described in Section 5.

3 The crankshaft must now be turned until the timing hole in the camshaft sprocket is aligned with the corresponding hole in the cylinder head. The holes are aligned when the camshaft sprocket hole is in the 2 o'clock position, when viewed from the right-hand end of the engine. The crankshaft can be turned by using a spanner on the crankshaft sprocket bolt, noting that it should always be rotated in a clockwise direction (viewed from the right-hand end of the engine). Turning the engine will be much easier if the spark plugs are removed first (see Chapter 1A).

4 With the camshaft sprocket hole correctly positioned, insert a 6 mm diameter bolt or drill bit through the hole in the front left-hand flange of the cylinder block, and locate it in the timing hole in the flywheel **(see illustration).** Note that it may be necessary to rotate the crankshaft slightly, to get the holes to align.

5 With the flywheel correctly positioned, insert a 10 mm diameter bolt or drill bit

through the timing hole in the camshaft sprocket, and locate it in the hole in the cylinder head **(see illustration).**

6 The crankshaft and camshaft are now locked in position, preventing unnecessary rotation.

16-valve engines

7 Disconnect the battery negative terminal (refer to *"Disconnecting the battery"* in the Reference Section of this manual).

8 Drain the cooling system as described in Chapter 1A.

9 Remove the air cleaner assembly as described in Chapter 4C.

10 Release the retaining clips and disconnect the radiator top hose.

11 Undo the bolts and remove the air cleaner intake duct for access to the exhaust manifold heat shield, then unbolt and remove the heat shield.

12 Remove the timing belt cover as described in Section 5.

13 Rotate the crankshaft pulley until the timing holes in both camshafts are aligned with their corresponding holes in the cylinder head. The holes are aligned when the inlet camshaft sprocket hole is in approximately the 5 o'clock position and the exhaust camshaft sprocket hole is in approximately the 7 o'clock position, when viewed from the right-hand end of the engine.

14 With the camshaft sprocket holes correctly positioned, insert a 6 mm diameter bolt or drill bit through the hole in the front left-hand flange of the cylinder block, and locate it in the timing hole in the flywheel. Note that it may be necessary to rotate the crankshaft slightly, to get the holes to align.

15 With the crankshaft locked in position, insert a suitable bolt, drill or dowel rod through the timing hole in each camshaft sprocket and locate it in the cylinder head **(see illustration).**

16 The crankshaft and camshafts are now locked in position, preventing rotation.

4.3 Disconnect the breather hose from the cylinder head cover . . .

4.4 . . . then slacken and remove the cover retaining nuts and washers (arrowed) . . .

4.5 . . . and lift off the cylinder head cover

17 On completion of the operations requiring the use of the timing pins, refit the components disturbed with reference to the relevant Sections and Chapters of this manual. Refill the cooling system as described in Chapter 1A, then reconnect the battery negative lead.

4 Cylinder head cover - removal and refitting

8-valve engines

Removal

1 Disconnect the battery negative terminal (refer to *"Disconnecting the battery"* in the Reference Section of this manual).
2 Where necessary, undo the bolts securing the HT lead retaining clips to the rear of the cylinder head cover, and position the clips clear of the cover.
3 Slacken the retaining clip, and disconnect the breather hose from the left-hand end of the cylinder head cover (see illustration). Where the original crimped-type hose clip is still fitted, cut it off and discard it. Use a standard worm-drive clip on refitting.
4 Undo the two retaining nuts, and remove the washer from each of the cylinder head cover studs (see illustration).
5 Lift off the cylinder head cover, and remove it along with its rubber seal (see illustration). Examine the seal for signs of damage and

deterioration, and if necessary, renew it.
6 Remove the spacer from each stud, and lift off the oil baffle plate (see illustrations).

Refitting

7 Carefully clean the cylinder head and cover mating surfaces, and remove all traces of oil.
8 Fit the rubber seal over the edge of the cylinder head cover, ensuring that it is correctly located along its entire length (see illustration).
9 Refit the oil baffle plate to the engine, and locate the spacers in their recesses in the baffle plate.
10 Carefully refit the cylinder head cover to the engine, taking great care not to displace the rubber seal. Check that the seal is correctly located, then refit the washers and cover retaining nuts, and tighten them to the specified torque.
11 Where necessary, refit the HT lead clips to the rear of the head cover, and securely tighten their retaining bolts.
12 Reconnect the breather hose to the cylinder head cover, securely tightening its retaining clip, and reconnect the battery negative terminal.

16-valve engines

Removal

13 Disconnect the battery negative terminal (refer to *"Disconnecting the battery"* in the Reference Section of this manual).
14 For improved access, remove the air cleaner assembly as described in Chapter 4C.

15 Slacken the retaining clip, and disconnect the breather hose from the left-hand end of the cylinder head cover.
16 Disconnect the wiring connector at the left-hand end of the ignition coil unit, located in the centre of the cylinder head covers. Undo the retaining bolts and lift the coil unit upwards, off the spark plugs and from its location between the cylinder head covers.
17 Working in a spiral sequence starting from the outside and working inwards, progressively slacken, then remove the retaining bolts of each cylinder head cover, noting the correct fitted position of any brackets or clips.
18 Lift off each cover in turn and remove it along with its rubber seal.

Refitting

19 Clean the cylinder head and cover mating surfaces, and remove all traces of oil.
20 Locate the rubber seal in the groove of each cover, ensuring that it is correctly located along its entire length.
21 Carefully refit the cylinder head covers to the engine, taking great care not to displace the rubber seals.
22 Check that the seal is correctly located, then refit the cover retaining bolts and, working in the sequence shown, tighten them evenly and progressively to the specified torque (see illustration).
23 Refit the ignition coil unit between the cylinder head covers. Refit the retaining bolts, tightening them securely, then reconnect the coil unit wiring connectors.

2A

4.6a Lift off the spacers (second one arrowed) . . .

4.6b . . . and remove the oil baffle plate

4.8 On refitting, ensure that the rubber seal is correctly located on the cylinder head cover

24 Reconnect the breather hose to the cylinder head cover, securely tightening its retaining clip.

25 Refit the air cleaner assembly.

26 Reconnect the battery negative terminal. On completion, start the engine and check the fuel hose unions for signs of leakage.

| 5 | Timing belt covers -
|---|
| | removal and refitting |

Removal - 8-valve engines

Upper cover

1 Slacken and remove the two retaining bolts (one at the front and one at the rear), and remove the timing belt upper cover from the cylinder head **(see illustrations)**.

Centre cover

Note: *On later engines the centre cover is combined with the lower cover and is not a separate component.*

2 Remove the upper cover as described in paragraph 1, then free the wiring from its retaining clips on the centre cover **(see illustration)**.

3 Slacken and remove the retaining bolts, and manoeuvre the centre cover out from the engine compartment **(see illustration)**.

Lower cover

4 Remove the auxiliary drivebelt as described in Chapter 1A.

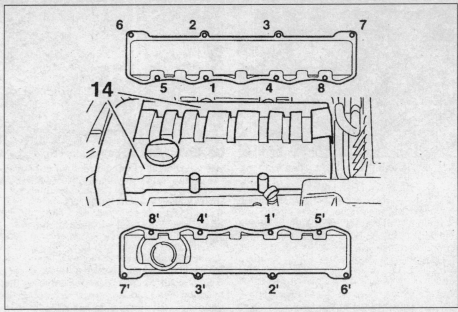

4.22 Refit the cylinder head covers (14) and tighten the bolts in the sequence shown - 16-valve engines

5 Remove the upper and, if applicable, centre covers as described in paragraphs 1 to 3.

6 Undo the three crankshaft pulley retaining bolts and remove the pulley, noting which way round it is fitted **(see illustrations)**.

7 Slacken and remove the remaining retaining bolt(s), and slide the lower cover off the end of the crankshaft **(see illustration)**.

Refitting - 8-valve engines

Upper cover

8 Refit the cover, ensuring that it is correctly located with the centre cover, and tighten its retaining bolts to the specified torque.

5.1a Undo the two retaining bolts (arrowed) . . .

5.1b . . . and remove the timing belt upper cover

5.2 Free the wiring loom from its retaining clip . . .

5.3 . . . then undo the three retaining bolts (locations arrowed) and remove the timing belt centre cover

5.6a Undo the three retaining bolts (arrowed) . . .

5.6b . . . and remove the crankshaft pulley

5.7 Undo the retaining bolt and remove the timing belt lower cover

Centre cover

9 Manoeuvre the centre cover back into position, ensuring that it is correctly located with the lower cover, and tighten its retaining bolts to the specified torque.

10 Clip the wiring loom into its retaining clips on the front of the centre cover, then refit the upper cover as described in paragraph 8.

Lower cover

11 Locate the lower cover over the timing belt sprocket, and tighten its retaining bolt(s) to the specified torque.

12 Fit the pulley to the end of the crankshaft, ensuring that it is fitted the correct way round, and tighten its retaining bolts to the specified torque.

13 Refit the centre and upper covers as described above, then refit and tension the auxiliary drivebelt as described in Chapter 1A.

Removal - 16-valve engines

Upper cover

14 Disconnect the battery negative terminal (refer to *"Disconnecting the battery"* in the Reference Section of this manual).

15 Remove the auxiliary drivebelt as described in Chapter 1A.

16 Remove the cover over the engine management ECU then lift the retaining clip and disconnect the wiring connector from the ECU. Slacken and remove the ECU retaining bolts, and remove it from the vehicle.

17 Move aside the double relay then remove the ECU mounting bracket.

18 Remove the deflector plate located in front of the timing belt cover.

19 On models with air conditioning, release the supply pipe from its retaining clips and move it aside as far as possible. Do not disconnect the pipe unions.

20 Undo the bolts and remove the alternator upper mounting bracket.

21 Undo the upper timing cover retaining bolts and remove the cover.

Lower cover

22 Remove the upper cover as described previously.

23 Undo the three crankshaft pulley retaining bolts and remove the pulley, noting which way round it is fitted.

24 Undo the remaining retaining bolts and remove the lower cover.

Refitting - 16-valve engines

Upper cover

25 Locate the upper cover in position and secure with the retaining bolts tightened to the specified torque.

26 Refit the alternator mounting bracket and, where applicable, locate the air conditioning pipe back in position.

27 Refit the deflector plate and ECU mounting bracket.

28 Refit the ECU and reconnect the wiring connector. Refit the ECU cover.

29 Refit and tension the auxiliary drivebelt as described in Chapter 1A, then reconnect the battery negative terminal.

Lower cover

30 Locate the lower cover in position and secure with the retaining bolts tightened to the specified torque.

31 Fit the pulley to the end of the crankshaft, ensuring that it is fitted the correct way round, and tighten its retaining bolts to the specified torque.

32 Refit the upper cover as described above, then refit and tension the auxiliary drivebelt as described in Chapter 1A.

---

6 Timing belt -
   general information,
   removal and refitting

General information

1 The timing belt drives the camshaft and coolant pump from a toothed sprocket on the front of the crankshaft. If the belt breaks or slips in service, the pistons are likely to hit the valve heads, resulting in extensive (and expensive) damage.

2 The timing belt should be renewed at the specified intervals (see Chapter 1A), or earlier if it is contaminated with oil, or if it is at all noisy in operation (a "scraping" noise due to uneven wear).

3 If the timing belt is being removed, it is a wise precaution to check the condition of the coolant pump at the same time (check for signs of coolant leakage). This may avoid the need to remove the timing belt again at a later stage, should the coolant pump fail.

Removal - 8-valve engines

Note: *Peugeot specify the use of a special electronic tool (SEEM C.TRONIC type 105 belt tensioning measuring tool, and valve rocker contact plate (-).0132 AE) to correctly set the timing belt tension. If access to this equipment cannot be obtained, an approximate setting can be achieved using the method described below. If the method described is used, the tension must be checked using the special electronic tool at the earliest possible opportunity. Do not drive the vehicle over large distances, or use high engine speeds, until the belt tension is known to be correct. Refer to a Peugeot dealer for advice.*

4 Disconnect the battery negative terminal (refer to *"Disconnecting the battery"* in the Reference Section of this manual).

5 Align the engine assembly/valve timing holes as described in Section 3, and lock both the camshaft sprocket and the flywheel in position. *Do not* attempt to rotate the engine whilst the locking tools are in position.

6 Remove the timing belt centre and lower covers as described in Section 5.

7 Loosen the timing belt tensioner pulley retaining nut. Pivot the pulley in a clockwise direction, using a square-section key fitted to the hole in the pulley hub, then retighten the retaining nut.

8 Slip the belt off the sprockets.

9 Check the timing belt carefully for any signs of uneven wear, splitting, or oil contamination. Pay particular attention to the roots of the teeth. Renew the belt if there is the slightest doubt about its condition. If the engine is undergoing an overhaul, and has covered more than 36 000 miles (60 000 km) with the existing belt fitted, renew the belt as a matter of course, regardless of its apparent condition. The cost of a new belt is nothing when compared to the cost of repairs, should the belt break in service. If signs of oil contamination are found, trace the source of the oil leak, and rectify it. Wash down the engine timing belt area and all related components, to remove all traces of oil **(see Haynes Hint).**

Refitting - 8-valve engines

10 Prior to refitting, thoroughly clean the timing belt sprockets. Check that the tensioner pulley rotates freely, without any sign of roughness. If necessary, renew the tensioner pulley as described in Section 7. Make sure that the locking tools are still in place, as described in Section 3.

11 Manoeuvre the timing belt into position, ensuring that the arrows on the belt are pointing in the direction of rotation (clockwise, when viewed from the right-hand end of the engine).

12 Do not twist the timing belt sharply while refitting it. Fit the belt over the crankshaft and

2A

If the timing belt is to be re-used, use white paint or similar to mark the direction of rotation on the belt (if markings do not already exist).

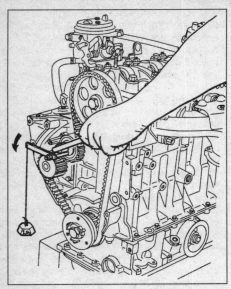

6.14 Using the Peugeot special tool to tension the timing belt

camshaft sprockets. Make sure that the "front run" of the belt is taut - ie, ensure that any slack is on the tensioner pulley side of the belt. Fit the belt over the coolant pump sprocket and tensioner pulley. Ensure that the belt teeth are seated centrally in the sprockets.

13 Loosen the tensioner pulley retaining nut. Pivot the pulley anti-clockwise to remove all free play from the timing belt, then retighten the nut. Tension the timing belt as described under the relevant sub-heading.

Tensioning without the special electronic measuring tool

Note: *If this method is used, ensure that the belt tension is checked by a Peugeot dealer at the earliest possible opportunity.*

14 Peugeot dealers use a special tool to tension the timing belt. A similar tool may be fabricated using a suitable square-section bar attached to an arm made from a metal strip; a hole should be drilled in the strip at a distance of 80 mm from the centre of the square-section bar. Fit the tool to the hole in the tensioner pulley, keeping the tool arm as close to the horizontal as possible, and hang a 1.5 kg (3.3 lb) weight (aluminium block engine) or 2.0 kg (4.4 lb) weight (cast-iron block engine) from the hole in the tool **(see illustration)**. In the absence of an object of the specified weight, a spring balance can be used to exert the required force, ensuring that the spring balance is held at 90° to the tool arm. Slacken the pulley retaining nut, allowing the weight or force exerted (as applicable) to push the tensioner pulley against the belt, then retighten the pulley nut.
15 If this special tool is not available, an approximate setting may be achieved by pivoting the tensioner pulley anti-clockwise until it is just possible to twist the timing belt through 90° by finger and thumb, midway

between the crankshaft and camshaft sprockets. The deflection of the belt at the mid-point between the sprockets should be approximately 6.0 mm.
16 Remove the locking tools from the camshaft sprocket and flywheel.
17 Using a suitable socket and extension bar on the crankshaft sprocket bolt, rotate the crankshaft through four complete rotations in a clockwise direction (viewed from the right-hand end of the engine). *Do not* at any time rotate the crankshaft anti-clockwise.
18 Slacken the tensioner pulley nut, re-tension the belt as described in paragraph 14 or 15, then tighten the tensioner pulley nut to the specified torque.
19 Rotate the crankshaft through a further two turns clockwise, and check that both the camshaft sprocket and flywheel timing holes are still correctly aligned.
20 If all is well, refit the timing belt covers as described in Section 5, and reconnect the battery negative terminal.

Tensioning using the special electronic measuring tool

21 Fit the special belt tensioning measuring equipment to the "front run" of the timing belt, approximately midway between the camshaft and crankshaft sprockets. Position the tensioner pulley so that the belt is tensioned to a setting of 44 units, then retighten its retaining nut.
22 Remove the locking tools from the camshaft sprocket and flywheel, and remove the measuring tool from the belt.
23 Using a suitable socket and extension bar on the crankshaft sprocket bolt, rotate the crankshaft through four complete rotations in a clockwise direction (viewed from the right-hand end of the engine). *Do not* at any time rotate the crankshaft anti-clockwise. Refit the locking tool to the flywheel and check that the camshaft sprocket timing hole is aligned.
24 Remove the cylinder head cover. Slacken the eight rocker arm contact bolts in the valve rocker contact plate (special tool (-).0132 AE) and fit the contact plate to the cylinder head, observing the correct fitted direction. Tighten each rocker arm contact bolt until the rockers are just free of the camshaft lobes. Do not over-tighten the contact bolts otherwise the valves will contact the pistons.
25 Refit the measuring tool to the belt, slacken the tensioner pulley retaining nut, and gradually release the tensioner pulley until a setting of between 29 and 33 units is indicated on the measuring tool. Retighten the tensioner pulley retaining nut.
26 Remove the measuring tool from the belt, the valve rocker contact plate from the cylinder head, and the locking tool from the flywheel. Rotate the crankshaft through another two complete rotations in a clockwise direction and check that both the camshaft sprocket and flywheel timing holes are realigned. *Do not* at any time rotate the crankshaft anti-clockwise.

27 With the belt tension correctly set, refit the cylinder head and timing belt covers, and reconnect the battery negative terminal.

Removal - 16-valve engines

Note: *Peugeot specify the use of a special electronic tool (SEEM C.TRONIC type 105.5 belt tensioning measuring tool) to correctly set the timing belt tension. If access to this equipment cannot be obtained, an approximate setting can be achieved using the method described below. If the method described is used, the tension must be checked using the special electronic tool at the earliest possible opportunity. Do not drive the vehicle over large distances, or use high engine speeds, until the belt tension is known to be correct. Refer to a Peugeot dealer for advice.*

28 Disconnect the battery negative terminal (refer to *"Disconnecting the battery"* in the Reference Section of this manual).
29 Align the engine assembly/valve timing holes as described in Section 3, and lock the camshaft sprockets and flywheel in position. *Do not* attempt to rotate the engine whilst the pins are in position.
30 Remove the timing belt covers as described in Section 5.
31 Loosen the timing belt tensioner pulley retaining bolt and pivot the pulley in a clockwise direction, using a suitable square-section key fitted to the hole in the pulley hub, then retighten the retaining bolt.
32 Check that the camshaft sprocket locking pins are still in position, then remove and inspect the belt as described in paragraphs 8 and 9.

Refitting - 16-valve engines

33 Before refitting, thoroughly clean the timing belt sprockets. Check that the tensioner and idler pulleys rotate freely, without any sign of roughness. If necessary, renew the pulleys as described in Section 7.
34 The timing belt is marked in three places with a paint line that indicates the position of teeth 1, 52 and 72 on the belt. When refitting, the paint marks on the belt must be positioned adjacent to the corresponding marks on the crankshaft and camshaft sprockets.
35 Ensure that the camshaft sprocket and flywheel locking pins are still in position, then without removing the locking pins, slacken the six camshaft sprocket retaining bolts (three on each sprocket). Check that both sprockets are free to move within the limits of their elongated bolt holes.
36 Manoeuvre the timing belt into position on the crankshaft sprocket and align the mark on the belt (indicating tooth 1) with the corresponding notch or mark on the crankshaft sprocket **(see illustration)**. Ensure that any arrows on the belt are pointing in the direction of rotation (clockwise when viewed from the right-hand end of the engine).
37 Turn each camshaft sprocket clockwise to the ends of their retaining bolt slots.

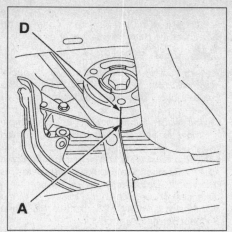

6.36 Align the timing belt mark (A) with the mark (D) on the crankshaft sprocket - 16-valve engines

38 With the timing belt engaged with the crankshaft sprocket and the marks aligned, keep the belt tight on its right-hand run and slip it over the idler pulley then up and into engagement with the exhaust camshaft sprocket. Ensure that the mark on the belt aligns with the corresponding notch or mark on the sprocket **(see illustration)**.

39 Keeping the belt tight, feed the belt over the inlet camshaft sprocket, again aligning the marks on the belt and sprocket, and taking care not to let the belt jump a tooth on the other sprockets as it is being fitted.

40 While still keeping the belt tight, feed it over the tensioner pulley and finally around the coolant pump.

41 If the special belt tension measuring equipment is available, proceed as described in paragraphs 42 to 48, and then to paragraph 55. If the tension is being set without the use of the special measuring equipment, proceed to paragraph 49.

42 If the special belt tension measuring equipment is available, it should be fitted to the "front run" of the timing belt. The tensioner pulley should be adjusted, by turning it anti-clockwise to give a belt pre-tensioning setting of 63 units. Hold the tensioner pulley in this position and tighten the retaining bolt to the specified torque.

43 Remove one retaining bolt from each camshaft sprocket and check that the sprockets are not at the end of their retaining bolt slots. If they are, repeat the refitting operation. If all is satisfactory, refit the two removed bolts, and tighten all six sprocket retaining bolts to the specified torque.

44 Remove the locking pins, then rotate the crankshaft through four complete rotations in a clockwise direction (viewed from the right-hand end of the engine). Realign the flywheel timing hole and refit the locking pin.

45 Slacken the six camshaft sprocket retaining bolts, then retighten them finger tight so that there is slight friction between the bolts and sprockets.

46 Refit the camshaft sprocket locking pins, then slacken the tensioner pulley retaining bolt once more. Refit the belt tension measuring equipment to the front run of the belt and turn the tensioner pulley to give a setting of 37 units on the tensioning gauge. Hold the tensioner pulley in this position and tighten the retaining bolt to the specified torque.

47 Retighten all six sprocket retaining bolts to the specified torque.

48 Remove the locking pins from the sprockets and flywheel.

49 If the tension is being set without the use of the special measuring equipment, the tensioner pulley should be adjusted, by turning it anti-clockwise until all free play is removed from the belt. Hold the tensioner pulley in this position and tighten the retaining bolt to the specified torque.

50 Remove one retaining bolt from each camshaft sprocket and check that the sprockets are not at the end of their retaining bolt slots. If they are, repeat the refitting operation. If all is satisfactory, refit the two removed bolts, and tighten all six sprocket retaining bolts to the specified torque.

51 Remove the locking pins, then rotate the crankshaft through four complete rotations in a clockwise direction (viewed from the right-hand end of the engine). Realign the timing hole and refit the locking pin to the flywheel.

52 Slacken the six camshaft sprocket retaining bolts, then retighten them finger tight so that there is slight friction between the bolts and sprockets.

53 Refit the camshaft sprocket locking pins, then slacken the tensioner pulley retaining bolt once more. Turn the tensioner pulley to tension the belt until, under moderate pressure from the thumb and forefinger, the belt can just be twisted through 45° at the mid-point between the inlet camshaft

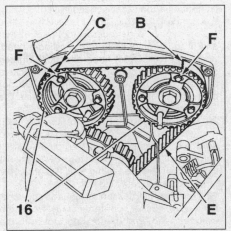

6.38 Camshaft sprocket and timing belt markings - 16-valve engines

16 Camshaft   C Timing belt marks
    sprockets   E Timing belt
B Timing belt marks   F Sprocket marks

sprocket and the idler pulley. Note that this method is only an initial setting and the belt tension must be checked at the earliest opportunity using the special belt tensioning equipment. Failure to do this could lead to the belt breaking (through over-tightening) or slipping (through slackness), resulting in serious engine damage. With the tension set, hold the tensioner pulley in this position and tighten the retaining bolt to the specified torque.

54 Retighten all six sprocket retaining bolts to the specified torque.

55 Refit the timing belt covers as described in Section 5, and reconnect the battery negative terminal.

---

7 Timing belt tensioner and sprockets - removal, inspection and refitting

Note: *This Section describes the removal and refitting of the components concerned as individual operations. If more than one of them is to be removed at the same time, start by removing the timing belt as described in Section 6; remove the actual component as described below, ignoring the preliminary dismantling steps.*

Removal - 8-valve engines

1 Disconnect the battery negative terminal (refer to *"Disconnecting the battery"* in the Reference Section of this manual).

Camshaft sprocket

2 On engines with a three-piece timing belt cover arrangement, remove the centre cover as described in Section 5. On engines with a two-piece cover, remove the lower cover.

3 Position the engine assembly/valve timing holes as described in Section 3, and lock both the camshaft sprocket and flywheel in position. *Do not* attempt to rotate the engine whilst the tools are in position.

4 Loosen the timing belt tensioner pulley retaining nut. Rotate the pulley in a clockwise direction, using a suitable square-section key fitted to the hole in the pulley hub, then retighten the retaining nut.

5 Disengage the timing belt from the sprocket, and move the belt clear, taking care not to bend or twist it sharply. Remove the locking pin from the camshaft sprocket.

6 Slacken the camshaft sprocket retaining bolt and remove it, along with its washer. *Do not* attempt to use the sprocket locking pin to prevent the sprocket from rotating whilst the bolt is slackened **(see Tool Tip overleaf)**.

7 With the retaining bolt removed, slide the sprocket off the end of the camshaft. If the locating peg is a loose fit in the rear of the sprocket, remove it for safe-keeping. Examine the camshaft oil seal for signs of oil leakage and, if necessary, renew it as described in Section 8.

To prevent the camshaft rotating as the bolt is slackened, a sprocket-holding tool will be required. In the absence of the special Peugeot tool, an acceptable substitute can be fabricated as follows. Use two lengths of steel strip (one long, the other short), and three nuts and bolts; one nut and bolt forms the pivot of a forked tool, with the remaining two nuts and bolts at the tips of the "forks" to engage with the sprocket spokes.

Crankshaft sprocket

8 Remove the centre and lower timing belt covers as described in Section 5, then position the engine assembly/valve timing holes as described in Section 3, and lock both the camshaft sprocket and flywheel in position. *Do not* attempt to rotate the engine whilst the tools are in position.

9 Loosen the timing belt tensioner pulley retaining nut. Rotate the pulley in a clockwise direction, using a suitable square-section key fitted to the hole in the pulley hub, then retighten the retaining nut.

10 To prevent crankshaft rotation whilst the sprocket retaining bolt is slackened, select top gear, and have an assistant apply the brakes firmly. If the engine has been removed from the vehicle, lock the flywheel ring gear, using an arrangement similar to that shown **(see illustration)**. *Do not* be tempted to use the flywheel locking pin to prevent the crankshaft from rotating; temporarily remove the locking pin from the rear of the flywheel prior to slackening the pulley bolt, then refit it once the bolt has been slackened.

11 Unscrew the retaining bolt and washer,

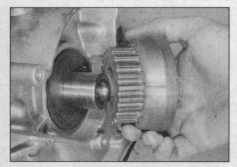

7.11b . . . then slide off the sprocket . . .

then slide the sprocket off the end of the crankshaft **(see illustrations)**. Refit the locating pin through the timing hole into the rear of the flywheel.

12 If the Woodruff key is a loose fit in the crankshaft, remove it and store it with the sprocket for safe-keeping. If necessary, also slide the flanged spacer off the end of the crankshaft **(see illustration)**. Examine the crankshaft oil seal for signs of oil leakage and, if necessary, renew as described in Section 16.

Tensioner pulley

13 Remove the centre timing belt cover as described in Section 5, then position the engine assembly/valve timing holes as described in Section 3, and lock both the camshaft sprocket and flywheel in position. *Do not* attempt to rotate the engine whilst the tools are in position.

14 Slacken and remove the timing belt tensioner pulley retaining nut, and slide the pulley off its mounting stud. Examine the mounting stud for signs of damage and, if necessary, renew it.

Removal - 16-valve engines

15 Disconnect the battery negative terminal (refer to *"Disconnecting the battery"* in the Reference Section of this manual).

Camshaft sprockets

16 Remove the cylinder head cover over the camshaft being worked on as described in Section 4.

17 Remove the timing belt upper cover as described in Section 5, then position the engine assembly/valve timing holes as

7.10 Use fabricated tool shown to lock flywheel ring gear and prevent the crankshaft rotating

7.12 . . . and remove the flanged spacer

described in Section 3, and lock the flywheel in position. *Do not* attempt to rotate the engine whilst the tool is in position.

18 Loosen the timing belt tensioner pulley retaining bolt and pivot the pulley in a clockwise direction, using a suitable square-section key fitted to the hole in the pulley hub, then retighten the retaining bolt.

19 Disengage the timing belt from the camshaft sprockets and position it clear, taking care not to bend or twist the belt sharply.

20 Slacken the sprocket hub centre retaining bolt. To prevent the sprocket rotating as the bolt is slackened, hold the camshaft using a suitable spanner engaged with the square section provided **(see illustration)**.

21 Remove the previously slackened hub retaining bolt and withdraw the sprocket and hub from the end of the camshaft. Suitably mark the sprockets "inlet" and/or "exhaust" if both are being removed.

Crankshaft sprocket

22 Remove the timing belt covers as described in Section 5.

23 Position the engine assembly/valve timing holes as described in Section 3, and lock both the camshaft sprocket and flywheel in position. *Do not* attempt to rotate the engine whilst the tools are in position.

7.11a Remove the crankshaft sprocket retaining bolt . . .

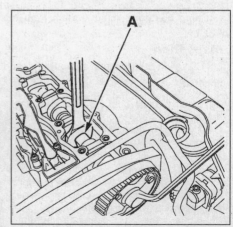

7.20 Using a spanner (A) to hold the camshaft as the sprocket bolt is slackened - 16-valve engines

24 Loosen the timing belt tensioner pulley retaining bolt and pivot the pulley in a clockwise direction, using a suitable square-section key fitted to the hole in the pulley hub, then retighten the retaining bolt.

25 To prevent crankshaft rotation whilst the sprocket retaining bolt is slackened, select top gear, and have an assistant apply the brakes firmly. If the engine has been removed from the vehicle, lock the flywheel ring gear, using an arrangement similar to that shown **(see illustration 7.10).** *Do not* be tempted to use the flywheel locking pin to prevent the crankshaft from rotating; temporarily remove the locking pin from the rear of the flywheel prior to slackening the pulley bolt, then refit it once the bolt has been slackened.

26 Unscrew the retaining bolt and washer, then slide the sprocket off the end of the crankshaft. Refit the locating pin to the rear of the timing hole in the rear of the flywheel.

27 If the Woodruff key is a loose fit in the crankshaft, remove it and store it with the sprocket for safe-keeping. If necessary, also slide the flanged spacer off the end of the crankshaft. Examine the crankshaft oil seal for signs of oil leakage and, if necessary, renew as described in Section 16.

Tensioner and idler pulleys

28 Remove the timing belt covers as described in Section 5.

29 Position the engine assembly/valve timing holes as described in Section 3, and lock both the camshaft sprocket and flywheel in position. *Do not* attempt to rotate the engine whilst the tools are in position.

30 Loosen the timing belt tensioner pulley retaining bolt and pivot the pulley in a clockwise direction, using a suitable square-section key fitted to the hole in the pulley hub, then retighten the retaining bolt.

31 Check that the camshaft sprocket locking pins are still in position, then disengage the timing belt from the camshaft sprockets and position it clear, taking care not to bend or twist the belt sharply.

32 Undo the tensioner and idler pulley retaining bolts and remove them from the engine.

Inspection

33 Clean the sprockets thoroughly, and renew any that show signs of wear, damage or cracks.

34 Clean the tensioner (and idler) assembly, but do not use any strong solvent which may enter the pulley bearing. Check that the pulley rotates freely about its hub, with no sign of stiffness or free play. Renew the tensioner/idler pulley if there is any doubt about its condition, or if there are any obvious signs of wear or damage.

Refitting - 8-valve engines

Camshaft sprocket

35 Refit the locating peg (where removed) to the rear of the sprocket, then locate the sprocket on the end of the camshaft. Ensure that the locating peg is correctly engaged with the cut-out in the end of the camshaft.

36 Refit the sprocket retaining bolt and washer. Tighten the bolt to the specified torque, whilst retaining the sprocket with the tool used on removal.

37 Realign the timing hole in the camshaft sprocket (see Section 3) with the corresponding hole in the cylinder head, and refit the locking pin.

38 Refit the timing belt to the camshaft sprocket. Ensure that the "front run" of the belt is taut - ie, ensure that any slack is on the tensioner pulley side of the belt. Do not twist the belt sharply while refitting it, and ensure that the belt teeth are seated centrally in the sprockets.

39 Loosen the tensioner pulley retaining nut. Rotate the pulley anti-clockwise to remove all free play from the timing belt, then retighten the nut.

40 Tension the belt as described under the relevant sub-heading of Section 6.

41 Refit the timing belt covers as described in Section 5.

Crankshaft sprocket

42 Where removed, locate the Woodruff key in the crankshaft end, then slide on the flanged spacer, aligning its slot with the Woodruff key.

43 Align the crankshaft sprocket slot with the Woodruff key, and slide it onto the end of the crankshaft.

44 Temporarily remove the locking pin from the rear of the flywheel, then refit the crankshaft sprocket retaining bolt and washer. Tighten the bolt to the specified torque, whilst preventing crankshaft rotation using the method employed on removal. Refit the locking pin to the rear of the flywheel.

45 Relocate the timing belt on the crankshaft sprocket. Ensure that the "front run" of the belt is taut - ie, ensure that any slack is on the tensioner pulley side of the belt. Do not twist the belt sharply while refitting it, and ensure that the belt teeth are seated centrally in the sprockets.

46 Loosen the tensioner pulley retaining nut. Rotate the pulley anti-clockwise to remove all free play from the timing belt, then retighten the nut.

47 Tension the belt as described under the relevant sub-heading of Section 6.

48 Refit the timing belt covers as described in Section 5.

Tensioner pulley

49 Refit the tensioner pulley to its mounting stud, and fit the retaining nut.

50 Ensure that the "front run" of the belt is taut - ie, ensure that any slack is on the tensioner pulley side of the belt. Check that the belt is centrally located on all its sprockets. Rotate the tensioner pulley anti-clockwise to remove all free play from the timing belt, then tighten the pulley retaining nut securely.

51 Tension the belt as described under the relevant sub-heading of Section 6.

52 Refit the timing belt covers as described in Section 5.

Refitting - 16-valve engines

Camshaft sprockets

53 Engage the sprocket hub with the camshaft, ensure that the correct sprocket is fitted to the relevant camshaft if both were removed.

54 Refit the sprocket retaining bolt and washer, and tighten it to the specified torque. Prevent rotation of the camshaft as the bolt is tightened using the spanner on the camshaft square section provided.

55 Turn the sprocket so that the locking pin can be engaged.

56 Relocate and tension the timing belt as described in Section 6.

Crankshaft sprocket

57 Refit the Woodruff key to its slot in the crankshaft end.

58 Slide on the crankshaft sprocket, aligning its slot with the Woodruff key.

59 Relocate and tension the timing belt as described in Section 6.

Tensioner and idler pulleys

60 Refit the tensioner and idler pulleys and secure with the retaining bolts.

61 Relocate and tension the timing belt as described in Section 6.

---

8 Camshaft oil seal - renewal

2A

Note: If the camshaft oil seal is to be renewed with the timing belt still in place, check first that the belt is free from oil contamination. (Renew the belt as a matter of course if signs of oil contamination are found; see Section 6.) Cover the belt to protect it from oil contamination while work is in progress. Ensure that all traces of oil are removed from the area before the belt is refitted.

1 On 8-valve engines, remove the camshaft sprocket as described in Section 7.

2 On 16-valve engines, remove both camshaft sprockets, the timing belt tensioner and the idler pulley. Unbolt and remove the timing belt inner cover.

3 Punch or drill two small holes opposite each other in the oil seal. Screw a self-tapping screw into each, and pull on the screws with pliers to extract the seal.

4 Clean the seal housing, and polish off any burrs or raised edges, which may have caused the seal to fail in the first place.

5 Lubricate the lips of the new seal with clean engine oil, and drive it into position until it seats on its locating shoulder. Use a suitable tubular drift, such as a socket, which bears only on the hard outer edge of the seal. Take care not to damage the seal lips during fitting. Note that the seal lips should face inwards.

9.5 Adjusting a valve clearance

6 On 8-valve engines, refit the camshaft sprocket(s) as described in Section 7.

7 On 16-valve engines, refit the timing belt inner cover, ensuring that the notch at the base of the cover locates correctly over the rib in the crankshaft oil seal carrier. Refit the idler and tensioner pulleys and the camshaft sprockets as described in Section 7.

9 Valve clearances (8-valve engines) - checking and adjustment

Note: *The valve clearances must be checked and adjusted only when the engine is cold.*

1 The importance of having the valve clearances correctly adjusted cannot be overstressed, as they vitally affect the performance of the engine. If the clearances are too big, the engine will be noisy (characteristic rattling or tapping noises) and engine efficiency will be reduced, as the valves open too late and close too early. A more serious problem arises if the clearances are too small, however. If this is the case, the valves may not close fully when the engine is hot, resulting in serious damage to the engine (eg. burnt valve seats and/or cylinder head warping/cracking). The clearances are checked and adjusted as follows.

2 Remove the cylinder head cover as described in Section 4.

3 The engine can now be turned using a suitable socket and extension bar fitted to the crankshaft sprocket/pulley bolt.

HAYNES HINT *Turning the engine will be easier if the spark plugs are removed first - see Chapter 1A.*

4 It is important that the clearance of each valve is checked and adjusted only when the valve is fully closed, with the rocker arm resting on the heel of the cam (directly opposite the peak). This can be ensured by carrying out the adjustments in the following sequence, (ex. = exhaust, in. = inlet) noting that No 1 cylinder is at the transmission end of the engine. The correct valve clearances are given in the Specifications at the start of this Chapter. The valve locations can be determined from the position of the manifolds.

Valve fully open	Adjust valves
No 1 ex.	No 3 in. and No 4 ex.
No 3 ex.	No 4 in. and No 2 ex.
No 4 ex.	No 2 in. and No 1 ex.
No 2 ex.	No 1 in. and No 3 ex.

5 With the relevant valve fully open, check the clearances of the two valves specified. Clearances are checked by inserting a feeler blade of the correct thickness between the valve stem and the rocker arm adjusting screw. The feeler blade should be a light, sliding fit. If adjustment is necessary, slacken the adjusting screw locknut, and turn the screw as necessary **(see illustration)**. Once the correct clearance is obtained, hold the adjusting screw and securely tighten the locknut. Recheck the valve clearance, and adjust again if necessary.

6 Rotate the crankshaft until the next valve in the sequence is fully open, and check the clearances of the next two specified valves.

7 Repeat the procedure until all eight valve clearances have been checked (and if necessary, adjusted), then refit the cylinder head cover as described in Section 4.

10 Camshaft and rocker arms (8-valve engines) - removal, inspection and refitting

General information

1 The rocker arm assembly is secured to the top of the cylinder head by the cylinder head

bolts. Although in theory it is possible to undo the head bolts and remove the rocker arm assembly without removing the head, in practice, this is not recommended. Once the bolts have been removed, the head gasket will be disturbed, and the gasket will almost certainly leak or blow after refitting. For this reason, removal of the rocker arm assembly cannot be done without removing the cylinder head and renewing the head gasket.

2 The camshaft is slid out of the right-hand end of the cylinder head, and it therefore cannot be removed without first removing the cylinder head, due to a lack of clearance.

Removal

Rocker arm assembly

3 Remove the cylinder head as described in Section 12.

4 To dismantle the rocker arm assembly, carefully prise off the circlip from the right-hand end of the rocker shaft; retain the rocker pedestal, to prevent it being sprung off the end of the shaft. Slide the various components off the end of the shaft, keeping all components in their correct fitted order **(see illustration)**. Make a note of each component's correct fitted position and orientation as it is removed, to ensure it is fitted correctly on reassembly.

5 To separate the left-hand pedestal and shaft, first unscrew the cylinder head cover retaining stud from the top of the pedestal; this can be achieved using a stud extractor, or two nuts locked together. With the stud removed, unscrew the grub screw from the top of the pedestal, and withdraw the rocker shaft **(see illustrations)**.

Camshaft

6 Remove the cylinder head as described in Section 12.

7 With the head on a bench, remove the locking pin, then remove the camshaft sprocket as described in Section 7.

8 Unbolt the housing from the left-hand end of the cylinder head, then undo the retaining bolt, and remove the camshaft thrust fork from the cylinder head **(see illustration)**.

9 Using a large flat-bladed screwdriver, carefully prise the oil seal out of the right-hand

10.4 Remove the circlip and slide the components off the end of the rocker arm

10.5a To remove the left-hand pedestal, lock two nuts together and unscrew the stud . . .

10.5b . . . then remove the grub screw

10.8 Undo the retaining bolt and remove the camshaft thrust fork (arrowed) . . .

10.9a . . . then prise out the oil seal . . .

10.9b . . . and slide out the camshaft

end of the cylinder head, then slide out the camshaft **(see illustrations).** Discard the seal - a new one must be used on refitting.

Inspection

Rocker arm assembly

10 Examine the rocker arm bearing surfaces which contact the camshaft lobes for wear ridges and scoring. Renew any rocker arms on which these conditions are apparent. If a rocker arm bearing surface is badly scored, also examine the corresponding lobe on the camshaft for wear, as both will likely be worn. On later engines, roller rocker arms are used incorporating a roller bearing at the camshaft lobe contact point. On this type of rocker, check for any sign of excess play of the roller bearing or any roughness as it is rotated. Renew worn components as necessary. The rocker arm assembly can be dismantled as described in paragraphs 4 and 5.

11 Inspect the ends of the (valve clearance) adjusting screws for signs of wear or damage, and renew as required.

12 If the rocker arm assembly has been dismantled, examine the rocker arm and shaft bearing surfaces for wear ridges and scoring. If there are obvious signs of wear, the relevant rocker arm(s) and/or the shaft must be renewed.

Camshaft

13 Examine the camshaft bearing surfaces and cam lobes for signs of wear ridges and scoring. Renew the camshaft if any of these conditions are apparent. Examine the condition of the bearing surfaces, both on the camshaft journals and in the cylinder head. If the head bearing surfaces are worn excessively, the cylinder head will need to be renewed. If the necessary measuring equipment is available, camshaft bearing journal wear can be checked by direct measurement, noting that No 1 journal is at the transmission end of the head.

14 Examine the thrust fork for signs of wear or scoring, and renew as necessary.

Refitting

Rocker arm assembly

15 If the rocker arm assembly was

dismantled, refit the rocker shaft to the left-hand pedestal, aligning its locating hole with the pedestal threaded hole. Refit the grub screw, and tighten it securely. With the grub screw in position, refit the cylinder head cover mounting stud to the pedestal, and tighten it securely. Apply a smear of clean engine oil to the shaft, then slide on all removed components, ensuring each is correctly fitted in its original position. Once all components are in position on the shaft, compress the right-hand pedestal and refit the circlip. Ensure that the circlip is correctly located in its groove on the shaft.

16 Refit the cylinder head and rocker arm assembly as described in Section 12.

Camshaft

17 Ensure that the cylinder head and camshaft bearing surfaces are clean, then liberally oil the camshaft bearings and lobes. Slide the camshaft back into position in the cylinder head. On carburettor engines, take care that the fuel pump operating lever is not trapped by the camshaft as it is slid into position. To prevent this, remove the fuel pump before refitting the camshaft, then refit it afterwards.

18 Locate the thrust fork with the left-hand end of the camshaft. Refit the fork retaining bolt, tightening it to the specified torque setting.

19 Ensure that the housing and cylinder head mating surfaces are clean and dry, then apply a smear of sealant to the housing mating surface. Refit the housing to the left-hand end of the head, and securely tighten its retaining bolts.

20 Lubricate the lips of the new seal with clean engine oil, then drive it into position until it seats on its locating shoulder. Use a suitable tubular drift, such as a socket, which bears only on the hard outer edge of the seal. Take care not to damage the seal lips during fitting. Note that the seal lips should face inwards.

21 Refit the camshaft sprocket as described in Section 7.

22 Refit the cylinder head as described in Section 12.

11 Camshaft and followers (16-valve engines) - removal, inspection and refitting

Removal

1 Disconnect the battery negative terminal (refer to *"Disconnecting the battery"* in the Reference Section of this manual).

2 Remove both cylinder head covers as described in Section 4.

3 Remove the oil seal from the camshaft to be removed as described in Section 8.

4 Progressively slacken, in a spiral sequence starting from the outside, the twelve bolts securing the camshaft bearing housing to the cylinder head. Only slacken the bolts sufficiently to separate the mating surfaces by a few millimetres at this stage.

5 Lightly tap the sprocket end of the camshaft, using a soft-faced mallet, to free the camshaft from its bearings.

6 Completely unscrew and remove the bearing housing retaining bolts, then lift off the housing.

7 As both camshafts are identical, suitably mark them inlet and exhaust, or front and rear before removal, if both are to be removed. Carefully lift the camshaft up and out of its location in the cylinder head.

8 If both camshafts are being removed, repeat the previous procedures on the remaining camshaft.

9 Obtain sixteen small, clean plastic containers (assuming both camshafts have been removed), and number them inlet 1 to 8 and exhaust 1 to 8; alternatively, divide a larger container into sixteen compartments and number each compartment accordingly. Using a rubber sucker, withdraw each hydraulic tappet in turn, and place it in its respective container. Do not interchange the tappets, or the rate of wear will be much-increased.

Inspection

10 Examine the camshaft bearing surfaces and cam lobes for signs of wear ridges and scoring. Renew the camshaft if any of these conditions are apparent. Examine the condition of the bearing surfaces, both on the camshaft

2A

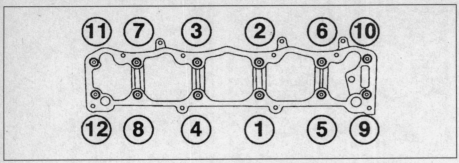

11.19 Camshaft bearing housing retaining bolt tightening sequence - 16-valve engines

journals and in the cylinder head/bearing caps. If the head bearing surfaces are worn excessively, the cylinder head will need to be renewed. If suitable measuring equipment is available, camshaft bearing journal wear can be checked by direct measurement (where the necessary specifications have been quoted by Peugeot), noting that No 1 journal is at the transmission end of the head.

11 Examine the cam follower/hydraulic tappet bearing surfaces which contact the camshaft lobes for wear ridges and scoring. Renew any follower/tappet on which these conditions are apparent. If a follower/tappet bearing surface is badly scored, also examine the corresponding lobe on the camshaft for wear, as it is likely that both will be worn. Renew worn components as necessary.

Refitting

12 Before refitting, remove all traces of oil from the bearing housing retaining bolt holes in the cylinder head, using a clean rag. Also ensure that both the cylinder head and bearing housing mating faces are clean and free from oil.

13 Remove the flywheel timing pin and turn the crankshaft one quarter turn so that the pistons are positioned half way down their bores.

14 Liberally oil the cylinder head hydraulic tappet bores and the tappets. Carefully refit the tappets to the cylinder head, ensuring that each tappet is refitted to its original bore. Some care will be required to enter the tappets squarely into their bores. Check that each tappet rotates freely in its bore.

15 Liberally oil the camshaft bearings in the cylinder head and the camshaft lobes, then refit the camshafts to the cylinder head. Turn the camshafts so that the groove at the timing belt end of each camshaft is positioned as follows:

Inlet camshaft groove at 7 o'clock
Exhaust camshaft groove positioned at 8 o'clock

16 Ensure that the four locating dowels are in position, one at each corner of the cylinder head.

17 Apply a bead of silicone based jointing compound around the perimeter of the mating faces and around the retaining bolt hole locations.

18 Liberally oil the camshaft bearings and carefully locate the bearing housings over the camshafts. Apply a suitable thread locking compound to the retaining bolt threads and refit the retaining bolts finger tight at this stage.

19 Working in the order shown, progressively tighten the bearing housing retaining bolts to the stage one torque setting then to the stage two setting **(see illustration)**.

20 Fit a new oil seal to each camshaft as described in Section 8.

21 Refit the timing belt inner cover, ensuring that the notch at the base of the cover locates correctly over the rib in the crankshaft oil seal carrier. Refit the idler and tensioner pulleys and the camshaft sprockets as described in Section 7.

22 Refit the cylinder head covers as described in Section 4.

12 Cylinder head (8-valve engines) - removal and refitting

Removal

1 Disconnect the battery negative terminal (refer to *"Disconnecting the battery"* in the Reference Section of this manual).

2 Drain the cooling system as described in Chapter 1A.

3 Remove the cylinder head cover as described in Section 4.

4 Align the engine assembly/valve timing holes as described in Section 3, and lock both the camshaft sprocket and flywheel in position. *Do not* attempt to rotate the engine whilst the tools are in position.

5 Note that the following text assumes that the cylinder head will be removed with both inlet and exhaust manifolds attached; this is easier, but makes it a bulky and heavy assembly to handle. If it is wished to remove the manifolds first, proceed as described in the relevant Part of Chapter 4.

6 Working as described in the relevant Part of Chapter 4, disconnect the exhaust system front pipe from the manifold. Where fitted, disconnect or release the lambda sensor wiring, so that it is not strained by the weight of the exhaust.

7 Remove the air cleaner housing and intake duct assembly as described in the relevant Part of Chapter 4.

8 On carburettor engines, disconnect the following from the carburettor and inlet manifold as described in Chapter 4A:

a) *Fuel feed hose from the pump and the return hose from the anti-percolation chamber (plug all openings, to prevent loss of fuel and the entry of dirt into the system).*

b) *Accelerator cable.*

c) *Choke cable.*

d) *Carburettor coolant hoses - 954 cc and 1124 cc models.*

e) *Carburettor heating element and idle cut-off solenoid wiring connector(s) - 1360 cc models.*

f) *Vacuum servo unit vacuum hose, coolant hose and all other relevant breather/vacuum hoses from the manifold.*

9 On fuel injection engines, carry out the following operations as described in the relevant Part of Chapter 4:

a) *Depressurise the fuel system, and disconnect the fuel feed and return hoses from the throttle body/fuel rail (plug all openings, to prevent loss of fuel and entry of dirt into the fuel system).*

b) *Disconnect the accelerator cable.*

c) *On single-point injection models, disconnect the relevant electrical connectors from the throttle body.*

d) *On multi-point injection models, disconnect the relevant electrical connectors from the throttle housing, fuel injectors and (where necessary) the idle speed auxiliary air valve.*

e) *Disconnect the vacuum servo unit hose, coolant hose(s) and all the other relevant/breather hoses from the manifold.*

10 Remove the centre and upper timing belt covers as described in Section 5.

11 Loosen the timing belt tensioner pulley retaining nut. Pivot the pulley in a clockwise direction, using a suitable square-section key fitted to the hole in the pulley hub, then retighten the retaining nut.

12 Disengage the timing belt from the camshaft sprocket, and position the belt clear of the sprocket. Ensure that the belt is not bent or twisted sharply.

13 Slacken the retaining clips, and disconnect the coolant hoses from the thermostat housing (on the left-hand end of the cylinder head).

14 Depress the retaining clip(s), and disconnect the wiring connector(s) from the electrical switch and/or sensor(s) which are screwed into the thermostat housing/cylinder head (as appropriate). Also, where necessary, release the TDC connector from its support on the distributor bracket on the left-hand end of the cylinder head.

Models with a distributor

15 Disconnect the LT wiring connectors from the distributor and HT coil. Release the TDC sensor wiring connector from the side of the coil mounting bracket, and disconnect the vacuum pipe from the distributor vacuum diaphragm unit. If the cylinder head is to be dismantled for overhaul, remove the distributor and ignition HT coil as described in Chapter 5B. If the cylinder numbers are not already marked on the HT leads, number each lead, to avoid the possibility of the leads being incorrectly connected on refitting. Disconnect the HT leads from the spark plugs, and remove the distributor cap and lead assembly.

Models with a distributorless ignition system

16 Disconnect the wiring connector from the ignition HT coil. If the cylinder head is to be dismantled for overhaul, remove the ignition HT coil as described in Chapter 5B. If the cylinder numbers are not already marked on the HT leads, number each lead, to avoid the possibility of the leads being incorrectly connected on refitting. Note that the HT leads should be disconnected from the spark plugs instead of the coil, and the coil and leads removed as an assembly.

All models

17 Slacken and remove the bolt securing the engine oil dipstick tube to the cylinder head.

18 Working in the *reverse* of the sequence shown in illustration 12.38a, progressively slacken the ten cylinder head bolts by half a turn at a time, until all bolts can be unscrewed by hand.

19 With all the cylinder head bolts removed, lift the rocker arm assembly off the cylinder head. Note the locating pins which are fitted to the base of each rocker arm pedestal. If any pin is a loose fit in the head or pedestal, remove it for safe-keeping.

20 On engines with a cast-iron cylinder block, lift the cylinder head away; seek assistance if possible, as it is a heavy assembly, especially if it is being removed complete with the manifolds.

21 On engines with an aluminium cylinder block, the joint between the cylinder head and gasket and the cylinder block/crankcase must now be broken without disturbing the wet liners. To break the joint, obtain two L-shaped metal bars which fit into the cylinder head bolt holes. Gently "rock" the cylinder head free towards the front of the car **(see illustration)**. Do not try to swivel the head on the cylinder block/crankcase; it is located by dowels, as well as by the tops of the liners. **Note:** *If care is not taken and the liners are moved, there is also a possibility of the bottom seals being disturbed, causing leakage after refitting the head.* When the joint is broken, lift the cylinder head away; seek assistance if possible, as it is a heavy assembly, especially if it is being removed complete with the manifolds.

22 On all models, remove the gasket from the top of the block, noting the two locating dowels.

23 If the locating dowels are a loose fit, remove them and store them with the head for safe-keeping. Do not discard the gasket - on some models it will be needed for identification purposes (see paragraphs 28 and 29).

Caution: On aluminium block engines, Do not attempt to rotate the crankshaft with the cylinder head removed, otherwise the wet liners may be displaced. Operations that require the rotation of the crankshaft (eg cleaning the piston crowns), should only be carried out once the cylinder liners are firmly clamped in position. In the absence of the special Peugeot liner clamps, the liners can be clamped in position using large flat washers positioned underneath suitable-length bolts. Alternatively, the original head bolts could be temporarily refitted, with suitable spacers fitted to their shanks.

24 If the cylinder head is to be dismantled for overhaul, remove the camshaft as described in Section 10, then refer to Part C of this Chapter.

Preparation for refitting

25 The mating faces of the cylinder head and cylinder block/crankcase must be perfectly clean before refitting the head. Use a hard plastic or wood scraper to remove all traces of gasket and carbon; also clean the piston crowns. Refer to paragraph 23 before turning the crankshaft on aluminium block engines. Take particular care during the cleaning operations, as aluminium alloy is easily damaged. Also, make sure that the carbon is not allowed to enter the oil and water passages - this is particularly important for the lubrication system, as carbon could block the oil supply to the engine's components. Using adhesive tape and paper, seal the water, oil and bolt holes in the cylinder block/crankcase. To prevent carbon entering the gap between the pistons and bores, smear a little grease in the gap. After cleaning each piston, use a small brush to remove all traces of grease and carbon from the gap, then wipe away the remainder with a clean rag. Clean all the pistons in the same way.

26 Check the mating surfaces of the cylinder block/crankcase and the cylinder head for nicks, deep scratches and other damage. If slight, they may be removed carefully with a file, but if excessive, machining may be the only alternative to renewal.

27 If warpage of the cylinder head gasket surface is suspected, use a straight-edge to check it for distortion. Refer to Part C of this Chapter if necessary.

28 When purchasing a new cylinder head gasket, it is essential that a gasket of the correct thickness is obtained. On some models only one thickness of gasket is available, so this is not a problem. However on all other models, there are two different thicknesses available - the standard gasket which is fitted at the factory, and a slightly thicker "repair" gasket (+ 0.2 mm), for use once the head gasket face has been machined. If the cylinder

12.21 Using two angled metal rods to free the cylinder head from the block

head has been machined, it should have the letter "R" stamped adjacent to the No 3 exhaust port, and the gasket should also have the letter "R" stamped adjacent to No 3 cylinder on its front upper face. The gaskets can also be identified as described in the following paragraph, using the cut-outs on the left-hand end of the gasket.

29 With the gasket fitted the correct way up on the cylinder block, there will be a single cut-out, or no cut-out at all, at the rear of the left-hand side of the gasket identifying the engine type (ie. TU engine). In the centre of the gasket there will likely be another series of between 0 and 4 cut-outs, identifying the manufacturer of the gasket and whether or not it contains asbestos (these cut-outs are of little importance). The important cut-out location is at the front of the gasket; on the standard gasket there will be no cut-out in this position, whereas on the thicker "repair" gasket there will be a single cut-out **(see illustration)**. Identify the gasket type, and

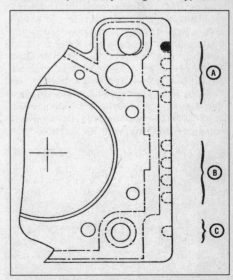

12.29 Cylinder head gasket identification markings

A *Engine type identification cut-outs*
B *Gasket manufacturer identification cut-outs*
C *Gasket thickness identification cut-out*

2A

12.33 Locate the cylinder head gasket on the block . . .

12.34 . . . then lower the cylinder head into position . . .

12.35 . . . and refit the rocker arm assembly

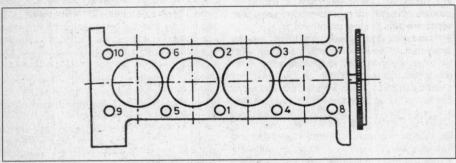

12.38a Cylinder head bolt tightening sequence - 8-valve engines

ensure that the new gasket obtained is of the correct thickness. If there is any doubt as to which gasket is fitted, take the old gasket along to your Peugeot dealer, and have him confirm the gasket type. Note that on engines manufactured from approximately mid-1996 onward, there are even more variations of gasket type. This is due to various changes that have been made to the cylinder head to meet the latest exhaust emission requirements, and vary according to specific engine type. If working on a post-1995 model it is essential that the engine type, code and serial numbers are taken to a Peugeot dealer to ensure that the correct gasket is obtained.

30 Check the condition of the cylinder head bolts, and particularly their threads, whenever they are removed. Wash the bolts in suitable solvent, and wipe them dry. Check each for any sign of visible wear or damage, renewing any bolt if necessary. Measure the length of each bolt, from the end of the thread to the underside of the bolt head, to check for stretching. If the length of any bolt exceeds 176.5 mm it must be renewed. It is strongly recommended that the bolts should be renewed as a complete set whenever they are disturbed.

31 On aluminium block engines, prior to refitting the cylinder head, check the cylinder liner protrusion as described in Part C of this Chapter.

Refitting

32 Wipe clean the mating surfaces of the cylinder head and cylinder block/crankcase. Check that the two locating dowels are in position at each end of the cylinder block/crankcase surface and, if necessary, remove the cylinder liner clamps.

33 Position a new gasket on the cylinder block/crankcase surface, ensuring that its identification cut-outs are at the left-hand end of the gasket **(see illustration)**.

34 Check that the flywheel and camshaft sprocket are still correctly locked in position with their respective tools then, with the aid of an assistant, carefully refit the cylinder head assembly to the block, aligning it with the locating dowels **(see illustration)**.

35 Ensure that the locating pins are in position in the base of each rocker pedestal, then refit the rocker arm assembly to the cylinder head **(see illustration)**.

36 Apply a smear of grease to the threads, and to the underside of the heads, of the cylinder head bolts. Peugeot recommend the use of Molykote G Rapid Plus grease (available from your Peugeot dealer - a sachet is supplied with the top-end gasket set); in the absence of the specified grease, a good-quality high-melting-point grease may be used.

37 Carefully enter each bolt into its relevant hole (do not drop them in) and screw in, by hand only, until finger-tight.

38 Working progressively and in the sequence shown, tighten the cylinder head bolts to their Stage 1 torque setting, using a torque wrench and suitable socket **(see illustrations)**.

39 Once all the bolts have been tightened to their Stage 1 setting, working again in the given sequence, angle-tighten the bolts through the specified Stage 2 angle, using a socket and extension bar. It is recommended that an angle-measuring gauge is used during this stage of the tightening, to ensure accuracy **(see illustration)**.

> **HAYNES HiNT**
> *If an angle-measuring gauge is not available, use white paint to make alignment marks between the bolt head and cylinder head prior to tightening; the marks can then be used to check that the bolt has been rotated through the correct angle during tightening.*

40 On cast-iron block engines, it will then be necessary to tighten the bolts through the specified Stage 3 angle setting.

12.38b Working in the specified sequence, tighten the head bolts first to the Stage 1 torque setting . . .

12.39 . . . then through the specified Stage 2 angle setting

41 With the cylinder head bolts correctly tightened, refit the dipstick tube retaining bolt and tighten it securely.

42 Refit the timing belt to the camshaft sprocket. Ensure that the "front run" of the belt is taut - ie, ensure that any slack is on the tensioner pulley side of the belt. Do not twist the belt sharply while refitting it, and ensure that the belt teeth are seated centrally in the sprockets.

43 Loosen the tensioner pulley retaining nut. Pivot the pulley anti-clockwise to remove all free play from the timing belt, then retighten the nut.

44 Tension the belt as described under the relevant sub-heading in Section 6, then refit the centre and upper timing belt covers as described in Section 5.

Models with a distributor

45 If the head was stripped for overhaul, refit the distributor and HT coil as described in Chapter 5B, ensuring that the HT leads are correctly reconnected. If the head was not stripped, reconnect the wiring connector and vacuum pipe to the distributor, and the HT lead to the coil; clip the TDC sensor wiring connector onto the coil bracket.

Models with a distributorless ignition system

46 If the head was stripped for overhaul, refit the ignition HT coil and leads as described in Chapter 5B, ensuring that the leads are correctly reconnected. If the head was not stripped, simply reconnect the wiring connector to the HT coil.

All models

47 Reconnect the wiring connector(s) to the coolant switch/sensor(s) on the left-hand end of the head.

48 Reconnect the coolant hoses to the thermostat housing, securely tightening their retaining clips.

49 Working as described in the relevant Part of Chapter 4, carry out the following tasks:

a) Refit all disturbed wiring, hoses and control cable(s) to the inlet manifold and fuel system components.

b) On carburettor models, reconnect and adjust the choke and accelerator cables.

c) On fuel injection models, reconnect and adjust the accelerator cable.

d) Reconnect the exhaust system front pipe to the manifold. Where applicable, reconnect the lambda sensor wiring connector.

e) Refit the air cleaner housing and intake duct.

50 Check and, if necessary, adjust the valve clearances as described in Section 9.

51 On completion, reconnect the battery, and refill the cooling system as described in Chapter 1A.

13 Cylinder head (16-valve engines) - removal and refitting

Removal

1 Disconnect the battery negative terminal (refer to *"Disconnecting the battery"* in the Reference Section of this manual).

2 Drain the cooling system (see Chapter 1A).

3 Remove the air cleaner assembly and intake ducting as described in Chapter 4C.

4 Align the engine assembly/valve timing holes as described in Section 3, locking both the camshaft sprockets and flywheel in position. *Do not* attempt to rotate the engine whilst the pins are in position.

5 Remove the cylinder head covers as described in Section 4.

6 Remove the inlet and exhaust manifolds as described in Chapter 4C.

7 Disconnect the coolant hoses and electrical connections from the thermostat housing.

8 Disconnect all remaining vacuum/breather hoses, and all electrical connector plugs from the cylinder head.

9 Release the timing belt tensioner and disengage the timing belt from the camshaft sprockets as described in Section 7.

10 Working in the *reverse* of the sequence shown in illustration 13.24, progressively slacken the ten cylinder head bolts by half a turn at a time, until all bolts can be unscrewed by hand. Remove the bolts along with their washers (where fitted).

11 With all the cylinder head bolts removed, the joint between the cylinder head and gasket and the cylinder block/crankcase must now be broken.

12 To break the joint, obtain two L-shaped metal bars which fit into the cylinder head bolt holes, and gently "rock" the cylinder head free towards the front of the car **(see illustration 12.21)**. *Do not* try to swivel the head on the cylinder block/crankcase; it is located by dowels.

13 When the joint is broken, lift the cylinder head away. Seek assistance if possible, as it is a heavy assembly. Remove the gasket from the top of the block, noting the two locating dowels. If the locating dowels are a loose fit, remove them and store them with the head for safe-keeping. Do not discard the gasket; it will be needed for identification purposes.

14 If the cylinder head is to be dismantled for overhaul, remove the camshaft(s) as described in Section 11, then refer to Part C of this Chapter.

Preparation for refitting

15 The mating faces of the cylinder head and cylinder block/crankcase must be perfectly clean before refitting the head. Use a hard plastic or wooden scraper to remove all traces of gasket and carbon; also clean the piston crowns. Take particular care, as the soft aluminium alloy is easily damaged. Make sure

that the carbon is not allowed to enter the oil and water passages - this is particularly important for the lubrication system, as carbon could block the oil supply to the engine's components. Using adhesive tape and paper, seal the water, oil and bolt holes in the cylinder block/crankcase. To prevent carbon entering the gap between the pistons and bores, smear a little grease in the gap. After cleaning each piston, use a small brush to remove all traces of grease and carbon from the gap, then wipe away the remainder with a clean rag. Clean all the pistons in the same way.

16 Check the mating surfaces of the cylinder block/crankcase and the cylinder head for nicks, deep scratches and other damage. If slight, they may be removed carefully with a file, but if excessive, machining may be the only alternative to renewal. If warpage of the cylinder head gasket surface is suspected, use a straight-edge to check it for distortion. Refer to Part C of this Chapter if necessary.

17 When purchasing a new cylinder head gasket, it is essential that a gasket of the correct thickness is obtained. On some models only one thickness of gasket is available, so this is not a problem. However on other models, there are different thicknesses available. As modifications to the cylinder head gasket material, type, and manufacturer are constantly taking place; seek the advice of a Peugeot dealer as to the latest recommendations.

18 Check the condition of the cylinder head bolts, and particularly their threads, whenever they are removed. Wash the bolts in a suitable solvent, and wipe them dry. Check each bolt for any sign of visible wear or damage, renewing them if necessary. Measure the length of each bolt (without the washer fitted) from the underside of its head to the end of the bolt. The bolts may be re-used if their length does not exceed 122.6 mm. If any one bolt is longer than the specified length, *all* of the bolts should be renewed as a complete set. Note that modifications to the cylinder head bolts are constantly taking place; seek the advice of a Peugeot dealer as to the latest recommendations. Considering the stress which the cylinder head bolts are under, it is highly recommended that they are renewed, regardless of their apparent condition.

Refitting

19 Wipe clean the mating surfaces of the cylinder head and cylinder block/crankcase. Check that the two locating dowels are in position at each end of the cylinder block/crankcase surface.

20 Position a new gasket on the cylinder block/crankcase surface, with its markings facing upward.

21 Check that the camshaft sprockets and flywheel are still locked in position with their respective pins. With the aid of an assistant, carefully refit the cylinder head assembly to the block, aligning it with the locating dowels.

2A

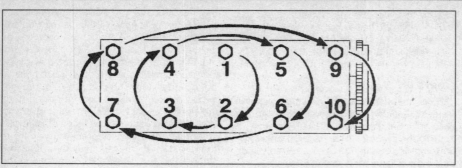

13.24 Cylinder head bolt tightening sequence - 16-valve engines

22 Apply a smear of grease to the threads, and to the underside of the heads, of the cylinder head bolts. Peugeot recommend the use of Molykote G Rapid Plus (available from your Peugeot dealer); in the absence of the specified grease, any good-quality high-melting-point grease may be used.

23 Carefully enter each bolt and washer into its relevant hole (*do not drop it in*) and screw it in finger-tight.

24 Working progressively and in the sequence shown, tighten the cylinder head bolts to their Stage 1 torque setting, using a torque wrench and suitable socket **(see illustration)**.

25 Once all the bolts have been tightened to their Stage 1 setting, working again in the given sequence, angle-tighten the bolts through the specified Stage 2 angle, using a socket and extension bar. It is recommended that an angle-measuring gauge is used during this stage of the tightening, to ensure accuracy (see **Haynes Hint** in Section 12).

26 Refit and tension the timing belt as described in Section 6.

27 The remainder of the refitting procedure is a reversal of removal, noting the following points:

a) *Ensure that all wiring is correctly routed, and that all connectors are securely reconnected to the correct components.*

b) *Ensure that the coolant hoses are correctly reconnected, and that their retaining clips are securely tightened.*

c) *Ensure that all vacuum/breather hoses are correctly reconnected.*

d) *Refit the inlet and exhaust manifolds, as described in Chapter 4C.*

e) *Refit the cylinder head covers as described in Section 4.*

f) *On completion, refill the cooling system as described in Chapter 1A, and reconnect the battery.*

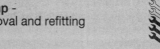

14 Sump -
removal and refitting

Removal

1 Disconnect the battery negative terminal (refer to *"Disconnecting the battery"* in the Reference Section of this manual). Chock the rear wheels then jack up the front of the vehicle and support it on axle stands (see *"Jacking and Vehicle Support"*).

2 Drain the engine oil, then clean and refit the engine oil drain plug, tightening it to the specified torque. If the engine is nearing its service interval when the oil and filter are due for renewal, it is recommended that the filter is also removed, and a new one fitted. After reassembly, the engine can then be refilled with fresh oil. Refer to Chapter 1A for further information.

3 Remove the exhaust system front pipe as described in the relevant Part of Chapter 4.

4 Progressively slacken and remove all the sump retaining nuts and bolts **(see illustration)**. On cast-iron block engines, it may be necessary to unbolt the flywheel cover plate from the transmission to gain access to the left-hand sump fasteners.

5 Break the joint by striking the sump with the palm of your hand, then lower the sump and withdraw it from underneath the vehicle **(see illustration)**.

6 While the sump is removed, take the opportunity to check the oil pump pick-up/strainer for signs of clogging or splitting. If necessary, remove the pump as described in Section 15, and clean or renew the strainer.

Refitting

7 Clean all traces of sealant from the mating surfaces of the cylinder block/crankcase and sump, then use a clean rag to wipe out the sump and the engine's interior.

8 Ensure that the sump and cylinder block/crankcase mating surfaces are clean and dry, then apply a coating of suitable sealant to the sump mating surface.

9 Offer up the sump, locating it on its retaining studs, and refit its retaining nuts and bolts. Tighten the nuts and bolts evenly and progressively to the specified torque.

10 Refit the exhaust front pipe as described in the relevant Part of Chapter 4.

11 Replenish the engine with oil as described in Chapter 1A.

15 Oil pump -
removal, inspection
and refitting

Removal

1 Remove the sump as described in Section 14.

2 Slacken and remove the three bolts securing the oil pump in position **(see illustration)**. Disengage the pump sprocket from the chain, and remove the oil pump. If the pump locating dowel is a loose fit, remove and store it with the retaining bolts for safe-keeping.

Inspection

3 Examine the oil pump sprocket for signs of damage and wear such as chipped or missing teeth. If the sprocket is worn, the pump assembly must be renewed, as the sprocket is not available separately. It is also recommended that the chain and drive sprocket, fitted to the crankshaft, is renewed at the same time. On aluminium block engines,

14.4 Slacken and remove the sump retaining nuts and bolts . . .

14.5 . . . then remove the sump from the engine

15.2 Oil pump is retained by three bolts

renewal of the chain and drive sprocket is an involved operation requiring the removal of the main bearing ladder, and therefore cannot be carried out with the engine still fitted to the vehicle. On cast-iron block engines, the oil pump drive sprocket and chain can be removed with the engine in situ, once the crankshaft sprocket has been removed and the crankshaft oil seal housing has been unbolted. Refer to Part C for further information.

4 Slacken and remove the bolts securing the strainer cover to the pump body, then lift off the strainer cover. Remove the relief valve piston and spring (and guide pin - cast-iron block engines only), noting which way round they are fitted.

5 Examine the pump rotors and body for signs of wear ridges and scoring. If worn, the complete pump assembly must be renewed.

6 Examine the relief valve piston for signs of wear or damage, and renew if necessary. The condition of the relief valve spring can only be measured by comparing it with a new one; if there is any doubt about its condition, it should also be renewed. Both the piston and spring are available individually.

7 Thoroughly clean the oil pump strainer with a suitable solvent, and check it for signs of clogging or splitting. If the strainer is damaged, the strainer and cover assembly must be renewed.

8 Locate the relief valve spring, piston and (where fitted) the guide pin in the strainer cover, then refit the cover to the pump body. Align the relief valve piston with its bore in the pump. Refit the cover retaining bolts, tightening them securely.

Refitting

9 Ensure that the locating dowel is in position, then engage the pump sprocket with its drive chain. Locate the pump on its dowel and refit the pump retaining bolts, tightening them to the specified torque setting.

10 Refit the sump as described in Section 14.

16 Crankshaft oil seals - renewal

Right-hand oil seal

1 Remove the crankshaft sprocket and flanged spacer as described in Section 7. Secure the timing belt clear of the working area, so that it cannot be contaminated with oil. Make a note of the correct fitted depth of the seal in its housing.

 HAYNES HINT *Punch or drill two small holes opposite each other in the seal. Screw a self-tapping screw into each, and pull on the screws with pliers to extract the seal.*

2 The seal can be levered out of position using a suitable flat-bladed screwdriver, taking great care not to damage the crankshaft shoulder or seal housing **(see illustration)**.

3 Clean the seal housing, and polish off any burrs or raised edges, which may have caused the seal to fail in the first place.

4 Lubricate the lips of the new seal with clean engine oil, and carefully locate the seal on the end of crankshaft. Note that its sealing lip must face inwards. Take care not to damage the seal lips during fitting.

5 Using a suitable tubular drift (such as a socket) which bears only on the hard outer edge of the seal, tap the seal into position, to the same depth in the housing as the original was prior to removal. The inner face of the seal must end up flush with the inner wall of the crankcase.

6 Wash off any traces of oil, then refit the crankshaft sprocket as described in Section 7.

Left-hand oil seal

7 Remove the flywheel/driveplate as described in Section 18.

8 Make a note of the correct fitted depth of the seal in its housing. Punch or drill two small holes opposite each other in the seal. Screw a self-tapping screw into each, and pull on the screws with pliers to extract the seal.

9 Clean the seal housing, and polish off any burrs or raised edges, which may have caused the seal to fail in the first place.

10 Lubricate the lips of the new seal with clean engine oil, and carefully locate the seal on the end of the crankshaft.

11 Using a suitable tubular drift, which bears only on the hard outer edge of the seal, drive the seal into position, to the same depth in the housing as the original was prior to removal.

12 Wash off any traces of oil, then refit the flywheel/driveplate as described in Section 18.

17 Oil cooler (1294 cc and some 1360 cc & 1587 cc models) - removal and refitting

Removal

1 Chock the rear wheels then jack up the front of the vehicle and support it on axle stands (see "*Jacking and Vehicle Support*").

2 Drain the cooling system as described in Chapter 1A. Alternatively, clamp the oil cooler coolant hoses directly above the cooler pipes, and be prepared for some coolant loss as the hoses are disconnected.

3 Position a suitable container beneath the oil filter, then unscrew the filter (using an oil filter removal tool if necessary), and drain the oil into the container. If the oil filter is damaged or disfigured during removal, it must be renewed and the engine should be filled with clean oil on refitting.

4 Release the hose clips, and disconnect the coolant hoses from the oil cooler.

5 Undo the bolt securing the oil cooler pipes

16.2 Using a screwdriver to lever out the crankshaft front oil seal

to the transmission, then unscrew the oil cooler/oil filter mounting bolt from the cylinder block, and withdraw the cooler. Discard the oil cooler sealing ring; a new one must be used on refitting.

Refitting

6 Fit a new sealing ring to the recess in the rear of the cooler, then offer up the cooler to the cylinder block. Refit the mounting bolt, and the bolt securing the pipes to the transmission, tightening them both securely.

7 Fit the oil filter, then lower the vehicle to the ground. Top-up the engine oil level as described in "*Weekly checks*".

8 Refill or top-up the cooling system (as applicable) as described in Chapter 1A or "*Weekly checks*", then start the engine and check the oil cooler for signs of leakage.

18 Flywheel/driveplate - removal, inspection and refitting

Removal

Flywheel (manual transmission models)

1 Remove the transmission as described in Chapter 7A, then remove the clutch assembly as described in Chapter 6.

2 Prevent the flywheel from turning by locking the ring gear teeth with a similar arrangement to that shown in illustration 7.10. Alternatively, bolt a strap between the flywheel and the cylinder block/crankcase. *Do not* attempt to lock the flywheel in position using the crankshaft pulley locking pin described in Section 3.

3 Slacken and remove the flywheel retaining bolts, and remove the flywheel from the end of the crankshaft. Be careful not to drop it; it is heavy. If the flywheel locating dowel is a loose fit in the crankshaft end, remove it and store it with the flywheel for safe-keeping. Discard the flywheel bolts; new ones must be used on refitting.

Driveplate (automatic transmission models)

4 Remove the transmission as described in Chapter 7B. Lock the driveplate as described

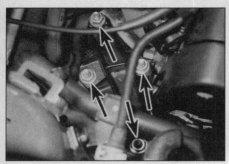

19.7a Undo the retaining nuts (arrowed) . . .

19.7b . . . and remove the right-hand engine/transmission mounting bracket (diesel engine shown)

in paragraph 2. Mark the relationship between the torque converter plate and the driveplate, and slacken all the driveplate retaining bolts.

5 Remove the retaining bolts, along with the torque converter plate and (where fitted) the two shims (one fitted on each side of the torque converter plate). Discard the driveplate retaining bolts; new ones must be used on refitting.

6 Remove the driveplate from the end of the crankshaft. If the locating dowel is a loose fit in the crankshaft end, remove it and store it with the driveplate for safe-keeping.

Inspection

7 On models with manual transmission, examine the flywheel for scoring of the clutch face, and for wear or chipping of the ring gear teeth. If the clutch face is scored, the flywheel may be surface-ground, but renewal is preferable. Seek the advice of a Peugeot dealer or engine reconditioning specialist to see if machining is possible. If the ring gear is worn or damaged, the flywheel must be renewed, as it is not possible to renew the ring gear separately.

8 On models with automatic transmission, check the torque converter driveplate carefully for signs of distortion. Look for any hairline cracks around the bolt holes or radiating outwards from the centre, and inspect the ring gear teeth for signs of wear or chipping. If any sign of wear or damage is found, the driveplate must be renewed.

Refitting

Flywheel (manual transmission models)

9 Clean the mating surfaces of the flywheel and crankshaft. Remove any remaining locking compound from the threads of the crankshaft holes, using the correct size of tap, if available.

If a suitable tap is not available, cut two slots along the threads of one of the old flywheel bolts, and use the bolt to remove the locking compound from the threads.

10 If the new flywheel retaining bolts are not supplied with their threads already pre-coated, apply a suitable thread-locking compound to the threads of each bolt.

11 Ensure that the locating dowel is in position. Offer up the flywheel, locating it on the dowel, and fit the new retaining bolts.

12 Lock the flywheel using the method employed on dismantling, and tighten the retaining bolts to the specified torque.

13 Refit the clutch as described in Chapter 6. Remove the flywheel locking tool, and refit the transmission as described in Chapter 7A.

Driveplate (automatic transmission models)

14 Carry out the operations described above in paragraphs 9 and 10, substituting "driveplate" for all references to the flywheel.

15 Locate the driveplate on its locating dowel.

16 Offer up the torque converter plate, with the shims (where fitted), and align the marks made prior to removal.

17 Fit the new retaining bolts, then lock the driveplate using the method employed on dismantling. Tighten the retaining bolts to the specified torque wrench setting (see Chapter 7B Specifications).

18 Remove the driveplate locking tool, and refit the transmission (see Chapter 7B).

---

19 Engine/transmission mountings - inspection and renewal

Inspection

1 If improved access is required, raise the front of the car and support it securely on axle stands (see *"Jacking and Vehicle Support"*).

2 Check the mounting rubber to see if it is cracked, hardened or separated from the metal at any point; renew the mounting if any such damage or deterioration is evident.

3 Check that all the mounting's fasteners are securely tightened; use a torque wrench to check if possible.

4 Using a large screwdriver or a crowbar, check for wear in the mounting by carefully levering against it to check for free play. Where

this is not possible, enlist the aid of an assistant to move the engine/transmission unit back and forth, or from side to side, while you watch the mounting. While some free play is to be expected even from new components, excessive wear should be obvious. If excessive free play is found, check first that the fasteners are correctly secured, then renew any worn components as described below.

Renewal

Right-hand mounting

5 Disconnect the battery negative terminal (refer to *"Disconnecting the battery"* in the Reference Section of this manual).

6 Place a jack beneath the engine, with a block of wood on the jack head. Raise the jack until it is supporting the weight of the engine.

7 Slacken and remove the three nuts securing the right-hand engine mounting upper bracket to the bracket on the cylinder block. Remove the nut(s) securing the bracket to the mounting rubber, and lift off the bracket **(see illustrations)**.

8 On 954 cc and 1124 cc models, slacken and remove the nut and bolt securing the rubber mounting to the vehicle body, and remove it from the vehicle.

9 On all other models, lift the buffer plate off the mounting rubber stud, then unscrew the nut and remove the mounting rubber from the body.

10 Check carefully for signs of wear or damage on all components, and renew them where necessary.

11 On reassembly, securely tighten the nut (or nut and bolt, as applicable) securing the mounting rubber to the body.

12 Refit the buffer plate (where fitted) to the mounting rubber stud, then install the mounting bracket.

13 Tighten the mounting bracket retaining nuts to the specified torque setting.

14 Remove the jack from underneath the engine, and reconnect the battery negative lead.

Left-hand mounting

15 Remove the battery as described in Chapter 5A.

16 Place a jack beneath the transmission, with a block of wood on the jack head. Raise the jack until it is supporting the weight of the transmission.

17 Slacken and remove the mounting rubber's centre nut, and the two bolts securing the bracket to the body. Remove the mounting rubber, and slide the spacer off the mounting bracket stud **(see illustrations)**.

18 Where necessary, unscrew the nuts and remove the bracket from the transmission.

19 Check carefully for signs of wear or damage on all components, and renew them where necessary.

20 Refit the bracket to the transmission, tightening its mounting nuts to the specified torque.

19.17a Remove the left-hand engine/transmission mounting centre nut and washer

19.17b Undo the two retaining bolts (arrowed) . . .

19.17c . . . then lift off the mounting . . .

21 Refit the spacer, then fit the mounting to the body, and tighten its retaining bolts to the specified torque. Refit the mounting centre nut, and tighten it to the specified torque.

22 Remove the jack from underneath the transmission, then refit the battery as described in Chapter 5A.

Rear mounting

23 If not already done, firmly apply the handbrake, then jack up the front of the vehicle and support it securely on axle stands (see *"Jacking and Vehicle Support"*).

24 Unscrew and remove the bolt securing the rear mounting link to the mounting on the rear of the transmission.

25 Remove the bolt securing the rear mounting link to the bracket on the underbody. Withdraw the link.

26 Unbolt the mounting from the rear of the transmission.

27 Check carefully for signs of wear or damage on all components, and renew them where necessary.

28 On reassembly, fit the rear mounting assembly to the rear of the transmission, and tighten its retaining bolts to the specified torque.

29 Refit the rear mounting link, and tighten both its bolts to the specified torque.

30 Lower the vehicle to the ground.

19.17d . . . and recover the spacer

2A

Chapter 2 Part B:
Diesel engine in-car repair procedures

Contents

Degrees of difficulty

Easy, suitable for novice with little experience	**Fairly easy,** suitable for beginner with some experience	**Fairly difficult,** suitable for competent DIY mechanic	**Difficult,** suitable for experienced DIY mechanic	**Very difficult,** suitable for expert DIY or professional 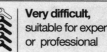

Specifications

Engine (general)
Designation:
1360 cc engine	TUD 3
1527 cc engine	TUD 5

Engine codes*:
1360 cc engine	K9B (TUD3L1)
1527 cc engine	VJY or VJZ (TUD5L/Y/L3)

*The engine code is stamped on a plate attached to the front left-hand end of the cylinder block. The code given in brackets is the factory identification number

Bore:
TUD 3	75.0 mm
TUD 5	77.0 mm

Stroke:
TUD 3	77.0 mm
TUD 5	82.0 mm
Direction of crankshaft rotation	Clockwise (viewed from right-hand side of vehicle)
No 1 cylinder location	At transmission end of block

Compression ratio:
TUD 3	22 : 1
TUD 5	23 : 1

Camshaft
Drive	Toothed belt
Number of bearings	3
Endfloat	0.025 to 0.114 mm

Valve clearances (engine cold)
Inlet	0.15 ± 0.075 mm
Exhaust	0.30 ± 0.075 mm

Cylinder head bolts
Maximum bolt length (refer to text):
TUD 3	185.9 mm
TUD 5	197.5 mm

Timing belt tension

Using a special Peugeot electronic measuring equipment

TUD 3:
    Stage 1 . . . . 50 units
    Stage 2 . . . . 39 units
    Final stage . . . . 51 ± 3 units

TUD 5:
    New belt:
        Stage 1 . . . . 98 units
        Stage 2 . . . . 54 units
        Final stage . . . . 54 ± 3 units
    Used belt:
        Stage 1 . . . . 75 units
        Stage 2 . . . . 44 units
        Final stage . . . . 44 ± 3 units

Lubrication system

Oil pump type . . . . Gear-type, chain-driven off the crankshaft
Minimum oil pressure at 90°C . . . . 4 bars at 4000 rpm
Oil pressure warning switch operating pressure . . . . 0.8 bars

Torque wrench settings

	Nm	lbf ft
Big-end bearing cap nuts	40	30
Camshaft bearing cap	20	15
Camshaft sprocket fastener(s):		
Camshaft sprocket retaining bolt - TUD 3 engines	80	59
Camshaft sprocket-to-hub bolts - TUD 5 engines	25	18
Camshaft sprocket hub retaining bolt - TUD 5 engines:		
Engines up to 31/12/98	80	59
Engines built after 1/1/99:		
Stage 1	40	30
Stage 2	Angle-tighten a further 20°	
Crankshaft pulley bolts	16	12
Crankshaft sprocket retaining bolt:		
TUD 3 engines, and TUD 5 engines up to 31/12/98	110	81
TUD 5 engines built after 1/1/99:		
Stage 1	70	52
Stage 2	Angle-tighten a further 45°	
Cylinder head bolts:		
TUD 3:		
Stage 1	60	44
Slacken all the bolts completely, then:		
Stage 2	20	15
Stage 3	Angle-tighten a further 160°	
Stage 4	Angle-tighten a further 160°	
TUD 5:		
Stage 1	40	30
Stage 2:		
Engines up to 31/12/98	Angle-tighten a further 260 ± 5°	
Engines built after 1/1/99	Angle-tighten a further 300 ± 5°	
Cylinder head cover bolts:		
TUD 3	7	5
TUD 5:		
Pre-tighten by	5	4
Then to	10	7
Engine-to-transmission bolts	35	26
Engine/transmission left-hand mounting:		
Mounting bracket-to-body bolts	30	22
Centre nut	85	63
Mounting bracket-to-transmission nuts	18	13
Engine/transmission rear mounting:		
Mounting link bolts	55	40
Mounting-to-transmission bolts	85	63
Engine/transmission right-hand mounting:		
Pre-July 1996 models:		
Mounting bracket-to-engine nuts	50	37
Mounting bracket-to-body 8 mm nut(s)	20	15
Mounting bracket-to-body 10 mm nut(s)	50	37

Torque wrench settings (continued)

	Nm	lbf ft
Engine/transmission right-hand mounting (continued):		
July 1996 models onward:		
Mounting bracket-to-engine nuts	45	33
Flexible mounting-to-mounting bracket bolt	28	21
Flexible mounting-to-body bolts	30	22
Flywheel retaining bolts	65	48
Injection pump sprocket fastener(s):		
Injection pump sprocket retaining nut - TUD 3 engines	50	37
Injection pump sprocket-to-hub bolts - TUD 5 engines	25	18
Injection pump sprocket hub retaining nut - TUD 5 engines	80	59
Main bearing ladder casting:		
11 mm bolts:		
Stage 1	20	15
Stage 2	Angle-tighten a further 45°	
6 mm bolts	8	6
Oil pump retaining bolts	8	6
Sump drain plug	30	22
Sump retaining nuts and bolts	8	6
Timing belt cover bolts:		
TUD 3 engine:		
Upper cover	5	5
Centre and lower covers	8	6
TUD 5 engines (all)	10	7
Timing belt tensioner pulley nut:		
TUD 3	15	11
TUD 5	20	15

1 General information

Using this Chapter

Chapter 2 is divided into three Parts: A, B and C. Repair operations that can be carried out with the engine in the vehicle are described in Parts A (TU series petrol engines) and B (TUD series diesel engines). Part C covers the removal of the engine/transmission as a unit, and describes the engine dismantling and overhaul procedures.

In Parts A and B, the assumption is made that the engine is installed in the vehicle, with all ancillaries connected. If the engine has been removed for overhaul, the preliminary dismantling information which precedes each operation may be ignored.

TUD series engine description

The diesel engine fitted to the Peugeot 106 is derived from the TU series of engines. The diesel version is a well-proven engine which has been fitted to several other Peugeot and Citroën vehicles. The bottom end of the engine is very similar to that of the TU petrol engine covered in Part A of this Chapter.

The 106 range is fitted with either a 1360 cc (TUD 3) or the 1527 cc (TUD 5) version of the engine (see illustration). The engine is of the in-line four-cylinder, overhead camshaft (OHC) type, mounted transversely at the front of the car. The clutch and transmission are attached to its left-hand end.

The crankshaft runs in five main bearings. Thrustwashers are fitted to No 2 main bearing (upper half) to control crankshaft endfloat.

The connecting rods rotate on horizontally-split bearing shells at their big-ends. The pistons are attached to the connecting rods by gudgeon pins, which are secured in position with circlips. The aluminium-alloy pistons are fitted with three piston rings - two compression rings and an oil control ring.

The cylinder bores on 1360 cc (TUD 3) engines have replaceable wet liners, whereas on the 1527 cc (TUD 5) engines, the cylinder

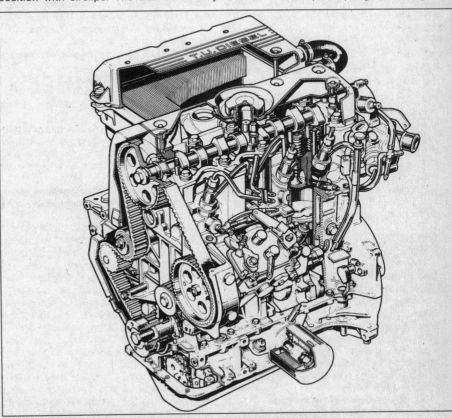

1.4 Cutaway view of the TUD diesel engine

bores are an integral part of the cylinder block. On TUD 3 engines, sealing O-rings are fitted at the base of each liner, to prevent the escape of coolant into the sump.

The inlet and exhaust valves are each closed by coil springs, and operate in guides pressed into the cylinder head. The valve seat inserts are also pressed into the cylinder head, and can be renewed separately if worn.

The camshaft is driven by a toothed timing belt, and operates the eight valves via bucket-type followers which are positioned directly below the camshaft. Valve clearance adjustment is by means of shims. The camshaft is supported by three bearings machined directly in the cylinder head.

Lubrication is by means of an oil pump, which is driven (via a chain and sprocket) off the right-hand end of the crankshaft. It draws oil through a strainer located in the sump, and then forces it through an externally-mounted filter into galleries in the cylinder block/crankcase. From there, the oil is distributed to the crankshaft (main bearings) and camshaft. The big-end bearings are supplied with oil via internal drillings in the crankshaft, while the camshaft bearings also receive a pressurised supply. The camshaft lobes and valves are lubricated by splash, as are all other engine components.

Throughout this manual, it is often necessary to identify the engines not only by their capacity, but also by their engine code which can be found on the left-hand end of the front face of the cylinder block. The code is stamped on a plate which is riveted to the block. The first part of the engine number gives the engine code - eg "K9B" **(see illustration)**.

Repair operations possible with the engine in the car

The following work can be carried out with the engine in the car:
a) Compression pressure and leakdown - testing.
b) Cylinder head cover - removal and refitting.
c) Timing belt covers - removal and refitting.
d) Timing belt - removal, refitting and adjustment.
e) Timing belt tensioner and sprockets - removal and refitting.
f) Camshaft oil seal - renewal.

1.11 The engine code is stamped on a plate (arrowed) attached to the front of the cylinder block - viewed from above

g) Camshaft and followers - removal, inspection and refitting.
h) Cylinder head - removal and refitting.
i) Cylinder head and pistons - decarbonising (refer to Part C of this Chapter).
j) Sump - removal and refitting.
k) Oil pump - removal, overhaul and refitting.
l) Crankshaft oil seals - renewal.
m) Engine/transmission mountings - inspection and renewal.
n) Flywheel - removal, inspection and refitting.

2 Compression and leakdown tests - description and interpretation

Compression test

Note: *A compression tester specifically designed for diesel engines must be used for this test.*

1 When engine performance is down, or if misfiring occurs which cannot be attributed to the fuel system, a compression test can provide diagnostic clues as to the engine's condition. If the test is performed regularly, it can give warning of trouble before any other symptoms become apparent.

2 A compression tester specifically intended for diesel engines must be used, because of the higher pressures involved. The tester is connected to an adapter which screws into the glow plug or injector hole. It is unlikely to be worthwhile buying such a tester for occasional use, but it may be possible to borrow or hire one - if not, have the test performed by a garage.

3 Unless specific instructions to the contrary are supplied with the tester, observe the following points:
a) The battery must be in a good state of charge, the air filter must be clean, and the engine should be at normal operating temperature.
b) All the injectors or glow plugs should be removed before starting the test. If removing the injectors, also remove the flame shield washers, otherwise they may be blown out.
c) The stop solenoid must be disconnected, to prevent the engine from running or fuel from being discharged.

4 There is no need to hold the accelerator pedal down during the test, because the diesel engine air inlet is not throttled.

5 Although Peugeot do not specify exact compression pressures, as a guide, any cylinder pressure of below 20 bars can be considered as less than healthy. Refer to a Peugeot dealer or other diesel specialist if in doubt as to whether a particular pressure reading is acceptable.

6 The cause of poor compression is less easy to establish on a diesel engine than on a petrol one. The effect of introducing oil into the cylinders ("wet" testing) is not conclusive, because there is a risk that the oil will sit in the swirl chamber or in the recess on the piston crown instead of passing to the rings. However, the following can be used as a rough guide to diagnosis.

7 All cylinders should produce very similar pressures; a difference of more than 4 bars between any two cylinders indicates the existence of a fault. Note that the compression should build up quickly in a healthy engine; low compression on the first stroke, followed by gradually-increasing pressure on successive strokes, indicates worn piston rings. A low compression reading on the first stroke, which does not build up during successive strokes, indicates leaking valves or a blown head gasket (a cracked head could also be the cause).

8 A low reading from two adjacent cylinders is almost certainly due to the head gasket having blown between them; the presence of coolant in the engine oil will confirm this.

9 If the compression reading is unusually high, the cylinder head surfaces, valves and pistons are probably coated with carbon deposits. If this is the case, the cylinder head should be removed and decarbonised (refer to Part C of this Chapter).

Leakdown test

10 A leakdown test measures the rate at which compressed air fed into the cylinder is lost. It is an alternative to a compression test, and in many ways it is better, since the escaping air provides easy identification of where pressure loss is occurring (piston rings, valves or head gasket).

11 The equipment needed for leakdown testing is unlikely to be available to the home mechanic. If poor compression is suspected, have the test performed by a suitably-equipped garage.

3 Location of TDC on No 1 cylinder - general information and usage

Caution: *Do not attempt to rotate the engine whilst the crankshaft, camshaft or injection pump are locked in position. If the engine is to be left in this state for a long period of time, it is a good idea to place warning notices inside the vehicle, and in the engine compartment. This will reduce the possibility of the engine being accidentally cranked on the starter motor, which is likely to cause damage with the locking tools in place.*

All engines

1 Timing holes are drilled in the camshaft sprocket, injection pump sprocket (or, on TUD5 engines, in their hubs) and in the flywheel. The holes are used to ensure that the crankshaft, camshaft and injection pump are correctly positioned when assembling the engine (to prevent the possibility of the valves contacting the pistons when refitting the cylinder head), or refitting the timing belt. When the timing holes are aligned with access holes, Suitable-diameter pins or bolts can be inserted to lock the camshaft, injection pump sprocket and crankshaft in position, preventing them from rotating. Proceed as follows. **Note:** *With*

3.4 Insert a 6 mm bolt (arrowed) through hole in cylinder block flange and into timing hole in the flywheel

3.5a Insert an 8 mm bolt (arrowed) through the camshaft sprocket timing hole, and screw it into the cylinder head . . .

3.5b . . . then insert two 8 mm bolts (arrowed) into the injection pump sprocket holes and screw them into the mounting bracket

the timing holes aligned, No 4 cylinder is at TDC on its compression stroke.

2 Remove the upper and centre timing belt covers as described in Section 5.

3 The crankshaft must now be turned until the timing holes in the camshaft sprocket and injection pump sprocket (or their hubs) are aligned with the corresponding holes in the cylinder head and pump mounting bracket (or body). The holes are aligned when the camshaft sprocket hole is in the 4 o'clock position, when viewed from the right-hand end of the engine. The crankshaft can be turned by using a spanner on the crankshaft sprocket bolt, noting that it should always be rotated in a clockwise direction (viewed from the right-hand end of the engine). If necessary, firmly apply the handbrake then jack up the front of the car, support it on axle stands (see *"Jacking and vehicle support"*)

4.1 Disconnect the breather hose from the left-hand end of the cylinder head cover

and remove the right-hand roadwheel and wheel arch liner (see chapter 11, section 23) to improve access to the crankshaft pulley.

 HAYNES HiNT *Turning the engine will be much easier if the glow plugs are removed first (see Chapter 5C).*

4 With the camshaft sprocket (or its hub) hole correctly positioned, insert a 6 mm diameter bolt or drill bit through the hole in the front left-hand flange of the cylinder block, and locate it in the timing hole in the flywheel **(see illustration)**. Note that it may be necessary to rotate the crankshaft slightly, to get the holes to align.

TUD 3 engines

5 With the flywheel correctly positioned, insert an 8 mm diameter bolt through the timing hole in the camshaft sprocket, and screw it into the hole on the cylinder head. Also insert an 8 mm diameter bolt through each of the two timing holes on the injection pump sprocket, and screw them into the holes in the mounting bracket **(see illustrations)**.

6 The crankshaft, camshaft and injection pump are now locked in position.

TUD 5 engines

7 With the flywheel correctly positioned, insert an 8 mm diameter bolt through the slot of the camshaft sprocket, along the groove in the hub and screw it into the cylinder head. Also insert an 6 mm diameter pin or drill bit

through the slot of the injection pump sprocket, along the groove in the hub, into the hole on the sump body.

8 The crankshaft, camshaft and injection pump are now locked in position .

Caution: On TUD 5 engines, the only way of ensure that the injection pump timing is correct is to lock the engine at TDC, as above. The sprocket hub timing must be perfectly aligned with the grooves corresponding holes in the cylinder head and pump body, so that there is minimum displacement when the locking bolt is put into place. An additional check will be required when the timing belt is put back on (see section 6)

4 Cylinder head cover - removal and refitting

2B

Removal

1 Disconnect the breather hose from the left-hand end of the cylinder head cover **(see illustration)**.

2 Remove the upper timing belt cover as described in Section 5.

3 Unscrew the eight retaining bolts in a spiral sequence starting from the outside. Note their correct fitted locations, as they are of two different lengths. Recover the washers from the bolts/cover **(see illustrations)**.

4 Lift the cover away from the engine **(see illustration)**, and recover the rubber seal.

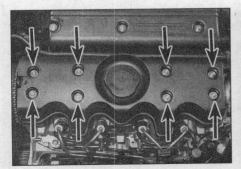

4.3a Unscrew the eight retaining bolts (arrowed) . . .

4.3b . . . and remove them along with their washers

4.4 Lift the cover away from the engine and recover the seal

4.6 Ensure that the rubber seal is correctly located in the cover groove prior to refitting

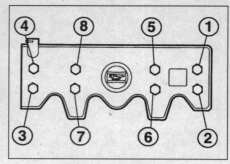

4.8 Cylinder head cover tightening sequence (TUD 5 engine)

5.1 Removing the timing belt upper cover

Examine the seal for signs of damage and deterioration, and if necessary, renew it.

Refitting

5 Carefully clean the cylinder head and cover mating surfaces, and remove all traces of oil.
6 Fit the rubber seal to the cylinder head cover groove, ensuring that it is correctly located along its entire length **(see illustration)**.
7 Carefully refit the cylinder head cover to the engine, taking great care not to displace the rubber seal.
8 Install the retaining bolts and washers, and tighten them to the specified torque setting. On TUD 5 engines, initially screw the bolts through to the head in the following order 8-5-7-6-4-1-3-2 **(see illustration)**. Then pre-tighten them (to the specified torque), in numerical sequence (1 through to 8) and then finally complete by tightening to the specified torque, again in numerical sequence.

9 Refit the upper timing belt cover as described in Section 5.
10 Reconnect the breather hose to the cylinder head cover, and securely tighten its retaining clip.

5 Timing belt covers - removal and refitting

Removal
Upper cover

1 Slacken and remove the three retaining screws, and remove the upper timing cover from the cylinder head **(see illustration)**.

Centre cover

2 Remove the upper cover as described in paragraph 1.

3 Turn the wheels onto full right-hand lock, then prise out the rubber plug from underneath the right-hand front wheel arch. Unscrew the timing belt cover bolt which is accessible through the hole in the wing valance **(see illustrations)**.
4 Unscrew the remaining bolt from the centre of the cover, then manoeuvre the cover out of position **(see illustration)**.

Lower cover

5 Remove the auxiliary drivebelt as described in Chapter 1B.
6 Remove the upper and centre covers as described above.
7 Undo the crankshaft pulley retaining bolts and remove the pulley, noting which way round it is fitted **(see illustrations)**.
8 Slacken and remove the three retaining bolts, and withdraw the lower cover over the crankshaft sprocket outer flange **(see illustration)**.

5.3a Remove the rubber plug from the right-hand wing valance . . .

5.3b . . . to gain access to the timing belt centre cover bolt (arrowed)

5.4 Unscrew the remaining bolt (location arrowed) and remove the centre cover

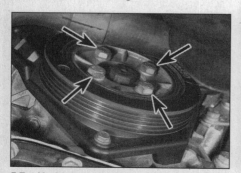

5.7a Undo the retaining bolts (arrowed) . . .

5.7b . . . and remove the crankshaft pulley from the engine

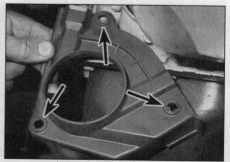

5.8 Undo the retaining bolts (locations arrowed) and remove the lower cover

Refitting

Upper cover

9 Refit the cover, ensuring that it is correctly located with the centre cover, and tighten its retaining screws to the specified torque.

Centre cover

10 Manoeuvre the centre cover back into position, ensuring that it is correctly located with the lower cover, then tighten its retaining bolts to the specified torque. Refit the rubber plug to the wing valance.
11 Refit the upper cover as described above.

Lower cover

12 Locate the lower cover over the crankshaft sprocket outer flange, and tighten its retaining bolts to the specified torque.
13 Fit the pulley onto the crankshaft sprocket flange, ensuring that it is fitted the correct way round, and tighten its retaining bolts to the specified torque.
14 Refit the centre and upper covers as described above, then refit and tension the auxiliary drivebelt as described in Chapter 1B.

---

6 Timing belt -
general information,
removal and refitting

Note: *Peugeot specify the use of a special electronic tool (SEEM belt tensioning measuring tool) to correctly set the timing belt tension. On TUD 3 engines and if access to this equipment cannot be obtained, an approximate setting can be achieved using the method described below. If the method described is used, the belt tension must be checked using the special electronic tool at the earliest possible opportunity. Do not drive the vehicle over large distances, or use high engine speeds, until the belt tension is known to be correct. Refer to a Peugeot dealer for advice.*

General information

1 The timing belt drives the camshaft, injection pump, and coolant pump from a toothed sprocket on the front of the crankshaft. If the belt breaks or slips in service, the pistons are likely to hit the valve heads, resulting in extensive (and expensive) damage.
2 The timing belt should be renewed at the specified intervals, or earlier if it is contaminated with oil, or at all noisy in operation (a "scraping" noise due to uneven wear).
3 If the timing belt is being removed, it is a wise precaution to check the condition of the coolant pump at the same time (check for signs of coolant leakage). This may avoid the need to remove the timing belt again at a later stage, should the coolant pump fail.

Removal

4 Disconnect the battery negative terminal (refer to "Disconnecting the battery" in the Reference Section of this manual).
5 Align the engine assembly/valve timing

holes, then lock the crankshaft, camshaft and fuel injection pump sprockets in position as described in Section 3. *Do not* attempt to rotate the engine whilst the locking tools are in position.
6 Remove the lower timing belt cover as described in Section 5.
7 Remove the right-hand headlight unit as described in Chapter 12.
8 Loosen the timing belt tensioner pulley retaining nut. Pivot the pulley in a clockwise direction, using a square-section key fitted to the hole in the pulley hub, then retighten the retaining nut.
9 Slip the belt off the sprockets, idler and tensioner, and remove it from the engine.
10 Check the timing belt carefully for any signs of uneven wear, splitting, or oil contamination. Pay particular attention to the roots of the teeth. Renew the belt if there is the slightest doubt about its condition. If the engine is under-going an overhaul, and has covered more than 36 000 miles (60 000 km) with the existing belt fitted, renew the belt as a matter of course, regardless of its apparent condition. The cost of a new belt is nothing when compared to the cost of repairs, should the belt break in service. If signs of oil contamination are found, trace the source of the oil leak, and rectify it. Wash down the engine timing belt area and all related components, to remove all traces of oil **(see Haynes Hint)**.

Refitting

11 Prior to refitting, thoroughly clean the timing belt sprockets. Check that both the tensioner and idler pulleys rotate freely, without any sign of roughness. If necessary, renew the damaged pulley(s) as described in Section 7. Make sure that the locking tools are still in place, as described in Section 3.

TUD 3 engines

12 Manoeuvre the timing belt into position, ensuring that the arrows on the belt are pointing in the direction of rotation (clockwise when viewed from the right-hand end of the engine). Do not twist the timing belt sharply while refitting it.
13 First locate the belt over the crankshaft sprocket then, keeping the belt taut, feed it over the idler pulley, around the injection pump sprocket, and over the camshaft sprocket **(see**

HAYNES
HiNT

If the timing belt is to be re-used, use white paint or similar to mark the direction of rotation on the belt (if markings do not already exist).

illustration). Locate the belt over the tensioner pulley, then finally over the coolant pump sprocket. Ensure that the belt teeth are seated centrally in the sprockets, and that any slack is in the section of the belt between the camshaft and coolant pump sprockets.
14 Loosen the tensioner pulley retaining nut. Pivot the pulley anti-clockwise to remove all freeplay from the timing belt, then retighten the nut **(see illustration).** Tension the timing belt as described under the relevant sub-heading.

TUD 5 engines

15 Slacken the six (three on each) camshaft and injection pump hub bolts **(see illustration).** Ensure that the sprockets move freely on their hubs. Finger tighten the six sprocket hub bolts, then slacken them all by just under a quarter of a turn.
16 Move the camshaft and injection pump sprockets to the bottom of their slot, by turning them in the direction of engine rotation (clockwise).
17 Locate the timing belt, fully taut, firstly on the crankshaft sprocket, then on the tension roller nearest to the injection pump. Wrap the belt around the injection pump sprocket, ensuring that the belt does not 'jump' on the crankshaft sprocket. If necessary move the injection pump sprocket, anti-clockwise by no more than one tooth to enable the belt to seat properly.

6.13 Engage the timing belt with the sprockets as described in text

6.14 Remove all freeplay from the belt, then securely tighten the tensioner pulley retaining nut

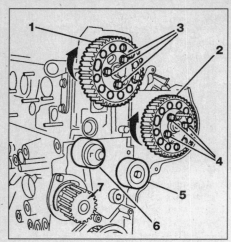

6.15 Camshaft and injection pump sprocket hub bolts (TUD 5 engines)

1 *Camshaft sprocket*
2 *Injection pump sprocket*
3 *Camshaft sprocket hub bolts*
4 *Injection pump sprocket hub bolts*
5 *Tension roller*
6 *Tension roller*
7 *Coolant pump sprocket*

18 Fit the belt on the camshaft sprocket in the same way. Feed the belt around the remaining tension roller and on around the coolant pump sprocket. Continue on to paragraph 28.

Tensioning without the special electronic measuring tool

Note: *If this method is used, ensure that the belt tension is checked by a Peugeot dealer at the earliest possible opportunity.*
19 Peugeot dealers use a special tool to tension the timing belt (see illustration 6.14 in Part A of this Chapter). A similar tool may be fabricated using a suitable square-section bar attached to an arm made from a metal strip; a hole should be drilled in the strip at a distance

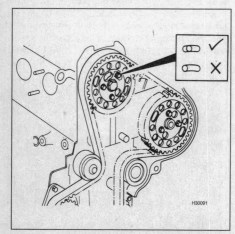

6.29 Correct location of camshaft and injection pump sprocket hub bolts (TUD 5 engines)

6.19 Using a home-made special tool and spring balance to tension the timing belt

of 80 mm from the centre of the square-section bar. Fit the tool to the hole in the tensioner pulley, keeping the tool arm as close to the horizontal as possible, and hang a 2.0 kg (4.4 lb.) weight from the hole in the tool. In the absence of an object of the specified weight, a spring balance can be used to exert the required force, ensuring that the spring balance is held at 90° to the tool arm **(see illustration)**. Slacken the pulley retaining nut, allowing the weight or force exerted (as applicable) to push the tensioner pulley against the belt. Now push down on the tool to exert some additional force, and retighten the pulley nut. This effectively "over-tensions" the belt, to allow it to settle in before the final tensioning.
20 If this special tool is not available, an approximate setting may be achieved by pivoting the tensioner pulley anti-clockwise until it is just possible to turn the timing belt through 45° by finger and thumb, midway between the camshaft and injection pump sprockets. Once the belt has been tensioned, securely tighten the pulley retaining nut.
21 Remove the locking tools from the camshaft sprocket, injection pump sprocket and flywheel.
22 Using a suitable socket and extension bar on the crankshaft sprocket bolt, rotate the crankshaft through four complete rotations in a clockwise direction (viewed from the right-hand end of the engine). *Do not* at any time rotate the crankshaft anti-clockwise.
23 Allow the belt to stand for approximately one minute, then slacken the tensioner pulley nut.
24 Where the special tool is being used, allow the weight of the tool to tension the belt, then tighten the pulley retaining nut to the specified torque. **Do not** exert any extra force on the tool this time (as in paragraph 15).
25 Where tensioning is being carried out without the special tool, re-tension the belt as described in paragraph 16, then tighten the tensioner pulley nut to the specified torque.
Note: *This method is only an initial setting. Do not drive the vehicle over large distances, or use high engine speeds, until the belt tension is known to be correct.*
26 Rotate the crankshaft through a further two turns clockwise, and check that the camshaft sprocket, injection pump and flywheel timing holes are still correctly aligned.

27 If all is well, refit the timing belt covers as described in Section 5, then refit the headlight as described in Chapter 12.

Tensioning using the special electronic measuring tool

28 Fit the special belt tensioning measuring equipment to the "front run" of the timing belt, midway between the camshaft and injection pump sprockets. Position the tensioner pulley so that the belt is tensioned to 'Stage 1' of the specified setting, then retighten its retaining nut without moving the tensioner.
29 On TUD 5 engines, ensure that the camshaft and injection sprocket hub bolts are located in the centre of the slot **(see illustration)**. If they are at either end, refit the timing belt. Fully tighten all six bolts to their correct torque.
30 Remove the locking tools from the camshaft sprocket, injection pump sprocket and flywheel, and remove the measuring tool from the belt.
31 Using a socket and extension bar on the crankshaft sprocket bolt, rotate the crankshaft through four (two on TUD 5 engines) complete rotations in a clockwise direction (viewed from the right-hand end of the engine). *Do not* at any time rotate the crankshaft anti-clockwise.
32 Refit the locking tools and allow the belt to stand for approximately one minute, then slacken the tensioner pulley retaining nut (and six sprocket hub bolts), and refit the measuring tool to the belt. Position the tensioner pulley so that the belt is tensioned to the 'Stage 2' setting, then tighten the pulley retaining nut to the specified torque setting. On TUD 5 engines tighten the six camshaft and injection pump hub sprockets bolts.
33 Remove the measuring tool from the belt. Then on TUD 3 engines, rotate the crankshaft through another two complete rotations in a clockwise direction, so that the camshaft and injection pump sprocket and flywheel timing holes are realigned. *Do not* at any time rotate the crankshaft anti-clockwise. Refit the measuring tool to the belt and check that the belt tension is as specified at the 'Final stage'.
34 If the belt tension is incorrect, repeat the procedures in paragraphs 32 and 33.
35 With the belt tension correctly set, remove the locking tools if applicable and refit the timing belt covers as described in Section 5. Refit the headlight (if applicable) as described in Chapter 12.

---

7 Timing belt tensioner and sprockets - removal, inspection and refitting

Removal

Note: *This Section describes the removal and refitting of the components concerned as individual operations. If more than one of them is to be removed at the same time, start by removing the timing belt as described in Section 6; remove the actual component as*

7.5 Remove the retaining bolt and washer, then remove the camshaft sprocket

described below, ignoring the preliminary dismantling steps.

1 Disconnect the battery negative terminal (refer to *"Disconnecting the battery"* in the Reference Section of this manual).
2 Align the engine assembly/valve timing holes as described in Section 3, and lock the camshaft sprocket, injection pump sprocket and flywheel in position. *Do not* attempt to rotate the engine whilst the locking tools are in position.

Camshaft sprocket

3 Loosen the timing belt tensioner pulley retaining nut. Rotate the pulley in a clockwise direction, using a suitable square-section key fitted to the hole in the pulley hub, then retighten the retaining nut.
4 Disengage the timing belt from the sprocket, and move the belt clear, taking care not to bend or twist it sharply. Remove the locking tool from the camshaft sprocket.
5 Slacken the camshaft sprocket retaining bolt and remove it, along with its washer. **(see illustration)**. *Do not* attempt to use the sprocket locking tool to prevent the sprocket from rotating whilst the retaining bolt is slackened **(see Haynes Hint)**.
6 With the retaining bolt removed, slide the sprocket off the end of the camshaft. Note that the key on the rear of the sprocket engages with a cut-out on the end of the camshaft. Examine the camshaft oil seal for signs of oil leakage and, if necessary, renew it as described in Section 8.

Crankshaft sprocket

7 Remove the lower timing belt cover as described in Section 5.
8 Loosen the timing belt tensioner pulley retaining nut. Rotate the pulley in a clockwise direction, using a suitable square-section key fitted to the hole in the pulley hub, then retighten the retaining nut.
9 Disengage the timing belt from the crankshaft sprocket, and move the belt clear, taking care not to bend or twist it sharply.
10 To prevent crankshaft rotation whilst the sprocket retaining bolt is slackened, select top gear, and have an assistant apply the brakes firmly. If the engine has been removed from the vehicle, lock the flywheel ring gear, using an arrangement similar to that shown in illus-

To prevent the camshaft rotating as the bolt is slackened, a sprocket-holding tool will be required. In the absence of the special Peugeot tool, an acceptable substitute can be fabricated as follows. Use two lengths of steel strip (one long, the other short), and three nuts and bolts; one nut and bolt forms the pivot of a forked tool, with the remaining two nuts and bolts at the tips of the "forks" to engage with the sprocket spokes.

tration 7.10 in Part A of this Chapter. *Do not* be tempted to use the flywheel locking pin/bolt to prevent the crankshaft from rotating; temporarily remove the pin/bolt from the rear of the flywheel prior to slackening the pulley bolt, then refit it once the bolt has been slackened.
11 Unscrew the retaining bolt and washer, then slide the sprocket off the end of the crankshaft. Refit the locking pin/bolt through the timing hole into the rear of the flywheel.
12 If the Woodruff key is a loose fit in the crankshaft, remove it and store it with the sprocket for safe-keeping. If necessary, also slide the flanged spacer off the end of the crankshaft. Examine the crankshaft oil seal for signs of oil leakage and, if necessary, renew as described in Section 16 in Part A of this Chapter.

Fuel injection pump sprocket

13 Loosen the timing belt tensioner pulley retaining nut. Rotate the pulley in a clockwise direction, using a suitable square-section key fitted to the hole in the pulley hub, then retighten the retaining nut.
14 Disengage the timing belt from the injection pump sprocket, and move the belt

7.17 Home-made injection pump sprocket removal tool in position on the sprocket

7.16 Using a home-made tool to hold the injection pump sprocket stationary whilst the retaining bolt is slackened - viewed through headlight aperture

clear, taking care not to bend or twist it sharply. If necessary, remove the right-hand headlight unit as described in Chapter 12 to improve access to the sprocket.
15 Unscrew the locking bolts from the pump sprocket.
16 Slacken the injection pump sprocket retaining nut whilst holding the sprocket stationary with a suitable peg spanner which engages with the sprocket holes, similar to that described in paragraph 5 **(see illustration)**. Unscrew the nut slightly so that it is clear of the sprocket.
17 A suitable tool will now be needed to free the sprocket from its taper on the pump shaft. In the absence of the special Peugeot clamp (No. 0157H), a suitable home-made alternative can be made out of a stout piece of steel strip and two 7 x 1 mm bolts which are approximately 40 mm in length. Drill two 8 mm holes in the strip, with their centres 45 mm apart. Align the holes in the strip with the two threaded holes in the sprocket, then screw in the bolts, tightening them evenly and progressively, until the sprocket is freed from the pump shaft taper **(see illustration)**. **Do not** be tempted to strike the pump with a hammer in an attempt to free the sprocket, as the pump internals will almost certainly be damaged.
18 Remove the bolts and the strip, then remove the sprocket retaining nut, and slide off the sprocket. If the Woodruff key is a loose fit in the pump shaft, remove it and store it with the sprocket for safe-keeping **(see illustrations)**.

7.18a Unscrew the retaining nut, then remove the sprocket . . .

2B

7.18b . . . and recover the Woodruff key (arrowed) from the injection pump shaft

7.19 Timing belt tensioner pulley retaining nut (arrowed)

7.21 Timing belt idler pulley retaining bolt (arrowed)

Tensioner pulley

19 Slacken and remove the timing belt tensioner pulley retaining nut, and slide the pulley off its mounting stud **(see illustration)**. Examine the mounting stud for signs of damage and, if necessary, renew it - it is removed by unscrewing it from the cylinder block.

Idler pulley

20 Loosen the timing belt tensioner pulley retaining nut. Rotate the pulley in a clockwise direction, using a suitable square-section key fitted to the hole in the pulley hub, then retighten the retaining nut. In order to provide some slack in the timing belt between the crankshaft and injection pump sprockets, it will be necessary to remove the locking tool from the flywheel and rotate the crankshaft slightly anti-clockwise.

21 Unscrew the bolt retaining the idler to the cylinder block **(see illustration)**, and withdraw the idler pulley. Carefully tie the timing belt up so that it is kept in full engagement with all of the sprockets.

Inspection

22 Clean the sprockets thoroughly, and renew any that show signs of wear, damage or cracks.

23 Clean the tensioner pulley and idler, but do not use any strong solvent which may enter the bearings. Check that each roller rotates freely about its hub, with no sign of stiffness or free play. Renew the tensioner pulley or idler if there is any doubt about its

condition, or if there are any obvious signs of wear or damage.

Refitting

Camshaft sprocket

24 Locate the sprocket on the end of the camshaft. Ensure that the locating key is correctly engaged with the cut-out in the camshaft end **(see illustration)**.

25 Refit the sprocket retaining bolt and washer (on TUD 5 engines, coat the bolt with Locite). Tighten the bolt to the specified torque, whilst retaining the sprocket with the tool used on removal.

26 Realign the timing hole in the camshaft sprocket (see Section 3) with the corresponding hole in the cylinder head, and refit the locking tool.

27 With the crankshaft, injection pump and camshaft locked in position, refit the timing belt to the camshaft sprocket. Ensure that the belt is taut around the crankshaft sprocket, idler pulley and injection pump sprocket, so that any slack is on the tensioner pulley side of the belt. Do not twist the belt sharply while refitting it, and ensure that the belt teeth are seated centrally in the sprockets.

28 Loosen the tensioner pulley retaining nut. Rotate the pulley anti-clockwise to remove all free play from the timing belt, then retighten the nut.

29 Tension the belt as described under the relevant sub-heading of Section 6.

30 Refit the timing belt covers as described in Section 5.

31 Reconnect the battery negative terminal.

Crankshaft sprocket

32 Where removed, locate the Woodruff key in the crankshaft end, then slide on the flanged spacer, aligning its slot with the Woodruff key.

33 Align the crankshaft sprocket slot with the Woodruff key, and slide it onto the end of the crankshaft.

34 Temporarily remove the locking tool from the rear of the flywheel, then refit the crankshaft sprocket retaining bolt and washer. Tighten the bolt to the specified torque, whilst preventing crankshaft rotation using the method employed on removal. Refit the locking tool to the rear of the flywheel.

35 With the crankshaft, injection pump and camshaft locked in position, refit the timing belt to the crankshaft sprocket. Ensure that the belt is taut between the crankshaft, idler pulley, injection pump and camshaft sprockets, so that any slack is on the tensioner pulley side of the belt. Do not twist the belt sharply while refitting it, and ensure that the belt teeth are seated centrally in the sprockets.

36 Loosen the tensioner pulley retaining nut. Rotate the pulley anti-clockwise to remove all free play from the timing belt, then retighten the nut.

37 Tension the belt as described under the relevant sub-heading of Section 6.

38 Refit the timing belt covers as described in Section 5.

Fuel injection pump sprocket

39 Where applicable, refit the Woodruff key to the pump shaft, ensuring that it is correctly located in its groove.

40 Locate the sprocket on the injection pump shaft, and engage it with the key **(see illustration)**.

41 Tighten the sprocket retaining nut to the specified torque, preventing the pump shaft from turning as during removal. Align the sprocket timing holes, and refit the locking tools.

42 With the crankshaft, injection pump and camshaft locked in position, refit the timing belt to the pump sprocket. Ensure that the belt is taut between the crankshaft, idler pulley, injection pump and camshaft sprockets, so

7.24 When refitting, ensure that the camshaft sprocket key and camshaft slot are correctly aligned (arrowed)

7.40 Align the sprocket groove (arrowed) with the Woodruff key when refitting the injection pump sprocket

that any slack is on the tensioner pulley side of the belt. Do not twist the belt sharply while refitting it, and ensure that the belt teeth are seated centrally in the sprockets.

43 Loosen the tensioner pulley retaining nut. Rotate the pulley anti-clockwise to remove all free play from the timing belt, then retighten the nut.

44 Tension the belt as described under the relevant sub-heading of Section 6.

45 Refit the timing belt covers as described in Section 5 and, where necessary, refit the headlight unit as described in Chapter 12.

Tensioner pulley

46 Check that the mounting stud is tightened in the cylinder block.

47 Locate the tensioner pulley on the stud, and lightly tighten its retaining nut.

48 With the crankshaft, injection pump and camshaft locked in position, ensure that the belt is taut between the crankshaft, idler pulley, injection pump and camshaft sprockets, so that any slack is on the tensioner pulley side of the belt.

49 Loosen the tensioner pulley retaining nut. Rotate the pulley anti-clockwise to remove all free play from the timing belt, then retighten the nut.

50 Tension the belt as described under the relevant sub-heading of Section 6.

51 Refit the timing belt covers as described in Section 5.

Idler pulley

52 Refit the idler pulley to the cylinder block, and tighten its retaining bolt securely.

53 Carefully turn the crankshaft clockwise until the locking tool can be inserted into the flywheel.

54 With the crankshaft, injection pump and camshaft locked in position, ensure that the belt is taut between the crankshaft, idler pulley, injection pump and camshaft sprockets, so that any slack is on the tensioner pulley side of the belt.

55 Loosen the tensioner pulley retaining nut. Rotate the pulley anti-clockwise to remove all free play from the belt, then retighten the nut.

56 Tension the belt as described under the relevant sub-heading of Section 6.

57 Refit the timing belt covers as described in Section 5.

---

8 Camshaft oil seal - renewal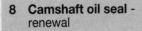

Note: *If the camshaft oil seal is to be renewed with the timing belt still in place, check first that the belt is free from oil contamination. (Renew the belt as a matter of course if signs of oil contamination are found; see Section 6.) Cover the belt to protect it from oil contamination while work is in progress. Ensure that all traces of oil are removed from the area before the belt is refitted.*

8.2 Removing the camshaft oil seal

1 Remove the camshaft sprocket as described in Section 7.

2 Punch or drill two small holes opposite each other in the oil seal. Screw a self-tapping screw into each, and pull on the screws with pliers to extract the seal **(see illustration)**.

3 Clean the seal housing, and polish off any burrs or raised edges, which may have caused the seal to fail in the first place.

4 Lubricate the lips of the new seal with clean engine oil, and drive or lever it into position until it seats on its locating shoulder. Use a suitable tubular drift, such as a socket, which bears only on the hard outer edge of the seal **(see illustration)**. Take care not to damage the seal lips during fitting. Note that the seal lips should face inwards.

5 Refit the camshaft sprocket as described in Section 7.

---

9 Camshaft and followers - removal, inspection and refitting

Removal

1 Remove the cylinder head cover as described in Section 4. On TUD 5 engines, remove the air cleaner assembly and intake pipe, as described in Chapter 4D.

2 Remove the camshaft sprocket (complete with hub on TUD 5 engines), as described in Section 7.

3 Remove the braking system vacuum pump from the left-hand end of the cylinder head as described in Chapter 9.

4 The camshaft bearing caps should be numbered 1 to 3, No 1 being at the transmission end of the engine **(see illustration)**. If not, make identification marks on the caps using white paint or a suitable marker pen. Also mark each cap in some way to indicate its correct fitted orientation. This will avoid the possibility of installing the centre cap the wrong way around on refitting.

5 Evenly and progressively slacken the camshaft bearing cap retaining nuts (or bolts) by one turn at a time, in a spiral pattern starting from the outside. This will relieve the pressure of the valve springs on the bearing caps gradually and evenly. Once the valve

8.4 Levering the camshaft oil seal into position with a suitable socket

spring pressure has been relieved, the nuts can be fully unscrewed and removed.

6 Note the correct fitted orientation of the bearing caps, then remove them from the cylinder head.

7 Lift the camshaft away from the cylinder head, and slide the oil seal off the camshaft end.

8 Obtain eight small, clean plastic containers, and number them 1 to 8. Alternatively, divide a larger container into eight compartments. Using a rubber sucker, withdraw each shim and follower in turn, and place it in its respective container. **Do not** interchange the cam followers, or the rate of wear will be much increased.

Inspection

9 Examine the camshaft bearing surfaces and cam lobes for signs of wear ridges and scoring. Renew the camshaft if any of these conditions are apparent. Examine the condition of the bearing surfaces both on the camshaft journals and in the cylinder head/bearing caps. If the head bearing surfaces are worn excessively, the cylinder head will need to be renewed. Since no dimensions are given by Peugeot, it is not possible to assess the amount of wear by direct measurement. Seek the advice of a Peugeot dealer or engine overhaul specialist before condemning the camshaft or cylinder head. On TUD 5 engines, if the camshaft or tappets are replacements, fit basic 3.20 mm shims.

9.4 Identification numbers (arrowed) are cast onto the camshaft bearing caps

2B

9.10 Oil the camshaft followers, and refit them to their original locations in the cylinder head

9.12 Thoroughly oil the camshaft bearing surfaces prior to installing the camshaft

9.13 Apply sealant to the shaded areas of Nos 1 and 3 bearing caps

Refitting

10 Liberally oil the cylinder head cam follower bores and the followers. Carefully refit the followers to the cylinder head, ensuring that each follower is refitted to its original bore **(see illustration)**. Some care will be required to enter the followers squarely into their bores.

11 Ensure that all the shims are correctly seated in the top of each follower.

12 Lubricate the camshaft bearing and lobe contact surfaces with clean engine oil, then refit the camshaft to the cylinder head **(see illustration)**. Temporarily refit the sprocket to the end of the shaft, and position it so that the sprocket timing hole is aligned with the threaded hole in the cylinder head (tips of No 4 cylinder cam lobes should be facing away from their followers). Also ensure that the crankshaft is still locked in position (see Section 3).

13 Ensure that the bearing cap and head mating surfaces are completely clean, unmarked, and free from oil. Apply a smear of suitable sealant to Nos 1 and 3 bearing caps as shown **(see illustration)**.

14 Refit the bearing caps, using the identification marks noted on removal to ensure that each is installed the correct way round and in its original location **(see illustration)**.

15 Evenly and progressively tighten the camshaft bearing cap nuts (or bolts) by one turn at a time in a spiral pattern, starting from

the inside until the caps touch the cylinder head. Then go round again and tighten all the nuts (or bolts) to the specified torque setting **(see illustrations)**. Work only as described, to impose the pressure of the valve springs gradually and evenly on the bearing caps.

16 Fit a new camshaft oil seal, using the information given in Section 8. Refit the camshaft sprocket as described in Section 7 and timing belt described in Section 6.

17 Check and, if necessary, adjust the valve clearances as described in Section 10.

18 Refit the braking system vacuum pump as described in Chapter 9.

19 Refit the cylinder head cover as described in Section 4. On TUD 5 engines refit the air cleaner assembly and intake pipe. Reconnect the battery negative terminal.

10 Valve clearances - checking and adjustment

Note: *This is not a routine operation. It should only be necessary at high mileage, after overhaul, or when investigating noise or power loss which may be attributable to the valve gear. Shims are available in thicknesses between 3.20 mm and 4.90 mm, in steps of 0.025 mm. On certain models the shims are located under the tappets, therefore if adjustment is necessary, the camshaft will have to be removed.*

1 The importance of having the valve

clearances correctly adjusted cannot be overstressed, as they vitally affect the performance of the engine. That being said, the check should not be regarded as routine maintenance, and should only be carried out when the valve gear has become noisy, after engine overhaul, or when trying to trace the cause of power loss which may be attributed to the valvegear. The clearances are checked as follows, noting that the engine must be cold for the check to be accurate.

2 Chock the rear wheels then jack up the front of the vehicle and support it on axle stands (see *"Jacking and Vehicle Support"*). Remove the right-hand front roadwheel.

3 The engine can then be turned over using a suitable socket and extension bar fitted to the crankshaft sprocket bolt. Where necessary, undo the retaining nut and free the coolant hoses from the bracket to improve access further.

> **HAYNES HiNT** *Turning the engine will be much easier if the glow plugs are removed first (see Chapter 5C).*

4 Remove the cylinder head cover as described in Section 4.

5 Draw the outline of the engine on a piece of paper, numbering the cylinders 1 to 4 (No 1 cylinder is at the transmission end of the engine). Show the position of each valve, together with the specified valve clearance (see paragraph 9). Above each valve, draw

9.14 Install the bearings caps, using the identification markings to ensure they are correctly positioned . . .

9.15a . . . and refit the retaining nuts . . .

9.15b . . . tightening them evenly and progressively to the specified torque setting

10.7 Checking a valve clearance

10.14a Shim thickness is stamped on the bottom face of the shim . . .

10.14b . . . however, shims should be measured to determine their true thickness

two lines for noting the actual clearance and the amount of adjustment required.

6 Turn the crankshaft until the inlet valve of No 1 cylinder (nearest the transmission) is fully closed, with the tip of the cam facing directly away from the cam follower.

7 Using feeler blades, measure the clearance between the base of the cam and the follower (see illustration). Record the clearance on the paper.

8 Repeat the measurement for the other seven valves, turning the crankshaft as necessary so that the cam lobe in question is always facing directly away from the relevant follower.

9 Calculate the difference between each measured clearance and the desired value, and record it on the piece of paper. Since the clearance is different for inlet and exhaust valves, make sure that you are aware which valve you are dealing with. The valve sequence from either end of the engine is:

TUD 3 engines: Ex–In–Ex–In–In–Ex–In–Ex
TUD 5 engines: In–Ex–In–Ex–Ex–In–Ex–In

10 Where a valve clearance differs from the specified value, then the shim for that valve must be replaced with a thinner or thicker shim accordingly.

11 To remove the shim, the follower has to be pressed down against valve spring pressure just far enough to allow the shim to be slid out. To do this, make sure that the cam lobe of the valve on which the shim is to be removed is pointing away from the follower, then rotate the follower so that its notch is at a right-angle to the camshaft centre-line.

12 Using a suitable C-spanner or stout screwdriver, carefully lever down between the camshaft and the edge of the follower, until the follower is depressed sufficiently to allow the shim to be slid out of position.

13 With the shim removed, slowly release the follower. If difficulty is experienced in removing the shims, it will be necessary to remove the camshaft as described in Section 9.

14 The shim size is stamped on the bottom face of the shim, but it is advisable to use a micrometer to measure the true thickness of any shim removed, as it may have been reduced by wear (see illustrations). The size of shim required is calculated as follows.

15 If the measured clearance is less than

specified, subtract the measured clearance from the specified clearance, and subtract the result from the thickness of the existing shim. For example:

**Sample calculation -
inlet valve clearance too small**
Clearance measured = 0.10 mm
Desired clearance = 0.15 mm
Difference = 0.05 mm
Shim thickness fitted = 3.70 mm
Shim thickness reqd. = 3.70 - 0.05 = 3.65 mm

16 If the measured clearance is greater than specified, subtract the specified clearance from the measured clearance, and add the result to the thickness of the existing shim. For example:

**Sample calculation -
exhaust valve clearance too big**
Clearance measured = 0.40 mm
Desired clearance = 0.30 mm
Difference = 0.10 mm
Shim thickness fitted = 3.45 mm
Shim thickness reqd. = 3.45 + 0.10 = 3.55 mm

17 Depress the follower, then slide the required size shim into position, with its marked face facing downwards. Ensure that the shim is correctly seated, then repeat the procedure (as required) for the remaining valve(s) which require adjustment.

18 Once all valves have been adjusted, rotate the crankshaft through at least four complete turns in the correct direction of rotation, to settle all disturbed shims in position, then recheck the clearances as described above.

19 With all valve clearances correctly adjusted, refit the cylinder head cover as described in Section 4.

20 Refit the roadwheel, then lower the vehicle to the ground and tighten the wheel bolts to the specified torque setting (see Chapter 1B Specifications). Refit the glow plugs, where applicable (see Chapter 5C). Where necessary, clip the coolant hoses into position, and securely tighten the bracket retaining nut.

HAYNES HiNT *It is worthwhile noting down all the valve shim thicknesses to save time when the engine is next overhauled; provided they are not worn or damaged, the shims can be moved to other locations.*

**11 Cylinder head -
removal and refitting**

HAYNES HiNT *To aid refitting, make notes on the locations of all relevant brackets, and the routing of hoses and cables, before removal.*

Removal

1 Disconnect the battery negative terminal (refer to "Disconnecting the battery" in the Reference Section of this manual).

2 Drain the cooling system as described in Chapter 1B.

3 Align the engine assembly/valve timing holes as described in Section 3, and lock the camshaft sprocket, injection pump sprocket and flywheel in position. Do not attempt to rotate the engine whilst the locking tools are in position.

4 Loosen the timing belt tensioner pulley retaining nut. Rotate the pulley in a clockwise direction, using a suitable square-section key fitted to the hole in the pulley hub, then retighten the retaining nut.

5 Disengage the timing belt from the camshaft sprocket, and move the belt clear, taking care not to bend or twist it sharply.

6 Working as described in the relevant Section of Chapter 4D, carry out the following operations:

a) Remove the air intake duct.
b) Remove the inlet manifold.
c) Disconnect the exhaust system front pipe from the exhaust manifold.
d) Disconnect the fast idle cable from the injection pump (so that the valve is free to be removed with the head).
e) Remove the injector pipes.

7 Loosen the retaining clip, and disconnect the vacuum pipe from the braking system vacuum pump located on the left-hand end of the cylinder head (see illustration).

8 Release the retaining clips, and disconnect the coolant hoses from the fuel filter/

2B

11.7 Slacken the retaining clip, and disconnect the hose from the braking system vacuum pump

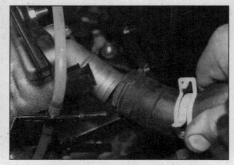

11.8a Disconnect the coolant hoses from the front . . .

11.8b . . . and rear of the fuel filter/thermostat housing

thermostat housing, noting their fitted positions **(see illustrations)**.

9 Slacken the retaining clips, and disconnect the fuel supply hose and pump feed hose from the fuel filter/thermostat housing, which is mounted onto the left-hand end of the cylinder head **(see illustration)**. Where the original crimped-type Peugeot hose clips are still fitted, cut and discard them. Use standard worm-drive clips on refitting.

10 Disconnect the fuel return pipe from No 1 cylinder injector, and position the pipe clear of the head so that it will not hinder removal.

11 Unscrew the retaining nut and disconnect the feed wire from No 1 cylinder glow plug **(see illustration)**. Screw the nut back onto the plug, for safe-keeping, and tighten it securely.

12 Disconnect the wiring from the temperature sender located on the front left-

hand end of the cylinder head **(see illustration)**.

13 Unscrew the bolt securing the engine oil dipstick tube to the front of the cylinder head **(see illustration)**.

14 Remove the cylinder head cover as described in Section 4.

15 Starting on the outside and working inwards in a spiral sequence, progressively loosen the cylinder head bolts, a half a turn at a time. Use the reverse sequence shown in paragraph 34 of this Section.

16 Lift out the cylinder head bolts, and recover the washers.

17 The joint between the cylinder head and gasket and the cylinder block/crankcase must now be broken. This is particularly important on TUD 3 engines as there is a risk of disturbing the seal at the bottom of the wet liners. Although these liners are better located

and sealed than on some other wet-liner engines, there is still a risk of coolant and foreign matter leaking into the sump if the cylinder head is lifted carelessly. If care is not taken and the liners are moved, there is also a possibility of the bottom seals being disturbed, causing leakage after refitting the head.

18 To break the joint, obtain two L-shaped metal bars which fit into the cylinder head bolt holes. Gently "rock" the cylinder head free towards the front of the car (see illustration 12.21 in Part A of this Chapter). Do not try to swivel the head on the cylinder block/crankcase; it is located by dowels, as well as by the tops of the liners.

19 When the joint is broken, lift the cylinder head away; seek assistance if possible, as it is a heavy assembly. Remove the gasket from the top of the block, noting the two locating dowels. If the locating dowels are a loose fit, remove them and store them with the head for safe-keeping. Do not discard the gasket - it will be needed for identification purposes.

20 On TUD 3 engines, *do not* attempt to rotate the crankshaft with the cylinder head removed, otherwise the wet liners may be displaced. Operations that require the rotation of the crankshaft (eg cleaning the piston crowns), should only be carried out once the cylinder liners are firmly clamped in position **(see illustration)**. In the absence of the special Peugeot liner clamps, the liners can be clamped in position using large flat washers positioned underneath suitable-length bolts. Alternatively, the original head bolts could be temporarily refitted, with suitable spacers fitted to their shanks.

11.9 Disconnect the fuel supply and pump feed hoses (arrowed) from the fuel filter/thermostat housing

11.11 Slacken the retaining nut and disconnect the feed wire from No 1 cylinder glow plug

11.12 Disconnect the wiring connector from the temperature sender unit . . .

11.13 . . . and unscrew the dipstick tube retaining bolt (arrowed)

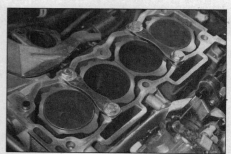

11.20 On TUD 3 engines, the cylinder liners must be clamped in position before the crankshaft is rotated

11.29 Ensure that the locating dowels (arrowed) are in position . . .

11.30 . . . and fit a new gasket

21 If the cylinder head is to be dismantled for overhaul, remove the camshaft and followers as described in Section 9, then refer to Part C of this Chapter.

Preparation for refitting

22 The mating faces of the cylinder head and cylinder block/crankcase must be perfectly clean before refitting the head. Use a hard plastic or wood scraper to remove all traces of gasket and carbon; also clean the piston crowns. Refer to paragraph 20 before turning the crankshaft. Take particular care during the cleaning operations, as the soft aluminium alloy is damaged easily. Also, make sure that the carbon is not allowed to enter the oil and water passages - this is particularly important for the lubrication system, as carbon could block the oil supply to the engine's components. Using adhesive tape and paper, seal the water, oil and bolt holes in the cylinder block/crankcase. Clean all the pistons in the same way.

> **HAYNES HINT** *To prevent carbon entering the gap between the pistons and bores, smear a little grease in the gap. After cleaning each piston, use a small brush to remove all traces of grease and carbon from the gap, then wipe away the remainder with a clean rag.*

23 Check the mating surfaces of the cylinder block/crankcase and the cylinder head for nicks, deep scratches and other damage. If slight, they may be removed carefully with a file, but if excessive, machining may be the only alternative to renewal.

24 If warpage of the cylinder head gasket surface is suspected, use a straight-edge to check it for distortion. Refer to Part C of this Chapter if necessary.

25 When purchasing a new cylinder head gasket, it is essential that a gasket of the correct thickness is obtained. There are two different thicknesses available - the standard gasket which is fitted at the factory, and a slightly thicker "repair" gasket (+ 0.1 mm), for use once the head gasket face has been machined. The gasket type can be identified as described in the following paragraph, using the cut-outs on the left-hand end of the gasket (see illustration 12.29 in Part A of this Chapter).

26 With the gasket fitted the correct way up on the cylinder block, there will be two cut-outs at the rear of the left-hand side of the gasket identifying the engine type (i.e. TUD engine). In the centre of the gasket, there may be another series of between 0 and 4 cut-outs, identifying the manufacturer of the gasket and whether or not it contains asbestos (these cut-outs are of little importance). The important cut-out location is at the front of the gasket; on the standard-thickness gasket, there will be no cut-out in this position, whereas on the thicker "repair" gasket, there will be a single cut-out. Identify the gasket type, and ensure that the new gasket obtained is of the correct thickness. If there is any doubt as to which gasket is fitted, take the old gasket along to your Peugeot dealer, and have him confirm the gasket type.

27 The manufacturers recommend that the cylinder head bolts are measured, to determine whether renewal is necessary. Measure the length of each bolt (without the washer fitted) from the underside of the head to the end of the bolt. If any one bolt is greater than specified length (refer to the Specifications), *all* of the bolts should be renewed as a complete set. As there have been numerous revisions to the bolt types on these engines, it is advisable to consult a Peugeot dealer as to the latest recommendations. Considering the stress which the cylinder head bolts are under, it is *highly* recommended that they are renewed, regardless of their apparent condition.

28 On TUD 3 engines, prior to refitting the cylinder head, check the cylinder liner protrusion as described in Part C of this Chapter.

Refitting

29 Wipe clean the mating surfaces of the cylinder head and cylinder block/crankcase. Check that the two locating dowels are in position at each end of the cylinder block/crankcase surface and, if necessary, remove the cylinder liner clamps **(see illustration)**. Note: *Ensure that the exhaust manifold is in position, as this can not be refitted with the head in position without disturbing the right-hand engine mounting (see Chapter 4D). On TUD 5 engines, clean the threads in the cylinder block with a M10 x 150 tap.*

30 Position a new gasket on the cylinder block/crankcase surface (makers name facing upwards), ensuring that its identification cut-outs are at the left-hand end of the gasket **(see illustration)**. Note: *Left- and right-hand are as seen from the driver's seat, throughout this manual.*

31 Check that the flywheel, injection pump sprocket and camshaft sprocket are still correctly locked in position then, with the aid of an assistant, carefully refit the cylinder head assembly to the block, aligning it with the locating dowels **(see illustration)**.

11.31 Ensure that all sprockets are correctly positioned, then refit the cylinder head assembly

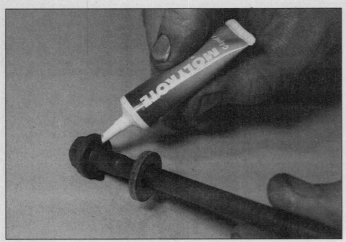

11.32 Apply a smear of the specified grease to the underside of the heads and to the threads of all cylinder head bolts

11.33 Screw the head bolts into position

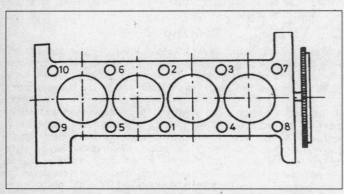

11.34a Head bolt tightening sequence for TUD 3 engine

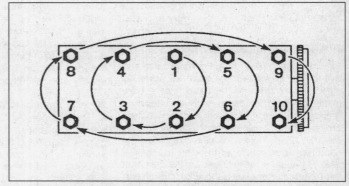

11.34b Head bolt tightening sequence for TUD 5 engine

32 Apply a smear of grease to the threads, and to the underside of the heads, of the cylinder head bolts. Peugeot recommend the use of Molykote G Rapid Plus grease (available from your Peugeot dealer - a sachet is supplied with the top-end gasket set); in the absence of the specified grease, a good-quality high-melting-point grease may be used **(see illustration)**.

33 Carefully enter each bolt and washer into its relevant hole (*do not drop them in*) and screw in, by hand only, until finger-tight **(see illustration)**.

34 Working progressively and in the sequence shown, tighten the cylinder head bolts to their Stage 1 torque setting, using a torque wrench and suitable socket **(see illustrations)**.

35 On TUD 5 engines using an angle gauge, tighten the bolts in the same sequence to the specified Stage 2 setting, then continue on to paragraph 38.

36 On TUD 3 engines, fully slacken the bolts, in the reverse order of tightening. Working again in the given sequence, tighten them to the specified Stage 2 torque setting. Once all the bolts have been tightened to their Stage 2 setting, working again in the specified sequence, angle-tighten the bolts through the specified Stage 3 angle, using a socket and extension bar. It is recommended that an angle-measuring gauge is used during this stage of the tightening, to ensure accuracy **(see illustration)**.

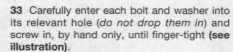

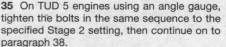

HAYNES HINT *If an angle-tightening gauge is not available, use white paint to make alignment marks between the bolt head and cylinder head prior to tightening; the marks can then be used to check that the bolt has been rotated through the correct angle during tightening.*

11.34c Tighten the head bolts through the various torque settings . . .

11.36 . . . and angle settings as described in text

37 With all bolts tightened through the specified Stage 3 angle, repeat the procedure and tighten the bolts through the specified Stage 4 angle setting.

38 With the cylinder head bolts correctly tightened, refit the dipstick tube retaining bolt, and tighten it securely.

39 Connect the wiring connector to the cylinder head temperature sender unit.

40 Connect the feed wire to No 1 cylinder glow plug, and securely tighten its retaining nut.

41 Ensure that all pipes and hoses are correctly routed, reconnect the fuel and coolant hoses to the filter/thermostat housing, and secure them in position with their retaining clips.

42 Connect the return pipe to No 1 cylinder injector ensuring that the pipe is correctly routed.

43 Connect the vacuum pipe to the braking system pump.

44 Carry out the following operations as described in Chapter 4D:
a) *Refit the injector pipes, and tighten the union nuts to the specified torque.*
b) *Reconnect and adjust the fast idle cable.*
c) *Reconnect the exhaust system to the manifold.*
d) *Refit the inlet manifold.*
e) *Refit the intake duct.*

45 With the crankshaft, injection pump and camshaft locked in position, refit the timing belt to the camshaft sprocket. Ensure that the belt is taut around the crankshaft sprocket, idler pulley and injection pump sprocket, so that any slack is on the tensioner pulley side of the belt. Do not twist the belt sharply while refitting it, and ensure that the belt teeth are seated centrally in the sprockets.

46 Loosen the tensioner pulley retaining nut. Rotate the pulley anti-clockwise to remove all free play from the timing belt, then retighten the nut.

47 Tension the belt as described under the relevant sub-heading of Section 6.

48 Check and, if necessary, adjust the valve clearances as described in Section 10.

49 Refit the cylinder head cover as described in Section 4.

50 Refill the cooling system as described in Chapter 1B.

51 Reconnect the battery negative terminal, then prime and bleed the fuel system as described in Chapter 4D.

12 Sump -
removal and refitting

Refer to Section 14 of Part A, noting that it is not necessary to remove the exhaust system front pipe.

13 Oil pump -
removal, inspection and refitting

Refer to Section 15 of Part A.

14 Crankshaft oil seals -
renewal

Refer to Section 16 of Part A.

15 Flywheel -
removal, inspection and refitting

Refer to Section 18 in Part A.

16 Engine/transmission mountings -
inspection and renewal

Refer to Section 19 of Part A. Note that on right-hand drive models, a reinforcement plate is fitted between the right-hand mounting bracket and the engine.

2B

Notes

Chapter 2 Part C:
Engine removal and overhaul procedures

Contents

Degrees of difficulty

Easy, suitable for novice with little experience	**Fairly easy,** suitable for beginner with some experience	**Fairly difficult,** suitable for competent DIY mechanic 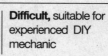	**Difficult,** suitable for experienced DIY mechanic	**Very difficult,** suitable for expert DIY or professional

Specifications

Note: *At the time of writing, very few specifications were available for the 1294 cc and 1587 cc petrol engines, and for some 1360 cc and 1527 cc engines. Where information is not available, refer to your Peugeot dealer for latest information.*

Cylinder head

Maximum gasket face distortion	0.05 mm
Cylinder head height:	
954 cc and 1124 cc engines	111.2 ± 0.8 mm
1360 cc engines:	
Petrol engine	111.2 ± 0.8 mm
Diesel engine	136.4 ± 0.1 mm
1294 cc and 1587 cc engines	Not available
1527 cc diesel engine	Not available
Swirl chamber protrusion - diesel engine only	0 to 0.035 mm

Cylinder block

Cylinder bore diameter:	
954 cc engine:	
Size group A	70.000 to 70.010 mm
Size group B	70.010 to 70.020 mm
Size group C	70.020 to 70.030 mm
1124 cc engine:	
Size group A	72.000 to 72.010 mm
Size group B	72.010 to 72.020 mm
Size group C	72.020 to 72.030 mm
1294 cc engine	Not available
1360 cc engines (petrol and diesel):	
Aluminium block engine:	
Size group A	75.000 to 75.010 mm
Size group B	75.010 to 75.020 mm
Size group C	75.020 to 75.030 mm
Cast-iron block engine	Not available
1527 cc diesel engine	Not available
1587 cc engine	Not available
Liner protrusion above block mating surface - aluminium block engine only:	
Standard:	
Petrol engine	0.03 to 0.10 mm
Diesel engine	0.05 to 0.10 mm
Maximum difference between any two liners	0.05 mm

2C

Valves

	Inlet	Exhaust
Valve head diameter (typical):		
954 cc engine	34.7 mm	27.7 mm
1124 cc engine	36.7 mm	29.2 mm
1360 cc engines:		
Petrol engine	36.8 mm	29.4 mm
Diesel engine	35.5 mm	30.55 mm
1294 and 1587 cc engines	Not available	Not available
1527 cc diesel engine	Not available	Not available
Valve stem diameter:		
954 cc engines	6.965 to 6.980 mm	6.960 to 6.975 mm
1124 cc engines	6.965 to 6.980 mm	6.945 to 6.960 mm
1360 cc engines:		
Petrol engine	6.965 to 6.980 mm	6.965 to 6.980 mm
Diesel engine	6.980 to 6.995 mm	6.980 to 6.995 mm
1294 cc and 1587 cc engines	Not available	Not available
1527 cc diesel engine	Not available	Not available
Overall length:		
954 cc and 1124 cc engines	112.76 mm	112.56 mm
1360 cc engines:		
Petrol engine	112.76 mm	112.56 mm
Diesel engine	108.43 mm	108.17 mm
1294 cc and 1587 cc engines	Not available	Not available
1527 cc diesel engine	Not available	Not available

Pistons

Piston diameter:
- 954 cc engine:
  - Size group A .... 69.960 to 69.970 mm
  - Size group B .... 69.970 to 69.980 mm
  - Size group C .... 69.980 to 69.990 mm
- 1124 cc engine:
  - Size group A .... 71.960 to 71.970 mm
  - Size group B .... 71.970 to 71.980 mm
  - Size group C .... 71.980 to 71.990 mm
- 1294 cc engine .... Not available
- 1360 cc petrol engine:
  - Aluminium block engine:
    - Size group A .... 74.960 to 74.970 mm
    - Size group B .... 74.970 to 74.980 mm
    - Size group C .... 74.980 to 74.990 mm
  - Cast-iron block engine .... Not available
- 1360 cc diesel engine:
  - Size group A .... 74.935 to 74.945 mm
  - Size group B .... 74.945 to 74.955 mm
  - Size group C .... 74.955 to 74.965 mm
- 1527 cc diesel engine .... Not available
- 1587 cc engine .... Not available

Piston protrusion above cylinder head (TUD 5 engines) .... 1.09 ± 0.05 mm

Piston rings

End gaps:
- Top compression ring:
  - 954 cc and 1124 cc engines .... 0.25 to 0.45 mm
  - 1360 cc engines:
    - Petrol engine .... 0.30 to 0.50 mm
    - Diesel engine .... 0.20 to 0.40 mm
  - 1527 cc diesel engine .... Not available
- Second compression ring:
  - 954 cc and 1124 cc engines .... 0.25 to 0.45 mm
  - 1360 cc engines:
    - Petrol engine .... 0.30 to 0.50 mm
    - Diesel engine .... 0.15 to 0.35 mm
  - 1527 cc diesel engine .... Not available
- Oil control ring:
  - 954 cc and 1124 cc engines .... 0.3 to 0.5 mm*
  - 1360 cc engines:
    - Petrol engine .... 0.3 to 0.5 mm*
    - Diesel engine .... 0.25 to 0.50 mm
  - 1527 cc diesel engine .... Not available

These are suggested figures, typical for this type of engine - no exact values are stated by Peugeot.

Crankshaft

Endfloat	0.07 to 0.32 mm
Main bearing journal diameter:	
954 cc, 1124 cc and 1360 cc engines:	
Standard	49.965 to 49.981 mm
Undersize	49.665 to 49.681 mm
1294 cc and 1587 cc engines	Not available
1527 cc diesel engine	Not available
Big-end bearing journal diameter:	
954 cc engine:	
Standard	37.992 to 38.008 mm
Undersize	36.992 to 37.008 mm
1124 cc and 1360 cc engines:	
Standard	44.975 to 44.991 mm
Undersize	44.675 to 44.691 mm
1294 cc and 1587 cc engines	Not available
1527 cc diesel engine	Not available
Maximum bearing journal out-of-round (all engines)	0.007 mm
Main bearing running clearance:	
954 cc, 1124 cc and 1360 cc engines*:	
Pre-February 1992 models	0.023 to 0.083 mm
February 1992-on models	0.023 to 0.048 mm
1294 cc and 1587 cc models**	0.025 to 0.050 mm
1527 cc diesel engine	Not available
Big-end bearing running clearance - all models**	0.025 to 0.050 mm

*On 954, 1124 cc and 1360 cc models, the main bearing shells were modified in February 1992, resulting in a reduction in the specified running clearance - see text for further information.

**These are suggested figures, typical for this type of engine - no exact values are stated by Peugeot.

Torque wrench settings

Petrol engines

Refer to Chapter 2A Specifications.

Diesel engines

Refer to Chapter 2B Specifications.

1 General information

Included in this Part of Chapter 2 are details of removing the engine from the vehicle, and general overhaul procedures for the cylinder head, cylinder block/crankcase, and all other engine internal components.

The information given ranges from advice concerning preparation for an overhaul and the purchase of replacement parts, to detailed step-by-step procedures covering removal, inspection, renovation and refitting of engine internal components.

After Section 6, all instructions are based on the assumption that the engine has been removed from the vehicle. For information concerning in-car engine repair, as well as the removal and refitting of those external components necessary for full overhaul, refer to Part A or B of this Chapter (as applicable) and to Section 6. Ignore any preliminary dismantling operations described in Part A (petrol engine) or Part B (diesel engine) that are no longer relevant once the engine has been removed from the vehicle.

Apart from torque wrench settings, which are given at the beginning of Part A or Part B, all specifications relating to engine overhaul are at the beginning of this Part of Chapter 2.

2 Engine overhaul - general information

It is not always easy to determine when, or if, an engine should be completely overhauled, as a number of factors must be considered.

High mileage is not necessarily an indication that an overhaul is needed, while low mileage does not preclude the need for an overhaul. Frequency of servicing is probably the most important consideration. An engine which has had regular and frequent oil and filter changes, as well as other required maintenance, should give many thousands of miles of reliable service. Conversely, a neglected engine may require an overhaul very early in its life.

Excessive oil consumption is an indication that piston rings, valve seals and/or valve guides are in need of attention. Make sure that oil leaks are not responsible before deciding that the rings and/or guides are worn. Perform a compression test, as described in Part A or B of this Chapter (as applicable), to determine the likely cause of the problem.

Check the oil pressure with a gauge fitted in place of the oil pressure switch, and compare it with that specified. If it is extremely low, the main and big-end bearings, and/or the oil pump, are probably worn out.

Loss of power, rough running, knocking or metallic engine noises, excessive valve gear noise, and high fuel consumption may also point to the need for an overhaul, especially if they are all present at the same time. If a complete service does not remedy the situation, major mechanical work is the only solution.

An engine overhaul involves restoring all internal parts to the specification of a new engine. During an overhaul, the cylinder liners (where applicable), the pistons and the piston rings are renewed. New main and big-end bearings are generally fitted; if necessary, the crankshaft may be reground, to restore the journals. The valves are also serviced as well, since they are usually in less-than-perfect condition at this point. While the engine is being overhauled, other components, such as the distributor, starter and alternator, can be overhauled as well. The end result should be an as-new engine that will give many trouble-free miles.

Note: *Critical cooling system components such as the hoses, thermostat and water pump should be renewed when an engine is overhauled. The radiator should be checked carefully, to ensure that it is not clogged or leaking. Also, it is a good idea to renew the oil pump whenever the engine is overhauled.*

2C

Before beginning the engine overhaul, read through the entire procedure, to familiarise yourself with the scope and requirements of the job. Overhauling an engine is not difficult if you follow all of the instructions carefully, have the necessary tools and equipment, and pay close attention to all specifications. It can, however, be time-consuming. Plan on the car being off the road for a minimum of two weeks, especially if parts must be taken to an engineering works for repair or reconditioning. Check on the availability of parts, and make sure that any necessary special tools and equipment are obtained in advance. Most work can be done with typical hand tools, although a number of precision measuring tools are required for inspecting parts to determine if they must be renewed. Often, the engineering works will handle the inspection of parts, and offer advice concerning reconditioning and renewal.

Note: *Always wait until the engine has been completely dismantled, and until all components (especially the cylinder block/crankcase and the crankshaft) have been inspected, before deciding what service and repair operations must be performed by an engineering works. The condition of these components will be the major factor to consider when determining whether to overhaul the original engine, or to buy a reconditioned unit. Do not, therefore, purchase parts or have overhaul work done on other components until they have been thoroughly inspected.* As a general rule, time is the primary cost of an overhaul, so it does not pay to fit worn or sub-standard parts.

As a final note, to ensure maximum life and minimum trouble from a reconditioned engine, everything must be assembled with care, in a spotlessly-clean environment.

3 Engine removal - methods and precautions

If you have decided that the engine must be removed for overhaul or major repair work, several preliminary steps should be taken.

Locating a suitable place to work is extremely important. Adequate work space, along with storage space for the vehicle, will be needed. If a workshop or garage is not available, at the very least, a flat, level, clean work surface is required.

Cleaning the engine compartment and engine/transmission before beginning the removal procedure will help keep tools clean and organised.

An engine hoist or A-frame will also be necessary. Make sure that the equipment is rated in excess of the combined weight of the engine and transmission. Safety is of primary importance, considering the potential hazards involved in lifting the engine/transmission out of the vehicle.

If this is the first time you have removed an

engine, an assistant should ideally be available. Advice and aid from someone more experienced would also be helpful. There are many instances when one person cannot simultaneously perform all of the operations required when lifting the engine out of the vehicle.

Plan the operation ahead of time. Before starting work, arrange for the hire of (or obtain) all of the tools and equipment you will need. Some of the equipment necessary to perform engine/transmission removal and installation safely and with relative ease (in addition to an engine hoist) is as follows: a heavy-duty trolley jack, complete sets of spanners and sockets, wooden blocks, and plenty of rags and cleaning solvent for mopping up spilled oil, coolant and fuel. If the hoist must be hired, make sure that you arrange for it in advance, and perform all of the operations possible without it beforehand. This will save you money and time.

Plan for the vehicle to be out of use for quite a while. An engineering works will be required to perform some of the work which the do-it-yourselfer cannot accomplish without special equipment. These places often have a busy schedule, so it would be a good idea to consult them before removing the engine, in order to accurately estimate the amount of time required to rebuild or repair components that may need work.

Always be extremely careful when removing and refitting the engine/transmission. Serious injury can result from careless actions. Plan ahead and take your time, and a job of this nature, although major, can be accomplished successfully.

The engine and transmission is removed from under the vehicle on all models described in this manual.

4 Engine and transmission - removal, separation and refitting

Removal - manual transmission

Note: *The engine can be removed from the car only as a complete unit with the transmission; the two are then separated for overhaul. The engine/transmission unit is lowered out of position. To allow adequate clearance underneath the vehicle to enable the unit to be withdrawn, there should be at least 75 cm between the front bumper and the ground when the vehicle is raised and supported.*

1 Park the vehicle on firm, level ground. Chock the rear wheels, then firmly apply the handbrake. Jack up the front of the vehicle, and securely support it on axle stands (see *"Jacking and Vehicle Support"*) and bearing in mind the note at the start of this Section.
2 Remove both front roadwheels.
3 Set the bonnet in the upright position, and remove the battery as described in Chapter 5A.

4 Drain the cooling system (see Chapter 1A or 1B), saving the coolant if it is fit for re-use.
5 Drain the transmission oil as described in Chapter 7A. Refit the drain and filler plugs, and tighten them to their specified torque settings.
6 If the engine is to be dismantled, drain the oil and (if required) remove the oil filter as described in Chapter 1A or 1B. Clean and refit the drain plug, tightening it securely.
7 Remove the alternator as described in Chapter 5A.
8 Where applicable, remove the power steering pump as described in Chapter 10.
9 On models with air conditioning, unbolt the compressor, and position it clear of the engine unit. Support the weight of the compressor by tying it to the vehicle body, to prevent any excess strain being placed on the compressor lines whilst the engine is removed. **Do not** disconnect the refrigerant lines from the compressor (see the warnings given in Chapter 3). On 16-valve engines, release the right-hand refrigerant pipe from its mounting bracket alongside the timing cover.
10 Proceed as described under the relevant sub-heading.

Petrol models

11 On models fitted with a carburettor, carry out the following operations using the information given in Chapter 4A:
a) *Remove the air cleaner housing and intake duct.*
b) *Disconnect the fuel feed hose from the anti-percolation chamber.*
c) *Disconnect the accelerator and choke cables from the carburettor.*
d) *Disconnect the braking system servo vacuum hose from the manifold.*
e) *Remove the complete exhaust system.*
12 On single-point fuel-injection models, carry out the following operations using the information given in Chapter 4B:
a) *Remove the air cleaner housing and intake duct (see illustrations).*
b) *Depressurise the fuel system, and disconnect the fuel feed and return hoses from the throttle body.*
c) *Disconnect the accelerator cable from the throttle body.*
d) *Disconnect the purge valve and/or braking system servo vacuum hoses from the manifold.*
e) *Remove the complete exhaust system.*
f) *Remove the plastic cover from the ECU mounting plate on the right-hand side of the engine compartment. Disconnect the wiring connectors from the ECU and its associated components. Release the harness from any relevant clips and ties, so that it is free to be removed with the engine/transmission.*
13 On multi-point fuel injected models, carry out the following operations using the information given in Chapter 4C:
a) *Remove the air cleaner housing and intake duct.*

b) *Depressurise the fuel system, and disconnect the fuel feed and return hoses from the fuel rail. Free the hoses from any relevant retaining clips.*

c) *Disconnect the accelerator cable from the throttle housing.*

d) *Disconnect the purge valve and braking system servo vacuum hoses from the manifold (as applicable). On 16-valve engines, disconnect the vacuum hose and wiring connector at the purge valve (located behind a flap under the right-hand wheel arch) and pull the wiring through into the engine compartment.*

e) *Remove the complete exhaust system.*

f) *Remove the plastic cover from the ECU mounting plate on the right-hand side of the engine compartment. Disconnect the wiring connectors from the ECU and its associated components. Release the harness from any relevant clips and ties, so that it is free to be removed with the engine/transmission.*

g) *On 16-valve engines, unbolt the ECU mounting bracket and move it to one side.*

14 Noting each hose's correct routing, slacken the retaining clips and disconnect the coolant hoses from the water pump housing on the rear of the engine, and from the thermostat housing on the left-hand end of the cylinder head. Where necessary, also disconnect the coolant hose from the inlet manifold.

Diesel models

15 On diesel models, carry out the following operations using the information in Chapter 4D:

a) *Remove the intake duct.*

**4.22a Disconnecting the main engine/
transmission unit wiring harness
connector . . .**

**4.22b . . . then disconnect the harness
leads . . .**

4.12a Remove the air cleaner housing . . .

b) *Disconnect the fuel supply hose from the fuel filter/thermostat housing and the return hose.*

c) *Disconnect the accelerator cable from the injection pump.*

d) *Disconnect the vacuum hose from the braking system vacuum pump.*

e) *Remove the complete exhaust system.*

16 Remove the preheating system control unit as described in Chapter 5C. Free the wiring harness from any relevant retaining clips, so that it is free to be removed with the engine/transmission.

17 Noting each hose's correct routing, slacken the retaining clips and disconnect the coolant hoses from the front and rear of the fuel filter/thermostat housing on the left-hand end of the cylinder head.

All models

18 Remove the radiator cooling fan as described in Chapter 3. On 16-valve engines with air conditioning, remove the radiator.

19 Remove both driveshafts as described in Chapter 8.

20 Disconnect the clutch cable from the transmission as described in Chapter 6.

21 Working as described in Chapter 7A, disconnect the gearchange linkage link rods and the speedometer cable from the transmission.

22 Trace the engine/transmission wiring harness back to its connector in the front, left-hand corner of the engine compartment. Release the wiring connector by twisting its locking ring anti-clockwise and disconnect it. Also trace the harness lead(s) back to the auxiliary fusebox, situated directly behind the

**4.22c . . . and earth lead (arrowed) from
the auxiliary fusebox**

**4.12b . . . and intake duct -
1360 cc model shown**

battery; disconnect the connectors and/or undo the nut(s) and release the lead(s) **(see illustrations)**. Check that all the relevant connectors have been disconnected, and that the wiring is released from any relevant clips or ties, so that it is free to be removed with the engine/transmission.

23 Manoeuvre the engine hoist into position, and attach it to the lifting brackets bolted onto the cylinder head. Raise the hoist until it is supporting the weight of the engine.

24 Slacken and remove the bolt securing the rear engine mounting link to the mounting on the transmission, then loosen the bolt securing the link to the body. Pivot the link away from the transmission, so that it will not hinder removal.

25 Slacken and remove the left-hand mounting rubber centre nut, and the two bolts securing the bracket to the body. Remove the mounting rubber, and slide the spacer off the mounting bracket stud.

26 Slacken and remove the nuts securing the right-hand engine mounting upper bracket to the mounting rubber and bracket on the cylinder block **(see illustration)**. Withdraw the bracket, and lift off the rubber buffer plate (where fitted) from the mounting stud. On diesel models, recover the reinforcement plate from the engine.

27 Make a final check that any components which would prevent the removal of the engine/transmission from the car have been removed or disconnected. Ensure that components such as the gearchange link rods are secured so that they cannot be damaged on removal.

**4.26 Right-hand engine mounting upper
bracket retaining nuts (arrowed)**

2C

28 If available, a low trolley should be placed under the engine/transmission assembly, to facilitate its easy removal from under the vehicle. Lower the engine/transmission assembly, making sure that nothing is trapped or damaged. Enlist the help of an assistant during this procedure, as it may be necessary to tilt the assembly slightly to clear the body panels. Great care must also be taken to ensure that the radiator (if not removed) is not damaged during the removal procedure.

29 Withdraw the assembly from under the vehicle.

Separation - manual transmission

30 With the engine/transmission assembly removed, support the assembly on suitable blocks of wood, on a workbench (or failing that, on a clean area of the workshop floor).

31 Unscrew the retaining bolts and remove the starter motor from the transmission.

32 Disconnect the wiring from the reversing light switch.

33 Ensure that both engine and transmission are adequately supported, then slacken and remove the bolts securing the transmission housing to the engine. Note the correct fitted positions of each bolt (and where fitted, the relevant brackets) as they are removed, to use as a reference on refitting. On cast-iron block engines, it will also be necessary to unbolt the flywheel cover plate from the transmission.

34 Carefully withdraw the transmission from the engine, ensuring that the weight of the transmission is not allowed to hang on the input shaft while it is engaged with the clutch friction disc.

35 If they are loose, remove the locating dowels from the engine or transmission, and keep them in a safe place.

Refitting - manual transmission

36 If the engine and transmission have been separated, perform the operations described below in paragraphs 37 to 42. If not, proceed as described from paragraph 43 onwards.

37 Apply a smear of high-melting-point grease to the splines of the transmission input shaft. Do not apply too much, otherwise there is a possibility of the grease contaminating the clutch friction plate.

38 Ensure that the locating dowels are correctly positioned in the engine or transmission, and that the release bearing is correctly engaged with the fork.

39 Carefully offer the transmission to the engine, until the locating dowels are engaged. Ensure that the weight of the transmission is not allowed to hang on the input shaft as it is engaged with the clutch friction plate.

40 Refit the transmission housing-to-engine bolts, ensuring that all the necessary brackets are correctly positioned, and tighten them to the specified torque setting. On cast-iron block engines, refit the flywheel cover plate and securely tighten its retaining bolts.

41 Reconnect the wire to the reversing light switch.

42 Refit the starter motor and tighten the retaining bolts.

43 Locate the engine/transmission assembly under the vehicle, then reconnect the hoist and lifting tackle to the engine lifting brackets.

44 With the aid of an assistant, lift the assembly up into the engine compartment. Make sure that it clears the surrounding components, and the radiator in particular.

45 Refit the rubber buffer plate (where fitted) and the right-hand engine mounting upper bracket to the body mounting and bracket, and lightly tighten its fasteners. On diesel models, do not omit the reinforcement plate from underneath the mounting bracket.

46 Refit the spacer, then install mounting to the body, and lightly tighten its retaining bolts. Refit the mounting centre nut again, tightening it lightly.

47 Reconnect the rear mounting link to the transmission mounting, and refit its centre bolt.

48 With engine/transmission mounting nuts and bolts lightly tightened, rock the engine/transmission unit to settle it in position, then go around and tighten all the mounting nuts and bolts to their specified torque settings. The hoist can then be detached from the engine unit and removed.

49 The remainder of the refitting procedure is a direct reversal of the removal sequence, noting the following points:

a) Ensure that the wiring harness is correctly routed and retained by all the relevant retaining clips, and that all connectors are correctly and securely reconnected.

b) Prior to refitting the driveshafts to the transmission, renew the driveshaft oil seals as described in Chapter 7A.

c) Ensure that all coolant hoses are correctly reconnected, and securely retained by their retaining clips.

d) Adjust the accelerator cable as described in the relevant Part of Chapter 4.

e) Connect and adjust the clutch cable as described in Chapter 6.

f) Refit and adjust the auxiliary drivebelt as described in Chapter 1A or 1B.

g) Refill the engine and transmission with the correct quantity and type of lubricant, as described in the relevant Sections of Chapter 1A or 1B.

h) Refill the cooling system as described in Chapter 1A or 1B.

i) On completion, start the engine and check for leaks. If the engine has been dismantled and overhauled, refer to Section 20 for further information.

Removal - automatic transmission

Note: *The engine can be removed from the car only as a complete unit with the transmission; the two are then separated for overhaul. The engine/transmission unit is lowered out of position. To allow adequate clearance underneath the vehicle to enable the unit to be* withdrawn, there should be at least 75 cm between the front bumper and the ground when the vehicle is raised and supported.

50 Carry out the operations described in paragraphs 1 to 9, noting that the transmission fluid draining procedure is given in Chapter 1A.

51 Carry out the following operations, using the information given in Chapter 4C:

a) Depressurise the fuel system, and disconnect the fuel feed and return hoses.

b) Disconnect the accelerator cable.

c) Disconnect the fuel system wiring connectors.

d) Disconnect the vacuum hose and wiring connector at the purge valve (located under the right-hand wheel arch) and pull the wiring through into the engine compartment.

e) Disconnect the remaining vacuum hoses from the inlet manifold (as applicable).

f) Remove the plastic cover from the ECU mounting plate on the right-hand side of the engine compartment. Disconnect the wiring connectors from the ECU and its associated components. Release the harness from any relevant clips and ties, so that it is free to be removed with the engine/transmission. Unbolt the ECU mounting bracket and move it to one side.

g) Remove the exhaust system front pipe.

52 Referring to Chapter 3, release the retaining clip and disconnect the heater matrix hoses from their connection on the engine compartment bulkhead.

53 Noting each hose's correct routing, slacken the retaining clips and disconnect the coolant hoses from the water pump housing on the rear of the engine, and from the thermostat housing on the left-hand end of the cylinder head. Where necessary, also disconnect the coolant hose from the inlet manifold.

54 Carry out the following operations, using the information given in Chapter 7B:

a) Disconnect the wiring connector and move aside the transmission ECU.

b) Disconnect the selector cable.

c) Disconnect the speedometer cable/wiring.

55 Remove both driveshafts as described in Chapter 8.

56 Remove the engine/transmission as described in paragraphs 22 to 29.

Separation - automatic transmission

57 With the engine/transmission assembly removed, support the assembly on suitable blocks of wood, on a workbench (or failing that, on a clean area of the workshop floor).

58 Undo the retaining bolts and remove the driveplate lower cover plate from the transmission, to gain access to the torque converter retaining bolts. Slacken and remove the visible bolt. Rotate the crankshaft using a socket and extension bar on the pulley bolt, and undo the remaining bolts securing the torque converter to the driveplate as they become accessible. There are three bolts in total.

59 Slacken and remove the retaining bolts, and remove the starter motor from the transmission.

60 To ensure that the torque converter does not fall out as the transmission is removed, secure it in position using a length of metal strip bolted to one of the starter motor bolt holes.

61 Ensure that both the engine and transmission are adequately supported, then slacken and remove the remaining bolts securing the transmission housing to the engine. Note the correct fitted positions of each bolt (and any relevant brackets) as they are removed, to use as a reference on refitting.

62 Carefully withdraw the transmission from the engine. If the locating dowels are a loose fit in the engine/transmission, remove them and keep them in a safe place.

Refitting - automatic transmission

63 If the engine and transmission have been separated, perform the operations described below in paragraphs 64 to 70. If not, proceed as described from paragraph 71 onwards.

64 Ensure that the bush fitted to the centre of the crankshaft is in good condition. Apply a little Molykote G1 grease (available from your Peugeot dealer) to the torque converter centring pin. Do not apply too much, otherwise there is a possibility of the grease contaminating the torque converter.

65 Ensure that the locating dowels are correctly positioned in the engine or transmission.

66 Carefully offer the transmission to the engine, until the locating dowels are engaged.

67 Refit the transmission housing-to-engine bolts, ensuring that all the necessary brackets are correctly positioned, and tighten them to the specified torque setting.

68 Remove the torque converter retaining strap installed prior to removal. Align the torque converter threaded holes with the retaining plate, and refit the three retaining bolts.

69 Tighten the torque converter retaining bolts to the specified torque setting (Chapter 7B), then refit the driveplate lower cover.

70 Refit the starter motor, and securely tighten its retaining bolts.

71 Refit the engine to the vehicle as described in paragraphs 43 to 48.

72 The remainder of the refitting procedure is a reversal of the removal sequence, noting the following points:

a) Ensure that the wiring loom is correctly routed, and retained by all the relevant retaining clips; all connectors should be correctly and securely reconnected.

b) Prior to refitting the driveshafts to the transmission, renew the driveshaft oil seals (see Chapter 7B).

c) Ensure that all coolant hoses are correctly reconnected, and securely retained by their retaining clips.

d) Adjust the selector cable as described in Chapter 7B.

e) Adjust the accelerator cable (see the relevant Part of Chapter 4).

f) Refill the engine and transmission with correct quantity and type of lubricant, as described in Chapter 1A.

g) Refill the cooling system (Chapter 1A).

5 Engine overhaul - dismantling sequence

1 It is much easier to dismantle and work on the engine if it is mounted on a portable engine stand. These stands can often be hired from a tool hire shop. Before the engine is mounted on a stand, the flywheel should be removed, so that the stand bolts can be tightened into the end of the cylinder block/crankcase.

2 If a stand is not available, it is possible to dismantle the engine with it blocked up on a sturdy workbench, or on the floor. Be extra-careful not to tip or drop the engine when working without a stand.

3 If you are going to obtain a reconditioned engine, all the external components must be removed first, to be transferred to the replacement engine (just as they will if you are doing a complete engine overhaul yourself). These components include the following:

a) Alternator mounting bracket (Chapter 5A).

b) On petrol engines, the distributor, HT leads and spark plugs, as applicable (Chapters 1A and 5B).

c) On diesel engines, the fuel injection pump and mounting bracket, the fuel injectors and glow plugs (Chapters 4D and 5C).

d) Thermostat housing, and coolant outlet chamber/elbow (Chapter 3). On diesel engines, the housing also includes the fuel filter housing.

e) Where applicable, the dipstick tube.

f) On petrol engines, the carburettor/fuel injection system components (Chapter 4A, 4B or 4C).

g) All electrical switches and sensors, and the engine wiring harness.

h) Inlet and exhaust manifolds (Chapter 4A, 4B, 4C or 4D).

i) Oil filter (Chapter 1A or 1B).

j) Fuel pump - carburettor petrol engines (Chapter 4A).

k) Engine mountings (Part A or B of this Chapter).

l) Flywheel/driveplate (Part A or B of this Chapter).

Note: When removing the external components from the engine, pay close attention to details that may be helpful or important during refitting. Note the fitted position of gaskets, seals, spacers, pins, washers, bolts, and other small items.

4 If you are obtaining a "short" engine (which consists of the engine cylinder block/crankcase, crankshaft, pistons and connecting rods

all assembled), then the cylinder head, sump, oil pump, and timing belt will have to be removed also.

5 If you are planning a complete overhaul, the engine can be dismantled, and the internal components removed, in the order given below, referring to Part A or B of this Chapter unless otherwise stated:

a) Inlet and exhaust manifolds (Chapter 4A, 4B, 4C or 4D).

b) Timing belt, sprockets and tensioner.

c) Cylinder head.

d) Flywheel/driveplate.

e) Sump.

f) Oil pump.

g) Piston/connecting rod assemblies.

h) Crankshaft.

6 Before beginning the dismantling and overhaul procedures, make sure that you have all of the correct tools necessary. Refer to *"Tools and working facilities"* at the end of this manual for further information.

6 Cylinder head - dismantling

Note: New and reconditioned cylinder heads are available from the manufacturer, and from engine overhaul specialists. Be aware that some specialist tools are required for the dismantling and inspection procedures, and new components may not be readily available. It may therefore be more practical and economical for the home mechanic to purchase a reconditioned head, rather than to dismantle, inspect and recondition the original head.

1 Remove the cylinder head as described in Part A or B of this Chapter (as applicable).

2 If not already done, remove the inlet and exhaust manifolds with reference to the relevant Part of Chapter 4.

3 Remove the camshaft(s) (and followers on diesel engines and 16-valve petrol engines) as described in Part A or B of this Chapter.

4 Using a valve spring compressor, compress each valve spring in turn until the split collets can be removed. Release the compressor, and lift off the spring retainer, spring and spring seat **(see illustration)**.

6.4 Using a valve spring compressor to compress the valve spring

6.5 Remove the valve stem oil seal using a pair of pliers

5 Using a pair of pliers, carefully extract the valve stem seal from the top of the guide **(see illustration)**.

HAYNES HiNT

If, when the valve spring compressor is screwed down, the spring retainer refuses to free and expose the split collets, gently tap the top of the tool, directly over the retainer, with a light hammer. This will free the retainer.

6 Withdraw the valve through the combustion chamber.
7 It is essential that each valve is stored together with its collets, retainer, spring, and spring seat **(see illustration)**. The valves should also be kept in their correct sequence, unless they are so badly worn that they are to be renewed. If they are going to be kept and used again, place each valve assembly in a labelled polythene bag or similar small container. Note that No 1 valve is nearest to the transmission (flywheel) end of the engine.

7 Cylinder head and valves - cleaning and inspection

1 Thorough cleaning of the cylinder head and valve components, followed by a detailed inspection, will enable you to decide how much valve service work must be carried out during the engine overhaul. **Note:** *If the engine has been severely overheated, it is best*

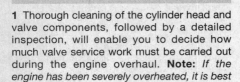

7.6 Checking the cylinder head gasket surface for distortion

6.7 Place each valve and its associated components in a labelled polythene bag

to assume that the cylinder head is warped - check carefully for signs of this.

Cleaning

2 Scrape away all traces of old gasket material from the cylinder head.
3 Scrape away the carbon from the combustion chambers and ports, then wash the cylinder head thoroughly with paraffin or a suitable solvent.
4 Scrape off any heavy carbon deposits that may have formed on the valves, then use a power-operated wire brush to remove deposits from the valve heads and stems.

Inspection

Note: *Be sure to perform all the following inspection procedures before concluding that the services of a machine shop or engine overhaul specialist are required. Make a list of all items that require attention.*

Cylinder head

5 Inspect the head very carefully for cracks, evidence of coolant leakage, and other damage. If cracks are found, a new cylinder head should be obtained.
6 Use a straight-edge and feeler blade to check that the cylinder head surface is not distorted **(see illustration)**. If it is, it may be possible to have it machined, provided that the cylinder head is not reduced to less than the specified height. **Note:** *On diesel engines, it will be necessary to recut the combustion chambers and valve seats if more than 0.1 mm has been machined off the cylinder head. This is necessary in order to maintain the correct*

7.10 Checking swirl chamber protrusion - diesel engine

dimensions between the valve heads, valve guides and cylinder head gasket face.
7 Examine the valve seats in each of the combustion chambers. If they are severely pitted, cracked, or burned, they will need to be renewed or re-cut by an engine overhaul specialist. If they are only slightly pitted, this can be removed by grinding-in the valve heads and seats with fine valve-grinding compound, as described below.
8 Check the valve guides for wear by inserting the relevant valve, and checking for side-to-side motion of the valve. A very small amount of movement is acceptable. If the movement seems excessive, remove the valve. Measure the valve stem diameter (see below), and renew the valve if it is worn. If the valve stem is not worn, the wear must be in the valve guide, and the guide must be renewed. The renewal of valve guides is best carried out by a Peugeot dealer or engine overhaul specialist, who will have the necessary tools available. Where no valve stem diameter is specified, seek the advice of a Peugeot dealer on the best course of action.
9 If renewing the valve guides, the valve seats should be re-cut or re-ground only *after* the guides have been fitted.
10 On diesel models, inspect the swirl chambers for burning or damage such as cracking. Small cracks in the chambers are acceptable; renewal of the chambers will only be required if chamber tracts are badly burned and disfigured, or if they are no longer a tight fit in the cylinder head. If there is any doubt as to the swirl chamber condition, seek the advice of a Peugeot dealer or a suitable repairer who specialises in diesel engines. Swirl chamber renewal should be entrusted to a specialist. Using a dial test indicator, check that the swirl chamber protrusion is within the limits given in the Specifications **(see illustration)**. Zero the dial test indicator on the gasket surface of the cylinder head, then measure the protrusion of the swirl chamber. If the protrusion is not within the specified limits, the advice of a Peugeot dealer or suitable repairer who specialises in diesel engines should be sought.

Valves

11 Examine the head of each valve for pitting, burning, cracks, and general wear. Check the valve stem for scoring and wear ridges. Rotate the valve, and check for any obvious indication that it is bent. Look for pits or excessive wear on the tip of each valve stem. Renew any valve that shows any such signs of wear or damage.
12 If the valve appears satisfactory at this stage, measure the valve stem diameter at several points using a micrometer **(see illustration)**. Any significant difference in the readings obtained indicates wear of the valve stem. Should any of these conditions be apparent, the valve(s) must be renewed.
13 If the valves are in satisfactory condition, they should be ground (lapped) into their

7.12 Measuring a valve stem diameter

7.15 Grinding-in a valve

Valve components

18 Examine the valve springs for signs of damage and discoloration. No minimum free length is specified by Peugeot, so the only way of judging valve spring wear is by comparison with a new component.

19 Stand each spring on a flat surface, and check it for squareness. If any of the springs are damaged, distorted or have lost their tension, obtain a complete new set of springs. It is normal to renew the valve springs as a matter of course if a major overhaul is being carried out.

20 Renew the valve stem oil seals regardless of their apparent condition.

respective seats, to ensure a smooth, gas-tight seal. If the seat is only lightly pitted, or if it has been re-cut, fine grinding compound *only* should be used to produce the required finish. Coarse valve-grinding compound should *not* be used, unless a seat is badly burned or deeply pitted. If this is the case, the cylinder head and valves should be inspected by an expert, to decide whether seat re-cutting, or even the renewal of the valve or seat insert (where possible) is required.

14 Valve grinding is carried out as follows. Place the cylinder head upside-down on a bench.

15 Smear a trace of (the appropriate grade of) valve-grinding compound on the seat face, and press a suction grinding tool onto the valve head **(see illustration)**. With a semi-rotary action, grind the valve head to its seat, lifting the valve occasionally to redistribute the grinding compound.

> **HAYNES HINT** *A light spring placed under the valve head will greatly ease the valve grinding operation.*

16 If coarse grinding compound is being used, work only until a dull, matt even surface is produced on both the valve seat and the valve, then wipe off the used compound, and repeat the process with fine compound. When a smooth unbroken ring of light grey matt finish is produced on both the valve and seat, the grinding operation is complete. Do not grind-in the valves any further than absolutely necessary, or the seat will be prematurely sunk into the cylinder head.

17 When all the valves have been ground-in, carefully wash off *all* traces of grinding compound using paraffin or a suitable solvent, before reassembling the cylinder head.

8 Cylinder head - reassembly

1 Lubricate the stems of the valves, and insert the valves into their original locations **(see illustration)**. If new valves are being fitted, insert them into the locations to which they have been ground.

2 Refit the spring seat then, working on the first valve, dip the new valve stem seal in fresh engine oil. Carefully locate it over the valve and onto the guide. Take care not to damage the seal as it is passed over the valve stem. Use a suitable socket or metal tube to press the seal firmly onto the guide **(see illustrations)**.

3 Locate the valve spring on top of its seat, then refit the spring retainer **(see illustrations)**.

4 Compress the valve spring, and locate the split collets in the recess in the valve stem. Release the compressor, then repeat the procedure on the remaining valves **(see illustrations)**.

> **HAYNES HINT** *Use a little dab of grease to hold the collets in position on the valve stem while the spring compressor is released.*

2C

8.1 Lubricate the valve stems prior to refitting

8.2a Refit the spring seat . . .

8.2b . . . then fit a new valve stem oil seal using a socket

8.3a Refit the valve spring . . .

8.3b . . . and the spring retainer . . .

8.4a . . . and compress the spring with a spring compressor

8.4b Locate the collets on the valve, using a dab of grease to hold them in position

8.5 Remove the spring compressor and tap the end of the valve to seat the collets in position

5 With all the valves installed, place the cylinder head flat on the bench and, using a hammer and interposed block of wood, tap the end of each valve stem to settle the components **(see illustration)**.

6 Refit the camshaft (and followers on diesel engines) as described in Part A or B (as applicable).

7 The cylinder head may now be refitted as described in Part A or B of this Chapter (as applicable).

9 Piston/connecting rod assembly - removal

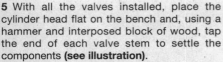

Note: *On engines with wet liners, clamp down the liners before turning the crankshaft (see Chapter 2B, Section 11, paragraph 20).*

1 Remove the cylinder head, sump and oil pump as described in Part A or B of this Chapter (as applicable).

2 If there is a pronounced wear ridge at the top of any bore, it may be necessary to remove it with a scraper or ridge reamer, to avoid piston damage during removal. Such a ridge indicates excessive wear of the cylinder bore.

3 Using a hammer and centre-punch, paint or similar, mark each connecting rod big-end bearing cap with its respective cylinder number on the flat machined surface provided; if the engine has been dismantled before, note carefully any identifying marks made previously **(see illustration)**. Note that

No 1 cylinder is at the transmission (flywheel) end of the engine.

4 Turn the crankshaft to bring pistons 1 and 4 to BDC (bottom dead centre).

5 Unscrew the nuts from No 1 piston big-end bearing cap. Take off the cap, and recover the bottom half bearing shell **(see illustration)**. If the bearing shells are to be re-used, tape the cap and the shell together.

6 To prevent the possibility of damage to the crankshaft bearing journals, tape over the connecting rod stud threads **(see illustration)**.

7 Using a hammer handle, push the piston up through the bore, and remove it from the top of the cylinder block. Recover the bearing shell, and tape it to the connecting rod for safe-keeping.

8 Loosely refit the big-end cap to the connecting rod, and secure with the nuts - this will help to keep the components in their correct order.

9 Remove No 4 piston assembly in the same way.

10 Turn the crankshaft through 180° to bring pistons 2 and 3 to BDC (bottom dead centre), and remove them in the same way.

10 Crankshaft - removal

1 Remove the crankshaft timing sprocket, the oil pump and the flywheel as described in Part A or B of this Chapter (as applicable).

2 Remove the pistons and connecting rods, as described in Section 9. **Note:** *If no work is to be done on the pistons and connecting rods, there is no need to remove the cylinder head, or to push the pistons out of the cylinder bores. The pistons should just be pushed far enough up the bores that they are positioned clear of the crankshaft journals.*

3 Check the crankshaft endfloat as described in Section 13, then proceed as follows.

Aluminium block engines

4 Work around the outside of the cylinder block, and unscrew all the small (6 mm) bolts securing the main bearing ladder to the base of the cylinder block. Note the correct fitted depth of both the front and rear crankshaft oil seals in the cylinder block/main bearing ladder.

5 Working in a diagonal sequence, evenly and progressively slacken the ten large (11 mm) main bearing ladder retaining bolts by a turn at a time. Once all the bolts are loose, remove them from the ladder.

6 With all the retaining bolts removed, carefully lift the main bearing ladder casting away from the base of the cylinder block. Recover the lower main bearing shells, and tape them to their respective locations in the casting. If the two locating dowels are a loose fit, remove them and store them with the casting for safe-keeping.

7 Lift out the crankshaft, and discard both the oil seals. Remove the oil pump drive chain from the end of the crankshaft, then slide off the drive sprocket and recover the Woodruff key.

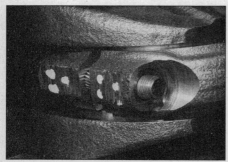

9.3 Connecting rod and big-end bearing cap marked for identification

9.5 Removing a big-end bearing cap and shell

9.6 To protect the crankshaft journals and cylinder bores, tape over the connecting rod stud threads prior to removal

10.9 On cast-iron block engines, remove the oil seal carrier from the front of the cylinder block . . .

10.10a . . . then remove the oil pump drive chain . . .

10.10b . . . and drive sprocket . . .

8 Recover the upper main bearing shells, and store them along with the relevant lower bearing shells. Also recover the two thrustwashers (one fitted either side of No 2 main bearing) from the cylinder block.

Cast-iron block engines

9 Unbolt and remove the crankshaft front and rear oil seal housings from each end of the cylinder block, noting the correct fitted locations of the locating dowels **(see illustration)**. If the locating dowels are a loose fit, remove them and store them with the housings for safe-keeping.

10 Remove the oil pump drive chain, and slide the drive sprocket off the end of the crankshaft. Remove the Woodruff key, and store it with the sprocket for safe-keeping **(see illustrations)**.

11 The main bearing caps should be numbered 1 to 5 from the transmission (flywheel) end of the engine **(see illustration)**. If not, mark them accordingly using a centre-punch or paint.

12 Unscrew and remove the main bearing cap retaining bolts, and withdraw the caps. Recover the lower main bearing shells, and tape them to their respective caps for safe-keeping.

13 Carefully lift out the crankshaft, taking care not to displace the upper main bearing shells **(see illustration)**.

14 Recover the upper bearing shells from the cylinder block, and tape them to their respective caps for safe-keeping. Remove the

thrustwasher halves from the side of No 2 main bearing, and store them with the bearing cap **(see illustration)**.

11 Cylinder block/crankcase - cleaning and inspection

Cleaning

1 Remove all external components and electrical switches/sensors from the block. For complete cleaning, the core plugs should ideally be removed. Drill a small hole in the plugs, then insert a self-tapping screw into the hole. Pull out the plugs by pulling on the screw with a pair of grips, or by using a slide hammer.

2 On aluminium block engines, remove the liners as described in paragraph 16.

3 On 1587 cc models, undo the retaining bolts and remove the piston oil jet spray tubes (there are four - one for each cylinder) from inside the cylinder block.

4 Scrape all traces of sealant from the cylinder block/crankcase, and from the main bearing ladder (where fitted), taking care not to damage the gasket/sealing surfaces.

5 Remove all oil gallery plugs (where fitted). The plugs are usually very tight - they may have to be drilled out, and the holes re-tapped. Use new plugs when the engine is reassembled.

6 If any of the castings are extremely dirty, all should be steam-cleaned.

10.10c . . . then remove the Woodruff key from the crankshaft

7 After the castings are returned, clean all oil holes and oil galleries one more time. Flush all internal passages with warm water until the water runs clear. Dry thoroughly, and apply a light film of oil to all mating surfaces, to prevent rusting. On cast-iron block engines, also oil the cylinder bores. If you have access to compressed air, use it to speed up the drying process, and to blow out all the oil holes and galleries.

⚠️ **Warning: Wear eye protection when using compressed air!**

8 If the castings are not very dirty, you can do an adequate cleaning job with hot (as hot as you can stand!), soapy water and a stiff brush. Take plenty of time, and do a thorough job. Regardless of the cleaning method used, be sure to clean all oil holes and galleries very thoroughly, and to dry all components well.

10.11 Main bearing cap identification markings (arrowed)

10.13 Lifting out the crankshaft

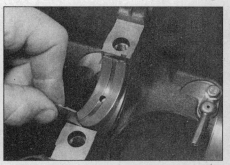

10.14 Remove the upper main bearing shells from the cylinder block/crankcase and store them with their lower shells

2C

11.9 Cleaning a cylinder block threaded hole using a suitable tap

On cast-iron block engines, protect the cylinder bores as described above, to prevent rusting.

9 All threaded holes must be clean, to ensure accurate torque readings during reassembly. To clean the threads, run the correct-size tap into each of the holes to remove rust, corrosion, thread sealant or sludge, and to restore damaged threads **(see illustration)**. If possible, use compressed air to clear the holes of debris produced by this operation.

> *A good alternative to compressed air is to inject an aerosol water-dispersant lubricant into each hole, using the long tube usually supplied.*
>
> *Warning: Wear eye protection when cleaning out these holes in this way!*

10 Apply suitable sealant to the new oil gallery plugs, and insert them into the holes in the block. Tighten them securely.

11 On 1587 cc engines, clean the threads of the piston oil jet retaining bolts, and apply a drop of suitable thread-locking compound to the bolt threads. Refit the piston oil jet spray tubes to the cylinder block, and tighten their retaining bolts to the specified torque setting.

12 If the engine is not going to be reassembled right away, cover it with a large plastic bag to keep it clean; protect all mating surfaces and the cylinder bores as described above, to prevent rusting.

11.16a On aluminium block engines, remove each liner . . .

Inspection

Cast-iron block engines

13 Visually check the casting for cracks and corrosion. Look for stripped threads in the threaded holes. If there has been any history of internal water leakage, it may be worthwhile having an engine overhaul specialist check the cylinder block/crankcase with special equipment. If defects are found, have them repaired if possible, or renew the assembly.

14 Check each cylinder bore for scuffing and scoring. Check for signs of a wear ridge at the top of the cylinder, indicating that the bore is excessively worn.

15 Since Peugeot do not state any specific wear limits for the cylinder bores or pistons, it is not possible to assess the amount of wear by direct measurement. If there is any doubt about the condition of the cylinder bores, seek the advice of a Peugeot dealer or engine reconditioning specialist. At the time of writing, it was not clear whether oversize pistons are available from Peugeot. Consult your Peugeot dealer for piston availability; if oversize pistons are available, the cylinders can be rebored, but if not, and the bores are worn, renewal of the block seems to be the only option. Seek the advice of an engine overhaul specialist as to the best course of action.

Aluminium cylinder block (with wet liners)

16 Remove the liner clamps (where used), then use a hardwood drift to tap out each liner from inside the cylinder block. When all the liners are released, tip the cylinder block/crankcase on its side and remove each liner from the top of the block. As each liner is removed, stick masking tape on its left-hand (transmission side) face, and write the cylinder number on the tape. No 1 cylinder is at the transmission (flywheel) end of the engine. Remove the O-ring from the base of each liner, and discard it **(see illustrations)**.

17 Check each cylinder liner for scuffing and scoring. Check for signs of a wear ridge at the top of the liner, indicating that the bore is excessively worn.

18 If the necessary measuring equipment is available, measure the bore diameter of each cylinder liner at the top (just under the wear

11.16b . . . and recover the bottom O-ring seal (arrowed)

ridge), centre, and bottom of the cylinder bore, parallel to the crankshaft axis.

19 Next, measure the bore diameter at the same three locations, at right-angles to the crankshaft axis. Compare the results with the figures given in the Specifications.

20 Repeat the procedure for the remaining cylinder liners.

21 If the liner wear exceeds the permitted tolerances at any point, or if the cylinder liner walls are badly scored or scuffed, then renewal of the relevant liner assembly will be necessary. If there is any doubt about the condition of the cylinder bores, seek the advice of a Peugeot dealer or engine reconditioning specialist.

22 If renewal is necessary, new liners, complete with pistons and piston rings, can be purchased from a Peugeot dealer. Note that it is not possible to buy liners individually - they are supplied only as a matched assembly complete with piston and rings.

23 To allow for manufacturing tolerances, on most engines, pistons and liners are separated into three size groups. The size group of each piston is indicated by a letter (A, B or C) stamped onto its crown, and the size group of each liner is indicated by a series of 1 to 3 notches on the upper lip of the liner; a single notch for group A, two notches for group B, and three notches for group C. Ensure that each piston and its respective liner are both of the same size group. It is permissible to have different size group piston and liner assemblies fitted to the same engine, but never fit a piston of one size group to a liner in a different group. On some later engines, pistons and liners are manufactured in only one size group.

24 Prior to installing the liners, thoroughly clean the liner mating surfaces in the cylinder block, and use fine abrasive paper to polish away any burrs or sharp edges which might damage the liner O-rings. Clean the liners and wipe dry, then fit a new O-ring to the base of each liner. To aid installation, apply a smear of oil to each O-ring and to the base of the liner.

25 If the original liners are being refitted, use the marks made on removal to ensure that each is refitted the correct way round, and is inserted into its original position. Insert each liner into the cylinder block, taking care not to damage the O-ring, and press it home as far as possible by hand. Using a hammer and a block of wood, tap each liner lightly but fully onto its locating shoulder. Wipe clean, then lightly oil, all exposed liner surfaces, to prevent rusting.

26 With all four liners correctly installed, use a dial gauge (or a straight-edge and feeler blade) to check that the protrusion of each liner above the upper surface of the cylinder block is within the limits given in the Specifications **(see illustration)**. The maximum difference between any two liners must not be exceeded.

27 If new liners are being fitted, it is permissible to interchange them to bring the

11.26 Checking cylinder liner protrusion - aluminium block engine

difference in protrusion within limits. Remember to keep each piston with its respective liner.

28 If liner protrusion cannot be brought within limits, seek the advice of a Peugeot dealer or engine reconditioning specialist before proceeding with the engine rebuild.

12 Piston/connecting rod assembly - inspection

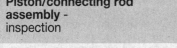

1 Before the inspection process can begin, the piston/connecting rod assemblies must be cleaned, and the original piston rings removed from the pistons.

2 Carefully expand the old rings over the top of the pistons. Be careful not to scratch the piston with the ends of the ring. The rings are brittle, and will snap if they are spread too far. They're also very sharp - protect your hands and fingers. Note that the third ring incorporates an expander. Always remove the rings from the top of the piston. Keep each set of rings with its piston if the old rings are to be re-used **(see Tool Tip)**.

3 Scrape away all traces of carbon from the top of the piston. A hand-held wire brush (or a piece of fine emery cloth) can be used, once the majority of the deposits have been scraped away.

4 Remove the carbon from the ring grooves in the piston, using an old ring. Break the ring in half to do this (be careful not to cut your fingers - piston rings are sharp). Be careful to remove only the carbon deposits - do not

remove any metal, and do not nick or scratch the sides of the ring grooves.

5 Once the deposits have been removed, clean the piston/connecting rod assembly with paraffin or a suitable solvent, and dry thoroughly. Make sure that the oil return holes in the ring grooves are clear.

6 If the pistons and cylinder bores are not damaged or worn excessively, and if the cylinder block does not need to be rebored (as applicable), the original pistons can be refitted. Normal piston wear shows up as even vertical wear on the piston thrust surfaces, and slight looseness of the top ring in its groove. New piston rings should always be used when the engine is reassembled.

7 Carefully inspect each piston for cracks around the skirt, around the gudgeon pin holes, and at the piston ring "lands" (between the ring grooves).

8 Look for scoring and scuffing on the piston skirt, holes in the piston crown, or burned areas at the edge of the crown. If the skirt is scored or scuffed, the engine may have been suffering from overheating, and/or abnormal combustion which caused excessively high operating temperatures. The cooling and lubrication systems should be checked thoroughly. Scorch marks on the sides of the pistons show that blow-by has occurred. A hole in the piston crown, or burned areas at the edge of the piston crown, indicates that abnormal combustion (pre-ignition, knocking, or detonation) has been occurring. If any of the above problems exist, the causes must be investigated and corrected, or the damage will occur again. The causes may include incorrect ignition/injection pump timing, or a faulty injector (as applicable).

9 Corrosion of the piston, in the form of pitting, indicates that coolant has been leaking into the combustion chamber and/or the crankcase. Again, the cause must be corrected, or the problem may persist in the rebuilt engine.

10 On aluminium-block engines with wet liners, it is not possible to renew the pistons separately; pistons are only supplied with piston rings and a liner, as a part of a matched assembly (see Section 11). On cast-iron block engines, replacement pistons are available separately but, on TUD 5 engines, the pistons

The use of two or three old feeler blades will be helpful in preventing the rings dropping into empty grooves.

must be of the correct height size group (see Section 19).

11 Examine each connecting rod carefully for signs of damage, such as cracks around the big-end and small-end bearings. Check that the rod is not bent or distorted. Damage is highly unlikely, unless the engine has been seized or badly overheated. Detailed checking of the connecting rod assembly can only be carried out by a Peugeot dealer or engine repair specialist with the necessary equipment.

12 On all 8-valve petrol engines (aluminium and cast-iron block), the gudgeon pins are an interference fit in the connecting rod small-end bearing. Therefore, piston and/or connecting rod renewal should be entrusted to a Peugeot dealer or engine repair specialist, who will have the necessary tooling to remove and install the gudgeon pins.

13 On diesel engines and 16-valve petrol engines, the gudgeon pins are of the floating type, secured in position by two circlips. On these engines, the pistons and connecting rods can be separated and reassembled as follows.

14 Using a small flat-bladed screwdriver, prise out the circlips, and push out the gudgeon pin. Hand pressure should be sufficient to remove the pin. Identify the piston, gudgeon pin and rod to ensure correct reassembly **(see illustrations)**. Discard the circlips - new ones *must* be used on refitting.

15 Examine the gudgeon pin and connecting rod small-end bearing for signs of wear or damage. Wear can be cured by renewing both

2C

12.14a On diesel engines and 16-valve petrol engines, prise out the circlip ...

12.14b ... withdraw the gudgeon pin ...

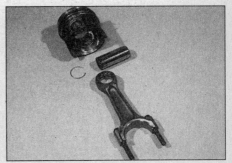

12.14c ... and separate the piston from the connecting rod

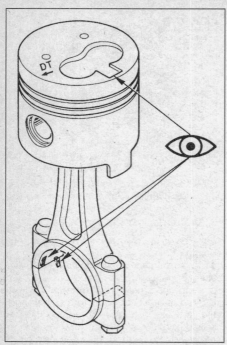

12.18 On diesel engines, ensure that the piston combustion recess is positioned as shown in relation to the connecting rod bearing shell cut-outs (arrowed)

the pin and bush. Bush renewal, however, is a specialist job - press facilities are required, and the new bush must be reamed accurately.

16 The connecting rods themselves should not need renewal, unless seizure or some other major mechanical failure has occurred. Check the alignment of the connecting rods visually, and if the rods are not straight, take them to an engine overhaul specialist for a more detailed check.

17 Examine all components, and obtain any new parts from your Peugeot dealer. **Note:** *Measure piston protrusion above the cylinder head on TUD5 engines to ensure the correct piston height size group is used (see Section 19). If new pistons are purchased, they will be supplied complete with gudgeon pins and circlips. Circlips can also be purchased individually.*

18 Position the piston so that the cloverleaf recess on the piston crown is positioned correctly in relation to the connecting rod big-end bearing shell cut-outs **(see illustration)**. Apply a smear of clean engine oil to the gudgeon pin. Slide it into the piston and through the connecting rod small-end. Check that the piston pivots freely on the rod, then secure the gudgeon pin in position with two new circlips. Ensure that each circlip is correctly located in its groove in the piston.

13 Crankshaft - inspection

Checking crankshaft endfloat

1 If the crankshaft endfloat is to be checked, this must be done when the crankshaft is still installed in the cylinder block/crankcase, but is free to move (see Section 10).

2 Check the endfloat using a dial gauge in contact with the end of the crankshaft. Push the crankshaft fully one way, and then zero the gauge **(see illustration)**. Push the crankshaft fully the other way, and check the endfloat. The result can be compared with the specified amount, and will give an indication as to whether new thrustwashers are required.

3 If a dial gauge is not available, feeler gauges can be used. First push the crankshaft fully towards the flywheel end of the engine, then use feeler blades to measure the gap between the No 1 crankpin web and No 2 main bearing thrustwasher **(see illustration)**.

Inspection

4 Clean the crankshaft using paraffin or a suitable solvent, and dry it, preferably with compressed air if available. Be sure to clean the oil holes with a pipe cleaner or similar probe, to ensure that they are not obstructed.

 Warning: Wear eye protection when using compressed air!

5 Check the main and big-end bearing journals for uneven wear, scoring, pitting and cracking.

6 Big-end bearing wear is accompanied by distinct metallic knocking when the engine is running (particularly noticeable when the

engine is pulling from low speed) and some loss of oil pressure.

7 Main bearing wear is accompanied by severe engine vibration and rumble - getting progressively worse as engine speed increases - and again by loss of oil pressure.

8 Check the bearing journal for roughness by running a finger lightly over the bearing surface. Any roughness (which will be accompanied by obvious bearing wear) indicates that the crankshaft requires regrinding (where possible) or renewal.

9 If the crankshaft has been reground, check for burrs around the crankshaft oil holes (the holes are usually chamfered, so burrs should not be a problem unless regrinding has been carried out carelessly). Remove any burrs with a fine file or scraper, and thoroughly clean the oil holes as described previously.

10 Using a micrometer, measure the diameter of the main and big-end bearing journals, and compare the results with the Specifications **(see illustration)**. By measuring the diameter at a number of points around each journal's circumference, you will be able to determine whether or not the journal is out-of-round. Take the measurement at each end of the journal, near the webs, to determine if the journal is tapered. Compare the results obtained with those given in the Specifications. Where no specified journal diameters are quoted, seek the advice of a Peugeot dealer.

11 Check the oil seal contact surfaces at each end of the crankshaft for wear and damage. If the seal has worn a deep groove in the surface of the crankshaft, consult an engine overhaul specialist. Repair may be possible, but otherwise a new crankshaft will be required.

12 It appears that Peugeot produce a set of undersize bearing shells for both the main bearings and big-end bearings for most engines; refer to your Peugeot dealer for further information on parts availability. If undersize bearing shells are available, and the crankshaft has worn beyond the specified limits, providing that the crankshaft journals have not already been reground, it may be possible to have the crankshaft reconditioned, and to fit the undersize shells. Seek the advice of your Peugeot dealer or engine specialist on the best course of action.

13.2 Checking crankshaft endfloat using a dial gauge

13.3 Checking crankshaft endfloat using feeler blades

13.10 Measuring a crankshaft big-end journal diameter

14 Main and big-end bearings - inspection

1 Even though the main and big-end bearings should be renewed during the engine overhaul, the old bearings should be retained for close examination, as they may reveal valuable information about the condition of the engine. The bearing shells are graded by thickness, the grade of each shell being indicated by the colour code marked on it.
2 Bearing failure can occur due to lack of lubrication, the presence of dirt or other foreign particles, overloading the engine, or corrosion **(see illustration)**. Regardless of the cause of bearing failure, the cause must be corrected (where applicable) before the engine is reassembled, to prevent it from happening again.
3 When examining the bearing shells, remove them from the cylinder block/crankcase, the main bearing ladder/caps (as appropriate), the connecting rods and the connecting rod big-end bearing caps. Lay them out on a clean surface in the same general position as their location in the engine. This will enable you to match any bearing problems with the corresponding crankshaft journal. *Do not* touch any shell's bearing surface with your fingers while checking it, or the delicate surface may be scratched.
4 Dirt and other foreign matter gets into the engine in a variety of ways. It may be left in the engine during assembly, or it may pass through filters or the crankcase ventilation system. It may get into the oil, and from there into the bearings. Metal chips from machining operations and normal engine wear are often present. Abrasives are sometimes left in engine components after reconditioning, especially when parts are not thoroughly cleaned using the proper cleaning methods. Whatever the source, these foreign objects often end up embedded in the soft bearing material, and are easily recognised. Large particles will not embed in the bearing, and will score or gouge the bearing and journal. The best prevention for this cause of bearing failure is to clean all parts thoroughly, and keep everything spotlessly-clean during engine assembly. Frequent and regular engine oil and filter changes are also recommended.
5 Lack of lubrication (or lubrication breakdown) has a number of interrelated causes. Excessive heat (which thins the oil), overloading (which squeezes the oil from the bearing face) and oil leakage (from excessive bearing clearances, worn oil pump or high engine speeds) all contribute to lubrication breakdown. Blocked oil passages, which usually are the result of misaligned oil holes in a bearing shell, will also oil-starve a bearing, and destroy it. When lack of lubrication is the cause of bearing failure, the bearing material is wiped or extruded from the steel backing of the bearing. Temperatures may increase to the point where the steel backing turns blue from overheating.

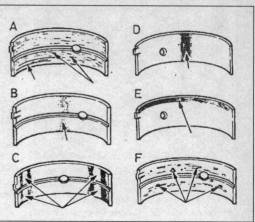

14.2 Typical bearing failures
A *Scratched by dirt; dirt embedded in bearing material*
B *Lack of oil; overlay wiped out*
C *Improper seating; bright (polished) sections*
D *Tapered journal; overlay gone from entire surface*
E *Radius ride*
F *Fatigue failure; craters or pockets*

6 Driving habits can have a definite effect on bearing life. Full-throttle, low-speed operation (labouring the engine) puts very high loads on bearings, tending to squeeze out the oil film. These loads cause the bearings to flex, which produces fine cracks in the bearing face (fatigue failure). Eventually, the bearing material will loosen in pieces, and tear away from the steel backing.
7 Short-distance driving leads to corrosion of bearings, because insufficient engine heat is produced to drive off the condensed water and corrosive gases. These products collect in the engine oil, forming acid and sludge. As the oil is carried to the engine bearings, the acid attacks and corrodes the bearing material.
8 Incorrect bearing installation during engine assembly will lead to bearing failure as well. Tight-fitting bearings leave insufficient bearing running clearance, and will result in oil starvation. Dirt or foreign particles trapped behind a bearing shell result in high spots on the bearing, which lead to failure.
9 *Do not* touch any shell's bearing surface with your fingers during reassembly; there is a risk of scratching the delicate surface, or of depositing particles of dirt on it.
10 As mentioned at the beginning of this Section, the bearing shells should be renewed as a matter of course during engine overhaul; to do otherwise is false economy. Refer to Section 17 for details of bearing shell selection.

15 Engine overhaul - reassembly sequence

1 Before reassembly begins, ensure that all new parts have been obtained, and that all necessary tools are available. Read through the entire procedure to familiarise yourself with the work involved, and to ensure that all items necessary for reassembly of the engine are at hand. In addition to all normal tools and materials, thread-locking compound will be needed. A suitable tube of liquid sealant will also be required for the joint faces that are fitted without gaskets. It is recommended that Peugeot's own product(s) are used, which are specially formulated for this purpose; the relevant product names are quoted in the text of each Section where they are required.
2 In order to save time and avoid problems, engine reassembly can be carried out in the following order:
  a) *Crankshaft (Section 17).*
  b) *Piston/connecting rod assemblies (Section 18).*
  c) *Oil pump.*
  d) *Sump (See Part A or B - as applicable).*
  e) *Flywheel (See Part A or B - as applicable).*
  f) *Cylinder head (See Part A or B - as applicable).*
  g) *Timing belt tensioner and sprockets, and timing belt (See Part A or B - as applicable).*
  h) *Engine external components.*
3 At this stage, all engine components should be absolutely clean and dry, with all faults repaired. The components should be laid out (or in individual containers) on a completely clean work surface.

16 Piston rings - refitting

1 Before fitting new piston rings, the ring end gaps must be checked as follows.
2 Lay out the piston/connecting rod assemblies and the new piston ring sets, so that the ring sets will be matched with the same piston and cylinder/liner during the end gap measurement and subsequent engine reassembly.
3 Insert the top ring into the first cylinder/liner, and push it down the bore using the top of the piston. This will ensure that the ring remains square with the cylinder walls. Position the ring near the bottom of the cylinder bore, at the lower limit of ring travel. Note that the top and second compression rings are different.
4 Measure the end gap using feeler gauges.

2C

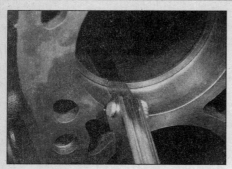

16.5 Measuring a piston ring end gap

5 Repeat the procedure with the ring at the top of the cylinder bore, at the upper limit of its travel, and compare the measurements with the figures given in the Specifications **(see illustration)**.

6 If the gap is too small (unlikely if genuine Peugeot parts are used), it must be enlarged, or the ring ends may contact each other during engine operation, causing serious damage. Ideally, new piston rings providing the correct end gap should be fitted. As a last resort, the end gap can be increased by filing the ring ends very carefully with a fine file. Mount the file in a vice equipped with soft jaws, slip the ring over the file with the ends contacting the file face, and slowly move the ring to remove material from the ends. Take care, as piston rings are sharp, and are easily broken.

7 With new piston rings, it is unlikely that the end gap will be too large. If the gaps are too large, check that you have the correct rings for your engine and for the particular cylinder bore size.

8 Repeat the checking procedure for each ring in the first cylinder, and then for the rings in the remaining cylinders. Remember to keep rings, pistons and cylinders matched up.

9 Once the ring end gaps have been checked and if necessary corrected, the rings can be fitted to the pistons.

10 Fit the piston rings using the same technique as for removal. Fit the bottom (oil control) ring first, and work up. When fitting the oil control ring, where applicable first insert the expander, then fit the ring with its gap positioned 180° from the expander gap. Ensure that the second compression ring is fitted the correct way up **(see illustrations)**. Arrange the gaps of the top and second compression rings 120° either side of the oil control ring gap. **Note:** *Always follow any instructions supplied with the new piston ring sets - different manufacturers may specify different procedures. Do not mix up the top and second compression rings, as they have different cross-sections.*

17 Crankshaft -
refitting and main bearing running clearance check

Selection of new bearing shells

Petrol engines

1 To ensure that the main bearing running clearance can be accurately set, the bearing shells are supplied in different thicknesses (grades).

2 On cast iron block engines there are three different grades of bearing shell, on aluminium block engines there are three different grades on early engines and six different grades on later engines. The grades are indicated by a colour-coding marked on the edge of each shell, which denotes the shell's thickness, as listed in the following table. The upper shell on all bearings is of the same size (class B, colour code black), and the running clearance is controlled by fitting a lower bearing shell of the required thickness.

Aluminium block engine - early models

Bearing colour code	Thickness (mm)	
	Standard	Undersize
Blue (class A)	1.823	1.973
Black (class B)	1.835	1.985
Green (class C)	1.848	1.998

Aluminium block engine - later models

Bearing colour code	Thickness (mm)	
	Standard	Undersize
Blue (class A)	1.823	1.973
Orange (class B)	1.829	1.979
Black (class C)	1.835	1.985
Yellow (class D)	1.841	1.991
Green (class E)	1.847	1.998
White (class F)	1.853	2.003

Cast-iron block engine

Bearing colour code	Thickness (mm)	
	Standard	Undersize
Blue (class A)	1.844	1.994
Black (class B)	1.858	2.008
Green (class C)	1.869	2.019

3 New bearing shells can be selected using the reference marks on the cylinder block/crankcase. The cylinder block marks identify the diameter of the bearing bores and the crankshaft marks, the diameter of the crankshaft journals.

4 The cylinder block reference marks are on the right-hand (timing belt) end of the block, and the crankshaft reference marks are on the right-hand (timing belt) end of the crankshaft, on the right-hand web of No 4 crankpin **(see illustration)**. These marks can be used to select bearing shells of the required thickness as follows.

5 On both the crankshaft and block there are two lines of identification: a bar code, which is

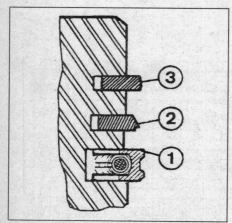

**16.10a Piston ring fitting diagram -
petrol engines**

1 Oil control ring
2 Second compression ring
3 Top compression ring

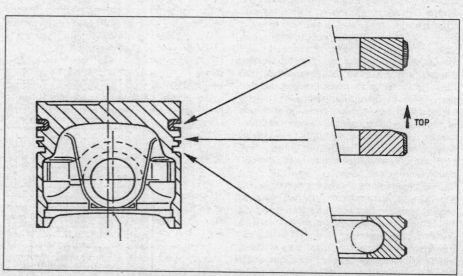

**16.10b Piston ring fitting diagram -
diesel engines**

used by Peugeot during production, and a row of five letters. The first letter in the sequence refers to the size of No 1 bearing (at the flywheel/driveplate end). The last letter in the sequence (which is followed by an arrow) refers to the size of No 5 main bearing. These marks can be used to select the required bearing shell grade as follows.

6 Obtain the identification letter of both the relevant crankshaft journal and the cylinder block bearing bore. Noting that the cylinder block letters are listed across the top of the chart, and the crankshaft letters down the side, trace a vertical line down from the relevant cylinder block letter, and a horizontal line across from the relevant crankshaft letter, and find the point at which both lines cross. This crossover point will indicate the grade of lower bearing shell required to give the correct main bearing running clearance. For example, illustration 17.6a shows cylinder block reference G, and crankshaft reference T, crossing at a point within the area of Class A, indicating that a blue-coded (Class A) lower bearing shell is required to give the correct main bearing running clearance **(see illustrations)**.

7 Repeat this procedure so that the required bearing shell grade is obtained for each of the five main bearing journals.

8 Seek the advice of your Peugeot dealer for the latest information on parts availability when ordering new bearing shells.

Diesel engine

9 The procedure is the same as that described in paragraphs 1 to 8. However, when the different grades were initially introduced, it was only possible to get blue-coded (Class A) lower bearing shells. This has now been extended, and it is now possible to get blue and black-coded lower bearing shells (Class A and B). Green-coded (Class C) lower bearing shells are not available.

Main bearing running clearance check

Aluminium block engines

10 On early engines, if the modified bearing shells are to be fitted, obtain a set of new black (Class B) upper bearing shells and new blue (Class A) lower bearing shells. On later engines where the modified bearing shells are already fitted, the running clearance check can be carried out using the original bearing shells. However, it is preferable to use a new set, since the results obtained will be more conclusive.

11 Clean the backs of the bearing shells, and the bearing locations in both the cylinder block/crankcase and the main bearing ladder.

12 Press the bearing shells into their locations, ensuring that the tab on each shell engages in the notch in the cylinder block/crankcase or main bearing ladder location. Take care not to touch any shell's bearing surface with your fingers. Note that the grooved bearing shells, both upper and lower, are fitted to Nos 2 and 4

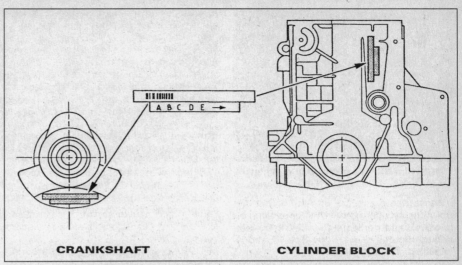

17.4 Cylinder block and crankshaft main bearing reference markings

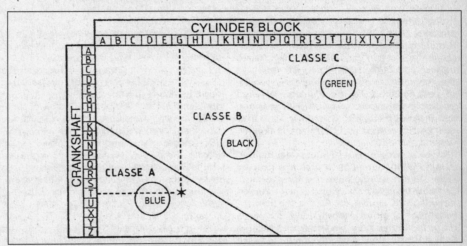

17.6a Three class main bearing shell selection chart - see text

2C

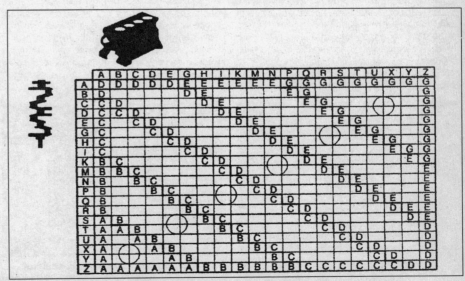

17.6b Six class main bearing shell selection chart - see text

17.12 Note that the grooved bearing shells are fitted to Nos 2 and 4 main bearing journals

17.16 Plastigage in place on a crankshaft main bearing journal

17.19 Measuring the width of the deformed Plastigage using the scale on the card provided

main bearings **(see illustration)**. If the original bearing shells are being used for the check, ensure that they are refitted in their original locations. The clearance can be checked in either of two ways.

13 One method (which will be difficult to achieve without a range of internal micrometers or internal/external expanding calipers) is to refit the main bearing ladder casting to the cylinder block/crankcase, with the bearing shells in place. With the casting retaining bolts correctly tightened, measure the internal diameter of each assembled pair of bearing shells. If the diameter of each corresponding crankshaft journal is measured and then subtracted from the bearing internal diameter, the result will be the main bearing running clearance.

14 The second (and more accurate) method is to use an American product known as "Plastigage". This consists of a fine thread of perfectly-round plastic, which is compressed between the bearing shell and the journal. When the shell is removed, the plastic is deformed, and can be measured with a special card gauge supplied with the kit. The running clearance is determined from this gauge. Plastigage should be available from your Peugeot dealer; otherwise, enquiries at one of the larger specialist motor factors should produce the name of a stockist in your area. The procedure for using Plastigage is as follows.

15 With the main bearing upper shells in place, carefully lay the crankshaft in position.

Do not use any lubricant; the crankshaft journals and bearing shells must be perfectly clean and dry.

16 Cut several lengths of the appropriate-size Plastigage (they should be slightly shorter than the width of the main bearings), and place one length on each crankshaft journal axis **(see illustration)**.

17 With the main bearing lower shells in position, refit the main bearing ladder casting, tightening its retaining bolts as described in paragraph 31. Take care not to disturb the Plastigage, and *do not* rotate the crankshaft at any time during this operation.

18 Remove the main bearing ladder casting, again taking great care not to disturb the Plastigage or rotate the crankshaft.

19 Compare the width of the crushed Plastigage on each journal to the scale printed on the Plastigage envelope, to obtain the main bearing running clearance **(see illustration)**. Compare the clearance measured with that given in the Specifications at the start of this Chapter.

20 If the clearance is significantly different from that expected, the bearing shells may be the wrong size (or excessively worn, if the original shells are being re-used). Before deciding that different-size shells are required, make sure that no dirt or oil was trapped between the bearing shells and the main bearing ladder or block when the clearance was measured. If the Plastigage was wider at one end than at the other, the crankshaft journal may be tapered.

21 If the clearance is not as specified, use the reading obtained, along with the shell thicknesses quoted above, to calculate the necessary grade of bearing shells required. When calculating the bearing clearance required, bear in mind that it is always better to have the running clearance slightly towards the lower end of the specified range, to allow for wear in use.

22 Where necessary, obtain the required grades of bearing shell, and repeat the running clearance checking procedure as described above.

23 On completion, carefully scrape away all traces of the Plastigage material from the crankshaft and bearing shells. Use your fingernail, or a wooden or plastic scraper which is unlikely to score the bearing surfaces.

Cast-iron block engine

24 The procedure is similar to that described in the previous paragraphs for the aluminium block engine, except that each main bearing has a separate cap, which must be fitted and the bolts tightened to the specified torques.

Final crankshaft refitting

Aluminium block engines

25 Carefully lift the crankshaft out of the cylinder block once more.

26 Using a little grease, stick the upper thrustwashers to each side of the No 2 main bearing upper location; ensure that the oilway grooves on each thrustwasher face outwards (away from the cylinder block) **(see illustration)**.

27 Place the bearing shells in their locations as described earlier. If new shells are being fitted, ensure that all traces of protective grease are cleaned off using paraffin. Wipe dry the shells and connecting rods with a lint-free cloth. Liberally lubricate each bearing shell in the cylinder block/crankcase with clean engine oil **(see illustration)**.

28 Refit the Woodruff key, then slide on the oil pump drive sprocket, and locate the drive chain on the sprocket **(see illustration)**. Lower the crankshaft into position so that Nos 2 and 3 cylinder crankpins are at TDC; Nos 1 and 4 cylinder crankpins will be at BDC, ready

17.26 Refitting a crankshaft thrustwasher

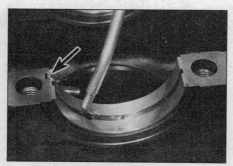

17.27 Ensure each bearing shell tab (arrowed) is correctly located and lubricate the shell with clean engine oil

17.28 Refitting the oil pump drive chain and sprocket

17.29 On aluminium block engines, apply a thin film of sealant to the cylinder block/crankcase mating surface . . .

17.30 . . . then lower the main bearing ladder into position

for fitting No 1 piston. Check the crankshaft endfloat as described in Section 13.

29 Thoroughly degrease the mating surfaces of the cylinder block/crankcase and the main bearing ladder. Apply a thin bead of suitable sealant to the cylinder block/crankcase mating surface of the main bearing ladder casting, then spread to an even film **(see illustration)**.

30 Lubricate the lower bearing shells with clean engine oil, then refit the main bearing ladder, ensuring that the shells are not displaced, and that the locating dowels engage correctly **(see illustration)**.

31 Install the ten 11 mm main bearing ladder retaining bolts, and tighten them all by hand only. Working progressively outwards from the centre bolts, tighten the ten bolts, by a turn at a time, to the specified Stage 1 torque wrench setting. Once all the bolts have been tightened to the Stage 1 setting, angle-tighten the bolts through the specified Stage 2 angle using a socket and extension bar. It is recommended that an angle-measuring gauge is used during this stage of the tightening, to ensure accuracy **(see illustrations)**. If a gauge is not available, use a dab of white paint to make alignment marks between the bolt head and casting prior to tightening; the marks can then be used to check that the bolt has been rotated sufficiently during tightening.

32 Refit all the 6 mm bolts securing the main bearing ladder to the base of the cylinder block, and tighten them to the specified torque. Check that the crankshaft rotates freely.

33 Refit the piston/connecting rod assemblies to the crankshaft as described in Section 18.

34 Ensuring that the drive chain is correctly located on the sprocket, refit the oil pump and sump as described in Part A or B (as applicable) of this Chapter.

35 Fit two new crankshaft oil seals as described in Part A or Part B (as applicable).

36 Refit the flywheel as described in Part A or B of this Chapter (as applicable).

37 Where removed, refit the cylinder head as described in Part A or Part B (as applicable). Also refit the crankshaft sprocket and timing belt as described in Part A or Part B (as applicable).

Cast-iron block engine

38 Carefully lift the crankshaft out of the cylinder block once more.

39 Using a little grease, stick the upper thrustwashers to each side of the No 2 main bearing upper location. Ensure that the oilway grooves on each thrustwasher face outwards (away from the cylinder block)

40 Place the bearing shells in their locations as described earlier. If new shells are being fitted, ensure that all traces of protective grease are cleaned off using paraffin. Wipe dry the shells and connecting rods with a lint-free cloth. Liberally lubricate each bearing shell in the cylinder block/crankcase and cap with clean engine oil.

41 Lower the crankshaft into position so that Nos 2 and 3 cylinder crankpins are at TDC;

Nos 1 and 4 cylinder crankpins will be at BDC, ready for fitting No 1 piston. Check the crankshaft endfloat as described in Section 13.

42 Lubricate the lower bearing shells in the main bearing caps with clean engine oil. Make sure that the locating lugs on the shells engage with the corresponding recesses in the caps.

43 Fit the main bearing caps to their correct locations, ensuring that they are fitted the correct way round (the bearing shell lug recesses in the block and caps must be on the same side). Insert the bolts loosely.

44 Tighten the main bearing cap bolts to the specified Stage 1 torque wrench setting **(see illustration)**. Once all the bolts have been tightened to the Stage 1 setting, angle-tighten the bolts through the specified Stage 2 angle, using a socket and extension bar. It is recommended that an angle-measuring gauge is used during this stage of the tightening, to ensure accuracy. If a gauge is not available, use a dab of white paint to make alignment marks between the bolt head and casting prior to tightening; the marks can then be used to check that the bolt has been rotated sufficiently during tightening.

45 Check that the crankshaft rotates freely.

46 Refit the piston/connecting rod assemblies to the crankshaft as described in Section 18.

47 Refit the Woodruff key to the crankshaft groove, and slide on the oil pump drive sprocket. Locate the drive chain on the sprocket.

2C

17.31a Tighten the ten 11 mm main bearing bolts to the Stage 1 torque setting . . .

17.31b . . . then angle-tighten them through the specified Stage 2 angle

17.44 On cast-iron block engines, tighten the main bearing cap retaining bolts to the specified Stage 1 torque

18.4 Fitting a bearing shell to a connecting rod - ensure that the tab (arrowed) engages with the recess in the connecting rod

48 Ensure that the mating surfaces of front oil seal housing and cylinder block are clean and dry. Note the correct fitted depth of the front oil seal then, using a large flat-bladed screwdriver, lever the seal out of the housing.

49 Apply a smear of suitable sealant to the oil seal housing mating surface, and make sure that the locating dowels are in position. Slide the housing over the end of the crankshaft, and into position on the cylinder block. Tighten the housing retaining bolts securely.

50 Repeat the operations in paragraphs 48 and 49, and fit the rear oil seal housing.

51 Fit a new front and rear crankshaft oil seal as described in Part A or B of this Chapter (as applicable).

52 Ensuring that the chain is correctly located on the drive sprocket, refit the oil pump and sump as described in Part A or B of this Chapter (as applicable).

53 Refit the flywheel as described in Part A or B of this Chapter (as applicable).

54 Where removed, refit the cylinder head and install the crankshaft sprocket and timing belt as described in the relevant Sections of Part A or B (as applicable).

18 Piston/connecting rod assembly - refitting and big-end bearing running clearance check

Selection of bearing shells

1 There are two sizes of big-end bearing shell produced by Peugeot; a standard size for use with the standard crankshaft, and an undersize for use once the crankshaft journals have been reground. When ordering shells, quote the diameter of the crankshaft big-end crankpins, to ensure that the correct set of shells are purchased.

2 Prior to refitting the piston/connecting rod assemblies, it is recommended that the big-end bearing running clearance is checked as follows.

Big-end bearing running clearance check

3 Clean the backs of the bearing shells, and the bearing locations in both the connecting rod and bearing cap.

4 Press the bearing shells into their locations, ensuring that the tab on each shell engages in the recess in the connecting rod and cap **(see illustration)**. Take care not to touch any shell's bearing surface with your fingers. If the original bearing shells are being used for the check, ensure that they are refitted in their original locations. The clearance can be checked in either of two ways.

5 One method is to refit the big-end bearing cap to the connecting rod, ensuring that they are fitted the correct way round (see paragraph 19), with the bearing shells in place. With the cap retaining nuts correctly tightened, use an internal micrometer or vernier caliper to measure the internal diameter of each assembled pair of bearing shells. If the diameter of each corresponding crankshaft journal is measured and then subtracted from the bearing internal diameter, the result will be the big-end bearing running clearance.

6 The second, and more accurate, method is to use Plastigage (see Section 17).

7 Ensure that the bearing shells are correctly fitted. Place a strand of Plastigage on each (cleaned) crankpin journal.

8 Refit the (clean) piston/connecting rod assemblies to the crankshaft, and refit the big-end bearing caps, using the marks made or noted on removal to ensure that they are fitted the correct way round.

9 Tighten the bearing cap nuts as described below in paragraph 20. Take care not to disturb the Plastigage, nor to rotate the connecting rod during the tightening sequence.

10 Dismantle the assemblies without rotating the connecting rods. Use the scale printed on the Plastigage envelope to obtain the big-end bearing running clearance.

11 If the clearance is significantly different from that expected, the bearing shells may be the wrong size (or excessively worn, if the original shells are being re-used). Make sure that no dirt or oil was trapped between the bearing shells and the caps or connecting rods when the clearance was measured. If the Plastigage was wider at one end than at the other, the crankpins may be tapered.

12 Note that Peugeot do not specify a recommended big-end bearing running clearance. The figure given in the

18.18 Tap the piston into the bore using a hammer handle

Specifications is a guide figure, which is typical for this type of engine. Before condemning the components concerned, refer to your Peugeot dealer or engine reconditioning specialist for further information on the specified running clearance. Their advice on the best course of action to be taken can then also be obtained.

13 On completion, carefully scrape away all traces of the Plastigage material from the crankshaft and bearing shells. Use your fingernail, or some other object which is unlikely to score the bearing surfaces.

Final piston/connecting rod refitting

Note: *Refer to Section 19 for the correct selection of pistons on TUD 5 engines.*

14 Note that the following procedure assumes that the cylinder liners (where fitted) are in position in the cylinder block/crankcase as described in Section 11, and that the crankshaft and main bearing ladder/caps are in place (see Section 17). It is possible to fit the pistons to the liners before fitting the liners to the cylinder block; the advantage of using this method is that the pistons enter the liner from the bottom end, which is tapered to allow easy entry of the piston rings (a piston ring compressor will still be required).

15 Ensure that the bearing shells are correctly fitted as described in paragraphs 3 and 4. If new shells are being fitted, ensure that all traces of the protective grease are cleaned off using paraffin. Wipe dry the shells and connecting rods with a lint-free cloth.

16 Lubricate the cylinder bores/liners, the pistons, and piston rings, then lay out each piston/connecting rod assembly in its respective position.

17 Start with assembly No 1. Make sure that the piston rings are still spaced as described in Section 16, then clamp them in position with a piston ring compressor.

18 Insert the piston/connecting rod assembly into the top of cylinder/liner No 1 as follows:

a) On diesel engines, ensure that the 'cloverleaf' cutout on the piston crown faces the oil filter side of the cylinder block.

b) On DOHC 16-valve petrol engines, ensure that the valve head cutouts on the piston crown face the side of the cylinder block **opposite** the oil filter.

c) On SOHC 8-valve petrol engines, ensure that the arrow on the piston crown is pointing towards the timing belt end of the engine.

Using a block of wood or hammer handle against the piston crown, tap the assembly into the cylinder/liner until the piston crown is flush with the top of the cylinder/liner **(see illustration)**.

19 Ensure that the bearing shell is still correctly installed. Liberally lubricate the crankpin and both bearing shells. Taking care not to mark the cylinder/liner bores, tap the piston/connecting rod assembly down the bore/liner and onto the crankpin. Refit the big-end bearing cap, tightening its retaining nuts finger-tight at first. Note that the faces with the identification marks must match (which means that the bearing shell locating tabs abut each other).

20 Tighten the bearing cap retaining nuts evenly and progressively to the specified torque setting **(see illustration)**.

21 Rotate the crankshaft. Check that it turns freely; some stiffness is to be expected if new components have been fitted, but there should be no signs of binding or tight spots.

22 Refit the remaining three piston/connecting rod assemblies in the same way. **Note:** *On engines with wet liners, clamp down the liners before turning the crankshaft (see Chapter 2B, Section 11, paragraph 20).*

23 Refit the cylinder head, oil pump and sump as described in Part A or B of this Chapter (as applicable).

19 Piston selection - TUD 5 engines

Note: *A special reference piston is required for checking piston protrusion. The following paragraphs are meant as a guide for use with this tool. If you do not have this tool, the check should be done by a Peugeot dealer.*

1 Before refitting the cylinder head, measure piston crown protrusion in relation to the upper face of the cylinder block, in order to determine the correct piston height size group. Proceeds as follows:

2 Fit the No 4 cylinder connecting rod to the reference piston. The reference piston does not have grooves for the gudgeon pin circlips.

3 Place a new bearing shell on the big-end bearing and slide the piston/connecting rod assembly into No 4 cylinder.

4 With a new bearing shell in place, refit the bearing cap. Tighten the cap retaining nuts uniformly and progressively to the specified torque wrench setting.

5 In order that the crankshaft can be turned, insert the timing belt sprocket retaining bolt temporarily.

6 Mount a dial gauge and stand on the cylinder head gasket surface of the cylinder block so that the probe touches the central boss of the reference piston.

7 Turn the crankshaft to bring the reference piston exactly to TDC, then set the dial gauge to zero.

8 Move the dial gauge and stand sideways so that the probe touches the cylinder block gasket surface, and note down the degree of piston protrusion displayed on the dial gauge.

9 Proceed as above for the three other cylinders, using the corresponding connecting rods.

18.20 Tighten the big-end bearing cap nuts to the specified torque setting

20 Choose the correct piston height size group from the table below. Note that the groups are identified by the letters stamped on their crown.

Reference piston protrusion (mm)	Piston group - original fitment
Above 2.5	*Non standard: check dimensions of individual components*
2.5 to 2.4	*A*
2.43 to 2.33	*B*
2.36 to 2.26	*C*
Below 2.26	*Non standard: check dimensions of individual components*

Reference piston protrusion (mm)	Piston group - repair components
Above 2.3	*Non standard: check dimensions of individual components*
2.3 to 2.2	*X*
2.23 to 2.13	*Y*
2.16 to 2.06	*Z*
Below 2.06	*Non standard: check dimensions of individual components*

21 After the height size group of each piston has been determined, fit the piston rings and connecting rods, and slide the piston/connecting rod assemblies into the cylinders (see Section 16).

20 Engine - initial start-up after overhaul

1 With the engine refitted in the vehicle, double-check the engine oil and coolant levels. Make a final check that everything has been reconnected, and that there are no tools or rags left in the engine compartment.

Petrol engine models

2 Remove the spark plugs. On models with a distributor, disable the ignition system by disconnecting the ignition HT coil lead from the distributor cap, and earthing it on the cylinder block. Use a jumper lead or similar wire to make a good connection. On models with a static (distributorless) ignition system, disable the ignition system by disconnecting the LT wiring connector from the ignition HT coil, referring to Chapter 5B for further information.

3 Turn the engine on the starter until the oil pressure warning light goes out. Refit the spark plugs and reconnect the spark plug (HT) leads, referring to Chapter 1A for further information. Reconnect any HT leads or wiring which was disconnected in paragraph 2.

Diesel engine models

4 Disconnect the wiring from the stop solenoid on the injection pump (see Chapter 4D), then turn the engine on the starter motor until the oil pressure warning light goes out. Reconnect the wire to the stop solenoid.

5 Prime the fuel system as described in Chapter 4D.

6 Fully depress the accelerator pedal, turn the ignition key to position "M", and wait for the preheating warning light to go out.

All models

7 Start the engine, noting that this may take a little longer than usual, due to the fuel system components having been disturbed.

8 While the engine is idling, check for fuel, water and oil leaks. Don't be alarmed if there are some odd smells and smoke from parts getting hot and burning off oil deposits.

9 Assuming all is well, keep the engine idling until hot water is felt circulating through the top hose, then switch off the engine.

10 Check the ignition timing (petrol engines) or injection pump timing (diesel engines), and the idle speed settings (as appropriate), then switch the engine off.

11 After a few minutes, recheck the oil and coolant levels as described in *"Weekly checks"*, and top-up as necessary.

12 If they were tightened as described, there is no need to re-tighten the cylinder head bolts once the engine has first run after reassembly.

13 If new pistons, rings or crankshaft bearings have been fitted, the engine must be treated as new, and run-in for the first 500 miles (800 km). *Do not* operate the engine at full-throttle, or allow it to labour at low engine speeds in any gear. It is recommended that the oil and filter be changed at the end of this period.

2C

Notes

Chapter 3
Cooling, heating and ventilation systems

Contents

Degrees of difficulty

Easy, suitable for novice with little experience		Fairly easy, suitable for beginner with some experience		Fairly difficult, suitable for competent DIY mechanic		Difficult, suitable for experienced DIY mechanic		Very difficult, suitable for expert DIY or professional	

Specifications

General

Maximum system pressure	2.0 bars (29 psi)
Expansion tank cap opening pressure:	
Orange cap	1.0 bar (14.5 psi)
Mauve cap	1.4 bars (20 psi)

Thermostat

Opening temperatures:	
Starts to open	88°C
Fully-open	100°C

Electric cooling fan

Cut-in temperature:	
Petrol models	97°C
Diesel models	101°C
Cut-out temperature:	
Petrol models	92°C
Diesel models	97°C

Torque wrench settings

	Nm	lbf ft
Smaller coolant pump housing securing bolts	30	22
Larger coolant pump housing securing bolts	65	48
Cooling fan thermostatic switch	45	33
Temperature gauge/temperature warning light sender	18	13

3

1 General information and precautions

General information

The cooling system is of pressurised type, comprising a coolant pump driven by the timing belt, an aluminium crossflow radiator, with integral expansion tank on petrol models, electric cooling fan, a thermostat, heater matrix and all associated hoses and switches. A separate remotely-mounted coolant expansion tank is fitted to diesel models **(see illustrations)**.

The system functions as follows. Cold coolant in the bottom of the radiator passes through the bottom hose to the coolant pump, where it is pumped around the cylinder block and head passages and through the oil cooler (where fitted). After cooling the cylinder bores, combustion surfaces and valve seats, the coolant reaches the underside of the thermostat, which is initially closed. The coolant passes through the heater and is returned via the cylinder block to the coolant pump.

When the engine is cold, the coolant circulates only through the cylinder block, cylinder head and heater. When the coolant reaches a predetermined temperature, the thermostat opens and the coolant passes through the top hose to the radiator. As the coolant circulates through the radiator, it is cooled by the inrush of air when the car is in forward motion. The airflow is supplemented by the action of the electric cooling fan when necessary. Upon reaching the bottom of the radiator, the coolant has now cooled and the cycle is repeated.

When the engine is at normal operating temperature, the coolant expands and some of it is displaced into the expansion tank. Coolant collects in the tank and is returned to the radiator when the system cools.

On some models, the coolant is also passed through the engine oil cooler and, where fitted, the automatic transmission heat exchanger.

The electric cooling fan(s) mounted in front of the radiator are controlled by a thermostatic switch. At a predetermined coolant temperature, the switch/sensor actuates the fan.

Precautions

⚠️ *Warning: Do not attempt to remove the expansion tank filler cap, or to disturb any part of the cooling system, while the engine is hot, as there is a high risk of scalding. If the expansion tank filler cap must be removed before the engine and radiator have fully cooled (even though this is not recommended), the pressure in the cooling system must first be relieved. Cover the cap with a thick layer of cloth, to avoid scalding and slowly unscrew the filler cap until a hissing sound is heard. When the hissing has stopped, indicating that the pressure has reduced, slowly unscrew the filler cap until it can be removed; if more hissing sounds are heard, wait until they have stopped before unscrewing the cap completely. At all times, keep well away from the filler cap opening and protect your hands.*

⚠️ *Warning: Do not allow antifreeze to come into contact with your skin, or with the painted surfaces of the vehicle. Rinse off spills immediately, with plenty of water. Never leave antifreeze lying around in an open container, or in a puddle in the driveway or on the garage floor. Children and pets are attracted by its sweet smell, but antifreeze can be fatal if ingested.*

⚠️ *Warning: If the engine is hot, the electric cooling fan may start rotating even if the engine is not running. Be careful to keep your hands, hair and any loose clothing well clear when working in the engine compartment.*

⚠️ *Warning: Refer to Section 10 for precautions to be observed when working on models with air conditioning.*

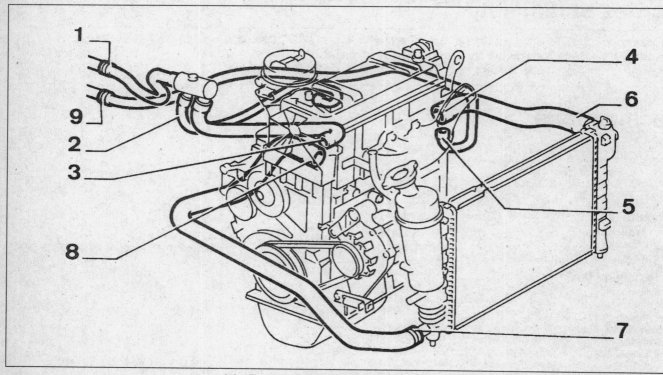

1.1a Typical cooling system layout - petrol engine

1 Heater matrix outlet	4 Engine outlet	7 Radiator outlet
2 Heater return to carburettor/throttle body	5 Engine outlet to heater matrix	8 Engine inlet
3 Heater return to engine	6 Radiator inlet	9 Heater matrix inlet

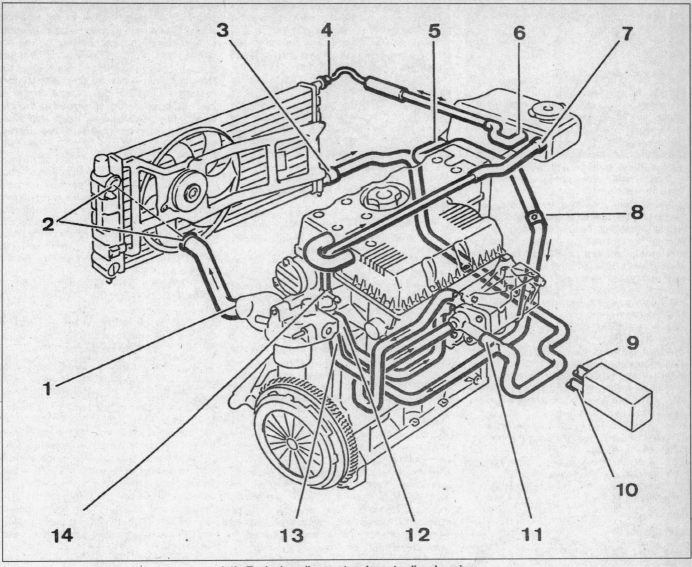

1.1b Typical cooling system layout - diesel engine

1 Engine outlet	7 Expansion tank inlet
2 Radiator inlet	8 Bleed screw
3 Radiator outlet	9 Heater matrix outlet
4 Radiator-to-expansion tank hose	10 Heater matrix inlet
5 Expansion tank-to-engine hose	11 Engine inlet
6 Expansion tank-to-radiator hose	12 By-pass outlet to heater matrix
	13 By-pass outlet to engine

---

2 Cooling system hoses - disconnection and renewal

1 The number, routing and pattern of hoses will vary according to model, but the same basic procedure applies. Before commencing work, make sure that the new hoses are to hand, along with new hose clips if needed. It is good practice to renew the hose clips at the same time as the hoses.

2 Drain the cooling system, as described in Chapter 1A or 1B, saving the coolant if it is fit for re-use. Squirt a little penetrating oil onto the hose clips if they are corroded.

3 Release the hose clips from the hose concerned. Three types of clip are used; worm-drive, spring and "sardine-can". The worm-drive clip is released by turning its screw anti-clockwise. The spring clip is released by squeezing its tags together with pliers, at the same time working the clip away from the hose stub **(see illustration)**. The "sardine-can" clip is not re-usable and is best cut off with snips or side cutters.

4 Unclip any wires, cables or other hoses which may be attached to the hose being removed. Make notes for reference when refitting if necessary.

2.3 Releasing a radiator top hose spring clip

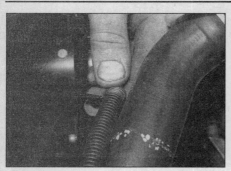

3.5 Release the wiring harness from the clips on the fan shroud

3.7 Disconnect the radiator hoses

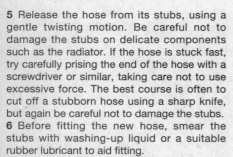

3.9a Unscrew the two securing bolts (arrowed) . . .

5 Release the hose from its stubs, using a gentle twisting motion. Be careful not to damage the stubs on delicate components such as the radiator. If the hose is stuck fast, try carefully prising the end of the hose with a screwdriver or similar, taking care not to use excessive force. The best course is often to cut off a stubborn hose using a sharp knife, but again be careful not to damage the stubs.

6 Before fitting the new hose, smear the stubs with washing-up liquid or a suitable rubber lubricant to aid fitting.

Caution: Do not use oil or grease, which may attack the rubber.

7 Fit the hose clips over the ends of the hose, then fit the hose over its stubs. Work the hose into position. When satisfied, locate and tighten the hose clips.

8 Refill the cooling system as described in Chapter 1A or 1B. Run the engine and check that there are no leaks.

9 Recheck the tightness of the hose clips on any new hoses after a few hundred miles.

10 Top-up the coolant level if necessary (see *"Weekly checks"*).

3 Radiator - removal, inspection and refitting

Note: *If the reason for removing the radiator is to cure a leak, it is worth trying the effect of a radiator sealing compound - this is added to the coolant and will often cure minor leaks with the radiator in situ.*

Removal

1 Disconnect the battery negative terminal (refer to *"Disconnecting the battery"* in the Reference Section of this manual).

2 Drain the cooling system as described in Chapter 1A or 1B.

3 Where applicable, to improve access, remove the exhaust manifold heat shield. On later models, move the power steering fluid reservoir to one side (where fitted).

4 Remove the air cleaner air intake ducting or the complete air cleaner assembly, as required, referring to the relevant Part of Chapter 4.

5 Disconnect the wiring plugs from the cooling fan and from the cooling fan switch, which is mounted in the top left-hand corner of the radiator. Where applicable, release the wiring harness from the clips on the fan shroud and move the harness to one side **(see illustration)**.

6 Remove the cooling fan shroud securing bolts, then disengage the shroud lugs from the brackets on the end of the radiator and lift the cooling fan and shroud assembly from the radiator. Note that on certain models, due to limited clearance, the fan/shroud assembly must be withdrawn from underneath the vehicle.

7 Disconnect the coolant hoses from the radiator, with reference to Section 2 if necessary **(see illustration)**.

8 On petrol models fitted with a radiator shield, remove the left-hand headlight as described in Chapter 12. Working through the headlight aperture, remove the left-hand radiator shield securing bolt. Working through the front body aperture, unscrew the right-hand radiator shield securing bolt from the front top right-hand corner of the radiator.

9 On diesel models, working through the front body aperture at the right-hand side of the radiator, unscrew the two radiator shield securing bolts and withdraw the shield **(see illustrations)**.

10 Using a suitable pair of pliers, release the upper radiator securing spring clips from the top of the radiator and the body front panel and withdraw the clips **(see illustrations)**. On later models, undo the bolts and release the radiator mounting brackets on each side.

11 The radiator can now be withdrawn from the engine compartment. On diesel and some petrol models, the radiator is most easily withdrawn from underneath the vehicle **(see illustration)**. On certain other models, the radiator must be withdrawn through the top of the engine compartment, in which case, it may be necessary to drill out the pop-rivets and remove the air intake tube from the front body panel.

Caution: Take care not to damage the radiator fins during removal.

12 On petrol models, if desired, remove the heat shield from the coolant expansion tank.

13 Where applicable, recover the lower mounting rubbers and lift out the radiator shield.

3.9b . . . and withdraw the radiator shield - diesel model

3.10a Using a pair of pliers, lift out the bottom of the clip . . .

3.10b . . . then release the top legs

3.11 Lower the radiator from the engine compartment - diesel model

3.19 Inspect the radiator mounting rubbers

3.20 Ensure that the spring clips are correctly engaged

Inspection

14 If the radiator has been removed due to suspected blockage, reverse-flush it as described in Chapter 1A or 1B. Clean dirt and debris from the radiator fins, using an air line (in which case, wear eye protection) or a soft brush.
Caution: Be careful, as the fins are sharp and easily damaged.

15 If necessary, a radiator specialist can perform a "flow test" on the radiator, to establish whether an internal blockage exists.

16 A leaking radiator must be referred to a specialist for permanent repair. Do not attempt to weld or solder a leaking radiator, as damage to the plastic components may result.

17 In an emergency, minor leaks from the radiator can be cured by using a suitable radiator sealant, in accordance with its manufacturer's instructions, with the radiator *in situ*.

18 If the radiator is to be sent for repair or renewed, remove all hoses and the cooling fan switch.

19 Inspect the condition of the radiator mounting rubbers and renew them if necessary **(see illustration)**.

Refitting

20 Refitting is a reversal of removal, bearing in mind the following points:
 a) *Ensure that the lower lugs on the radiator are correctly engaged with the mounting rubbers in the body panel.*

b) *Ensure that the upper radiator securing spring clips are correctly engaged* **(see illustration)**.

 HAYNES HiNT *Fit the clips to the body panel before pushing the radiator forwards to engage the clips with the recesses in the top of the radiator.*

 c) *Where applicable, refit the headlight with reference to Chapter 12.*
 d) *Reconnect the hoses with reference to Section 2.*
 e) *Where applicable, refit the air intake tube using new pop-rivets.*
 f) *On completion, refill the cooling system as described in Chapter 1A or 1B.*

4 Thermostat - removal, testing and refitting

Removal

1 Drain the cooling system as described in Chapter 1A or 1B.

2 If desired for improved access, remove the air cleaner and/or the air intake ducting as described in the relevant Part of Chapter 4. Similarly, remove the battery as described in Chapter 5A.

3 Where necessary, release any relevant wiring and hoses from the retaining clips and position clear of the thermostat housing to improve access.

4 Unscrew the retaining bolts and carefully withdraw the thermostat housing cover to expose the thermostat. Take care not to strain the coolant hose(s) connected to the cover **(see illustrations)**.

5 Lift the thermostat from the housing, noting which way round the thermostat is fitted and recover the sealing ring **(see illustration)**.

Testing

6 A rough test of the thermostat may be made by suspending it with a piece of string in a container full of water. Heat the water to bring it to the boil - the thermostat must open by the time the water boils. If not, renew it.

7 If a thermometer is available, the precise opening temperature of the thermostat may be determined; compare with the figures given in the Specifications. The opening temperature is also marked on the thermostat.

8 A thermostat which fails to close as the water cools must also be renewed.

Refitting

9 Refitting is a reversal of removal, bearing in mind the following points:
 a) *Examine the sealing ring for signs of damage or deterioration and if necessary, renew.*
 b) *Ensure that the thermostat is fitted the correct way round, as noted before removal.*
 c) *Where applicable, refit the air cleaner and/or the air intake ducting, with reference to the relevant Part of Chapter 4.*
 d) *On completion, refill the cooling system as described in Chapter 1A or 1B.*

3

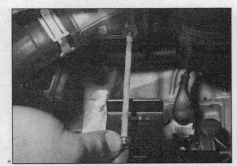

4.4a Unscrew the retaining bolts . . .

4.4b . . . and withdraw the thermostat housing cover

4.5 Lift the thermostat from the housing

5.9a Remove the securing bolt (arrowed) . . .

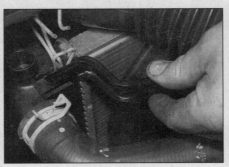

5.9b . . . and disengage the cooling fan shroud legs from the radiator brackets

5.10 Removing the cooling fan blades securing clip

5 Electric cooling fan(s) - testing, removal and refitting

Testing

1 Current supply to the cooling fan is via the ignition switch (see Chapter 5A) and a fuse (see Chapter 12). The circuit is completed by the cooling fan thermostatic switch, which is mounted in the upper left-hand corner of the radiator. On models with air conditioning, the cooling fan is also controlled by the coolant temperature sensor, via the air conditioning control unit - see Section 6.

2 If the fan does not appear to work, run the engine until normal operating temperature is reached, then allow it to idle. The fan should cut in within a few minutes (before the temperature gauge needle enters the red section, or before the coolant temperature warning light comes on). If not, switch off the ignition and disconnect the wiring plug from the cooling fan switch. Bridge the two contacts in the wiring plug using a length of spare wire and switch on the ignition. If the fan now operates, the switch is probably faulty and should be renewed.

3 If the fan still fails to operate, check that battery voltage is available at the feed wire to the switch; if not, then there is a fault in the feed wire (possibly due to a fault in the fan motor, or a blown fuse). If there is no problem with the feed, check that there is continuity between the switch earth terminal and a good earth point on the body; if not, then the earth connection is faulty and must be re-made.

4 If the switch and the wiring are in good condition, the fault must lie in the motor itself. The motor can be checked by disconnecting it from the wiring loom and connecting a 12-volt supply directly to it.

Removal

5 Disconnect the battery negative terminal (refer to *"Disconnecting the battery"* in the Reference Section of this manual).

6 Remove the air cleaner air intake ducting as described in the relevant Part of Chapter 4. If necessary for improved access, drill out the pop-rivets and remove the air intake tube from the front body panel.

7 Where applicable, remove the heat shield from the exhaust manifold. On 1587 cc (16-valve) models, remove the front bumper as described in Chapter 11.

8 Disconnect the wiring plug(s) from the cooling fan(s).

9 Remove the cooling fan shroud securing bolt(s), then disengage the shroud legs from the brackets on the end of the radiator and lift the cooling fan and shroud assembly from the radiator **(see illustrations)**.

10 If desired, the fan blades can be removed from the end of the motor shaft after removing the securing clip **(see illustration)**. The motor can be removed from the shroud assembly after drilling out the securing rivets.

Refitting

11 Refitting is a reversal of removal. Where applicable, use new rivets to secure the fan motor and/or the air intake tube.

6 Cooling system electrical switches - testing, removal and refitting

Electric cooling fan thermostatic switch

Testing

1 Testing of the switch is described in Section 5 as part of the electric cooling fan test procedure.

6.5 Disconnecting the cooling fan switch wiring plug (radiator top hose disconnected for clarity)

Removal

Note: *Suitable sealing compound or a new sealing ring (as applicable) will be required on refitting.*

2 The switch is located in the top left-hand corner of the radiator. The engine and radiator should be cold before removing the switch.

3 Disconnect the battery negative terminal (refer to *"Disconnecting the battery"* in the Reference Section of this manual).

4 Partially drain the cooling system to just below the level of the switch (as described in Chapter 1A or 1B). Alternatively, have ready a suitable bung to plug the switch aperture in the radiator when the switch is removed. If this method is used, take great care not to damage the radiator and do not use anything which will allow foreign matter to enter the radiator.

5 Disconnect the wiring plug from the switch **(see illustration)**.

6 Carefully unscrew the switch from the radiator and recover the sealing ring (where applicable). If the system has not been drained, plug the switch aperture to prevent further coolant loss.

Refitting

7 If the switch was originally fitted using sealing compound, clean the switch threads thoroughly and coat them with fresh sealing compound.

8 If the switch was originally fitted using a sealing ring, use a new sealing ring on refitting.

9 Refitting is a reversal of removal. Tighten the switch to the specified torque and refill (or top-up) the cooling system as described in Chapter 1A or 1B (or *"Weekly checks"*).

10 On completion, start the engine and run it until it reaches normal operating temperature. Continue to run the engine and check that the cooling fan cuts in and out correctly.

Coolant temperature gauge/ temperature warning light sender

Testing

11 On petrol models without air conditioning, the sender is located in the gearbox end of the cylinder head. On diesel models and petrol models with air conditioning, the sender is located in the thermostat housing (see illustration).

12 The temperature gauge (where fitted) is fed with a stabilised voltage from the instrument panel feed (via the ignition switch and a fuse). The gauge earth is controlled by the sender. The sender contains a thermistor - an electronic component whose electrical resistance decreases at a predetermined rate as its temperature rises. When the coolant is cold, the sender resistance is high, current flow through the gauge is reduced and the gauge needle points towards the blue (cold) end of the scale. As the coolant temperature rises and the sender resistance falls, current flow increases and the gauge needle moves towards the upper end of the scale. If the sender is faulty, it must be renewed.

13 On models with a temperature warning light, the light is fed with a voltage from the instrument panel. The light earth is controlled by the sender. The sender is effectively a switch, which operates at a predetermined temperature to earth the light and complete the circuit. If the light is fitted in addition to a gauge, on certain models, the senders for the gauge and light are incorporated in a single unit, with two wires, one each for the light and gauge earths.

14 If the gauge develops a fault, first check the other instruments; if they do not work at all, check the instrument panel electrical feed. If the readings are erratic, there may be a fault in the voltage stabiliser, which will necessitate renewal of the stabiliser (the stabiliser is integral with the instrument panel printed circuit board - see Chapter 12). If the fault lies in the temperature gauge alone, check it as follows.

15 If the gauge needle remains at the "cold" end of the scale when the engine is hot, disconnect the sender wiring plug and earth the relevant wire to the cylinder head. If the needle then deflects when the ignition is switched on, the sender unit is proved faulty and should be renewed. If the needle still does not move, remove the instrument panel (Chapter 12) and check the continuity of the wire between the sender unit and the gauge and the feed to the gauge unit. If continuity is shown and the fault still exists, then the gauge is faulty and the gauge unit should be renewed.

16 If the gauge needle remains at the "hot" end of the scale when the engine is cold, disconnect the sender wire. If the needle then returns to the "cold" end of the scale when the ignition is switched on, the sender unit is proved faulty and should be renewed. If the needle still does not move, check the remainder of the circuit as described previously.

17 The same basic principles apply to testing the warning light. The light should illuminate when the relevant sender wire is earthed.

6.11 Coolant temperature gauge/temperature warning light sender (arrowed) - diesel model

Removal and refitting

18 The procedure is similar to that described previously in this Section for the electric cooling fan thermostatic switch. On some models, access to the switch is poor and other components may need to be removed (or hoses, wiring, etc moved to one side) before the sender unit can be reached.

Fuel injection system coolant temperature sensor

Testing

19 The coolant temperature sensor is located in the thermostat housing.

20 The sensor is a thermistor (see paragraph 12). The fuel injection/engine management ECU supplies the sensor with a set voltage and then, by measuring the current flowing in the sensor circuit, it determines the engine temperature. This information is then used, in conjunction with other inputs, to control the injector opening time (pulse width). On some models, the idle speed and/or ignition timing settings are also temperature-dependent.

21 If the sensor circuit should fail to provide adequate information, the ECU back-up facility will override the sensor signal. In this event, the ECU assumes a predetermined setting which will allow the fuel injection/engine management system to run, albeit at reduced efficiency. When this occurs, the engine warning light on the instrument panel will come on and the advice of a Peugeot dealer should be sought. The sensor itself can only be tested using special Peugeot diagnostic equipment.

7.4a Withdraw the coolant pump . . .

Caution: Do not attempt to test the circuit using any other equipment, as there is a high risk of damaging the ECU.

Removal and refitting

22 The procedure is similar to that described previously in this Section for the electric cooling fan thermostatic switch. On some models, access to the switch is poor and other components may need to be removed (or hoses, wiring, etc moved to one side) before the sensor can be reached.

Air conditioning system coolant temperature sensor

Testing

23 The sensor is located at the transmission end of the cylinder head, in the position normally occupied by the coolant temperature gauge/temperature warning light sender. The sensor provides information to the air conditioning system electronic control unit.

24 The operation of the sensor is similar to the operation of the engine coolant temperature sensor described previously in this Section.

25 The sensor itself can only be tested using special Peugeot diagnostic equipment.

Caution: Do not attempt to test the circuit using any other equipment, as there is a high risk of damaging the air conditioning ECU.

Removal and refitting

26 The procedure is similar to that described previously in this Section for the electric cooling fan thermostatic switch. On some models, access to the switch is poor and other components may need to be removed (or hoses, wiring, etc moved to one side) before the sensor can be reached.

---

7 Coolant pump -
   removal and refitting

Models with aluminium cylinder block

Note: *A new impeller assembly O-ring and where applicable, a new impeller housing O-ring, will be required on refitting.*

Removal

1 The coolant pump is driven by the timing belt and is located in a housing at the timing belt end of the engine.

2 Drain the cooling system as described in Chapter 1A or 1B.

3 Remove the timing belt as described in Chapter 2A or 2B.

4 Remove the securing bolts and withdraw the pump impeller assembly from the pump housing. Manipulate the pump past the engine mounting and withdraw it from the top of the engine compartment. Recover the O-ring (see illustrations).

**7.4b . . . and recover the O-ring -
1360 cc diesel engine shown**

5 If desired, the pump impeller housing can be removed from the rear of the coolant pump housing. Access is most easily obtained from underneath the vehicle (it may be necessary to remove the exhaust heat shield). Disconnect the coolant hoses from the impeller housing (be prepared for coolant spillage), then remove the securing bolts and withdraw the impeller housing. Again, recover the O-ring.

Refitting

6 Ensure that all mating faces are clean.
7 Where applicable, refit the impeller housing to the rear of the coolant pump housing, using a new O-ring. Reconnect the coolant hoses.
8 Refit the impeller assembly to the pump housing, using a new O-ring.
9 Refit the timing belt as described in Chapter 2A or 2B.
10 Refill the cooling system as described in Chapter 1A or 1B.

Models with cast-iron cylinder block

Note: *A new pump O-ring must be used on refitting.*
11 The pump is driven by the timing belt and is located directly in the cylinder block.
12 Proceed as described previously for models with an aluminium cylinder block, but note that there is no separate impeller housing.

8	Heating/ventilation system - general information

The heating/ventilation system consists of a four-speed blower motor (housed behind the facia), face level vents in the centre and at each end of the facia and air ducts to the front footwells.

The control unit is located in the facia and the controls operate flap valves to deflect and mix the air flowing through the various parts of the heating/ventilation system. The flap valves are contained in the air distribution housing, which acts as a central distribution unit, passing air to the various ducts and vents.

Cold air enters the system through the grille at the rear of the engine compartment. If required, the airflow is boosted by the blower and then flows through the various ducts, according to the settings of the controls. Stale air is expelled through ducts at the rear of the vehicle. If warm air is required, the cold air is passed over the heater matrix, which is heated by the engine coolant.

On models fitted with air conditioning, a recirculation switch enables the outside air supply to be closed off, while the air inside the vehicle is recirculated. This can be useful to prevent unpleasant odours entering from outside the vehicle, but should only be used briefly, as the recirculated air inside the vehicle will soon become stale.

9	Heating/ventilation system components - removal and refitting	

Heating/ventilation control unit

1 With the exception of the heater blower motor switch, the heater controls are integral with the heater assembly. The controls are operated by levers pushed through the heater control panel, which engage with the control levers on the heater assembly. Removal of the blower motor switch and the heater illumination bulb is described in Chapter 12.

Complete heater assembly

Removal

2 Drain the cooling system as described in Chapter 1A or 1B.
3 Remove the complete facia assembly as described in Chapter 11.
4 Disconnect the air ducts from each side of the heater assembly **(see illustration)**.
5 Where applicable, release the speedometer cable from the clips on the rear of the heater assembly. Note the routing of the cable to aid refitting **(see illustration)**.
6 Working in the engine compartment, disconnect the heater coolant hoses from the heater matrix pipes at the bulkhead. On diesel models, it will be necessary to remove the inlet manifold, as described in Chapter 4D, to gain access **(see illustration)**.
7 Working inside the vehicle, remove the lower heater assembly securing nut **(see illustration)**.
8 Carefully pull the heater assembly rearwards from its location, until the heater pipe grommet is free from the bulkhead **(see illustration)**. Withdraw the assembly from the vehicle. Be prepared for coolant spillage from the heater matrix.

9.4 Disconnect the heater ducts

9.5 Speedometer cable clip (arrowed) on rear of heater assembly

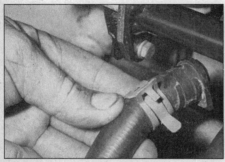
9.6 Disconnecting a heater coolant hose from the matrix pipe

9.7 Lower heater assembly securing nut (arrowed)

9.8 Withdrawing the heater assembly

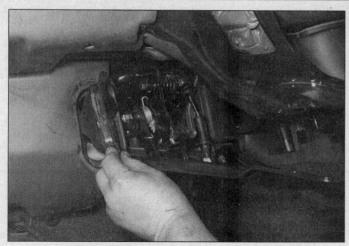

9.9 Fitting the heater pipe grommet to the bulkhead

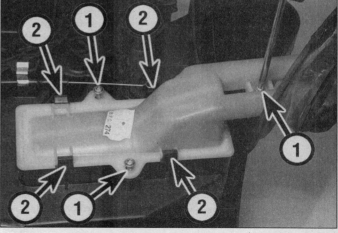

9.11 Remove the securing screws (1) and release the clips (2) . . .

Refitting

9 Refitting is a reversal of removal, bearing in mind the following points:

a) *Before refitting the assembly, pull the heater pipe grommet from the pipes and refit the grommet to the bulkhead (see illustration).*

 Lubricate the heater pipe grommet with washing-up liquid to ease fitting.

b) *As the assembly is refitted, push the heater pipes through the grommet.*
c) *On diesel models, refit the inlet manifold as described in Chapter 4D.*
d) *Ensure that the speedometer cable is correctly routed behind the heater assembly.*
e) *Refit the facia assembly with reference to Chapter 11.*
f) *On completion, refill the cooling system as described in Chapter 1A or 1B.*

Heater matrix

Removal

10 Remove the complete heater assembly, as described previously in this Section.

11 Remove the three screws securing the heater matrix to the heater assembly (see illustration).

12 Release the securing clips and withdraw the heater matrix from the heater assembly. Be prepared for coolant spillage (see illustration).

Refitting

13 Refitting is a reversal of removal. Refit the heater assembly as described previously in this Section and refit the facia assembly as described in Chapter 11. On completion, refill the cooling system as described in Chapter 1A or 1B.

Heater blower motor

Removal - right-hand-drive models

14 Remove the complete facia assembly as described in Chapter 11.

15 Disconnect the wiring plug from the heater blower motor.

16 Remove the windscreen wiper arms as described in Chapter 12.

17 Open the bonnet.

18 Remove the securing screw and the two nuts and withdraw the windscreen cowl panel from the scuttle. Note the panel clips around the edge of the windscreen and the front wings.

19 Remove the securing nuts and unclip the plastic cover panel from the right-hand end of the scuttle to expose the heater blower motor securing bolts.

20 Unscrew the securing bolts and lower the heater blower assembly into the vehicle interior.

Refitting

21 Refitting is a reversal of removal. Refit the windscreen wiper arms and the facia assembly as described in Chapters 12 and 11 respectively.

Removal - left-hand-drive models

22 Disconnect the battery negative terminal (refer to *"Disconnecting the battery"* in the Reference Section of this manual).

23 Working inside the vehicle, remove the two securing screws and withdraw the glovebox assembly.

24 Reach up through the glovebox aperture and disconnect the air trunking from the blower motor casing.

25 On models with air conditioning, working under the facia, unscrew the securing nut and withdraw the motor assembly securing bracket. Recover the spacer if it is loose.

26 Proceed as described in paragraphs 16 to 19 (see illustration).

27 Unscrew the securing bolts and manipulate the assembly out through the glovebox aperture (see illustration).

Refitting

28 Refitting is a reversal of removal.

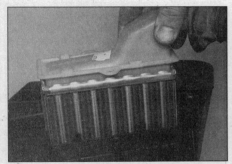

9.12 . . . and withdraw the heater matrix

9.26 Removing the heater blower motor cover panel . . .

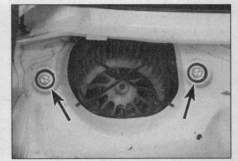

9.27 . . . to expose the blower motor securing bolts (arrowed) - left-hand-drive model

3

10 Air conditioning system -
general information and
precautions

General information

An air conditioning system is available on
certain models **(see illustration)**. It enables
the temperature of incoming air to be lowered
and also dehumidifies the air, which makes for
rapid demisting and increased comfort.

The cooling side of the system works in the
same way as a domestic refrigerator.
Refrigerant gas is drawn into a belt-driven
compressor and passes into a condenser
mounted on the front of the radiator, where it
loses heat and becomes liquid. The liquid
passes through an expansion valve to an
evaporator, where it changes from liquid
under high pressure to gas under low
pressure. This change is accompanied by a
drop in temperature, which cools the
evaporator. The refrigerant returns to the
compressor and the cycle begins again.

Air blown through the evaporator passes to
the air distribution unit, where it is mixed with
hot air blown through the heater matrix, to
achieve the desired temperature in the
passenger compartment.

The heating side of the system works in the
same way as on models without air
conditioning (see Section 8).

The operation of the system is controlled by
an electronic control unit, which controls the
electric cooling fan, the compressor and the
facia-mounted warning light. Any problems
with the system should be referred to a
Peugeot dealer.

Precautions

When an air conditioning system is fitted, it
is necessary to observe special precautions
whenever dealing with any part of the system,
or its associated components. If for any
reason the system must be disconnected,
entrust this task to your Peugeot dealer or a
refrigeration engineer.

⚠️ *Warning: The refrigeration circuit
contains a liquid refrigerant and it
is therefore dangerous to
disconnect any part of the system without
specialised knowledge and equipment.*

⚠️ *Warning: The refrigerant is
potentially dangerous and should
only be handled by qualified
persons. If it is splashed onto the skin, it
can cause frostbite. It is not itself
poisonous, but in the presence of a naked
flame (including a cigarette) it forms a*
*poisonous gas. Uncontrolled discharging
of the refrigerant is dangerous and
potentially damaging to the environment.*

*Caution: Do not operate the air
conditioning system if it is known to be
short of refrigerant, as this may damage
the compressor.*

**11 Air conditioning system
components -**
removal and refitting

⚠️ *Warning: Do not attempt to open
the refrigerant circuit. Refer to
the precautions given in Section 10.*

1 The only operation which can be carried out
easily without discharging the refrigerant is
renewal of the compressor drivebelt. This is
described in Chapter 1A, Section 16 or
Chapter 1B, Section 12. All other operations
must be referred to a Peugeot dealer or an air
conditioning specialist.

2 If necessary for access to other
components, the compressor can be
unbolted and moved aside, without
disconnecting its flexible hoses, after
removing the drivebelt.

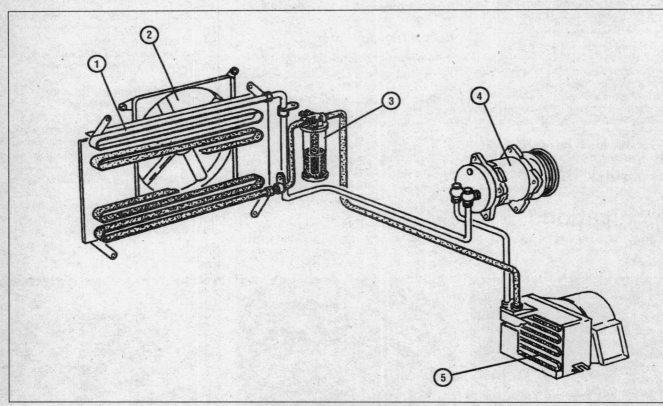

10.1 Air conditioning system components

1 *Condenser*	3 *Dehydrator reservoir*	5 *Evaporator*
2 *Electric cooling fan*	4 *Compressor*	

Chapter 4 Part A:
Fuel/exhaust systems - carburettor petrol models

Contents

Degrees of difficulty

Easy, suitable for novice with little experience	**Fairly easy,** suitable for beginner with some experience	**Fairly difficult,** suitable for competent DIY mechanic	**Difficult,** suitable for experienced DIY mechanic	**Very difficult,** suitable for expert DIY or professional

4A

Specifications

Fuel pump
Type .... Mechanical, driven by eccentric on camshaft

Carburettor
Type:
  954 and 1124 cc models .... Solex 32 PBISA 16
  1360 cc models:
    Engine code K2D .... Solex 32-34 Z2
    Engine code K5A .... Solex 32-34 CISAC
Designation:
  954 cc models .... 32 PBISA 16 412/2
  1124 cc models:
    Engine code H1A .... 32 PBISA 16 411/3
    Engine code H3A .... 32 PBISA 16 439/1
  1360 cc models:
    Engine code K2D .... 32-34 Z2 - 528
    Engine code K5A .... 32-34 CISAC 528/5
Choke type .... Manual, cable-operated

Carburettor data

Solex 32 PBISA 16 - 954 cc models

Venturi diameter	25 mm
Main jet	130
Idle jet	47
Idle air jet	140
Air correction jet	160
Emulsion tube	N12
Accelerator pump	40
Needle valve	1.6
Float height setting	See text
Throttle valve fast idle setting	0.6 mm
Choke pull-down setting	3.0 mm
Idle speed	700 ± 50 rpm
Idle mixture CO content	1.3 ± 0.5 %

Solex 32 PBISA 16 - 1124 cc models (code H1A)

Venturi diameter	25 mm
Main jet	132
Idle jet	43
Idle air jet	145
Air correction jet	165
Emulsion tube	37
Accelerator pump	40
Needle valve	1.6
Float height setting	See text
Throttle valve fast idle setting	0.6 mm
Choke pull-down setting	3.0 mm
Idle speed	700 ± 50 rpm
Idle mixture CO content	1.3 ± 0.5 %

Solex 32 PBISA 16 - 1124 cc models (code H3A)

Venturi diameter	25 mm
Main jet	127.5
Idle jet	44
Idle air jet	135
Air correction jet	175
Emulsion tube	-
Accelerator pump	40
Needle valve	1.6
Float height setting	See text
Throttle valve fast idle setting	0.6 mm
Choke pull-down setting	3.0 mm
Idle speed	700 ± 50 rpm
Idle mixture CO content	1.3 ± 0.5 %

Solex 32-34 Z2 - 1360 cc models (code K2D)

	Primary	Secondary
Venturi diameter	24 mm	25 mm
Main jet	120	122
Idle jet	40	100
Idle air jet	150	150
Air correction jet	175	180
Emulsion tube	6Z	ZC
Accelerator pump	35	
Pneumatic enrichment device	45	
Needle valve	1.8	
Float height setting	See text	
Throttle valve fast idle setting	0.5 mm	
Choke pull-down setting	3.0 mm	
Idle speed	750 ± 50 rpm	
Idle mixture CO content	1.5 ± 0.5 %	

Solex 32-34 CISAC - 1360 cc models (code K5A)

	Primary	Secondary
Venturi diameter	24 mm	25 mm
Main jet	117	120
Idle jet	43	70
Idle air jet	155	160
Air correction jet	155	160
Emulsion tube	7Z	ZC

Solex 32-34 CISAC - 1360 cc models (code K5A) (continued)	Primary	Secondary
Accelerator pump	40	35
Pneumatic enrichment device	35	
Needle valve	1.8	
Float height setting	See text	
Throttle valve fast idle setting	0.5 mm	
Choke pull-down setting	4.0 mm	
Idle speed	750 ± 50 rpm	
Idle mixture CO content	1.5 ± 0.5 %	

Recommended fuel

Minimum octane rating	95 RON unleaded or 97 RON leaded

Torque wrench settings

	Nm	lbf ft
Fuel pump retaining bolts	16	12
Inlet manifold retaining nuts	8	6
Exhaust manifold retaining nuts (see text, Section 16):		
Long nuts (early models)	16	12
Short nuts (later models)	25	18
Exhaust system fasteners:		
Front pipe-to-manifold nuts	30	22
Front pipe-to-intermediate pipe	10	7
Clamping ring nuts	15	11

1 General information and precautions

The fuel system consists of a fuel tank mounted under the rear of the car, a mechanical fuel pump and a carburettor. The fuel pump is operated by an eccentric on the camshaft and is mounted on the rear of the cylinder head. The air cleaner contains a disposable paper filter element and incorporates a flap valve air temperature control system; this allows cold air from the outside of the car and warm air from the exhaust manifold, to enter the air cleaner in the correct proportions.

The fuel pump lifts fuel from the fuel tank via a filter, which is mounted underneath the vehicle and supplies it to the carburettor via an anti-percolation chamber. The anti-percolation chamber ensures that the supply of fuel to the carburettor is kept at a constant pressure and is free of air bubbles. Excess fuel is returned from the anti-percolation chamber to the fuel tank.

Mixture enrichment for cold starting is by a cable-operated choke control.

Refer to Section 17 for information on the exhaust system.

⚠ **Warning: Many of the procedures in this Chapter require the removal of fuel lines and connections, which may result in some fuel spillage. Before carrying out any operation on the fuel system, refer to the precautions given in "Safety first!" at the beginning of this manual and follow them implicitly. Petrol is a highly dangerous and volatile liquid and the precautions necessary when handling it cannot be overstressed.**

2 Air cleaner assembly - removal and refitting

Removal

1 Slacken the retaining clips (where fitted) and disconnect the vacuum hose and breather hose from the front of the air cleaner housing-to-carburettor duct **(see illustration)**. Where the crimped-type hose clips or ties are fitted, cut and discard them; replace them with standard worm-drive hose clips or new cable ties when refitting.

2 Slacken the retaining clips, then lift the duct off the top of the carburettor and air cleaner housing. Disconnect the air temperature control valve hose from the end of the duct and remove the duct from the engine compartment **(see illustrations)**. Recover the rubber sealing ring(s) from the top of the carburettor and/or air cleaner housing (as applicable).

3 Disconnect the intake duct from the front of the air cleaner housing and remove the air cleaner housing from the engine compartment.

4 To remove the intake duct assembly, drill out the rivets securing the duct to the crossmember, then release the fastener securing the rear of the duct to the cylinder head **(see illustration)**. Disconnect the hot-air intake hose from the exhaust manifold shroud and remove the duct and hose assembly from the engine compartment.

4A

2.1 Disconnect the vacuum and breather hoses (arrowed) from the front of the duct . . .

2.2a . . . then slacken the retaining clips . . .

2.2b . . . and remove the duct, disconnecting the air temperature control valve hose (arrowed)

2.4 Release the rear fastener and remove the duct assembly

2.5 When refitting, ensure that the air cleaner housing peg is correctly located in its mounting rubber (arrowed)

Refitting

5 Refitting is a reversal of the removal procedure, noting the following points:

a). *Examine the rubber sealing ring(s) for signs of damage or deterioration and if necessary renew. Note that, on some models, the carburettor seal is fitted with an O-ring; this should also be renewed if it is damaged.*

b) *Ensure the air cleaner housing locating peg is correctly engaged with its mounting on the top of the transmission* (see illustration).

c) *Prior to tightening the air cleaner-to-carburettor duct retaining clips, ensure the duct is correctly seated on both the air cleaner housing and carburettor flanges.*

d) *Secure the duct to the crossmember (where removed) with new pop rivets.*

3.8a Remove the retaining clip . . .

3.8b . . . and seal . . .

3 Air cleaner air temperature control system - information and component renewal

Information

1 The system is controlled by a heat-sensitive vacuum switch, mounted in the end of the air cleaner housing-to-carburettor duct. When the engine is started from cold, the switch is open, allowing inlet manifold depression to act on the air temperature control valve diaphragm in the intake duct. This vacuum causes the diaphragm to rise, drawing a flap valve across the cold-air intake, thus allowing only (warmed) air from the exhaust manifold to enter the air cleaner.

2 As the temperature of the exhaust-warmed air in the air cleaner-to-carburettor duct rises, the wax capsule in the vacuum switch deforms and closes the switch, cutting off the vacuum supply to the air temperature control valve assembly. As the vacuum supply is cut, the flap is gradually lowered across the hot-air intake until, when the engine is fully warmed-up to normal operating temperature, only cold air from the front of the car is entering the air cleaner.

3 To check the system, allow the engine to cool down completely, then disconnect the intake duct from the front of the control valve assembly; the flap valve in the duct should be securely seated across the hot-air intake. Start the engine; the flap should immediately rise to close off the cold-air intake and should then lower steadily as the engine warms up,

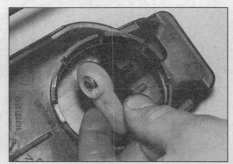

3.8c . . . then withdraw the vacuum switch from inside the duct

until it is eventually seated across the hot-air intake again.

4 To check the vacuum switch, disconnect the vacuum pipe from the control valve when the engine is running and place a finger over the pipe end. When the engine is cold, full inlet manifold vacuum should be present in the pipe and when the engine is at normal operating temperature, there should be no vacuum in the pipe.

5 To check the air temperature control valve assembly, disconnect the intake duct from the front of the valve assembly; the flap valve should be securely seated across the hot-air intake. Disconnect the vacuum pipe and suck hard at the control valve stub; the flap should rise to shut off the cold-air intake.

6 If either component is faulty, it must be renewed.

Vacuum switch - renewal

7 Remove the air cleaner housing-to-carburettor duct, as described in paragraphs 1 and 2 of Section 2.

8 Bend up the tangs on the switch retaining clip, then remove the clip, along with its seal and withdraw the switch from inside the duct (see illustrations). Examine the seal for signs of damage or deterioration and renew if necessary.

9 On refitting, ensure the switch and duct mating surfaces are clean and dry and position the switch inside the duct.

10 Fit the seal over the switch unions and refit the retaining clip. Ensure the switch is pressed firmly against the duct and secure it in position by bending down the retaining clip tangs.

11 Refit the duct as described in Section 2.

Air temperature control valve - renewal

12 Disconnect the vacuum pipe from the air temperature control valve, then slacken the retaining clips securing the intake ducts to the valve (see illustration).

13 Disconnect both intake ducts and the hot-air intake hose from the control valve assembly and remove it from the vehicle.

14 Refitting is the reverse of the removal procedure, noting that the air temperature control valve assembly can only be renewed as a complete unit.

3.12 Air temperature control valve assembly

4.3 Arrows on fuel pump unions indicate the direction of fuel flow

5.3 Remove the plastic access cover . . .

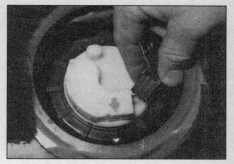

5.4 . . . and disconnect the wiring connector from the fuel gauge sender unit (fuel-injected model shown)

4 Fuel pump - testing, removal and refitting

Note: *Refer to the warning note in Section 1 before proceeding.*

Testing

1 To test the fuel pump on the engine, disconnect the outlet pipe which leads to the carburettor. Hold a wad of rag by the pump outlet while an assistant spins the engine on the starter. *Keep your hands away from the electric cooling fan.* Regular spurts of fuel should be ejected as the engine turns. Be careful not to spill fuel onto hot engine components.

2 The pump can also be tested after removing it. With the pump outlet pipe disconnected but the inlet pipe still connected, hold the wad of rag by the outlet. Operate the pump lever by hand, moving it in and out; if the pump is in a satisfactory condition, the lever should move and return smoothly and a strong jet of fuel should be ejected.

Removal

3 Identify the pump inlet and outlet hoses and slacken both retaining clips **(see illustration)**. Where crimped-type hose clips are fitted, cut the clips and discard them; use standard worm-drive hose clips when refitting. Place wads of rag beneath the hose unions to catch any spilled fuel, then disconnect both hoses from the pump; plug the hose ends to minimise fuel loss.

4 Slacken and remove the bolts securing the pump to the rear of the cylinder head. Remove the pump along with its gasket. Discard the gasket; a new one must be used when refitting.

Refitting

5 Ensure the pump and cylinder head mating surfaces are clean and dry, then offer up the new gasket and refit the pump to the cylinder head. Tighten the pump retaining bolts to the specified torque.

6 Reconnect the inlet and outlet hoses to the relevant pump unions and securely tighten their retaining clips.

5 Fuel gauge sender unit - removal and refitting

Note: *Refer to the warning note in Section 1 before proceeding.*

Removal

1 Disconnect the battery negative terminal (refer to *"Disconnecting the battery"* in the Reference Section of this manual).

2 For access to the sender unit, fold the rear seat cushion forwards.

3 Using a screwdriver, carefully prise the plastic access cover from the floor to expose the sender unit. It is located under the left-hand cover **(see illustration)**.

4 Disconnect the wiring connector from the sender unit and tape the connector to the vehicle body to prevent it from disappearing behind the tank **(see illustration)**.

5 Mark the hoses for identification purposes, then slacken the feed and return hose retaining clips. Where the crimped-type hose clips are fitted, cut the clips and discard them; use worm-drive hose clips on refitting. Disconnect both hoses from the top of the sender unit and plug the hose ends.

6 On some models, quick-release fittings may be fitted to the fuel hoses; these are released by depressing their metal collars with a small flat-bladed screwdriver.

7 Noting the alignment marks on the tank, sender unit and the locking ring, unscrew the ring and remove it from the tank. This is best accomplished by using a screwdriver on the raised ribs of the locking ring. Carefully tap the screwdriver to turn the ring anti-clockwise until it can be unscrewed by hand **(see illustrations)**.

8 Carefully lift the sender unit from the top of the fuel tank, taking great care not to bend the sender unit float arm, or to spill fuel onto the interior of the vehicle. Recover the rubber sealing ring and discard it - a new one must be used on refitting **(see illustrations)**.

4A

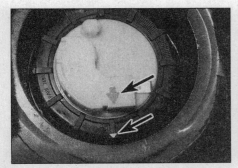

5.7a Note the position of the sender unit and locking ring alignment marks . . .

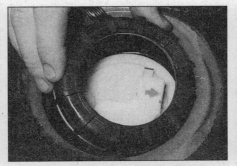

5.7b . . . then unscrew the locking ring

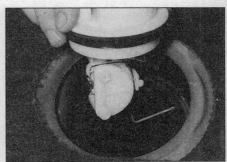

5.8a Withdraw the sender unit from the tank . . .

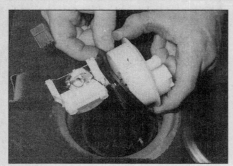

5.8b . . . and remove the rubber sealing ring

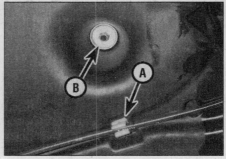

6.3 Fuel tank handbrake cable retaining clip (A) and retaining nut (B)

6.6a Disconnect the main breather hose (arrowed) from the filler neck . . .

Refitting

9 Refitting is a reversal of the removal procedure, noting the following points:

   a) *Prior to refitting, fit a new rubber sealing ring to the sender unit.*

   b) *Refit the sender unit to the tank, aligning its arrow with the centre of the three alignment marks on the fuel tank. Secure the sender in position with the locking ring and check that the locking ring, sender unit and fuel tank marks are all correctly aligned.*

   c) *Ensure the feed and return hoses are correctly reconnected and securely retained by their clips.*

6 Fuel tank - removal and refitting

Note: *Refer to the warning note in Section 1 before proceeding.*

Removal

1 Before removing the fuel tank, all fuel must be drained from the tank. Since a fuel tank drain plug is not provided, it is therefore preferable to carry out the removal operation when the tank is nearly empty. Before proceeding, disconnect the battery negative terminal (refer to *"Disconnecting the battery"* in the Reference Section of this manual) and syphon or hand-pump the remaining fuel from the tank.

2 Remove the exhaust system as described in Section 17.

3 Free both handbrake cables from their

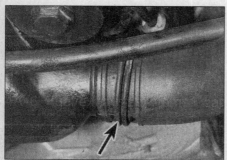

6.6b . . . and the main filler hose (arrowed) from the fuel tank

retaining clips on the base of the fuel tank **(see illustration)**.

4 Disconnect the wiring connector and fuel hoses from the fuel gauge sender unit as described in paragraphs 2 to 5 of Section 5.

5 Unclip the fuel filter retaining strap and free the filter from the left-hand side of the fuel tank.

6 Working at the right-hand side of the fuel tank, release the retaining clips then disconnect the filler neck vent pipe and main filler neck hose from the fuel tank/filler neck. Where necessary, also disconnect the breather hose(s). Some breather hoses are joined to the tank with quick-release fittings; to disconnect these fittings, slide the cover along the hose then depress the centre ring and pull the hose out of its fitting **(see illustrations)**.

7 Place a trolley jack with an interposed block of wood beneath the tank, then raise the jack until it is supporting the weight of the tank.

8 Slacken and remove the two retaining nuts and washers, then slowly lower the fuel tank out of position, disconnecting any other relevant vent pipes as they become accessible (where necessary). Remove the tank from underneath the vehicle and recover the tank mounting rubbers, noting their correct fitted positions.

9 If the tank is contaminated with sediment or water, remove the sender unit (Section 5) and swill the tank out with clean fuel. The tank is injection-moulded from a synthetic material - if seriously damaged, it should be renewed.

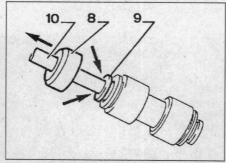

6.6c Fuel tank breather hose quick-release connector

8 *Cover*	10 *Hose*
9 *Centre ring*	

However, in certain cases, it may be possible to have small leaks or minor damage repaired. Seek the advice of a specialist.

Refitting

10 Refitting is the reverse of the removal procedure, noting the following points:

   a) *When lifting the tank back into position, make sure that the mounting rubbers are correctly positioned and take great care to ensure that none of the hoses become trapped between the tank and vehicle body.*

   b) *Ensure all pipes and hoses are correctly routed and securely held in position with their retaining clips.*

   c) *On completion, refill the tank with a small amount of fuel and check for signs of leakage prior to taking the vehicle out on the road.*

7 Accelerator cable - removal, refitting and adjustment

Removal

1 Where necessary, prise out the retaining clip and remove the plastic cover to gain access to the carburettor **(see illustrations)**.

2 Free the accelerator inner cable from the carburettor throttle cam **(see illustration)**, then pull the outer cable out from its mounting bracket rubber grommet. Slide the flat washer off the end of the cable and remove the spring clip.

7.1a Where necessary, prise out the retaining clip . . .

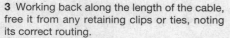

7.1b . . . and remove the plastic cover (arrowed) to gain access to the carburettor

7.2 Free the accelerator cable from the throttle cam and withdraw the outer cable from its mounting bracket

7.16 Adjusting the accelerator cable

3 Working back along the length of the cable, free it from any retaining clips or ties, noting its correct routing.

4 Working from inside the vehicle, undo the retaining nuts and remove the undercover panel from the driver's side of the facia.

5 Reach up behind the facia, then depress the retaining clips and detach the inner cable from the top of the accelerator pedal.

6 Displace the rubber grommet from the end of the outer cable retainer and tie a length of string to the end of the inner cable.

7 Return to the engine compartment and release the outer cable retainer from the engine compartment bulkhead. Withdraw the cable from the bulkhead until the end of the cable appears, then untie the string and leave it in position. The string can then be used to draw the cable back into position when refitting.

Refitting

8 Tie the string to the end of the cable, then use the string to draw the cable into position through the bulkhead. Once the cable end is visible, untie the string.

9 Align the outer cable retainer lug with the cut-out in the bulkhead, then securely clip the retainer into position. Check that the retainer is securely fitted, then slide the rubber grommet over the retainer end and clip the inner cable into position in the pedal.

10 Make sure that the cable is securely retained, then refit the undercover panel to the facia.

11 From within the engine compartment, ensure the outer cable is correctly seated in the bulkhead grommet, then work along the cable, securing it in position with the retaining clips and ties and ensuring that the cable is correctly routed.

12 Slide the flat washer onto the cable end and refit the spring clip.

13 Pass the outer cable through its carburettor mounting bracket grommet and reconnect the inner cable to the throttle cam. Adjust the cable as described below.

Adjustment

14 If not already done, prise out the retaining clip and remove the plastic cover (where fitted) from the carburettor.

15 Remove the spring clip from the accelerator outer cable. Ensuring that the throttle cam is fully against its stop, gently pull the cable out of its grommet until all free play is removed from the inner cable.

16 With the cable held in this position, ensure that the flat washer is pressed securely against the grommet and fit the spring clip to the last exposed outer cable groove in front of the rubber grommet and washer. When the clip is refitted and the outer cable is released, there should be only a small amount of free play in the inner cable **(see illustration)**.

17 Have an assistant depress the accelerator pedal and check that the throttle cam opens fully and returns smoothly to its stop.

18 Where necessary, clip the carburettor plastic cover back into position and refit its retaining clip.

---

8 Accelerator pedal - removal and refitting

Removal

1 Undo the retaining nuts and remove the undercover panel from the driver's side of the facia.

2 Depress the retaining clips and detach the inner cable from the top of the accelerator pedal.

3 Slacken and remove the two nuts securing the pedal mounting bracket to the bulkhead. Slide off the outer part of the mounting clamp,

9.2a Release the choke cable from its linkage . . .

then withdraw the pedal from behind the facia and slide off the inner part of the clamp.

4 Examine the mounting bracket and pedal pivot points for signs of wear and renew as necessary.

Refitting

5 Refitting is a reversal of the removal procedure, applying a little multi-purpose grease to the pedal pivot point. On completion, adjust the accelerator cable as described in Section 7.

---

9 Choke cable - removal, refitting and adjustment

Removal

1 Where necessary, prise out the retaining clip and remove the plastic cover to gain access to the carburettor.

2 Free the choke inner cable from the carburettor linkage, then slacken and remove the retaining bolt and remove the outer cable retaining clamp **(see illustrations)**.

3 Slacken the retaining clip securing the rubber collar to the outer cable and slide the collar off the cable. Where the original crimped-type hose clip is still fitted, cut the clip and discard it; use a standard worm-drive hose clip on refitting.

4 Working back along the length of the cable, free it from any retaining clips or ties, noting its correct routing. Tie a length of string to the end of the choke inner cable.

9.2b . . . then undo the retaining bolt and remove the choke cable retaining clip

4A

9.11 Cutting the original crimped-type hose clip from the choke cable rubber collar

5 Working from inside the vehicle, pull the choke lever fully out and unclip the lever from the facia. Withdraw the lever and cable assembly from the facia, disconnecting the wiring from the lever warning light switch (where fitted) as it becomes accessible. Once the end of the cable appears through the lever aperture, untie the string and leave it in position in the vehicle - it can then be used to draw the cable back into position on refitting.

Refitting

6 Tie the string to the end of the choke cable, then use the string to draw the cable into position through the bulkhead into the engine compartment. Once the cable end is fully in position, untie the string.
7 Reconnect the wiring connector (where fitted) and clip the choke lever in its facia panel aperture.

8 From within the engine compartment, ensure the outer cable is correctly seated in the bulkhead grommet. Work along the cable, securing it in position with all the relevant retaining clips and ties and ensuring that the cable is correctly routed.
9 Slide the rubber collar and retaining clip onto the end of the cable, then engage the inner end of the cable with the carburettor linkage. Align the rubber collar with the carburettor bracket, then refit the retaining clip and securely tighten its retaining bolt. Adjust the cable as described below.

Adjustment

10 If not already done, prise out the retaining clip and remove the plastic cover (where fitted) from the carburettor.
11 Slacken the retaining clip securing the rubber collar to the outer cable. Where the crimped-type hose clip is still fitted, cut the clip and discard it; use a standard worm-drive hose clip on refitting (see illustration).
12 Ensuring that the choke lever is flush with the facia panel and the carburettor linkage is fully against its stop, move the outer cable in the rubber collar until the position is found where there is only a small amount of free play present in the inner cable. Hold the outer cable in this position and securely tighten the clip securing the rubber collar to the outer cable.
13 Have an assistant operate the choke lever and check that the choke linkage closes fully and returns smoothly to its stop. If necessary, repeat the adjustment procedure.
14 Where necessary, clip the plastic cover back into position and refit its retaining clip.

10 Unleaded petrol - general information and usage

Note: *The information given in this Chapter is correct at the time of writing. If updated information is thought to be required, check with a Peugeot dealer. If travelling abroad, consult one of the motoring organisations (or a similar authority) for advice on the fuel available.*

The fuel recommended by Peugeot is given in the Specifications Section of this Chapter.
All Peugeot 106 carburettor models are designed to run on 95 (RON) octane petrol. Both leaded and unleaded petrol can be used without modification.

11 Carburettor - general information

Solex 32 PBISA carburettor - 954 and 1124 cc models

1 The Solex PBISA carburettor is a downdraught single-venturi instrument with a manually-controlled choke (see illustration). The carburettor consists of three main components. These are the upper body, the main body and the throttle body (which contains the throttle valve assembly). An insulating block placed between the carburettor body and throttle body prevents excess heat transfer from the manifold to the main body.

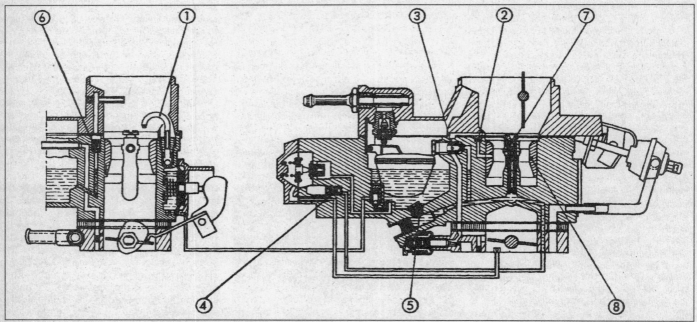

11.1 Sectional view of the Solex 32 PBISA carburettor fitted to 954 cc and 1124 cc models

1 Accelerator pump tube	*3 Idle jet*	*5 Main jet*	*7 Air correction jet*
2 Idle ventilator	*4 Enrichment jet*	*6 Fuel econostat*	*8 Venturi*

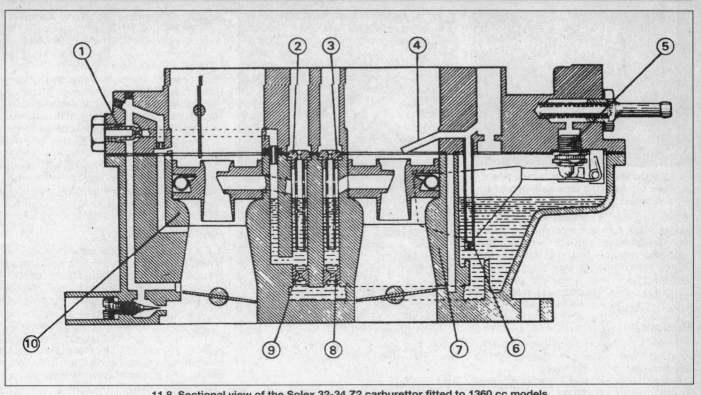

11.8 Sectional view of the Solex 32-34 Z2 carburettor fitted to 1360 cc models

1 Idle jet	3 Secondary air correction	5 Needle valve
2 Primary air correction	jet/emulsion tube	6 Bypass jet
jet/emulsion tube	4 Secondary fuel jet	7 Secondary venturi

8 Secondary main jet	
9 Primary main jet	
10 Primary venturi	

2 The throttle body contain a drilling through which the engine coolant runs. The engine coolant warms the carburettor body quickly on cold starts, improving atomisation of the fuel/air mixture and preventing carburettor icing during warm-up.

3 During slow running and at idle, fuel from the float chamber passes into the idle channel through a metered idle jet. Here it is mixed with a small amount of air from a calibrated air bleed. The resulting mixture is drawn through a channel, to be discharged from the idle orifice under the throttle valve. A tapered mixture screw is used to vary the outlet, allowing fine control of the idle mixture.

4 A progression slot provides extra enrichment as it is uncovered by the opening of the throttle valve during initial acceleration.

5 Under normal operating conditions, fuel is drawn through a calibrated main jet into the base of the auxiliary venturi. An emulsion tube is placed in the auxiliary venturi, capped with an air correction jet. The fuel is mixed with air, drawn in through the holes in the emulsion tube. The resulting mixture is discharged into the main airstream via four orifices, spaced at 90° apart, in the upper part of the auxiliary venturi.

6 The carburettor also has an accelerator pump to provide an initial spurt of extra fuel during sudden acceleration. The accelerator pump is controlled by a diaphragm and is mechanically operated by a lever and rod which is connected to the throttle linkage.

7 The idle speed is set by an adjustable screw. The adjustable mixture screw is sealed during production with a tamperproof plug, to prevent unnecessary adjustment.

Solex 32-34 Z2 and CISAC carburettor - 1360 cc models

8 The Solex 32-34 Z2 and CISAC carburettors are similar in design and operation and are both downdraught progressive twin-venturi instruments **(see illustration)**. The throttle linkages are arranged so that the secondary throttle valve will not start to open until the primary valve is about two-thirds open, but at full throttle both valves are fully open. The choke control is manual.

9 An electrical heating element is fitted to the base of the throttle body. The heater warms the carburettor body quickly on cold starts, improving atomisation of the fuel/air mixture and preventing carburettor icing

10 During slow running and at idle, fuel from the float chamber passes into the idle channel through a metered idle jet. Here it is mixed with a small amount of air from a calibrated air bleed. The resulting mixture is drawn through a channel, to be discharged from the idle orifice under the primary throttle plate. A tapered mixture screw is used to vary the outlet, allowing fine control of the idle mixture.

11 On some models, an idle cut-off valve is used to prevent run-on when the engine is switched off. The valve uses a solenoid plunger to block the idle jet when the ignition is switched off.

12 A progression slot provides extra enrichment as it is uncovered by the opening of the throttle valve during initial acceleration.

13 Under normal operating conditions, the amount of fuel discharged into the airstream is controlled by a calibrated main jet. Fuel is drawn through the main jet. The fuel is then mixed with air, drawn in through the air correction jet and through the holes in the emulsion tube. The resulting mixture is discharged from the main orifice through an auxiliary vent.

14 The carburettor also has an accelerator pump to provide an initial spurt of extra fuel during sudden acceleration. During acceleration, fuel is pumped through a ball valve located in the pump injector and is discharged into both the primary and secondary venturis.

15 The idle speed is set by an adjustable screw. The adjustable mixture screw is sealed during production with a tamperproof plug, to prevent unnecessary adjustment.

4A

12.4 On 954 cc and 1124 cc models, slacken the retaining clips and disconnect the coolant hoses (arrowed) from the carburettor

12.7 Disconnect the idle cut-off solenoid wiring connector (1124 cc model shown)

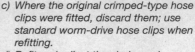

12 Carburettor - removal and refitting

Note: *Refer to the warning note in Section 1 before proceeding.*

Removal

1 Disconnect the battery negative terminal (refer to *"Disconnecting the battery"* in the Reference Section of this manual).
2 Remove the air cleaner-to-carburettor duct as described in paragraphs 1 and 2 of Section 2.
3 Where necessary, prise out the retaining clip and remove the plastic cover from the carburettor.
4 On 954 and 1124 cc models, slacken the retaining clips and disconnect the coolant hoses from the base of the carburettor **(see illustration)**. Plug the hose ends to minimise coolant loss and mop up any spilt coolant immediately.
5 On all models, free the accelerator inner cable from the throttle cam, then pull the outer cable out from its mounting bracket rubber grommet, along with its flat washer and spring clip.
6 Disconnect the choke inner cable from the carburettor linkage, then undo the retaining bolt and remove the retaining clamp. Position the cable clear of the carburettor.
7 Disconnect the wiring connector from the carburettor heating element and/or the idle

cut-off solenoid **(see illustration)**.
8 Slacken the retaining clip and disconnect the fuel feed hose from the carburettor **(see illustration)**. Place wads of rag around the union to catch any spilled fuel and plug the hose as soon as it is disconnected, to minimise fuel loss.
9 Make a note of the correct fitted positions of all the relevant vacuum pipes and breather hoses, to ensure they are correctly positioned on refitting, then release the retaining clips (where fitted) and disconnect them from the carburettor.
10 Unscrew the two or four nuts and washers securing the carburettor to the inlet manifold and remove the carburettor assembly from the car **(see illustration)**. Remove the insulating spacer and/or gasket(s). Discard the gasket(s); new ones must be used on refitting. Plug the inlet manifold port with a wad of clean cloth, to prevent the possible entry of foreign matter.

Refitting

11 Refitting is the reverse of the removal procedure, noting the following points:
a) *Ensure the carburettor and inlet manifold sealing faces are clean and flat. Fit a new gasket/gaskets and insulating spacer (as applicable) and securely tighten the carburettor retaining nuts.*
b) *Use the notes made on dismantling to ensure all hoses are refitted to their original positions and, where necessary, are securely held by their retaining clips.*

c) *Where the original crimped-type hose clips were fitted, discard them; use standard worm-drive hose clips when refitting.*
d) *Refit and adjust the choke and accelerator cables as described in Sections 7 and 9.*
e) *Refit the air cleaner duct (Section 2).*
f) *On completion, check and, if necessary, adjust the idle speed and mixture settings as described in Chapter 1A.*

13 Solex 32 PBISA carburettor - fault finding, overhaul and adjustments

Fault finding

1 If a carburettor fault is suspected, always check first that the ignition timing is correctly set, that the spark plugs are in good condition and correctly gapped, that the accelerator and choke cables are correctly adjusted and that the air cleaner filter element is clean; refer to the relevant Sections of Chapter 1A, Chapter 5B or this Chapter. If the engine is running very roughly, first check the valve clearances as described in Chapter 2A, then check the compression pressures as described in Chapter 2A.
2 If careful checking of all the above produces no improvement, the carburettor must be removed for cleaning and overhaul.
3 Prior to overhaul, check the availability of component parts before starting work; note that most sealing washers, screws and gaskets are available in kits, as are some of the major sub-assemblies. In most cases, it will be sufficient to dismantle the carburettor and to clean the jets and passages.

Overhaul

Note: *Refer to the warning note in Section 1 before proceeding.*
4 Remove the carburettor from the vehicle as described in Section 12.
5 Disconnect the vacuum hose from the choke pull-down diaphragm.
6 Disconnect the choke spring (where necessary), then undo the six screws and lift off the carburettor upper body.
7 Tap out the float pivot pin and remove the float assembly, needle valve and float chamber gasket. Check that the needle valve anti-vibration ball is free in the valve end, then examine the needle valve tip and seat for wear or damage. Examine the float assembly and pivot pin for signs of wear and damage. The float assembly must be renewed if it appears to be leaking.
8 Unscrew the fuel inlet union and inspect the fuel filter. Clean the filter housing of debris and dirt and renew the filter if it is blocked.
9 Undo the screws, detach the accelerator pump cover and remove the pump diaphragm and spring, noting which way around they are fitted. Examine the diaphragm for signs of

12.8 Carburettor fuel feed hose union (1124 cc model shown)

12.10 Carburettor retaining nuts - two of four arrowed (1360 cc model shown)

damage and deterioration and renew if necessary.

10 Unscrew the idle jet from the main body.

11 Unscrew the main jet from the float chamber. Note that it may be necessary to remove a plug in the float chamber body to expose an opening through which the main jet can be withdrawn.

12 Remove the combined air correction jet and emulsion tube from the auxiliary venturi.

13 Remove the two screws, then separate the carburettor main body and throttle body assemblies. Recover the insulating spacer. Examine the throttle valve spindle and throttle bore for signs of wear or damage and, if necessary, renew the throttle body assembly.

14 Remove the idle mixture adjustment screw tamperproof cap. Screw the screw in until it seats lightly, counting the **exact** number of turns required to do this, then unscrew and remove it. When refitting, turn the screw in until it seats lightly, then back the screw off by the number of turns noted on removal, to return the screw to its original location.

15 Clean the jets, carburettor body assemblies, float chamber and internal drillings. An air line may be used to clear the internal passages once the carburettor is fully dismantled.

⚠️ *Warning: If high pressure air is directed into drillings and passages where a diaphragm is fitted, the diaphragm is likely to be damaged. Aerosol cans of carburettor cleaner are widely available and can prove very useful in helping to clear internal passages of stubborn obstructions.*

16 Use a straight edge to check all carburettor body assembly mating surfaces for distortion.

17 On reassembly, renew any worn components and fit a complete set of new gaskets and seals. A jet kit and a gasket and seal kit, are available from your Peugeot dealer.

18 Reassembly is a reversal of the dismantling procedure. Ensure that all jets are securely locked in position, but take great care not to overtighten them. Ensure that all mating surfaces are clean and dry and that all body sections are correctly assembled with their fuel and air passages correctly aligned. Prior to refitting the carburettor to the vehicle, set the throttle valve fast idle and choke pull-down settings as described below.

Adjustments

Idle speed and mixture

19 Refer to Chapter 1A.

Float height setting

20 To accurately check the float height setting, a special float height checking gauge is required. Therefore, this task must be entrusted to a Peugeot dealer. As a guide, with the carburettor body inverted (so that the float is at the top and the needle valve is depressed) the distance between the upper edge of the float and the sealing face of the upper body (with its gasket fitted) should be approximately 38 mm. To adjust the float height setting, **carefully** bend the pivot arm.

Throttle valve fast idle setting

21 Invert the carburettor and operate the carburettor choke linkage to fully close the choke valve. The fast idle screw will butt against the fast idle cam and force open the throttle valve slightly.

22 Using the shank of an appropriate diameter twist drill, measure the clearance between the edge of the throttle valve and bore and compare this to the specified clearance given in the Specifications. If necessary, adjust by turning the fast idle adjustment screw in the appropriate direction until the specified clearance is obtained **(see illustration)**.

Choke pull-down setting

23 Operate the carburettor choke linkage to fully close the choke valve and hold the linkage in this position.

24 Attach a hand-held vacuum pump to the choke pull-down diaphragm and apply a vacuum to the diaphragm so that the diaphragm rod is pulled fully into the diaphragm body. In the absence of a vacuum pump, the rod can be pushed into the diaphragm using a small screwdriver.

25 With the rod fully retracted, use the shank of a suitable twist drill to measure the clearance between the edge of the choke valve and bore and compare this to the specified clearance given in the Specifications. If necessary, remove the plug from the diaphragm cover and adjust by turning the adjustment screw **(see illustration)**. Once the pull-down setting is correctly adjusted, refit the plug to the diaphragm cover and remove the vacuum pump (where used).

4A

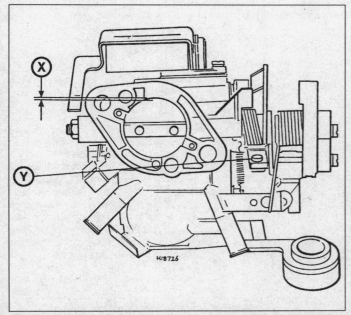

13.22 Throttle valve fast idle setting - Solex 32 PBISA carburettor fitted to 954 cc and 1124 cc models

Adjust screw Y until clearance X is as given in the Specifications

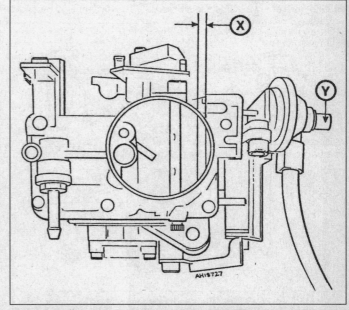

13.25 Choke pull-down setting - Solex 32 PBISA carburettor fitted to 954 cc and 1124 cc models

Adjust screw Y until clearance X is as given in the Specifications

14 Solex 32-34 Z2 and CISAC carburettor - fault finding, overhaul and adjustments

Fault finding

1 Refer to Section 13.

Overhaul

Note: *Refer to the warning note in Section 1 before proceeding.*

2 Remove the carburettor from the vehicle as described in Section 12.

3 Unscrew the idle cut-off solenoid from the carburettor body and remove it along with its plunger and spring. To test the solenoid, connect a 12-volt battery to it (positive terminal to the solenoid terminal, negative terminal to the solenoid body) and check that the plunger is retracted fully into the body. Disconnect the battery and check that the plunger is pushed out by spring pressure. If the valve does not perform as expected and cleaning does not improve the situation, the solenoid valve must be renewed.

4 Remove the five screws and lift off the carburettor upper body.

5 Tap out the float pivot pin and remove the float assembly, needle valve and float chamber gasket. Check that the needle valve anti-vibration ball is free in the valve end, then examine the needle valve tip and seat for wear or damage. Examine the float assembly and pivot pin for signs of wear and damage. The float assembly must be renewed if it appears to be leaking - shake the float to detect the presence of fuel inside.

6 Unscrew the fuel inlet union and inspect the fuel filter. Clean the filter housing of debris and dirt and renew the filter if it is blocked.

7 Undo the four screws, detach the accelerator pump cover and remove the pump diaphragm and spring, noting which way around they are fitted. Examine the diaphragm for signs of damage and deterioration and renew if necessary. Remove the choke pull-down diaphragm and part-load enrichment diaphragms and examine them in the same way.

8 Unscrew the idle jet from the upper body.

9 Unscrew both the primary and secondary combined air correction jets and emulsion tubes.

10 Using a long thin screwdriver, unscrew the main jets from the bottom of the emulsion tube drillings. Invert the carburettor and catch the jets as they fall out of the drillings.

11 Remove the idle mixture adjustment screw tamperproof cap. Screw the screw in until it seats lightly, counting the **exact** number of turns required to do this, then unscrew it. On refitting, screw the screw in until it seats lightly, then back the screw off by the number of turns noted on removal, to return the screw to its original position.

12 Examine the carburettor components as described in paragraphs 15 to 17 of Section 13.

13 To test the carburettor heating element, connect a multimeter, set to the resistance function, between the heater wiring terminal and the carburettor body. A resistance reading of approximately 0.25 to 0.5 ohms should be obtained. If an open-circuit is present, or an extremely high resistance reading is obtained, it is likely that the heating element is faulty. To remove the element, undo the retaining screw and plate, then slide the element noting the correct locations of the insulators positioned on each side of the element.

14 Reassembly is a reversal of the dismantling procedure. Ensure that all jets are securely locked in position, but take great care not to overtighten them. Ensure all mating surfaces are clean and dry and that all body sections are correctly assembled with their fuel and air passages correctly aligned. If the heating element has been disturbed, ensure that the insulators are correctly fitted so that the element is in no danger of contacting the carburettor body. Prior to refitting the carburettor to the vehicle, set the float height, throttle valve fast idle and choke pull-down settings as described below.

Adjustments

Idle speed and mixture

15 Refer to Chapter 1A.

Float height setting

16 To accurately check the float height setting, a special float height checking gauge is required. Therefore, this task must be entrusted to a Peugeot dealer. As a guide, with the carburettor body inverted (so that the float is at the top and the needle valve is depressed) the distance between the upper edge of the float and the sealing face of the upper body (with its gasket fitted) should be approximately 35 mm.

17 If necessary the float height can be adjusted by **carefully** bending the small tang on the float arm which contacts the needle valve.

Throttle valve fast idle setting

18 Invert the carburettor and pull the carburettor choke linkage to fully close the choke valve. The fast idle screw will butt against the fast idle cam and force the throttle valve open slightly.

19 Using the shank of a twist drill, measure the clearance between the edge of the throttle valve and bore and compare this to the

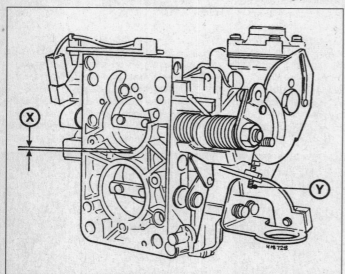

**14.19 Throttle valve fast idle setting -
Solex 32-34 Z2 carburettor fitted to 1360 cc models**

Adjust screw Y until clearance X is as given in the Specifications

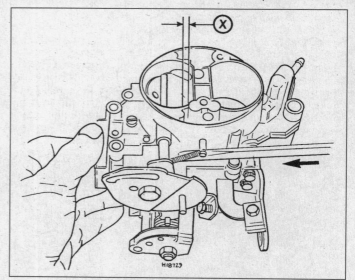

**14.22 Choke pull-down setting
(using a screwdriver to retract the diaphragm rod) -
Solex 32-34 Z2 carburettor fitted to 1360 cc models**

Adjust as ahown in text until clearance X is as given in the Specifications

clearance given in the Specifications at the start of this Chapter. If necessary, adjust by turning the fast idle adjustment screw in the appropriate direction until the specified clearance is obtained **(see illustration)**.

Choke pull-down setting

20 Pull the carburettor choke linkage to fully close the choke valve and hold the linkage in this position.

21 Attach a hand-held vacuum pump to the choke pull-down diaphragm and apply a vacuum to the diaphragm so that the diaphragm rod is pulled fully into the diaphragm body. In the absence of a vacuum pump, the rod can be pushed into the diaphragm with a small screwdriver.

22 With the rod fully retracted, use the shank of a twist drill to measure the clearance between the edge of the choke valve and bore and compare this to the clearance given in the Specifications **(see illustration)**. If necessary, remove the plug from the diaphragm cover and adjust by turning the adjustment screw. Once the pull-down setting is correctly adjusted, refit the plug to the diaphragm cover and remove the vacuum pump (where used).

15 Inlet manifold - removal and refitting

Note: *Refer to the warning note in Section 1 before proceeding.*

Removal

1 Remove the carburettor as described in Section 12.

2 Drain the cooling system as described in Chapter 1A.

3 Undo the bolt(s) securing the anti-percolation chamber mounting bracket to the manifold **(see illustration)** and position the chamber clear of the manifold so that it does not hinder removal.

4 Slacken the retaining clips, then disconnect the vacuum servo unit hose from the left-hand side of the manifold and the coolant hose from the base of the manifold.

5 Make a final check that all the necessary vacuum/breather hoses have been disconnected from the manifold.

6 Unscrew the six retaining nuts, then manoeuvre the manifold away from the head and out of the engine compartment. Note that there is no manifold gasket.

Refitting

7 Refitting is the reverse of the removal procedure, noting the following points:

a) *Ensure that the manifold and cylinder head mating surfaces are clean and dry and apply a thin coating of suitable sealing compound to the manifold mating surface. Install the manifold and tighten its retaining nuts to the specified torque setting.*

b) *Ensure all relevant hoses are reconnected to their original positions and are securely held (where necessary) by their retaining clips.*

c) *Refit the carburettor as described in Section 12.*

d) *On completion, refill the cooling system as described in Chapter 1A.*

16 Exhaust manifold - removal and refitting

Removal

1 Disconnect the hot-air intake hose from the manifold shroud and remove it from the vehicle **(see illustration)**.

2 Slacken and remove the three retaining screws and remove the shroud from the top of the exhaust manifold **(see illustration)**.

3 Chock the rear wheels then jack up the front of the vehicle and support it on axle stands (see *"Jacking and Vehicle Support"*).

4 Undo the nuts securing the exhaust front pipe to the manifold, then remove the bolt securing the front pipe to its mounting bracket. Disconnect the front pipe from the manifold and recover the gasket. Note that on 1360 cc models, it may be necessary to remove the bolt securing the front pipe to its mounting bracket in order to disconnect the exhaust.

5 Undo the eight retaining nuts securing the manifold to the head **(see illustration)**. Manoeuvre the manifold out of the engine compartment and collect the manifold gaskets.

15.3 Anti-percolation chamber retaining bolt (arrowed)

6 Examine the exhaust manifold and all the manifold studs and nuts for signs of damage and corrosion. Remove all traces of corrosion and repair or renew any damaged studs. Note that on later models the manifold retaining nuts have been modified and what are termed "short nuts" are now fitted in place of the earlier "long nuts". To determine the type fitted, temporarily refit the manifold and gaskets over the studs and screw on a retaining nut. If the long nuts are fitted, there will be virtually no stud thread protruding past the end of the nut. With the short nuts there will be two or three turns of stud thread visible. If any nuts are damaged, all eight should be replaced with the later type short nuts. Note also that the torque setting for each type is different (see Specifications).

7 Ensure that the manifold and cylinder head sealing faces are clean and flat and obtain new manifold gaskets prior to refitting. On early engines, fibre gaskets are used, whereas on later units, the gaskets are of stainless steel. Note that the two types must not be mixed on an engine.

Refitting

8 Refitting is the reverse of the removal procedure, noting the following points:

a) *If the later type stainless steel gaskets are being used, ensure that the gasket is fitted with the raised sealing surface on the gasket face toward the manifold. Tighten the manifold retaining nuts to the specified torque.*

b) *Reconnect the front pipe to the manifold using the information given in Section 17.*

4A

16.1 Remove the hot-air intake hose . . .

16.2 . . . then undo the three retaining bolts (arrowed) and remove the exhaust manifold shroud

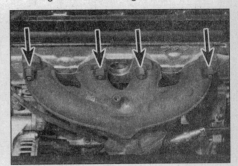

16.5 Exhaust manifold is retained by eight nuts (upper four arrowed)

17 Exhaust system - general information and component renewal

General information

1 On 954 and 1124 cc models, the exhaust system consists of two sections - the front pipe and a tailpipe. The front pipe is secured to the manifold by nuts and to the silencer by a clamping ring.

2 On 1360 cc models, the exhaust system consists of three sections - the front pipe, the intermediate pipe and silencer box and the tailpipe and main silencer box. All exhaust sections are joined by a flanged joint. The front pipe joints are secured by nuts and bolts, while the intermediate pipe joint is of the spring-loaded ball type, to allow for movement in the exhaust system. The intermediate pipe-to-tailpipe joint is secured by a clamping ring.

3 The system is suspended throughout its entire length by rubber mountings.

Removal

4 Each exhaust section can be removed individually; alternatively, the complete system can be removed as a unit.

5 To remove the system or a part of the system, first jack up the front or rear of the car and support it on axle stands (see *"Jacking and Vehicle Support"*). Alternatively, position the car over an inspection pit, or on car ramps.

Front pipe - 954 and 1124 cc models

6 Undo the nuts securing the front pipe flange joint to the manifold, then separate the flange joint and collect the gasket.

7 Slacken the front pipe-to-tailpipe clamping ring bolt, then disengage the clamp from the flange joint and manoeuvre the front pipe out from underneath the vehicle.

Front pipe - 1360 cc models

8 Undo the nuts securing the front pipe to the manifold and the bolt securing the front pipe to its mounting bracket. Separate the front pipe from the manifold and collect the gasket.

9 Slacken and remove the two nuts securing the front pipe flange joint to the intermediate pipe and recover the spring cups and springs. Remove the bolts, then withdraw the front pipe from underneath the vehicle and recover the wire-mesh gasket.

Intermediate pipe - 1360 cc models

10 Undo the two nuts securing the front pipe flange joint to the intermediate pipe. Recover the springs and spring cups and withdraw the bolts.

11 Slacken the intermediate pipe-to-tailpipe clamping ring bolts and disengage the clamp from the flange joint.

12 Free the intermediate pipe from its mounting rubbers, then withdraw it from underneath the vehicle and recover the wire mesh gasket from the front pipe joint.

Tailpipe

13 Slacken the intermediate pipe-to-tailpipe clamping ring bolt(s) and disengage the clamp from the flange joint.

14 Unhook the tailpipe from its mounting rubbers and remove it from the vehicle.

Complete system

15 On 954 and 1124 cc models, disconnect the front pipe from the manifold as described in paragraph 6. On 1360 cc models, disconnect the front pipe from the manifold as described in paragraph 8.

16 On all models, with the aid of an assistant, free the system from all its mounting rubbers and manoeuvre it out from underneath the vehicle.

Heat shield(s)

17 The heat shields (where fitted) are secured to the underside of the body by a mixture of nuts and bolts. Each shield can be removed once the relevant exhaust section has been removed. If the shield is being removed to gain access to a component located behind it, in some cases it may prove sufficient to remove the retaining nuts and/or bolts and simply lower the shield, without disturbing the exhaust system.

Refitting

18 Each section is refitted by a reverse of the removal sequence, noting the following points:

a) Ensure that all traces of corrosion have been removed from the flanges and renew all necessary gaskets.

b) Inspect the rubber mountings for signs of damage or deterioration and renew as necessary.

c) On 1360 cc models, prior to assembling the front pipe-to-intermediate pipe joint, a smear of high-temperature grease should be applied to the joint mating surfaces.

d) In the case of the front pipe/intermediate pipe-to-tailpipe joint, apply a smear of exhaust system jointing paste to the flange joint, to ensure a gas-tight seal. On 1360 cc models, tighten the clamping ring nuts evenly and progressively to the specified torque, so that the clearance between the clamp halves remains equal on either side.

e) Prior to tightening the exhaust system fasteners, ensure that all rubber mountings are correctly located and that there is adequate clearance between the exhaust system and the vehicle underbody.

Chapter 4 Part B:
Fuel/exhaust systems - single-point petrol injection models

Contents

Degrees of difficulty

Easy, suitable for novice with little experience	**Fairly easy,** suitable for beginner with some experience	**Fairly difficult,** suitable for competent DIY mechanic	**Difficult,** suitable for experienced DIY mechanic	**Very difficult,** suitable for expert DIY or professional 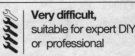

Specifications

System type

954 cc (CDY and CDZ engine) models:
  Pre-July 1996 models . . . . Bosch Monopoint MA3.0
  July 1996-on models . . . . Bosch Monopoint MA3.1
1124 cc (HDY and HDZ engine) models:
  Pre-July 1992 models . . . . Bosch Monopoint A2.2
  July 1992 to July 1996 models . . . . Magneti Marelli G6
  July 1996-on models . . . . Bosch Monopoint MA3.1
1360 cc models:
  KDY engine . . . . Bosch Monopoint A2.2
  KDX engine . . . . Bosch Monopoint MA3.0
Note: *Refer to Chapter 2A for further information on engine code identification.*

Fuel system data

Fuel pump type . . . . Electric, immersed in tank
Fuel pump regulated constant pressure (approximate):
  Bosch system . . . . 1.0 bar
  Magneti Marelli system . . . . 0.8 ± 0.1 bars
Specified idle speed (not adjustable) . . . . 850 ± 50 rpm (controlled by ECU)
Idle mixture CO content:
  Bosch system (not adjustable) . . . . Less than 1.0 % (controlled by ECU)
  Magneti Marelli system* . . . . Less than 1.0 % (controlled by ECU)
On the Magneti Marelli system, idle mixture adjustment is possible, but only using special electronic equipment - see text

Recommended fuel

Minimum octane rating . . . . 95 RON unleaded **only**

Torque wrench settings

	Nm	lbf ft
Inlet manifold retaining nuts	8	6
Exhaust manifold retaining nuts:		
Long nuts (early models)	16	12
Short nuts (later models)	25	18
Exhaust system fasteners:		
Front pipe-to-manifold nuts	30	22
Front pipe-to-intermediate pipe/catalytic converter nuts	10	7
Clamping ring nuts	15	11

4B

4.3 Adjust the accelerator cable as described in text

1 General information and precautions

The fuel system consists of a fuel tank mounted under the rear of the car (with an electric fuel pump immersed in it), a fuel filter, fuel feed and return lines, the throttle body assembly (which incorporates the single fuel injector and the fuel pressure regulator), as well as the Electronic Control Unit (ECU) and the various sensors, electrical components and related wiring. The air cleaner contains a disposable paper filter element and incorporates a flap valve air temperature control system, which allows cold air from the outside of the car and air warmed by the exhaust manifold, to enter the air cleaner in the correct proportions.

Refer to Section 7 for further information on the operation of each relevant fuel injection system and to Section 18 for information on the exhaust system. Throughout this Chapter, it is occasionally necessary to identify vehicles by their engine codes rather than engine capacity. Refer to Chapter 2A for further information on engine code identification.

⚠️ **Warning: Many of the procedures in this Chapter require the removal of fuel lines and connections, which may result in some fuel spillage. Before carrying out any operation on the fuel system, refer to the precautions given in "Safety first!" at the beginning of this manual and follow them implicitly. Petrol is a highly-dangerous and volatile liquid and the precautions necessary when handling it cannot be overstressed.**
Note: Residual pressure will remain in the fuel lines long after the vehicle was last used. Before disconnecting any fuel line, depressurise the fuel system as described in Section 8.

2 Air cleaner assembly - removal and refitting

Refer to Chapter 4A, Section 2, substituting "throttle body" for all references to the carburettor.

3 Air cleaner air temperature control system - information and component renewal

Refer to Chapter 4A, Section 3, substituting "throttle body" for all references to the carburettor.

4 Accelerator cable - removal, refitting and adjustment

Removal and refitting

1 Refer to Chapter 4A, Section 7, substituting "throttle body" for all references to the carburettor. Adjust the cable as described below.

Adjustment

2 Remove the spring clip from the accelerator outer cable then, ensuring that the throttle cam is fully against its stop, gently pull the cable out of its grommet until all free play is removed from the inner cable.
3 With the cable held in this position, ensure that the flat washer is pressed securely against the grommet, then fit the spring clip to the third outer cable groove visible in front of the rubber grommet and washer **(see illustration)**. This will leave a fair amount of freeplay in the inner cable, which is necessary to ensure correct operation of the idle control stepper motor.
4 Have an assistant depress the accelerator pedal and check that the throttle cam opens fully and returns smoothly to its stop.

5 Accelerator pedal - removal and refitting

Refer to Chapter 4A, Section 8.

6 Unleaded petrol - general information and usage

Note: The information given in this Chapter is correct at the time of writing. If updated information is thought to be required, check with a Peugeot dealer. If travelling abroad, consult one of the motoring organisations (or a similar authority) for advice on the fuel available and their suitability for your vehicle.

The fuel recommended by Peugeot is given in the Specifications Section of this Chapter.

All Peugeot 106 single-point injection models are designed to run on fuel with a minimum octane rating of 95 (RON). All models are equipped with catalytic converters and therefore must be run on unleaded fuel **only**.
Caution: Under no circumstances should leaded fuel be used, as this may damage the catalytic converter.

7 Fuel injection systems - general information

Note: The fuel injection ECU is of the "self-learning" type, meaning that as it operates, it also monitors and stores the settings which give optimum engine performance under all operating conditions. When the battery is disconnected, these settings are lost and the ECU reverts to the base settings programmed into its memory at the factory. On restarting, this may lead to the engine running/idling roughly for a short while, until the ECU has re-learned the optimum settings. This process is best accomplished by taking the vehicle on a road test (for approximately 15 minutes), covering all engine speeds and loads, concentrating mainly in the 2,500 to 3,500 rpm region.

Bosch Monopoint A2.2 system

The Bosch Monopoint A2.2 fuel injection system incorporates a closed-loop catalytic converter and an evaporative emission control system and complies with pre-1996 emission standards. The system operates as follows.

The fuel pump, immersed in the fuel tank, pumps fuel from the fuel tank to the fuel injector, via a filter mounted underneath the rear of the vehicle. Fuel supply pressure is controlled by the pressure regulator in the throttle body assembly, which lifts to allow excess fuel to return to the tank when the optimum operating pressure of the fuel system is exceeded.

The electrical control system consists of the ECU, along with the following sensors and actuators:

a) Throttle potentiometer - informs the ECU of the throttle valve position and the rate of throttle opening/closing.
b) Coolant temperature sensor - informs the ECU of engine temperature.
c) Inlet air temperature sensor - informs the ECU of the temperature of the air passing through the throttle body.
d) Lambda sensor - informs the ECU of the oxygen content of the exhaust gases (explained in greater detail in Part E of this Chapter).
e) Throttle position switch (built into idle control stepper motor) - informs the ECU when the throttle valve is closed (ie when the accelerator pedal is released).
f) Idle control stepper motor - controls the position of the throttle during idling to maintain a constant engine idle speed.
g) Ignition HT coil - ECU monitors the coil low-tension (LT) circuit to determine the engine speed.

All the above signals are compared by the ECU and, based on this information, the ECU selects the response appropriate to those values and controls the fuel injector (varying its pulse width - the length of time the injector is held open - to provide a richer or weaker mixture, as appropriate). The mixture and idle speed are constantly varied by the ECU, to provide the best settings for cranking, starting (with either a hot or cold engine) and engine warm-up, idle, cruising and acceleration.

The ECU also has full control over the engine idle speed, via a stepper motor which is fitted to the throttle body. The motor pushrod rests against a cam on the throttle valve spindle. When the throttle valve is closed (accelerator pedal released), the ECU uses the motor to vary the opening of the throttle valve and so control the idle speed.

The ECU also controls the exhaust and evaporative emission control systems, which are described in detail in Part E of this Chapter.

If there is an abnormality in any of the readings obtained from either the coolant temperature sensor, the inlet air temperature sensor or the lambda sensor, the ECU enters its back-up mode. If this happens, it ignores the sensor signal and assumes a pre-programmed value which will allow the engine to continue running, albeit at reduced efficiency. If the ECU enters this back-up mode, the warning light on the instrument panel will be illuminated and the relevant fault code will be stored in the ECU memory.

If the warning light comes on, the vehicle should be taken to a Peugeot dealer at the earliest opportunity. Once there, a complete test of the engine management system can be carried out, using a special electronic diagnostic test unit which is simply plugged into the system's diagnostic connector.

Bosch Monopoint MA3.0 and MA3.1 systems

The Bosch Monopoint MA3.0 and MA3.1 engine management systems differ from the earlier A2.2 system in that they control both the fuel injection system and ignition system, thus providing full engine management under all operating conditions. Both systems incorporate a closed-loop catalytic converter and an evaporative emission control system and comply with the latest emission standards. Refer to Chapter 5B for information on the ignition side of the system.

The fuel injection side of the system is very similar to the A2.2 system described above, with the following differences.

A crankshaft sensor is fitted to the engine, to inform the ECU of engine speed and crankshaft position. The crankshaft sensor is needed since the ECU also controls the ignition side of the system and cannot use the ignition low-tension (LT) circuit to calculate engine speed. The sensor works in conjunction with a reluctor ring fixed to the rear of the flywheel. The reluctor ring originally has a total of 60 teeth, which are equally spaced at intervals of 6°. Of these 60 teeth, two adjacent teeth are removed to leave a gap of 18°. The ECU uses the reluctor ring gap to establish where TDC is and calculates engine speed from the frequency of teeth passing the crankshaft sensor.

On 1360 cc models, a vehicle speed sensor is also incorporated into the system. The vehicle speed sensor is fitted to the transmission and informs the ECU of the actual speed of the vehicle.

On the MA3.1 system an inlet manifold heater is fitted, to raise the temperature of the inlet manifold and minimise fuel condensation.

Magneti Marelli G6 system

The Magneti Marelli G6 engine management system controls both the fuel injection and ignition systems and incorporates a closed-loop catalytic converter and an evaporative emission control system to comply with the latest emission standards.

The fuel injection side of the system operates as follows. Refer to Chapter 5B for information on the ignition side of the system.

The fuel pump, immersed in the fuel tank, pumps fuel from the fuel tank to the fuel injector via a filter. Fuel supply pressure is controlled by the pressure regulator in the throttle body assembly, which lifts to allow excess fuel to return to the tank when the optimum operating pressure of the fuel system is exceeded. To reduce emissions and to improve driveability when the engine is cold, an electrical heating element is fitted to the throttle body, to quickly warm it up on cold starts.

The electrical control system consists of the ECU, along with the following sensors and actuators:

a) *Manifold absolute pressure (MAP) sensor - informs the ECU of load on engine.*
b) *Crankshaft sensor - informs the ECU of crankshaft position and engine speed.*
c) *Throttle potentiometer - informs the ECU of the throttle valve position and the rate of throttle opening/closing.*
d) *Coolant temperature sensor - informs the ECU of engine temperature.*
e) *Inlet air temperature sensor - informs the ECU of the temperature of the air passing through the throttle body.*
f) *Lambda (oxygen) sensor - informs the ECU of the oxygen content of the exhaust gases (explained in greater detail in Part E of this Chapter).*
g) *Idle control stepper motor - controls the position of the throttle during idling to maintain a constant engine idle speed.*

In addition, the ECU senses battery voltage (adjusting the injector pulse width to suit and using the stepper motor to increase the idle speed and, therefore, the alternator output if it is too low). The ECU has short-circuit protection and diagnostic capabilities and can both receive and transmit information via the engine management circuit diagnostic connector, thus permitting engine diagnosis and tuning by special diagnostic equipment.

All the above signals are compared by the ECU, using digital techniques, with set values pre-programmed (mapped) into its memory; based on this information, the ECU selects the response appropriate to those values and

controls the ignition HT coil (see Chapter 5B) and the fuel injector (varying its pulse width - the length of time the injector is held open - to provide a richer or weaker mixture, as appropriate). The mixture, idle speed and ignition timing are constantly varied by the ECU to provide the best settings for cranking, starting (with either a hot or cold engine) and engine warm-up, idle, cruising and acceleration.

The ECU regulates the engine idle speed via a stepper motor which is fitted to the throttle body. The motor has a pushrod which controls the opening of an air passage which bypasses the throttle valve. When the throttle valve is closed, the ECU controls the movement of the motor pushrod, which regulates the amount of air which flows through the throttle body passage and so controls the idle speed. The bypass passage is also used as an additional air supply during cold starting.

The ECU also controls the exhaust and evaporative emission control systems, which are described in detail in Part E of this Chapter.

If there is an abnormality in any of the readings obtained from any of engine management circuit sensors, the ECU enters a back-up mode. If this happens, it ignores the sensor signal and assumes a pre-programmed value which will allow the engine to continue running, albeit at reduced efficiency. On entering the back-up mode, the engine management warning light in the instrument panel will come on, informing the driver of the fault and the relevant fault code will be stored in the ECU memory.

If the warning light comes on, the vehicle should be taken to a Peugeot dealer at the earliest opportunity. Once there, a complete test of the engine management system can be carried out, using a special electronic diagnostic test unit which is simply plugged into the system's diagnostic connector.

8 Fuel system - depressurisation

Note: *Refer to the warning note in Section 1 before proceeding.*

⚠️ *Warning: The following procedure will merely relieve the pressure in the fuel system - remember that fuel will still be present in the system components and take precautions accordingly before disconnecting any of them.*

1 The fuel system referred to in this Section is defined as the tank-mounted fuel pump, the fuel filter, the fuel injector and the pressure regulator in the injector housing and the metal pipes and flexible hoses of the fuel lines between these components. All these contain fuel, which will be under pressure while the engine is running and/or while the ignition is

4B

9.4 Disconnect the wiring connector, then release the fuel feed and return hoses (arrowed) from the fuel pump

9.6 Unscrew the locking ring . . .

9.7a . . . then lift out the fuel pump . . .

switched on. The pressure will remain for some time after the ignition has been switched off and must be relieved before any of these components are disturbed for servicing work.

2 Disconnect the battery negative terminal (refer to "Disconnecting the battery" in the Reference Section of this manual).

3 Place a suitable container beneath the relevant connection/union to be disconnected and have a large rag ready to soak up any escaping fuel not being caught by the container.

4 Slowly loosen the connection or union nut (as applicable) to avoid a sudden release of pressure and position the rag around the connection to catch any fuel spray which may be expelled. Once the pressure is released, disconnect the fuel line. Plug the openings, to minimise fuel loss and prevent the entry of dirt into the fuel system.

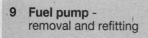

9 Fuel pump - removal and refitting

Note: *Refer to the warning note in Section 1 before proceeding.*

Removal

1 Disconnect the battery negative terminal (refer to "Disconnecting the battery" in the Reference Section of this manual).

2 For access to the fuel pump, fold the rear seat cushion forwards.

3 Using a screwdriver, carefully prise the plastic access cover from the floor to expose the fuel pump. Where two access covers are fitted, the pump is located under the right-hand cover.

4 Disconnect the wiring connector from the fuel pump **(see illustration)**. Tape the connector to the vehicle body, to prevent it disappearing behind the tank.

5 Mark the hoses for identification purposes, then slacken the feed and return hose retaining clips. Where crimped-type hose clips are fitted, cut the clips and discard them; replace them with standard worm-drive hose clips when refitting. Disconnect both hoses from the top of the pump and plug the hose ends **(see illustration 9.4)**.

6 Noting the alignment marks on the tank, pump cover and the locking ring, unscrew the ring and remove it from the tank. This is best accomplished by using a screwdriver on the raised ribs of the locking ring. Carefully tap the screwdriver to turn the ring anti-clockwise until it can be unscrewed by hand **(see illustration)**.

7 Carefully lift the fuel pump assembly out of the fuel tank, taking great care not to damage the filter, or to spill fuel onto the interior of the vehicle. Recover the rubber sealing ring and discard it; a new one must be used on refitting **(see illustrations)**.

8 Note that the fuel pump assembly is only available as a complete assembly; no individual components are available separately.

Refitting

9 Ensure that the fuel pump pick-up filter is clean and free of debris. Fit a new sealing ring to the top of the fuel tank.

10 Carefully manoeuvre the pump assembly into the fuel tank, aligning the mark noted on removal.

11 Refit the locking ring, tightening it so that its mark is correctly aligned with the line on the fuel tank, as noted prior to removal **(see illustration)**.

12 Reconnect the feed and return hoses to the top of the fuel pump, using the marks made on removal to ensure that they are correctly reconnected and securely tighten their retaining clips.

13 Reconnect the pump wiring connector.

14 Reconnect the battery negative terminal and start the engine. Check the fuel pump feed and return hose unions for signs of leakage.

15 If all is well, refit the plastic access cover and fold back the rear seat cushion.

10 Fuel gauge sender unit - removal and refitting

1 On pre-July 1996 models, refer to Chapter 4A, Section 5, noting that there are no fuel pipe connections to the sender unit **(see illustration)**.

2 On July 1996 models onward, the sender unit is integral with the fuel pump - refer to Section 9 of this Chapter.

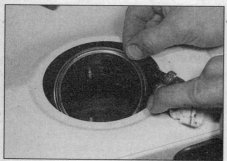

9.7b . . . and recover the rubber sealing ring

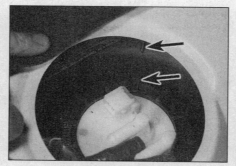

9.11 When refitting, tighten the locking ring until it is correctly aligned with the fuel tank mark (arrowed)

10.1 Removing the fuel gauge sender unit

12.3a Disconnect the wiring connectors from the throttle potentiometer . . .

12.3b . . . the injector cap and the stepper motor

12.4 Fuel feed and return hose connections (arrowed) - later model shown

11 Fuel tank - removal and refitting

Refer to Chapter 4A, Section 6, noting that it will be necessary to depressurise the fuel system as the feed and return hoses are disconnected from the fuel pump (see Section 8). It will also be necessary to disconnect the wiring connector from the fuel pump prior to lowering the tank out of position.

12 Throttle body - removal and refitting

Note: *Refer to the warning note in Section 1 before proceeding.*

Removal

1 Disconnect the battery negative terminal (refer to *"Disconnecting the battery"* in the Reference Section of this manual).
2 Remove the air cleaner housing-to-throttle body duct, using the information given in Section 2.
3 Depress the retaining clips and disconnect the wiring connectors from the throttle potentiometer, the idle control stepper motor and the injector wiring loom connector, which is situated on the side of the throttle body **(see illustration)**. On later 1124 cc models (with the Magneti Marelli system) the injector, heating element and inlet air temperature

sensor wiring are all joined to one large connector.
4 Bearing in mind the information given in Section 8 about depressurising the fuel system, release the retaining clips and disconnect the fuel feed and return hoses from the throttle body assembly **(see illustration)**. If the original crimped-type clips are still fitted, cut the clips and discard them; replace them with standard worm-drive hose clips on refitting.
5 Disconnect the accelerator inner cable from the throttle cam, then withdraw the outer cable from the mounting bracket, along with its flat washer and spring clip.
6 Where necessary, disconnect the distributor vacuum hose, idle control auxiliary air valve and/or purge valve hose from the throttle body (as applicable).
7 Slacken and remove the bolts securing the throttle body assembly to the inlet manifold **(see illustration)**, then remove the assembly along with its gasket.
8 If necessary, with the throttle body removed, undo the retaining screws and separate the upper and lower sections, noting the insulating spacer and gaskets, or the single gasket (as applicable) fitted between the two.

Refitting

9 Refitting is a reverse of the removal procedure, bearing in mind the following points:
a) *Where applicable, ensure that the mating surfaces of the upper and lower throttle body sections are clean and dry, then fit the insulating spacer and new gaskets, or a new gasket (as applicable) and reassemble the two, tightening the retaining screws securely.*
b) *Ensure that the mating surfaces of the manifold and throttle body are clean and dry, then fit a new gasket. Securely tighten the throttle body retaining bolts.*
c) *Ensure that all hoses are correctly reconnected and, where necessary, that their retaining clips are securely tightened.*
d) *On completion, adjust the accelerator cable using the information given in Section 4.*

13 Fuel injection system - testing and adjustment

Testing

1 If a fault appears in the fuel injection system, first ensure that all the system wiring connectors are securely connected and free of corrosion. Then ensure that the fault is not due to poor maintenance; ie, check that the air cleaner filter element is clean, the spark plugs are in good condition and correctly gapped, the valve clearances are correctly adjusted, the cylinder compression pressures are correct, the ignition timing is correct and that the engine breather hoses are clear and undamaged, referring to Chapters 1A, 2A and 5B for further information.
2 If these checks fail to reveal the cause of the problem, the vehicle should be taken to a suitably equipped Peugeot dealer for testing. A wiring block connector is incorporated in the engine management circuit, into which a special electronic diagnostic tester can be plugged. On pre-1997 models, the connector is clipped onto the side of the ECU mounting bracket **(see illustration)**; on later models the connector is located in the passenger compartment on the driver's side. The tester will locate the fault quickly and simply, alleviating the need to test all the system components individually, which is a time-consuming operation that carries a high risk of damaging the ECU.

4B

12.7 Throttle body retaining screws (arrowed)

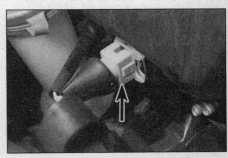

13.2 Diagnostic wiring connector (arrowed) clipped onto the side of the ECU mounting bracket on early models

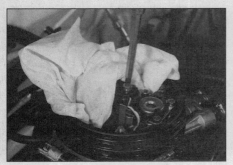

14.3a Undo the injector cap retaining screw, noting the use of rag to catch fuel spray . . .

14.3b . . . then lift off the cap and withdraw the injector

14.4 On refitting, ensure the cap terminals are correctly aligned with the injector pins (arrowed)

Adjustment

3 Experienced home mechanics with a considerable amount of skill and equipment (including a good-quality tachometer and a good-quality, carefully-calibrated exhaust gas analyser) may be able to *check* the exhaust CO level and the idle speed. However, if these are found to be in need of *adjustment*, the car **must** be taken to a suitably-equipped Peugeot dealer.

4 On the Bosch Monopoint system, no adjustment is possible. Should the idle speed or exhaust gas CO level be incorrect, then a fault must be present in the fuel injection system.

5 On the Magneti Marelli system, it is possible to adjust the mixture setting (exhaust gas CO level) and ignition timing. However, adjustments can be made only by re-programming the ECU using special diagnostic equipment connected to the system via the diagnostic connector.

14 Bosch Monopoint system components - removal and refitting

Note: *Check the availability of individual components with your Peugeot dealer before dismantling.*

Fuel injector

Note: *Refer to the warning note in Section 1 before proceeding. If a faulty injector is suspected, before condemning the injector, it*

is worth trying the effect of one of the proprietary injector-cleaning treatments.

1 Disconnect the battery negative terminal (refer to *"Disconnecting the battery"* in the Reference Section of this manual).

2 Remove the air cleaner-to-throttle body duct using the information given in Section 2, then proceed as described under the relevant sub-heading.

A2.2 system

3 Undo the injector cap retaining screw, then lift off the cap and withdraw the injector, noting its sealing ring locations. As the cap screw is slackened and the injector is withdrawn, place a rag over the injector, to catch any fuel spray which may be released **(see illustrations)**.

4 Refitting is a reversal of the removal procedure, ensuring that the injector sealing ring(s) and injector cap O-ring are in good condition. When refitting the injector cap, ensure that the injector pins are correctly aligned with the cap terminals; the terminals are marked "+" and "-" for identification **(see illustration)**.

MA3.0 and MA3.1 systems

5 Remove the inlet air temperature sensor as described later in this Section.

6 Lift out the injector and recover its lower sealing ring.

7 Refitting is a reversal of the removal procedure, ensuring that the injector sealing ring(s) and injector cap O-ring are in good condition. When refitting the injector cap, ensure that the injector pins are correctly

aligned with the cap terminals; the terminals are marked "+" and "-" for identification.

Fuel pressure regulator

Note: *Refer to the warning note in Section 1 before proceeding. At the time of writing, the fuel pressure regulator assembly is not available separately. If the fuel pressure regulator assembly is faulty, the complete throttle body assembly must be renewed. Refer to a Peugeot dealer for further information on parts availability. Although the unit can be dismantled for cleaning, if required, it should not be disturbed unless absolutely necessary.*

8 Disconnect the battery negative terminal (refer to *"Disconnecting the battery"* in the Reference Section of this manual).

9 Remove the air cleaner-to-throttle body duct using the information given in Section 2.

10 Using a suitable marker pen, make alignment marks between the regulator cover and throttle body, then slacken and remove the cover retaining screws **(see illustration)**. As the screws are slackened, place a rag over the cover, to catch any fuel spray which may be released.

11 Lift off the cover, then remove the spring and withdraw the diaphragm, noting its correct fitted orientation. Remove all traces of dirt and examine the diaphragm for signs of splitting; renew if necessary.

12 Refitting is a reverse of the removal procedure, ensuring that the diaphragm and cover are fitted the correct way around and the retaining screws are securely tightened.

Idle control stepper motor

Note: *On some later models, at the time of writing, the idle control stepper motor is not available separately. If the motor is faulty, the complete throttle body assembly must be renewed. Refer to your Peugeot dealer for further information on parts availability.*

13 Disconnect the battery negative terminal (refer to *"Disconnecting the battery"* in the Reference Section of this manual).

14 Depress the retaining clip and disconnect the wiring connector from the idle control stepper motor.

15 Undo the retaining screws and remove the motor from the throttle body **(see illustration)**.

14.10 Fuel pressure regulator retaining screws (arrowed)

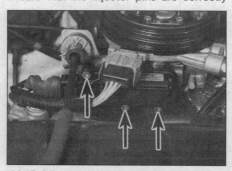

14.15 Idle control stepper motor retaining screws (arrowed)

14.19a Undo the three retaining screws (arrowed) . . .

14.19b . . . then lift off the plastic ring. Recover the sealing ring

14.20 Disconnecting the injector wiring connector. Injector retaining screw is arrowed

16 Refitting is a reverse of the removal procedure, ensuring that the motor retaining screws are securely tightened.

Throttle potentiometer

17 The throttle potentiometer is a sealed unit and under no circumstances should it be disturbed. For this reason, on some models, it is secured to the throttle body assembly by tamperproof screws. If the throttle potentiometer is faulty, the complete throttle body assembly must be renewed. Refer to your Peugeot dealer for further information.

Inlet air temperature sensor

Note: *Refer to the warning note in Section 1 before proceeding. On some later models, at the time of writing, the inlet air temperature sensor is not available separately. If the sensor is faulty, the complete throttle body assembly*

must be renewed. Refer to your Peugeot dealer for further information on parts availability.

18 The inlet air temperature sensor is an integral part of the throttle body injector cap. To remove the cap, first disconnect the battery negative terminal (refer to *"Disconnecting the battery"* in the Reference Section of this manual), then remove the air cleaner-to-throttle body duct using the information given in Section 2.

19 Undo the three retaining screws and remove the circular plastic ring from the top of the throttle body. Recover its sealing ring **(see illustrations)**.

20 Depress the retaining clip and disconnect the wiring connector from the injector wiring connector **(see illustration)**.

21 Undo the injector cap retaining screw, then lift off the cap and recover the gasket and/or sealing ring (as applicable). As the cap screw is slackened, place a rag over the injector, to catch any fuel spray which may be released. On models fitted with the A2.2 system, it will be necessary to release the injector cap connector from the throttle body as the cap is removed **(see illustration)**.

22 Refitting is a reversal of the removal procedure, ensuring that the injector cap gasket and/or O-ring is in good condition. Take care to ensure that the cap terminals are correctly aligned with the injector pin and securely tighten the cap retaining screw.

Coolant temperature sensor

23 Refer to Chapter 3.

Electronic control unit (ECU)

24 The ECU is located on the right-hand side of the engine compartment, underneath a large plastic cover.

25 Disconnect the battery negative terminal (refer to *"Disconnecting the battery"* in the Reference Section of this manual).

26 Unclip the cover from the mounting plate, then lift the retaining clip and disconnect the wiring connector from the ECU. Slacken and remove the ECU retaining bolts and remove it from the vehicle **(see illustrations)**.

27 Refitting is a reverse of the removal procedure, ensuring that the wiring connector is securely reconnected.

Fuel injection system relay unit

28 The relay unit is clipped onto the underside of the ECU mounting plate, on the right-hand side of the engine compartment.

29 Disconnect the battery negative terminal (refer to *"Disconnecting the battery"* in the Reference Section of this manual).

30 Unclip the relay unit from the mounting plate, disconnect the wiring connector and remove the unit from the vehicle **(see illustration)**.

31 Refitting is the reverse of removal, ensuring that the relay unit is securely held in position by its retaining clip.

Injector resistor

32 The injector resistor is fixed to the underside of the ECU mounting plate, on the right-hand side of the engine compartment.

4B

14.21 On models with the A2.2 system, the injector wiring connector is a push-fit in the throttle body

14.26a Unclip the plastic cover to gain access to the ECU . . .

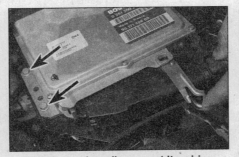

14.26b . . . then disconnect its wiring connector and undo the two retaining bolts (arrowed)

14.30 Removing the fuel injection system relay unit from the ECU mounting plate

33 Disconnect the battery negative terminal (refer to *"Disconnecting the battery"* in the Reference Section of this manual).
34 Unscrew the resistor retaining nut, then disconnect the wiring connector and remove the resistor from the vehicle. On some models, the resistor maybe riveted in position. If this is the case, drill out or cut the rivets to release it from the mounting plate **(see illustration)**.
35 Refitting is a reversal of the removal procedure. Where the resistor was riveted in positioned secure it in position with either a suitable nut and bolt or new pop rivets.

Crankshaft sensor (MA3.0 and MA3.1 systems)

36 The crankshaft sensor is situated on the front face of the transmission clutch housing.
37 Disconnect the battery negative terminal (refer to *"Disconnecting the battery"* in the Reference Section of this manual).
38 Trace the wiring back from the sensor to the wiring connector and disconnect it from the main harness.
39 Prise out the rubber grommet, then undo the retaining bolt and withdraw the sensor from the transmission.
40 Refitting is a reverse of the removal procedure. Ensure that the sensor retaining bolt is securely tightened and that the grommet is correctly seated in the transmission housing.

Vehicle speed sensor (MA3.0 and MA3.1 systems)

41 The vehicle speed sensor is an integral part of the speedometer drive housing. Refer to Chapter 7A or 7B for removal and refitting details.

Inlet manifold heater (MA3.1 system)

42 Remove the inlet manifold as described in Section 16.
43 Release the circlip and withdraw the heater from the underside of the manifold casting.
44 Refitting is a reversal of removal.

15 Magneti Marelli system components - removal and refitting

Note: *Check the availability of individual components with your Peugeot dealer before dismantling.*

Fuel injector

Note: *Refer to the warning note at the start of this Section before proceeding.*
Note: *If a faulty injector is suspected, before condemning the injector, it is worth trying the effect of one of the proprietary injector-cleaning treatments. If this fails, the vehicle should be taken to a Peugeot dealer for testing using the appropriate specialist*

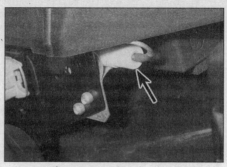

14.34 The injector resistor (arrowed) is mounted onto the ECU mounting plate

equipment. At the time of writing, it appears that neither the fuel injector or its seals are available separately and, if faulty, the complete upper throttle body assembly must be renewed. Refer to your Peugeot dealer for further information on parts availability.
1 Disconnect the battery negative terminal (refer to *"Disconnecting the battery"* in the Reference Section of this manual).
2 Remove the air cleaner-to-throttle body duct, using the information given in Section 2.
3 Release the retaining tangs and disconnect the injector wiring connector.
4 Undo the retaining screw, then remove the retaining clip and lift the injector out of the housing, noting its sealing ring. As the screw is slackened, place a rag over the injector, to catch any fuel spray which may be released.
5 Refitting is a reverse of the removal procedure, ensuring that the injector sealing ring is in good condition.

Fuel pressure regulator

Note: *Refer to the warning note at the start of this Section before proceeding.*
Note: *At the time of writing, it appears that the fuel pressure regulator is not available separately. If the fuel pressure regulator assembly is faulty, the complete upper throttle body assembly must be renewed. Refer to a Peugeot dealer for further information on parts availability. Although the unit can be dismantled for cleaning, if required, it should not be disturbed unless absolutely necessary.*
6 Disconnect the battery negative terminal (refer to *"Disconnecting the battery"* in the Reference Section of this manual).
7 Remove the air cleaner-to-throttle body duct, using the information given in Section 2.
8 Using a suitable marker pen, make alignment marks between the regulator cover and throttle body, then undo the four retaining screws. As the screws are slackened, place a rag over the cover, to catch any fuel spray which may be released.
9 Lift off the cover, then remove the spring and withdraw the diaphragm, noting its correct fitted orientation. Remove all traces of dirt and examine the diaphragm for signs of splitting. If damage is found, it may be necessary to renew the complete upper throttle body assembly, as described in Section 12.

10 Refitting is a reverse of the removal procedure. Ensure that the diaphragm and cover are fitted the correct way around and that the retaining screws are securely tightened.

Idle control stepper motor

11 Disconnect the battery negative terminal (refer to *"Disconnecting the battery"* in the Reference Section of this manual).
12 To remove the stepper motor, depress the retaining tabs and disconnect the wiring connector. Undo the two retaining screws and withdraw the motor from the side of the throttle body assembly.
13 Refitting is a reverse of removal.

Throttle potentiometer

14 Disconnect the battery negative terminal (refer to *"Disconnecting the battery"* in the Reference Section of this manual), then depress the retaining tabs and disconnect the wiring connector from the throttle potentiometer.
15 Undo the two retaining screws and remove the throttle potentiometer from the side of the throttle body assembly.
16 Refitting is a reversal of the removal procedure, ensuring that the throttle potentiometer tang is correctly engaged with the throttle spindle.

Inlet air temperature sensor

17 The inlet air temperature sensor is screwed into the underside of the upper throttle body, on the left-hand side of the fuel injector.
18 Disconnect the battery negative terminal (refer to *"Disconnecting the battery"* in the Reference Section of this manual).
19 Disconnect the wiring connector, then undo the retaining screw and remove the inlet air temperature sensor from the throttle body.
Note: *The sensor retaining screw is very difficult to reach. If it proves impossible to unscrew, the throttle body will have to be removed to permit sensor removal.*
20 Refitting is a reverse of the removal procedure.

Manifold absolute pressure (MAP) sensor

21 The MAP sensor is mounted onto a bracket on the engine compartment bulkhead, behind the throttle body.
22 Disconnect the battery negative terminal (refer to *"Disconnecting the battery"* in the Reference Section of this manual).
23 Slacken and remove the three retaining bolts, then free the MAP sensor from the bracket. Disconnect the wiring connector and vacuum hose and remove the sensor from the engine compartment.
24 Refitting is a reverse of the removal procedure.

Coolant temperature sensor

25 Refer to Chapter 3.

Crankshaft sensor

26 Refer to paragraphs 36 to 40 of Section 14.

Electronic control unit (ECU)

27 Refer to paragraphs 24 to 27 of Section 14.

Fuel injection system relay unit

28 Refer to paragraphs 28 to 31 of Section 14.

Throttle body heating element

29 The throttle body heating element is situated in the front of the throttle body.

30 Disconnect the battery negative terminal (refer to *"Disconnecting the battery"* in the Reference Section of this manual).

31 Remove the air cleaner housing-to-throttle body duct, using the information given in Section 2.

32 Disconnect the wiring connectors from the inlet air temperature sensor and the injector. Also disconnect the main wiring connector from the throttle body and free the connector from its mounting bracket.

33 Undo the retaining screws and free the accelerator cable mounting bracket from the throttle body. As the bracket is released, recover the spring from the front of the heating element.

34 Ease the heating element out from the throttle housing and remove it along with the wiring connector and wiring harness. Examine the O-ring for signs of damage or deterioration and renew if necessary.

35 Refitting is a reversal of the removal procedure, using a new O-ring where necessary.

16 Inlet manifold - removal and refitting

Removal

1 Remove the throttle body as described in Section 12.

2 Drain the cooling system as described in Chapter 1A.

3 Slacken the retaining clip and disconnect the coolant hose(s) from the manifold.

4 Similarly disconnect the vacuum servo unit hose from the left-hand side of the manifold.

5 Make a final check that all the necessary vacuum/breather hoses have been disconnected from the manifold.

6 Unscrew the six retaining nuts, then manoeuvre the manifold away from the head and out of the engine compartment. Note that there is no manifold gasket.

Refitting

7 Refitting is the reverse of the removal procedure, noting the following points:

a) *Ensure that the manifold and cylinder head mating surfaces are clean and dry and apply a thin coating of suitable sealing compound to the manifold mating surface. Install the manifold and tighten its retaining nuts to the specified torque setting.*

b) *Ensure that all relevant hoses are reconnected to their original positions and are securely held (where necessary) by their retaining clips.*

c) *Refit the throttle body as described in Section 12.*

d) *On completion, refill the cooling system as described in Chapter 1A.*

17 Exhaust manifold - removal and refitting

Refer to Chapter 4A, Section 16, noting that the lambda (oxygen) sensor wiring connectors must either be disconnected, or care must be taken to support the front pipe to avoid any strain being placed on the sensor wiring.

18 Exhaust system - general information and component renewal

General information

1 On 954 and 1124 cc models, the exhaust system consists of three sections; the front pipe, the intermediate pipe and catalytic converter and the tailpipe and main silencer box. All exhaust sections are connected by a flanged joint. The front pipe joints are secured by nuts and bolts, the intermediate pipe joint being of the spring-loaded ball type, to allow

for movement in the exhaust system. The intermediate pipe-to-tailpipe joint is secured by a clamping ring.

2 On 1360 cc models, the exhaust system consists of four sections; the front pipe, the catalytic converter, the intermediate pipe and the tailpipe and main silencer box. All exhaust sections are joined by a flanged joint. The front pipe joints are secured by nuts and bolts, the catalytic converter joint being of the spring-loaded ball type, to allow for movement in the exhaust system. The catalytic converter-to-intermediate pipe joint and the intermediate pipe-to-silencer joint are secured by a clamping ring.

3 The system is suspended throughout its entire length by rubber mountings.

Removal

4 Each exhaust section can be removed individually or, alternatively, the complete system can be removed as a unit.

5 To remove the system or part of the system, first jack up the front or rear of the car and support it on axle stands. Alternatively, position the car over an inspection pit, or on car ramps.

Front pipe

6 Trace the wiring back from the lambda (oxygen) sensor to its wiring connectors, which are clipped onto the top of the transmission and disconnect them from the main wiring harness.

7 Undo the nuts securing the front pipe flange joint to the manifold and, where necessary, the single bolt securing the front pipe to its mounting bracket **(see illustrations)**. Separate the flange joint and collect the gasket.

8 Slacken and remove the two nuts securing the front pipe to the catalytic converter/intermediate pipe (as applicable) and recover the spring cups and springs **(see illustration)**. Remove the bolts, then withdraw the front pipe from underneath the vehicle, taking great care not to damage the lambda sensor. Recover the wire-mesh gasket from the joint.

Catalytic converter - 1360 cc models

9 Undo the two nuts securing the front pipe flange joint to the catalytic converter. Recover the springs and spring cups and withdraw the bolts.

4B

18.7a Front pipe-to-manifold retaining nuts (arrowed) . . .

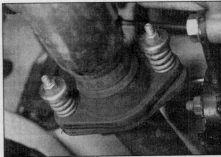

18.7b . . . and front pipe mounting bolt (arrowed)

18.8 Front pipe-to-catalytic converter joint

10 Slacken the catalytic converter-to-intermediate pipe clamping ring bolts and disengage the clamp from the flange joint.

11 Free the catalytic converter from the intermediate pipe, then withdraw it from underneath the vehicle. Do not drop the catalytic converter, as it contains a fragile ceramic element. Recover the wire-mesh gasket from the front pipe joint.

Intermediate pipe - 954 and 1124 cc models

12 Undo the two nuts securing the front pipe flange joint to the intermediate pipe. Recover the springs and spring cups and withdraw the bolts.

13 Slacken the clamping ring bolts and disengage the clamp from the intermediate pipe-to-tailpipe flange joint **(see illustration)**.

14 Free the intermediate pipe from its mounting rubbers, then disengage it from the tailpipe and the front pipe and remove it from underneath the vehicle. Recover the wire-mesh gasket from the front pipe joint.

Intermediate pipe - 1360 cc models

15 Slacken the clamping ring bolts and disengage the clamps from both the intermediate pipe flange joints.

16 Free the intermediate pipe from its mounting rubbers, then disengage it first from the tailpipe then the catalytic converter and remove it from underneath the vehicle.

Tailpipe

17 Slacken the intermediate pipe-to-tailpipe clamping ring bolts and disengage the clamp from the flange joint.

18 Unhook the tailpipe from its mounting rubbers and remove it from the vehicle.

18.13 Intermediate pipe-to-tailpipe clamping ring

Complete system

19 Disconnect the front pipe from the manifold as described in paragraphs 6 and 7.

20 With the aid of an assistant, free the system from its mounting rubbers and manoeuvre it out from underneath the vehicle.

Heat shield(s)

21 The heat shields are secured to the underside of the body by a mixture of nuts and bolts. Each shield can be removed once the relevant exhaust section has been removed. If the shield is being removed to gain access to a component located behind it, in some cases it may prove sufficient to remove the retaining nuts and/or bolts and simply lower the shield, without disturbing the exhaust system.

Refitting

22 Each section is refitted by a reverse of the removal sequence, noting the following points:

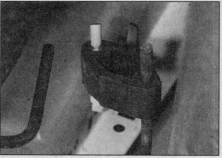

18.22 Ensure that the exhaust system is correctly located on its rubber mountings before tightening its fasteners securely

a) *Ensure that all traces of corrosion have been removed from the flanges and renew all necessary gaskets.*

b) *Inspect the rubber mountings for signs of damage or deterioration and renew as necessary.*

c) *Prior to assembling the spring-loaded ball type joint, a smear of high-temperature grease should be applied to the joint mating surfaces.*

d) *On joints which are secured by clamping rings, apply a smear of exhaust system jointing paste to the joint mating surfaces, to ensure an air-tight seal. Tighten the clamping ring nuts evenly and progressively to the specified torque, so that the clearance between the clamp halves is equal on either side.*

e) *Prior to tightening the exhaust system fasteners, ensure that all rubber mountings are correctly located and that there is adequate clearance between the exhaust system and vehicle underbody* **(see illustration)**.

Chapter 4 Part C:
Fuel/exhaust systems - multi-point petrol injection models

Contents

Degrees of difficulty

Easy, suitable for novice with little experience	**Fairly easy,** suitable for beginner with some experience	**Fairly difficult,** suitable for competent DIY mechanic	**Difficult,** suitable for experienced DIY mechanic	**Very difficult,** suitable for expert DIY or professional

Specifications

System type
1294 cc (MFZ engine) models . . . . Magneti Marelli 8P
1360 cc models:
  K6B and KFZ engines . . . . Bosch Motronic MP3.1
  KFX engine . . . . Magneti Marelli 1AP
1587 cc (8-valve) models:
  NFY engines . . . . Bosch Motronic MP5.1
  NFZ engines (pre-July 1996) . . . . Bosch Motronic MP5.1
  NFZ engines (July-1996 on) . . . . Bosch Motronic MP5.2
  NFW engines . . . . Magneti Marelli 8P
1587 cc (16-valve) models:
  NFX engines . . . . Magneti Marelli 1AP
Note: *Refer to Chapter 2A for further information on engine code identification.*

Fuel system data
Fuel pump type . . . . Electric, immersed in tank
Fuel pump regulated constant pressure (approximate) . . . . - 2.5 to 3.0 bars
Specified idle speed . . . . 900 ± 50 rpm (not adjustable - controlled by ECU)
Idle mixture CO content:
  1360 cc (K6B engine) models . . . . 1.0 to 2.0 % (adjustable via mixture potentiometer)
  All other models . . . . Less than 1.0 % (not adjustable - controlled by ECU)

Recommended fuel
Minimum octane rating:
  1360 cc (K6B engine) models . . . . 95 RON unleaded or 97 RON leaded
  All other models . . . . 95 RON unleaded **only**

4C

Torque wrench settings

	Nm	lbf ft
Inlet manifold retaining nuts		
8-valve models	8	6
16-valve models	10	7
Exhaust manifold retaining nuts - 1294 and 1587 cc (8-valve) models	16	12
Exhaust manifold retaining nuts - 1360 cc models (see Section 16):		
Long nuts (early models)	16	12
Short nuts (later models)	25	18
Exhaust manifold retaining nuts - 16-valve models:		
Stage 1	10	7
Stage 2	20	15
Exhaust system fasteners:		
Front pipe-to-manifold nuts	30	22
Front pipe-to-intermediate pipe/catalytic converter nuts	10	7
Clamping ring nuts	15	11

1 General information and precautions

The fuel system consists of a fuel tank mounted under the rear of the car (with an electric fuel pump immersed in it), a fuel filter, fuel feed and return lines. The fuel pump supplies fuel to the fuel rail, which acts as a reservoir for the four fuel injectors which inject fuel into the inlet tracts. A fuel filter is incorporated in the feed line from the pump to the fuel rail, to ensure that the fuel supplied to the injectors is clean.

Refer to Section 6 for further information on the operation of the relevant fuel injection system and Section 17 for information on the exhaust system. Throughout this Section, it is occasionally necessary to identify vehicles by their engine codes rather than engine capacity. Refer to Chapter 2A for further information on engine code identification.

⚠ *Warning: Many of the procedures in this Chapter require the removal of fuel lines and connections, which may result in some fuel spillage. Before carrying out any operation on the fuel system, refer to the precautions given in "Safety first!" at the beginning of this manual and follow them implicitly. Petrol is a highly-dangerous and volatile liquid and the precautions necessary when handling it cannot be overstressed.*
Note: *Residual pressure will remain in the fuel*

2.1 Slacken the retaining clip and disconnect the duct from the air cleaner housing - 1294 cc model

lines long after the vehicle was last used. Before disconnecting any fuel line, depressurise the fuel system as described in Section 7.

2 Air cleaner assembly - removal and refitting

Removal

1294 cc models

1 Slacken the retaining clip and disconnect the throttle housing duct from the air cleaner housing **(see illustration)**. Where a crimped-type hose clip or tie is fitted, cut and discard it; replace it with a standard worm-drive hose clip or new cable tie (as applicable) on refitting.
2 Slacken and remove the air cleaner housing retaining nuts and bolts and lift the housing out of the engine compartment.

1360 and 1587 cc models

3 Slacken the retaining clips (where fitted) and disconnect the vacuum and breather hoses from the top of the air cleaner housing. Where crimped-type hose clips or ties are fitted, cut and discard them; replace them with standard worm-drive hose clips or new cable ties when refitting.
4 Slacken the retaining clips or ties and free the throttle housing duct from the top of the air cleaner housing. Also remove the inlet duct from the side of the housing. If necessary, free the duct from the throttle housing and remove it, along with its sealing ring.
5 Lift the air cleaner housing assembly out of the engine compartment.
6 To remove the inlet duct assembly, drill out the rivets securing the duct to the crossmember, then release the fastener securing the rear of the duct to the cylinder head and remove the duct and hose assembly from the engine compartment.

Refitting

1294 cc models

7 Refitting is a reversal of the removal procedure.

1360 and 1587 cc models

8 Refitting is a reversal of the removal

procedure. Ensure that all hoses are properly reconnected and that all ducts are correctly seated and securely held by their retaining clips. Also note the following:
a) Ensure that the air cleaner housing locating peg is correctly engaged with its mounting on the top of the transmission.
b) If the inlet duct was removed, secure it to the crossmember with new pop-rivets.

3 Accelerator cable - removal, refitting and adjustment

Refer to Chapter 4A, Section 7, substituting "throttle housing" for all references to the carburettor.

4 Accelerator pedal - removal and refitting

Refer to Chapter 4A, Section 8.

5 Unleaded petrol - general information and usage

Note: *The information given in this Chapter is correct at the time of writing. If updated information is thought to be required, check with a Peugeot dealer. If travelling abroad, consult one of the motoring organisations (or a similar authority) for advice on the petrols available and their suitability for your vehicle.*

The fuel recommended by Peugeot is given in the Specifications Section of this Chapter.

All Peugeot 106 multi-point injection models are designed to run on fuel with a minimum octane rating of 95 (RON). With the exception of the 1360 cc (K6B engine) model which does not have a catalytic converter, all models have catalytic converters and must therefore be run on unleaded fuel **only**. Under no circumstances should leaded fuel be used on a catalytic converter-equipped vehicle. On the 1360 cc model without a catalytic converter, however, both unleaded and leaded fuel can be used without modification.

6 Fuel injection systems - general information

Note: *The fuel injection ECU is of the "self-learning" type, meaning that as it operates, it also monitors and stores the settings which give optimum engine performance under all operating conditions. When the battery is disconnected, these settings are lost and the ECU reverts to the base settings programmed into its memory at the factory. On restarting, this may lead to the engine running/idling roughly for a short while, until the ECU has re-learned the optimum settings. This process is best accomplished by taking the vehicle on a road test (for approximately 15 minutes), covering all engine speeds and loads, concentrating mainly in the 2,500 to 3,500 rpm region.*

Magneti Marelli 1AP system

The Magneti Marelli 1AP engine management (fuel injection/ignition) system is fitted to 1360 cc models from July 1996 onward and to 1587 cc (16-valve) models. The system incorporates a closed-loop catalytic converter and an evaporative emission control system and complies with the very latest emission control standards. Refer to Chapter 5B for information on the ignition side of the system; the fuel side of the system operates as follows.

The fuel pump supplies fuel from the tank to the fuel rail, via a replaceable cartridge filter mounted underneath the rear of the vehicle. The pump itself is mounted inside the fuel tank, the pump motor is permanently immersed in fuel, to keep it cool. The fuel rail is mounted directly above the fuel injectors and acts as a fuel reservoir.

Fuel rail supply pressure is controlled by the pressure regulator, mounted at the end of the fuel rail. The regulator contains a spring-loaded valve, which lifts to allow excess fuel to return to the tank when the optimum operating pressure of the fuel system is exceeded (eg during low speed, light load cruising). The regulator also contains a diaphragm which is supplied with vacuum from the inlet manifold. This allows the regulator to reduce the fuel supply pressure during light load, high manifold depression conditions (e.g. during idling or deceleration) to prevent excess fuel being 'sucked' through the open injectors. Note that on later models, a fuel pressure regulator is not fitted; a fuel pressure monitoring point is provided at the left hand end of the fuel rails

The fuel injectors are electromagnetic pintle valves, which spray atomised fuel into the combustion chambers under the control of the engine management system ECU. There are four injectors, one per cylinder, mounted in the inlet manifold close to the cylinder head. Each injector is mounted at an angle that allows it to spray fuel directly onto the back of the inlet valve(s). The ECU controls the volume of fuel injected by varying the length of time for which each injector is held open.

The fuel injection system is of the semi-sequential type, whereby fuel is injected into each cylinder's inlet tract twice per engine cycle; once during the power stroke and once during the induction stroke.

The electrical control system consists of the ECU, along with the following sensors:
a) *Throttle potentiometer - informs the ECU of the throttle valve position and the rate of throttle opening/closing.*
b) *Coolant temperature sensor - informs the ECU of engine temperature.*
c) *Inlet air temperature sensor - informs the ECU of the temperature of the air passing through the throttle housing.*
d) *Lambda sensor - informs the ECU of the oxygen content of the exhaust gases (explained in greater detail in Part E of this Chapter).*
e) *Manifold Absolute Pressure (MAP) sensor - informs the ECU of the load on the engine (expressed in terms of inlet manifold vacuum).*
f) *Crankshaft sensor - informs the ECU of engine speed and crankshaft angular position.*
g) *Vehicle speed sensor - informs the ECU of the vehicle speed.*
h) *Knock sensor - informs the ECU of pre-ignition (detonation) within the cylinders.*

Signals from each of the sensors are compared by the ECU and, based on this information, the ECU selects the response appropriate to those values and controls the fuel injectors (varying the pulse width - the length of time the injectors are held open - to provide a richer or weaker air/fuel mixture, as appropriate). The air/fuel mixture is constantly varied by the ECU, to provide the best settings for cranking, starting (with either a hot or cold engine) and engine warm-up, idle, cruising and acceleration.

The ECU also has full control over the engine idle speed, via a stepper motor fitted to the throttle body. The stepper motor pushrod controls the amount of air passing through a by-pass drilling at the side of the throttle. When the throttle valve is closed (accelerator pedal released), the ECU uses the motor to alter the position of the pushrod, controlling the amount of air bypassing the throttle valve and so controlling the idle speed. The ECU also carries out 'fine tuning' of the idle speed by varying the ignition timing to increase or reduce the torque of the engine as it is idling. This helps to stabilise the idle speed when electrical or mechanical loads (such as headlights, air conditioning etc) are switched on and off.

On certain models, the throttle housing is fitted with an electric heating element. The heater is supplied with current by the ECU, warming the throttle body on cold starts to help prevent icing of the throttle valve.

The exhaust and evaporative loss emission control systems are described in more detail in Chapter 4E.

If there is any abnormality in any of the readings obtained from either the coolant temperature sensor, the inlet air temperature sensor or the lambda sensor, the ECU enters its 'back-up' mode. If this happens, the erroneous sensor signal is overridden and the ECU assumes a pre-programmed 'back-up' value, which will allow the engine to continue running, albeit at reduced efficiency. If the ECU enters this mode, the warning lamp on the instrument panel will be illuminated and the relevant fault code will be stored in the ECU memory.

If the warning light illuminates, the vehicle should be taken to a Peugeot dealer at the earliest opportunity. Once there, a complete test of the engine management system can be carried out, using a special electronic diagnostic test unit, which is plugged into the system's diagnostic connector.

Magneti Marelli 8P system

The Magneti Marelli 8P engine management (fuel injection/ignition) system is fitted to all 1294 cc models and to 1587 cc (NFW engine) models. The system is very similar in operation to the Magneti Marelli 1AP system described previously but in addition, on all models, the throttle housing is fitted with an electric heating element. The heater is supplied with current by the ECU, warming the throttle body on cold starts to help prevent icing of the throttle valve.

Bosch Motronic MP3.1 system

The Bosch Motronic MP3.1 engine management (fuel injection/ignition) system is fitted to all 1360 cc models; however, there are two different versions of the system available. On later models (fitted with the KFZ engine) the system incorporates a closed-loop catalytic converter and an evaporative emissions control system and complies to the very latest emission control standards. Earlier models (fitted with the K6B engine) are not fitted with either a catalytic converter or the evaporative emission control system. Refer to Chapter 5B for information on the ignition side of the system. The fuel side of the system operates as follows.

The fuel pump, immersed in the fuel tank, pumps fuel from the fuel tank to the fuel rail, via a filter mounted underneath the rear of the vehicle. Fuel supply pressure is controlled by the pressure regulator in the fuel rail, which lifts to allow excess fuel to return to the tank when the optimum operating pressure of the fuel system is exceeded.

The electrical control system consists of the ECU, along with the following sensors:
a) *Throttle potentiometer - informs the ECU of the throttle valve position and the rate of throttle opening/closing.*
b) *Coolant temperature sensor - informs the ECU of engine temperature.*

4C

c) *Inlet air temperature sensor - informs the ECU of the temperature of the air passing through the air cleaner housing.*

d) *Crankshaft sensor - informs the ECU of the crankshaft position and speed of rotation.*

e) *Manifold Absolute Pressure (MAP) sensor - informs the ECU of the load on the engine.*

f) *Lambda (oxygen) sensor (KFZ engine only) - informs ECU of oxygen content of the exhaust gases (explained in greater detail in Part E of this Chapter).*

All the above signals are compared by the ECU to values programmed (mapped) in its memory. Based on this information, the ECU selects the response appropriate to those values and controls the fuel injectors (varying their pulse width - the length of time the injectors are held open) - to provide a richer or weaker mixture, as appropriate. The mixture and idle speed are constantly monitored by the ECU, to provide the best settings for cranking, starting (with either a hot or cold engine) and engine warm-up, idle, cruising and acceleration.

The ECU also has full control over the engine idle speed, via an auxiliary air valve which bypasses the throttle valve. When the throttle valve is closed, the ECU controls the opening of the valve, which in turn regulates the amount of air entering the manifold and so controls the idle speed.

The throttle housing is fitted with an electric heating element; the heater is supplied with current by the ECU and warms the throttle housing on cold starts to prevent possible icing of the throttle valve.

On KFZ engine models, the ECU also controls the exhaust and evaporative emission control systems which are described in detail in Part E of this Chapter.

If there is an abnormality in any of the readings from the system sensors, the ECU enters a back-up mode. If this happens, it ignores the sensor signal and assumes a pre-programmed value which will allow the engine to continue running, albeit at reduced efficiency. If the ECU enters this back-up mode, the warning light on the instrument panel will be illuminated and the relevant fault code will be stored in the ECU memory.

If the warning light comes on, the vehicle should be taken to a Peugeot dealer at the earliest opportunity. Once there, a complete test of the engine management system can be carried out, using a special electronic diagnostic test unit which is simply plugged into the system's diagnostic connector.

Bosch Motronic MP5.1 and MP 5.2 systems

1587 cc (NFY and NFZ engine) models are equipped with the Bosch Motronic MP5.1 or MP5.2 engine management (fuel injection/ ignition) system. The MP5.1 system was fitted to all NFY engine models and to NFZ engine models up to approximately July 1996. The MP5.2 system replaced the MP5.1 system on later NFZ engine models. Both systems are very similar in operation to the Magneti Marelli 1AP system described previously, but with the following differences.

The MP5.1 and MP5.2 systems employ 'banked' fuel injection, where all four injectors are activated simultaneously. Fuel is injected into each cylinder's inlet tract on every engine stroke and is then drawn into the combustion chamber during the induction stroke.

On the MP5.1 system, ECU control of the engine idle speed is by means of an auxiliary air valve which bypasses the throttle valve. When the throttle valve is closed, the ECU controls the opening of the air valve, which in turn regulates the amount of air entering the manifold and so controls the idle speed.

On both systems the throttle housing is fitted with an electric heating element. The heater is supplied with current by the ECU, warming the throttle body on cold starts to help prevent icing of the throttle valve.

The MP5.1 system is not fitted with a knock sensor.

7 Fuel system - depressurisation

Note: *Refer to the warning note in Section 1 before proceeding.*

⚠ **Warning: The following procedure will merely relieve the pressure in the fuel system - remember that fuel will still be present in the system components and take precautions accordingly before disconnecting any of them.**

1 The fuel system referred to in this Section is defined as the tank-mounted fuel pump, the fuel filter, the fuel injectors, the fuel rail and the pressure regulator and the metal pipes and flexible hoses of the fuel lines between these components. All these contain fuel, which will be under pressure while the engine is running and/or while the ignition is switched on. The pressure will remain for some time after the ignition has been switched off and must be relieved before any of these components are disturbed for servicing work.

2 Disconnect the battery negative terminal (refer to *"Disconnecting the battery"* in the Reference Section of this manual).

3 Place a suitable container beneath the relevant connection/union to be disconnected and have a large rag ready to soak up any escaping fuel not being caught by the container.

4 Slowly loosen the connection or union nut (as applicable) to avoid a sudden release of pressure and position the rag around the connection to catch any fuel spray which may be expelled. Once the pressure is released, disconnect the fuel line. Plug the openings, to minimise fuel loss and prevent the entry of dirt into the fuel system.

8 Fuel pump - removal and refitting

Refer to Chapter 4B, Section 9.

9 Fuel gauge sender unit - removal and refitting

Refer to Chapter 4A, Section 5 noting that there are no fuel pipe connections to the sender unit.

10 Fuel tank - removal and refitting

Refer to Chapter 4A, Section 6, noting that it will be necessary to depressurise the fuel system as the feed and return hoses are disconnected (see Section 7). It will also be necessary to disconnect the wiring connector from the fuel pump, prior to lowering the tank out of position.

11 Fuel injection systems - testing and adjustment

Testing

1 If a fault appears in the fuel injection system, first ensure that all the system wiring connectors are securely connected and free of corrosion. Then ensure that the fault is not due to poor maintenance; ie, check that the air cleaner filter element is clean, the spark plugs are in good condition and correctly gapped, the cylinder compression pressures are correct, the ignition timing is correct and that the engine breather hoses are clear and undamaged, referring to Chapters 1A, 2A and 5B for further information.

2 If these checks fail to reveal the cause of the problem, the vehicle should be taken to a suitably-equipped Peugeot dealer for testing. A wiring block connector is incorporated in the engine management circuit, into which a special electronic diagnostic tester can be plugged; the connector is clipped onto the side of the ECU mounting bracket. The tester will locate the fault quickly and simply, alleviating the need to test all the system components individually, which is a time-consuming operation that carries a high risk of damaging the ECU.

Adjustment

3 On 1360 cc (K6B engine) models without a catalytic converter, the idle mixture (exhaust gas CO level) is adjustable. Refer to Chapter 1A for information on the adjustment procedure. The engine idle speed is not adjustable and is fully under the control of the ECU.

4 On all other models, experienced home mechanics with a considerable amount of skill and equipment (including a good-quality tachometer and a good-quality, carefully-calibrated exhaust gas analyser) may be able to *check* the exhaust CO level and the idle speed. However, if these are found to be in need of *adjustment*, the car **must** be taken to a suitably-equipped Peugeot dealer. Neither the mixture (exhaust gas CO level) or idle speed are adjustable and should either be incorrect, a fault must be present in the fuel injection system.

12 Throttle housing - removal and refitting

Removal

1 Disconnect the battery negative terminal (refer to *"Disconnecting the battery"* in the Reference Section of this manual).

2 Slacken the retaining clip, then disconnect the inlet duct from the throttle housing and recover the sealing ring. Where a crimped-type hose clip or tie fitted, cut and discard it; replace it with a standard worm-drive hose clip or new cable tie on refitting. According to engine, it may be beneficial to remove the complete air cleaner assembly as described in Section 2 for improved access to the throttle housing.

3 Disconnect the accelerator inner cable from the throttle cam, then withdraw the outer cable from the mounting bracket, along with its flat washer and spring clip.

4 Depress the retaining clips and disconnect the wiring connectors from the throttle potentiometer, the electric heating element, the air temperature sensor and idle control stepper motor (as applicable).

5 Release the retaining clips (where fitted) and disconnect all the relevant vacuum and breather hoses from the throttle housing. Make identification marks on the hoses, to ensure they are connected correctly on refitting.

6 Slacken and remove the three retaining screws and remove the throttle housing from the inlet manifold. Where fitted, recover the O-ring from manifold and discard it; a new one must be used when refitting.

Refitting

7 Refitting is a reversal of the relevant removal procedure, noting the following points:
a) On 1294 cc models, ensure that the inlet manifold and insulating spacer mating surfaces are clean and dry, then apply a smear of suitable sealant to the spacer surface. Refit the throttle housing and securely tighten its retaining screws.
b) On 1360 cc and 1587 cc models, fit a new O-ring to the manifold, then refit the throttle housing and securely tighten its screws.

c) Ensure that all hoses are correctly reconnected and, where necessary, are securely held in position by the retaining clips.
d) Ensure that all wiring is correctly routed and the connectors are securely reconnected.
e) On completion, adjust the accelerator cable using the information in Section 3.

13 Bosch Motronic system components - removal and refitting

Fuel rail and injectors

Note: *Refer to the warning note in Section 1 before proceeding.*
Note: *If a faulty injector is suspected, before condemning the injector, it is worth trying the effect of one of the proprietary injector-cleaning treatments.*

1 Disconnect the battery negative terminal (refer to *"Disconnecting the battery"* in the Reference Section of this manual).

2 Disconnect the vacuum pipe from the fuel pressure regulator.

3 Bearing in mind the information given in Section 7, slacken the retaining clips and disconnect the fuel feed and return hoses from either end of the fuel rail. Where the original crimped-type hose clips are still fitted, cut them off and discard; replace them with standard worm-drive hose clips on refitting.

4 Depress the retaining tangs and disconnect the wiring connectors from the four injectors.

5 Slacken and remove the fuel rail retaining bolts and the two retaining nuts, then carefully ease the fuel rail and injector assembly out from the inlet manifold and remove it from the vehicle. Remove the O-rings from the end of each injector and discard them; they must be renewed whenever they are disturbed.

6 Slide out the retaining clip(s) and remove the relevant injector(s) from the fuel rail. Remove the upper O-ring from each disturbed injector and discard; any O-rings which are disturbed during removal must be renewed.

7 Refitting is a reversal of the removal procedure, noting the following points:
a) Fit new O-rings to all injector unions disturbed on removal.
b) Apply a smear of engine oil to the O-rings to aid installation, then ease the injectors and fuel rail into position, ensuring that none of the O-rings are displaced.
c) On completion, start the engine and check for fuel leaks.

Fuel pressure regulator

Note: *Refer to the warning note in Section 1 before proceeding.*

8 Disconnect the vacuum pipe from the regulator.

9 Place a wad of rag over the regulator, to catch any fuel spray which may be released, then remove the retaining clip and ease the regulator out from the fuel rail.

10 Refitting is a reversal of the removal procedure. Examine the regulator seal for signs of damage or deterioration and renew if necessary.

Throttle potentiometer

11 Disconnect the battery negative terminal (refer to *"Disconnecting the battery"* in the Reference Section of this manual).

12 Depress the retaining clip and disconnect the wiring connector from the throttle potentiometer.

13 Slacken and remove the two retaining screws, then disengage the potentiometer from the throttle valve spindle and remove it from the vehicle.

14 Refitting is a reverse of the removal procedure, ensuring that the potentiometer is correctly engaged with the throttle valve spindle.

Electronic Control Unit (ECU)

15 The ECU is located on the right-hand side of the engine compartment, underneath a large plastic cover.

16 Disconnect the battery negative terminal (refer to *"Disconnecting the battery"* in the Reference Section of this manual).

17 Unclip the cover from the mounting plate, then lift the retaining clip and disconnect the wiring connector from the ECU. Slacken and remove the ECU retaining bolts and remove it from the vehicle. On 1360 cc models, it will also be necessary to disconnect the vacuum hose.

18 Refitting is a reverse of the removal procedure, ensuring that the wiring connector is securely reconnected.

Idle speed mixture adjustment potentiometer - 1360 cc (K6B engine) models

19 The idle speed mixture adjustment potentiometer is situated on the right-hand side of the engine compartment, on the underside of the ECU bracket. To remove it, first disconnect the battery negative terminal (refer to *"Disconnecting the battery"* in the Reference Section of this manual).

20 Depress the retaining tangs and disconnect the wiring connector, then undo the retaining screw and remove the potentiometer from the vehicle.

21 Refitting is the reverse of removal. On completion check and, if necessary, adjust the idle mixture setting (exhaust gas CO level) as described in Chapter 1A.

Idle speed auxiliary air valve

22 The auxiliary air valve is mounted on the underside of the inlet manifold.

23 Disconnect the battery negative terminal (refer to *"Disconnecting the battery"* in the Reference Section of this manual).

24 Depress the retaining clip and disconnect the wiring connector from the air valve.

25 Slacken the retaining clips and disconnect both vacuum hoses from the end of the auxiliary air valve.

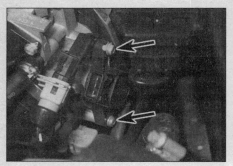

14.3 Throttle potentiometer retaining screws (arrowed)

26 Slide the valve out from its mounting rubber and remove it from the engine compartment.

27 Refitting is a reversal of the removal procedure. Examine the mounting rubber for signs of deterioration and renew it if necessary.

Manifold absolute pressure (MAP) sensor

1360 cc models

28 On 1360 cc models, the MAP sensor is an integral part of the electronic control unit (ECU). Refer to paragraphs 15 to 18 for removal and refitting details.

1587 cc models

29 On 1587 cc models, the MAP sensor is mounted on the right-hand side of the engine compartment bulkhead. To remove it, first disconnect the battery negative terminal (refer to *"Disconnecting the battery"* in the Reference Section of this manual).

30 Undo the retaining nut and free the sensor from its mounting bracket.

31 Disconnect the wiring connector and vacuum hose and remove the MAP sensor from the engine compartment.

32 Refitting is the reverse of the removal procedure.

Coolant temperature sensor

33 Refer to Chapter 3, Section 6.

Inlet air temperature sensor

34 The inlet air temperature sensor is

14.7 . . . then undo the two screws (arrowed) and remove the stepper motor from the throttle housing

14.6 Disconnect the wiring connector (arrowed) . . .

screwed into the top of the air cleaner housing. To remove the sensor, first disconnect the battery negative terminal (refer to *"Disconnecting the battery"* in the Reference Section of this manual).

35 Disconnect the wiring connector, then unscrew the sensor and remove it from the vehicle.

36 Refitting is the reverse of removal.

Crankshaft sensor

37 The crankshaft sensor is situated on the front face of the transmission clutch housing.

38 To remove the sensor, first disconnect the battery negative terminal (refer to *"Disconnecting the battery"* in the Reference Section of this manual).

39 Trace the wiring back from the sensor to the wiring connector and disconnect it from the main harness.

40 Prise out the rubber grommet, then undo the retaining bolt and withdraw the sensor from the transmission.

41 Refitting is reverse of the removal procedure, ensuring that the sensor retaining bolt is securely tightened and the grommet is correctly seated in the transmission housing.

Fuel injection system relay unit

42 The relay unit is clipped onto the underside of the ECU mounting plate, on the right-hand side of the engine compartment.

43 To remove the relay unit, first disconnect the battery negative lead (refer to *"Disconnecting the battery"* in the Reference Section of this manual).

14.9 The MAP sensor is mounted on the engine compartment bulkhead

44 Unclip the relay unit from the mounting plate, disconnect the wiring connector and remove the unit from the vehicle.

45 Refitting is the reverse of removal, ensuring that the relay unit is securely held in position by its retaining clip.

14 Magneti Marelli system components - removal and refitting

Fuel rail and injectors

1 On 1294 cc, 1360 cc and 1587 cc (8-valve) models, refer to Section 13, paragraphs 1 to 7. On 1587 cc (16-valve) models, remove the upper section of the inlet manifold as described in Section 15, then proceed as described in Section 13, paragraphs 1 to 7.

Fuel pressure regulator

2 Refer to Section 13, paragraphs 8 to 10.

Throttle potentiometer

3 Refer to Section 13, paragraphs 11 to 14 (see illustration).

Electronic Control Unit (ECU)

4 Refer to Section 13, paragraphs 15 to 18.

Idle speed control stepper motor

5 The idle speed control stepper motor is located on the top of the throttle housing assembly. To remove the motor, first disconnect the battery negative terminal (refer to *"Disconnecting the battery"* in the Reference Section of this manual).

6 Release the retaining clip and disconnect the wiring connector from the motor (see illustration).

7 Slacken and remove the two retaining screws and withdraw the motor from the throttle housing (see illustration).

8 Refitting is a reversal of the removal procedure.

Manifold absolute pressure (MAP) sensor

9 The MAP sensor is mounted either on the engine compartment bulkhead, just behind the inlet manifold (see illustration), or alternatively it may be mounted directly on the inlet manifold casting. To remove the sensor, first disconnect the battery negative terminal (refer to *"Disconnecting the battery"* in the Reference Section of this manual).

10 Where the sensor is mounted on the bulkhead, undo the retaining nut and free the sensor from its location. On some models, the sensor may be riveted to the bulkhead; if this is the case, drill out the rivet. Where the sensor is mounted on the inlet manifold, remove the securing screws and withdraw the sensor from the manifold, recovering the sealing ring.

11 Depress the retaining clip and disconnect the wiring connector and vacuum hose from the sensor. Remove the sensor from the engine compartment.

12 Refitting is a reversal of the removal procedure. Where necessary, secure the sensor in position with a new rivet (or a suitable self-tapping screw).

Coolant temperature sensor

13 Refer to Chapter 3, Section 6.

Inlet air temperature sensor

14 The inlet air temperature sensor is located in the base of the throttle housing.

15 Trace the wiring back from the sensor and disconnect it at the wiring connector.

16 Undo the two retaining screws and remove the sensor from the throttle housing. Examine the sensor O-ring for signs of damage or deterioration and renew if necessary.

17 Refitting is a reversal of the removal procedure; where necessary, use a new O-ring.

Crankshaft sensor

18 Refer to Section 13, paragraphs 37 to 41. Remove the air cleaner housing to improve access to the sensor.

Fuel injection system relay unit

19 Refer to Section 13, paragraphs 42 to 45.

Knock sensor

20 The knock sensor is screwed onto the rear face of the cylinder block.

21 To gain access to the sensor, firmly apply the handbrake, then jack up the front of the vehicle and support it on axle stands (see "Jacking and vehicle support"). Access to the sensor can then be gained from underneath the vehicle.

22 Trace the wiring back from the sensor to its wiring connector and disconnect it from the main loom.

23 Slacken and remove the bolt securing the sensor to the cylinder block and remove it from underneath the vehicle.

24 Refitting is a reversal of the removal procedure, ensuring that the sensor wiring is correctly routed and its retaining bolt securely tightened.

Throttle housing heating element

25 The throttle housing heating element is fitted to the top of the throttle housing. To remove the element, first disconnect the battery negative terminal (refer to "Disconnecting the battery" in the Reference Section of this manual).

26 Disconnect the accelerator inner cable from the throttle cam, then withdraw the outer cable from the mounting bracket, along with its flat washer and spring clip **(see illustration)**.

27 Disconnect the element wiring connector, then undo the retaining screw and free the wiring connector from the throttle housing **(see illustration)**.

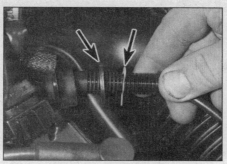

14.26 Free the accelerator cable from its mounting bracket and recover the washer and spring clip (arrowed)

28 Undo the four screws securing the accelerator cable bracket to the side of the throttle housing **(see illustration)**. Carefully remove the bracket and recover the spring from the top of the heating element.

29 Ease the heating element out from the throttle housing. Examine the O-ring for signs of damage or deterioration and renew if necessary.

30 Refitting is a reversal of the removal procedure; where necessary, use a new O-ring.

Vehicle speed sensor

31 The vehicle speed sensor is an integral part of the speedometer drive housing. Refer to Chapter 7A or 7B for removal and refitting details.

15 Inlet manifold - removal and refitting

Removal

1 Disconnect the battery negative terminal (refer to "Disconnecting the battery" in the Reference Section of this manual).

2 Carry out the operations listed in paragraphs 2 to 5 of Section 12. Proceed as described under the relevant sub-heading.

1294 cc models

3 Release the retaining clips (where fitted) and disconnect all the relevant vacuum and

14.28 Accelerator cable bracket is retained by four screws (arrowed)

14.27 Disconnect the wiring connector, then undo the retaining screw and free the connector from its mounting bracket

breather hoses from the manifold. Make identification marks on the hoses to ensure that they are connected correctly on refitting.

4 Bearing in mind the information given in Section 7, slacken the retaining clips and disconnect the fuel feed and return hoses from the fuel rail. Where the original crimped-type Peugeot hose clips are still fitted, cut them off and discard; replace them with standard worm-drive hose clips on refitting.

5 Depress the retaining tangs and disconnect the wiring connectors from the four injectors. Free the wiring from any relevant retaining clips and position it clear of the manifold.

6 Undo the retaining bolts and remove the support brackets from the right- and left-hand ends of the manifold.

7 Undo the manifold retaining nuts and withdraw the manifold from the engine compartment. Recover the manifold gaskets and discard them; new ones must be used on refitting.

1360 and 1587 cc (8-valve) models

8 Depress the retaining clip and disconnect the wiring connector from the idle speed auxiliary air valve, which is mounted on the underside of the manifold. Slacken the retaining clip and disconnect the vacuum hose connecting the valve to the inlet duct, leaving the valve free to be removed with the manifold.

9 Release the retaining clips (where fitted) and disconnect all the relevant vacuum and breather hoses from the manifold. Make identification marks on the hoses, to ensure that they are connected correctly on refitting.

10 Bearing in mind the information given in Section 7, slacken the retaining clips and disconnect the fuel feed and return hoses from the fuel rail. Where the original crimped-type Peugeot hose clips are still fitted, cut them off and discard; replace them with standard worm-drive hose clips on refitting.

11 Depress the retaining tangs and disconnect the wiring connectors from the four injectors. Free the wiring from any relevant retaining clips and position it clear of the manifold.

12 Where necessary, undo the retaining bolts and remove the support bracket from the underside of the manifold.

4C

13 Undo the manifold retaining nuts and withdraw the manifold from the engine compartment. Recover the four manifold seals and discard them; new ones must be used on refitting.

1587 cc (16-valve) models

14 Chock the rear wheels then jack up the front of the vehicle and support it on axle stands (see *"Jacking and Vehicle Support"*).

15 Working under the vehicle and using a socket and long extension bar, undo the two rear bolts securing the inlet manifold upper part to the lower part.

16 From above, undo the centre bolt and the two remaining bolts, one each side, then lift off the upper part of the inlet manifold, complete with throttle housing.

17 Bearing in mind the information given in Section 7, slacken the retaining clips and disconnect the fuel feed and return hoses from the fuel rail. Where the original crimped-type hose clips are still fitted, cut them off and discard; replace them with standard worm-drive hose clips on refitting.

18 Depress the retaining tangs and disconnect the wiring connectors from the four injectors. Free the wiring from any relevant retaining clips and position it clear of the manifold.

19 Slacken and remove the fuel rail retaining bolts/nuts, then carefully ease the fuel rail and injector assembly out from the inlet manifold and remove it from the vehicle. Remove the O-rings from the end of each injector and discard them; they must be renewed whenever they are disturbed.

20 Release the retaining clamps and free the fuel supply pipes from the rear of the manifold lower part.

21 Undo the retaining nuts securing the manifold lower part to the cylinder head and withdraw the manifold from the engine compartment. Recover the gasket(s) or manifold seals according to fitment and discard them; new ones must be used on refitting.

Refitting

22 Refitting is a reverse of the relevant removal procedure, noting the following points:

a) Ensure that the manifold and cylinder head mating surfaces are clean and dry.

b) On 1294 cc models, fit the new gaskets onto the studs, then refit the manifold and tighten its retaining nuts to the specified torque.

c) On 1360 and 1587 cc models, locate the new seals in their recesses in the manifold. Refit the manifold and tighten its retaining nuts to the specified torque.

d) On 1587 cc (16-valve) models, fit new O-rings to all injector unions disturbed on removal. Apply a smear of engine oil to the O-rings to aid installation, then ease the injectors and fuel rail into position, ensuring that none of the O-rings are displaced.

e) Ensure that all relevant hoses are reconnected to their original positions and are securely held (where necessary) by the retaining clips.

16 Exhaust manifold - removal and refitting

Removal

1294 cc models

1 Remove the air cleaner housing as described in Section 2.

2 Slacken and remove the retaining screws and remove the shroud from the top of the exhaust manifold.

3 Chock the rear wheels then jack up the front of the vehicle and support it on axle stands (see *"Jacking and Vehicle Support"*).

4 Slacken and remove the bolt securing the front pipe in position.

5 Undo the nuts securing the exhaust front pipe to the manifold, then free the front pipe and recover the gasket.

6 Undo the eight retaining nuts securing the manifold to the head.

7 Manoeuvre the manifold out of the engine compartment and discard the manifold gaskets.

1360 cc models

8 Slacken and remove the retaining screws and remove the shroud from the top of the exhaust manifold.

9 Chock the rear wheels then jack up the front of the vehicle and support it on axle stands (see *"Jacking and Vehicle Support"*).

10 Unscrew the nut securing the front pipe to its mounting stud and recover the spring cup and spring.

11 Undo the nuts securing the exhaust front pipe to the manifold, then free the front pipe and recover the gasket.

12 Undo the eight retaining nuts securing the manifold to the head. Manoeuvre the manifold out of the engine compartment and discard the manifold gaskets.

13 Note that on later models the manifold retaining nuts have been modified and what are termed "short nuts" are now fitted in place of the earlier "long nuts". To determine the type fitted, temporarily refit the manifold and gaskets over the studs and screw on a retaining nut. If the long nuts are fitted, there will be virtually no stud thread protruding past the end of the nut. With the short nuts there will be two or three turns of stud thread visible. If any nuts are damaged, all eight should be replaced with the later type short nuts. Note also that the torque setting for each type is different (see Specifications).

1587 cc (8-valve) models

14 Slacken and remove the retaining screws and remove the shroud from the top of the exhaust manifold.

15 Chock the rear wheels then jack up the front of the vehicle and support it on axle stands (see *"Jacking and Vehicle Support"*).

16 Slacken and remove the bolt securing the front pipe in position.

17 Undo the nuts securing the exhaust front pipe to the manifold, then free the front pipe and recover the gasket.

18 Undo the eight retaining nuts securing the manifold to the head. Manoeuvre the manifold out of the engine compartment and discard the manifold gaskets.

1587 cc (16-valve) models

19 Remove the air cleaner housing as described in Section 2.

20 Slacken and remove the retaining screws and remove the shroud from the top of the exhaust manifold.

21 Pull out the dipstick then remove the upper section of the dipstick tube.

22 Chock the rear wheels then jack up the front of the vehicle and support it on axle stands (see *"Jacking and Vehicle Support"*).

23 Remove the catalytic converter as described in Section 17.

24 Undo the four nuts securing the front pipe to the manifold.

25 Unscrew the nut securing the front pipe to the transmission mounting stud and recover the spring cup and spring. Move the front pipe so that the mounting stud engages with the elongated slot on the mounting bracket then withdraw the front pipe from under the car. Recover the pipe-to-manifold gasket.

26 Trace the wiring back from the lambda (oxygen) sensor to its wiring connector and disconnect the connector from the main wiring harness.

27 Undo the ten retaining nuts securing the manifold to the cylinder head. Manoeuvre the manifold out of the engine compartment and discard the manifold gasket.

Refitting

28 Refitting is the reverse of the removal procedure, noting the following points:

a) Examine all the exhaust manifold studs for signs of damage and corrosion. Remove all traces of corrosion and repair or renew any damaged studs. On 1360 cc models, refer to the information contained in paragraph 13 above concerning the different nut types.

b) Ensure that the manifold and cylinder head sealing faces are clean and flat and fit the new manifold gaskets. On early 1360 cc and 1587 cc (8-valve) models, fibre gaskets are used, whereas on later units the gaskets are of stainless steel. Note that the two types must not be mixed on an engine.

c) If the later type stainless steel gaskets are being used, ensure that the gasket is fitted with the raised sealing surface on the gasket face toward the manifold.

d) Tighten the manifold retaining nuts to the specified torque. On 1587 cc (16-valve) models, tighten the nuts in the sequence shown **(see illustration)**.

e) Reconnect the front pipe to the manifold using the information given in Section 17.

17 Exhaust system - general information and component renewal

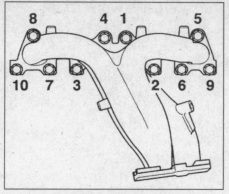

16.28 Exhaust manifold retaining nut tightening sequence - 1587 cc (16-valve) models

General information

1 On 1360 cc models without a catalytic converter, the exhaust system consists of three sections; the front pipe, the intermediate pipe and silencer box and the tailpipe and main silencer box. All exhaust sections are joined by a flanged joint. The front pipe joints are secured by nuts and bolts, the intermediate pipe joint being of the spring-loaded ball type, to allow for movement in the exhaust system. The intermediate pipe-to-tailpipe joint is secured by a clamping ring.

2 On all other models, the exhaust system consists of four sections; the front pipe, the catalytic converter, the intermediate pipe and silencer box and the tailpipe and main silencer box. All exhaust sections are connected by flanged joints. The front pipe joints are secured by nuts and bolts, the catalytic converter joint being of the spring-loaded ball type, to allow for movement in the exhaust system. The catalytic converter-to-intermediate pipe joint and the intermediate pipe-to-silencer joint are secured by a clamping ring.

3 On all models, the system is suspended throughout its entire length by rubber mountings.

Removal

4 Each exhaust section can be removed individually or, alternatively, the complete system can be removed as a unit.

5 To remove the system or part of the system, first jack up the front or rear of the car and support it on axle stands (see *"Jacking and Vehicle Support"*). Alternatively, position the car over an inspection pit, or on car ramps.

Front pipe

6 On models with a catalytic converter, trace the wiring back from the lambda (oxygen) sensor to its wiring connectors, which are clipped on top of the transmission and disconnect them from the main wiring harness.

7 On 1587 cc (16-valve) models, first remove the catalytic converter as described below, to allow clearance for the front pipe to be removed rearwards. On 1360 cc and 1587 cc (16-valve) models, unscrew the nut securing

the front pipe to its mounting stud and recover the spring cup and spring.

8 On 1294 and 1587 cc (8-valve) models, slacken and remove the bolt securing the front pipe in position.

9 On all models, undo the nuts securing the exhaust front pipe to the manifold, then free the front pipe and recover the gasket.

10 Slacken and remove the two nuts securing the front pipe to the catalytic converter/intermediate pipe (as applicable) and recover the spring cups and springs. Remove the bolts, then withdraw the front pipe from underneath the vehicle, taking great care not to damage the lambda sensor (where fitted). Recover the wire-mesh gasket from the joint.

Catalytic converter

11 Undo the two nuts securing the front pipe flange joint to the catalytic converter. Recover the springs and spring cups and withdraw the bolts.

12 Slacken the catalytic converter-to-intermediate pipe clamping ring bolts and disengage the clamp from the flange joint.

13 Free the catalytic converter from the intermediate pipe, then withdraw it from underneath the vehicle. Do not drop the catalytic converter, as it contains a fragile ceramic element. Recover the wire-mesh gasket from the front pipe joint.

Intermediate pipe - models without a catalytic converter

14 Undo the two nuts securing the front pipe flange joint to the intermediate pipe. Recover the springs and spring cups and withdraw the bolts.

15 Slacken the clamping ring bolts and disengage the clamp from the intermediate pipe-to-tailpipe flange joint.

16 Free the intermediate pipe from its mounting rubbers, then disengage it from the tailpipe and the front pipe and remove it from underneath the vehicle. Recover the wire-mesh gasket from the front pipe joint.

Intermediate pipe - models with a catalytic converter

17 Slacken the clamping ring bolts and disengage the clamps from both the intermediate pipe flange joints.

18 Free the intermediate pipe from its mounting rubbers, then disengage it first from the tailpipe then the catalytic converter and remove it from underneath the vehicle.

Tailpipe

19 Slacken the intermediate pipe-to-tailpipe clamping ring bolts and disengage the clamp from the flange joint.

20 Unhook the tailpipe from its mounting rubbers and remove it from the vehicle.

Complete system

21 Disconnect the front pipe from the manifold as described in paragraphs 6 to 9.

22 With the aid of an assistant, free the system from all its mounting rubbers and manoeuvre it out from underneath the vehicle.

Heat shield(s)

23 The heat shields are secured to the underside of the body by a mixture of nuts and bolts. Each shield can be removed once the relevant exhaust section has been removed. If the shield is being removed to gain access to a component located behind it, in some cases, it may prove sufficient to remove the retaining nuts and/or bolts and simply lower the shield, without disturbing the exhaust system.

Refitting

24 Each section is refitted by a reverse of the removal sequence, noting the following points:

a) Ensure that all traces of corrosion have been removed from the flanges and renew all necessary gaskets.

b) Inspect the rubber mountings for signs of damage or deterioration and renew as necessary.

c) Prior to assembling the spring-loaded ball type joint, a smear of high-temperature grease should be applied to the joint mating surfaces.

d) On joints which are secured by clamping rings, apply a smear of exhaust system jointing paste to the joint mating surfaces, to ensure a gas-tight seal. Tighten the clamping ring nuts evenly and progressively to the specified torque, so that the clearance between the clamp halves is equal on either side.

e) Prior to tightening the exhaust system fasteners, ensure that all rubber mountings are correctly located and that there is adequate clearance between the exhaust system and vehicle underbody.

4C

Notes

Chapter 4 Part D:
Fuel/exhaust systems - diesel models

Contents

Degrees of difficulty

Easy, suitable for novice with little experience		Fairly easy, suitable for beginner with some experience		Fairly difficult, suitable for competent DIY mechanic		Difficult, suitable for experienced DIY mechanic		Very difficult, suitable for expert DIY or professional	

Specifications

General

System type	Rear-mounted fuel tank, distributor fuel injection pump with integral transfer pump, indirect injection
Firing order	1-3-4-2 (No 1 at transmission end)

Fuel

Type	Commercial diesel fuel for road vehicles (DERV)
Fuel tank capacity	45 litres

Injection pump (Lucas)

Direction of rotation	Clockwise, viewed from timing belt end
Static timing:	
Engine position	No 4 cylinder at TDC (engine assembly/valve timing holes aligned - see text)
Pump position	
TUD 3	Value shown on pump (see text)
TUD 5	Sprocket hub timing groove must be aligned with the corresponding hole on the pump body
Dynamic timing (at specified idle speed):	
TUD 3	12° BTDC
TUD 5	Not available
Idle speed and anti-stall speed	See Chapter 1B
Fast idle speed:	
TUD 3	950 ± 50 rpm
TUD 5	1000 ± 100 rpm
Maximum speed:	
TUD 3	5500 rpm
TUD 5	5450 ± 100 rpm
Fast idle lever travel (between cold and hot positions)	6.0 mm

Injection pump (Bosch)

Direction of rotation	Clockwise, viewed from timing belt end
Static timing:	
Engine position	No 4 piston at TDC (engine assembly/valve timing holes aligned - see text)
Pump position	
TUD 3	Value shown on pump (see text)
TUD 5	Sprocket hub timing groove must be aligned with the corresponding hole on the pump body
Idle speed and anti-stall speed	See Chapter 1B
Fast idle speed	1000 ± 100 rpm
Maximum speed	5450 ± 125 rpm
Fast idle lever travel (between cold and hot positions)	6.0 mm

Injectors

Type	Pintle
Opening pressure:	
Models with Lucas fuel injection pump:	
TUD 3	125 to 130 bars
TUD 5	130 to 135 bars
Models with Bosch fuel injection pump	119.5 to 124.5 bars

Torque wrench settings

	Nm	lbf ft
Exhaust manifold nuts		
TUD 3	18	12
TUD 5	20	15
Exhaust system fasteners:		
Front pipe-to-manifold nut	35	26
Front pipe-to-intermediate pipe/catalytic converter nuts	10	7
Clamping ring nuts	15	11
Injector pipe union nuts:		
TUD 3	20	15
TUD 5	25	18
Injection pump fixings:		
TUD 3:		
Front mounting nuts	18	12
Rear mounting bolt	23	17
TUD 5	20	15
Injection pump union bolts	25	18
Injectors:		
TUD 3	70	52
TUD 5	55	40
Inlet manifold nuts and bolts:		
TUD 3	16	11
TUD 5	20	15

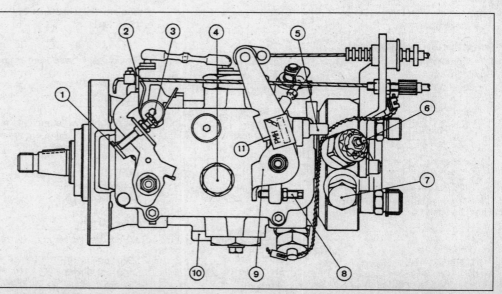

1.1a Lucas fuel injection pump adjustment points and other features

1 Stop lever
2 Fast idle lever
3 Idle speed adjustment screw
4 Fuel return hose union
5 Maximum speed adjustment screw
6 Stop solenoid
7 Fuel inlet hose union
8 Anti-stall adjustment screw
9 Accelerator lever
10 & 11   Injection pump timing value location(s)

1 General information and precautions

The fuel system consists of a rear-mounted fuel tank, a fuel filter with integral water separator, a fuel injection pump, injectors and associated components **(see illustrations)**. As the fuel passes through the filter, the fuel is heated by coolant flowing through the filter housing.

The exhaust system is conventional, but on certain models, an unregulated catalytic converter may be fitted to reduce exhaust gas emissions.

Fuel is drawn from the fuel tank to the fuel injection pump by a vane-type transfer pump incorporated in the fuel injection pump. Before reaching the pump, the fuel passes through a fuel filter, where foreign matter and water are removed. Excess fuel lubricates the moving components of the pump and is then returned to the tank.

The fuel injection pump is driven at half-crankshaft speed by the timing belt. The high pressure required to inject the fuel into the compressed air in the swirl chambers is achieved by a cam plate acting on a single piston on the Bosch pump, or by two opposed pistons forced together by rollers running in a cam ring on the Lucas pump. The fuel passes through a central rotor with a single outlet drilling which aligns with ports leading to the injector pipes.

Fuel metering is controlled by a centrifugal governor, which reacts to accelerator pedal position and engine speed. The governor is linked to a metering valve which increases or decreases the amount of fuel delivered at each pumping stroke.

Basic injection timing is determined when the pump is fitted. When the engine is running, it is varied automatically to suit the prevailing engine speed by a mechanism which turns the cam plate or ring.

The four fuel injectors produce a homogeneous spray of fuel into the swirl chambers located in the cylinder head. The injectors are calibrated to open and close at critical pressures to provide efficient and even combustion. Each injector needle is lubricated by fuel, which accumulates in the spring chamber and is channelled to the injection pump return hose by leak-off pipes.

Bosch or Lucas fuel system components may be fitted, depending on the model. Components from the latter manufacturer are marked either "CAV", "Roto-Diesel" or "Con-Diesel", depending on their date and place of manufacture. With the exception of the fuel filter assembly, replacement components must be of the same make as those originally fitted.

Cold starting is assisted by preheater or "glow" plugs fitted to each swirl chamber (see Chapter 5C for further details).

The fast idle system is operated by a thermostatic valve which is screwed into the fuel filter/thermostat housing. The valve operates a fast idle lever on the injection pump, via a cable, to increase the idle speed when the engine is cold.

A stop solenoid cuts the fuel supply to the injection pump rotor when the ignition is switched off. On some pumps, there is also a hand-operated stop lever for use in an emergency.

Provided that the specified maintenance is carried out, the fuel injection equipment will give long and trouble-free service. The injection pump itself may well outlast the engine. The main potential cause of damage to the injection pump and injectors is dirt or water in the fuel.

Servicing of the injection pump and injectors is very limited for the home mechanic and any dismantling or adjustment other than that described in this Chapter must be entrusted to a Peugeot dealer or fuel injection specialist.

Note: *The fuel system component photographs appearing throughout this Chapter depict the Lucas fuel injection pump and associated equipment which is fitted to the majority of TUD 3 and TUD 5 models. The Bosch fuel injection pump is an alternative fitment on 1997-on TUD 5 models for certain territories. At the time of writing very little specific information exists on the Bosch equipment but the procedures contained in the text are applicable to both, unless otherwise stated.*

⚠ **Warning: It is necessary to take certain precautions when working on the fuel system components, particularly the fuel injectors. Before carrying out any operations on the fuel system, refer to the precautions given in "Safety first!" at the beginning of this manual and to any additional warning notes at the start of the relevant Sections.**

4D

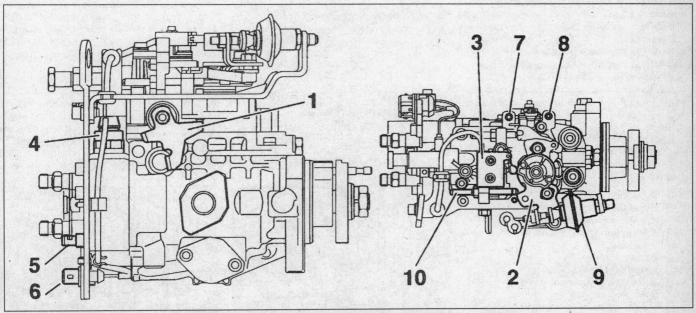

1.1b Bosch fuel injection pump adjustment points and other features

1 Stop lever
2 Load lever
3 Load lever switch

4 Stop solenoid
5 Stop solenoid wiring
   connector

6 Load lever switch connector
7 Idle speed adjustment screw
8 Fast idle adjustment screw

9 Damping vacuum capsule
10 Residual flow adjustment
    screw

3.3 Adjusting the accelerator cable

6.3 Remove the right-hand access cover to reveal the fuel pick-up unit

6.4a Where quick-release type fittings are used, depress their metal centre collars to release them . . .

2 Air cleaner housing - removal and refitting

Removal

TUD3 engine

1 The air cleaner housing is built into the inlet manifold. Cover and element removal are described in Chapter 1B.

2 If necessary, the inlet duct can be removed once its retaining clip has been slackened, the nut securing it to the cylinder head has been removed and the two pop-rivets securing it to the crossmember have been drilled out.

TUD5 engines

3 Detach the ventilation pipe from the rear of the cylinder head cover.

4 Slacken the retaining clip and detach the connecting tube with the inlet manifold air distributor housing from the air cleaner housing cover.

5 Free the connecting tube from the inlet manifold air distributor housing, turning it anti-clockwise to release its fastenings.

6 Slacken the retaining clip and detach the inlet duct at the front of the air cleaner housing cover.

7 Slacken the bolt, then remove the air cleaner housing from its bracket. Recover any displaced rubber fastening rings.

Refitting

8 Refitting is the reverse of removal. On TUD 3 engines, tighten the inlet duct retaining clip securely, then fix the duct in position with the pop-rivets.

3 Accelerator cable - removal, refitting and adjustment

Removal and refitting

1 Refer to Chapter 4A, Section 7, substituting "injection pump" for all references to a carburettor. Adjust the cable as described below.

Adjustment

2 Remove the spring clip from the accelerator outer cable then, ensuring that the pump accelerator lever is fully against the anti-stall screw, gently pull the cable out of its grommet until all free play is removed from the inner cable.

3 With the cable held in this position, ensure that the flat washer is pressed securely against the grommet, then fit the spring clip to the first outer cable groove visible in front of the rubber grommet and washer **(see illustration)**.

4 Have an assistant depress the accelerator pedal and check that the accelerator lever opens fully, so that it contacts the maximum speed screw and returns smoothly to its stop against the anti-stall screw.

4 Accelerator pedal - removal and refitting

Refer to Chapter 4A, Section 8.

5 Fuel gauge sender unit - removal and refitting

Refer to Chapter 4A, Section 5.

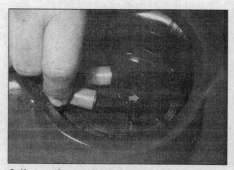

6.4b . . . then pull the hoses away from the pick-up unit

6 Fuel pick-up unit - removal and refitting

Removal

1 Disconnect the battery negative terminal (refer to *"Disconnecting the battery"* in the Reference Section of this manual).

2 For access to the fuel pick-up unit, fold the rear seat cushion forwards.

3 Using a screwdriver, carefully prise the plastic access cover from the floor to expose the fuel pump. Where two access covers are fitted, the pump is located under the right-hand cover (viewed facing towards the front of the vehicle) **(see illustration)**.

4 Mark the hoses for identification purposes, then slacken the feed and return hose retaining clips. Where crimped-type hose clips are fitted, cut the clips and discard them, replace them with standard worm-drive hose clips on refitting. On later models, quick-release fittings may be fitted to the fuel hoses; these are released by depressing their metal collars with a small, flat-bladed screwdriver **(see illustrations)**.

5 Disconnect both hoses from the top of the pick-up unit and plug the hose ends.

6 Noting the alignment marks on the tank, pick-up unit and the locking ring, unscrew the ring and remove it from the tank **(see illustration)**. This is best accomplished by using a screwdriver on the raised ribs of the locking ring. Carefully tap the screwdriver to

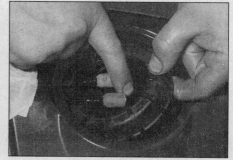

6.6 Unscrew the locking ring . . .

6.7 . . . then lift out the pick-up unit and recover the rubber sealing ring

6.11 Tighten the sealing ring until its mark is aligned with the centre of the three ribs on the fuel tank (arrowed)

8.3 Fuel system bleed screw (arrowed) is located on the top of the fuel filter/thermostat housing

turn the ring anti-clockwise until it can be unscrewed by hand.

7 Carefully lift the fuel pick-up assembly out of the fuel tank, taking great care not to damage the filter, or to spill fuel onto the interior of the vehicle. Recover the rubber sealing ring and discard it; a new one must be used on refitting **(see illustration)**.

8 Note that the fuel pick-up assembly is only available as a complete assembly; no individual components are available separately.

Refitting

9 Ensure that the fuel pick-up filter is clean and free of debris. Fit the new sealing ring to the top of the fuel tank.

10 Carefully manoeuvre the pick-up unit into the fuel tank, aligning the mark noted on removal.

11 Refit the locking ring, tightening it until its mark is correctly aligned with the centre of the three lines on the fuel tank, as noted prior to removal **(see illustration)**.

12 Reconnect the feed and return hoses, using the marks made on removal to ensure that they are correctly reconnected and (where necessary) securely tighten their retaining clips.

13 Reconnect the battery negative terminal and start the engine. Check the fuel feed and return hose unions for signs of leakage.

14 If all is well, refit the plastic access cover and fold back the rear seat cushion.

7 Fuel tank -
removal, repair and refitting

Refer to Chapter 4A, Section 6, ignoring the remark about the fuel filter and disconnecting the fuel hoses from the pick-up unit.

8 Fuel system -
priming and bleeding

1 After disconnecting part of the fuel supply system or running out of fuel, it is necessary to prime the system and bleed off any air

which may have entered the system components.

2 All models are fitted with a hand-operated priming pump, consisting of a rubber bulb, which is clipped onto the side of the left-hand suspension strut turret.

3 To prime the system, first loosen the bleed screw located on the top of the fuel filter/thermostat housing, mounted on the left-hand end of the cylinder head **(see illustration)**. If no bleed screw is fitted, use the outlet union itself (either at the filter/thermostat housing or at the injection pump).

4 Pump the priming plunger until fuel free from air bubbles emerges from the outlet union or bleed screw (as applicable). Retighten the bleed screw or outlet union.

5 Switch on the ignition (to activate the stop solenoid) and continue pumping the priming plunger until firm resistance is felt, then pump a few more times.

6 If a large amount of air has entered the pump, place a wad of rag around the fuel return union on the pump (to absorb spilt fuel), then slacken the union. Operate the priming plunger (with the ignition switched on to activate the stop solenoid), or crank the engine on the starter motor in 10-second bursts, until fuel free from air bubbles emerges from the fuel union. Tighten the union and mop up spilt fuel.

> **Warning: Be prepared to stop the engine if it should fire, to avoid excessive fuel spray and spillage.**

7 If air has entered the injector pipes, place wads of rag around the injector pipe unions at

9.1 Maximum engine speed adjustment screw (arrowed) is locked in position and should not be disturbed

the injectors (to absorb spilt fuel), then slacken the unions. Crank the engine on the starter motor until fuel emerges from the unions, then stop cranking the engine and retighten the unions. Mop up spilt fuel.

> **Warning: Be prepared to stop the engine if it should fire, to avoid excessive fuel spray and spillage.**

8 Start the engine with the accelerator pedal fully depressed. Additional cranking may be necessary to finally bleed the system before the engine starts.

9 Maximum engine speed -
checking and adjustment

Caution: The maximum speed adjustment screw is sealed by the manufacturers at the factory using locking wire and a lead seal and should not be disturbed (see illustration).

1 Run the engine to normal operating temperature. If the vehicle is not equipped with a tachometer (rev counter), connect a suitable instrument in accordance with its manufacturer's instructions.

2 Have an assistant fully depress the accelerator pedal and check that the maximum engine speed is as given in the Specifications. Do not keep the engine at maximum speed for more than two or three seconds.

3 If adjustment is necessary, the vehicle should be taken to a Peugeot dealer or suitable diesel specialist. Adjustment should not be attempted by the home mechanic.

10 Fast idle thermostatic valve -
renewal, testing and adjustment

Removal

1 Disconnect the battery negative terminal (refer to *"Disconnecting the battery"* in the Reference Section of this manual).

2 Partially drain the cooling system as described in Chapter 1B.

3 Loosen the clamp nut and slide the fast idle

4D

10.3 Slacken the clamp nut and slide the end fitting off the fast idle cable

10.5a Unscrew the fast idle valve (arrowed) from the cylinder head . . .

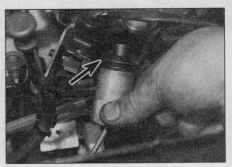

10.5b . . . and remove it along with its sealing washer (arrowed)

10.10 Adjust the fast idle cable as described in text

10.12 Fine adjustment of the fast idle cable can be made using the adjuster on the mounting bracket

cable end fitting off the injection pump end of the inner cable **(see illustration)**.

4 Free the fast idle cable from the bracket on the fuel injection pump.

5 Using a suitable spanner, unscrew the thermostatic valve from the cylinder head and remove the valve and cable assembly. Recover the sealing washer **(see illustrations)**.

Refitting

6 Fit a new sealing washer to the valve and screw the valve into position in the cylinder head, tightening it securely.

7 Insert the cable through the pump bracket and pass the inner cable through the fast idle lever. Slide the end fitting onto the inner and lightly tighten its clamp nut.

8 Refill the cooling system as described in Chapter 1B.

9 Adjust the cable as follows.

11.4a Remove the rubber cover . . .

Testing and adjustment

10 With the engine cold, push the fast idle lever fully to the end of its travel (towards the rear of the pump). Hold it in this position and slide the cable end fitting along the cable until it abuts the fast idle lever; securely tighten its clamp nut **(see illustration)**.

11 Start the engine and warm it up to its normal operating temperature. As the engine warms up, the fast idle cable should extend so that the fast idle lever returns to is stop.

12 Wait until the cooling fan has cut in and cut out, then switch off the engine. Measure the clearance between the fast idle lever and the cable end fitting. There should be a gap of approximately 0.5 to 1 mm. If not, slacken the clamp nut, move the end fitting to the correct position, then securely retighten the screw or nut. Note that fine adjustment of the cable can

11.4b . . . then unscrew the retaining nut and disconnect the stop solenoid wiring connector

be made using the adjuster on the mounting bracket **(see illustration)**.

13 With the cable correctly adjusted, allow the engine to cool. As it cools, the fast idle cable should be drawn back into the valve, pulling the fast idle lever back against its stop.

---

11 Stop solenoid - description, removal and refitting

Description

1 The stop solenoid is located on the top of the fuel injection pump. Its purpose is to cut the fuel supply when the ignition is switched off. If an open-circuit occurs in the solenoid or its electrical supply, it will be impossible to start the engine, as the fuel will not be allowed to pass through the injection pump. The same applies if the solenoid jams shut. If the solenoid jams open, the engine will not stop when the ignition is switched off.

2 If the solenoid has failed and the engine will not run, a temporary repair may be made by removing the solenoid as described in the following paragraphs. Refit the solenoid body without the plunger and spring and tape up its feed wire so that it cannot touch earth. The engine can then be started as usual, but it will be necessary to use the manual stop lever on the injection pump, or to stall the engine in gear, to stop it.

Removal

3 Disconnect the battery negative terminal (refer to *"Disconnecting the battery"* in the Reference Section of this manual).

4 Remove the rubber cover (where fitted), then slacken and remove the retaining nut and washer and disconnect the solenoid wiring connector **(see illustrations)**.

5 Unscrew the solenoid valve from the pump and recover the plunger, spring and sealing ring. Take great care not to allow dirt to enter the pump **(see illustrations)**.

Refitting

6 Refitting is a reversal of removal, using a new sealing ring.

11.5a Unscrew the stop solenoid from the pump and recover the O-ring (arrowed)

11.5b Remove the solenoid and withdraw the plunger and spring

12.6 Loosen the clamp nut and remove the end fitting from the fast idle cable

12 Fuel injection pump - removal and refitting

Caution: *Be careful not to allow dirt into the injection pump or injector pipes during this procedure. New sealing rings should be used on the fuel pipe banjo unions when refitting.*

Removal

Note: *When refitting the pump it will be necessary to set the injection pump timing as described in Section 14. The information contained in Section 14 applies to the Lucas fuel injection pump fitted to the majority of diesel models covered by this manual. The Bosch fuel injection pump is an alternative fitment on 1997-on TUD 5 models for certain territories. At the time of writing very little information exists as to the static timing setting, or the Peugeot special tool (timing probe and bracket) required to check the setting. On models fitted with Bosch equipment, it is recommended that fuel injection pump removal and refitting is entrusted to a Peugeot dealer or other suitably-equipped specialist. If, however, accurate alignment marks are made during removal, it should be possible to refit the pump with an approximate timing setting. This will allow the vehicle to be driven to a dealer or specialist to enable accurate timing adjustment to be carried out.*

1 Disconnect the battery negative terminal (refer to *"Disconnecting the battery"* in the Reference Section of this manual).

2 Remove the right-hand headlight unit as described in Chapter 12.

3 Remove the upper and centre timing belt covers as described in Chapter 2B.

4 Align the engine assembly/valve timing holes as described in Chapter 2B, Section 3 and lock the crankshaft, camshaft sprocket and injection pump sprocket in position. *Do not* attempt to rotate the engine whilst the pins are in position.

5 Remove the injection pump sprocket as described in Chapter 2B, Section 7.

6 Loosen the clamp nut and slide the fast idle cable end fitting off the injection pump end of

12.7a Free the accelerator inner cable from the pump lever . . .

the inner cable **(see illustration)**. Free the fast idle cable from the bracket on the fuel injection pump.

7 Free the accelerator inner cable from the pump lever, then pull the outer cable out from its mounting bracket rubber grommet. Slide the flat washer off the end of the cable and remove the spring clip **(see illustrations)**.

8 Wipe clean the fuel feed and return unions on the injection pump. Cover the alternator with a clean cloth or plastic bag, to guard against fuel being spilt onto it during the following operations.

9 Slacken and remove the fuel feed hose union bolt from the pump. Recover the sealing washer from each side of the hose union and position the hose clear of the pump. Screw the union bolt back into position on the pump for safe-keeping and cover both the hose end

12.7b . . . then withdraw the outer cable from the mounting bracket and recover the washer and spring clip (arrowed)

and union bolt to prevent the ingress of dirt into the fuel system.

10 Detach the fuel return hose from the pump as described in the previous paragraph **(see illustration)**. **Note:** *The injection pump feed and return hose union bolts are not interchangeable.*

11 Wipe clean the pipe unions, then slacken the union nut securing the injector pipes to the top of each injector and the four union nuts securing the pipes to the rear of the injection pump; as each pump union nut is slackened, retain the adapter with a suitable open-ended spanner to prevent it being unscrewed from the pump. With all the union nuts undone, remove the injector pipes from the engine (the pipes are removed in pairs) **(see illustrations)**.

12 Remove the rubber cover (where fitted), then undo the retaining nut and disconnect

12.10 Unscrew the fuel return hose union bolt and recover the sealing washer from each side of the hose union

12.11a Unscrew the union nuts securing the injector pipes to the injectors . . .

4D

12.11b . . . and the pump. Whilst slackening the pump nuts, retain the pump adapters with an open-ended spanner

12.11c Remove the injector pipes in pairs

12.12 Disconnecting the wiring from the injection pump stop solenoid

12.13a Remove the cover panel from the side of the radiator to improve access . . .

12.13b . . . then make alignment marks (arrowed) between the injection pump and mounting bracket

the wiring from the injection pump stop solenoid **(see illustration)**.

13 Using a scriber or suitable marker pen, make alignment marks between the injection pump front flange and the front mounting bracket. These marks can then be used to ensure that the pump is correctly positioned on refitting. To improve access to the pump, undo the two screws and remove the cover panel from the right-hand side of the radiator **(see illustrations)**.

14 Unscrew the bolt securing the injection pump rear mounting bracket to the cylinder block **(see illustration)**.

15 Slacken and remove the three nuts and washers securing the pump to its front mounting bracket, then manoeuvre the pump out of the engine compartment **(see illustrations)**.

Refitting

16 If a new pump is being installed, transfer the alignment mark from the original pump onto the mounting flange of the new pump.

17 Manoeuvre the pump into position and refit its three front washers and mounting nuts and the rear mounting bolt. Align the marks made prior to removal, then securely tighten the retaining nuts and bolt.

18 Refit the injection pump sprocket as described in Chapter 2B, Section 7. Align the sprocket timing holes with those in the mounting plate and lock the sprocket in position with the two timing bolts.

19 Check the crankshaft, camshaft and injection pump sprockets are all correctly positioned, then engage the timing belt and tension it as described in Chapter 2B, Section 6. With the timing belt correctly fitted, remove the pins/bolts from the sprockets.

20 Set the injection pump timing as described in Section 14.

21 With the pump timing correctly set, reconnect the wiring to the stop solenoid and securely tighten its retaining nut. Refit the rubber boot.

22 Reconnect the fuel feed and return hose unions to the pump, not forgetting to fit the filter to the feed hose union. Position a new sealing washer on each side of both unions and tighten the union bolts to the specified torque setting.

23 Refit the injector pipes and tighten their union nuts to the specified torque setting.

24 Mop up any spilt fuel, then remove the cover from the alternator.

25 Reconnect the accelerator cable and adjust as described in Section 3.

26 Reconnect the fast idle valve cable and adjust as described in Section 10.

27 Refit the right-hand headlight unit as described in Chapter 12.

28 Reconnect the battery negative terminal.

29 Bleed the fuel system as described in Section 8.

30 On completion, start the engine and adjust the idle speed and anti-stall speed as described in Chapter 1B.

13 Injection timing - checking methods

Checking the injection timing is not a routine operation. It should only be necessary after the injection pump has been disturbed.

Dynamic timing equipment does exist, but it is unlikely to be available to the home mechanic. The equipment works by converting pressure pulses in an injector pipe into electrical signals. If such equipment is available, use it in accordance with its maker's instructions.

12.14 Unscrew the rear mounting bracket bolt (arrowed) . . .

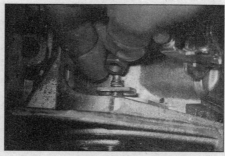

12.15a . . . then unscrew the front mounting nuts and washer . . .

12.15b . . . and remove the injection pump from the engine

TUD 3 engine

Static timing as described in this Chapter gives good results if carried out carefully. A dial test indicator will be needed, with probes and adapters appropriate to the type of injection pump. Read through the procedures before starting work, to find out what is involved.

TUD 5 engines

Injection pumps (Bosch or Lucas) have non-adjustable fastenings, so their static timing is fixed and cannot be adjusted by swivelling their body round in relation to the engine. The only way to ensure that the pump timing is correct is to position the engine at TDC as described in Chapter 2B, Section 3. In this position, the sprocket hub timing groove must be aligned with the corresponding hole on the pump body, in order that the locking tool can be inserted. If these holes do not align, this indicates that the timing belt has not been properly fitted.

If you suspect that the pump timing is out - eg, if there is smoke, abnormal engine noise, a change in pulling power, or high fuel consumption - the fault may well be in the pump itself and the vehicle should be inspected by a Peugeot dealer or other suitably-equipped diesel specialist.

14 Fuel Injection pump - checking and adjustment

Caution: The maximum engine speed and transfer pressure settings, together with timing access plugs, are sealed by the manufacturers at the factory, using locking wire and lead seals. Do not disturb the wire if the vehicle is still within the warranty period, otherwise the warranty will be invalidated. Furthermore, do not attempt the timing procedure unless accurate instrumentation is available. Suitable special tools for carrying out pump timing should be available from larger motor factors or your Peugeot dealer. Refer to the precautions given in Section 1 of this Chapter before proceeding.

Injection timing

TUD3 engine - Lucas pump

Note: *To check the injection pump timing, a special timing probe and mounting bracket (Peugeot tool No 0117AM) is required (see illustration 14.4). Without access to this piece of equipment, injection pump timing should be entrusted to a Peugeot dealer or other suitably-equipped specialist.*

1 If the injection timing is being checked with the pump in position on the engine, rather than as part of the pump refitting procedure, disconnect the battery negative lead and cover the alternator with a clean cloth or plastic bag, to guard against fuel being spilt onto it. Remove the injector pipes as described in paragraph 11 of Section 12.
2 Referring to Chapter 2B, Section 3, align the

14.3 Injection pump timing access plug (arrowed)

engine assembly/valve timing holes. Ensure that all locking tools are removed, then turn the crankshaft **backwards** (anti-clockwise) approximately a quarter of a turn. Turning the engine will be much easier if the glow plugs are removed first - see Chapter 5C.
3 Unscrew the access plug from the guide on the top of the pump body and recover the sealing washer **(see illustration)**. Insert the special timing probe into the guide, making sure it is correctly seated against the guide sealing washer surface. **Note:** *The timing probe must be seated against the guide sealing washer surface and not the upper lip of the guide, for the measurement to be accurate.*
4 Mount the bracket on the pump guide (Peugeot tool No. 0117AM) and securely mount the dial gauge (dial test indicator) in the bracket, so that its tip is in contact with the bracket linkage **(see illustration)**. Position the dial gauge so that its plunger is at the mid-point of its travel and zero the gauge.
5 Rotate the crankshaft slowly in the correct direction of rotation (clockwise) until the crankshaft locking tool (paragraph 2) can be re-inserted.
6 With the crankshaft locked in position, read the dial gauge; the reading should correspond to the value marked on the pump (there is a tolerance of ± 0.04 mm). The timing value may be marked on a plastic disc attached to the front of the pump, or alternatively on a tag attached to the pump accelerator lever **(see illustration)**.
7 If adjustment is necessary, slacken the right-hand pump mounting nuts and the left-

14.6 Injection pump timing value is usually on a tag attached to the pump accelerator lever

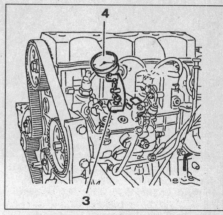

14.4 Peugeot injection pump timing gauge (4) and mounting bracket (3) in position on the injection pump

hand mounting bolt, then slowly rotate the pump body until the point is found where the specified reading is obtained on the dial gauge. When the pump is correctly positioned, tighten both its right-hand mounting nuts and the left-hand bolt to their specified torque settings. To improve access to the pump nuts, undo the two screws and remove the cover panel from the side of the radiator, if not already done.
8 Withdraw the timing probe slightly, so that it is positioned clear of the pump rotor dowel and remove the crankshaft locking tool. Rotate the crankshaft through one and three-quarter rotations in the normal direction of rotation.
9 Slide the timing probe back into position, ensuring that it is correctly seated against the guide sealing washer surface, not the upper lip, then zero the dial gauge.
10 Rotate the crankshaft slowly in the correct direction of rotation, until the crankshaft locking tool can be re-inserted. Recheck the timing measurement.
11 If adjustment is necessary, slacken the pump mounting nuts and bolt and repeat the operations in paragraphs 7 to 10.
12 When the pump timing is correctly set, remove the dial gauge and mounting bracket and withdraw the timing probe.
13 Refit the screw and sealing washer to the guide and tighten it securely.
14 If the procedure is being carried out as part of the pump refitting sequence, proceed as described in Section 12.
15 If the procedure is being carried out with the pump fitted to the engine, refit the injector pipes, tightening their union nuts to the specified torque setting. Reconnect the battery, then prime and bleed the fuel system as described in Section 8. Refit the glow plugs, if removed. Start the engine and adjust the idle speed and anti-stall speed as described in Chapter 1B.

TUD 5 engines

16 The only way to ensure that the pump timing is correct is to position the engine at TDC as described in Chapter 2B, Section 3. In

15.6 Unscrew the injector and remove it from the cylinder head - note cover over the pipe opening, secured with an elastic band

this position, the sprocket hub timing groove must be aligned with the corresponding hole on the pump body, in order that the locking tool can be inserted. If these holes do not align, this indicates that the timing belt has not been properly fitted.

Fast idle speed

Bosch pump

17 Start the engine and allow it to idle. Operate the fast idle lever by hand until it contacts the fast idle screw. Hold the lever in this position, and adjust the fast idle screw until the specified fast idle speed is obtained. Release the lever.

18 Slacken the fast idle cable end fitting clamp nut. With the engine cold, operate the fast idle lever until it contacts the fast idle screw. Hold the lever in this position, and slide the cable end fitting along the cable until its abuts the fast idle lever. Securely tighten the end fitting clamp nut.

19 Start the engine, and warm it up to its normal operating temperature. As the engine warms up, the fast idle cable should extend so that the fast idle lever moves away from the fast idle screw.

20 Wait until the cooling fan has cut in and cut out, then switch off the engine. Measure the total travel of the fast idle lever between the cold and hot positions and compare it with the figure given in the Specifications. If the measured travel is incorrect, slacken the clamp nut, move the end fitting to achieve the correct travel, then securely retighten the screw or nut. Fine adjustment of the cable can be carried out by turning the knurled adjustment collar at the end of the fast idle cable outer sleeve.

21 With the cable correctly adjusted, allow the engine to cool. As it cools, the fast idle cable should be drawn back into the valve, pulling the fast idle lever back against its stop.

Lucas pump

22 With the engine cold, check that the fast idle lever rests against the stop on the top of the fuel injection pump. If this is not the case, slacken the fast idle cable end fitting clamp nut, move the end fitting to achieve the correct lever travel, then securely retighten the screw or nut.

23 Start the engine, and warm it up to its normal operating temperature. As the engine warms up, the fast idle cable should extend so that the fast idle lever moves away from its stop.

24 Wait until the cooling fan has cut in and cut out, then switch off the engine. Measure the total travel of the fast idle lever between the cold and hot positions and compare it with the figure given in the Specifications. If the measured travel is incorrect, slacken the clamp nut, move the end fitting to achieve the correct travel, then securely retighten the screw or nut. Fine adjustment of the cable can be carried out by turning the knurled collar at the end of the fast idle cable outer sleeve.

Manual stop lever

25 Both types of fuel injection pump (Bosch and Lucas) fitted to the TUD5 engine are equipped with a manual stop lever. This device cuts off the fuel supply from the injection pump, allowing the engine to be stopped in an emergency if required. The operation of the manual stop lever should be checked regularly.

26 On Bosch injection pumps, the manual stop lever is located on the rear of the pump body, between the pump and the engine. On Lucas injection pumps, the manual stop lever is located on the front of the pump body below the fast idle lever. To check the operation of the manual stop lever, start the engine and allow it to idle. Rotate the manual stop lever fully to the end of its travel; the engine should stop immediately. If the engine continues to run, adjust the anti-stall speed as described in Chapter 1B, Section 10. If the problem persists, then a fault may exist within the fuel injection pump - refer to a Peugeot dealer, or diesel fuel injection specialist for further advice.

15 Fuel injectors - testing, removal and refitting

⚠️ *Warning: Exercise extreme caution when working on the fuel injectors. Never expose the hands (or any part of the body) to injector spray, as the high working pressure can cause the fuel to penetrate the skin, with possibly fatal results. You are strongly advised to have any work which involves testing the*

15.10a Fit the new flame shield washer to the cylinder head . . .

injectors under pressure carried out by a dealer or fuel injection specialist. Refer to the precautions given in Section 1 of this Chapter before proceeding.

Testing

1 Injectors do deteriorate with prolonged use and it is reasonable to expect them to need reconditioning or renewal after 60 000 miles (100 000 km) or so. Accurate testing, overhaul and calibration of the injectors must be left to a specialist. A defective injector which is causing knocking or smoking can be located without dismantling, as follows.

2 Run the engine at a fast idle. Slacken each injector union in turn, placing rag around the union to catch spilt fuel and *being careful not to expose the skin to any spray*. When the union on the defective injector is slackened, the knocking or smoking will stop.

Removal

Caution: Take great care not to allow dirt into the injectors or fuel pipes during this procedure. Do not drop the injectors, or allow the needles at their tips to become damaged. The injectors are precision-made to fine limits and must not be handled roughly. In particular, do not mount them in a bench vice.

3 Disconnect the battery negative terminal (refer to *"Disconnecting the battery"* in the Reference Section of this manual). Cover the alternator with a clean cloth or plastic bag, to guard against fuel being spilt onto it.

4 Carefully clean around the injectors and pipe union nuts and disconnect the return pipe from the injector.

5 Wipe clean the pipe unions, then slacken the union nut securing the relevant injector pipes to each injector. Slacken the relevant union nuts securing the pipes to the rear of the injection pump (the pipes are removed in pairs). As each pump union nut is slackened, retain the adapter with a suitable open-ended spanner, to prevent it being unscrewed from the pump. With the union nuts undone, remove the relevant injector pipes from the engine. Note the position of any clips attached to the pipes, for use when refitting. Cover the injector and pipe unions, to prevent the entry of dirt into the system.

6 Unscrew the injector, using a deep socket or box spanner and remove it from the cylinder head **(see illustration)**.

7 Recover the sealing and flame shield washers. Also remove the injector sleeve if it is a loose fit in the cylinder head.

Refitting

8 Obtain a new sealing washer and flame shield washer. Where removed, also renew the injector sleeve if it is damaged.

9 Where necessary, refit the injector sleeve to the cylinder head.

10 Fit the new flame shield washer to the sleeve, noting that it must be fitted with its convex side facing upwards (towards the injector) **(see illustrations)**.

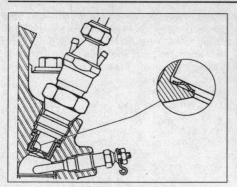

15.10b . . . making sure that its convex side is facing towards the injector (see inset)

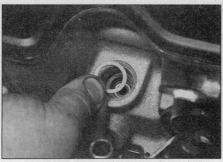

15.11 Fit a new sealing washer . . .

15.12 . . . then refit the injector and tighten it to the specified torque setting

11 Fit the new sealing washer to the top of the sleeve **(see illustration).**

12 Screw the injector into position and tighten it to the specified torque **(see illustration).**

13 Refit the injector pipes and tighten the union nuts to the specified torque setting. Position any clips attached to the pipes as noted before removal.

14 Reconnect the return pipe securely to the injector.

15 Reconnect the battery and start the engine. If difficulty is experienced, bleed the fuel system as described in Section 8.

16 Inlet manifold - removal and refitting

TUD 3 engine

Removal

1 Disconnect the battery negative terminal (refer to *"Disconnecting the battery"* in the Reference Section of this manual).

2 Remove the air cleaner element as described in Chapter 1B.

3 Slacken the retaining clip and disconnect the air inlet duct from the left-hand side of the manifold **(see illustration).**

4 Unscrew the three manifold retaining bolts and the two retaining nuts, then manoeuvre the manifold away from the head and out of the engine compartment. Note that there is no manifold gasket.

Refitting

5 Ensure that the manifold and cylinder head mating surfaces are clean and dry and apply a thin coating of suitable sealing compound to the manifold mating surface.

6 Manoeuvre the manifold into position and refit its retaining nuts and bolts. Tighten them evenly and progressively to the specified torque setting **(see illustration).**

7 Refit the air cleaner element as described in Chapter 1B.

8 Connect the air inlet duct to the manifold, tighten its retaining clip securely and reconnect the battery.

16.3 Slacken the retaining clip and disconnect the air inlet duct from the left side of the manifold

TUD 5 engines

Removal

9 Disconnect the battery negative terminal.

10 Remove the air cleaner housing and ducts (see Section 2)

11 Where appropriate, remove the exhaust gas recycling valve.

12 Remove the retaining clips and lift off the air distributor housing bracket, below the inlet manifold.

13 Remove the retaining bolts and separate the air distributor housing from the inlet manifold.

14 Progressively unscrew the retaining bolts and nuts and manoeuvre the manifold away from the cylinder head and out of the engine compartment. Note that there is no manifold gasket.

Refitting

15 Ensure that the manifold and cylinder head mating surfaces are clean and dry and apply a coating of suitable sealing compound to the manifold mating surface.

16 Manoeuvre the manifold into position and refit its retaining nuts and bolts. Tighten them evenly and progressively to the specified torque setting.

17 Apply a thin coating of suitable sealing compound to the mating surface, the refit the air distributor housing to the manifold and tighten the retaining bolts securely

18 Insert the bracket retaining bolts below the manifold and tighten them securely.

19 Refit the air cleaner housing and ducts as described in Section 2.

16.6 When refitting, tighten the manifold fasteners to the specified torque setting

17 Exhaust manifold - removal and refitting

Removal

1 Chock the rear wheels then jack up the front of the vehicle and support it on axle stands (see *"Jacking and Vehicle Support"*).

2 Remove the inlet manifold as described in Section 16.

3 Place a jack beneath the engine, with a block of wood on the jack head. Raise the jack until it is supporting the weight of the engine.

4 Slacken and remove the four nuts securing the right-hand engine mounting upper bracket to the cylinder block and body and lift off the bracket. Lift the buffer plate off the mounting stud **(see illustrations)**

17.4a Unscrew the four retaining nuts (arrowed) . . .

4D

17.4b . . . then lift off the mounting bracket . . .

17.4c . . . and recover the buffer plate from the mounting stud

17.6 Remove the manifold along with its gasket

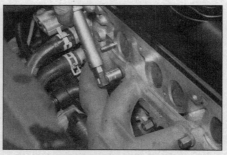

17.7 When refitting, tighten the manifold retaining nuts to the specified torque

5 Unscrew the bolt securing the front pipe to its mounting, then undo the nuts securing the exhaust front pipe to the manifold. Free the front pipe from the manifold and recover the gasket.

6 Undo the eight retaining nuts securing the manifold to the head. Manoeuvre the manifold out of the engine compartment and discard the manifold gasket(s) **(see illustration)**.

Refitting

7 Refitting is the reverse of the removal procedure, noting the following points:
 a) *Examine all the exhaust manifold studs for signs of damage and corrosion. Remove all traces of corrosion and repair or renew any damaged studs.*
 b) *Ensure that the manifold and cylinder head sealing faces are clean and flat and fit the new manifold gaskets. Tighten the manifold retaining nuts to the specified torque **(see illustration)**.*

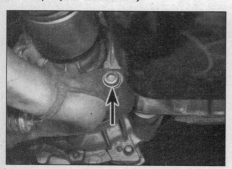

18.6 Exhaust front pipe-to-transmission bolt (arrowed)

 c) *Refit the right-hand engine mounting bracket and tighten its retaining nuts to the specified torque (see Chapter 2B).*
 d) *Reconnect the front pipe to the manifold using the information given in Section 18.*

18 Exhaust system - general information and component renewal

General information

1 On models without a catalytic converter, the exhaust system consists of three sections: the front pipe, the intermediate pipe and silencer box and the tailpipe and main silencer box. All exhaust sections are connected by flanged joints. The front pipe joints are secured by nuts and bolts, the intermediate pipe joint being of the spring-loaded ball type, to allow for movement in the exhaust system. The intermediate pipe-to-tailpipe joint is secured by a clamping ring.

18.8a Remove the front pipe-to-intermediate pipe/catalytic converter fasteners, noting the correct fitted location of each component . . .

2 On all models with a catalytic converter, the exhaust system consists of four sections: the front pipe, the catalytic converter, the intermediate pipe and silencer box and the tailpipe and main silencer box. All exhaust sections are connected by flanged joints. The front pipe joints are secured by nuts and bolts, the catalytic converter joint being of the spring-loaded ball type, to allow for movement in the exhaust system. The catalytic converter-to-intermediate pipe joint and the intermediate pipe-to-silencer joint are secured by a clamping ring.

3 On all models, the system is suspended throughout its entire length by rubber mountings.

Removal

4 Each exhaust section can be removed individually or, alternatively, the complete system can be removed as a unit.

5 To remove the system or part of the system, first jack up the front or rear of the car and support it on axle stands (see *"Jacking and Vehicle Support"*). Alternatively, position the car over an inspection pit, or on car ramps.

Front pipe

6 Slacken and remove the bolt securing the front pipe to its mounting **(see illustration)**.

7 Undo the nuts securing the exhaust front pipe to the manifold, then free the front pipe from the manifold and recover the gasket. If necessary, undo the two bolts and remove the heat shield to improve access to the nuts.

8 Slacken and remove the two nuts securing the front pipe to the catalytic converter/intermediate pipe (as applicable) and recover the spring cups and springs. Remove the bolts, then withdraw the front pipe from underneath the vehicle. Recover the wire-mesh gasket from the joint **(see illustrations)**.

Catalytic converter

9 Undo the two nuts securing the front pipe flange joint to the catalytic converter. Recover the springs and spring cups and withdraw the bolts.

10 Slacken the catalytic converter-to-intermediate pipe clamping ring bolts and disengage the clamp from the flange joint.

11 Free the catalytic converter from the intermediate pipe, then withdraw it from

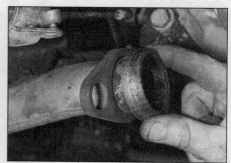

18.8b . . . then remove the front pipe and recover the gasket

underneath the vehicle. Do not drop the catalytic converter, as it contains a fragile ceramic element. Recover the wire-mesh gasket from the front pipe joint.

Intermediate pipe - models without a catalytic converter

12 Undo the two nuts securing the front pipe flange joint to the intermediate pipe. Recover the springs and spring cups and withdraw the bolts.
13 Slacken the clamping ring bolts and disengage the clamp from the intermediate pipe-to-tailpipe flange joint.
14 Free the intermediate pipe from its mounting rubbers, then disengage it from the tailpipe and the front pipe and remove it from underneath the vehicle. Recover the wire-mesh gasket from the front pipe joint.

Intermediate pipe - models with a catalytic converter

15 Slacken the clamping ring bolts and disengage the clamps from both the intermediate pipe flange joints.
16 Free the intermediate pipe from its mounting rubbers, then disengage it first from the tailpipe then the catalytic converter and remove it from underneath the vehicle.

Tailpipe

17 Slacken the intermediate pipe-to-tailpipe clamping ring bolts and disengage the clamp from the flange joint **(see illustration)**.
18 Unhook the tailpipe from its mounting rubbers and remove it from the vehicle.

Complete system

19 Disconnect the front pipe from the manifold as described in paragraphs 6 and 7.
20 With the aid of an assistant, free the system from all its mounting rubbers and manoeuvre it out from underneath the vehicle.

Heat shield(s)

21 The heat shields are secured to the underside of the body by a mixture of nuts and bolts. Each shield can be removed once the relevant exhaust section has been removed. If the shield is being removed to gain access to a component located behind it, in some cases, it may prove sufficient to remove the retaining nuts and/or bolts and simply lower the shield, without disturbing the exhaust system.

Refitting

22 Each section is refitted by a reverse of the removal sequence, noting the following points:
  a) Ensure that all traces of corrosion have been removed from the flanges and renew all necessary gaskets.
  b) Inspect the rubber mountings for signs of damage or deterioration and renew as necessary.
  c) Prior to assembling the spring-loaded ball

18.17 Intermediate pipe-to-tailpipe clamp

type joint, a smear of high-temperature grease should be applied to the joint mating surfaces.
  d) On joints which are secured by clamping rings, apply a smear of exhaust system jointing paste to the joint mating surfaces, to ensure an air-tight seal. Tighten the clamping ring nuts evenly and progressively to the specified torque, so that the clearance between the clamp halves is equal on either side.
  e) Prior to tightening the exhaust system fasteners, ensure that all rubber mountings are correctly located and that there is adequate clearance between the exhaust system and vehicle underbody.

4D

Chapter 4 Part E:
Emission control systems

Contents

Degrees of difficulty

Easy, suitable for novice with little experience	**Fairly easy,** suitable for beginner with some experience	**Fairly difficult,** suitable for competent DIY mechanic	**Difficult,** suitable for experienced DIY mechanic	**Very difficult,** suitable for expert DIY or professional

1 General information

All petrol models have the ability to use unleaded petrol and also have various other features built into the fuel system to help minimise harmful emissions. On top of this, all models have the crankcase emission control system described below. All later petrol models have a catalytic converter and some are also fitted with exhaust and evaporative emission control systems (see Chapter 4B or 4C for further information).

Diesel engine models are also designed to meet strict emission requirements and have a crankcase emission control system. Certain models may also be fitted with a catalytic converter, to reduce exhaust emissions.

The emission control systems function as follows.

Crankcase emission control

To reduce the emissions of unburned hydrocarbons from the crankcase into the atmosphere, the engine is sealed and the blow-by gases and oil vapour are drawn from inside the crankcase, through a wire-mesh oil separator, into the inlet tract, to be burned by the engine during normal combustion.

Under conditions of high manifold depression (idling, deceleration) the gases will be sucked positively out of the crankcase. Under conditions of low manifold depression (acceleration, full-throttle running) the gases are forced out of the crankcase by the (relatively) higher crankcase pressure; if the engine is worn, the raised crankcase pressure (due to increased blow-by) will cause some of the flow to return under all manifold conditions.

Exhaust emission control - petrol models

To minimise the amount of pollutants which escape into the atmosphere, some models are fitted with a catalytic converter in the exhaust system. On all models where a catalytic converter is fitted, the system is of the closed-loop type, in which a lambda sensor in the exhaust system provides the fuel-injection/ignition system ECU with constant feedback on the oxygen content of the exhaust gases. This enables the ECU to adjust the mixture to provide the best possible conditions for the converter to operate.

The lambda sensor has a built-in heating element, controlled by the ECU through the lambda sensor relay, to quickly bring the sensor's tip to an efficient operating temperature. The sensor's tip is sensitive to oxygen and sends the ECU a varying voltage depending on the amount of oxygen in the exhaust gases; if the intake air/fuel mixture is too rich, the exhaust gases are low in oxygen, so the sensor sends a low-voltage signal, the voltage rising as the mixture weakens and the amount of oxygen in the exhaust gases rises. Peak conversion efficiency of all major pollutants occurs if the intake air/fuel mixture is maintained at the chemically-correct ratio for the complete combustion of petrol - 14.7 parts (by weight) of air to 1 part of fuel (the "stoichiometric" ratio). The sensor output voltage alters in a large step at this point, the ECU using the signal change as a reference point and correcting the intake air/fuel mixture accordingly, by altering the fuel injector pulse width (injector opening time).

4E

2.3a Undo the retaining screw (arrowed) . . .

2.3b . . . then prise out the retaining clips . . .

2.3c . . . and remove the right-hand front wheelarch liner to gain access to the charcoal canister

Exhaust emission control - diesel models

To minimise the level of exhaust pollutants released into the atmosphere, a catalytic converter is fitted in the exhaust system on some models.

The catalytic converter is a canister containing a fine mesh impregnated with a catalyst material, over which the hot exhaust gases pass. The catalyst speeds up the oxidation of harmful carbon monoxide, unburnt hydrocarbons and soot, effectively reducing the quantity of harmful products released into the atmosphere via the exhaust gases.

Evaporative emission control - petrol models

To minimise the escape into the atmosphere of unburned hydrocarbons, an evaporative emission control system is fitted to models equipped with a catalytic converter. The fuel tank filler cap is sealed and a charcoal canister is mounted underneath the right-hand wing, to collect the petrol vapours generated in the tank when the car is parked. It stores them until they can be cleared from the canister (under the control of the fuel injection/ignition system ECU) via the purge valve(s) into the inlet tract, to be burned by the engine during normal combustion.

To ensure that the engine runs correctly when it is cold and/or idling and to protect the catalytic converter from the effects of an over-rich mixture, the purge control valve(s) is/are not opened by the ECU until the engine has warmed-up and the engine is under load; the valve solenoid is then modulated on and off to allow the stored vapour to pass into the inlet tract.

| 2 | Emission control systems - testing and component renewal |

Crankcase emission control

1 The components of this system require no attention, other than to check that the hose(s) are clear and undamaged at regular intervals.

Evaporative emission control - petrol models

Testing

2 If the system is thought to be faulty, disconnect the hoses from the charcoal canister and purge control valve and check that they are clear by blowing through them. If the purge control valve(s) or charcoal canister are thought to be faulty, they must be renewed.

Charcoal canister - renewal

3 The charcoal canister is located behind the right-hand front wing. To gain access to the canister, undo the retaining screw from the base of the wheelarch liner, then prise out the retaining clips and remove the liner from underneath the wing (see illustrations).

4 Slacken and remove the clamp bolt (see illustration), then free the canister from its mounting clamp and lower it out from underneath the wing. Mark the hoses for identification purposes.

5 Slacken the retaining clips, then disconnect both hoses and remove the canister from the vehicle (see illustration). Where crimped-type hose clips are fitted, cut the clips and discard them; replace them with standard worm-drive hose clips when refitting.

6 Refitting is a reverse of the removal procedure, ensuring that the hoses are correctly reconnected.

Purge valve(s) - renewal

7 Either a single purge valve is used, or a twin purge valve arrangement is fitted, depending on model. The purge valve(s) is/are located in the right-hand rear corner of the engine compartment (see illustration).

8 To renew a purge valve, first disconnect the battery negative terminal (refer to "Disconnecting the battery" in the Reference Section of this manual). Depress the retaining clip and disconnect the wiring connector from the valve.

9 Disconnect the hoses from either end of the valve, then release the valve from its retaining clip and remove it from the engine compartment, noting which way around it is fitted.

2.4 Unscrew the mounting clamp bolt (arrowed) . . .

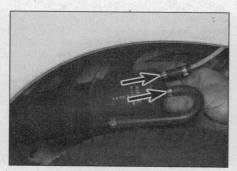

2.5 . . . then lower the canister out of position and disconnect its hoses (arrowed)

2.7 The purge valve(s) can be found in the right-hand rear corner of the engine compartment

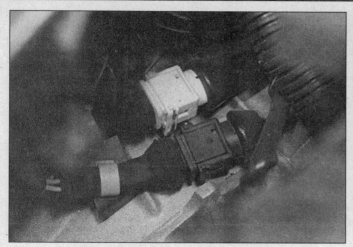

2.15 Trace the lambda sensor wiring back to the top of the transmission, then disconnect the connectors . . .

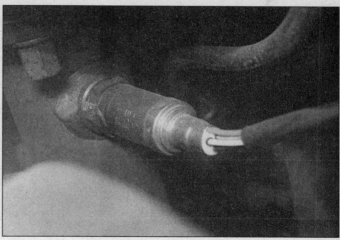

2.16 . . . and unscrew the sensor from the exhaust front pipe or manifold

10 Refitting is a reversal of the removal procedure, ensuring that the valve is fitted the correct way around and the hoses are securely connected.

Exhaust emission control

Testing

11 The performance of the catalytic converter can be checked only by measuring the exhaust gases using a good-quality, carefully-calibrated exhaust gas analyser as described in Chapter 1A, Section 14.

12 On petrol models, if the CO level at the tailpipe is too high, the vehicle should be taken to a Peugeot dealer. Once there, the fuel injection and ignition systems, including the lambda sensor, can be thoroughly checked using the special diagnostic equipment. Once these have been checked and are known to be free from faults, the fault must be in the catalytic converter, which must be renewed as described in Part B or C of this Chapter (as applicable).

13 On diesel models, if the catalytic converter is thought to be faulty, before assuming the catalytic converter is faulty, it is worth checking the problem is not due to a faulty injector(s). Refer to your Peugeot dealer for further information.

Catalytic converter - renewal

14 Refer to Part B, C or D of this Chapter (as applicable).

Lambda sensor (petrol models only) - renewal

Caution: The lambda sensor is delicate and will not work if it is dropped or knocked, if its power supply is disrupted, or if any cleaning materials are used on it.

15 Trace the wiring back from the lambda sensor, which is screwed into the top of the exhaust front pipe or exhaust manifold, to the top of the transmission. Disconnect both wiring connectors and free the wiring from any relevant retaining clips or ties **(see illustration)**.

16 Unscrew the sensor from the exhaust system front pipe or manifold and remove it along with its sealing washer **(see illustration)**.

17 Refitting is a reverse of the removal procedure, using a new sealing washer. Prior to installing the sensor, apply a smear of high-temperature grease to the sensor threads. Ensure that the sensor is securely tightened. Make certain that the wiring is correctly routed and in no danger of contacting either the exhaust system or the engine.

---

3 Catalytic converter - general information and precautions

The catalytic converter is a reliable and simple device, which needs no maintenance in itself, but there are some facts of which an owner should be aware if the converter is to function properly for its full service life.

Petrol models

a) DO NOT use leaded petrol in a car equipped with a catalytic converter - the lead will coat the precious metals, reducing their converting efficiency and will eventually destroy the converter.

b) Always keep the ignition and fuel systems well-maintained in accordance with the manufacturer's schedule (see Chapter 1A).

c) If the engine develops a misfire, do not drive the car at all (or at least as little as possible) until the fault is cured.

d) DO NOT push- or tow-start the car - this will soak the catalytic converter in unburned fuel, causing it to overheat when the engine does start.

e) DO NOT switch off the ignition at high engine speeds, ie do not "blip" the throttle immediately before switching off.

f) DO NOT use fuel or engine oil additives - these may contain substances harmful to the catalytic converter.

g) DO NOT continue to use the car if the engine burns oil to the extent of leaving a visible trail of blue smoke.

h) Remember that the catalytic converter operates at very high temperatures. DO NOT, therefore, park the car in dry undergrowth, over long grass or piles of dead leaves, after a long run.

i) Remember that the catalytic converter is FRAGILE - do not strike it with tools during servicing work.

j) In some cases, a sulphurous smell (like that of rotten eggs) may be noticed from the exhaust. This is common to many catalytic converter-equipped cars. Once the car has covered a few thousand miles, the problem should disappear.

k) The catalytic converter, used on a well-maintained and well-driven car, should last for between 50 000 and 100 000 miles - if the converter is no longer effective, it must be renewed.

Diesel models

The advice given in paragraphs (f), (g), (h) and (i) above applies equally to the converter fitted to diesel models.

4E

Chapter 5 Part A:
Starting and charging systems

Contents

Degrees of difficulty

Easy, suitable for novice with little experience	**Fairly easy,** suitable for beginner with some experience	**Fairly difficult,** suitable for competent DIY mechanic	**Difficult,** suitable for experienced DIY mechanic	**Very difficult,** suitable for expert DIY or professional

Specifications

System type .... 12-volt, negative earth

Battery
Type .... Fulmen, Delco or Steco
Charge condition:
  Poor .... 12.5 volts
  Normal .... 12.6 volts
  Good .... 12.7 volts

Alternator
Type .... Valeo or Bosch (depending on model)

Starter motor
Type .... Valeo or Bosch (depending on model)

1 General information and precautions

General information

Because of their engine-related functions, the components of the starting and charging systems are covered separately from the body electrical devices such as the lights, instruments, etc (which are covered in Chapter 12). On petrol models, refer to Part B of this Chapter for information on the ignition system. On diesel models, refer to Part C for information on the preheating system.

The electrical system is of the 12-volt negative earth type.

The battery is of the low-maintenance or "maintenance-free" (sealed for life) type and is charged by the alternator, which is belt-driven from the crankshaft pulley.

The starter motor is of the pre-engaged type, incorporating an integral solenoid. On starting, the solenoid moves the drive pinion into engagement with the flywheel ring gear before the starter motor is energised. Once the engine has started, a one-way clutch prevents the motor armature being driven by the engine until the pinion disengages from the flywheel.

Precautions

Further details of the various systems are given in the relevant Sections of this Chapter. While some repair procedures are given, the usual course of action is to renew the component concerned. The owner whose interest extends beyond mere component renewal should obtain a copy of the "Automotive Electrical & Electronic Systems Manual", available from the publishers of this manual.

It is necessary to take extra care when working on the electrical system, to avoid damage to semi-conductor devices (diodes and transistors) and to avoid the risk of personal injury. In addition to the precautions given in "Safety first!" at the beginning of this manual, observe the following when working on the system:

Always remove rings, watches, etc before working on the electrical system. Even with the battery disconnected, capacitive discharge could occur if a component's live terminal is earthed through a metal object. This could cause a shock or nasty burn.

Do not reverse the battery connections. Components such as the alternator, electronic control units, or any other components having semi-conductor circuitry could be irreparably damaged.

If the engine is being started using jump leads and a slave battery, connect the batteries positive-to-positive and negative-to-negative (see "Jump starting"). This also applies when connecting a battery charger.

Never disconnect the battery terminals, the alternator, any electrical wiring or any test instruments, when the engine is running.

5A

Do not allow the engine to turn the alternator when the alternator is not connected.

Never "test" for alternator output by "flashing" the output lead to earth.

Never use an ohmmeter of the type incorporating a hand-cranked generator for circuit or continuity testing.

Always ensure that the battery negative lead is disconnected when working on the electrical system.

Before using electric-arc welding equipment on the car, disconnect the battery, alternator and components such as the fuel injection/ignition electronic control unit, to protect them from the risk of damage.

Several systems fitted to the vehicle require battery power to be available at all times, either to ensure their continued operation (such as the clock) or to maintain control unit memories or security codes which would be wiped if the battery were to be disconnected. To ensure that there are no unforeseen consequences of this action, Refer to "Disconnecting the battery" in the Reference Section of this manual for further information.

2 Electrical fault-finding - general information

Refer to Chapter 12.

3 Battery - testing and charging

Standard and low-maintenance battery - testing

1 If the vehicle covers a small annual mileage, it is worthwhile checking the specific gravity of the electrolyte every three months, to determine the state of charge of the battery. Use a hydrometer to make the check and compare the results with the following table. Note that the specific gravity readings assume an electrolyte temperature of 15°C (60°F); for every 10°C (18°F) below 15°C (60°F), subtract 0.007. For every 10°C (18°F) above 15°C (60°F), add 0.007.

	Temp. above 25°C (77°F)	Temp. below 25°C (77°F)
Fully-charged	1.210 to 1.230	1.270 to 1.290
70% charged	1.170 to 1.190	1.230 to 1.250
Discharged	1.050 to 1.070	1.110 to 1.130

2 If the battery condition is suspect, first check the specific gravity of electrolyte in each cell. A variation of 0.040 or more between any cells indicates loss of electrolyte or deterioration of the internal plates.

3 If the specific gravity variation is 0.040 or

more, the battery should be renewed. If the cell variation is satisfactory but the battery is discharged, it should be charged as described later in this Section.

Maintenance-free battery - testing

4 In cases where a "sealed for life" maintenance-free battery is fitted, topping-up and testing of the electrolyte in each cell is not possible. The condition of the battery can therefore only be tested using a battery condition indicator or a voltmeter.

5 Certain models may be fitted with a "Delco" type maintenance-free battery, with a built-in charge condition indicator. The indicator is located in the top of the battery casing and indicates the condition of the battery from its colour. If the indicator shows green, then the battery is in a good state of charge. If the indicator turns darker, eventually to black, then the battery requires charging, as described later in this Section. If the indicator shows clear/yellow, then the electrolyte level in the battery is too low to allow further use and the battery should be renewed.

Caution: Do not attempt to charge, load or jump start a battery when the indicator shows clear/yellow.

6 If testing the battery using a voltmeter, connect the voltmeter across the battery and compare the results with those given in the Specifications under "charge condition". The test is only accurate if the battery has not been subjected to any kind of charge for the previous six hours, including charging by the alternator. If this is not the case, switch on the headlights for 30 seconds, then wait four to five minutes after switching off the headlights before testing the battery. All other electrical circuits must be switched off, so check (for instance) that the doors and tailgate are fully shut when making the test.

7 If the voltage reading is less than 12.2 volts, then the battery is discharged, whilst a reading of 12.2 to 12.4 volts indicates a partially-discharged condition.

8 If the battery is to be charged, remove it from the vehicle (Section 4) and charge it as described later in this Section.

Standard and low-maintenance battery - charging

Note: *The following is intended as a guide only. Always refer to the manufacturer's recommendations (often printed on a label attached to the battery) before charging a battery.*

9 Charge the battery at a rate of 3.5 to 4 amps and continue to charge the battery at this rate until no further rise in specific gravity is noted over a four-hour period.

10 Alternatively, a trickle charger charging at the rate of 1.5 amps can safely be used overnight.

11 Specially rapid "boost" charges, which are claimed to restore the power of the battery in 1 to 2 hours, are not recommended, as they

can cause serious damage to the battery plates through overheating.

12 While charging the battery, note that the temperature of the electrolyte should never exceed 37°C (100°F).

Maintenance-free battery - charging

Note: *The following is intended as a guide only. Always refer to the manufacturer's recommendations (often printed on a label attached to the battery) before charging a battery.*

13 This battery type takes considerably longer to fully recharge than the standard type, the time taken being dependent on the extent of discharge, but it can take anything up to three days.

14 A constant-voltage type charger is required, to be set, when connected, to 13.9 to 14.9 volts with a charger current below 25 amps. Using this method, the battery should be usable within three hours, giving a voltage reading of 12.5 volts, but this is for a partially-discharged battery and, as mentioned, full charging can take considerably longer.

15 If the battery is to be charged from a fully-discharged state (condition reading less than 12.2 volts), have it recharged by your Peugeot dealer or local automotive electrician, as the charge rate is higher and constant supervision during charging is necessary.

4 Battery - removal and refitting

Note: *Refer to "Disconnecting the battery" in the Reference Section of this manual before proceeding.*

Removal

1 The battery is located on the left-hand side of the engine compartment.

2 Disconnect the lead(s) at the negative (earth) terminal. There are two possible types of battery terminal fixings fitted on these models. With the first type, the leads are secured to a stud on the top of the terminal with a wing nut, on the second, a conventional fitting is used, secured in position by a clamp bolt and nut.

3 Remove the insulation cover (where fitted) and disconnect the positive terminal lead(s) in the same way.

4 Unscrew the nut/bolt (as applicable) and remove the battery retaining clamp.

5 Lift the battery out of the engine compartment and, where necessary, remove the insulation plate(s).

Refitting

6 Refitting is a reversal of removal, but smear petroleum jelly on the terminals when reconnecting the leads and always reconnect the positive lead first and the negative lead last.

7.3 Undo the retaining nuts (arrowed) and disconnect the wiring from the rear of the alternator

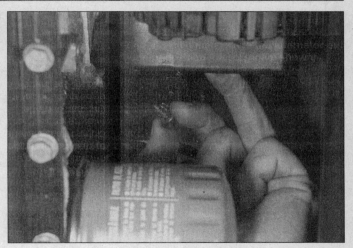

7.4a On diesel models, to improve access to the upper bolt, remove the fastener and lift the alternator cover slightly

5 Charging system - testing

Note: *Refer to the warnings given in "Safety first!" and in Section 1 of this Chapter before starting work.*

1 If the ignition/no-charge warning light does not come on when the ignition is switched on, first check the alternator wiring connections for security. If satisfactory, check that the warning light bulb has not blown and that the bulbholder is secure in its location in the instrument panel. If the light still does not come on, check the continuity of the warning light feed wire from the alternator to the bulbholder. If all is satisfactory, the alternator is at fault and should be renewed or taken to an auto-electrician for testing and repair.

2 If the ignition warning light comes on when the engine is running, stop the engine and check that the drivebelt is correctly tensioned (see the relevant Part of Chapter 1) and that the alternator connections are secure. If all is so far satisfactory, check the alternator brushes and slip rings as described in Section 8. If the fault persists, the alternator should be renewed, or taken to an auto-electrician for testing and repair.

3 If the alternator output is suspect even though the warning light functions correctly, the regulated voltage may be checked as follows.

4 Connect a voltmeter across the battery terminals and start the engine.

5 Increase the engine speed until the voltmeter reading remains steady; the reading should be approximately 12 to 13 volts and no more than 14 volts.

6 Switch on as many electrical accessories (eg, the headlights, heated rear window and heater blower) as possible and check that the alternator maintains the regulated voltage at around 13 to 14 volts.

7 If the regulated voltage is not as stated, the fault may be due to worn brushes, weak brush springs, a faulty voltage regulator, a faulty diode, a severed phase winding, or worn or damaged slip rings. The brushes and slip rings may be checked (see Section 8), but if the fault persists, the alternator should be renewed, or taken to an auto-electrician for testing and repair.

6 Alternator drivebelt - removal, refitting and tensioning

Refer to the procedure given for the auxiliary drivebelt in the relevant Part of Chapter 1.

7 Alternator - removal and refitting

Removal

1 Disconnect the battery negative terminal (refer to *"Disconnecting the battery"* in the Reference Section of this manual).

2 Slacken the auxiliary drivebelt as described

in the relevant Part of Chapter 1 and disengage it from the alternator pulley.

3 Remove the rubber covers (where fitted) from the alternator terminals, then unscrew the retaining nuts and disconnect the wiring from the rear of the alternator **(see illustration)**.

4 Unscrew the alternator upper and lower mounting bolts, then manoeuvre the alternator away from its mounting brackets and out of position. On diesel models, prise out the cover shield fastener to allow the cover to be lifted slightly to improve access to the upper bolt **(see illustrations)**.

Refitting

5 Refitting is a reversal of removal, ensuring that the alternator mountings are securely tightened and tensioning the auxiliary drivebelt as described in the relevant Part of Chapter 1.

8 Alternator brushes and regulator - inspection and renewal

5A

1 Remove the alternator as described in Section 7. Proceed as described below the relevant sub-heading.

7.4b Unscrew the upper and lower mounting bolts . . .

7.4c . . . then manoeuvre the alternator out of position (diesel model shown)

8.3a On the Valeo alternator, undo the retaining nuts (arrowed) . . .

8.3b . . . and lift off the rear cover

8.5 Pull the plastic cover to reveal the armature shaft

8.6 Regulator/brush holder retaining nuts and screw (arrowed)

8.7 Check the protrusion of the brushes (arrowed) from the holder

Valeo alternator

2 Where applicable, scrape the sealing compound from the rear plastic cover to expose the three rear cover retaining nuts.

3 Undo the retaining nuts and remove the rear cover **(see illustrations)**.

4 If necessary, scrape the sealing compound from the rear of the alternator to expose the regulator/brush holder assembly fixings. The assembly is retained by two nuts and a single screw.

5 Pull the plastic cover from the rear of the armature shaft **(see illustration)**.

8.9 Clean the armature slip rings and examine them for signs of damage

6 Undo the retaining nuts and the screw and withdraw the regulator/brush holder assembly from the rear of the alternator **(see illustration)**.

7 Measure the protrusion of each brush from the its holder. No minimum dimension is specified by the manufacturers, but excessive wear should be self-evident **(see illustration)**. If either brush requires renewal, the complete regulator/brush holder assembly must be renewed. It is not possible to renew the brushes separately.

8 If the brushes are still serviceable, clean them with a petrol-moistened cloth. Check that the brush spring tension is equal for both brushes and provides a reasonable pressure. The brushes must move freely in their holders.

9 Clean the alternator slip rings with a petrol-moistened cloth. Check for signs of scoring, burning or severe pitting on the surface of the slip rings. It may be possible to have the slip rings renovated by an electrical specialist **(see illustration)**.

10 Refit the regulator/brush holder assembly using a reverse of the removal procedure.

11 Refit the alternator as described in Section 7.

Bosch alternator

12 Unclip the cover from the rear of the alternator.

13 If necessary, scrape the sealing compound from the rear of the alternator to expose the regulator/brush holder assembly retaining screws. Slacken and remove the two retaining screws and remove the regulator/brush holder from the rear of the alternator.

14 Examine the alternator components as described above in paragraphs 7 to 9.

15 Refit the regulator/brush holder assembly and securely tighten its retaining screws.

16 Clip the rear cover onto the alternator and refit the alternator as described in Section 7.

9 Starting system - testing

Note: *Refer to the precautions given in "Safety first!" and in Section 1 of this Chapter before starting work.*

1 If the starter motor fails to operate when the ignition key is turned to the appropriate position, the following possible causes may be to blame:

a) *The battery is faulty.*

b) *The electrical connections between the switch, solenoid, battery and starter motor are somewhere failing to pass the necessary current from the battery through the starter to earth.*

10.3a On diesel models, remove the exhaust system heat shield . . .

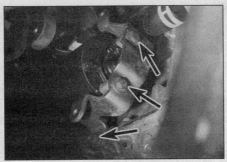

10.3b . . . then undo the retaining bolts (three arrowed) and remove the rear mounting bracket from the starter

c) The solenoid is faulty.
d) The starter motor is mechanically or electrically defective.

2 To check the battery, switch on the headlights. If they dim after a few seconds, this indicates that the battery is discharged - recharge (see Section 3) or renew the battery. If the headlights glow brightly, operate the ignition switch and observe the lights. If they dim, then this indicates that current is reaching the starter motor, therefore the fault must lie in the starter motor. If the lights continue to glow brightly (and no clicking sound can be heard from the starter motor solenoid), this indicates that there is a fault in the circuit or solenoid - see following paragraphs. If the starter motor turns slowly when operated, but the battery is in good condition, then this indicates that either the starter motor is faulty, or there is considerable resistance somewhere in the circuit.

3 If a fault in the circuit is suspected, disconnect the battery leads (including the earth connection to the body), the starter/solenoid wiring and the engine/transmission earth strap. Thoroughly clean the connections and reconnect the leads and wiring, then use a voltmeter or test light to check that full battery voltage is available at the battery positive lead connection to the solenoid and that the earth is sound. Smear petroleum jelly around the battery terminals to prevent corrosion - corroded connections are amongst the most frequent causes of electrical system faults.

4 If the battery and all connections are in good condition, check the circuit by disconnecting the wire from the solenoid blade terminal. Connect a voltmeter or test light between the wire end and a good earth (such as the battery negative terminal) and check that the wire is live when the ignition switch is turned to the "start" position. If it is, then the circuit is sound - if not, the circuit wiring can be checked as described in Chapter 12.

5 The solenoid contacts can be checked by connecting a voltmeter or test light between the battery positive feed connection on the starter side of the solenoid and earth. When the ignition switch is turned to the "start" position, there should be a reading or lighted bulb, as applicable. If there is no reading or lighted bulb, the solenoid is faulty and should be renewed.

6 If the circuit and solenoid are proved sound, the fault must lie in the starter motor. Begin checking the starter motor by removing it (see Section 10) and checking the brushes (see Section 11). If the fault does not lie in the brushes, the motor windings must be faulty. In this event, it may be possible to have the starter motor overhauled by a specialist, but check on the availability and cost of spares before proceeding, as it may prove more economical to obtain a new or exchange motor.

10 Starter motor - removal and refitting

Removal

1 Disconnect the battery negative terminal (refer to "Disconnecting the battery" in the Reference Section of this manual).

2 So that access to the motor can be gained both from above and below, firmly apply the handbrake, then jack up the front of the vehicle and support it on axle stands (see "Jacking and vehicle support").

3 On diesel models, although not strictly necessary, access to the starter motor is considerably improved if the exhaust system front pipe is first removed as described in Chapter 4D. Undo the retaining bolts and remove the heat shield from the rear of the starter motor. Slacken and remove the retaining bolts and remove the rear mounting bracket **(see illustrations)**.

4 On all models, slacken and remove the two retaining nuts and disconnect the wiring from the starter motor solenoid. Recover the washers under the nuts **(see illustration)**.

5 Undo the three mounting bolts (two at the rear of the motor and one which comes through from the top of the transmission housing), supporting the motor as the bolts are withdrawn **(see illustration)**. Recover the washers from under the bolt heads and note the locations of any wiring or hose brackets secured by the bolts.

5A

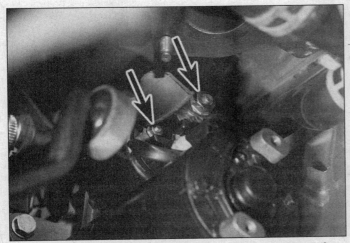

10.4 Unscrew the retaining nuts (arrowed) and disconnect the wiring from the starter motor solenoid

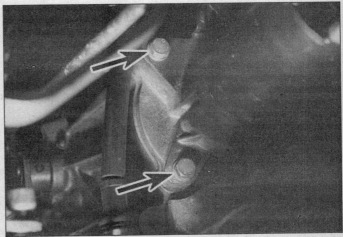

10.5 Undo the starter motor retaining bolts (rear two arrowed) and remove the motor from the vehicle

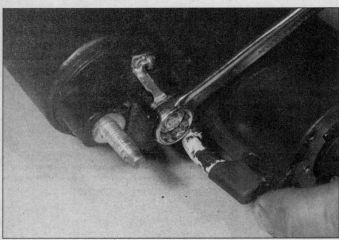

11.17 Where the brush plate assembly is supplied complete, undo the nut and disconnect its supply wire from the solenoid

11.21a On the Bosch starter motor, undo the two screws . . .

6 Manoeuvre the starter motor out from underneath the engine and recover the locating dowel(s) from the motor/transmission (as applicable).

Refitting

7 Refitting is a reversal of removal, ensuring that the locating dowel(s) are correctly positioned. Also make sure that any wiring or hose brackets are in place under the bolt heads, as noted prior to removal.

11 Starter motor - brush renewal

Note: *Consult your Peugeot dealer on the cost and availability of spare parts before stripping the starter motor, as spare parts for certain starter motors may not be available.*

1 Note that no minimum brush length is specified by the manufacturers, but it should be self-evident if the brushes are worn to the extent where renewal is required. With the motor removed as described in Section 10, proceed as described under the relevant sub-heading.

Valeo starter motor

Diesel models

2 Carefully prise the plastic cap from the end of the armature shaft, using a screwdriver or similar tool.
3 Prise the C-clip from the end of the armature shaft and recover the shim.
4 Unscrew the two through-bolts, then withdraw the end cover from the motor casing and recover the shim from the armature shaft. Do not mix up the shim with the one removed in the previous paragraph.
5 Carefully pull the brush plate from the end of the armature.
6 Using a suitable screwdriver, release the brush retainers and withdraw the brushes from the brush holders.

7 Unsolder the brush leads or release them from the clips on the brush plate, as applicable.
8 Fit the new brushes. Solder the leads into position, or secure them to the brush plate by bending the securing clips into position, as applicable. Where the brush plate is supplied as a complete assembly, undo the terminal nut and remove the old brush plate, then install the new assembly and securely tighten the terminal nut.
9 Fit the brush plate over the end of the armature shaft, leaving enough clearance to fit the brushes Note that when finally fitted, the lug on the brush plate must locate in the corresponding hole in the motor casing.
10 Push the brushes into their holders, so that they rest against the commutator on the armature shaft.
11 Carefully fit the brush retainers, complete with springs and secure them to retain the brushes.
12 Check that the brushes are seated on the commutator, then slide the brush plate down the armature shaft until the lug on the brush plate engages with the hole in the motor casing.
13 Further refitting is a reversal of removal, ensuring that the shims are fitted to the armature shaft, as noted before removal.

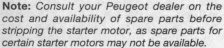

11.21b . . . and remove the centre cap from the end cover

Petrol models

14 Undo the retaining nuts, then withdraw the end cover from the armature. Recover any shims which may be fitted to the armature end, noting their correct fitted positions.
15 Carefully pull the brush plate from the end of the armature.
16 Using a suitable screwdriver, lift the brush springs and withdraw the brushes from the brush holders. Unsolder the brush leads, or release them from the clips on the brush plate, as applicable.
17 Fit the new brushes. Solder the leads into position, or secure them to the brush plate by bending the securing clips into position, as applicable. Lift the springs and slide the brushes into position. Position the springs on the side of each brush, so that the brushes are jammed in the holders. Where the brush plate is supplied as a complete assembly, undo the terminal nut and remove the old brush plate, then install the new assembly and securely tighten the terminal nut **(see illustration)**.
18 Locate the brush plate over the end of the armature shaft, then push the brushes fully into their holders. Ensure that the springs are correctly located against the end of each brush. Check that each brush is seated against the commutator and is free to move easily in its holder.
19 Refit the shim(s) to the end of the armature shaft.
20 Slide the rear cover fully into position and securely tighten its retaining nuts.

Bosch starter motor

21 Undo the two retaining screws and remove the centre cap from the starter motor rear cover **(see illustrations)**.
22 Prise the C-clip from the end of the armature shaft and recover the shims, noting their correct fitted positions **(see illustrations)**.
23 Unscrew the two through-bolts, then withdraw the end cover from the motor casing

11.22a Slide out the C-clip . . .

11.22b . . . and recover the shim(s) from the armature

and recover any relevant shims from the armature shaft **(see illustrations)**. Do not mix up the shim with the ones removed in the previous paragraph.

24 Carefully pull the brush plate from the end of the armature.

25 Fit the new brushes as described above in paragraphs 16 to 18.

26 Refit any relevant shims to the armature end, then install the rear cover and secure it in position with the through-bolts.

27 Refit the outer shims in their correct order and secure them in position with the C-clip. Install the centre cap and securely tighten its screws.

11.23a Undo the two through-bolts . . .

11.23b . . . and remove the end cover from the motor

12 Ignition switch -
removal and refitting

The ignition switch is integral with the steering column lock and can be removed as described in Chapter 10.

13 Oil pressure warning light switch -
removal and refitting

Removal

1 The switch is located at the front of the cylinder block, above the oil filter mounting. On some models, access to the switch may be improved if the vehicle is jacked up and supported on axle stands, so that the switch can be reached from underneath (see *"Jacking and vehicle support"*).

2 Disconnect the battery negative terminal (refer to *"Disconnecting the battery"* in the Reference Section of this manual).

3 Remove the protective sleeve from the wiring plug (where applicable), then disconnect the wiring from the switch.

4 Unscrew the switch from the cylinder block and recover the sealing washer. Be prepared for oil spillage; if the switch is to be left removed from the engine for any length of time, plug the hole in the cylinder block.

Refitting

5 Examine the sealing washer for signs of damage or deterioration and if necessary renew it.

6 Refit the switch, complete with washer and tighten it securely. Reconnect the wiring connector.

7 Lower the vehicle to the ground. Check and, if necessary, top-up the engine oil as described in *"Weekly checks"*.

14 Oil level sensor -
removal and refitting

1 The sensor is located on the front side of the cylinder block, just to the right of the oil filter.

2 The removal and refitting procedure is as described for the oil pressure switch in Section 13. Access is most easily obtained from underneath the vehicle.

15 Oil temperature sensor -
removal and refitting

Removal

1 The oil temperature sensor is screwed into the rear of the sump.

2 To gain access to the sensor, chock the rear wheels then jack up the front of the vehicle and support it on axle stands (see *"Jacking and Vehicle Support"*).

3 Drain the engine oil into a clean container, then refit the drain plug and tighten it to the specified torque setting (see the relevant Part of Chapter 1).

4 Disconnect the wiring connector, then unscrew the sensor from the sump and remove it from underneath the vehicle along with its sealing washer.

Refitting

5 Examine the sealing washer for signs of damage or deterioration and if necessary renew it.

6 Refit the sensor, tightening it securely and reconnect the wiring connector.

7 Lower the vehicle to the ground. Refill the engine with oil as described in the relevant Part of Chapter 1.

5A

Notes

Chapter 5 Part B:
Ignition system (petrol models)

Contents

Degrees of difficulty

Easy, suitable for novice with little experience	**Fairly easy,** suitable for beginner with some experience	**Fairly difficult,** suitable for competent DIY mechanic	**Difficult,** suitable for experienced DIY mechanic	**Very difficult,** suitable for expert DIY or professional

Specifications

System type
Carburettor models	Breakerless electronic ignition system
Fuel-injected models:	
954 cc models	Static (distributorless) ignition system controlled by engine management ECU
1124 cc models:	
Early (pre-July 1992) models	Breakerless electronic ignition system
Later (July 1992-on) models	Static (distributorless) ignition system controlled by engine management ECU
1294 cc models	Static (distributorless) ignition system controlled by engine management ECU
1360 cc single-point injection models:*	
KDY engine models	Breakerless electronic ignition system
KDX engine models	Static (distributorless) ignition system controlled by engine management ECU
1360 cc multi-point injection models	Static (distributorless) ignition system controlled by engine management ECU
1587 cc models	Static (distributorless) ignition system controlled by engine management ECU

Refer to Chapter 2A for further information on engine codes.

Firing order
Firing order	1-3-4-2 (No 1 cylinder at transmission end)

Ignition timing
Models with a distributor	8° BTDC @ 750 rpm
Models with static (distributorless) ignition	Controlled by the ECU - see text

Ignition HT coil resistances:*
Models with a distributor:	
Primary windings	0.8 ohms
Secondary windings	6.5 k ohms
Models with static (distributorless) ignition:	
Primary windings	0.5 to 0.8 ohms
Secondary windings - Bosch coil	14.6 k ohms
Secondary windings - Valeo coil	8.6 k ohms

The above results are approximate values and are accurate only when the coil is at 20°C. See text for further information

Torque wrench setting
	Nm	lbf ft
Distributor mounting nuts	8	6

1 General information

Carburettor models

On all carburettor models, a breakerless electronic ignition system is used. The system comprises solely of the HT ignition coil and the distributor, both of which are mounted on the left-hand end of the cylinder head, the distributor being driven off the end of the camshaft.

The distributor contains a reluctor mounted onto its shaft and a magnet and stator fixed to its body. The ignition amplifier unit is also mounted onto the side of the distributor body. The system operates as follows.

When the ignition is switched on but the engine is stationary, the transistors in the amplifier unit prevent current flowing through the ignition system primary (LT) circuit.

As the crankshaft rotates, the reluctor moves through the magnetic field created by the stator. When the reluctor teeth are in alignment with the stator projections, a small AC voltage is created. The amplifier unit uses this voltage to switch the transistors in the unit and completes the ignition system primary (LT) circuit.

As the reluctor teeth move out of alignment with the stator projections the AC voltage changes and the transistors in the amplifier unit are switched again to interrupt the primary (LT) circuit. This causes a high voltage to be induced in the coil secondary (HT) windings which then travels down the HT lead to the distributor and onto the relevant spark plug.

A TDC sensor is fitted to the rear of the flywheel, but the sensor is not part of the ignition system. It is there to be used for diagnostic purposes only.

Early 1124 cc and 1360 cc fuel-injected models

On early (pre-July 1992) 1124 cc models and 1360 cc (KDY engine) fuel-injected models with the Bosch Monopoint A2.2 fuel injection system (see Chapter 4B), a breakerless electronic ignition system is fitted. This operates in the same way as that described above for the carburettor models above.

In addition to system components described above, the system is equipped with an ignition timing retard system. This reduces the nitrous oxide (NOx) content of the exhaust gases. This is achieved by reducing the temperature at the end of the combustion, by reducing the ignition advance at certain engine temperatures. This system is controlled by the fuel injection ECU. The ECU has control over an electrically-operated solenoid valve, mounted in the engine compartment, which is fitted in the vacuum pipe linking the distributor vacuum diaphragm unit to the inlet manifold. At certain engine temperatures, the ECU switches off the solenoid valve, which then cuts off the vacuum supply to the distributor vacuum diaphragm, thereby reducing the ignition advance.

A TDC sensor is fitted to the rear of the flywheel, but the sensor is not part of the ignition system. It is there to be used for diagnostic purposes only.

All other fuel-injected (8-valve) models

On all other (8-valve) models, the ignition system is integrated with the fuel injection system, to form a combined engine management system under the control of one ECU (see the relevant Part of Chapter 4 for further information).

The ignition side of the system is of the static (distributorless) type, consisting only of a four-output ignition coil. The ignition coil actually consists of two separate HT coils, which supply two cylinders each (one coil supplies cylinders 1 and 4 and the other cylinders 2 and 3). Under the control of the ECU, the ignition coil operates on the "wasted spark" principle. The spark plugs are fired in two pairs, twice for each complete cycle of the engine. One plug of each pair will fire on a compression stroke and one on an exhaust stroke; the spark on the exhaust stroke has no effect on the running of the engine and is therefore "wasted". The ECU uses inputs from various sensors to calculate the required ignition advance setting and coil charging time.

On certain models, a knock sensor is incorporated into the ignition system. The sensor is mounted on the cylinder block and prevents the engine "pinking" under load. The sensor is sensitive to vibration and detects the knocking which occurs when the engine starts to "pink" (pre-ignite). The knock sensor sends an electrical signal to the ECU, which in turn retards the ignition advance setting until the "pinking" ceases.

1587 cc (16-valve) models

On 16-valve models, the ignition side of the system is also of the static (distributorless) type and consists primarily of four ignition coils located in an ignition coil unit fitted to the centre of the cylinder head cover. The coils are integral with the spark plug caps and are pushed directly onto the spark plugs, one for each plug. This removes the need for any HT leads connecting the coils to the plugs. The ECU uses the inputs from the various sensors to calculate the required ignition advance setting and calculate the coil charging time.

2 Ignition system - testing

⚠️ **Warning: Voltages produced by an electronic ignition system are considerably higher than those produced by conventional ignition systems. Extreme care must be taken when working on the system if the ignition is switched on. Persons with surgically-implanted cardiac pacemaker devices should keep well clear of the ignition circuits, components and test equipment**

Models with a distributor

Note: *Refer to the precautions given in Section 1 of Part A of this Chapter before starting work. Always switch off the ignition before disconnecting or connecting any component and when using a multi-meter to check resistances.*

General

1 The components of electronic ignition systems are normally very reliable; most faults are far more likely to be due to loose or dirty connections, or to "tracking" of HT voltage due to dirt, dampness or damaged insulation, than to the failure of any of the system's components. **Always** check all wiring thoroughly before condemning an electrical component and work methodically to eliminate all other possibilities before deciding that a particular component is faulty.

2 The old practice of checking for a spark by holding the live end of an HT lead a short distance away from the engine is **not** recommended; not only is there a high risk of a powerful electric shock, but the HT coil or amplifier unit will be damaged. Similarly, **never** try to "diagnose" misfires by pulling off one HT lead at a time.

Engine will not start

3 If the engine either will not turn over at all, or only turns very slowly, check the battery and starter motor. Connect a voltmeter across the battery terminals (meter positive probe to battery positive terminal), disconnect the ignition coil HT lead from the distributor cap and earth it, then note the voltage reading obtained while turning over the engine on the starter for (no more than) ten seconds. If the reading obtained is less than approximately 9.5 volts, first check the battery, starter motor and charging system as described in the relevant Sections of Chapter 5A.

4 If the engine turns over at normal speed but will not start, check the HT circuit by connecting a timing light (following its manufacturer's instructions) and turning the engine over on the starter motor; if the light flashes, voltage is reaching the spark plugs, so these should be checked first. If the light does not flash, check the HT leads themselves, followed by the distributor cap, carbon brush and rotor arm, using the information given in Chapter 1A.

5 If there is a spark, check the fuel system for faults, referring to the relevant part of Chapter 4 for further information.

6 If there is still no spark, check the voltage at the ignition HT coil "+" terminal; it should be the same as the battery voltage (ie, at least 11.7 volts). If the voltage at the coil is more than 1 volt less than that at the battery, check

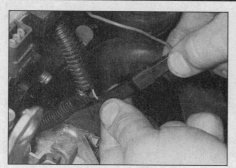

3.3 On models with a distributor, disconnect the capacitor wiring connector and release the TDC sensor connector . . .

3.4a . . . then disconnect the HT lead . . .

plugged. The tester will locate the fault quickly and simply, alleviating the need to test all the system components individually, which is a time-consuming operation that carries a high risk of damaging the ECU.

17 The only ignition system checks which can be carried out by the home mechanic are those in Chapter 1A, relating to the spark plugs and the ignition coil test described in this Chapter. If necessary, the system wiring and wiring connectors can be checked as described in Chapter 12, ensuring that the ECU wiring connector(s) have first been disconnected.

the feed back through the fusebox and ignition switch to the battery and its earth until the fault is found.

7 If the feed to the HT coil is sound, check the coil's primary and secondary winding resistance as described later in this Section. If faulty, a new coil should be fitted. However, check carefully the condition of the LT connections themselves before doing so, to ensure that the fault is not due to dirty or poorly-fastened connectors.

8 If the HT coil is in good condition, the fault is probably within the amplifier unit or distributor stator assembly. Testing of these components should be entrusted to a Peugeot dealer.

Engine misfires

9 An irregular misfire suggests either a loose connection or intermittent fault on the primary circuit, or an HT fault on the coil side of the rotor arm.

10 With the ignition switched off, check carefully through the system, ensuring that all connections are clean and securely fastened. If the equipment is available, check the LT circuit as described above.

11 Check that the HT coil, the distributor cap and the HT leads are clean and dry. Check the leads themselves and the spark plugs (by substitution, if necessary), then check the distributor cap, carbon brush and rotor arm as described in Chapter 1A.

12 Regular misfiring is almost certainly due to a fault in the distributor cap, HT leads or spark plugs. Use a timing light (paragraph 4 above) to

check whether HT voltage is present at all leads.

13 If HT voltage is not present on any particular lead, the fault will be in that lead, or in the distributor cap. If HT is present on all leads, the fault will be in the spark plugs; check and renew them if there is any doubt about their condition.

14 If no HT is present, check the HT coil; its secondary windings may be breaking down under load.

Models with a static (distributorless) ignition system

15 If a fault appears in the engine management (fuel injection/ignition) system, first ensure that the fault is not due to a poor electrical connection or poor maintenance; ie, check that the air cleaner filter element is clean, the spark plugs are in good condition and correctly gapped and that the engine breather hoses are clear and undamaged, referring to Chapter 1A for further information. Also check that the accelerator cable is correctly adjusted, as described in the relevant Part of Chapter 4. If the engine is running very roughly, check the compression pressures and the valve clearances as described in Chapter 2A.

16 If these checks fail to reveal the cause of the problem, the vehicle should be taken to a suitably-equipped Peugeot dealer for testing. A wiring block connector is incorporated in the engine management circuit, into which a special electronic diagnostic tester can be

3 Ignition HT coil - removal, testing and refitting

Removal

Models with a distributor

1 Disconnect the battery negative terminal (refer to *"Disconnecting the battery"* in the Reference Section of this manual).

2 Disconnect the hot-air intake hose from the exhaust manifold shroud and air temperature control valve and remove it from the engine. Release the intake duct fastener and position the duct clear of the coil.

3 Disconnect the wiring connector from the capacitor mounted on the coil mounting bracket and release the TDC sensor wiring connector from the front of the bracket **(see illustration)**.

4 Disconnect the HT lead from the coil, then depress the retaining clip and disconnect the coil wiring connector **(see illustrations)**.

5 Slacken and remove the two retaining bolts and remove the coil and mounting bracket from the cylinder head. Where necessary, slacken and remove the four screws and nuts and separate the HT coil and mounting bracket **(see illustrations)**.

8-valve models with a static (distributorless) ignition system

6 Disconnect the battery negative terminal (refer to *"Disconnecting the battery"* in the Reference Section of this manual).

5B

3.4b . . . and wiring connector (arrowed) from the ignition HT coil

3.5a Undo the two retaining bolts (arrowed) . . .

3.5b . . . and remove the coil and mounting bracket from the engine

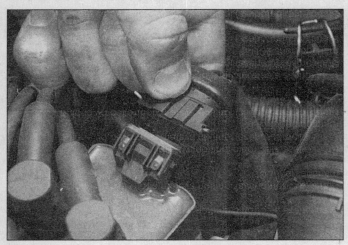

3.7 On models with a static (distributorless) ignition system, disconnect the wiring connector from the HT coil . . .

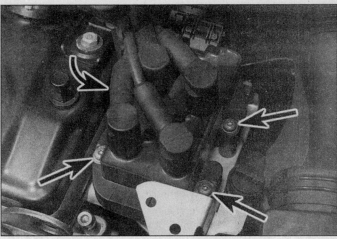

3.9 . . . then disconnect the HT leads from the coil. Undo the four retaining screws (arrowed) and remove the coil

7 The ignition HT coil is mounted on the left-hand end of the cylinder head. Depress the retaining clip and disconnect the wiring connector from the HT coil (see illustration).

8 Make a note of the correct fitted positions of the HT leads, then disconnect them from the coil terminals (see illustration 3.9).

9 Undo the four retaining screws securing the coil to its mounting bracket and remove it from the engine compartment (see illustration).

16-valve models

10 Disconnect the battery negative terminal (refer to "Disconnecting the battery" in the Reference Section of this manual).

11 There are four separate ignition HT coils, one on the top of each spark plug. To gain access to the coils, disconnect the wiring connectors at the left-hand end of the coil unit, then undo the retaining bolts and lift the coil unit upwards, off the spark plugs and from its location in the cylinder head cover. The individual coils can now be removed as required.

Testing

8-valve models

12 Testing of the coil is carried out using a multi-meter set to its resistance function, to check the primary (LT "+" to "-" terminals) and secondary (LT "+" to HT lead terminal) windings for continuity. Bear in mind that on the four-output, static type HT coil, there are two sets of each windings. Compare the results obtained to those given in the Specifications at the start of this Chapter. The resistance of the coil windings will vary slightly according to the coil temperature - the results in the Specifications are approximate values for when the coil is at 20°C.

13 Check that there is no continuity between the HT lead terminal and the coil body/mounting bracket.

14 If the coil is thought to be faulty, have your findings confirmed by a Peugeot dealer before renewing the coil.

16-valve models

15 The circuitry arrangement of the ignition coils and the coil unit on these engines is such that testing of an individual coil in isolation from the remainder of the engine management system is unlikely to prove effective in diagnosing a particular fault. Should there be any reason to suspect a faulty individual coil, the engine management system should be tested by a Peugeot dealer using diagnostic test equipment (see Section 2).

Refitting

16 Refitting is a reversal of the relevant removal procedure. Ensure that the wiring connectors and the HT lead(s) are securely reconnected.

4 Distributor - removal and refitting

Removal

1 Disconnect the battery negative terminal (refer to "Disconnecting the battery" in the Reference Section of this manual). If necessary, to improve access to the distributor, remove the ignition HT coil as described in Section 3 and the intake duct as described in Chapter 4A.

2 Peel back the waterproof cover, then slacken and remove the distributor cap retaining screws. Remove the cap and place it clear of the distributor body (see illustrations). Recover the seal from the cap.

3 Depress the retaining clip and disconnect the wiring connector from the distributor. Disconnect the hose from the vacuum diaphragm unit (see illustrations).

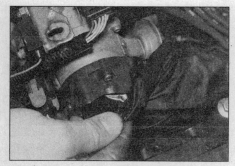

4.2a Peel back the waterproof cover . . .

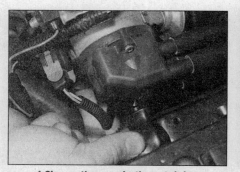

4.2b . . . then undo the retaining screws . . .

4.2c . . . and remove the cap from the end of the distributor

4.3a Disconnect the distributor wiring connector . . .

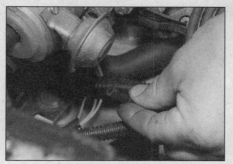

4.3b . . . and the vacuum diaphragm hose . . .

4.4 . . . then undo the retaining nuts and remove the distributor

4 Check the cylinder head and distributor flange for signs of alignment marks. If no marks are visible, using a scriber or suitable marker pen, mark the relationship of the distributor body to the cylinder head. Slacken and remove the two mounting nuts and withdraw the distributor from the cylinder head **(see illustration)**. Remove the O-ring from the end of the distributor body and discard it; a new one must be used on refitting.

Refitting

5 Lubricate the new O-ring with a smear of engine oil and fit it to the groove in the distributor body. Examine the distributor cap seal for wear or damage and renew if necessary.

6 Align the distributor rotor shaft drive coupling key with the slots in the camshaft end, noting that the slots are offset to ensure that the distributor can only be fitted in one position. Carefully insert the distributor into the cylinder head, rotating the rotor arm slightly to ensure that the coupling is correctly engaged.

7 Align the marks noted or made (as applicable) on removal. Install the distributor retaining nuts, tightening them only lightly at this stage.

8 Ensure that the seal is correctly located in its groove, then refit the cap assembly to the distributor and tighten its retaining screws securely. Fold the waterproof cover back over

the distributor cap, ensuring that it is correctly located.

9 Reconnect the vacuum hose to the diaphragm unit and the distributor wiring connector. Where necessary, refit the ignition HT coil as described in Section 3 and the intake duct as described in Chapter 4A.

10 Check and, if necessary, adjust the ignition timing as described in Section 6, then tighten the distributor mounting nuts to the specified torque.

---

5 Ignition system amplifier unit - removal and refitting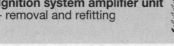

Removal

1 Disconnect the battery negative terminal (refer to *"Disconnecting the battery"* in the Reference Section of this manual).

2 The amplifier unit is mounted on the side of the distributor body **(see illustration)**. To improve access to the unit, disengage the hot-air intake hose from the control valve and the exhaust manifold shroud and remove it from the vehicle.

3 Disconnect the wiring connector, then undo the two retaining screws and remove the amplifier unit.

Refitting

4 Refitting is a reverse of the removal procedure.

---

6 Ignition timing - checking and adjustment

Models with a distributor

1 To check the ignition timing, a stroboscopic timing light will be required. It is also recommended that the flywheel timing mark is highlighted as follows.

2 Remove the plug from the aperture on the front of the transmission clutch housing. Using a socket and suitable extension bar on the crankshaft pulley bolt, slowly turn the engine over until the timing mark (a straight line) scribed on the edge of the flywheel appears in the aperture. Highlight the line with quick-drying white paint - typist's correction fluid is ideal **(see illustrations)**.

3 Start the engine, allow it to warm up to normal operating temperature, then switch off.

4 Disconnect the vacuum hose from the distributor diaphragm and plug the hose end.

5 Connect the timing light to No 1 cylinder (nearest the transmission) plug lead as described in the timing light manufacturer's instructions.

6 Start the engine, allowing it to idle at the specified speed and point the timing light at the transmission housing aperture. The flywheel timing mark should be aligned with the relevant notch on the timing plate (refer to

5B

5.2 The ignition amplifier unit is secured to the side of the distributor by two screws

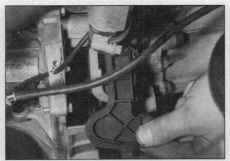

6.2a On models with a distributor, remove the plug from the transmission housing . . .

6.2b . . . to reveal the timing plate and flywheel timing mark (arrowed)

the Specifications for the correct timing setting); the numbers on the plate indicate degrees Before Top Dead Centre (BTDC).

7 If adjustment is necessary, slacken the two distributor mounting nuts, then slowly rotate the distributor body as required until the flywheel mark and relevant timing plate notch are brought into alignment. Once the marks are correctly aligned, hold the distributor stationary and tighten its mounting nuts to the specified torque. Recheck the timing marks are still correctly aligned and, if necessary, repeat the adjustment procedure.

8 When the timing is correctly set, increase engine speed and check that the pulley mark advances to beyond the beginning of the timing plate reference marks, returning to close to the specified mark when the engine is allowed to idle. This check shows that the centrifugal advance mechanism is at least functioning - a detailed check must be left to a Peugeot dealer who has the necessary equipment. Reconnect the vacuum hose to the distributor and repeat the check. The rate of advance should significantly increase if the vacuum diaphragm is functioning correctly, but again, a detailed check must be left to a Peugeot dealer.

9 When the ignition timing is correct, stop the engine and disconnect the timing light.

Models with static (distributorless) ignition systems

10 On models with static (distributorless) ignition systems, Peugeot do not quote any specified timing settings. Therefore, it is not possible for the home mechanic to check the ignition timing.

11 The timing setting is constantly being monitored and adjusted by the engine management ECU and, therefore, nominal values cannot be given. The only way to check the ignition timing is using special electronic test equipment which is connected to the engine management system diagnostic connector (see the relevant Part of Chapter 4 for further information).

12 On later (July 1992-on) 1124 cc and all 1294 cc models with a Magneti Marelli engine management system (see relevant Part of Chapter 4), adjustment of the ignition timing is possible. However, adjustments can be made only by re-programming the ECU using the special electronic test equipment.

13 On all other models, no adjustment of the ignition timing is possible. Should the ignition timing be incorrect, a fault must be present in the engine management system and the vehicle should be taken to a Peugeot dealer for testing.

Chapter 5 Part C:
Preheating system (diesel models)

Contents

Degrees of difficulty

Easy, suitable for novice with little experience	**Fairly easy,** suitable for beginner with some experience	**Fairly difficult,** suitable for competent DIY mechanic	**Difficult,** suitable for experienced DIY mechanic	**Very difficult,** suitable for expert DIY or professional

Specifications

Torque wrench setting	Nm	lbf ft
Glow plugs	22	16

5C

1 Preheating system - description and testing

Description

Each swirl chamber has a heater plug (commonly called a glow plug) screwed into it. The plugs are electrically operated before start-up by the preheating control unit.

A warning light in the instrument panel tells the driver that preheating is taking place. When the light goes out, the engine is ready to be started. If no attempt is made to start, the timer then cuts off the supply, in order to avoid draining the battery and overheating the glow plugs.

Testing

If the system malfunctions, testing is ultimately by substitution of known good units, but some preliminary checks may be made as follows.

Connect a voltmeter or 12-volt test light between the glow plug supply cable and earth (engine or vehicle metal). Make sure that the live connection is kept clear of the engine and bodywork.

Have an assistant switch on the ignition and check that voltage is supplied to the glow plugs. Note the time for which the warning light is lit and the total time for which voltage is supplied before the system cuts out. Switch off the ignition.

If all is well, voltage will be supplied and the warning light will stay on for approximately 5 to 6 seconds.

If there is no supply at all, the control unit or associated wiring is at fault.

To locate a defective glow plug, disconnect the main supply cable and interconnecting wire from the top of the glow plugs.
Caution: Be careful not to drop the nuts and washers.

Use a continuity tester, or a 12-volt test light connected to the battery positive terminal, to check for continuity between each glow plug terminal and earth. The resistance of a glow plug in good condition is very low (less than 1 ohm), so if the test light does not come on, or if the continuity tester shows a high resistance, the glow plug is certainly defective.

If an ammeter is available, the current draw of each glow plug can be checked. After an initial surge of around 15 to 20 amps, each plug should draw around 10 amps. Any plug which draws much more or less than this is probably defective.

As a final check, the glow plugs can be removed and inspected as described in Section 2.

2.2a Unscrew the nut (arrowed) . . .

2.2b . . . and disconnect the wiring from the glow plug

2.4 Unscrew the glow plug and remove it from the cylinder head

2 Glow plugs - removal, inspection and refitting

Removal

Caution: If the preheating system has just been energised, or if the engine has been running, the glow plugs will be very hot.

1 Disconnect the battery negative terminal (refer to *"Disconnecting the battery"* in the Reference Section of this manual).

2 Unscrew the nut from the relevant glow plug terminal(s) and recover the washer(s). Note that the main supply cable is connected to No 1 cylinder glow plug (at the transmission end) and an interconnecting wire is fitted between the four plugs **(see illustrations)**.

3 Where applicable, carefully move any obstructing pipes or wires to one side, to gain access to the relevant glow plug(s).

4 Unscrew the glow plug(s) and remove from the cylinder head **(see illustration)**.

Inspection

5 Inspect each glow plug for physical damage. Burnt or eroded glow plug tips can be caused by a bad injector spray pattern. Have the injectors checked if this sort of damage is found.

6 If the glow plugs are in good physical condition, check them electrically using a 12-volt test light or continuity tester as described in the previous Section.

7 The glow plugs can be energised by applying 12 volts to them, to verify that they heat up evenly and in the required time. Observe the following precautions:

a) *Support the glow plug by clamping it carefully in a vice or self-locking pliers.* **Remember - it will become red-hot**.

b) *Make sure that the power supply or test lead incorporates a fuse or overload trip, to protect against damage from a short-circuit.*

c) *After testing, allow the glow plug to cool for several minutes before attempting to handle it.*

8 A glow plug in good condition will start to glow red at the tip after drawing current for 5 seconds or so. Any plug which takes much longer to start glowing, or which starts glowing in the middle instead of at the tip, is defective.

Refitting

9 Refit by reversing the removal operations. Apply a smear of copper-based anti-seize compound to the plug threads and tighten the glow plugs to the specified torque. Do not overtighten, as this can damage the glow plug element.

3 Preheating system control unit - removal and refitting

Removal

1 The unit is located on the right-hand side of the engine compartment, on the coolant expansion tank.

2 Disconnect the battery negative terminal (refer to *"Disconnecting the battery"* in the Reference Section of this manual).

3 Unscrew the retaining bolt securing the unit to the coolant expansion tank **(see illustration)**.

4 Disconnect the wiring connector from the base of the unit. Unscrew the two retaining nuts and free the main feed and supply wires from the unit - note their locations for use when refitting **(see illustrations)**. Remove the unit from the engine compartment.

Refitting

5 Refitting is a reversal of removal, ensuring that all wiring is securely connected to its original location, as noted on removal.

3.3 Unscrew the preheating unit retaining bolt (arrowed) and free the unit from the expansion tank

3.4a Disconnect the wiring connector . . .

3.4b . . . then undo the two nuts securing the feed and supply wires to the unit

Chapter 6
Clutch

Contents

Degrees of difficulty

Easy, suitable for novice with little experience	Fairly easy, suitable for beginner with some experience	Fairly difficult, suitable for competent DIY mechanic	Difficult, suitable for experienced DIY mechanic	Very difficult, suitable for expert DIY or professional

Specifications

Type .... Single dry plate with diaphragm spring. Cable-operated release mechanism

Clutch pedal travel* .... 140 ± 5 mm
On later models the clutch cable is automatically adjusted and therefore the pedal travel is not adjustable - see text

Friction plate diameter
954 cc models:
  Pre-March 1993 models .... 160 mm
  March 1993-on models .... 180 mm
1124 cc carburettor models:
  Pre-March 1993 models .... 160 mm
  March 1993-on models .... 180 mm
1124 cc fuel-injected models .... 180 mm
1294 cc and 1360 cc models .... 180 mm
1527 cc models .... 180 mm
1587 cc models .... 200 mm

Torque wrench setting	Nm	lbf ft
Pressure plate retaining bolts	20	15

1 General information

The clutch consists of a friction plate, a pressure plate assembly, a release bearing and the release mechanism; all of these components are contained in the large cast aluminium alloy bellhousing, sandwiched between the engine and the transmission. The release mechanism is mechanical, being operated by a cable.

The friction plate is fitted between the engine flywheel and the clutch pressure plate and is allowed to slide on the transmission input shaft splines. It consists of two circular facings of friction material riveted in position to provide the clutch bearing surface and a spring-cushioned hub to damp out transmission shocks.

The pressure plate assembly is bolted to the engine flywheel and is located by three dowel pins. When the engine is running, drive is transmitted from the crankshaft via the flywheel to the friction plate (these components being clamped securely together by the pressure plate assembly) and from the friction plate to the transmission input shaft.

To interrupt the drive, the spring pressure must be relaxed. This is achieved by a sealed release bearing fitted concentrically around the transmission input shaft; when the driver depresses the clutch pedal, the release bearing is pressed against the fingers at the centre of the diaphragm spring. Since the spring is held by rivets between two annular fulcrum rings, the pressure at its centre causes it to deform so that it flattens and thus releases the clamping force it exerts, at its periphery, on the pressure plate.

Depressing the clutch pedal pulls the control cable inner wire and this in turn rotates the release fork by acting on the lever at the fork's upper end, above the bellhousing. The fork itself is clipped to the left of the release bearing.

As the friction plate facings wear, the pressure plate moves towards the flywheel; this causes the diaphragm spring fingers to push against the release bearing, thus reducing the clearance which must be present in the mechanism. On early models, to ensure correct operation, the clutch must be regularly adjusted. On later models the clutch cable has an automatic adjuster built into the cable.

6

2.2 To check clutch cable adjustment, measure the clutch pedal travel as described in text

2 Clutch - adjustment

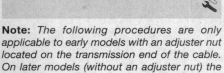

Note: *The following procedures are only applicable to early models with an adjuster nut located on the transmission end of the cable. On later models (without an adjuster nut) the cable is self-adjusting.*

1 The clutch adjustment is checked by measuring the clutch pedal travel.

2 Ensuring that there are no obstructions beneath the clutch pedal, depress the clutch pedal fully to the floor, measuring the distance that the centre of the clutch pedal pad travels through from the at-rest position to the floor **(see illustration)**. Using a ruler for this check might prove awkward - as an alternative, mark the at-rest and fully-depressed positions on a strip of wood and measure the distance (the pedal travel) between them. If this is less than the specified distance given in the Specifications at the start of this Chapter, adjust the clutch as follows.

3 The clutch cable is adjusted by means of the adjuster nut on the transmission end of the cable. Access to the locknut is limited and, if required, the battery can be removed to improve access. Refer to Chapter 5A for further information. Alternatively, easy access to the adjuster nut can be gained from underneath. Chock the rear wheels then jack up the front of the vehicle and support it on axle stands (see *"Jacking and Vehicle Support"*).

4 Slacken the locknut from the end of the

2.4 Adjusting the clutch cable - viewed from above with battery removed

clutch cable. Adjust the position of the adjuster nut **(see illustration)**, then re-measure the clutch pedal travel. Repeat this procedure until the clutch pedal travel is as specified.

5 Once the adjuster nut is correctly positioned and the pedal travel is correctly set, securely tighten the cable locknut. Where applicable, refit the battery as described in Chapter 5A and lower the vehicle to the ground.

3 Clutch cable - removal and refitting

Removal

1 Working in the engine compartment, release the inner cable and outer cable fittings from the clutch release lever and mounting bracket and free the cable from the transmission housing. On early models, where necessary, fully slacken the locknut and adjuster nut from the end of the clutch cable to aid removal. On some models, access to the nuts is limited and, if required, the battery can be removed to improve access. Refer to Chapter 5A for further information. Alternatively, easy access to the adjuster nut can be gained from underneath. Chock the rear wheels then jack up the front of the vehicle and support it on axle stands (see *"Jacking and Vehicle Support"*).

2 Working inside the vehicle, undo the retaining nuts and remove the under-facia trim panel from the driver's side of the facia.

3 Unhook the clutch inner cable from the top of the clutch pedal. Note that access to the top of the pedal is very poor.

4 Return to the engine compartment and slacken and remove the nut (where fitted) securing the outer cable to the engine compartment bulkhead.

5 Withdraw the cable forwards through the bulkhead, releasing it from any relevant retaining clips and guides and noting its correct routing and remove it from the vehicle.

6 Examine the cable, looking for worn end fittings or a damaged outer casing and for signs of fraying of the inner wire. Check the cable's operation - the inner wire should move smoothly and easily through the outer casing. Remember, however, that a cable that appears serviceable when tested off the car may well be much heavier in operation, when compressed into its working position. Renew the cable if it shows any signs of excessive wear or of damage.

Refitting

7 Apply a thin smear of multi-purpose grease to the cable end fittings, then pass the cable through the engine compartment bulkhead. Clip the cable into position and, where necessary, refit the cable retaining nut and tighten it securely.

8 From inside the vehicle, hook the inner cable over the clutch pedal end and check that it is securely retained. Refit the under-facia trim panel and securely tighten its retaining nuts.

9 Refit the plastic locating collar to the release

lever and ensure that the rubber spacer is correctly located on the transmission end of the outer cable.

10 Ensuring that the cable is correctly routed and retained by all the relevant retaining clips and guides, pass the lower end through the release lever/mounting bracket and engage the inner cable with the clutch release lever/mounting bracket (as applicable). Refit the rubber spacer and flat washer to the end of the inner cable and screw on the adjuster nut and locknut (where applicable).

11 On models with an adjustable cable, adjust the clutch cable as described in Section 2.

4 Clutch pedal - removal and refitting

Note: *Access to the pedal pivot bolt is very poor, and can only be significantly improved by removing the facia as described in Chapter 11.*

Removal

Right-hand drive models

1 With the use of an assistant, unscrew a couple of brake caliper bleeding nipples to enable the brake pedal to be pressed to the floor. Make sure that you catch any leaking brake fluid, as it attacks plastics.

2 While the brake pedal is pressed out of the way, unhook the cable from the upper end of the clutch pedal (see Section 3 for details).

3 Slacken and remove the nut and pivot bolt, then withdraw the clutch pedal from the vehicle, along with its assister spring.

4 Carefully clean all components, renewing any that are worn or damaged; check the bearing surfaces of the pivot bushes and bolt with particular care; the bushes can be renewed separately if worn.

Left-hand drive models

5 Working as described in Section 2, slacken the clutch cable locknut and adjuster nut to obtain maximum freeplay in the cable.

6 Working inside the vehicle, undo the retaining nuts and remove the under-facia trim panel from the driver's side of the facia.

7 Unhook the clutch inner cable from the top of the clutch pedal.

8 Unscrew the nut from the pedal pivot bolt.

9 Noting the correct fitted position of the clutch pedal assister spring, withdraw the pivot bolt sufficiently to allow the pedal, spring and spacer to be removed.

10 Carefully clean all components, renewing any that are worn or damaged; check the bearing surfaces of the pivot bush and bolt with particular care; the bushes can be renewed separately if worn.

Refitting

Right-hand drive models

11 Press the pivot bushes into the pedal bore, then apply a smear of multi-purpose grease to their bearing surfaces.

12 Refit the pedal and spring to the vehicle, and install the pivot bolt. Refit the pivot bolt nut, and tighten it securely.

13 Check that the pedal pivots smoothly, tighten the brake caliper bleed nipples. Top up the brake fluid and, if necessary, bleed the brake system (see Chapter 9)

14 On completion check and, if necessary, adjust the clutch cable as described in Section 2.

Left-hand drive models

15 Press the pivot bush into the pedal bore, then apply a smear of multi-purpose grease to its bearing surface.

16 Refit the pedal, spring and spacer to the vehicle, and install the pivot bolt. Ensure that the bolt is correctly engaged with the brake pedal, then refit the pivot bolt nut and tighten it securely.

17 Hook the clutch cable onto the end of the pedal, then adjust the clutch cable as described in Section 2.

18 With the clutch cable correctly adjusted, refit the under-facia trim panel to the driver's side of the facia.

---

5 Clutch assembly -
removal, inspection
and refitting

⚠ *Warning: Dust created by clutch wear and deposited on the clutch components may contain asbestos, which is a health hazard. DO NOT blow it out with compressed air or inhale any of it. DO NOT use petrol or petroleum-based solvents to clean off the dust. Brake system cleaner or methylated spirit should be used to flush the dust into a suitable receptacle. After the clutch components are wiped clean with rags, dispose of the contaminated rags and cleaner in a sealed, marked container. Although some friction materials may no longer contain asbestos, it is safest to assume that they DO and to take precautions accordingly.*

Removal

1 Unless the engine/transmission is to be removed from the car and separated for major overhaul (Chapter 2C), the clutch can be reached by removing the transmission alone, as described in Chapter 7A.

2 Before disturbing the clutch, use chalk or a marker pen to mark the relationship of the pressure plate assembly to the flywheel.

3 Working in a diagonal sequence, slacken the pressure plate bolts by half a turn at a time, until spring pressure is released and the bolts can be unscrewed by hand.

4 Prise the pressure plate assembly off its locating dowels and collect the friction plate, noting which way round the friction plate is fitted **(see illustration)**.

Inspection

Note: *Due to the amount of work necessary to gain access to the clutch components, it is usually considered good practice to renew the*

clutch friction plate, pressure plate assembly and release bearing as a matched set, even if only one of these is actually worn enough to require renewal.

5 Remove the clutch assembly.

6 When cleaning clutch components, read first the warning at the beginning of this Section; remove any dust using a clean, dry cloth and working in a well-ventilated atmosphere.

7 Check the friction plate facings for signs of wear, damage or oil contamination. If the friction material is cracked, burnt, scored or damaged, or if it is contaminated with oil or grease (shown by shiny black patches), the friction plate must be renewed.

8 If the friction material is still serviceable, check that the centre boss splines are unworn, that the torsion springs are in good condition and securely fastened and that all the rivets are tightly fastened. If any wear or damage is found, the friction plate must be renewed.

9 If the friction material is fouled with oil, this must be due to an oil leak from the crankshaft left-hand oil seal, from the sump-to-cylinder block joint, or from the transmission input shaft. If a leak is evident, renew the seal or repair the joint (as appropriate) as described in the relevant Part of Chapter 2 or 7, before installing the new friction plate.

10 Check the pressure plate assembly for obvious signs of wear or damage. Shake it to check for loose rivets or damaged fulcrum rings; check that the drive straps securing the pressure plate to the cover do not show signs (such as a deep yellow or blue discoloration) of overheating. If the diaphragm spring is worn or damaged, or if its pressure is in any way suspect, the pressure plate assembly should be renewed.

11 Examine the machined bearing surfaces of the pressure plate and of the flywheel; they should be clean, completely flat and free from scratches or scoring (minor damage of this nature can sometimes be polished away using emery paper). If either is discoloured from excessive heat, or shows signs of cracking, it should be renewed.

12 Check that the release bearing contact surface rotates smoothly and easily, with no

5.4 Remove the pressure plate and friction plate, noting which way around the friction plate is fitted

sign of noise or roughness and that the surface itself is smooth and unworn, with no signs of cracks, pitting or scoring. If there is any doubt about its condition, the bearing must be renewed.

Refitting

13 On reassembly, ensure that the bearing surfaces of the flywheel and pressure plate are completely clean, smooth and free from oil or grease. Use solvent to remove any protective grease from new components.

14 Fit the friction plate so that its spring hub assembly faces away from the flywheel; there may also be a marking showing which way round the plate is to be refitted.

15 Refit the pressure plate assembly, aligning the marks made on dismantling (if the original pressure plate is re-used) and locating the pressure plate on its three locating dowels. Fit the pressure plate bolts, but tighten them only finger-tight, so that the friction plate can still be moved.

16 The friction plate must now be centralised, so that when the transmission is refitted, its input shaft will pass through the splines at the centre of the friction plate.

17 Centralisation can be achieved by passing a screwdriver or other long bar through the friction plate and into the hole in the crankshaft; the friction plate can then be moved around until it is centred on the crankshaft hole **(see Haynes Hint)**.

A clutch-aligning tool can be used to eliminate the guesswork when fitting the friction plate; these can be obtained from most accessory shops, or can be made up from a length of metal rod or wooden dowel which fits closely inside the crankshaft hole, and has insulating tape wound around it to match the diameter of the friction plate splined hole.

6

5.18 Once the friction plate is centralised, tighten the pressure plate retaining bolts to the specified torque

18 When the friction plate is centralised, tighten the pressure plate bolts evenly and in a diagonal sequence to the specified torque setting **(see illustration)**.

6.2a Using a hammer and suitable punch . . .

19 Apply a thin smear of high-melting point grease to the splines of the friction plate and the transmission input shaft, also to the release bearing bore and release fork shaft.
20 Refit the transmission as described in Chapter 7A.

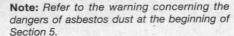

6 Clutch release mechanism -
removal, inspection and refitting

Note: *Refer to the warning concerning the dangers of asbestos dust at the beginning of Section 5.*

Removal

1 Unless the engine/transmission is to be removed from the car and separated for major overhaul (Chapter 2C), the clutch release mechanism can be reached by removing the transmission alone, as described in Chapter 7A.
2 Unhook the release bearing from the fork and slide it off the input shaft. Drive out the retaining pin or unscrew the retaining bolt (as applicable) and remove the release lever from the top of the release fork shaft **(see illustrations)**.
3 Depress the retaining tabs, then slide the upper bush off the end of the release fork shaft, then disengage the shaft from its lower bush and manoeuvre it out from the transmission **(see illustrations)**. Depress the retaining tabs and remove the lower pivot bush from the transmission housing.

Inspection

4 Check the release mechanism, renewing any component which is worn or damaged. Carefully check all bearing surfaces and points of contact.
5 Check the release bearing itself, noting that it is often considered worthwhile to renew it as a matter of course. Check that the contact surface rotates smoothly and easily, with no sign of noise or roughness and that the surface itself is smooth and unworn, with no signs of cracks, pitting or scoring. If there is any doubt about its condition, the bearing must be renewed.

Refitting

6 Apply a smear of high-melting point grease to the shaft pivot bushes and the contact surfaces of the release fork.
7 Locate the lower pivot bush in the transmission, ensuring that it is securely retained by its locating tangs and refit the release fork **(see illustration)**. Slide the upper bush down the shaft and clip it into position in the transmission housing.
8 Refit the release lever to the shaft. Align the lever with the shaft hole and secure it in position by tapping in the retaining pin or securely tightening its retaining bolt (as applicable). Slide the release bearing onto the input shaft and engage it with the release fork **(see illustration)**.
9 Refit the transmission as described in Chapter 7A.

6.2b . . . tap out the retaining pin . . .

6.2c . . . then remove the release lever from the top of the release fork shaft

6.3a Release the upper pivot bush and slide it off the shaft . . .

6.3b . . . then withdraw the release fork shaft and remove the lower bush (arrowed)

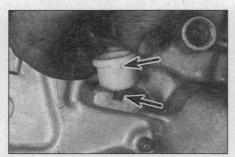

6.7 On refitting, ensure that the bush lug and housing recess (arrowed) are correctly aligned

6.8 Install the release bearing, ensuring that its hooks are correctly engaged with the release fork

Chapter 7 Part A:
Manual transmission

Contents

Degrees of difficulty

Easy, suitable for novice with little experience		Fairly easy, suitable for beginner with some experience		Fairly difficult, suitable for competent DIY mechanic		Difficult, suitable for experienced DIY mechanic		Very difficult, suitable for expert DIY or professional	

Specifications

General

Type .... Manual, four or five forward speeds and reverse. Synchromesh on all forward speeds

Designation:
Four-speed transmission MA4
Five-speed transmission MA5

Gear ratios

MA4 transmission:
1st	3.417 : 1 (12/41 teeth)
2nd	1.810 : 1 (21/38 teeth)
3rd	1.130 : 1 (31/35 teeth)
4th	0.810 : 1 (35/43 teeth)
Reverse	3.583 : 1 (12/43 teeth)
Final drive (typical)	4.286 : 1 (14/60 teeth)

MA5 transmission:
1st	3.417 : 1 (12/41 teeth)
2nd	1.950 : 1 (20/39 teeth)
3rd	1.360 : 1 (28/38 teeth)
4th	1.050 : 1 (37/39 teeth)
5th	0.850 : 1 (41/35 teeth)
Reverse	3.583 : 1 (12/43 teeth)
Final drive (typical)	4.286 : 1 (14/60 teeth)

Lubrication

Recommended oil type .... See "Lubricants and fluids"

Torque wrench settings

	Nm	lbf ft
Oil filler/level plug	25	18
Oil drain plug	25	18
Clutch release bearing guide sleeve bolts	12	9
Reversing light switch	25	18
Left-hand engine/transmission mounting:		
Mounting bracket-to-body bolts	30	22
Centre nut	85	63
Engine/transmission rear mounting:		
Mounting link bolts	55	40
Mounting-to-transmission bolts	85	63
Engine-to-transmission fixing bolts	35	26

7A

2.3 Unscrew the filler/level plug from the transmission and recover the sealing washer

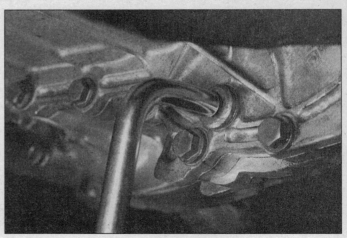

2.4 Using the special square-section wrench to unscrew the transmission drain plug

1 General information

The transmission is contained in a cast aluminium alloy casing bolted to the engine's left-hand end and consists of the gearbox and final drive differential, often called a transaxle.

Drive is transmitted from the crankshaft via the clutch to the input shaft, which has a splined extension to accept the clutch friction plate and rotates in sealed ball-bearings. From the input shaft, drive is transmitted to the output shaft, which rotates in a roller bearing at its right-hand end and a sealed ball-bearing at its left-hand end. From the output shaft, the drive is transmitted to the differential crownwheel, which rotates with the differential case and planetary gears, thus driving the sun gears and driveshafts. The rotation of the planetary gears on their shaft allows the inner roadwheel to rotate at a slower speed than the outer roadwheel when the car is cornering.

The input and output shafts are arranged side by side, parallel to the crankshaft and driveshafts, so that their gear pinion teeth are in constant mesh. In the neutral position, the output shaft gear pinions rotate freely, so that drive cannot be transmitted to the crownwheel.

Gear selection is via a floor-mounted lever and selector rod mechanism. The selector rod causes the appropriate selector fork to move its respective synchro-sleeve along the shaft, to lock the gear pinion to the synchro-hub. Since the synchro-hubs are splined to the output shaft, this locks the pinion to the shaft so that drive can be transmitted. To ensure that gear-changing can be made quickly and quietly, a synchromesh system is fitted to all forward gears, consisting of baulk rings and spring-loaded fingers as well as the gear pinions and synchro-hubs; the synchromesh cones are formed on the mating faces of the baulk rings and gear pinions.

2 Manual transmission - draining and refilling

Note: *A suitable square-section wrench may be required to undo the transmission filler/level and drain plugs on some models. These wrenches can be obtained from most motor factors, or from your Peugeot dealer.*

1 This operation is much quicker and more effective if the car is first taken on a journey of sufficient length to warm the engine/transmission up to normal operating temperature.
2 Park the car on level ground, switch off the ignition and apply the handbrake firmly. For improved access, jack up the front of the car and support it securely on axle stands (see *"Jacking and vehicle support"*). Note that the car must be lowered to the ground and level, to ensure accuracy, when refilling and checking the oil level.
3 Wipe clean the area around the filler/level plug, which is situated on the left-hand end of the transmission, next to the end cover. Unscrew the filler/level plug from the transmission and recover the sealing washer **(see illustration)**.
4 Position a suitable container under the drain plug, situated on the left-hand side of the differential housing and unscrew the plug from the transmission **(see illustration)**.
5 Allow the oil to drain completely into the container. If the oil is hot, take precautions against scalding. Clean both the filler/level and the drain plugs, being especially careful to wipe any metallic particles off the magnetic inserts. Discard the original sealing washers; they should be renewed whenever they are disturbed.
6 When the oil has finished draining, clean the drain plug threads and those of the transmission casing. Fit a new sealing washer and refit the drain plug, tightening it to the specified torque wrench setting. It the car was raised for the draining operation, now lower it to the ground.

7 Refilling the transmission is an extremely awkward operation. Above all, allow plenty of time for the oil level to settle properly before checking the level. Note that the car must be parked on flat level ground when checking the oil level.
8 Refill the transmission with the exact amount of the specified type of oil, then check the oil level as described in Chapter 1A or 1B. If the correct amount was poured into the transmission and a large amount flows out on checking the level, refit the filler/level plug and take the car on a short journey. When the new oil is distributed fully around the transmission components, check the level again on your return and top-up if necessary.

3 Gearchange linkage - general information and adjustment

General information

1 If a stiff, sloppy or imprecise gearchange leads you to suspect that a fault exists within the linkage, dismantle it completely and check it for wear or damage as described in Section 4. Reassemble the linkage, applying a smear of multi-purpose grease to all bearing surfaces.
2 If this does not cure the fault, the car should be examined by an expert, as the fault must lie within the transmission itself. There is no adjustment as such in the linkage.
3 While the length of the link rods can be altered as described below, this is for initial setting-up only and is not intended to provide a form of compensation for wear. If the link rods have been renewed, or if the length of the originals is incorrect, adjust them as follows.

Adjustment

4 Chock the rear wheels, then jack up the front of the vehicle and support it on axle stands (see *"Jacking and Vehicle Support"*). Access to the link rods is poor, but they can be reached both from above and below the vehicle.

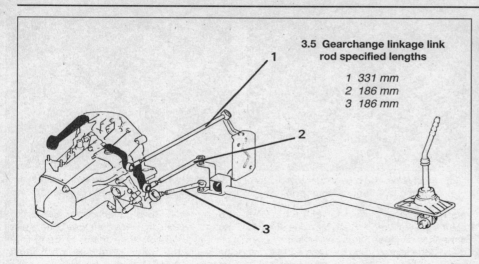

3.5 Gearchange linkage link rod specified lengths

1 331 mm
2 186 mm
3 186 mm

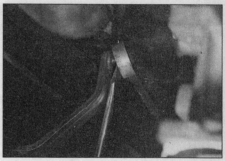

3.6a Carefully lever the link rods off their balljoints using a large flat-bladed screwdriver

3.6b When refitting, securely press the link rod back onto its balljoint

5 Working in (or under) the engine compartment, measure the length of each link rod and compare this to the relevant specified length **(see illustration)**. Note the measurements given are the distances between the centre points of the link rod balljoints and not the total length of the rod.

6 If adjustment is necessary, slacken the locknut, then carefully lever the relevant link rod off its balljoint on the transmission unit. Screw or unscrew (as applicable) the end of the rod until the specified distance between the link rod balljoint centres is obtained, then press the disconnected end of the rod firmly back onto its balljoint and securely tighten the link rod locknut **(see illustrations)**.

7 Once all link rod lengths are correctly set, check that all gears can be selected and that the gearchange lever returns properly to its correct at-rest position.

4 Gearchange linkage - removal and refitting

Removal

1 Firmly apply the handbrake, then jack up the front of the vehicle and support it on axle stands (see "*Jacking and vehicle support*").

2 Slacken and remove the nut and withdraw the pivot bolt securing the selector rod to the base of the gearchange lever.

3 Using a flat-bladed screwdriver, carefully lever the two selector rod link rods off their balljoints on the transmission. Disengage the selector rod from bellcrank pivot and remove it, complete with link rods, from underneath the vehicle.

4 Carefully lever the bellcrank link rod balljoint off the transmission lever, then undo the two retaining nuts and remove the bellcrank assembly from the bulkhead **(see illustration)**.

5 Inspect all the linkage components for signs of wear or damage, paying particular attention to the pivot bushes and link rod balljoints and renew worn components as necessary. If necessary, the gearchange lever can also be removed as follows.

6 Remove the centre console as described in Chapter 11, then undo the four retaining nuts and remove the gearchange lever, complete with rubber mounting plate, from the vehicle. The lever can be separated from its baseplate after the retaining ring has been unclipped **(see illustrations)**.

7 Examine the lever components for signs of wear or damage, paying particular attention to the rubber gaiters and renew components as necessary.

Refitting

8 Refitting is a reversal of the removal procedure, noting the following points:

a) Prior to refitting check and, if necessary, adjust the link rod lengths as described in Section 3.

b) Apply a smear of multi-purpose grease to the gearchange lever pivot ball, the link rod balljoints and the bellcrank ball and pivot bushes.

c) Ensure that all link rods are securely pressed onto their balljoints.

7A

4.4 Gearchange linkage bellcrank is secured to the bulkhead by two nuts (arrowed)

4.6a Gearchange lever retaining nuts (arrowed)

4.6b The gearchange lever can be separated from its baseplate once its retaining ring has been unclipped

5.4 Use a large flat-bladed screwdriver to prise the driveshaft oil seal out of position . . .

5.5 . . . and tap the new seal into position using a suitable tubular drift

5.9 Clutch release bearing guide sleeve is retained by three bolts (arrowed)

5 Oil seals - renewal

Driveshaft oil seal

1 Chock the rear wheels then jack up the front of the vehicle and support it on axle stands (see *"Jacking and Vehicle Support"*). Remove the appropriate front roadwheel.
2 Drain the transmission oil as described in Section 2.
3 Working as described in Chapter 8, free the inner end of the driveshaft from the transmission and place it clear of the seal. There is no need to unscrew the driveshaft retaining nut; the driveshaft can be left secured to the hub. Support the driveshaft, to avoid placing any strain on the driveshaft joints or gaiters.
4 Carefully prise the oil seal out of the transmission, using a large flat-bladed screwdriver **(see illustration)**.
5 Remove all traces of dirt from the area around the oil seal aperture, then apply a smear of grease to the outer lip of the new oil seal. Fit the new seal into its aperture and drive it squarely into position until it abuts its locating shoulder. Use a suitable tubular drift (such as a socket) which bears only on the hard outer edge of the seal **(see illustration)**. If the seal was supplied with a plastic protector sleeve, leave this in position until the driveshaft has been refitted.
6 Refit the driveshaft as described in Chapter 8.
7 Refill the transmission with the specified type and amount of oil as described in Section 2.

Input shaft oil seal

8 Remove the transmission from the car as described in Section 8.
9 Undo the three bolts securing the clutch release bearing guide sleeve in position and slide the guide off the input shaft along with its O-ring or gasket (as applicable) **(see illustration)**. Recover any relevant thrust-washers which have stuck to the rear of the guide sleeve and refit them to the input shaft.

10 Before fitting a new seal, check the input shaft's seal rubbing surface for signs of burrs, scratches or other damage which may have caused the seal to fail in the first place. It may be possible to polish away minor defects of this sort using fine abrasive paper; however, more serious defects will require the renewal of the input shaft. Ensure that the input shaft is clean and greased to protect the seal lips on refitting.
11 Fit a new O-ring or gasket (as applicable) to the rear of the guide sleeve, then carefully slide the sleeve into position over the input shaft. Refit the retaining bolts and tighten them to the specified torque setting.
12 Refit the transmission to the car as described in Section 8.

Selector shaft oil seal

13 To renew the selector shaft seal, the transmission unit must be dismantled. This task should therefore be entrusted to a Peugeot dealer.

6 Reversing light switch - testing, removal and refitting

Testing

1 The reversing light circuit is controlled by a plunger-type switch screwed into the top of the transmission casing. If a fault develops in the circuit, first ensure that the circuit fuse has not blown.
2 To test the switch, disconnect the wiring

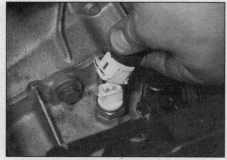

6.4 Disconnecting the wiring connector from the reversing light switch

connector and use a multi-meter (set to the resistance function) or a battery-and-bulb test circuit to check that there is continuity between the switch terminals only when reverse gear is selected. If this is not the case and there are no obvious breaks or other damage to the wires, the switch is faulty and must be renewed.

Removal

3 To improve access to the switch, remove the battery as described in Chapter 5A.
4 Disconnect the wiring connector from the switch **(see illustration)**. Unscrew it from the transmission casing and remove it along with its sealing washer.

Refitting

5 Fit a new sealing washer to the switch, then screw it back into position in the top of the transmission housing, tightening it to the specified torque setting. Reconnect the wiring connector, then refit the battery and test the operation of the circuit.

7 Speedometer drive - removal and refitting

Removal

1 Chock the rear wheels then jack up the front of the vehicle and support it on axle stands (see *"Jacking and Vehicle Support"*). The speedometer drive is situated on the rear of the transmission housing, next to the inner end of the right-hand driveshaft.
2 Pull out the speedometer cable retaining pin and disconnect the cable from the speedometer drive **(see illustrations)**. Where necessary, disconnect the wiring connector from the speedometer drive.
3 Slacken and remove the retaining bolt and withdraw the speedometer drive and driven pinion assembly from the transmission housing, along with its O-ring.
4 Examine the pinion for signs of damage and renew if necessary. Renew the housing O-ring as a matter of course. On models where the speedometer drive is also the fuel injection system vehicle speed sensor (these are easily

7.2a Withdraw the rubber retaining pin (arrowed) . . .

identified by the wiring connector on the housing) the drive assembly is a sealed unit. However, on all other models, the speedometer drive can be dismantled and the driven pinion and oil seal renewed individually.

5 If the driven pinion is worn or damaged, also examine the drive pinion in the transmission housing for signs of wear or damage. To renew the drive pinion, the transmission must be dismantled and the differential gear removed. This task should therefore be entrusted to a Peugeot dealer.

Refitting

6 Fit a new O-ring to the speedometer drive. Refit the drive to the transmission, ensuring that the pinions are correctly engaged.

7 Refit the retaining bolt and tighten it securely. Where necessary, reconnect the wiring connector to the speedometer drive.

8.6 Free the clutch cable from the release lever and place it clear of the transmission

8.11 Disconnect the driveshafts from the transmission, noting that it is not necessary to disconnect them from the hubs

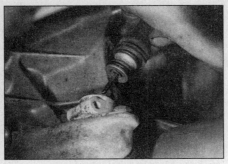

7.2b . . . then disconnect the speedometer cable from its drive

8 Apply a smear of oil to the speedometer cable O-rings, then reconnect the cable to the drive, securing it in position with the rubber retaining pin. Lower the vehicle to the ground.

8 Manual transmission - removal and refitting

Removal

1 Chock the rear wheels then jack up the front of the vehicle and support it on axle stands (see *"Jacking and Vehicle Support"*). Remove the front roadwheels.

2 Drain the transmission oil as described in Section 2, then refit the drain and filler/level plugs and tighten them to their specified torque settings.

8.7 Undo the retaining nut and release the earth straps from the top of the transmission housing

8.12 Take the weight of the engine with an engine support bar . . .

3 Remove the battery (see Chapter 5A).

4 If necessary, to improve access to the top of the transmission, remove the air cleaner housing and/or intake duct (as applicable), as described in the relevant Part of Chapter 4.

5 Remove the starter motor as described in Chapter 5A.

6 Fully slacken the clutch cable locknut and adjuster nut (where fitted), then free the inner and outer cable end fittings from the mounting bracket and release lever **(see illustration)**. Release the cable from any relevant retaining clips and place it clear of the transmission.

7 Disconnect the wiring connectors from the reversing light switch, TDC sensor and speedometer drive housing (as applicable). Undo the retaining nut and disconnect the earth straps from the top of the transmission housing **(see illustration)**. Free the wiring from any relevant retaining clips and place it clear of the transmission.

8 Using a flat-bladed screwdriver, carefully lever the three gearchange mechanism link rods off their respective balljoints on the transmission. Position the rods clear of the transmission unit.

9 Withdraw the rubber retaining pin and disconnect the speedometer cable from the drive housing, freeing it from any relevant retaining clips.

10 On cast-iron block engines, unbolt the flywheel cover plate from the base of the transmission and remove it from the vehicle.

11 Working as described in Chapter 8, free the inner end of each driveshaft from the transmission and position them clear of the transmission **(see illustration)**. Note that there is no need to unscrew the driveshaft retaining nuts; each driveshaft can be left secured to the hub. Support the driveshafts, however, to avoid placing any strain on the driveshaft joints or gaiters.

12 Place a jack with interposed block of wood beneath the engine, to take the weight of the engine. Alternatively, attach a hoist or support bar to the engine lifting eyes and take the weight of the engine **(see illustration)**.

13 Place a trolley jack and block of wood beneath the transmission and raise the jack to take the weight of the transmission **(see illustration)**.

7A

8.13 . . . and position a jack with interposed block of wood underneath the transmission

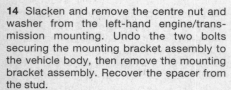

8.15a Unscrew the two bolts securing the rear mounting to the transmission . . .

8.15b . . . then undo the bolt securing the mounting link to the body and remove the mounting assembly from the vehicle

8.19 Carefully release the transmission from the engine and lower it out of position

14 Slacken and remove the centre nut and washer from the left-hand engine/transmission mounting. Undo the two bolts securing the mounting bracket assembly to the vehicle body, then remove the mounting bracket assembly. Recover the spacer from the stud.

15 Slacken and remove the two bolts securing the rear engine mounting to the transmission. Unscrew the nut and bolt securing the mounting link to the vehicle body and remove the mounting assembly from the vehicle **(see illustrations)**.

16 With the jack beneath the transmission taking its weight, slacken and remove the remaining bolts securing the transmission housing to the engine. Note the correct fitted positions of each bolt and the necessary brackets, as they are removed, to use as a reference on refitting. On diesel models, it may be necessary to remove the fuel filter to gain access to the upper transmission-to-engine unit bolts (see Chapter 1B); if the filter is damaged on removal, a new one must be used on refitting.

17 Make a final check that all necessary components have been disconnected and are positioned clear of the transmission so that they will not hinder the removal procedure.

18 With the bolts removed, move the trolley jack and transmission to the left to free it from its locating dowels.

19 Once the transmission is free, lower the jack and manoeuvre the unit out from under

the car **(see illustration)**. If they are loose, remove the locating dowels from the transmission or engine and keep them in a safe place.

Refitting

20 The transmission is refitted using a reversal of the removal procedure, bearing in mind the following points:

a) Apply a little high-melting point grease to the splines of the transmission input shaft. Do not apply too much, otherwise there is a possibility of the grease contaminating the clutch friction plate.

b) Ensure that the locating dowels are correctly positioned prior to installation.

c) Tighten all nuts and bolts to the specified torque (where given).

d) Renew the driveshaft oil seals using the information given in Section 5.

e) On completion, refill the transmission with the specified type and quantity of oil as described in Section 2.

9 Manual transmission overhaul - general information

Overhauling a manual transmission is a difficult and involved job for the DIY home mechanic. In addition to dismantling and reassembling many small parts, clearances must be precisely measured and, if

necessary, changed by selecting shims and spacers. Internal transmission components are also often difficult to obtain and in many instances, extremely expensive. Because of this, if the transmission develops a fault or becomes noisy, the best course of action is to have the unit overhauled by a specialist repairer, or to obtain an exchange reconditioned unit.

Nevertheless, it is not impossible for the more experienced mechanic to overhaul the transmission, provided the special tools are available and the job is done in a deliberate step-by-step manner, so that nothing is overlooked.

The tools necessary for an overhaul include internal and external circlip pliers, bearing pullers, a slide hammer, a set of pin punches, a dial test indicator and possibly a hydraulic press. In addition, a large, sturdy workbench and a vice will be required.

During dismantling of the transmission, make careful notes of how each component is fitted, to make reassembly easier and more accurate.

Before dismantling the transmission, it will help if you have some idea what area is malfunctioning. Certain problems can be closely related to specific areas in the transmission, which can make component examination and replacement easier. Refer to the *Fault Finding* Section at the end of this manual for more information.

Chapter 7 Part B:
Automatic transmission

Contents

Degrees of difficulty

Easy, suitable for novice with little experience	Fairly easy, suitable for beginner with some experience	Fairly difficult, suitable for competent DIY mechanic	Difficult, suitable for experienced DIY mechanic	Very difficult, suitable for expert DIY or professional 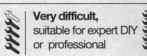

Specifications

General
Type . . . . Automatic, 3 forward speeds and reverse
Designation MB3

Lubrication
Recommended fluid . . . . See "Lubricants and fluids"

Torque wrench settings

	Nm	lbf ft
Engine-to-transmission securing bolts	35	26
Left-hand engine/transmission mounting:		
Mounting bracket-to-body bolts	30	22
Centre nut	85	63
Engine/transmission rear mounting:		
Mounting link bolts	55	40
Mounting-to-transmission bolts	85	63
Torque converter-to-driveplate bolts	25	18

1 General information

Some models covered in this manual have an electronically controlled three-speed fully-automatic transmission, consisting of a torque converter, an epicyclic geartrain and electro-hydraulically-operated clutches and brakes.

The torque converter provides a fluid coupling between engine and transmission, which acts as an automatic clutch and also provides a degree of torque multiplication when accelerating.

The epicyclic geartrain provides either of the three forward or one reverse gear ratios, according to which of its component parts are held stationary or allowed to turn. The components of the geartrain are held or released by brakes and clutches which are activated hydraulically according to signals from the transmission electronic control unit (ECU). A fluid pump within the transmission provides the necessary hydraulic pressure to operate the brakes and clutches.

Automatic operation of the transmission is controlled by an electronic control unit which receives signals on vehicle operating conditions from various sensors. The sensors typically provide information on vehicle speed, selector lever position, throttle position and engine speed, enabling the ECU to select the appropriate gear ratio and gear change point.

Driver control of the transmission is by a six-position selector lever. The transmission has a "drive" position and a "hold" facility on the first two gear ratios. The "drive" position "D" provides automatic changing throughout the range of all three gear ratios and is the one to select for normal driving. An automatic kickdown facility shifts the transmission down a gear if the accelerator pedal is fully depressed. The "hold" facility is very similar, but limits the number of gear ratios available - ie when the selector lever is in the "2" position, only the first two ratios can be selected; in the "1" position, only first can be selected. The "hold" facility is useful for providing engine braking when travelling down steep gradients, or for preventing unwanted selection of top gear on twisty roads. Note, however, that the transmission should *never* be shifted down a position if the engine speed exceeds 4000 rpm.

Due to the complexity of the automatic transmission, any repair or overhaul work must be left to a Peugeot dealer with the necessary special equipment for fault diagnosis and repair. The contents of the following Sections are therefore confined to supplying general information and any service information and instructions that can be used by the owner.

7B

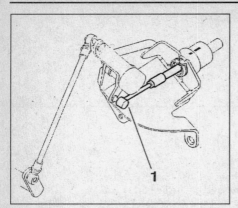

2.3 Lever the selector lever inner cable end fitting (1) off the bellcrank balljoint

2 Selector cable - adjustment

1 Remove the air cleaner assembly as described in the relevant Part of Chapter 4.
2 Move the selector lever in the car to the "1" (rearmost) position.
3 Using a large flat-bladed screwdriver, carefully lever the selector inner cable end fitting off the transmission bellcrank balljoint, whilst ensuring that the lever does not move **(see illustration)**.
4 Check that the selector lever on the transmission is fully up against its top stop (1st gear position)
5 With both the selector levers in the "1" (1st gear) position, the selector cable end fitting should be correctly aligned with the transmission bellcrank balljoint, so that the cable can be connected to the lever without the balljoint moving. If necessary, adjust the cable as follows.
6 Unlock the outer cable end fitting at the bracket on the transmission.
7 Check that the selector lever in the car is still in the "1" position and the transmission selector lever is fully up against its top stop.
8 Refit the selector inner cable end fitting to

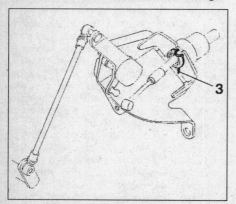

3.5 Extract the circlip (3) securing the selector outer cable to the transmission bracket

the bellcrank balljoint whilst ensuring that the selector levers do not move.
9 Lock the outer cable end fitting at the transmission by turning the outer cable a quarter turn. In this position the coloured marks on the cable and end fitting should be in alignment.
10 Refit the air cleaner assembly then road test the car and check the gear selection operation.

3 Selector lever and cable assembly - removal and refitting

Removal

1 Remove the air cleaner assembly as described in the relevant Part of Chapter 4.
2 Move the selector lever in the car to the "1" (rearmost) position.
3 Using a large flat-bladed screwdriver, carefully lever the selector inner cable end fitting off the transmission bellcrank balljoint, whilst ensuring that the lever does not move.
4 Unlock the outer cable end fitting at the bracket on the transmission.
5 Extract the circlip securing the selector outer cable to the transmission bracket **(see illustration)**.
6 Chock the rear wheels then jack up the front of the vehicle and support it on axle stands (see "*Jacking and Vehicle Support*").
7 Remove the exhaust system front pipe and heat shield as described in the relevant Part of Chapter 4.
8 Detach the selector cable from the bracket on the transmission tunnel.
9 From inside the car undo the two screws securing the selector lever knob to the lever **(see illustration)**. Depress the knob detent button, then rotate the knob through 90° anti-clockwise, lift the assembly up and rotate it back 90° clockwise to release the detent button from the selector lever pushrod.
10 Remove the gear selection indicator from the console by releasing the clip at the front and disengaging the two rear locating tags.
11 Remove the gear selector console then unbolt the selector lever assembly.
12 Release the selector cable from any clips in the engine compartment, then withdraw the assembly from the car.

Refitting

13 Ensuring that the cable is correctly routed, manoeuvre the lever and cable assembly back into position. Secure the assembly, refit the console and clip the selection indicator back into position.
14 Check that the selector lever in the car is still in the "1" position and the transmission selector lever is fully up against its top stop.
15 Secure the selector cable to the bracket on the transmission tunnel.
16 Engage the outer cable with the transmission bracket, then refit the inner cable

end fitting to the bellcrank balljoint whilst ensuring that the selector levers do not move.
17 Refit the circlip securing the outer cable to the transmission bracket.
18 Lock the outer cable end fitting at the transmission by turning the outer cable a quarter turn. In this position the coloured marks on the cable and end fitting should be in alignment.
19 Keeping the detent button depressed, slide the knob onto the selector lever then, exerting light downward pressure on the knob, rotate the knob through 90°, release the button, then turn the knob back 90° until the detent button is in its correct position. Refit the two knob retaining screws and tighten them securely. Check the operation of the selector lever detent button before proceeding.
20 Check the operation of the selector mechanism then refit the heat shield, exhaust front pipe and air cleaner.

4 Speedometer drive - removal and refitting

Refer to Chapter 7A.

5 Oil seals - renewal

Driveshaft oil seals

1 Refer to Chapter 7A.

Torque converter oil seal

2 Remove the transmission from the car as described in Section 8.
3 Remove the retaining strap then carefully slide the torque converter off the transmission shaft.
4 Note the fitted depth of the seal as a guide to refitting. Punch or drill two small holes opposite each other in the seal. Screw a self-

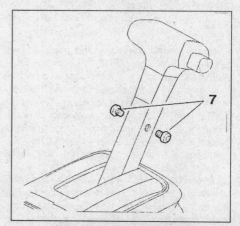

3.9 Selector lever knob retaining screws (7)

tapping screw into each and pull on the screws with pliers to extract the seal.

5 Using a suitable tubular drift (such as a socket) which bears only on the hard outer edge of the seal, tap the seal into position, to the same depth in the housing as the original was prior to removal.

6 Lubricate the lips of the new seal with clean transmission fluid and carefully locate the torque converter back into position.

7 Refit the transmission to the car as described in Section 8.

6 Heat exchanger - removal and refitting

Removal

1 The fluid cooler is mounted on the top of the transmission housing. To gain access to the fluid cooler, remove the air cleaner assembly and intake duct as described in the relevant Part of Chapter 4 and the battery as described in Chapter 5A. Where the transmission ECU is mounted adjacent to the battery, remove the ECU cover.

2 Using a hose clamp or similar, clamp both the heat exchanger coolant hoses to minimise coolant loss during subsequent operations.

3 Slacken the retaining clips and disconnect both coolant hoses from the heat exchanger - be prepared for some coolant spillage (see illustration). Wash off any spilt coolant immediately with cold water and dry the surrounding area before proceeding further.

4 Slacken and remove the two heat exchanger retaining bolts and recover the two copper washers from each bolt (one located on each side of the heat exchanger. Remove the unit from the transmission.

Refitting

5 Lubricate the new copper washers with clean automatic transmission fluid, then refit the heat exchanger. Ensure that the copper washers are fitted on each side of the heat exchanger and tighten the bolts securely.

6 Reconnect the coolant hoses to the fluid cooler and securely tighten their retaining clips. Remove the hose clamps.

7 Refit the battery, ECU cover and intake duct/air cleaner housing components.

8 On completion, top-up the cooling system (see "Weekly checks") and check the automatic transmission fluid level as described in Chapter 1A.

7 Transmission electronic control components - removal and refitting

Note: Whenever a new ECU is fitted, the unit must be initialised using Peugeot diagnostic equipment before the transmission will function. If the following procedures are being undertaken with the intention of ECU renewal, this work should be entrusted to a Peugeot dealer.

General

1 The transmission electronic control components described in this Section consist of the electronic control unit (ECU), a multi-function switch and a speed sensor. The multi-function switch and speed sensor are connected to the ECU by an integral wiring harness and the three components therefore form one assembly. The multi-function switch and speed sensor are located on the transmission assembly, while the ECU is mounted above the transmission, adjacent to the battery on early models and in front of the transmission on later models.

Removal

2 Disconnect the battery negative terminal (refer to "Disconnecting the battery" in the Reference Section of this manual).

3 Where the ECU is mounted above the transmission, remove the air cleaner assembly and intake duct as described in the relevant Part of Chapter 4 and the battery as described in Chapter 5A.

4 Remove the ECU cover (where applicable) and remove any cable ties from the wiring

harness in the vicinity of the ECU wiring connector. Disconnect the wiring connector, remove the retaining strap and withdraw the ECU from its location. Disconnect the remaining connectors from the base of the unit (see illustration).

5 Trace the wiring harness to the speed sensor and multi-function switch and make notes of the harness routing for refitting. Release any cable ties or clips encountered.

6 Undo the retaining bolt and earth lead bolt and withdraw the multi-function switch from the transmission (see illustration). Recover the switch O-ring.

7 Undo the wiring harness clamp retaining bolt and the speed sensor mounting bolt and withdraw the speed sensor from the transmission (see illustration). Recover the O-ring.

8 Carefully feed the components and cables out from their locations and remove them from the transmission.

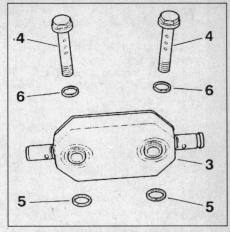

6.3 Heat exchanger components

3 Heat exchanger
4 Mounting bolts
5 Inner copper washers
6 Outer copper washers

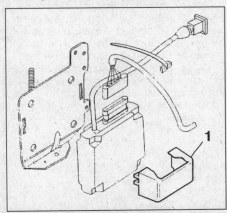

7.4 ECU retaining strap (1) and mounting components

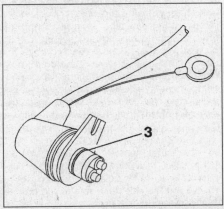

7.6 Multi-function switch (3) location on the transmission

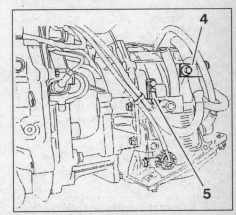

7.7 Speed sensor wiring harness clamp (4) and speed sensor (5)

7B

Refitting

9 Refitting is a reversal of removal noting the following points:

a) *Use a new O-ring on the speed sensor and multi-function switch.*

b) *Ensure that the wiring is routed and correctly clipped back into place as noted during removal.*

c) *Refit all remaining components disturbed during removal.*

8 Automatic transmission - removal and refitting

Removal

1 Chock the rear wheels, apply the handbrake and place the selector lever in the "1" (1st gear) position. Jack up the front of the vehicle and securely support it on axle stands (see *"Jacking and Vehicle Support"*). Remove both front roadwheels.

2 Drain the transmission fluid as described in Chapter 1A, then refit the drain plugs, tightening them securely.

3 Remove the battery and battery tray as described in Chapter 5A.

4 Remove the air cleaner and intake duct(s) as described in the relevant Part of Chapter 4.

5 Remove the ECU cover (where applicable) and remove any cable ties from the wiring harness in the vicinity of the ECU wiring connector. Disconnect the wiring connector, remove the retaining strap and withdraw the ECU from its location. Disconnect the remaining connectors from the base of the unit. Lay the ECU on top of the transmission and suitably retain it in place.

6 Where applicable, remove the ECU mounting bracket.

7 Remove the exhaust system front pipe from the manifold as described in the relevant Part of Chapter 4.

8 Remove the starter motor as described in Chapter 5A.

9 Remove the dipstick from the transmission.

10 Using a hose clamp or similar, clamp both the heat exchanger coolant hoses to minimise coolant loss. Slacken the retaining clips and disconnect both coolant hoses from the heat exchanger - be prepared for some coolant spillage. Wash off any spilt coolant immediately with cold water.

11 Using a large flat-bladed screwdriver, carefully lever the selector inner cable end fitting off the transmission bellcrank balljoint, whilst ensuring that the lever does not move.

12 Unlock the outer cable end fitting at the bracket on the transmission.

13 Extract the circlip securing the selector outer cable to the transmission bracket.

14 Undo the retaining bolts and remove the lower driveplate cover plate from the transmission, to gain access to the torque converter retaining bolts. Slacken and remove the visible bolt then, using a socket and extension bar to rotate the crankshaft pulley, undo the remaining bolts securing the torque converter to the driveplate as they become accessible. There are three bolts in total.

15 To ensure that the torque converter does not fall out as the transmission is removed, secure it in position using a length of metal strip bolted to one of the starter motor bolt holes.

16 Withdraw the rubber retaining pin, disconnect the speedometer cable from the drive and free it from any retaining clips.

17 Disconnect the remaining wiring connectors and vacuum hoses likely to impede transmission removal.

18 Remove the driveshafts as described in Chapter 8.

19 Place a jack with a block of wood beneath the engine, to take the weight of the engine. Alternatively, attach a couple of lifting eyes to the engine and fit a hoist or support bar to take the weight of the engine.

20 Place a jack and block of wood beneath the transmission and raise the jack to take the weight of the transmission.

21 Slacken and remove the centre nut and washer from the left-hand engine/transmission mounting. Undo the two bolts securing the mounting bracket assembly to the vehicle body, then remove the mounting bracket assembly. Recover the spacer from the stud.

22 Slacken and remove the two bolts securing the rear engine mounting to the transmission. Unscrew the nut and bolt securing the mounting link to the vehicle body and remove the mounting assembly from the vehicle.

23 With the jack positioned beneath the transmission taking the weight, slacken and remove the remaining bolts securing the transmission housing to the engine. Note the correct fitted positions of each bolt as it is removed, to use as a reference on refitting. Make a final check that all necessary components have been disconnected and positioned clear of the transmission so that they will not hinder the removal procedure.

24 With the bolts removed, move the trolley jack and transmission to the left, to free it from its locating dowels.

25 Once the transmission is free, lower the jack and manoeuvre the unit out from under the car. If they are loose, remove the locating dowels from the transmission or engine and keep them in a safe place.

Refitting

26 The transmission is refitted by a reversal of the removal procedure, bearing in mind the following points:

a) *Ensure that the bush fitted to the centre of the crankshaft is in good condition and apply a little Molykote G1 grease to the torque converter centring pin. Do not apply too much, otherwise there is a possibility of the grease contaminating the torque converter.*

b) *Ensure that the engine/transmission locating dowels are correctly positioned prior to installation.*

c) *Once the transmission and engine are correctly joined, refit the securing bolts, tightening them to the specified torque setting, then remove the metal strip used to retain the torque converter.*

d) *Tighten all nuts and bolts to the specified torque (where given).*

e) *Renew the driveshaft oil seals using the information given in Chapter 7A and refit the driveshafts to the transmission as described in Chapter 8.*

f) *Adjust the selector cable as described in Section 2.*

g) *On completion, top-up the cooling system (see "Weekly checks"), then refill the transmission with the specified type and quantity of fluid as described in Chapter 1A.*

9 Automatic transmission overhaul - general information

In the event of a fault occurring with the transmission, it is first necessary to determine whether it is of an electrical, mechanical or hydraulic nature and to do this, special test equipment is required. It is therefore essential to have the work carried out by a Peugeot dealer if a transmission fault is suspected.

Do not remove the transmission from the car for possible repair before professional fault diagnosis has been carried out, since most tests require the transmission to be in the vehicle.

Chapter 8
Driveshafts

Contents

Degrees of difficulty

Easy, suitable for novice with little experience	Fairly easy, suitable for beginner with some experience	Fairly difficult, suitable for competent DIY mechanic	Difficult, suitable for experienced DIY mechanic	Very difficult, suitable for expert DIY or professional

Specifications

General

Lubrication (overhaul only) . . . . Use only special grease supplied in sachets with gaiter kits - joints are otherwise pre-packed with grease and sealed

Torque wrench settings

	Nm	lbf ft
Driveshaft intermediate bearing bracket securing bolts	45	33
Driveshaft intermediate bearing securing nuts	10	7
Driveshaft nut*	245	181
Front anti-roll bar drop link securing nuts*	30	22
Front anti-roll bar end clamp-to-lower arm bolts	25	18
Lower arm balljoint-to-hub carrier nut and clamp bolt*	50	37

*Use a new nut.

1 General information

Drive is transmitted from the differential to the front wheels by means of two solid-steel driveshafts of unequal length (see illustration).

Both driveshafts are splined at their outer ends, to accept the wheel hubs and are threaded so that each hub can be fastened to the driveshaft by a large nut. The inner end of each driveshaft is also splined, to accept the differential sun gear.

Constant velocity (CV) joints are fitted to each end of the driveshafts, to ensure the smooth and efficient transmission of power at all suspension and steering angles. The inner and outer constant velocity joints are of the spider-and-yoke type.

On later 1294 cc, 1360 cc and 1587 cc engine models (from approximately July 1993-on), due to the length of the right-hand driveshaft, the inner constant velocity joint is situated approximately halfway along the length of the shaft and an intermediate bearing is mounted in a bracket bolted to the rear of the cylinder block. The inner section of the driveshaft passes through the bearing, which prevents lateral flexing of the driveshaft.

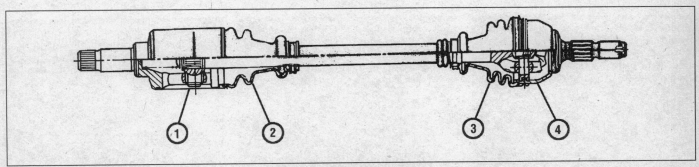

1.1 Typical driveshaft

1 Inner constant velocity joint   *2 Inner joint gaiter*   *3 Outer joint gaiter*   *4 Outer constant velocity joint*

8

2.4 Relieving the staking on the driveshaft nut

2 Driveshafts - removal and refitting

Note: *A balljoint separator tool will be required for this operation. A new driveshaft nut, a new track-rod end-to-steering arm nut and a new hub carrier-to-lower arm balljoint clamp nut, must be used on refitting.*

Removal

1 Chock the rear wheels then jack up the front of the vehicle and support it on axle stands (see *"Jacking and Vehicle Support"*). Remove the appropriate front roadwheel.

2 Drain the transmission oil/fluid as described in Chapter 7A (manual transmission) or Chapter 1A (automatic transmission).

3 Where applicable, to avoid any possibility

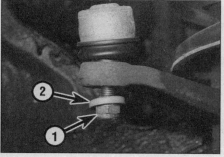

2.8a Unscrew the nut (1). Note the washer (2)

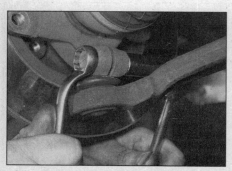

2.9a Undo the nut, while counterholding the bolt . . .

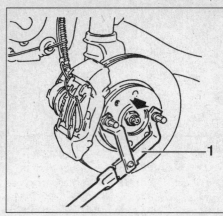

2.5 Using a suitable tool (1) to hold the front hub whilst loosening the driveshaft nut (arrowed)

of damage during the following procedure, remove the ABS wheel sensor from the hub carrier as described in Chapter 9.

4 Using a hammer and a suitable cold chisel or punch, relieve the staking on the driveshaft nut **(see illustration)**.

 Warning: Wear suitable eye protection.

5 The front hub must now be held stationary in order to loosen the driveshaft nut. Ideally, the hub should be held by a suitable tool bolted into place using two of the wheel bolts **(see illustration)**. Alternatively, refit at least two wheel bolts, tighten them securely, then

2.8b Using a balljoint separator tool to separate the track-rod end from the steering arm

2.9b . . . and withdraw the bolt. Note that the bolt fits from the front of the strut

have an assistant firmly apply the brake pedal to prevent the hub from rotating. Using a socket and extension bar, slacken and remove the driveshaft nut.

⚠ *Warning: Take care that the vehicle is adequately supported, as the nut is very tight! Discard the nut - a new one must be used on refitting.*

6 If removing the left-hand driveshaft on automatic transmission models, unscrew the three bolts securing the driveshaft gaiter retaining plate to the transmission casing.

7 On models where the anti-roll bar is connected to the suspension strut body, undo the nut and washer securing the drop link to the strut and position the link clear of the strut. On models where the anti-roll bar is connected directly to the lower arm, remove the two screws and washers securing the anti-roll bar end clamp to the lower arm. Remove the clamp and the rubber bush.

8 Partially unscrew the nut securing the track-rod end to the steering arm on the suspension strut. Using a balljoint separator tool, separate the track-rod end from the steering arm. Remove the nut and washer **(see illustrations)**.

9 Undo the nut (while counterholding the bolt) and withdraw the hub carrier-to-lower arm clamp bolt, noting which way round it is fitted **(see illustrations)**.

10 Using a suitable metal bar, lever the lower arm downwards just enough to release the balljoint shank from the lower arm. If the balljoint is a tight fit in the hub carrier, use a large flat-bladed screwdriver to carefully open up the clamp a little. Recover the balljoint rubber gaiter protector if it is loose.

11 Release the hub from the driveshaft splines by pulling the strut/hub carrier assembly outwards **(see illustration)**. If necessary, the shaft can be tapped out of the hub using a soft-faced mallet. Support the driveshaft with a piece of string or wire - do not allow the end of the driveshaft to hang down, or the joint may be damaged.

All except right-hand driveshaft with intermediate bearing

12 Support the driveshaft, then withdraw the inner constant velocity joint from the transmission, taking care not to damage the

2.11 Releasing the driveshaft from the hub

driveshaft oil seal (see illustration). If removing the left-hand driveshaft on automatic transmission models, take care not to allow the inner joint rollers to drop off the tripod as the joint is withdrawn from the transmission. Remove the driveshaft from the vehicle.

Right-hand driveshaft with intermediate bearing

13 Loosen the two intermediate bearing retaining bolt nuts, then rotate the bolts through 90°, so that their offset heads are clear of the bearing outer race.

14 Support the outer end of the driveshaft, then pull on the inner end of the shaft to free the intermediate bearing from its mounting bracket.

15 Once the driveshaft end is free from the transmission, slide the dust seal off the inner end of the shaft, noting which way around it is fitted and remove the driveshaft from the vehicle.

Refitting

16 Before installing the driveshaft, examine the driveshaft oil seal in the transmission for signs of damage or deterioration and, if necessary, renew it, referring to Chapter 7A or 7B for further information (it is advisable to renew the seal as a matter of course).

17 Thoroughly clean the driveshaft splines and the apertures in the transmission and hub assembly. Apply a thin film of grease to the oil seal lips and to the driveshaft splines and shoulders. Check that all driveshaft gaiter clips are securely fastened.

All except right-hand driveshaft with intermediate bearing

18 Offer up the driveshaft and engage the joint splines or the tripod rollers with the differential sun gear, taking great care not to damage the oil seal. Push the joint fully into position. Support the driveshaft until both ends have been refitted.

19 Ensure that the driveshaft splines and the corresponding splines in the hub are clean, then engage the driveshaft with the hub. Fit a new driveshaft nut, tightening it by hand only at this stage.

20 Ensure that the protector plate is in place over the lower arm balljoint, then engage the balljoint taper with the hub carrier (see illustration). If necessary, lever the arm downwards just enough to engage the balljoint, as during removal. Similarly, use a screwdriver to open up the clamp a little if necessary.

21 Fit the hub carrier-to-lower arm clamp bolt (inserting the bolt from the front of the strut) and a new nut and tighten to the specified torque.

22 Reconnect the track-rod end to the steering arm and fit the washer and a new nut. Tighten the nut to the specified torque.

23 Reconnect the anti-roll bar to the lower arm, or the anti-roll bar drop link to the strut, as applicable. Ensure that the washers are in place, then tighten the fixings to the specified torque.

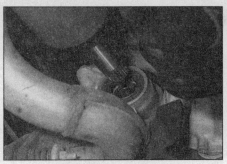

2.12 Withdraw the driveshaft from the transmission

24 Grease the driveshaft nut contact face on the hub bearing and the threads of the driveshaft nut, then hold the hub stationary as during removal and tighten the new driveshaft nut to the specified torque. Stake the nut into position.

25 If the left-hand driveshaft on automatic transmission models is being refitted, locate the driveshaft gaiter retaining plate on the transmission casing and secure with the three bolts.

26 Where applicable, refit the ABS wheel sensor, then refit the roadwheel and lower the vehicle to the ground.

27 Refill the transmission with oil or fluid as described in Chapter 7A or 1A as applicable.

Right-hand driveshaft with intermediate bearing

28 Check that the intermediate bearing rotates smoothly, without any sign of roughness or undue free play between its inner and outer races. If necessary, renew the bearing as described in Section 5. Examine the dust seal for signs of damage or deterioration and renew if necessary.

29 Apply a smear of grease to the outer race of the intermediate bearing and to the inner lip of the dust seal.

30 Pass the inner end of the shaft through the bearing mounting bracket, then carefully slide the dust seal into position on the driveshaft, ensuring that its flat surface is facing the transmission (see illustration).

31 Carefully engage the inner driveshaft splines with those of the differential sun gear, taking care not to damage the oil seal. Align

2.30 Slide the dust seal into position

2.20 Ensure that the balljoint protector plate is in place

the intermediate bearing with its mounting bracket and push the driveshaft fully into position. If necessary, use a soft-faced mallet to tap the outer race of the bearing into position in the mounting bracket. Support the driveshaft until it is completely refitted.

32 Ensure that the driveshaft splines and the corresponding splines in the hub are clean, then engage the driveshaft with the hub. Fit a new driveshaft nut, tightening it by hand only at this stage.

33 Ensure that the intermediate bearing is correctly seated, then rotate its retaining bolts back through 90°, so that their offset heads are resting against the bearing outer race. Tighten the retaining nuts to the specified torque. Ensure that the dust seal is tight against the driveshaft oil seal (see illustration).

34 Carry out the operations described previously in paragraphs 20 to 27 (with the exception of paragraph 25).

3 Driveshaft rubber gaiters - renewal

Manual transmission models

Outer joint

1 Remove the driveshaft as described in Section 2.

2 Remove the inner constant velocity joint and gaiter as described in paragraphs 13 to 20. It is recommended that the inner gaiter is also renewed, regardless of its apparent condition.

2.33 Ensure that the dust seal is tight against the driveshaft oil seal

8

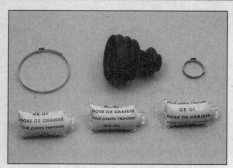

3.6 Driveshaft outer joint gaiter repair kit components

3.7 Sliding the outer joint gaiter onto the driveshaft

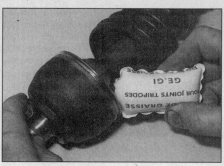

3.8 Pack the joint with the grease supplied in the repair kit

3 Release the two outer gaiter retaining clips, then slide the gaiter off the inner end of the driveshaft.

4 Thoroughly clean the outer constant velocity joint using paraffin, or a suitable solvent and dry it thoroughly. Carry out a visual inspection of the joint.

5 Check the driveshaft spider and outer member yoke for signs of wear, pitting or scuffing on their bearing surfaces. Also check that the outer member pivots smoothly and easily, with no traces of roughness.

6 If on inspection, the spider or outer member reveal signs of wear or damage, it will be necessary to renew the complete driveshaft as an assembly, since no components are available separately. If the joint components are in satisfactory condition, obtain a repair kit from your Peugeot dealer, consisting of a new gaiter, retaining clips and the correct type and quantity of grease **(see illustration)**.

7 Tape over the splines on the inner end of the driveshaft, then carefully slide the outer gaiter onto the shaft **(see illustration)**.

8 Pack the joint with the grease supplied in the repair kit **(see illustration)**. Work the grease well into the bearing tracks whilst twisting the joint and fill the rubber gaiter with any excess.

9 Ease the gaiter over the joint and ensure that the gaiter lips are correctly located in the grooves on both the driveshaft and constant velocity joint. Lift the outer sealing lip of the gaiter, to equalise air pressure within the gaiter.

10 Fit the large metal retaining clip to the gaiter. Remove any slack in the gaiter retaining clip by carefully compressing the raised section of the clip. In the absence of the special tool, a pair of side cutters may be used. Secure the small retaining clip using the same procedure **(see illustration)**. Check that the constant velocity joint moves freely in all

directions before proceeding further.

11 Refit the inner constant velocity joint as described in paragraphs 21 to 28.

Inner joint

12 Remove the driveshaft as described in Section 2.

13 Secure the driveshaft in a vice equipped with soft jaws then, using a suitable pair of pliers, carefully peel back the lip of the constant velocity joint outer member cover **(see illustration)**.

14 Once the lip of the cover is fully released, pull the joint outer member out from the cover and recover the spring and thrust cap from the end of the shaft. Remove the O-ring from the outside of the outer member and discard it.

15 Fold the gaiter back and wipe away the excess grease from the tripod joint. If the rollers are not secured to the joint with circlips, wrap adhesive tape around the joint to hold them in position.

16 Using a dab of paint, or a hammer and punch, mark the relative position of the tripod joint in relation to the driveshaft. Using circlip pliers, extract the circlip securing the joint to the driveshaft **(see illustration)**.

17 The tripod joint can now be removed. If it is tight, draw the joint off the driveshaft end, using a two- or three-legged bearing puller. Ensure that the legs of the puller are located behind the joint inner member and do not contact the joint rollers **(see illustrations)**. Alternatively, support the inner member of the tripod joint and press the shaft out of the joint using a hydraulic press, ensuring that no load is applied to the joint rollers.

3.10 Securing a gaiter securing clip using side cutters

3.13 Peeling back the lip of the joint outer member cover

3.16 Removing the inner tripod joint securing circlip

3.17a Using a three-legged puller to remove the inner tripod joint

3.17b Withdrawing the inner tripod joint. Note the alignment marks (made in the previous paragraph)

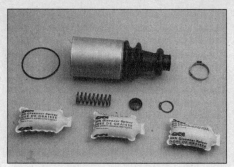

3.20 Driveshaft inner joint gaiter repair kit components

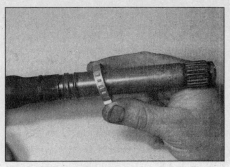

3.21a Slide on the inner retaining collar . . .

3.21b . . . and the gaiter/cover assembly

18 With the tripod joint removed, slide the gaiter and inner retaining collar off the end of the driveshaft.

19 Thoroughly clean the constant velocity joint components using paraffin, or a suitable solvent and dry them thoroughly - take great care not to remove the alignment marks made on dismantling, especially if paint was used. Carry out a visual inspection of the joint.

20 Examine the tripod joint, rollers and outer member for any signs of scoring or wear and for smoothness of movement of the rollers on the tripod stems. If any component is worn, the complete driveshaft assembly must be renewed; no joint components are available separately. If the joint components are in good condition, obtain a repair kit from your Peugeot dealer, consisting of a new rubber gaiter and outer cover assembly, circlip, thrust cap, spring, O-ring and the correct quantity of the special grease **(see illustration)**.

21 Tape over the splines on the end of the driveshaft and carefully slide the inner retaining collar and gaiter/cover assembly onto the shaft **(see illustrations)**.

22 Remove the tape then, aligning the marks made on dismantling, engage the tripod joint with the driveshaft splines. Use a hammer and soft metal drift (or a suitable tube or socket) to tap the joint onto the shaft, taking great care not to damage the driveshaft splines or joint rollers **(see illustration)**.

23 Secure the tripod joint in position with the new circlip, ensuring that it is correctly located in the driveshaft groove.

24 Remove the tape and evenly distribute the special grease contained in the repair kit around the tripod joint and outer member **(see illustration)**. Pack the gaiter/cover with more grease, then draw the cover over the tripod joint. Leave one sachet of grease to lubricate the outer member as the joint is fitted.

25 Fit the new spring, thrust cap and O-ring to the joint outer member **(see illustrations)**.

26 Position the outer member assembly over the tripod joint and locate the thrust cap against the end of the driveshaft. Apply the remainder of the grease to the joint, then push the outer member onto the shaft, compressing the spring and locate it inside the outer cover. Secure the outer member in position by peening the end of the cover evenly over the joint outer edge **(see illustrations)**.

27 Briefly lift the inner gaiter lip, using a blunt instrument such as a knitting needle, to equalise the air pressure within the gaiter. Secure the inner clip in position **(see illustration)**.

28 Check that the constant velocity joint moves freely in all directions, then refit the driveshaft to the vehicle as described in Section 2.

3.22 Using a hammer and a socket to tap the joint onto the driveshaft

3.24 Pack the joint and gaiter/cover with grease

3.25a Fit the new spring . . .

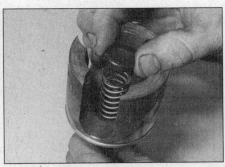

3.25b . . . thrust cap . . .

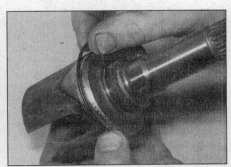

3.25c . . . and O-ring

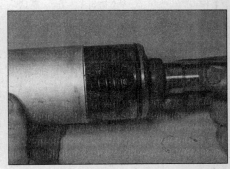

3.26a Position the outer member over the tripod joint . . .

8

3.26b . . . then apply the remainder of the grease . . .

3.26c . . . and peen over the end of the cover

3.27 Securing the inner gaiter clip in position

Automatic transmission models

29 The procedure for renewal of the inner and outer joint gaiters on the right-hand driveshaft is as described previously for manual transmission models.

30 At the time of writing no information was available for the renewal of the left-hand driveshaft inner joint gaiter on these models. If inner or outer joint gaiter renewal is necessary, the driveshaft should be removed from the vehicle and taken to a Peugeot dealer.

4 Driveshaft overhaul - general information

If any of the checks described in Chapter 1A or 1B reveal wear in any driveshaft joint, first remove the roadwheel trim or centre cap (as appropriate).

If the staking is still effective, the driveshaft nut should be correctly tightened; if in doubt, relieve the staking, then tighten the nut to the specified torque and restake it into the driveshaft grooves. Refit the roadwheel trim or centre cap (as applicable) and repeat the check on the remaining driveshaft nut.

Road test the vehicle and listen for a metallic clicking from the front as the vehicle is driven slowly in a circle on full-lock. If a clicking noise is heard, this indicates wear in the outer constant velocity joint.

If vibration, consistent with road speed, is felt through the car when accelerating, there is a possibility of wear in the inner constant velocity joints.

To check the joints for wear, remove the driveshafts, then dismantle them as described in Section 3. If any wear or free play is found, the complete driveshaft assembly must be renewed, as the joints are not available separately. Refer to a Peugeot dealer for information on the availability of driveshaft components.

5 Right-hand driveshaft intermediate bearing - renewal

Note: *A suitable bearing puller will be required, to draw the bearing and collar off the driveshaft end.*

1 Remove the right-hand driveshaft as described in Section 2.

2 Check that the bearing outer race rotates smoothly and easily, without any signs of roughness or undue free play between the inner and outer races. If necessary, renew the bearing as follows.

3 Using a long-reach universal bearing puller,

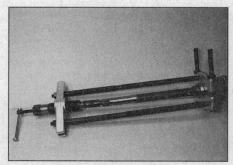

5.3 Using a long-reach bearing puller to remove the intermediate bearing from the right-hand driveshaft

carefully draw the collar and intermediate bearing off the driveshaft inner end **(see illustration)**. Apply a smear of grease to the inner race of the new bearing, then fit the bearing over the end of the driveshaft. Using a hammer and a suitable long piece of tubing which bears only on the bearing inner race, tap the new bearing into position on the driveshaft, until it abuts the constant velocity joint outer member. Once the bearing is correctly positioned, tap the bearing collar onto the shaft until it contacts the bearing inner race.

4 Check that the bearing rotates freely, then refit the driveshaft as described in Section 2.

Chapter 9
Braking system

Contents

Degrees of difficulty

Easy, suitable for novice with little experience	Fairly easy, suitable for beginner with some experience	Fairly difficult, suitable for competent DIY mechanic 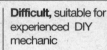	Difficult, suitable for experienced DIY mechanic	Very difficult, suitable for expert DIY or professional

Specifications

General

System type . . . . Dual hydraulic circuit, split diagonally. Anti-lock braking system (ABS) available as an option. Front disc brakes (ventilated on certain models) and rear drum or disc brakes according to model. Vacuum servo-assistance on all models, vacuum provided by camshaft-driven pump on diesel models. Cable-operated handbrake acting on rear wheels.

Front brakes

Type . . . . Disc, with single-piston sliding caliper
Disc diameter:
    954 cc and 1124 cc engine models:
        Non-ABS models with standard suspension . . . . 238.0 mm
        Models with ABS and/or uprated suspension . . . . 247.0 mm
    1294 cc, 1360 cc, 1527 cc and 1587 cc engine models . . . . 247.0 mm

Disc thickness:	New	Minimum thickness (1.0 mm max. variation between sides)
238.0 mm diameter disc	8.0mm	6.0 mm
247.0 mm diameter disc:		
Solid discs	10.0 mm	8.0 mm
Ventilated discs	20.4 mm	18.4 mm
Maximum disc run-out (no value specified, typical value given)	0.1 mm	
Minimum pad friction material thickness	2.0 mm	

Rear drum brakes

Drum diameter:	New	Maximum diameter after machining
954 cc and 1124 cc engine models:		
Non-ABS models with standard suspension	165.0 mm	166.2 mm
Models with ABS and/or uprated suspension	203.0 mm	204.2 mm
1294cc, 1360 cc 1527cc and 1587 cc engine models:		
Non-ABS models with standard suspension	180.0 mm	181.2 mm
Models with ABS and/or uprated suspension	203.0.mm	204.2 mm
Minimum shoe lining thickness	1.5 mm	

Rear disc brakes

Disc diameter	247.0 mm
Disc thickness:	
New	8.0 mm
Minimum thickness	6.0 mm
Maximum disc run-out (no value specified, typical value given)	0.1 mm
Brake pad minimum thickness	2.0 mm

Torque wrench settings

	Nm	lbf ft
ABS wheel sensor securing stud*	10	7
Backplate to hub	30	22
Brake disc to hub	10	7
Brake fluid pipe union nuts	15	11
Brake pedal bracket-to-bulkhead nuts	5	4
Brake pedal fastening to pedal bracket	20	15
Brake vacuum pump	20	15
Front brake caliper bolts:		
ATE caliper:		
M12 bolts*	105	77
M8 bolts	32	24
Bendix caliper:		
M12 bolts*	120	88
M8 bolts	32	24
Handbrake lever securing bolts	15	11
Hydraulic system bleed screws	3	2
Load-sensitive brake compensator to crossmember	10	7
Master cylinder-to-servo nuts	14	10
Rear brake caliper bolts:		
M12 bolts	120	88
M8 bolts	40	30
Rear hub nut**	140	103
Roadwheel bolts	85	63
Vacuum servo securing nuts	15	11
Wheel cylinder to backplate	15	11

*Use suitable thread-locking compound.
**Use a new nut.

1 General information

The braking system is of the servo-assisted, dual-circuit hydraulic type. The arrangement of the hydraulic system is such that each circuit operates one front and one rear brake from a tandem master cylinder. Under normal circumstances, both circuits operate in unison. However, in the event of hydraulic failure in one circuit, full braking force will still be available at two diagonally-opposite wheels (see illustration).

Some large-capacity engine models have disc brakes all round as standard; all other models are fitted with front disc brakes and rear drum brakes. An anti-lock braking system (ABS) is available as an option on certain models (refer to Section 23 for further information on ABS operation).

The front disc brakes are actuated by single-piston sliding type calipers, which ensure that equal pressure is applied to each disc pad (see illustration).

The rear drum brakes incorporate leading and trailing shoes, which are actuated by twin-piston wheel cylinders (see illustration). On models without ABS, the wheel cylinders incorporate integral pressure-regulating valves, which control the hydraulic pressure applied to the rear brakes. The regulating valves help to prevent rear wheel lock-up during emergency braking. On models with ABS, a load-sensitive rear pressure-regulating valve is fitted. A self-adjust mechanism is incorporated, to automatically compensate for brake shoe wear. As the brake shoe linings wear, the footbrake operation automatically operates the adjuster mechanism, which effectively lengthens the shoe strut and repositions the brake shoes, to remove the lining-to-drum clearance.

On models with rear disc brakes, the brakes are actuated by single-piston sliding calipers which incorporate mechanical handbrake mechanisms. A pressure-regulating valve is situated in the brake line to each rear caliper. The regulating valve is similar to that fitted to the rear wheel cylinders on drum brake models, and helps to prevent rear wheel lock-up during emergency braking. On models with ABS, a load-sensitive rear pressure-regulating valve is fitted, linked to the rear axle.

On all models, the handbrake provides an independent mechanical means of rear brake application.

On diesel models, there is insufficient vacuum in the inlet manifold to operate the braking system servo effectively. To overcome this problem, a vacuum pump is fitted to the engine, to provide vacuum to the servo unit. The vacuum pump is mounted on the end of the cylinder head and is driven directly from the camshaft.

Note: When servicing any part of the system, work carefully and methodically; also observe scrupulous cleanliness when overhauling any part of the hydraulic system. Always renew components (in axle sets, where applicable) if in doubt about their condition and use only genuine Peugeot replacement parts, or at least those of known good quality. Note the warnings given in "Safety first" and at relevant points in this Chapter concerning the dangers of asbestos dust and hydraulic fluid.

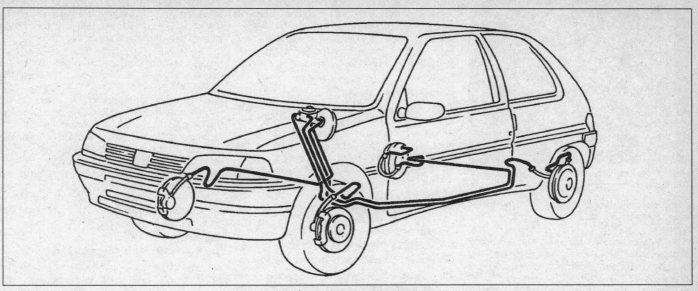

1.1 Brake hydraulic circuit layout

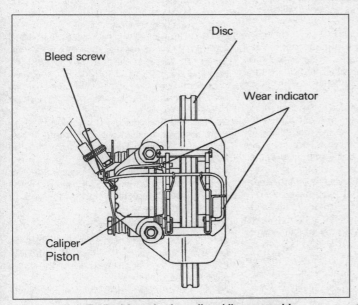

1.3 Typical front brake caliper/disc assembly

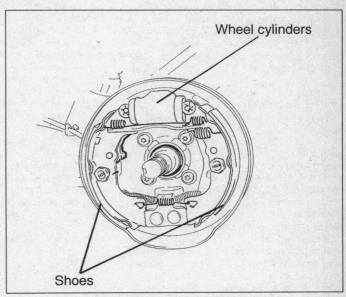

1.4 Typical rear drum brake assembly

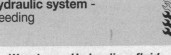

2 Hydraulic system - bleeding

⚠️ **Warning: Hydraulic fluid is poisonous; wash off immediately and thoroughly in the case of skin contact and seek immediate medical advice if any fluid is swallowed or gets into the eyes. Certain types of hydraulic fluid are inflammable and may ignite when allowed into contact with hot components; when servicing any hydraulic system, it is safest to assume that the fluid IS inflammable and to take precautions against the risk of fire as though it is petrol that is being handled. Finally, it is hygroscopic (it absorbs moisture from the air). The more moisture is absorbed by the fluid, the lower its boiling point becomes, leading to a dangerous loss of braking under hard use. Old fluid may be contaminated and unfit for further use. When topping-up or renewing the fluid, always use the recommended type and ensure that it comes from a freshly-opened sealed container.**

Caution: Hydraulic fluid is an effective paint stripper and will attack plastics; if any is spilt, it should be washed off immediately, using copious quantities of fresh water.

Non-ABS models

General

1 The correct operation of any hydraulic system is only possible after removing all air from the components and circuit; and this is achieved by bleeding the system.

2 During the bleeding procedure, add only clean, fresh hydraulic fluid of the recommended type; never re-use fluid that has already been bled from the system. Ensure that sufficient fluid is available before starting work.

3 If there is any possibility of incorrect fluid being already in the system, the brake components and circuit must be flushed

9

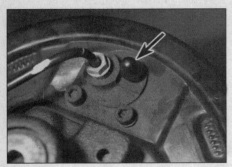

2.14 Rear brake bleed screw dust cap (arrowed)

completely with uncontaminated, correct fluid and new seals should be fitted throughout the system.

4 If hydraulic fluid has been lost from the system, or air has entered because of a leak, ensure that the fault is cured before proceeding further.

5 Park the vehicle on level ground, switch off the engine and select first or reverse gear (or P on automatic transmission models). Chock the wheels and release the handbrake.

6 Check that all pipes and hoses are secure, unions tight and bleed screws closed. Remove the dust caps (where applicable) and clean any dirt from around the bleed screws.

7 Unscrew the master cylinder reservoir cap and top the master cylinder reservoir up to the "MAX" level line. Refit the cap loosely and remember to maintain the fluid level at least above the "MIN" level line throughout the procedure, otherwise there is a risk of further air entering the system.

8 There are a number of one-man, do-it-yourself brake bleeding kits currently available from motor accessory shops. It is recommended that one of these kits is used whenever possible, as they greatly simplify the bleeding operation and also reduce the risk of expelled air and fluid being drawn back into the system. If such a kit is not available, the basic (two-man) method must be used, which is described in detail below.

9 If a kit is to be used, prepare the vehicle as described previously and follow the kit manufacturer's instructions, as the procedure may vary slightly according to the type being

2.22 Bleeding a front brake caliper using a one-way valve kit

used; generally, they are as outlined below in the relevant sub-section.

10 Whichever method is used, the same sequence must be followed (paragraphs 11 and 12) to ensure the removal of all air from the system.

Bleeding sequence

11 If the system has been only partially disconnected and suitable precautions were taken to minimise fluid loss, it should be necessary to bleed only that part of the system (ie the primary or secondary circuit).

12 If the complete system is to be bled, then it should be done working in the following sequence:

a) *Right-hand rear wheel.*
b) *Left-hand rear wheel.*
c) *Right-hand front wheel.*
d) *Left-hand front wheel.*

Bleeding - basic (two-man) method

13 Collect a clean glass jar, a suitable length of plastic or rubber tubing which is a tight fit over the bleed screw and a ring spanner to fit the screw. The help of an assistant will also be required.

14 Remove the dust cap from the first screw in the sequence (if not already done) **(see illustration)**. Fit a suitable spanner and tube to the screw. Place the other end of the tube in the jar and pour in sufficient fluid to cover the end of the tube.

15 Ensure that the master cylinder reservoir fluid level is maintained at least above the "MIN" level line throughout the procedure.

16 Have the assistant fully depress the brake pedal several times to build up pressure, then maintain it on the final downstroke.

17 While pedal pressure is maintained, unscrew the bleed screw (approximately one turn) and allow the compressed fluid and air to flow into the jar. The assistant should maintain pedal pressure, following the pedal down to the floor if necessary and should not release the pedal until instructed to do so. When the flow stops, tighten the bleed screw again, have the assistant release the pedal slowly and recheck the reservoir fluid level.

18 Repeat the steps given in paragraphs 16 and 17 until the fluid emerging from the bleed screw is free from air bubbles. If the master cylinder has been drained and refilled and air is being bled from the first screw in the sequence, allow approximately five seconds between cycles for the master cylinder passages to refill.

19 When no more air bubbles appear, tighten the bleed screw securely, remove the tube and spanner and refit the dust cap (where applicable). Do not overtighten the bleed screw.

20 Repeat the procedure on the remaining screws in the sequence, until all air is removed from the system and the brake pedal feels firm again.

Bleeding - using a one-way valve kit

21 As their name implies, these kits consist

of a length of tubing with a one-way valve fitted, to prevent expelled air and fluid being drawn back into the system; some kits include a translucent container, which can be positioned so that the air bubbles can be more easily seen flowing from the end of the tube.

22 The kit is connected to the bleed screw, which is then opened. The user returns to the driver's seat, depresses the brake pedal with a smooth, steady stroke and slowly releases it; this is repeated until the expelled fluid is clear of air bubbles **(see illustration)**.

23 Note that these kits simplify work so much that it is easy to forget the master cylinder reservoir fluid level; ensure that this is maintained at least above the "MIN" level line at all times.

Bleeding - using a pressure-bleeding kit

24 These kits are usually operated by the reservoir of pressurised air contained in the spare tyre. However, note that it will probably be necessary to reduce the pressure to a lower level than normal; refer to the instructions supplied with the kit.

25 By connecting a pressurised, fluid-filled container to the master cylinder reservoir, bleeding can be carried out simply by opening each screw in turn (in the specified sequence) and allowing the fluid to flow out until no more air bubbles can be seen in the expelled fluid.

26 This method has the advantage that the large reservoir of fluid provides an additional safeguard against air being drawn into the system during bleeding.

27 Pressure-bleeding is particularly effective when bleeding "difficult" systems, or when bleeding the complete system at the time of routine fluid renewal.

All methods

28 When bleeding is complete and firm pedal feel is restored, wash off any spilt fluid, tighten the bleed screws securely and refit their dust caps (where applicable).

29 Check the hydraulic fluid level in the master cylinder reservoir and top-up if necessary (see "*Weekly checks*").

30 Discard any hydraulic fluid that has been bled from the system; it will not be fit for re-use.

31 Check the feel of the brake pedal. If it feels at all spongy, air must still be present in the system and further bleeding is required. Failure to bleed satisfactorily after a reasonable repetition of the bleeding procedure may be due to worn master cylinder seals.

Anti-lock braking system (ABS)

⚠ *Warning: On ABS models, ensure that the ignition is switched off before starting the bleeding procedure, to avoid any possibility of voltage being applied to the modulator before the bleeding procedure is* completed. *Ideally, the battery should be disconnected. If voltage is applied to the modulator before the bleeding procedure is complete, this will effectively drain the hydraulic fluid in the modulator, rendering the unit unserviceable. Note that internal bleeding of the modulator solenoid valves, low-pressure circuit, pump and high-pressure circuit is not possible without the use of special equipment available to a Peugeot dealer.*

32 Proceed as described previously for non-ABS models, but after bleeding the system at the front calipers and rear wheel cylinders (see paragraph 12), the hydraulic modulator assembly must be bled in a similar manner.

33 Connect a bleed tube to one of the bleed screws on the top of the modulator assembly and bleed the modulator circuit as described previously for the front calipers and rear wheel cylinders (see illustration).

34 Repeat the procedure for the remaining hydraulic modulator bleed screw, then proceed as described in paragraphs 28 to 31 inclusive.

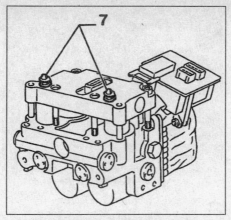

2.33 ABS hydraulic modulator bleed screws (7)

3 Hydraulic pipes and hoses - renewal

Note: *Before starting work, refer to the warning at the beginning of Section 2 concerning the dangers of hydraulic fluid.*

1 If any pipe or hose is to be renewed, minimise fluid loss by first removing the master cylinder reservoir cap, then tightening it down onto a piece of polythene to obtain an airtight seal. Alternatively, flexible hoses can be sealed, if required, using a proprietary brake hose clamp; metal brake pipe unions can be plugged (if care is taken not to allow dirt into the system) or capped immediately they are disconnected. Place a wad of rag under any union that is to be disconnected, to catch any spilt fluid.

2 If a flexible hose is to be disconnected, unscrew the brake pipe union nut before removing the spring clip which secures the hose to its mounting bracket (see illustration).

3 To unscrew the union nuts, it is preferable to obtain a brake pipe spanner of the correct size; these are available from most large motor accessory shops. Failing this, a close-fitting open-ended spanner will be required, though if the nuts are tight or corroded, their flats may be rounded-off if the spanner slips. In such a case, a self-locking wrench is often the only way to unscrew a stubborn union, but it follows that the pipe and the damaged nuts must be renewed on reassembly. Always clean a union and surrounding area before disconnecting it. If disconnecting a component with more than one union, make a careful note of the connections before disturbing any of them.

4 If a brake pipe is to be renewed, it can be obtained, cut to length and with the union nuts and end flares in place, from Peugeot dealers. All that is then necessary is to bend it to shape, following the line of the

original, before fitting it to the vehicle. Alternatively, most motor accessory shops can make up brake pipes from kits, but this requires very careful measurement of the original, to ensure that the replacement is of the correct length. The safest answer is usually to take the original to the shop as a pattern.

5 On refitting, do not overtighten the union nuts. It is not necessary to exercise brute force to obtain a sound joint.

6 Ensure that the pipes and hoses are correctly routed, with no kinks and that they are secured in the clips or brackets provided. After fitting, remove the polythene from the reservoir and bleed the hydraulic system as described in Section 2. Wash off any spilt fluid and check carefully for fluid leaks.

4 Front brake pads - renewal (solid disc)

⚠️ **Warning: Renew BOTH sets of front brake pads at the same time - NEVER renew the pads on only one wheel, as uneven braking may result. Note that the dust created by wear of the pads may contain asbestos, which is a health hazard. Never blow it out with compressed air and don't inhale any of it. An approved filtering mask should be worn when working on the brakes. DO NOT use petrol or petroleum-based solvents to clean brake parts; use brake cleaner or methylated spirit only.**

1 Chock the rear wheels then jack up the front of the vehicle and support it on axle stands (see *"Jacking and Vehicle Support"*). Remove the front roadwheels.

2 Trace the brake pad wear sensor wiring back from the pads and disconnect it from the wiring connector (see illustration). Note the routing of the wiring and free it from any relevant retaining clips.

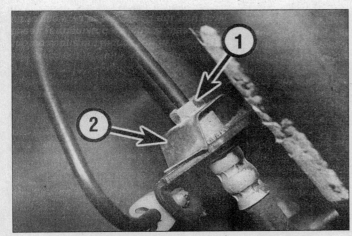

3.2 Brake pipe union nut (1) and hose spring clip (2)

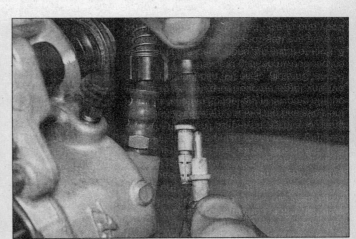

4.2 Disconnecting the brake pad wear sensor wiring - ATE caliper

4.5a Extract the spring clip (arrowed) . . .

4.5b . . . and slide out the pad retaining plate - Bendix caliper

3 Push the piston into its bore by pulling the caliper outwards.

4 There are different types of front brake caliper fitted to the models covered in this manual. Identify the relevant caliper by reference to the accompanying illustrations (the manufacturer's name is usually stamped on part of the caliper, in any case), then proceed as described under the relevant sub-heading. The procedure for vented discs is given in Section 27.

Bendix caliper

5 Using pliers, extract the small spring clip from the pad retaining plate and then slide the plate out of the caliper (it will probably be necessary to tap the plate from the caliper) **(see illustrations)**.

6 Withdraw the pads from the caliper **(see illustrations)**, then make a note of the correct fitted position of each anti-rattle spring and remove the spring from each pad (where applicable, unclip the pad wear sensor wiring). It may be necessary to push the inboard pad back against the piston, to retract the piston into its bore, before the pad can be removed.

7 First measure the thickness of each brake pad's friction material. If either pad is worn at any point to the specified minimum thickness or less, *all four* pads must be renewed. Also, the pads should be renewed if any are fouled with oil or grease; there is no satisfactory way of degreasing friction material, once contaminated. If any of the brake pads are worn unevenly, or are fouled with oil or grease, trace and rectify the cause before reassembly. New brake pads and spring kits

are available from Peugeot dealers.

8 If the brake pads are still serviceable, carefully clean them using a clean, fine wire brush or similar, paying particular attention to the sides and back of the metal backing. Clean out the grooves in the friction material and pick out any large embedded particles of dirt or debris. Carefully clean the pad locations in the caliper body/mounting bracket.

9 Prior to fitting the pads, check that the guide pins are free to slide easily in the caliper body/mounting bracket and check that the rubber guide pin gaiters are undamaged. Brush the dust and dirt from the caliper and piston, but *do not* inhale it, as it is injurious to health. Inspect the dust seal around the piston for damage and the piston for evidence of fluid leaks, corrosion or damage. If attention to any of these components is necessary, refer to Section 10.

10 If new brake pads are to be fitted, the caliper piston must be pushed back into the cylinder to make room for them. Either use a G-clamp or similar tool, or use suitable pieces of wood as levers. Provided that the master cylinder reservoir has not been overfilled with hydraulic fluid, there should be no spillage, but keep a careful watch on the fluid level while retracting the piston. If the fluid level rises above the "MAX" level line at any time, the surplus should be syphoned off or ejected via a plastic tube connected to the bleed screw (see Section 2).

> ⚠️ *Warning: Do not syphon the fluid by mouth, as it is poisonous; use a syringe or an old poultry baster.*

11 Apply a little copper-based brake grease to the pad backing plates, but take great care not to allow any grease onto the pad friction linings.

12 Fit the anti-rattle springs to the pads, so that when the pads are installed in the caliper, the spring end will be located at the opposite end of the pad in relation to the pad retaining plate.

13 Locate the pads in the caliper, ensuring that the friction material of each pad is against the brake disc and check that the anti-rattle spring ends are at the opposite end of the pad to which the retaining plate is to be inserted.

14 Slide the retaining plate into place and install the new small spring clip at its inner end. It may be necessary to file an entry chamfer on the edge of the retaining plate, to enable it to be fitted without difficulty.

15 Reconnect the brake pad wear sensor wiring connectors, ensuring that the outer wire is correctly routed through the anti-rattle spring loops and that both wires pass through the loop of the bleed screw cap **(see illustration)**.

16 Depress the brake pedal repeatedly, until the pads are pressed into firm contact with the brake disc and normal (non-assisted) pedal pressure is restored.

17 Repeat the above procedure on the remaining front brake caliper.

18 Refit the roadwheels, then lower the vehicle to the ground and tighten the roadwheel bolts to the specified torque.

19 Check the hydraulic fluid level as described in "Weekly checks".

ATE caliper

20 Note the location and orientation of the pad anti-rattle spring (note the routing of the brake pad wear sensor wiring through the anti-rattle spring), then remove the pad retaining pins by tapping them from the caliper using a suitable pin-punch. Note that the pad retaining spring will be released as the pins are removed **(see illustrations)**.

21 Withdraw the pad retaining spring.

22 Withdraw the pads from the caliper. It may be necessary to push the inboard pad back against the piston, to retract the piston into its bore, before the pad can be removed **(see illustrations)**.

4.6a Withdraw the outer . . .

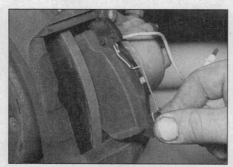

4.6b . . . and inner pads - Bendix caliper

4.15 Brake pad wear sensor wiring is routed through anti-rattle springs (1) and bleed screw cap (2)

4.20a Note the orientation of the pad anti-rattle spring (arrowed) - ATE caliper

4.20b Free the pad retaining pins from the caliper using a pin-punch . . .

4.20c . . . then withdraw the upper . . .

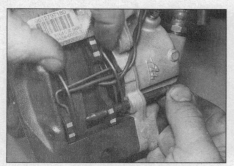

4.20d . . . and lower pins - ATE caliper

4.22a Withdraw the inner . . .

4.22b . . . and outer brake pads - ATE caliper

23 Proceed as described in paragraphs 7 to 11 inclusive.
24 Slide the pads into position in the caliper, ensuring that the friction material of each pad is against the brake disc.
25 Locate the anti-rattle spring on the pads,

as noted before removal and ensure that the pad wear sensor wiring is correctly routed through the spring **(see illustration)**.
26 Fit the upper pad retaining pin, ensuring that the top arms of the pad retaining spring locate behind the pin, then tap the pin into

position in the caliper.
27 Refit the lower pad retaining pin, ensuring that it passes through the anti-rattle spring, then tap the pin into position in the caliper **(see illustration)**.
28 Reconnect the brake pad wear sensor wiring connectors, ensuring that the wiring is correctly routed.
29 Proceed as described in paragraphs 16 to 19 inclusive.

4.25 Ensure that the pad wear sensor wiring is correctly routed through the spring - ATE caliper

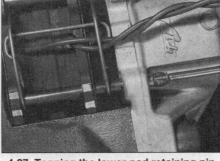

4.27 Tapping the lower pad retaining pin into position - ATE caliper

5 Rear brake pads - renewal

⚠️ **Warning: Renew both sets of rear brake pads at the same time - never renew the pads on only one wheel, as uneven braking may result. Dust created by wear of the pads may contain asbestos, which is a health hazard. Never blow it out with compressed air and don't inhale any of it. An approved filtering mask should be worn when working on the brakes. DO NOT use petrol or petroleum-based solvents to clean brake parts; use brake cleaner or methylated spirit only.**

1 Chock the front wheels, then jack up the rear of the vehicle and support it on axle stands (see *"Jacking and Vehicle Support"*). Remove the rear wheels.
2 Extract the small spring clip from the pad retaining plate and then slide the plate out of the caliper **(see illustrations)**. Discard the spring clip - a new one must be used on refitting.

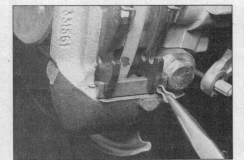

5.2a Extract the spring clip . . .

5.2b . . . then slide out the pad retaining plate . . .

9

5.3 . . . and withdraw the brake pads from the caliper

3 Using pliers if necessary, withdraw both the inner and outer pads from the caliper **(see illustration)**. Make a note of the correct fitted position of the anti-rattle springs and remove the springs from each pad.

4 First measure the thickness of the friction material of each brake pad. If either pad is worn at any point to the specified minimum thickness or less, all four pads must be renewed. Also, the pads should be renewed if any are fouled with oil or grease; there is no satisfactory way of degreasing friction material, once contaminated. If any of the brake pads are worn unevenly, or fouled with oil or grease, trace and rectify the cause before reassembly. New brake pads and spring kits are available from Peugeot dealers.

5 If the brake pads are still serviceable, carefully clean them using a clean, fine wire brush or similar, paying particular attention to the sides and back of the metal backing. Clean out the grooves in the friction material and pick out any large embedded particles of dirt or debris. Carefully clean the pad locations in the caliper body.

6 Prior to fitting the pads, check that the guide sleeves are free to slide easily in the caliper body and check that the rubber guide sleeve gaiters are undamaged. Brush the dust and dirt from the caliper and piston, but **do not**

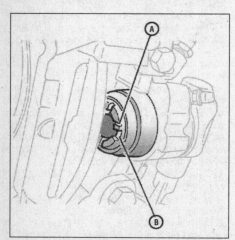

5.8 . . . and position the piston so that the reference slot (A) is positioned horizontally above or below the piston groove (B)

5.7 Retract the piston using a square-section bar . . .

inhale it, as it is injurious to health. Inspect the dust seal around the piston for damage and the piston for evidence of fluid leaks, corrosion or damage. If attention to any of these components is necessary, refer to Section 11.

7 If new brake pads are to be fitted, it will be necessary to retract the piston fully into the caliper bore, by rotating it in a clockwise direction. This can be achieved using a suitable square-section bar, such as the shaft of a screwdriver, which locates snugly in the caliper piston slots **(see illustration)**. Provided that the master cylinder reservoir has not been overfilled with hydraulic fluid, there should be no spillage, but keep a careful watch on the fluid level while retracting the piston. If the fluid level rises above the "MAX" level line at any time, the surplus should be siphoned off, or ejected via a plastic tube connected to the bleed screw (see Section 2).

> ⚠️ *Warning: Do not syphon the fluid by mouth, as it is poisonous; use a syringe or an old poultry baster.*

8 Position the caliper piston so that its piston reference slot (A) is positioned horizontally, above or below the piston groove (B); this is necessary to ensure that the lug on the inner pad will locate with the caliper piston slot on installation **(see illustration)**.

9 The brake pad with the lug on its backing plate is the inner pad. Refit the anti-rattle springs to the pads, so that when the pads are fitted in the caliper, the spring end will be located at the opposite end of the pad, in relation to the pad retaining plate **(see illustration)**.

10 Locate the outer brake pad in the caliper body, ensuring that its friction material is against the brake disc. Slide the inner pad into position in the caliper, ensuring that the lug on its backing plate is aligned with the slot in the caliper piston **(see illustration)**.

11 Ensure that the anti-rattle spring ends on both pads are correctly positioned, then slide the retaining plate into place and secure it in position with a new spring clip. It may be necessary to file an entry chamfer on the edge of the retaining plate, to enable it to be fitted without difficulty.

12 Depress the brake pedal repeatedly until the pads are pressed into firm contact with the brake disc and normal (non-assisted) pedal pressure is restored. Check that the inner pad lug is correctly engaged with one of the caliper piston slots.

13 Repeat the above procedure on the remaining rear brake caliper.

14 Check the handbrake cable adjustment as described in Chapter 1A or 1B, then refit the roadwheels and lower the vehicle to the ground. Tighten the roadwheel bolts to the specified torque setting.

15 Check the hydraulic fluid level as described in *"Weekly checks"*.

16 New pads will not give full braking efficiency until they have bedded in. Be prepared for this and avoid hard braking as far as possible for the first hundred miles or so after pad renewal.

6 Rear brake shoes - renewal

> ⚠️ *Warning: Renew BOTH sets of rear brake shoes at the same time - NEVER renew the shoes on only one wheel, as uneven braking may result. Note that the dust created by wear of the shoes may contain asbestos, which is a health hazard. Never blow it out with compressed air and don't inhale any of it. An approved filtering mask should be worn when working on the brakes. DO NOT use petrol or petroleum-based solvents to clean brake parts; use brake cleaner or methylated spirit only.*

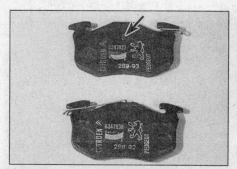

5.9 Inner brake pad can be identified by its locating lug (arrowed). Note the correct fitted positions of the anti-rattle springs

5.10 Install the inner pad, ensuring its locating lug is correctly engaged in the piston slot

6.3 Rear brake shoes and components. Note the locations of the springs

6.4a Use pliers . . .

6.4b . . . to remove the outer hold-down spring cups

1 Remove the rear brake drums (Section 9).

2 Working on one side of the vehicle, brush the dirt and dust from the brake backplate and drum. **Do not** inhale the dust, as it may be a health hazard.

6.6a Pull the leading brake shoe forwards . . .

3 Note the position of each shoe and the location of the return and steady springs **(see illustration)**.

4 Remove the shoe hold-down springs. Use pliers to depress the outer spring cups and turn them through 90° **(see illustrations)**.

5 Recover the springs and cups and remove the spring retainer pins from the backplate.

6 Carefully pull the leading brake shoe forwards from the backplate and using a suitable pair of pliers, unhook and remove the lower return spring **(see illustrations)**.

7 Disengage the lower ends of the shoes from the bottom anchor and pull the upper ends of the shoes from the wheel cylinder, then withdraw the shoe assembly and unhook the handbrake cable from the lever on the trailing brake shoe **(see illustration)**.

8 If necessary, position a rubber band or a cable-tie over the wheel cylinder, to prevent

the pistons from being ejected **(see illustration)**. If there is any evidence of fluid leakage from the wheel cylinder, renew it or overhaul it as described in Section 12.

9 Unhook the upper return spring from the shoes and unhook the adjuster strut spring.

10 Working on the leading brake shoe, prise the adjuster lever retaining plate over the pivot pin on the adjuster lever, then pull the adjuster lever forwards to allow the adjuster strut to be removed **(see illustrations)**.

11 Transfer the handbrake and automatic adjuster levers to the new shoes, as required (prise off the spring clips to remove the levers) **(see illustration)**. Note that the levers and strut on each rear wheel are different and that the leading and trailing shoes are fitted with different grade linings. New shoes will be supplied complete with the adjuster retaining plate riveted to the leading shoe.

6.6b . . . and remove the lower return spring

6.7 Unhooking the handbrake cable from the lever on the trailing shoe

6.8 Rubber band positioned over wheel cylinder to retain pistons

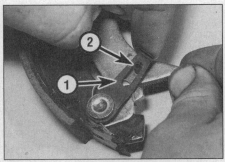

6.10a Prise the retaining plate (1) over the pivot pin (2) . . .

6.10b . . . and remove the adjuster strut

6.11 Prising off the spring clip to remove the adjuster lever from the trailing shoe

9

6.14 Fit the adjuster strut spring (arrowed) between the shoe and the adjuster strut

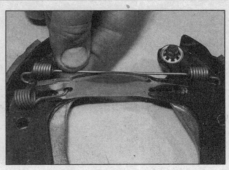

6.15a Fit the upper return spring to the shoes . . .

6.15b . . . then engage the adjuster strut

12 Place the shoes on the bench in their correct positions and lay the adjuster strut in position.

13 With the adjuster strut engaged with the leading shoe, push the adjuster lever back towards the shoe and clip the adjuster lever retaining plate over the pivot pin on the adjuster lever.

14 Fit the adjuster strut spring between the trailing shoe and the adjuster strut **(see illustration)**, but do not fully engage the adjuster strut with the trailing shoe at this stage.

15 Fit the upper return spring to the shoes, then carefully manipulate the adjuster strut into position to engage it with the slot in the trailing shoe **(see illustrations)**.

16 Apply copper-based brake grease sparingly to the shoe contact areas of the brake backplate. Where applicable, remove the rubber band or cable tie from the wheel cylinder **(see illustration)**.

17 Offer the shoes into position and reconnect the handbrake cable to the handbrake lever on the trailing shoe.

18 Position the shoes on the backplate and lever the upper ends of the shoes apart to engage them with the wheel cylinder.

19 Carefully refit the lower return spring to the shoes **(see illustration)**, then lever the lower ends of the shoes apart to engage them with the lower anchor.

20 Insert the steady spring retainer pins in the backplate and through the holes in the shoes, then fit the hold-down springs and the cups.

21 Move the serrated automatic adjuster

lever quadrant against the spring tension, to set the shoes at their minimum diameter.

22 Check that the handbrake lever on the trailing brake shoe is positioned with the lug on the edge of the shoe web and not behind the shoe.

23 Repeat the procedure on the remaining side of the vehicle, then refit the brake drums as described in Section 9.

24 On completion, check the handbrake adjustment as described in Chapter 1A or 1B.

7 Front brake disc - inspection, removal and refitting

Note: *Before starting work, refer to the warning at the beginning of Section 4 concerning the dangers of asbestos dust.*

Inspection

Note: *If either disc requires renewal, BOTH should be renewed at the same time, to ensure even and consistent braking. New brake pads should also be fitted.*

1 Chock the rear wheels then jack up the front of the vehicle and support it on axle stands (see *"Jacking and Vehicle Support"*). Remove the appropriate front roadwheel.

2 Slowly rotate the brake disc so that the full area of both sides can be checked; remove the brake pads (see Section 4 or 27) if better access is required to the inboard surface. Light scoring is normal in the area swept by the brake pads, but if heavy scoring or cracks are found, the disc must be renewed.

3 It is normal to find a lip of rust and brake dust around the disc's perimeter; this can be scraped off if required. If, however, a lip has formed due to excessive wear of the brake pad swept area, then the disc's thickness must be measured using a micrometer. Take measurements at several places around the disc, at the inside and outside of the pad swept area; if the disc has worn at any point to the specified minimum thickness or less, the disc must be renewed.

4 If the disc is thought to be warped, it can be checked for run-out. Either use a dial gauge mounted on any convenient fixed point, while the disc is slowly rotated, or use feeler blades to measure (at several points all around the disc) the clearance between the disc and a fixed point, such as the caliper mounting bracket. If the measurements obtained are at the specified maximum or beyond, the disc is excessively warped and must be renewed; however, it is worth checking first that the hub bearing is in good condition (Chapters 1A or 1B and/or 10). Also try the effect of removing the disc and turning it through 180°, to reposition it on the hub; if the run-out is still excessive, the disc must be renewed.

5 Check the disc for cracks, especially around the wheel bolt holes and any other wear or damage and renew if necessary.

Removal

6 Remove the brake pads as described in Section 4 or 27.

7 On certain models, it may be necessary to remove the brake caliper as described in Section 10 in order to allow sufficient clearance to remove the disc. Note that in this case there is no need to disconnect the brake fluid hose from the caliper. Support the caliper with wire or string, taking care not to strain the hose.

8 Use chalk or paint to mark the relationship of the disc to the hub, then remove the screws securing the brake disc to the hub and withdraw the disc **(see illustrations)**. Note that it may be necessary to use an impact screwdriver to free the disc securing screws. If the disc is tight, lightly tap its rear face with a hide or plastic mallet. Where applicable (if the brake caliper is still fitted), tilt the disc as necessary to clear the hub and caliper.

6.16 Apply copper-based brake grease to the shoe contact areas

6.19 Refitting the lower return spring

7.8a Using an impact screwdriver to free a brake disc securing screw

7.8b Removing a brake disc - model with Bendix caliper

Refitting

9 Ensure that the mating faces of the disc and the hub are clean and flat. If necessary, wipe the mating surfaces clean.

10 Refit the disc, then refit and securely tighten the disc retaining screws.

11 If a new disc has been fitted, use a suitable solvent to wipe any preservative coating from the disc.

12 Where applicable, refit the caliper as described in Section 10.

13 Refit the brake pads as described in Section 4 or 27.

8 Rear brake disc - inspection, removal and refitting

Note: *Before starting work, refer to the note at the beginning of Section 5 concerning the dangers of asbestos dust.*

9.4a Remove the hub nut . . .

Inspection

Note: *If either disc requires renewal, BOTH should be renewed at the same time, to ensure even and consistent braking. New brake pads should also be fitted.*

1 Firmly chock the front wheels, then jack up the rear of the car and support it on axle stands (see *"Jacking and Vehicle Support"*). Remove the appropriate rear roadwheel.

2 Inspect the disc as described in Section 7.

Removal

3 Remove the brake pads as described in Section 5.

4 Use chalk or paint to mark the relationship of the disc to the hub, then remove the screw securing the brake disc to the hub and remove the disc. If it is tight, lightly tap its rear face with a hide or plastic mallet.

Refitting

5 Refitting is the reverse of the removal procedure, noting the following points:

  a) *Ensure that the mating surfaces of the disc and hub are clean and flat.*

  b) *Align (if applicable) the marks made on removal and securely tighten the disc retaining screws.*

  c) *If a new disc has been fitted, use a suitable solvent to wipe any preservative coating from the disc, before refitting the caliper.*

  d) *Refit the brake pads as described in Section 5.*

  e) *Refit the roadwheel, then lower the vehicle to the ground and tighten the roadwheel bolts to the specified torque.*

9 Rear brake drum - removal, inspection and refitting

Note: *Before starting work, refer to the warning at the beginning of Section 6 concerning the dangers of asbestos dust.*
Note: *A new rear hub nut and dust cap must be used on refitting.*

Removal

1 Chock the front wheels then jack up the rear of the vehicle and support it on axle stands (see *"Jacking and Vehicle Support"*). Remove the appropriate rear roadwheel.

2 Using a hammer and a large flat-bladed screwdriver, carefully tap and prise the dust cap out of the centre of the brake drum. Discard the cap - a new one must be used on refitting.

3 Using a hammer and a suitable cold chisel or punch, relieve the staking on the driveshaft nut.

⚠️ **Warning: Wear suitable eye protection.**

4 Using a socket and long bar, slacken and remove the rear hub nut and withdraw the thrustwasher **(see illustrations)**. Discard the hub nut - a new nut must be used on refitting.

5 It should now be possible to withdraw the brake drum assembly from the stub axle by hand **(see illustration)**. It may be difficult to remove the drum, due to the tightness of the hub bearing on the stub axle, or due to the brake shoes binding on the inner circumference of the drum. If the bearing is tight, tap the periphery of the drum using a hide or plastic mallet, or use a universal puller, secured to the drum with the wheel bolts, to pull it off. If the brake shoes are binding, first check that the handbrake is fully released, then proceed as follows.

6 Insert a screwdriver through one of the wheel bolt holes in the brake drum, so that it contacts the handbrake shoe adjuster lever on the leading brake shoe. Push the lever to release the ratchet until the brake shoes are fully retracted **(see illustration)**. The brake drum can now be withdrawn.

9.4b . . . and withdraw the thrustwasher

9.5 Withdrawing the brake drum

9.6 Using a screwdriver to release the shoe adjuster mechanism and retract the shoes

9

9.13 Ensure that the handbrake lever stop peg (arrowed) is positioned against the edge of the shoe web

9.14a Tighten the hub nut to the specified torque . . .

9.14b . . . then stake the nut in position

Inspection

Note: *If either drum requires renewal, BOTH should be renewed at the same time, to ensure even and consistent braking. New brake shoes should also be fitted.*

7 Working carefully, remove all traces of brake dust from the drum, but *avoid inhaling the dust, as it is a health hazard.*

8 Clean the outside of the drum and check it for obvious signs of wear or damage, such as cracks around the roadwheel bolt holes; renew the drum if necessary.

9 Carefully examine the inside of the drum. Light scoring of the friction surface is normal, but if heavy scoring is found, the drum must be renewed. It is usual to find a lip on the drum's inboard edge which consists of a mixture of rust and brake dust; this should be scraped away, to leave a smooth surface which can be polished with fine (120- to 150-grade) emery paper. If, however, the lip is due to the friction surface being recessed by excessive wear, then the drum must be renewed.

10 If the drum is thought to be excessively worn, or oval, its internal diameter must be measured at several points using an internal micrometer. Take measurements in pairs, the second at right-angles to the first and compare the two, to check for signs of ovality. Provided that it does not enlarge the drum to beyond the specified maximum diameter, it may be possible to have the drum refinished by skimming or grinding; if this is not possible,

the drums on both sides must be renewed. Note that if the drum is to be skimmed, BOTH drums must be refinished, to maintain a consistent internal diameter on both sides.

11 Check the condition of the oil seal on the stub axle and renew if necessary. To renew the oil seal, simply prise the old seal from the stub axle, then push the new seal into position until it is seated on the spacer. At the same time, check the condition of the oil seal seating ring in the rear of the drum and if any signs of wear or damage are present, renew the ring (if the surface of the ring is damaged, this is likely to quickly result in damage to the oil seal).

Refitting

12 If a new brake drum is to be installed, use a suitable solvent to remove any preservative coating that may have been applied to its internal friction surfaces. Note that it may also be necessary to shorten the adjuster strut length, by rotating the strut wheel, to allow the drum to pass over the brake shoes.

13 Ensure that the handbrake lever stop peg is correctly repositioned against the edge of the brake shoe web **(see illustration)**, then apply a smear of clean engine oil to the stub axle and slide on the drum assembly.

14 Fit the thrustwasher and new hub nut and tighten the hub nut to the specified torque. Stake the nut firmly into the groove on the stub axle, to secure it in position **(see illustrations)**.

15 Tap the new dust cover into place in the centre of the brake drum.

16 Depress the footbrake several times to operate the self-adjusting mechanism.

17 Repeat the above procedure on the remaining rear brake assembly (where necessary), then check and, if necessary, adjust the handbrake cable as described in Chapter 1A or 1B.

18 On completion, refit the roadwheel(s), then lower the vehicle to the ground and tighten the roadwheel bolts to the specified torque.

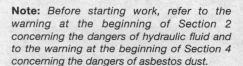

10 Front brake caliper - removal, overhaul and refitting

Note: *Before starting work, refer to the warning at the beginning of Section 2 concerning the dangers of hydraulic fluid and to the warning at the beginning of Section 4 concerning the dangers of asbestos dust.*

Removal

1 Chock the rear wheels then jack up the front of the vehicle and support it on axle stands (see *"Jacking and Vehicle Support"*). Remove the appropriate front roadwheel.

2 Minimise fluid loss by first removing the master cylinder reservoir cap, then tightening it down onto a piece of polythene, to obtain an airtight seal. Alternatively, use a brake hose clamp, a G-clamp or a similar tool to clamp the flexible hose running to the caliper.

3 Remove the brake pads as described in Section 4 or 27.

4 Clean the area around the union, then loosen the brake hose union nut.

5 Where applicable, remove the dust cover(s) from the caliper securing bolts, then slacken the two bolts securing the caliper assembly to the hub carrier and remove them. On models with Bendix calipers, recover the mounting plate from the bolts, noting which way around the plate is fitted **(see illustrations)**.

6 Lift the caliper assembly away from the brake disc **(see illustration)** and unscrew it from the end of the brake hose.

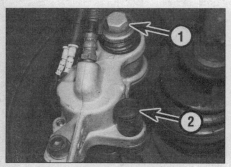

10.5a ATE brake caliper mountings

1 Upper (M12) mounting bolt
2 Lower (M8) mounting bolt dust cover

10.5b Removing a brake caliper mounting bolt - Bendix caliper

10.6 Withdrawing a brake caliper

Overhaul

7 With the caliper on the bench, wipe away all traces of dust and dirt, but *avoid inhaling the dust, as it is a health hazard.*

8 Where necessary, use a small flat-bladed screwdriver to carefully prise the dust seal retaining clip out of the caliper bore **(see illustration)**.

9 Withdraw the partially-ejected piston from the caliper body and remove the dust seal. The piston can be withdrawn by hand, or if necessary pushed out by applying compressed air to the brake hose union hole. Only low pressure should be required, such as is generated by a foot pump.

Caution: The piston may be ejected with some force.

10 Using a small screwdriver, extract the piston hydraulic seal, taking great care not to damage the caliper bore.

11 Where applicable, prise off the retaining clips, then withdraw the guide sleeves/pins from the caliper body/mounting bracket (as applicable) and remove the rubber gaiters.

12 Thoroughly clean all components, using only methylated spirit, isopropyl alcohol or clean hydraulic fluid as a cleaning medium. Never use mineral-based solvents such as petrol or paraffin, as they will attack the hydraulic system's rubber components. Dry the components immediately, using compressed air or a clean, lint-free cloth. Use compressed air to blow clear the fluid passages.

 Warning: Wear eye protection when using compressed air!

13 Check all components and renew any that are worn or damaged. Check particularly the cylinder bore and piston; these should be renewed (note that this means the renewal of the complete body assembly) if they are scratched, worn or corroded in any way. Similarly check the condition of the guide sleeves/pins and their bores in the caliper body/mounting bracket (as applicable); both sleeves/pins should be undamaged and (when cleaned) a reasonably tight sliding fit in the body/mounting bracket bores. If there is any doubt about the condition of any component, renew it.

14 If the assembly is fit for further use, obtain the appropriate repair kit; the components are available from Peugeot dealers in various combinations.

15 Renew all rubber seals, dust covers and caps disturbed on dismantling as a matter of course; these should never be re-used.

16 On reassembly, ensure that all components are absolutely clean and dry.

17 Soak the piston and the new piston (fluid) seal in clean hydraulic fluid. Smear clean fluid on the cylinder bore surface.

18 Fit the new piston (fluid) seal, using only your fingers (no tools) to manipulate it into the cylinder bore groove. Fit the new dust seal to the piston and refit the piston to the cylinder bore using a twisting motion; ensure that the piston enters squarely into the bore. Press the piston fully into the bore, then press the dust seal into the caliper body.

19 Where fitted, install the dust seal retaining clip, ensuring that it is correctly seated in the caliper groove.

20 Apply the grease supplied in the repair kit, or a copper-based high-temperature brake grease or anti-seize compound (eg Duckhams Copper 10), to the guide sleeves/pins. Fit the guide sleeves/pins to the caliper body/mounting bracket and fit the new rubber gaiters, ensuring that they are correctly located in the grooves on both the sleeve/pin and body/mounting bracket (as applicable).

Refitting

21 Screw the caliper fully onto the flexible hose union, then position the caliper over the brake disc.

22 If the threads of the new caliper mounting bolts are not already pre-coated with locking compound, apply a suitable locking

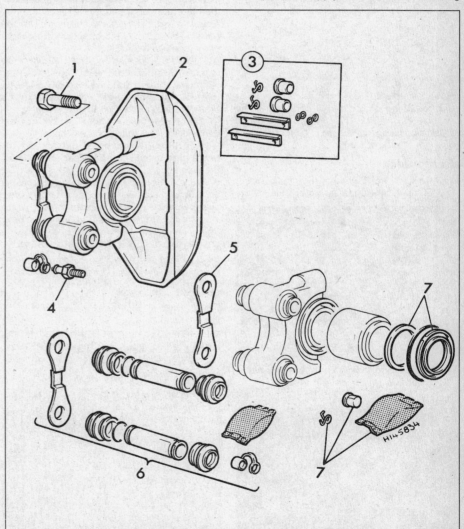

10.8 Bendix brake caliper components

1 Mounting bolt	4 Bleed screw	7 Caliper repair kit with
2 Caliper assembly	5 Mounting plate	grease
3 Pad retaining plate	6 Guide pin kit with grease	

compound to them. Refit the bolts, along with the mounting plate on models with Bendix calipers, ensuring that the plate is fitted so that its bend curves away from the caliper body **(see illustration)**. Tighten the caliper bolts to the specified torque. Where applicable, refit the dust cover(s) to the bolt(s).

23 Securely tighten the brake hose union nut, then refit the brake pads as described in Section 4 or 27.

24 Remove the brake hose clamp, or remove the polythene from the fluid reservoir, as applicable and bleed the hydraulic system as described in Section 2. Note that, providing the precautions described were taken to minimise brake fluid loss, it should only be necessary to bleed the relevant front brake circuit.

25 Refit the roadwheel, then lower the vehicle to the ground and tighten the roadwheel bolts to the specified torque.

11 Rear brake caliper - removal, overhaul and refitting

Note: *Before starting work, refer to the note at the beginning of Section 2 concerning the dangers of hydraulic fluid and to the warning at the beginning of Section 5 concerning the dangers of asbestos dust.*

Removal

1 Chock the front wheels, then jack up the rear of the vehicle and support on axle stands

11.3a Disconnect the handbrake inner cable from the caliper lever . . .

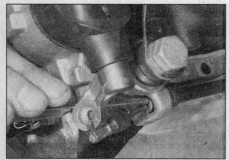

11.3b . . . then tap the outer cable out from the caliper body

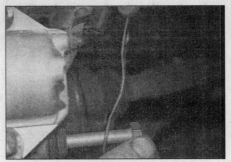

10.22 The mounting plate fits with the bend curving away from the caliper body - Bendix caliper

(see *"Jacking and Vehicle Support"*). Remove the relevant rear wheel.

2 Remove the brake pads (see Section 5).

3 Ensure that the handbrake is fully released, then free the handbrake inner cable from the caliper handbrake operating lever. Tap the outer cable out of its bracket on the caliper body **(see illustrations)**.

4 Minimise fluid loss by first removing the master cylinder reservoir cap and then tightening it down onto a piece of polythene, to obtain an airtight seal. Alternatively, use a brake hose clamp, a G-clamp or a similar tool to clamp the flexible hose at the nearest convenient point to the brake caliper.

5 Wipe away all traces of dirt around the brake pipe union on the caliper and slacken the union nut.

6 Slacken the two bolts securing the caliper assembly to the trailing arm and remove them along with the mounting plate, noting which way around the plate is fitted. Lift the caliper assembly away from the brake disc and unscrew it from the end of the brake hose.

Overhaul

7 The caliper can be overhauled after obtaining the relevant repair kit from a Peugeot dealer. Ensure that the correct repair

kit is obtained for the caliper being worked on. Note the locations of all components (this applies particularly if the handbrake mechanism is dismantled) to ensure correct refitting and lubricate the new seals using brake fluid **(see illustration)**. Follow the assembly instructions supplied with the repair kit.

Refitting

8 Screw the caliper fully onto the brake hose, then position the caliper over the brake disc. If the threads of the new caliper mounting bolts are not already pre-coated with locking compound, apply a suitable locking compound to them. Install the new caliper mounting bolts and the mounting plate, noting that the mounting plate must be fitted so that its bend curves away from the caliper body. With the plate correctly positioned, tighten the caliper bolts to the specified torque.

9 Tighten the brake hose union securely, then remove the clamp from the flexible brake hose, or the polythene from the master cylinder reservoir (as applicable).

10 Insert the handbrake cable through its bracket on the caliper and tap the outer cable into position using a hammer and suitable pin punch. Reconnect the inner cable to the caliper operating lever.

11 Refit the brake pads (see Section 5).

12 Bleed the hydraulic system as described in Section 2. Note that, providing the precautions described were taken to minimise brake fluid loss, it should only be necessary to bleed the relevant rear brake.

13 Repeatedly apply the brake pedal until normal (non-assisted) pedal pressure returns. Check and if necessary adjust the handbrake cable as described in Chapter 1A or 1B.

14 Refit the roadwheel, then lower the vehicle to the ground and tighten the wheel bolts to the specified torque. Finally, check the fluid level as described in *"Weekly checks"*.

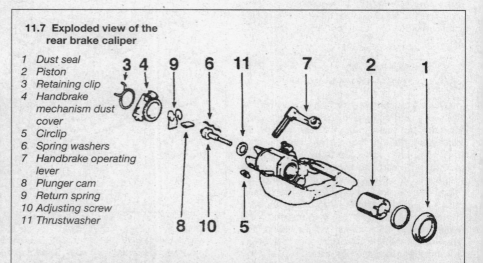

11.7 Exploded view of the rear brake caliper

1 Dust seal
2 Piston
3 Retaining clip
4 Handbrake mechanism dust cover
5 Circlip
6 Spring washers
7 Handbrake operating lever
8 Plunger cam
9 Return spring
10 Adjusting screw
11 Thrustwasher

12 Rear wheel cylinder -
removal, overhaul and refitting

Removal

1 Remove the brake drum as described in Section 9.

2 Using pliers, carefully unhook the brake shoe upper return spring and remove it from both brake shoes (note the orientation of the spring, to ensure correct refitting). Pull the upper ends of the shoes away from the wheel cylinder, to disengage them from the pistons.

> **HAYNES HiNT** *Pull the handbrake lever on the trailing shoe fully forwards, so that the upper ends of the shoes are clear of the wheel cylinder. Wedge the lever in this position using a block of wood.*

3 Minimise fluid loss by first removing the master cylinder reservoir cap, then tightening it down onto a piece of polythene, to obtain an airtight seal. Alternatively, use a brake hose clamp, a G-clamp or a similar tool to clamp the flexible hose (connected between the metal pipe sections on the rear axle and trailing arm) at the nearest convenient point to the wheel cylinder **(see illustration)**.

4 Wipe away all traces of dirt around the brake pipe union at the rear of the wheel cylinder and unscrew the union nut **(see illustration)**. Carefully ease the pipe out of the wheel cylinder and plug or tape over its end to prevent dirt entry. Wipe off any spilt fluid immediately.

5 Unscrew the two wheel cylinder retaining bolts from the rear of the backplate and remove the cylinder, taking great care not to allow surplus hydraulic fluid to contaminate the brake shoe linings.

Overhaul

Non-ABS models

6 On non-ABS models, the rear brake pressure-regulating valves are integral with the rear wheel cylinders and the cylinders **must not** be dismantled. No spare parts are available and if a cylinder is faulty or damaged, the complete assembly must be renewed.

ABS models

7 Clean the exterior of the cylinder to remove all traces of dirt and brake dust.

8 Pull the dust seals from the ends of the cylinder **(see illustration)**.

9 Extract the pistons, seals spring seats and return spring, noting the locations of all components to ensure correct refitting.

10 Examine the surfaces of the cylinder bore and pistons for signs of scoring and corrosion and if evident, renew the complete wheel cylinder. If the components are in good condition, discard the seals and obtain a

12.3 To minimise fluid loss, fit a brake hose clamp to the flexible hose

repair kit, which will contain all the necessary renewable components.

11 Clean the pistons and the cylinder with methylated spirit or clean brake fluid and reassemble in the reverse order to dismantling, making sure that the components are fitted in the correct sequence and orientated correctly, as noted before removal. Ensure that the lips of the seals face into the cylinder.

12 On completion, wipe the outer surfaces of the dust seals to remove any excess brake fluid.

Refitting

13 Clean the backplate, then place the wheel cylinder in position and refit the securing bolts.

14 Reconnect the brake pipe to the rear of the wheel cylinder, taking care not to allow dirt into the system.

15 Where applicable, release the handbrake lever on the trailing shoe and reposition the upper ends of the shoes to engage them with the wheel cylinder pistons.

16 Refit the brake shoe upper return spring, ensuring that it is orientated as noted before removal.

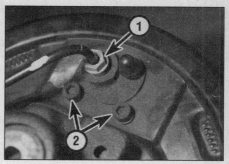

12.4 Wheel cylinder brake pipe union nut (1) and wheel cylinder retaining bolts (2)

17 Refit the brake drum as described in Section 9.

18 On completion, remove the brake hose clamp, or remove the polythene from the fluid reservoir, as applicable and bleed the hydraulic system as described in Section 2. Note that, providing the precautions described were taken to minimise brake fluid loss, it should only be necessary to bleed the relevant rear brake circuit.

13 Master cylinder -
removal, overhaul and refitting

Note: *Before starting work, refer to the warning at the beginning of Section 2 concerning the dangers of hydraulic fluid.*

Removal

1 Remove the master cylinder fluid reservoir cap and syphon the hydraulic fluid from the reservoir. **Note:** *Do not syphon the fluid by mouth, as it is poisonous; use a syringe or an old poultry baster.* Alternatively, open any convenient bleed screw in the system and gently pump the brake pedal to expel the fluid

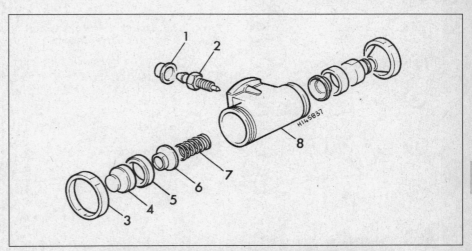

12.8 Exploded view of rear wheel cylinder - ABS model

1 Bleed screw dust cover	3 Dust seal	6 Spring seat
2 Bleed screw	4 Piston	7 Return spring
	5 Seal	8 Cylinder body

13.1 Disconnecting the brake fluid level sender wiring plug

through a plastic tube connected to the screw (see Section 2). Disconnect the wiring connector from the brake fluid level sender unit **(see illustration)**.

2 Wipe clean the area around the brake pipe unions on the side of the master cylinder and place absorbent rags beneath the pipe unions to catch any surplus fluid. Make a note of the correct fitted positions of the unions, then unscrew the union nuts and carefully withdraw the pipes. Plug or tape over the pipe ends and master cylinder orifices, to minimise the loss of brake fluid and to prevent the entry of dirt into the system. Wash off any spilt fluid immediately with cold water.

3 Slacken and remove the two nuts securing the master cylinder to the vacuum servo unit, then withdraw the unit from the engine compartment.

4 Where applicable, recover the seal from the rear of the master cylinder and discard it.

Overhaul

5 Pull the fluid reservoir from the top of the master cylinder. Prise the reservoir seals from the reservoir or the master cylinder, as applicable **(see illustration)**.

6 Using a wooden dowel, press the piston assembly into the master cylinder body, then extract the circlip from the end of the master cylinder bore.

7 Noting the order of removal and the direction of fitting of each component, withdraw the washer and the piston assemblies with their springs and seals, tapping the body on to a clean wooden surface to dislodge them. If necessary, clamp the master cylinder body in a vice (fitted with soft jaw covers) and use compressed air (applied through the secondary circuit fluid port) to assist the removal of the secondary piston assembly.

> ⚠️ **Warning: Wear eye protection when using compressed air!**

8 Thoroughly clean all components, using only methylated spirit, isopropyl alcohol or clean hydraulic fluid as a cleaning medium. Never use mineral-based solvents such as petrol or paraffin, as they will attack the hydraulic system's rubber components. Dry the components immediately, using compressed air or a clean, lint-free cloth.

9 Check all components and renew any that are worn or damaged. Check particularly the cylinder bores and pistons; the complete assembly should be renewed if these are scratched, worn or corroded. If there is any doubt about the condition of the assembly or of any of its components, renew it. Check that the cylinder body fluid passages are clear.

10 If the assembly is fit for further use, obtain a repair kit from your Peugeot dealer; the kit consists of both piston assemblies and springs, complete with all seals and washers. Never re-use the old components.

11 Before reassembly, soak the pistons and the new seals in clean hydraulic fluid. Smear clean fluid into the cylinder bore.

12 Insert the piston assemblies into the cylinder bore, using a twisting motion to avoid trapping the seal lips. Ensure that all components are refitted in the correct order and the right way round, then fit the washer to the end of the primary piston. Where applicable, follow the assembly instructions supplied with the repair kit.

13 Press the piston assemblies fully into the bore using a clean wooden dowel and secure them in position with the new circlip. Ensure that the circlip is correctly located in the groove in the cylinder bore.

14 Examine the fluid reservoir seals and if necessary renew them. Fit the reservoir seals to the master cylinder body, then refit the reservoir.

Refitting

15 Remove all traces of dirt from the master cylinder and servo unit mating surfaces and where applicable, fit a new seal between the master cylinder body and the servo.

16 Fit the master cylinder to the servo unit, ensuring that the servo unit pushrod enters the master cylinder bore centrally. Refit the master cylinder mounting nuts and tighten them to the specified torque.

17 Wipe clean the brake pipe unions, then refit them to the correct master cylinder ports, as noted before removal and tighten the union nuts securely.

18 Refill the master cylinder reservoir with new fluid and bleed the complete hydraulic system as described in Section 2.

14 Brake pedal - removal and refitting

Removal

1 Remove retaining clips from the fabric panel at the bottom of the dashboard and remove the panel.

2 Remove the pivot bolt which secures the pedal to its mounting bracket and recover the return spring.

3 Withdraw the brake pedal-to-pushrod clevis pin before the brake pedal is removed.

Refitting

4 Refitting is the reverse of removal, but make sure that the return spring is fitted correctly.

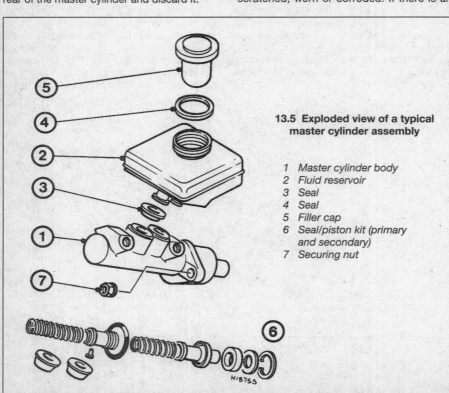

13.5 Exploded view of a typical master cylinder assembly

1 Master cylinder body
2 Fluid reservoir
3 Seal
4 Seal
5 Filler cap
6 Seal/piston kit (primary and secondary)
7 Securing nut

H18755

15.5 Remove the linkage crosstube securing bolts (arrowed)

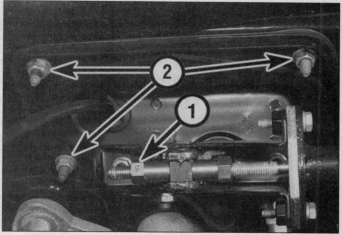

15.6 Link rod end nut (1) and three of the pedal bracket securing nuts (2)

15 Brake pedal-to-servo linkage (RHD models) - renewal and overhaul

Removal

1 Removal of the servo-end linkage and the main crossover linkage, is described in Section 16 as part of the vacuum servo unit removal and refitting procedure.

2 To remove the brake pedal bracket and linkage, proceed as follows.

3 Remove the brake and clutch pedals, with reference to Section 14 and Chapter 6.

4 On diesel models, remove the inlet manifold as described in Chapter 4D.

5 Remove the linkage crosstube securing bolts (two at each end of the tube) **(see illustration)**.

6 Unclip the plastic cover from the pedal end of the linkage, then slacken the link rod end nut sufficiently to disconnect the link rod end fitting from the pedal relay lever **(see illustration)**. Do not move the inner nut on the link rod (this should be left in position to preserve the link rod adjustment).

7 Working in the engine compartment, unscrew the four nuts securing the pedal bracket to the bulkhead and withdraw the bracket and linkage into the engine compartment.

Overhaul

8 If desired, the linkage can be dismantled with reference to the accompanying illustration, but if the link rod is to be removed, mark the position of the adjuster nuts before removal, to ensure that the adjustment is maintained on reassembly **(see illustration)**.

9 Individual spare parts can be obtained from a Peugeot dealer.

10 When reassembling the linkage, grease all moving parts sparingly and ensure that the adjustment nuts are refitted to the link rod in the positions noted before removal.

Refitting

11 Refitting is a reversal of removal, bearing in mind the following points:

a) *On diesel models, refit the inlet manifold as described in Chapter 4D.*

b) *Where applicable, refit the brake and clutch pedals with reference to Chapter 6.*

c) *Where applicable, refit the servo-end linkage and the main crossover linkage, as described in Section 16.*

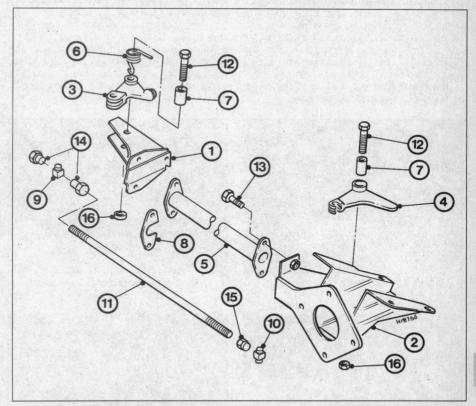

15.8 Exploded view of brake pedal-to-servo linkage - right-hand drive models

1 Bracket	6 Return spring	12 Bolt
2 Servo mounting bracket	7 Spacer	13 Bolt
3 Pedal relay lever	8 Shim	14 Adjuster nuts
4 Servo relay lever	9 Cross-shaft barrel	15 Adjuster nut
5 Cross-shaft housing	10 Cross-shaft barrel	16 Nut
	11 Link rod	

9

16.8 Pulling the non-return valve from the brake servo

16.10a Unscrew the securing nuts . . .

16.10b . . . and detach the master cylinder from the servo

16 Vacuum servo unit - testing, removal and refitting

Right-hand-drive models

Testing

1 To test the operation of the servo unit, with the engine switched off, depress the footbrake several times to exhaust the vacuum. Keep the pedal firmly depressed and start the engine. As the engine starts, there should be a noticeable "give" in the brake pedal as the vacuum builds up. Allow the engine to run for at least two minutes, then switch it off. If the brake pedal is now depressed, it should feel normal, but further applications should result in the pedal feeling firmer, with the pedal stroke decreasing on each application.

2 If the servo does not operate as described, first inspect the servo unit check valve as described in Section 17. On diesel models, also check the operation of the vacuum pump, as described in Section 26.

3 If the servo unit still fails to operate satisfactorily, the fault lies within the unit itself. Repairs to the unit are not possible - if faulty, the servo unit must be renewed.

Removal

Note: *A new spring clip must be fitted to the servo pushrod clevis pin on refitting.*

4 To improve access, remove the battery as described in Chapter 5A.

5 Unclip any relevant hoses and/or wiring from the fusebox bracket in front of the servo, then remove the nut securing the bracket to the wheel arch and move the bracket clear of the working area.

6 Where applicable, remove the air cleaner assembly as described in the relevant Part of Chapter 4.

7 On diesel models, remove the inlet manifold as described in Chapter 4D.

8 Carefully pull the non-return valve from the servo, leaving the vacuum hose connected **(see illustration)**.

9 Working under the servo, unclip the master cylinder brake fluid pipes from the supporting brackets.

10 Unscrew the two master cylinder securing nuts and detach the master cylinder from the servo. Where applicable, recover the seal **(see illustrations)**.

11 Carefully pull the master cylinder forwards from the servo, taking care not to strain the fluid pipes.

12 Unclip the plastic cover from the pedal end of the linkage, then slacken the link rod end nut sufficiently to disconnect the link rod end fitting from the pedal relay lever. **Do not** move the inner nut on the link rod (this should be left in position, to preserve the link rod adjustment) **(see illustration)**.

13 Remove the linkage crosstube securing bolts (two at each end of the tube) and remove the spacer plate from the pedal end of the crosstube **(see illustrations)**.

14 Slide the link rod end fitting from the pedal relay lever.

15 Unscrew the four nuts securing the servo mounting bracket to the bulkhead, then carefully manipulate the servo and crossover linkage assembly from the engine compartment, taking care not to strain the master cylinder brake pipes **(see illustrations)**.

16.12 Slacken the link rod end nut

16.13a Unscrewing a linkage crosstube securing bolt

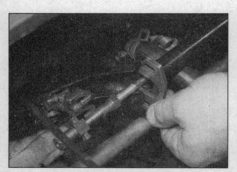

16.13b Removing the spacer plate from the crosstube

16.15a Unscrewing a servo mounting bracket securing nut

16.15b Removing the servo and crossover linkage assembly

16 Prise off the spring clip and withdraw the clevis pin securing the servo pushrod to the crossover linkage.
17 Unscrew the four securing nuts and withdraw the servo from the mounting bracket.

Refitting

18 Refitting is a reversal of removal, bearing in mind the following points:
  a) Tighten all fixings to the specified torque (where given).
  b) Where applicable, refit the inlet manifold as described in Chapter 4D.
  c) Where applicable, refit the servo-end linkage and the main crossover linkage

Left-hand-drive models

Testing

19 Proceed as described in paragraphs 1 to 3 inclusive.

Removal

Note: *A new spring clip must be fitted to the servo pushrod clevis pin on refitting.*
20 Proceed as described in paragraphs 4 to 10 inclusive, then proceed as follows.
21 Working inside the vehicle, unclip the front edge of the under-facia trim panel from the facia and lower the panel. Unscrew the two nuts securing the trim panel to the studs in the footwell, then withdraw the panel from the footwell.
22 Working in the footwell, unscrew the securing nut from the lower column pinch-bolt, then carefully tap the pinch-bolt from the universal joint. Pull off the metal clip securing the column to the steering gear pinion (see Chapter 10, Section 12, paragraph 5)
23 Make alignment marks on the universal joint and the steering gear pinion, then push the universal joint upwards to separate it from the pinion. Manipulate the lower steering column as necessary for access to the brake pedal assembly.
24 Remove the spring clip from the end of the brake servo pushrod-to-brake pedal clevis pin, then withdraw the clevis pin.
25 Working in the engine compartment, remove the four securing nuts from the studs at the rear of the servo, then remove the servo from its mounting bracket.

Refitting

26 Refit the servo to its mounting bracket and tighten the securing nuts.
27 Reconnect the servo pushrod to the pedal and fit the clevis pin. Secure the clevis pin with a new spring clip.
28 Slide the column universal joint over steering gear pinion, ensuring that the marks made before removal are still aligned then refit the metal clips.
29 Fit a new lower column pinch-bolt and nut, ensuring that the lugs on the bolt engage with the cut-outs in the universal joint and tighten the nut to the specified torque (see Chapter 10 Specifications).
30 Refit the under-facia trim panel.
31 Further refitting is a reversal of removal,

but tighten all fixings to the specified torque. On diesel models, refit the inlet manifold as described in Chapter 4D.

17 Vacuum servo unit check valve - removal, testing and refitting

Removal

1 Slacken the retaining clip (where fitted) and disconnect the vacuum hose from the servo unit check valve.
2 Withdraw the valve from its rubber sealing grommet, using a pulling and twisting motion. Remove the grommet from the servo.

Testing

3 Examine the check valve for signs of damage and renew if necessary. The valve may be tested by blowing through it in both directions. Air should flow through the valve in one direction only - when blown through from the servo unit end of the valve. Renew the valve if this is not the case.
4 Examine the rubber sealing grommet and flexible vacuum hose for signs of damage or deterioration and renew as necessary.

Refitting

5 Fit the sealing grommet into position in the servo unit.
6 Carefully ease the check valve into position, taking great care not to displace or damage the grommet. Reconnect the vacuum hose to the valve and, where necessary, securely tighten its retaining clip.
7 On completion, start the engine and check the check valve-to-servo unit connection for signs of air leaks. Test the servo operation as described at the start of Section 16.

18 Handbrake lever - removal and refitting

Removal

1 Chock the front wheels then jack up the rear of the vehicle and support it on axle stands (see *"Jacking and Vehicle Support"*). Working under the vehicle, slacken the adjuster nut on the cable equaliser assembly until the rear handbrake cables can be disengaged from the equaliser plate.
2 If desired, to improve access, remove the front seats as described in Chapter 11. Working inside the vehicle, pull the carpet panel back for access to the two handbrake lever securing bolts **(see illustration)**.
3 Unscrew the securing bolts, then lift the lever assembly from the floor. Disengage the cable grommet from the floor, then feed the front section of the cable/rod through into the passenger compartment and withdraw the assembly from the vehicle.

Refitting

4 Refitting is a reversal of removal. Ensure

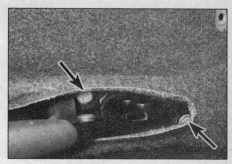

18.2 Handbrake lever securing bolts (arrowed)

that the cable grommet is correctly located in the aperture in the floor and on completion, adjust the handbrake mechanism as described in Chapter 1A or 1B.

19 Handbrake cables - removal and refitting

Front cable/rod

1 The front cable or rod is integral with the handbrake lever assembly and must be removed complete with the lever assembly, as described in Section 18. The cable/rod cannot be renewed individually and if faulty, the complete lever assembly must be renewed.

Rear cables

Removal

2 Chock the front wheels then jack up the rear of the vehicle and support it on axle stands (see *"Jacking and Vehicle Support"*). Remove the relevant rear roadwheel(s).
3 Working under the vehicle, slacken the adjuster nut on the cable equaliser assembly until the handbrake rear cables can be disengaged from the equaliser plate.
4 Remove the brake drum as described in Section 9.
5 Remove the trailing brake shoe and unhook the end of the handbrake cable from the shoe, as described in Section 6.
6 Feed the cable through the rear brake backplate. If necessary, prise the cable outer from the backplate **(see illustration)**.

19.6 Removing the handbrake cable outer from the rear brake backplate

7 Unhook the cable from the clips and brackets under the vehicle **(see illustrations)**, noting the cable routing, then withdraw the cable from the vehicle. Note that on certain models, it may be necessary to lower the exhaust heat shield to allow the cable to be removed.

Refitting

8 Attach the cable to the brackets and clips under the rear of the vehicle, ensuring that it is routed as noted before removal.

9 Feed the cable through the rear brake backplate (if necessary, tap the cable outer into position in the backplate), then hook the end of the cable onto the trailing brake shoe and refit the shoe as described in Section 6.

10 Refit the brake drum as described in Section 9.

11 Refit the rear wheel(s).

12 Reconnect the front of the cable to the equaliser plate, then adjust the handbrake as described in Chapter 1A or 1B.

13 On completion, lower the vehicle to the ground.

19.7a Unhook the handbrake cable from the clips (arrowed) on the rear suspension . . .

and to prevent the entry of dirt into the system. Wash off any spilt fluid immediately with cold water.

Refitting

6 Refitting is a reverse of the removal procedure, ensuring that the pipe union nuts are securely tightened. On completion, bleed the complete braking system (see Section 2).

Anti-lock braking system (ABS)

Adjustment

7 On models with ABS, a load-sensitive pressure-regulating valve is fitted, which is connected to the rear axle assembly to sense the load on the rear of the vehicle.

8 To carry out a complete check on the valve, pressure-testing equipment must be used, but a simple check on the condition of the valve spring can be made as follows.

9 The check must be made with a ride height of 210 mm, measured from the rear jacking point cut-out to the ground. If necessary, ballast the rear of the vehicle to give the required ride height.

10 With the ride height correctly set, refer to the accompanying illustration and measure the clearance between the end face of the bolt (1) and the lever (2) **(see illustration)**.

11 If the clearance is not as specified, adjust by turning the bolt (1) until the correct clearance is obtained.

19.7b . . . and the body

Removal

12 To remove the valve, simply unhook the spring, then remove the two screws securing the assembly to the rear suspension.

Refitting

13 Refitting is a reversal of removal, but on completion, check the valve adjustment as described previously in this Section.

21	**Stop-light switch -** adjustment, removal and refitting

Adjustment

1 With the brake pedal at rest, adjust the position of the stop-light switch in its mounting bracket to obtain the clearance shown between the end of the switch plunger and the stop on the brake pedal **(see illustration)**. On

20	**Rear brake pressure-regulating valves -** adjustment, removal and refitting

Conventional braking system - rear drum brakes

1 On models with a conventional braking system, the pressure-regulating valves are integral with the rear wheel cylinders. The cylinders must not be dismantled and if a fault is suspected, the complete wheel cylinder must be renewed as described in Section 12.

Conventional braking system - rear disc brakes

Removal

Note: *Before starting work, refer to the warning at the beginning of Section 2 concerning the dangers of hydraulic fluid.*

2 The pressure-regulating valves are located just in front of the rear axle assembly; there are two valves, one for each rear brake caliper.

3 Firmly chock the front wheels, then jack up the rear of the vehicle and support it on axle stands (see *"Jacking and vehicle support"*).

4 Minimise fluid loss by first removing the master cylinder reservoir cap, and then tightening it down onto a piece of polythene, to obtain an airtight seal.

5 Wipe clean the area around the brake pipe unions on the relevant valve, and place absorbent rags beneath the pipe unions to catch any surplus fluid. Retain the relevant pressure-regulating valve with a suitable open-ended spanner, then slacken the union nuts, disconnect both brake pipes, and remove the valve from underneath the vehicle. Plug or tape over the pipe ends and valve orifices, to minimise the loss of brake fluid,

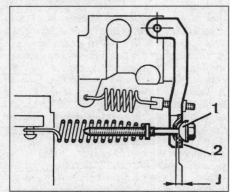

20.5 Rear brake pressure-regulating valve - ABS model

1	Bolt	J	1.0 ± 0.5 mm
2	Lever		

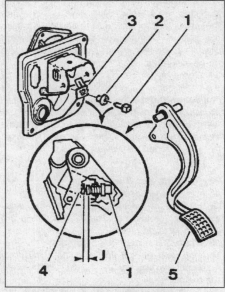

21.1 Stop-light switch adjustment (left-hand-drive model shown)

1	Stop-light switch	4	Stop on brake pedal
2	Mounting clip	5	Brake pedal
3	Pedal bracket	J	2.0 to 3.0 mm

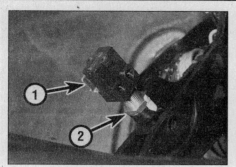

21.6 Stop-light switch (1) and locknut (2) - right-hand-drive model viewed with facia removed

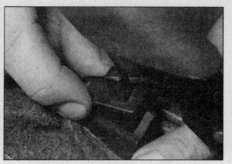

22.3a Prise out the handbrake "on" warning light switch . . .

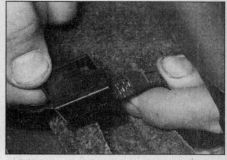

22.3b . . . and disconnect the wiring plug

some models, the switch is screwed into the mounting bracket and a locknut must be loosened before the switch can be moved (it will also be necessary to disconnect the wiring before the switch is rotated).

2 The switch must operate the stop-lights when the pedal has travelled a maximum of 5.0 mm.

Removal

3 Disconnect the battery negative terminal (refer to *"Disconnecting the battery"* in the Reference Section of this manual).

4 Working in the driver's footwell, unclip the front edge of the under-facia trim panel from the facia and lower the panel. Unscrew the two nuts securing the trim panel to the studs in the footwell, then withdraw the panel from the footwell.

5 Reach up and disconnect the wiring from the switch.

6 Where applicable, release the securing clip and pull the switch from the pedal bracket assembly. Alternatively, where the switch is screwed into position, loosen the locknut and unscrew the switch from the bracket **(see illustration)**.

Refitting

7 Refitting is a reversal of removal. On completion, check the adjustment of the switch as described previously in this Section.

22 Handbrake "on" warning light switch - removal and refitting

Removal

1 Disconnect the battery negative terminal (refer to *"Disconnecting the battery"* in the Reference Section of this manual).

2 Lift the carpet panel for access to the switch.

3 Carefully prise out the switch and disconnect the wiring plug **(see illustrations)**.

Refitting

4 Refitting is a reversal of removal.

23 Anti-lock Braking System (ABS) - general information

The Bendix "additional" Anti-lock Braking System is available as an option on certain models **(see illustration)**.

The system is fail-safe and is fitted in addition to the conventional braking system, which allows the vehicle to retain conventional braking in the event of ABS failure.

To prevent wheel locking, the system provides pressure modulation in the braking circuits. To achieve this, sensors mounted at each front wheel monitor the rotational speeds of the wheels and are thus able to detect when there is a risk of wheel locking (low rotational speed). Solenoid valves are positioned in the brake circuits to the front wheels and the solenoid valves are incorporated in a modulator assembly, which is controlled by an electronic control unit (ECU). The ECU controls modulation of the braking effort applied to each front wheel, according to the information supplied by the wheel sensors.

Should a fault develop in the system, a self-

diagnostic facility is incorporated in the ECU, which can be used in conjunction with special diagnostic equipment available to a Peugeot dealer, to determine the nature of the fault.

The braking system components used on models fitted with ABS are similar to those used on models with a conventional braking system. Rear drum or disc brakes are fitted to models with ABS, as on those with a conventional system.

Note that when bleeding the brake hydraulic system, the modulator assembly must also be bled, as described in Section 2.

24 Anti-lock Braking System (ABS) components - removal and refitting

Modulator assembly

Note: *Before starting work, refer to the warning at the beginning of Section 2 concerning the dangers of hydraulic fluid.*

Removal

1 Disconnect the battery negative terminal

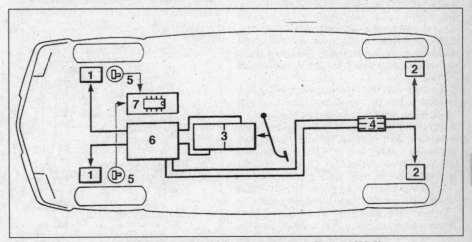

23.1 Schematic layout of Anti-lock Braking System (ABS)

1   Front brake calipers
2   Rear brake wheel cylinders
3   Master cylinder
4   Rear brake pressure-regulating valve
5   Wheel sensors
6   Modulator assembly
7   Electronic control unit

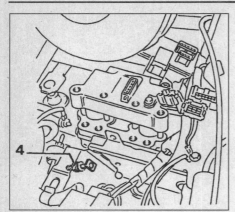

24.6 ABS modulator mounting bracket upper securing nut (4) (left-hand drive model shown)

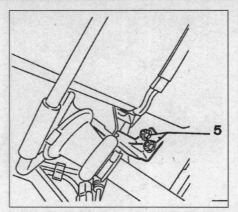

24.7 ABS modulator mounting bracket lower mounting nuts (5) (left-hand drive model shown)

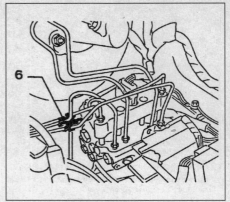

24.9 ABS hydraulic modulator fluid pipe clip (6)

(refer to *"Disconnecting the battery"* in the Reference Section of this manual).

2 Remove the master cylinder as described in Section 13.

3 Remove the brake servo as described in Section 16.

4 Mark the locations of the hydraulic fluid pipes to ensure correct refitting, then unscrew the union nuts and disconnect the pipes from the modulator assembly. Be prepared for fluid spillage and plug the open ends of the pipes and the modulator, to prevent dirt ingress and further fluid loss. Note the position of the clip on the brake pipes to ensure correct refitting.

5 Disconnect the wiring connectors from the modulator assembly.

6 Remove the upper securing nut from the modulator mounting bracket **(see illustration)**.

7 Working under the modulator mounting bracket, unscrew the two lower mounting nuts, then withdraw the assembly, complete with the mounting bracket **(see illustration)**.

Refitting

⚠️ **Warning: Do not reconnect the wiring connectors to the modulator until the hydraulic circuits have been bled as described in Section 2.**

8 Commence refitting by positioning the assembly in the engine compartment and refitting the upper and lower securing nuts.

9 Reconnect the fluid pipes to the assembly, as noted before removal, ensuring that no dirt enters the system. Ensure that the brake pipe clip is fitted as noted before removal **(see illustration)**.

10 Refit the brake servo as described in Section 16.

11 Refit the master cylinder as described in Section 13.

12 Bleed the complete hydraulic system as described in Section 2.

13 Reconnect the modulator assembly wiring plugs.

14 Reconnect the battery negative terminal.

Electronic control unit
Removal

15 The unit is mounted on a bracket on the left-hand side of the engine compartment, next to the battery **(see illustration)**.

16 Disconnect the battery negative terminal (refer to *"Disconnecting the battery"* in the Reference Section of this manual).

17 Release the securing clips and withdraw the cover from the control unit.

18 Release the securing clip and/or remove the securing screw, as applicable and disconnect the control unit wiring plug.

19 Unscrew the securing nuts and withdraw the control unit from the mounting bracket.

Refitting

20 Refitting is a reversal of removal.

Wheel sensor

Note: *Suitable thread-locking compound must be applied to the sensor securing stud on refitting.*

Removal

21 Disconnect the battery negative terminal

(refer to *"Disconnecting the battery"* in the Reference Section of this manual).

22 Chock the rear wheels then jack up the front of the vehicle and support it on axle stands (see *"Jacking and Vehicle Support"*). If desired, remove the appropriate front roadwheel to improve access.

23 Follow the wiring back from the sensor and separate the two halves of the wiring connector. Release the wiring from the securing clips, noting its routing.

24 Unscrew the securing nut and withdraw the shield from the sensor **(see illustration)**.

25 Unscrew the securing stud and withdraw the sensor from its mounting bracket.

Refitting

26 Refitting is a reversal of removal, bearing in mind the following points:

a) *Ensure that the mating faces of the sensor and the mounting bracket are clean and apply a little grease to the mounting bracket bore before refitting.*

24.15 ABS electronic control unit location

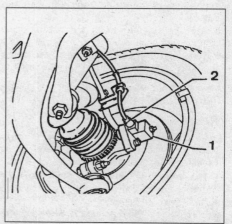

24.24 ABS wheel sensor shield (1) and sensor (2)

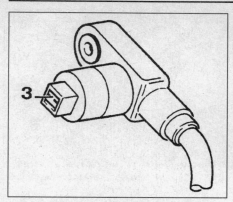

24.26 Ensure that the end face (3) of the sensor is clean

b) *Ensure that the end face of the sensor is clean (see illustration).*
c) *Apply thread-locking compound the threads of the sensor securing stud and tighten to the specified torque.*
d) *Ensure that the sensor wiring is routed as noted before removal.*

25 Vacuum pump (diesel models) - removal and refitting

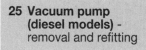

Removal

Note: *A new O-ring should be used on refitting.*

1 The pump is located at the transmission end of the cylinder head.
2 Where applicable, release the securing clip and disconnect the vacuum hose from the pump **(see illustration)**.
3 Slacken and remove the two securing bolts and washers, then withdraw the pump from the cylinder head. Recover the O-ring **(see illustrations)**.

Refitting

4 Fit a new O-ring to the pump, then align the pump drive dogs with the slots in the end of the camshaft and refit the pump to the cylinder head.
5 Refit the securing bolts and washers and tighten them securely.
6 Reconnect the vacuum hose to the pump and (where applicable) tighten the retaining clip.

26 Vacuum pump (diesel models) - testing and overhaul

Testing

1 The operation of the braking system vacuum pump can be checked using a suitable vacuum gauge.
2 Disconnect the vacuum hose from the pump and connect the gauge to the pump union using a suitable length of hose.

25.2 Disconnecting the vacuum hose from the brake vacuum pump - diesel model

3 Start the engine and allow it to idle, then measure the vacuum created by the pump. As a guide, after one minute, a minimum of approximately 500 mmHg should be recorded. If the vacuum registered is significantly less than this, it is likely that the pump is faulty. However, seek the advice of a Peugeot dealer before condemning the pump.

Overhaul

4 Overhaul of the vacuum pump is not possible, since no components are available separately for it. If faulty, the pump must be renewed complete.

27 Front brake pads - renewal (vented discs)

⚠ *Warning: Renew BOTH sets of front brake pads at the same time - NEVER renew the pads on only one wheel, as uneven braking may result. Note that the dust created by wear of the pads may contain asbestos, which is a health hazard. Never blow it out with compressed air and don't inhale any of it. An approved filtering mask should be worn when working on the brakes. DO NOT use petrol or petroleum-based solvents to clean brake parts; use brake cleaner or methylated spirit only.*

1 Chock the rear wheels then jack up the front of the vehicle and support it on axle stands (see "*Jacking and Vehicle Support*"). Remove the front roadwheels. Trace the brake

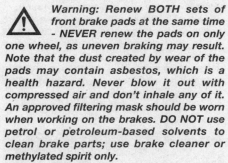

27.2 Using a screwdriver, carefully prise out the brake pad retaining spring from the caliper

25.3a Remove the brake vacuum pump . . .

25.3b . . . and recover the O-ring

pad wear sensor wiring back from the pads and disconnect it from the wiring connector. Note the routing of the wiring and free it from any relevant retaining clips.
2 Using a screwdriver, prise the pad retaining spring from the outer edge of the caliper, noting its correct fitted position **(see illustration)**.
3 Prise out the two guide bolt dust caps from the inner edge of the caliper **(see illustration)**.
4 Unscrew the guide bolts from the caliper, and lift the caliper and inner pad away from the mounting bracket. Tie the caliper to the suspension strut using a suitable piece of wire **(see illustrations)**. Do not allow the caliper to hang unsupported on the flexible brake hose.
5 Remove the inner pad from the caliper piston, noting that it is retained by a clip attached to the pad backing plate, and recover the outer pad from the mounting bracket.

27.3 Remove the guide bolt dust caps . . .

9

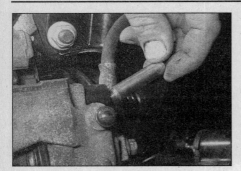

27.4a . . . then unscrew the guide bolts . . .

27.4b . . . and slide off the caliper and inner pad assembly

27.11 Clip the pad securely into the caliper piston . . .

6 First measure the thickness of each brake pad's friction material. If either pad is worn at any point to the specified minimum thickness or less, *all four* pads must be renewed. Also, the pads should be renewed if any are fouled with oil or grease; there is no satisfactory way of degreasing friction material, once contaminated. If any of the brake pads are worn unevenly, or are fouled with oil or grease, trace and rectify the cause before reassembly. New brake pads and spring kits are available from Peugeot dealers.

7 If the brake pads are still serviceable, carefully clean them using a clean, fine wire brush or similar, paying particular attention to the sides and back of the metal backing. Clean out the grooves in the friction material and pick out any large embedded particles of dirt or debris. Carefully clean the pad locations in the caliper body/mounting bracket.

8 Prior to fitting the pads, check that the guide pins are free to slide easily in the caliper body/mounting bracket and check that the rubber guide pin gaiters are undamaged. Brush the dust and dirt from the caliper and piston, but *do not* inhale it, as it is injurious to health. Inspect the dust seal around the piston

for damage and the piston for evidence of fluid leaks, corrosion or damage. If attention to any of these components is necessary, refer to Section 10.

9 If new brake pads are to be fitted, the caliper piston must be pushed back into the cylinder to make room for them. Either use a G-clamp or similar tool, or use suitable pieces of wood as levers. Provided that the master cylinder reservoir has not been overfilled with hydraulic fluid, there should be no spillage, but keep a careful watch on the fluid level while retracting the piston. If the fluid level rises above the "MAX" level line at any time, the surplus should be syphoned off or ejected via a plastic tube connected to the bleed screw (see Section 2).

 Warning: Do not syphon the fluid by mouth, as it is poisonous; use a syringe or an old poultry baster.

10 Apply a little copper-based brake grease to the pad backing plates, but take great care not to allow any grease onto the pad friction linings.

11 Fit the inner pad to the caliper, ensuring that its clip is correctly located in the caliper piston (see illustration).

12 Fit the outer pad to the caliper mounting

bracket, ensuring that its friction material is facing the brake disc (see illustration).

13 Slide the caliper and inner pad into position over the outer pad, and locate it in the mounting bracket.

14 Install the caliper guide bolts, and tighten them to the specified torque (see illustration).

15 Refit the guide bolt dust caps to the caliper.

16 Refit the pad retaining spring to the caliper, ensuring that its ends are correctly located in the caliper holes (see illustration).

17 Depress the brake pedal repeatedly, until normal (non-assisted) pedal pressure is restored, and the pads are pressed into firm contact with the brake disc.

18 Repeat the above procedure on the remaining front brake caliper.

19 Reconnect the brake pad wear sensor wiring connectors, ensuring that the wiring is correctly routed, as noted before removal.

20 Refit the roadwheels, then lower the vehicle to the ground and tighten the road-wheel bolts to the specified torque setting.

21 Check the hydraulic fluid level as described in "Weekly checks".

27.12 . . . and fit the outer pad to the caliper mounting bracket

27.14 Slide the caliper into position and install the guide bolts, tightening them to the specified torque setting

27.16 When refitting, ensure that the pad retainer spring ends are correctly located in the caliper holes (arrowed)

Chapter 10
Suspension and steering

Contents

Degrees of difficulty

Easy, suitable for novice with little experience	**Fairly easy,** suitable for beginner with some experience	**Fairly difficult,** suitable for competent DIY mechanic	**Difficult,** suitable for experienced DIY mechanic	**Very difficult,** suitable for expert DIY or professional

Specifications

Front suspension

Type .... Independent by MacPherson struts, with inclined coil springs and integral shock absorbers. Certain models have anti-roll bar linked to the lower arms or struts (depending on model)

Front ride height:
  Models with 145/70 R 13 T tyres:
    Normal suspension .... 140.0 mm
    Heavy-duty suspension .... 185.0 mm
  Models with 155/70 R 13 T tyres .... 146.0 mm
  Models with 165/65 R 13 T tyres:
    Normal suspension .... 144.0 mm
    Heavy-duty suspension .... 185.0 mm
  Models with 175/60 R14 H tyres .... 154.0 mm

Rear suspension

Type .... Trailing arms with transverse torsion bars and telescopic shock absorbers. Certain models have rear anti-roll bar running through axle tube, linking both trailing arms

Rear ride height:
  Models with 145/70 R 13 T tyres:
    Normal suspension .... 135.0 mm
    Heavy-duty suspension .... 179.0 mm
  Models with 155/70 R 13 T tyres .... 143.0 mm
  Models with 165/65 R 13 T tyres:
    Normal suspension .... 140.0 mm
    Heavy-duty suspension .... 179.0 mm
  Models with 175/60 R14 H tyres .... 150.0 mm

Steering

Type .... Rack-and-pinion, power-assisted on certain models
Power steering fluid type .... See *"Lubricants and fluids"*

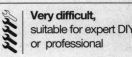

Wheel alignment and steering angles

Front wheel toe setting:

954 cc and 1124 cc engine models	0.5 ± 0.5 mm (0°4' ± 4') toe-out
All other models	0.5 ± 0.5 mm (0°4' ± 4') toe-in

Roadwheels

Type	Pressed-steel or aluminium alloy (depending on model)
Size	4.5B x 13, 5B x 13, 5J x 13, 5J x 14, 5.5J x 14 or 6J x 14 (depending on model)

Tyres

Size	145/70 R 13 T, 155/70 R 13 T, 165/65 R 13 T, 165/70 R 13 T, 165/65 R 14 H, 175/60 R 14 H or 185/55 R 14 H (depending on model)
Pressures	Refer to end of "Weekly checks".

Torque wrench settings

	Nm	lbf ft
Front suspension		
Driveshaft nut*	245	181
Front suspension strut upper mounting-to-body nuts	20	15
Front suspension strut damper rod nut*	60	44
Lower arm balljoint-to-hub carrier nut and clamp bolt*	50	37
Lower arm-to-body front mounting nut and through-bolt	85	63
Lower arm rear mounting bracket-to-body nuts	40	30
Front anti-roll bar mounting clamp-to-body bolts	55	41
Front anti-roll bar end clamp-to-lower arm screws	25	18
Front anti-roll bar drop-link securing nuts*	30	22
Rear suspension		
Rear hub nut*	140	103
Rear shock absorber upper mounting bolt and nut	90	66
Rear shock absorber lower mounting bolt and nut	110	81
Rear suspension assembly-to-body mounting bolts	85	63
Rear torsion bar retaining bolts	20	15
Steering		
Steering wheel nut*	40	30
Track-rod end-to-steering arm nut*	35	26
Lower steering column pinch-bolt and nut**	25	18
Steering column securing bolts	20	15
Steering gear-to-bulkhead bolts:		
15 mm retaining bolt thread length	25	18
26 mm retaining bolt thread length	40	30
Track-rod balljoint locknuts	45	33
Track-rod-to-steering gear bolts and nuts	25	18
Steering yoke-to-steering gear bolts and nuts	25	18
Roadwheels		
Roadwheel bolts	85	63

*Use a new nut.
**Use a new nut and bolt.

---

1 General information

The independent front suspension is of the MacPherson strut type, incorporating coil springs and integral telescopic shock absorbers. The MacPherson struts are located by transverse lower suspension arms, which utilise rubber inner mounting bushes and incorporate a balljoint at the outer ends. The front hub carriers, which carry the wheel bearings, brake calipers and the hub/disc assemblies, are integral with the MacPherson struts and are connected to the lower arms via the balljoints. A front anti-roll bar is fitted to certain models. The anti-roll bar is rubber-mounted onto the subframe and is either connected to both lower suspension arms or directly to the front suspension struts, depending on the model (see illustration).

The rear suspension is of the independent trailing arm type, which consists of two trailing arms, linked by a tubular crossmember. Torsion bars linking the trailing arms are situated in front of and behind the crossmember and on certain models, an anti-roll bar linking the arms passes through the centre of the crossmember (see illustration).

The complete rear axle assembly is mounted onto the vehicle underbody by four rubber mountings.

The steering column has a universal joint fitted at its lower end, which is clamped to the steering gear pinion by means of a clamp bolt and nut.

The steering gear is mounted on the engine compartment bulkhead. It is connected by two track-rods (with balljoints at their inner and outer ends) to the steering arms projecting rearwards from the suspension struts. The track-rod ends are threaded, to facilitate steering angle adjustment.

Power-assisted steering is fitted as standard on some models and is available as an option on all others. The hydraulic steering system is powered by a belt-driven pump, which is driven from the crankshaft pulley, or by an electric pump mounted in the engine compartment.

1.1 Front suspension assembly (models with anti-roll bar mounted directly on lower arms)

1 Suspension strut
2 Coil spring
3 Steering gear
4 Track-rod
5 Driveshafts
6 Hub carrier
7 Lower arm
8 Anti-roll bar (not fitted to all models)

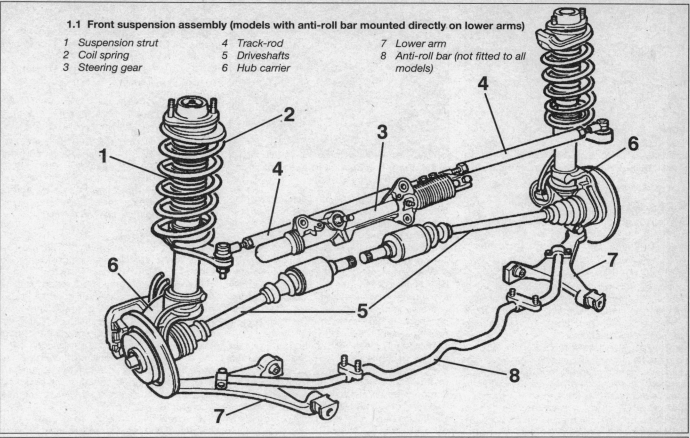

1.2 Rear suspension assembly

1 Flexible bushes
2 Torsion bars
3 Trailing arm
4 Shock absorber
5 Anti-roll bar (not fitted to all models)

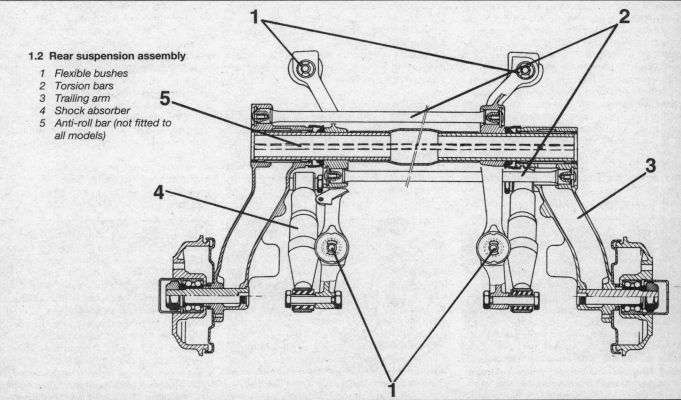

10

2.3 Driving the hub flange from the front hub bearing

2 Front hub bearings - renewal

Note: *The bearing is a sealed, pre-adjusted and pre-lubricated, double-row roller type and is intended to last the vehicle's entire service life without maintenance or attention. Never overtighten the driveshaft nut beyond the specified torque wrench setting in an attempt to "adjust" the bearing.*

Note: *Peugeot special tools are available to carry out this operation, in which case the task can be carried out without removing the suspension strut. The procedure described in this Section assumes that the special tools are not available, in which case the task can be accomplished using improvised tools, once the suspension strut assembly has been removed.*

Note: *A press will be required to dismantle and rebuild the assembly; if such a tool is not available, a large bench vice and spacers (such as large sockets) will serve as an adequate substitute. The bearing's inner races are an interference fit on the hub; if the inner race remains on the hub when it is pressed out of the hub carrier, a knife-edged bearing puller will be required to remove it.*

1 Remove the relevant front suspension strut assembly, as described in Section 3.
2 If not already done, remove the securing screw(s) and withdraw the brake disc from the hub.
3 Support the strut assembly securely on blocks or in a vice. Using a tubular spacer which bears only on the inner end of the hub

2.4 Front hub bearing retaining circlip (arrowed)

flange, press or drive the hub flange out of the bearing **(see illustration)**. If the bearing outboard inner race remains on the hub, remove it using a bearing puller (see note above).
4 Extract the bearing retaining circlip from the inner end of the hub carrier **(see illustration)**.
5 Where necessary, refit the bearing inner race back in position over the ball cage and securely support the inner face of the hub carrier. Using a tubular spacer which bears only on the bearing inner race, press or drive the complete bearing assembly out of the hub carrier.
6 Thoroughly clean the hub and hub carrier, removing all traces of dirt and grease and polish away any burrs or raised edges which might hinder reassembly. Check the components for cracks or any other signs of wear or damage and renew them if necessary. Renew the bearing retaining circlip, regardless of its apparent condition.
7 Commence reassembly by applying a light film of oil to the bearing outer race and the contact faces of the hub, to aid installation of the bearing.
8 Securely support the hub carrier and locate the bearing in the hub. Press the bearing fully into position, ensuring that it enters the hub squarely, using a tubular spacer which bears only on the bearing outer race.
9 Once the bearing is correctly seated, fit a new bearing retaining circlip, ensuring that it is correctly located in the groove in the hub carrier.
10 Securely support the outer face of the hub and the suspension strut and locate the hub carrier bearing inner race over the end of the hub. Press the bearing onto the hub, using a

tubular spacer which bears only on the inner race of the bearing, until the bearing seats against the hub shoulder. Check that the hub rotates freely and wipe off any excess oil or grease.
11 Refit the suspension strut assembly as described in Section 3.

3 Front suspension strut - removal, overhaul and refitting

Note: *A balljoint separator tool will be required for this operation. A new driveshaft nut, a new track-rod end-to-steering arm nut and a new hub carrier-to-lower arm balljoint clamp nut, must be used on refitting.*

Removal

1 Chock the rear wheels then jack up the front of the vehicle and support it on axle stands (see *"Jacking and Vehicle Support"*). Remove the appropriate front roadwheel.
2 Disconnect the driveshaft from the hub, as described in Chapter 8. Note that there is no need to remove the driveshaft completely - the inner end can be left engaged with the gearbox. Support the driveshaft by suspending it from the vehicle body using wire or string - do not allow the end of the driveshaft to hang down.
3 Unscrew the bolt securing the brake pad wear sensor earth lead to the hub carrier **(see illustration)**.
4 Unscrew the two bolts securing the brake caliper to the hub carrier, then remove the bolts, along with the mounting plate (noting which way round the plate is fitted), where applicable. Slide the caliper off the disc (if necessary, remove the brake pads first, with reference to Chapter 9). Using a piece of wire or string, suspend the caliper from the body, to avoid placing any strain on the hydraulic brake hose **(see illustration)**.
5 Ensure that any wires or hoses attached to the strut are released from the clips or brackets and moved to one side to facilitate strut removal. Note the locations of any clips or brackets.
6 Have an assistant support the strut from under the wheel arch, then slacken and remove the suspension strut upper mounting nuts **(see illustration)**. There may be two or

3.3 Unscrew the bolt securing the brake pad wear sensor earth lead to the hub carrier

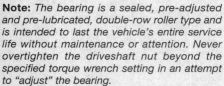

3.4 Suspend the caliper from the body

3.6 Remove the suspension strut upper mounting nuts (three on this model)

three nuts, depending on model - **do not** attempt to slacken the large central nut at this stage. Note the positions of the upper mounting nuts to ensure correct refitting (there are four holes in the body, three of which may be used), as the positions differ for models with manual and power steering.

7 Carefully lower the suspension strut and withdraw it from under the wheel arch **(see illustration)**.

Overhaul

⚠️ *Warning: Before attempting to dismantle the front suspension strut, suitable tools to hold the coil spring in compression must be obtained. Adjustable coil spring compressors are readily available and are recommended for this operation. Any attempt to dismantle the strut without such a tool is likely to result in damage or personal injury.*

Note: *A new damper rod nut must be used on reassembly.*

8 With the strut removed from the vehicle as described previously in this Section, clean away all external dirt, then mount the strut upright in a vice.

9 Fit the spring compressors and compress the coil spring until all tension is relieved from the upper spring seat **(see illustration)**.

10 Hold the strut damper rod using a T40 Torx bit and unscrew the strut top nut. Discard the nut - a new nut must be used when refitting.

11 Withdraw the upper spring seat and associated components, the spring, complete

3.7 Withdrawing the suspension strut

with the compressors, then the rubber gaiter, thrustwasher (where applicable), bump rubber and bump rubber collar. Remove the compressors from the spring.

12 With the strut now dismantled, examine all the components for wear, damage or deformation and check the upper bearing for smoothness of operation. Renew any of the components as necessary.

13 Examine the strut for signs of fluid leakage. Check the strut piston for signs of pitting along its entire length and check the strut body for signs of damage. While holding it in an upright position, test the operation of the strut by moving the piston through a full stroke and then through short strokes of 50 to 100 mm. In both cases, the resistance felt should be smooth and continuous. If the resistance is jerky, or uneven, or if there is any visible sign of wear or damage to the strut, renewal is necessary. The strut damper

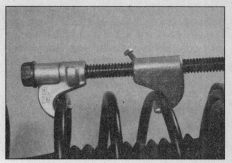

3.9 Coil spring compressor fitted to suspension strut coil spring

cartridge can be renewed independently of the strut, but a special tool is required to unscrew the damper nut. This nut is very tight and it is not possible to safely improvise a suitable tool. Unless the Peugeot special tool is available (Tool No (-).0618A), the strut should be taken to a Peugeot dealer for renewal of the damper cartridge.

14 If any doubt exists about the condition of the coil spring, carefully remove the spring compressors and check the spring for distortion and signs of cracking. Renew the spring if it is damaged or distorted, or if there is any doubt as to its condition.

15 Inspect all other components for signs of damage or deterioration and renew any that are suspect.

16 To reassemble the strut, follow the accompanying photo sequence, beginning with illustration 3.16a. Be sure to follow each step in sequence and carefully read the caption underneath each photo **(see illustrations)**. Compress the spring sufficiently to allow the top mounting components to be refitted and if necessary pull on the end of the piston rod to extend the damper.

Refitting

17 Manoeuvre the strut assembly into position under the wheel arch, passing the mounting studs through the holes in the body turret, then refit the upper mounting nuts and tighten them to the specified torque.

⚠️ *Warning: It is essential to ensure that the upper mounting nuts are fitted in their correct positions as shown (if necessary, turn the upper*

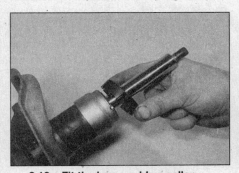

3.16a Fit the bump rubber collar . . .

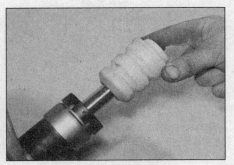

3.16b . . . the bump rubber . . .

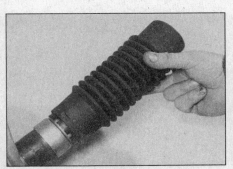

3.16c . . . and the rubber gaiter

3.16d Slide the spring, complete with compressors, onto the strut . . .

3.16e . . . ensuring that the end of the spring locates against the stop on the lower seat

10

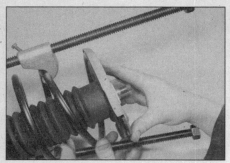

3.16f Fit the upper spring seat . . .

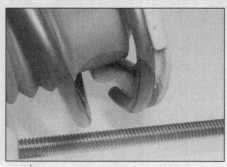

3.16g . . . again ensuring that the end of the spring locates against the stop

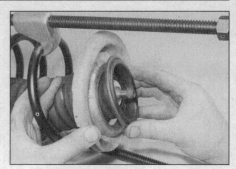

3.16h Fit the spring seat collar . . .

3.16i . . . the top mounting lower seat . . .

3.16j . . . the top mounting plate . . .

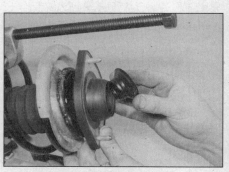

3.16k . . . and the top mounting upper seat . . .

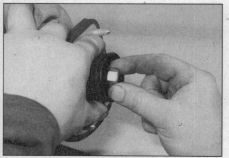

3.16l . . . then refit the top nut . . .

3.16m . . . and tighten using a spanner, whilst counterholding the piston rod

mounting on the strut until the studs line up with the relevant holes) - if the strut is fitted incorrectly, the castor angle will be incorrect and there is a risk of contact between the track-rods and the wheel arches (see illustration).

18 Ensure that the driveshaft splines and the corresponding splines in the hub are clean, then reconnect the driveshaft to the hub as described in Chapter 8.

19 Refit the brake caliper to the hub carrier, noting that (where applicable) the mounting plate fits so that its bend curves away from the caliper body and tighten the mounting bolts to the specified torque (see Chapter 9). Where applicable, refit the brake pads as described in Chapter 9.

20 Refit the bolt securing the brake pad wear sensor wiring to the hub carrier.

21 Clip any relevant wires or hoses back into position on the strut.

22 Refit the roadwheel and lower the vehicle to the ground.

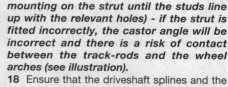
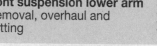

4 Front suspension lower arm
- removal, overhaul and refitting

Note: *A new hub carrier-to-lower arm balljoint clamp nut must be used on refitting.*

Removal

1 Chock the rear wheels then jack up the front of the vehicle and support it on axle stands (see *"Jacking and Vehicle Support"*). Remove the appropriate front roadwheel.

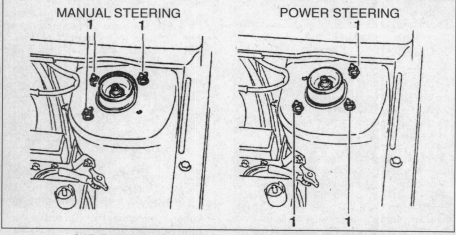

3.17 Front suspension strut upper mounting nut positions (1)

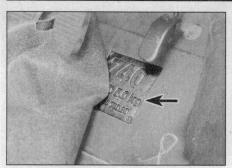

4.5a Lift the carpet and the insulation panel (arrowed) . . .

4.5b . . . and pull off the foam sealing panel for access to the lower arm bracket securing nuts

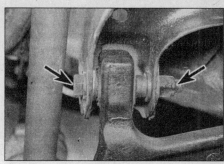

4.6 Lower arm front securing bolt and nut (arrowed)

2 On models where the anti-roll bar is mounted onto the suspension lower arm, remove the two screws and washers securing the anti-roll bar end clamp to the lower arm. Remove the clamp and the rubber bush.

3 Undo the nut and withdraw the hub carrier-to-lower arm clamp bolt, noting which way round it is fitted.

4 Using a suitable metal bar, lever the lower arm downwards just enough to release the balljoint taper from the lower arm. If the taper is a tight fit in the hub carrier, use a large flat-bladed screwdriver to carefully open up the clamp a little.

5 Working inside the passenger compartment, release the securing clips (and the throttle pedal stop, where applicable) and lift the carpet and sound insulation panels for access to the two lower arm rear bracket securing nuts. Where applicable, unbolt the bonnet release lever to enable the carpet panel to be released. On certain models, it may be necessary to pull the foam sealing panel from the floor for access to the nuts. Unscrew the securing nuts (see illustrations).

6 Working under the vehicle, unscrew the nut and remove the through-bolt securing the front of the lower arm to the bracket on the body (see illustration).

7 Pull the lower arm down to disengage the front mounting studs from the holes in the body and withdraw the lower arm from under the vehicle.

Overhaul

8 It is possible to renew the lower arm pivot bushes, but due to the requirement for Peugeot special tools (a suitable press, positioning jig and socket adapter will be required), it is recommended that the job is entrusted to a Peugeot dealer. Similarly, it is also possible to renew the lower arm balljoint, which is a press-fit in the end of the lower arm.

Refitting

9 Commence refitting by ensuring that the bushes, the bush contact faces on the body and the lower arm securing bolt and studs, are clean.

10 Place the lower arm in position under the vehicle, then refit the front through-bolt and nut and tighten to the specified torque.

11 Working inside the passenger compartment, refit the rear bracket securing nuts and tighten them to the specified torque. Fit the carpet and sound insulation panels back in position.

12 Ensure that the protector plate is in place over the lower arm balljoint, then engage the balljoint taper with the hub carrier. If necessary, lever the arm downwards just enough to engage the balljoint, as during removal. Similarly, use a screwdriver to open up the clamp a little if necessary.

13 Fit the hub carrier-to-lower arm clamp bolt (insert the bolt from the front of the strut) and a new nut and tighten to the specified torque.

14 Where applicable, refit the anti-roll bar end clamp and bush. Position the end of the anti-roll bar on the lower arm and refit the securing screws and washers. Tighten the screws to the specified torque.

15 Refit the roadwheel and lower the vehicle to the ground.

16 If the driver's side lower arm has been removed, ensure that the sound insulation and carpet panels have been correctly refitted. Check the operation of the throttle pedal and check that the pedal can be depressed smoothly to the full-throttle position (check that full-throttle is available at the engine with the pedal fully depressed - see the relevant Part of Chapter 4 as applicable).

5 Front suspension anti-roll bar - removal and refitting

Anti-roll bar

Note: *On models where the anti-roll bar is connected to the suspension struts by drop-links, new drop-link-to-anti-roll bar nuts must be used on refitting.*

Removal

1 Chock the rear wheels then jack up the front of the vehicle and support it on axle stands (see *"Jacking and Vehicle Support"*). Remove the front roadwheels.

2 On models where the anti-roll bar is mounted onto the lower arms, working at each end of the anti-roll bar, remove the screws and washers securing the anti-roll bar end clamps to the lower arms. Remove the clamps and the rubber bushes (see illustration).

3 On models where the anti-roll bar has drop-links connecting the ends of the bar to the suspension struts, remove the nuts securing the lower ends of the drop-links to the anti-roll bar (see illustration).

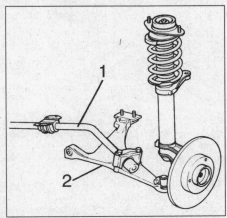

5.2 Front suspension layout for models with anti-roll bar mounted directly on lower arms

1 Anti-roll bar   2 Lower arm

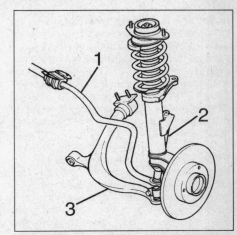

5.3 Front suspension layout for models with anti-roll bar incorporating drop-links

1 Anti-roll bar
2 Drop link (to rear of suspension strut)
3 Lower arm

10

4 Remove the bolts securing the anti-roll bar mounting clamps to the body. Withdraw the clamps.

5 Manipulate the anti-roll bar out from under the vehicle.

Refitting

6 Examine the condition of the anti-roll bar mounting bushes and renew if necessary. The anti-roll bar-to-body clamp bushes can be renewed by sliding the old bushes from the bar and sliding the new bushes into position. Before removing the old bushes, mark their fitted positions on the bar, so that the new bushes can be fitted in the same position.

7 Manipulate the bar into position under the vehicle, then refit the mounting clamps. Fit the mounting clamp securing bolts, but do not fully tighten them at this stage.

8 On models where the anti-roll bar is connected to the suspension struts by drop-links, reconnect the drop-links to the ends of the bar and fit new securing nuts. Tighten the nuts to the specified torque.

9 On models where the anti-roll bar is mounted onto the lower arms, refit the rubber bushes and the clamps, then refit the washers and the screws. Tighten the screws to the specified torque.

10 Finally tighten the anti-roll bar clamp-to-body bolts to the specified torque.

11 Refit the roadwheels and lower the vehicle to the ground. Tighten the roadwheel bolts to the specified torque.

Drop-link (models with strut-mounted anti-roll bar)

Note: *New drop-link securing nuts must be used on refitting.*

Removal

12 Chock the rear wheels then jack up the front of the vehicle and support it on axle stands (see *"Jacking and Vehicle Support"*). Remove the appropriate front roadwheel.

13 Unscrew the nut securing the lower end of the drop-link to the end of the anti-roll bar.

14 If necessary, using a suitable metal bar, carefully lever the end of the anti-roll bar down, to separate it from the end of the drop-link.

15 Unscrew the nut securing the drop-link to the suspension strut and remove the drop-link from the vehicle.

Refitting

16 Check the drop-link balljoints for excessive wear and check the condition of the balljoint rubber gaiters. If the balljoints or gaiters are worn or damaged, the complete drop-link must be renewed, as the components cannot be renewed individually. Note that wear in the drop-links is often indicated by a "clonking" noise produced when driving over bumps or cornering.

17 Refitting is a reversal of removal, but use new securing nuts.

7.2 Extracting the rear wheel bearing circlip

6 Rear hub assembly - removal and refitting

Rear drum brake models

1 The rear hub is integral with the brake drum. Refer to Chapter 9 for details of brake drum removal and refitting.

Rear disc brake models

Note: *Do not remove the hub assembly unless it is absolutely necessary. A puller will be required to draw the hub assembly off the stub axle and the hub bearing will be damaged by the removal procedure. As the bearing is not available separately, it will be necessary to obtain a complete new rear hub assembly prior to refitting. A new hub nut and a new hub cap will also be required.*

Removal

2 Remove the rear brake disc as described in Chapter 9.

3 Using a hammer and a large flat-bladed screwdriver, carefully tap and prise the cap out of the centre of the hub. Discard the cap - a new one must be used on refitting. Using a hammer and a chisel-nosed tool, tap up the staking securing the hub retaining nut to the groove in the stub axle.

4 Using a socket and long bar, slacken and remove the rear hub nut and withdraw the thrustwasher. Discard the hub nut - a new nut must used on refitting.

7.3 Prising the oil seal seating ring from the rear hub

5 Using a puller, draw the hub assembly off the stub axle, along with the outer bearing race. With the hub removed, use the puller to draw the inner bearing race off the stub axle, then remove the hub spacer, noting which way around it is fitted.

6 The bearing must be renewed as a matter of course as it will have been damaged during removal. This means that the complete hub assembly must be renewed, since it is not possible to obtain the bearing separately.

7 Examine the stub axle shaft for signs of wear or damage. The shaft is an integral part of the trailing arm and if worn or damaged, the complete trailing arm must be renewed. Refer to Section 9 for further details.

Refitting

8 Lubricate the stub axle shaft with clean engine oil, then slide on the spacer, ensuring it is fitted the correct way round.

9 Slide the hub assembly onto the stub axle and tap it into position using a hammer and tubular drift in contact with the bearing inner race. Once sufficient thread is exposed on the stub axle, the old hub nut can be used to draw the hub assembly fully into position.

10 Remove the old hub nut and lightly grease the face and threads of the new hub nut. Fit the thrustwasher and new hub nut and tighten the nut to the specified torque. Stake the nut firmly into the groove on the stub axle to secure it in position, then tap the new hub cap into place in the centre of the hub.

11 Refit the rear brake disc (see Chapter 9).

7 Rear hub bearings - renewal

Rear drum brake models

Note: *The bearing is intended to last the vehicle's entire service life without maintenance or attention. Never overtighten the hub nut beyond the specified torque wrench setting, in an attempt to "adjust" the bearings.*

1 Remove the rear brake drum as described in Chapter 9.

2 Using circlip pliers, extract the bearing retaining circlip from the centre of the brake drum **(see illustration)**.

3 Prise the oil seal seating ring from the rear of the hub **(see illustration)**.

4 Securely support the drum hub, then press or drive the bearing out of position, using a tubular drift which bears on the bearing inner race. Alternatively, the bearing can be removed using an improvised tool made up from a suitable socket or tube, washers, nut and a suitable long bolt or threaded rod **(see illustration)**.

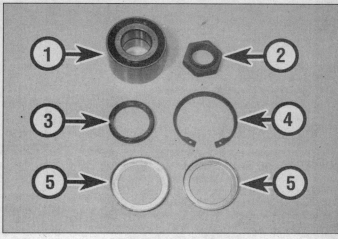

7.4 Drawing the hub bearing from the hub using improvised tools

7.5 Rear hub bearing kit

1 Bearing
2 Hub nut
3 Oil seal

4 Circlip
5 Oil seal seating rings
   (alternative sizes)

5 Thoroughly clean the hub, removing all traces of dirt and grease and polish away any burrs or raised edges which might hinder reassembly. Check the hub for cracks or any other signs of wear or damage and renew them if necessary. The bearing and its circlip must be renewed whenever they are disturbed. Obtain a new bearing kit from a Peugeot dealer **(see illustration)**.

6 Carefully prise the oil seal from the stub axle and fit the new seal supplied in the bearing kit. Note the spacer fitted behind the oil seal **(see illustration)**.

7 Examine the stub axle shaft for signs of wear or damage. The shaft is an integral part of the trailing arm and if worn or damaged, the complete trailing arm must be renewed. Refer to Section 9 for further details.

8 On reassembly, apply a light film of clean engine oil to the bearing outer race, to aid installation of the bearing.

9 Securely support the drum and locate the bearing in the hub. Press the bearing fully into position, ensuring that it enters the hub squarely, using a tubular spacer which bears only on the bearing outer race. Alternatively, the bearing can be drawn into position with the improvised tool used previously, but note that a different socket or tube will be required, to bear on the bearing outer race **(see illustrations)**.

10 Ensure that the bearing is correctly seated against the hub shoulder and secure it in position with the new circlip. Ensure that the circlip is correctly seated in its hub groove.

11 Tap the new oil seal seating ring into position in the rear of the hub, taking care not to damage the oil seal seating surface **(see illustrations)**. Note that two different-size oil seal seating rings may be supplied in the bearing kit - ensure that the correct ring is used.

12 Refit the brake drum as described in Chapter 9.

Rear disc brake models

13 On models with rear disc brakes, it is not possible to renew the rear hub bearing separately. If the bearing is worn, the complete rear hub assembly must be renewed. Refer to Section 6 for hub removal and refitting procedures.

7.6 Fitting a new oil seal to the stub axle. Note spacer (arrowed)

7.9a Locate the bearing in the hub . . .

7.9b . . . then draw the bearing into position

7.11a Fit the new oil seal seating ring . . .

7.11b . . . and tap it into position

10

8.3 Counterhold the bolts when unscrewing the rear shock absorber mounting nuts

8.4a Remove the upper . . .

8.4b . . . and lower rear shock absorber mounting bolts

8 Rear shock absorber - removal, testing and refitting

Removal

1 Chock the front wheels then jack up the rear of the vehicle and support it on axle stands (see *"Jacking and Vehicle Support"*). Remove the relevant rear roadwheel.

2 Using a trolley jack, raise the trailing arm until the shock absorber is slightly compressed.

3 Slacken and remove the nuts from both the upper and lower shock absorber mounting bolts. Note that it will be necessary to counterhold the bolts **(see illustration)**.

4 Withdraw the mounting bolts, noting which way around they are fitted and manoeuvre the shock absorber out from underneath the vehicle **(see illustrations)**.

Testing

5 Examine the shock absorber for signs of fluid leakage or damage. Test the operation of the shock absorber, while holding it in an upright position, by moving the piston through a full stroke and then through short strokes of 50 to 100 mm. In both cases, the resistance felt should be smooth and continuous. If the resistance is jerky, or uneven, or if there is any visible sign of wear or damage, renewal is necessary. Also check the rubber mounting bushes for damage and deterioration. Renew the complete unit if any damage or excessive wear is evident; the mounting bushes are not available separately. Inspect the shanks of the mounting bolts for signs of wear or damage and renew as necessary.

Refitting

6 Prior to refitting the shock absorber, mount it upright in the vice and operate it fully through several strokes in order to prime it. Apply a smear of multi-purpose grease to both the shock absorber mounting bolts.

7 Manoeuvre the shock absorber into position and insert the mounting bolts. Ensure that the upper bolt is inserted from the outside of the trailing arm and the lower bolt from the inside, as noted on removal.

8 Refit the nuts, tightening them by hand only at this stage.

9 Refit the roadwheel, then lower the vehicle to the ground and tighten the roadwheel bolts to the specified torque.

10 With the vehicle standing on its wheels, rock the vehicle to settle the shock absorber in position, then tighten both the upper and lower mountings to the specified torque setting.

9 Rear suspension assembly - general

The operations in the following list can be carried out using suitable special tools, but due to the difficulty in improvising such tools easily, these procedures are considered to be beyond the scope of the home mechanic and should be referred to a Peugeot dealer:

a) *Removal and refitting of torsion bars.*

b) *Removal and refitting of rear anti-roll bar (where applicable).*

c) *Removal and refitting of trailing arms.*

d) *Renewal of suspension bushes and bearings.*

e) *Adjustment of rear suspension ride height.*

10 Steering wheel - removal and refitting

Note: *A new steering wheel securing nut must be used on refitting.*

Models without air bag

Removal

1 Set the front wheels in the straight-ahead position and release the steering lock by inserting the ignition key.

2 Carefully prise out the steering wheel centre pad, then slacken and remove the steering wheel retaining nut. Recover the washers **(see illustrations)**.

3 Mark the steering wheel and steering column shaft in relation to each other, then lift the steering wheel off the column splines. If it is tight, tap it up near the centre, using the palm of your hand, or twist it from side to side, whilst pulling upwards to release it from the shaft splines. If the wheel is particularly tight, a suitable puller should be used.

Refitting

4 Refitting is a reversal of removal, bearing in mind the following points:

a) *Ensure that the indicator switch is in the central, cancelled position and make sure*

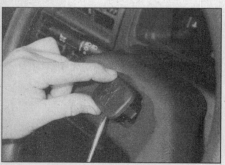

10.2a Prise out the centre pad for access . . .

10.2b . . . then remove the steering wheel retaining nut . . .

10.2c . . . and recover the washer

the lug on the steering wheel engages with the switch lever (see illustration).

b) Align the marks made on the wheel and the column shaft before removal.

c) Make sure that the washer is in position and use a new retaining nut tightened to the specified torque.

5 Note that if necessary, the position of the steering wheel on the column shaft can be altered in order to centralise the wheel, by moving the wheel the required number of splines on the shaft. Ensure that the front roadwheels are pointing in the straight-ahead position. If the wheel cannot be centralised this way, it is likely that the problem arose due to the front wheel alignment having been inexpertly set up. Have the alignment checked by a qualified specialist.

Models with an air bag

⚠ **Warning: Refer to the precautions given in Chapter 12 before proceeding. Note that the air bag control unit is integral with the steering wheel.**

Additionally, note the following points:

a) Do not drop the steering wheel, or subject it to impacts.

b) Do not try to dismantle the steering wheel.

c) Do not attempt to fit a steering wheel from another model of vehicle (even a different model of Peugeot 106), as the air bag control module is calibrated for each particular model.

Removal

6 Remove the air bag unit (see Chapter 12).

7 Set the front wheels in the straight-ahead

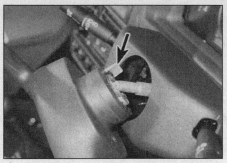

10.4 Make sure that the lug (arrowed) engages with the indicator switch lever

position and engage the steering lock.

8 Unscrew the steering wheel retaining nut by several threads.

9 Release the steering wheel from the column splines. If the wheel is particularly tight, a suitable puller should be used.

10 Separate the two halves of the air bag control unit wiring connector.

11 Remove the steering wheel retaining nut and recover the washer.

12 Carefully withdraw the steering wheel, feeding the wiring harness (connecting the rotary connector to the air bag control unit) through the wheel as it is withdrawn. Do not disturb the air bag control unit wiring connector (located in the steering wheel).

Refitting

13 Refitting is a reversal of removal, noting the points listed in paragraph 4. On completion, refit the air bag unit (Chapter 12).

11 Ignition switch/ steering column lock - removal and refitting

Removal

1 Disconnect the battery negative terminal (refer to "Disconnecting the battery" in the Reference Section of this manual).

2 Working under the steering column, remove the three steering column shroud securing screws. Unclip and lift off the upper shroud, then withdraw the lower shroud. Note that the lower shroud clips over a metal bracket on the steering column and the shroud must be slid from the bracket before it can be removed. On certain models, it may be necessary to remove the steering wheel in order to facilitate removal of the steering column shrouds (see illustrations).

3 Unclip the ignition switch wiring connectors from the steering column bracket or the facia, as applicable. Note the location of the connectors, so that they can be refitted in their original positions. Separate the two halves of each connector (see illustration).

4 Unscrew the lock retaining screw and recover the washer from the side of the lock.

5 Insert the key and rotate it so that it is aligned with the mark positioned between the "A" and "S" marks on the barrel.

6 Using a small flat-bladed screwdriver, or a suitable pin-punch, depress either of the lock retaining lugs, then withdraw the lock assembly from the steering column (see illustrations).

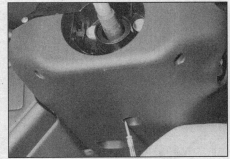

11.2a Remove the securing screws . . .

11.2b . . . and withdraw the upper . . .

11.2c . . . and lower steering column shrouds

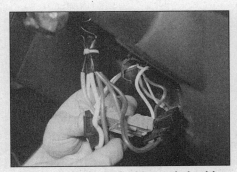

11.3 Disconnect the ignition switch wiring connectors

11.6a Depress the lock retaining lug . . .

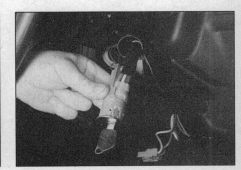

11.6b . . . then withdraw the lock assembly

10

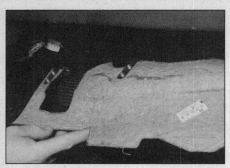

12.3 Withdraw the under-facia trim panel

Refitting

7 Refitting is a reversal of the removal procedure, ensuring that the lock assembly is securely held in position by its retaining lugs. Before refitting the steering column shrouds, remove the ignition key and check that the steering lock functions correctly.

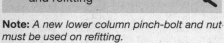

12 Steering column - removal, inspection and refitting

Note: *A new lower column pinch-bolt and nut must be used on refitting.*

Removal

1 Disconnect the battery negative terminal (refer to *"Disconnecting the battery"* in the Reference Section of this manual).

2 Remove the steering wheel as described in Section 10.

3 Unclip the front edge of the under-facia trim panel from the facia and lower the panel. Unscrew the two nuts securing the trim panel to the studs in the footwell, then withdraw the panel from the footwell **(see illustration)**.

4 Working under the steering column, remove the three steering column shroud securing screws. Unclip and lift off the upper shroud, then withdraw the lower shroud. Note that the lower shroud clips over a metal bracket on the steering column and the shroud must be slid from the bracket before it can be removed.

5 Working in the footwell, unscrew the securing nut from the lower column pinch-bolt, then carefully tap the pinch-bolt from the universal joint. Pull off the metal clip securing the column to the steering gear pinion **(see illustrations)**.

6 Make alignment marks on the universal joint and the steering gear pinion, then push the universal joint upwards to separate it from the pinion.

7 Disconnect the wiring plugs from the steering column combination switches.

8 Unclip the ignition switch wiring connectors from the steering column bracket or the facia, as applicable, Note the location of the connectors, so that they can be refitted in their original positions. Separate the two halves of each connector.

9 Ensure that all wiring has been moved clear of the column to facilitate removal.

10 Working under the steering column, unscrew the two steering column securing bolts, then lift the steering column from the facia and withdraw it from the vehicle.

Inspection

11 The steering column incorporates a telescopic safety feature. In the event of a front-end crash, the shaft collapses, reducing the chance of the steering wheel injuring the driver. Before refitting the steering column, examine the column assembly for signs of damage and deformation and renew as necessary.

12 Check the steering shaft for signs of free play in the column bushes and check the universal joints for signs of damage or roughness in the joint bearings. If any damage or wear is found on the steering column universal joints or shaft bushes, the column must be renewed as an assembly.

Refitting

13 Offer the steering column into position and refit the securing bolts. Tighten the bolts to the specified torque.

14 Reconnect the ignition switch wiring connectors and the combination switch wiring plugs. Fasten the ignition switch wiring connectors in position as noted before removal.

15 Refit the metal clip, then slide the column universal joint over the steering gear pinion, ensuring that the marks made before removal are still aligned.

16 Fit a new lower column pinch-bolt and nut, ensuring that the lugs on the bolt engage with the cut-outs in the universal joint. Tighten the nut to the specified torque.

17 Refit the steering column shrouds and the under-facia trim panel.

18 Refit the steering wheel as described in Section 10.

19 Reconnect the battery negative terminal.

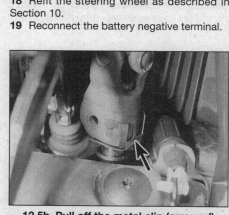

12.5b Pull off the metal clip (arrowed) securing the column to the pinion

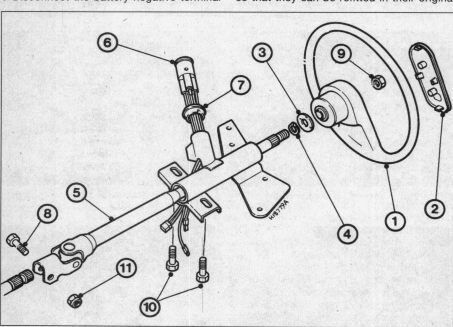

12.5a Steering column and associated components

1 Steering wheel	6 Steering lock/ignition
2 Centre pad	switch assembly
3 Bowl washer	7 Gasket
4 Stop-ring	8 Pinch-bolt
5 Column	

9 Steering wheel securing nut
10 Steering column securing bolts
11 Pinch-bolt nut

13.7 Two of the steering gear securing bolts (arrowed)

13 Steering gear assembly - removal, overhaul and refitting

Note: *New track-rod end balljoint nuts and a new lower steering column pinch-bolt and nut must be used on refitting.*

Manual steering gear

Removal

1 Ensure that the steering lock is engaged.
2 Unclip the front edge of the under-facia trim panel from the facia and lower the panel. Unscrew the two nuts securing the trim panel to the studs in the footwell, then withdraw the panel from the footwell.
3 Working in the footwell, unscrew the securing nut from the lower column pinch-bolt, then carefully tap the pinch-bolt from the universal joint. Pull off the metal clip securing the column to the steering gear pinion.
4 Make alignment marks on the universal joint and the steering gear pinion, then push the universal joint upwards to separate it from the pinion.
5 Chock the rear wheels then jack up the front of the vehicle and support it on axle stands (see *"Jacking and Vehicle Support"*). Remove the front roadwheels.
6 Working on each side of the vehicle in turn, unscrew the nut securing the track-rod end to the steering arm on the suspension strut and recover the washer. Using a balljoint separator tool, separate the track-rod end from the steering arm.
7 Working through the right-hand wheel arch, unscrew the three Torx bolts securing the steering gear to the engine compartment bulkhead **(see illustration)** and recover the washers. Withdraw the steering gear, complete with the track-rods, through the right-hand wheel arch.

Overhaul

8 Examine the steering gear assembly for signs of wear or damage. Check that the rack moves freely throughout the full length of its travel, with no signs of roughness or excessive free play between the steering gear pinion and rack. It is possible to overhaul the steering gear assembly housing components,

but this task should be entrusted to a Peugeot dealer. The only components which can be renewed easily by the home mechanic are the steering gear rubber gaiter, the track-rod balljoints and the track-rods. Steering gear rubber gaiter, track-rod balljoint and track-rod renewal procedures are covered in Sections 14, 17 and 18 respectively.

Refitting

9 Before refitting the steering gear, the rack must be centralised as follows.
10 Make a mark on the rack housing, corresponding with the centre-line of the steering gear securing bolt hole nearest the steering gear rubber gaiter.
11 Move the rack to its full extent of movement, so that the steering gear rubber gaiter is fully extended. Measure the distance from the mark made on the rack housing to the end of the steering gear rubber gaiter nearest the track-rod sleeve **(see illustration)**. Call this dimension "Y".
12 Move the rack to its full extent of movement in the opposite direction, until the rubber gaiter is fully compressed. Again, measure the distance from the mark made on the rack housing to the end of the steering gear rubber gaiter nearest the track-rod sleeve **(see illustration)**. Call this dimension "X".
13 Calculate the dimension between the mark on the rack housing and the end of the steering gear rubber gaiter, which corresponds to the mid-position of the rack. Call this dimension "Z". Dimension "Z" can be calculated as follows:

a) Subtract "X" from "Y" and divide the result by 2.
b) Add "X" to the result of the previous calculation, to give dimension "Z". ie:
$$Z = (Y - X)/2 + X$$

14 Set the steering gear to dimension "Z", then proceed with the refitting procedure as follows, ensuring that the rack position is not altered during the refitting procedure.
15 Check the condition of the pinion shaft seal located in the engine compartment bulkhead. Ensure that the seal is correctly located and renew the seal if there are any signs of damage or wear.
16 Offer the steering gear into position through the right-hand wheel arch.
17 Check the routing of the clutch cable, making sure that the cable is not trapped between the steering gear and the track-rod.
18 Locate the steering gear on the bulkhead, ensuring that the dowels on the bulkhead engage with the corresponding holes in the steering gear.
19 Fit the steering gear securing bolts and tighten them to the specified torque.
20 Reconnect the track-rods to the steering arms, then fit the washers and new nuts and tighten the nuts to the specified torque.

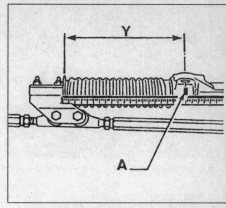

13.11 Steering rack centralisation - rack at maximum-travel position (left-hand drive steering gear shown)

A *Mark on rack housing*
Y *Maximum movement of rack - gaiter fully extended*

21 Refit the metal clip and slide the column universal joint over the steering gear pinion, ensuring that the marks made before removal are still aligned.
22 Fit a new lower column pinch-bolt and nut, ensuring that the lugs on the bolt engage with the cut-outs in the universal joint. Tighten the nut to the specified torque.
23 Refit the under-facia trim panel.
24 Refit the roadwheels and lower the vehicle to the ground.
25 Have the front wheel alignment checked at the earliest opportunity (refer to Section 19 for details) and check that the steering wheel is centralised (if necessary, the steering wheel position can be altered by removing the wheel and moving it the required number of splines on the column shaft before refitting - see Section 10).

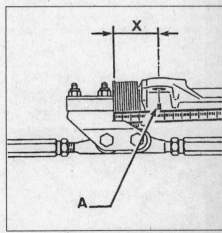

13.12 Steering rack centralisation - rack at minimum-travel position (left-hand drive steering gear shown)

A *Mark on rack housing*
X *Minimum movement of rack - gaiter fully compressed*

10

14.2 Remove the track-rod securing bolts

14.3a Unscrew the securing bolts . . .

14.3b . . . and remove the upper . . .

Power steering gear

Removal

26 Using suitable clamps, clamp both the fluid supply and return hoses near the power steering fluid reservoir. This will minimise fluid loss during subsequent operations.

27 Mark the unions to ensure that they are correctly positioned on reassembly, then unscrew the feed and return pipe union nuts from the steering gear assembly; be prepared for fluid spillage and position a suitable container beneath the pipes whilst unscrewing the union nuts. Disconnect both pipes and plug the pipe ends and steering gear orifices, to prevent fluid leakage and to keep dirt out of the hydraulic system.

28 Free the power steering pipes from any retaining clips and position them clear of the steering gear so that they will not hinder the removal procedure.

29 Remove the steering gear as described in paragraphs 1 to 7 inclusive.

Overhaul

30 Refer to paragraph 8, but additionally, inspect all the steering gear fluid unions for signs of leakage and check that all union nuts are securely tightened. Also examine the steering gear hydraulic ram for signs of fluid leakage or damage and if necessary renew it.

Refitting

31 Refitting is as described in paragraphs 9 to 25 inclusive, but additionally, note the following:

a) *Reconnect the fluid pipes to the steering gear, ensuring that they are correctly*

14.3c . . . and lower sections of the track-rod bracket

reconnected as noted before removal.
b) *Ensure that the pipes are repositioned correctly in any relevant clips and correctly routed to avoid straining the pipes.*
c) *On completion, bleed the power steering hydraulic system as described in Section 15 and if necessary top-up the fluid level (see "Weekly checks").*

14 Steering gear rubber gaiter - renewal

1 On diesel models, to improve access, remove the inlet manifold as described in Chapter 4D.
2 Unscrew the securing bolts (while counterholding the nuts) and disconnect the inner ends of the track-rods from the steering gear (see illustration).
3 Unscrew the two securing bolts and remove the upper and lower sections of the track-rod bracket (see illustrations).
4 Release the securing clip from the pinion end of the gaiter, then slide the gaiter from the steering gear (see illustration).
5 Fit the new gaiter using a reversal of the removal procedure. Tighten all fixings to the specified torque and (where applicable) refit the inlet manifold as described in Chapter 4D.

15 Power steering hydraulic system - bleeding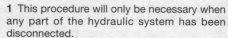

1 This procedure will only be necessary when any part of the hydraulic system has been disconnected.
2 Referring to *"Weekly checks"*, remove the fluid reservoir filler cap and top-up with the specified fluid to the maximum level mark.
3 With the engine stopped, slowly move the steering from lock-to-lock several times to purge out any trapped air, then top-up the level in the fluid reservoir. Repeat this procedure until the fluid level in the reservoir does not drop any further.
4 Start the engine, then slowly move the steering from lock-to-lock several times, to purge out any remaining air in the system.

Repeat this procedure until bubbles cease to appear in the fluid reservoir.
5 If, when turning the steering, an abnormal noise is heard from the fluid lines, it indicates that there is still air in the system. Check this by turning the wheels to the straight-ahead position and switching off the engine. If the fluid level in the reservoir rises, then air is present in the system and further bleeding is necessary.
6 Once all traces of air have been removed from the power steering hydraulic system, stop the engine and allow the system to cool. Once cool, check that the fluid level is up to the maximum mark on the reservoir. Top-up if necessary.

16 Power steering pump - removal and refitting

General

1 On early models without air conditioning, a belt-driven mechanical power steering pump is fitted, which is driven from the crankshaft via the auxiliary drivebelt (see Chapter 1A or 1B).
2 On early models with air conditioning, there is insufficient space in the engine compartment to fit a mechanical pump, due to the location of the air conditioning compressor. On these models, a remotely-mounted electric pump is therefore used.
3 On all later models (except diesel models without air conditioning) a remotely-mounted electric pump is used (see illustrations).

14.4 Slide the gaiter from the steering gear

Mechanical pump

Removal

4 Chock the rear wheels then jack up the front of the vehicle and support it on axle stands (see *"Jacking and Vehicle Support"*).

5 Slacken the auxiliary drivebelt as described in Chapter 1A or 1B and slip the belt from the power steering pump pulley.

6 Remove the alternator as described in Chapter 5A.

7 Using suitable clamps, clamp both the fluid supply and return hoses near the power steering fluid reservoir. This will minimise fluid loss during subsequent operations.

8 Slacken the union nut and disconnect the fluid supply hose from the pump. Be prepared for fluid spillage and plug the open ends of the hose and pump, to minimise fluid loss and to prevent the entry of dirt into the system.

9 Similarly, loosen the securing clamp and disconnect the fluid return hose from the pump.

10 Free the power steering hoses from any retaining clips and/or brackets and position them clear of the pump so that they will not hinder the removal procedure.

11 Remove the securing bolts and withdraw the power steering pump pulley. It may be necessary to counterhold the pulley, using an old drivebelt for example, when unscrewing the bolts.

12 Unscrew the front and rear securing bolts and withdraw the pump from the mounting brackets.

Refitting

13 Refitting is a reversal of removal, bearing in mind the following points:

a) *Refit the alternator with reference to Chapter 5A.*

b) *Refit and tighten the auxiliary drivebelt as described in Chapter 1A or 1B.*

c) *On completion, bleed the power steering hydraulic system as described in Section 15.*

Electric pump

Removal - U-shaped mounting bracket pump

14 The power steering pump may be mounted inside its own plastic housing - where necessary, to gain access to the top of the pump, remove the screws and clips, and lift off the top cover.

15 Disconnect the battery negative lead.

16 Using suitable clamps, clamp both the fluid supply and return hoses near the power steering fluid reservoir (which is attached to the top of the radiator). This will minimise fluid loss during subsequent operations.

17 Apply the handbrake, then raise and support the front of the car on axle stands (see *"Jacking and Vehicle Support"*).

18 Disconnect the wiring from the pump body - some models have a multi-plug connector, on others, the wiring is secured to the pump body by two nuts. Note the location of the wires, for use when refitting.

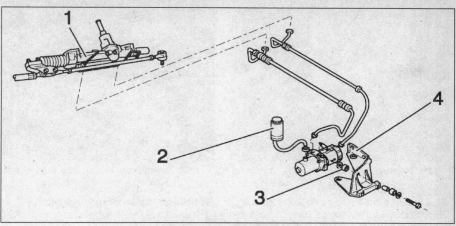

16.3a Steering assembly layout

1 Steering rack	3 Electric pump
2 Fluid reservoir	4 Pump mounting bracket

19 Disconnect the low-pressure fluid return hose, and place the end in a clean container. Turn the steering from lock to lock a few times, to purge the fluid from the pump and further minimise spillage.

20 Disconnect the high-pressure supply hose leading to the rack, and plug the pump hole to minimise fluid loss and prevent dirt entry.

21 Support the mounting bracket from below, then loosen (do not remove) the mounting bracket-to-body bolts.

22 Loosen and remove the pump mounting bolts. If required, unclip the steering fluid reservoir from its mounting, and remove the pump and reservoir from the engine compartment.

Removal - collar-mounted pump

23 The power steering pump may be mounted inside its own plastic housing - where necessary, to gain access to the top of the pump, remove the screws and clips, and lift off the top cover.

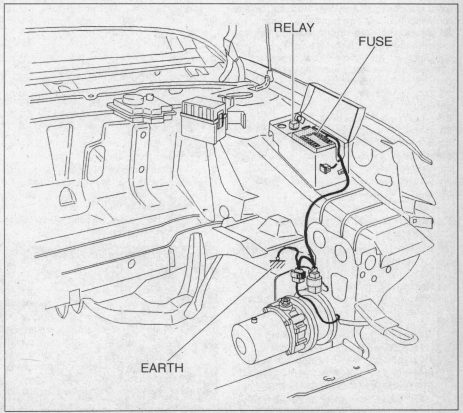

16.3b Wiring layout for the electric pump

10

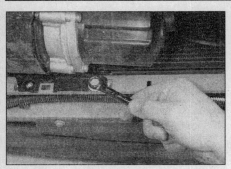

16.31 Removing the power steering pump mounting bolts

24 Disconnect the battery negative lead.

25 Using suitable clamps, clamp both the fluid supply and return hoses near the power steering fluid reservoir (which is attached to the top of the radiator). This will minimise fluid loss during subsequent operations.

26 Apply the handbrake, then raise and support the front of the car on axle stands (see *"Jacking and Vehicle Support"*).

27 On models with automatic transmission, remove the transmission ECU support bracket to improve access to the pump.

28 Disconnect the low-pressure fluid return hose, and place the end in a clean container. Turn the steering from lock to lock a few times, to purge the fluid from the pump and further minimise spillage.

29 Disconnect the high-pressure supply hose leading to the rack, and plug the pump hole to minimise fluid loss and prevent dirt entry.

30 Unclip the relay and the wiring harness from the top of the pump mounting.

31 Support the pump from below, then unscrew and remove the pump mounting-to-body bolts **(see illustration)**.

32 Disconnect the wiring connector and unclip the pipework around the pump, noting its routing **(see illustration)**.

33 If required, unclip the steering fluid reservoir from its mounting, and remove the pump and reservoir from the engine compartment.

34 Loosen the clamp bolts, and release the pump from its mounting clamp.

Refitting - U-shaped mounting bracket pump

35 Refitting is a reversal of removal, noting the following points:

a) Before refitting the pump, check the condition of the mounting bracket rubber bushes, and renew if necessary.

b) Tighten all fixings and fluid unions securely, and ensure that the wiring connections are securely re-made.

c) Fill and bleed the power steering system, taking care to ensure that as much air as possible is bled out before the engine is started. If preferred, pre-fill the steering pump with fluid before finally connecting and tightening the unions.

16.32 Unclip the wiring and the hoses from the top of the pump

Refitting - collar-mounted pump

36 Refitting is a reversal of removal, noting the following points:

a) Fit the pump into its collar, and tighten the clamp screws securely.

b) Tighten all fixings and fluid unions securely, and ensure that the wiring connections are securely re-made.

c) Fill and bleed the power steering system, taking care to ensure that as much air as possible is bled out before the engine is started. If preferred, pre-fill the steering pump with fluid before finally connecting and tightening the unions.

17 Track-rod balljoint - removal and refitting

Inner balljoint

Removal

1 Remove the track-rod as described in Section 18.

2 Note the number of exposed threads on the balljoint shank, then loosen the locknut and unscrew the balljoint from the end of the track-rod.

Refitting

3 Screw the balljoint onto the end of the track-rod to leave the same number of threads exposed as noted during removal, then tighten the locknut. Ensure that the bolt hole in the balljoint is vertical - ie parallel to the outer track-rod balljoint pin.

18.3 Track-rod-to-steering gear bolts (arrowed)

4 Refit the track-rod as described in Section 18.

Outer balljoint

Note: *A new track-rod end balljoint nut must be used on refitting.*

Removal

5 Chock the rear wheels then jack up the front of the vehicle and support it on axle stands (see *"Jacking and Vehicle Support"*). Remove the relevant front roadwheel.

6 Unscrew the nut securing the track-rod end to the steering arm on the suspension strut and recover the washer. Using a balljoint separator tool, separate the track-rod end from the steering arm.

7 Note the number of exposed threads on the balljoint shank, then loosen the locknut and unscrew the balljoint from the end of the track-rod.

Refitting

8 Screw the balljoint onto the end of the track-rod, to leave the same number of threads exposed as noted during removal, then tighten the locknut. Ensure that the balljoint pin is pointing vertically downwards.

9 Reconnect the track-rod to the steering arms, then fit the washer and new nut and tighten the nut to the specified torque.

10 Refit the roadwheel and lower the vehicle to the ground.

11 Have the front wheel alignment checked at the earliest opportunity (refer to Section 19 for details). Check also that the steering wheel is centralised (if necessary, the steering wheel position can be altered by removing the wheel and moving it the required number of splines on the column shaft before refitting - see Section 10).

18 Track-rod - removal and refitting

Note: *A new track-rod outer end balljoint nut and a new track-rod-to-steering gear nut, must be used on refitting.*

Removal

1 Chock the rear wheels then jack up the front of the vehicle and support it on axle stands (see *"Jacking and Vehicle Support"*). Remove the relevant front roadwheel.

2 Unscrew the nut securing the track-rod end to the steering arm on the suspension strut and recover the washer. Using a balljoint separator tool, separate the track-rod end from the steering arm.

3 Working in the engine compartment, unscrew the bolt securing the inner end of the track-rod to the steering gear **(see illustration)**. It will be necessary to counterhold the nut as the bolt is unscrewed. Recover the washer from under the nut.

4 Withdraw the track-rod through the wheel arch.

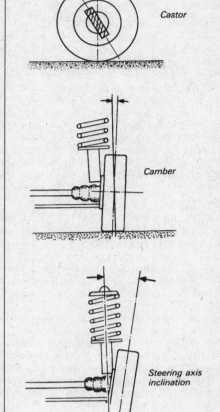

19.1 Wheel alignment and steering angles

(Labels in illustration: Castor; Camber; Steering axis inclination; FRONT; Toe-out; H23815)

Refitting

5 Refitting is a reversal of removal, bearing in mind the following points:
a) Use a new track-rod outer end balljoint nut.
b) Use a new track-rod-to-steering gear nut.
c) Tighten all fixings to the specified torques.
d) On completion, have the front wheel alignment checked at the earliest opportunity (refer to Section 19 for details) and check that the steering wheel is centralised (if necessary, the steering wheel position can be altered by removing the wheel and moving it the required number of splines on the column shaft before refitting - see Section 10).

19 Wheel alignment and steering angles - general information

General

1 A car's steering and suspension geometry is defined in four basic settings - all angles are expressed in degrees (toe settings are also expressed as a measurement); the relevant settings are camber, castor, steering axis inclination and toe-setting **(see illustration overleaf)**. With the exception of front wheel toe-setting, none of these settings are adjustable.

Front wheel toe setting - checking and adjusting

2 Due to the special measuring equipment necessary to check the wheel alignment and the skill required to use it properly, the checking and adjustment of these settings is best left to a Peugeot dealer or similar expert. Note that most tyre-fitting centres now possess sophisticated checking equipment. The following is provided as a guide, should the owner decide to carry out a DIY check.
3 The front wheel toe setting is checked by measuring the distance between the front and rear inside edges of the roadwheel rims. Proprietary toe measurement gauges are available from motor accessory shops.
4 For **accurate** checking, the vehicle **must** be at the kerb weight, ie unladen and with a full tank of fuel and the ride height must be correct (see Section 9).
5 Before starting work, check first that the

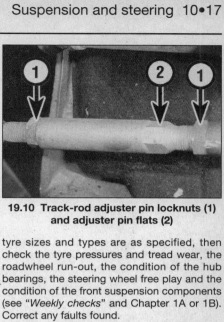

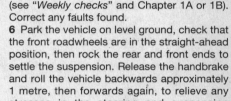

19.10 Track-rod adjuster pin locknuts (1) and adjuster pin flats (2)

tyre sizes and types are as specified, then check the tyre pressures and tread wear, the roadwheel run-out, the condition of the hub bearings, the steering wheel free play and the condition of the front suspension components (see "Weekly checks" and Chapter 1A or 1B). Correct any faults found.
6 Park the vehicle on level ground, check that the front roadwheels are in the straight-ahead position, then rock the rear and front ends to settle the suspension. Release the handbrake and roll the vehicle backwards approximately 1 metre, then forwards again, to relieve any stresses in the steering and suspension components.
7 Measure the distance between the front edges of the wheel rims and the rear edges of the rims. Subtract the rear measurement from the front measurement and check that the result is within the specified range.
8 Make sure that the steering is in the straight-ahead position when taking measurements.
9 If adjustment is found to be necessary, clean the ends of the track-rods in the areas of the adjustment pin locknuts.
10 Slacken the locknuts (one at the inner and outer end of each adjustment pin) and turn the adjustment pin on each track-rod by equal amounts in the same direction **(see illustration)**. Only turn each pin by a quarter of a turn at a time before rechecking.
11 Check that the track-rod end balljoints are centralised and not forced to the limit of movement in any direction.
12 When adjustment is correct, tighten the locknuts.
13 Check that the track-rod lengths are equal and that the steering wheel spokes are in the straight-ahead position.

10

Chapter 11
Bodywork and fittings

Contents

Degrees of difficulty

Easy, suitable for novice with little experience	**Fairly easy,** suitable for beginner with some experience	**Fairly difficult,** suitable for competent DIY mechanic	**Difficult,** suitable for experienced DIY mechanic	**Very difficult,** suitable for expert DIY or professional

Specifications

Torque wrench settings	Nm	lbf ft
Seat rail-to-floor securing bolts	25	18
Seat belt mounting bolts	20	15

1 General information

The bodyshell is made of pressed-steel sections and is available in both three- and five-door Hatchback versions. Most components are welded together, but some use is made of structural adhesives; the front wings are bolted on.

The bonnet, door and some other vulnerable panels are made of zinc-coated metal and are further protected by being coated with an anti-chip primer, prior to being sprayed.

Extensive use is made of plastic materials, mainly in the interior, but also in exterior components. The front and rear bumpers are injection-moulded from a synthetic material which is very strong and yet light. Plastic components such as wheel arch liners are fitted to the underside of the vehicle, to improve the body's resistance to corrosion.

2 Maintenance - bodywork and underframe

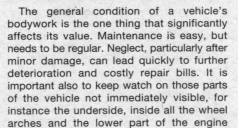

The general condition of a vehicle's bodywork is the one thing that significantly affects its value. Maintenance is easy, but needs to be regular. Neglect, particularly after minor damage, can lead quickly to further deterioration and costly repair bills. It is important also to keep watch on those parts of the vehicle not immediately visible, for instance the underside, inside all the wheel arches and the lower part of the engine compartment.

The basic maintenance routine for the bodywork is washing - preferably with a lot of water, from a hose. This will remove all the loose solids which may have stuck to the vehicle. It is important to flush these off in such a way as to prevent grit from scratching the finish. The wheel arches and underframe need washing in the same way, to remove any accumulated mud, which will retain moisture and tend to encourage rust. Paradoxically enough, the best time to clean the underframe and wheel arches is in wet weather, when the mud is thoroughly wet and soft. In very wet weather, the underframe is usually cleaned of large accumulations automatically and this is a good time for inspection.

Periodically, except on vehicles with a wax-based underbody protective coating, it is a good idea to have the whole of the underframe of the vehicle steam-cleaned, engine compartment included, so that a thorough inspection can be carried out to see what minor repairs and renovations are necessary. Steam-cleaning is available at many garages and is necessary for the removal of the accumulation of oily grime, which sometimes is allowed to become thick in certain areas. If steam-cleaning facilities are not available, there are some excellent grease solvents available which can be brush-

11

applied; the dirt can then be simply hosed off. Note that these methods should not be used on vehicles with wax-based underbody protective coating, or the coating will be removed. Such vehicles should be inspected annually, preferably just prior to Winter, when the underbody should be washed down and any damage to the wax coating repaired. Ideally, a completely fresh coat should be applied. It would also be worth considering the use of such wax-based protection for injection into door panels, sills, box sections, etc, as an additional safeguard against rust damage, where such protection is not provided by the vehicle manufacturer.

After washing paintwork, wipe off with a chamois leather to give an unspotted clear finish. A coat of clear protective wax polish will give added protection against chemical pollutants in the air. If the paintwork sheen has dulled or oxidised, use a cleaner/polisher combination to restore the brilliance of the shine. This requires a little effort, but such dulling is usually caused because regular washing has been neglected. Care needs to be taken with metallic paintwork, as special non-abrasive cleaner/polisher is required to avoid damage to the finish. Always check that the door and ventilator opening drain holes and pipes are completely clear, so that water can be drained out. Brightwork should be treated in the same way as paintwork. Windscreens and windows can be kept clear of the smeary film which often appears, by the use of proprietary glass cleaner. Never use any form of wax or other body or chromium polish on glass.

3 Maintenance - upholstery and carpets

Mats and carpets should be brushed or vacuum-cleaned regularly, to keep them free of grit. If they are badly stained, remove them from the vehicle for scrubbing or sponging and make quite sure they are dry before refitting. Seats and interior trim panels can be kept clean by wiping with a damp cloth and a proprietary upholstery cleaner. If they do become stained (which can be more apparent on light-coloured upholstery), use a little liquid detergent and a soft nail brush to scour the grime out of the grain of the material. Do not forget to keep the headlining clean in the same way as the upholstery. When using liquid cleaners inside the vehicle, do not over-wet the surfaces being cleaned. Excessive damp could get into the seams and padded interior, causing stains, offensive odours or even rot. If the inside of the vehicle gets wet accidentally, it is worthwhile taking some trouble to dry it out properly, particularly where carpets are involved. *Caution: Do not leave oil or electric heaters inside the vehicle for this purpose.*

4 Minor body damage - repair

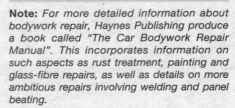

Note: *For more detailed information about bodywork repair, Haynes Publishing produce a book called "The Car Bodywork Repair Manual". This incorporates information on such aspects as rust treatment, painting and glass-fibre repairs, as well as details on more ambitious repairs involving welding and panel beating.*

Repairs of minor scratches in bodywork

If the scratch is very superficial and does not penetrate to the metal of the bodywork, repair is very simple. Lightly rub the area of the scratch with a paintwork renovator, or a very fine cutting paste, to remove loose paint from the scratch and to clear the surrounding bodywork of wax polish. Rinse the area with clean water.

Apply touch-up paint to the scratch using a fine paint brush; continue to apply fine layers of paint until the surface of the paint in the scratch is level with the surrounding paintwork. Allow the new paint at least two weeks to harden, then blend it into the surrounding paintwork by rubbing the scratch area with a paintwork renovator or a very fine cutting paste. Finally, apply wax polish.

Where the scratch has penetrated right through to the metal of the bodywork, causing the metal to rust, a different repair technique is required. Remove any loose rust from the bottom of the scratch with a penknife, then apply rust-inhibiting paint to prevent the formation of rust in the future. Using a rubber or nylon applicator, fill the scratch with bodystopper paste. If required, this paste can be mixed with cellulose thinners to provide a very thin paste which is ideal for filling narrow scratches. Before the stopper-paste in the scratch hardens, wrap a piece of smooth cotton rag around the top of a finger. Dip the finger in cellulose thinners and quickly sweep it across the surface of the stopper-paste in the scratch; this will ensure that the surface of the stopper-paste is slightly hollowed. The scratch can now be painted over as described earlier in this Section.

Repairs of dents in bodywork

When deep denting of the vehicle's bodywork has taken place, the first task is to pull the dent out, until the affected bodywork almost attains its original shape. There is little point in trying to restore the original shape completely, as the metal in the damaged area will have stretched on impact and cannot be reshaped fully to its original contour. It is better to bring the level of the dent up to a point which is about 3 mm below the level of the surrounding bodywork. In cases where the dent is very shallow anyway, it is not worth trying to pull it out at all. If the underside of the dent is accessible, it can be hammered out gently from behind, using a mallet with a wooden or plastic head. Whilst doing this, hold a suitable block of wood firmly against the outside of the panel, to absorb the impact from the hammer blows and thus prevent a large area of the bodywork from being "belled-out".

Should the dent be in a section of the bodywork which has a double skin, or some other factor making it inaccessible from behind, a different technique is called for. Drill several small holes through the metal inside the area - particularly in the deeper section. Then screw long self-tapping screws into the holes, just sufficiently for them to gain a good purchase in the metal. Now the dent can be pulled out by pulling on the protruding heads of the screws with a pair of pliers.

The next stage of the repair is the removal of the paint from the damaged area and from an inch or so of the surrounding "sound" bodywork. This is accomplished most easily by using a wire brush or abrasive pad on a power drill, although it can be done just as effectively by hand, using sheets of abrasive paper. To complete the preparation for filling, score the surface of the bare metal with a screwdriver or the tang of a file, or alternatively, drill small holes in the affected area. This will provide a really good "key" for the filler paste.

To complete the repair, see the Section on filling and respraying.

Repairs of rust holes or gashes in bodywork

Remove all paint from the affected area and from an inch or so of the surrounding "sound" bodywork, using an abrasive pad or a wire brush on a power drill. If these are not available, a few sheets of abrasive paper will do the job most effectively. With the paint removed, you will be able to judge the severity of the corrosion and therefore decide whether to renew the whole panel (if this is possible) or to repair the affected area. New body panels are not as expensive as most people think and it is often quicker and more satisfactory to fit a new panel than to attempt to repair large areas of corrosion.

Remove all fittings from the affected area, except those which will act as a guide to the original shape of the damaged bodywork (eg headlight shells etc). Then, using tin snips or a hacksaw blade, remove all loose metal and any other metal badly affected by corrosion. Hammer the edges of the hole inwards, in order to create a slight depression for the filler paste.

Wire-brush the affected area to remove the powdery rust from the surface of the remaining metal. Paint the affected area with rust-inhibiting paint, if the back of the rusted area is accessible, treat this also.

Before filling can take place, it will be necessary to block the hole in some way. This can be achieved by the use of aluminium or plastic mesh, or aluminium tape.

Aluminium or plastic mesh, or glass-fibre matting, is probably the best material to use for a large hole. Cut a piece to the approximate size and shape of the hole to be filled, then position it in the hole so that its edges are below the level of the surrounding bodywork. It can be retained in position by several blobs of filler paste around its periphery.

Aluminium tape should be used for small or very narrow holes. Pull a piece off the roll, trim it to the approximate size and shape required, then pull off the backing paper (if used) and stick the tape over the hole; it can be overlapped if the thickness of one piece is insufficient. Burnish down the edges of the tape with the handle of a screwdriver or similar, to ensure that the tape is securely attached to the metal underneath.

Bodywork repairs - filling and respraying

Before using this Section, see the Sections on dent, deep scratch, rust holes and gash repairs.

Many types of bodyfiller are available, but generally speaking, those proprietary kits which contain a tin of filler paste and a tube of resin hardener are best for this type of repair. A wide, flexible plastic or nylon applicator will be found invaluable for imparting a smooth and well-contoured finish to the surface of the filler.

Mix up a little filler on a clean piece of card or board - measure the hardener carefully (follow the maker's instructions on the pack), otherwise the filler will set too rapidly or too slowly. Using the applicator, apply the filler paste to the prepared area; draw the applicator across the surface of the filler to achieve the correct contour and to level the surface. As soon as a contour that approximates to the correct one is achieved, stop working the paste - if you carry on too long, the paste will become sticky and begin to "pick-up" on the applicator. Continue to add thin layers of filler paste at 20-minute intervals, until the level of the filler is just proud of the surrounding bodywork.

Once the filler has hardened, the excess can be removed using a metal plane or file. From then on, progressively-finer grades of abrasive paper should be used, starting with a 40-grade production paper and finishing with a 400-grade wet-and-dry paper. Always wrap the abrasive paper around a flat rubber, cork, or wooden block - otherwise the surface of the filler will not be completely flat. During the smoothing of the filler surface, the wet-and-dry paper should be periodically rinsed in water. This will ensure that a very smooth finish is imparted to the filler at the final stage.

At this stage, the "dent" should be surrounded by a ring of bare metal, which in turn should be encircled by the finely "feathered" edge of the good paintwork. Rinse the repair area with clean water, until all of the dust produced by the rubbing-down operation has gone.

Spray the whole area with a light coat of primer - this will show up any imperfections in the surface of the filler. Repair these imperfections with fresh filler paste or bodystopper and once more smooth the surface with abrasive paper. Repeat this spray-and-repair procedure until you are satisfied that the surface of the filler and the feathered edge of the paintwork, are perfect. Clean the repair area with clean water and allow to dry fully.

 HAYNES HiNT *If bodystopper is used, it can be mixed with cellulose thinners to form a really thin paste which is ideal for filling small holes.*

The repair area is now ready for final spraying. Paint spraying must be carried out in a warm, dry, windless and dust-free atmosphere. This condition can be created artificially if you have access to a large indoor working area, but if you are forced to work in the open, you will have to pick your day very carefully. If you are working indoors, dousing the floor in the work area with water will help to settle the dust which would otherwise be in the atmosphere. If the repair area is confined to one body panel, mask off the surrounding panels; this will help to minimise the effects of a slight mis-match in paint colours. Bodywork fittings (eg chrome strips, door handles etc) will also need to be masked off. Use genuine masking tape and several thicknesses of newspaper, for the masking operations.

Before commencing to spray, agitate the aerosol can thoroughly, then spray a test area (an old tin, or similar) until the technique is mastered. Cover the repair area with a thick coat of primer; the thickness should be built up using several thin layers of paint, rather than one thick one. Using 400-grade wet-and-dry paper, rub down the surface of the primer until it is really smooth. While doing this, the work area should be thoroughly doused with water and the wet-and-dry paper periodically rinsed in water. Allow to dry before spraying on more paint.

Spray on the top coat, again building up the thickness by using several thin layers of paint. Start spraying at one edge of the repair area and then, using a side-to-side motion, work until the whole repair area and about 2 inches of the surrounding original paintwork is covered. Remove all masking material 10 to 15 minutes after spraying on the final coat of paint.

Allow the new paint at least two weeks to harden, then, using a paintwork renovator, or a very fine cutting paste, blend the edges of the paint into the existing paintwork. Finally, apply wax polish.

Plastic components

With the use of more and more plastic body components by the vehicle manufacturers (eg bumpers, spoilers and in some cases major body panels), rectification of more serious damage to such items has become a matter of either entrusting repair work to a specialist in this field, or renewing complete components. Repair of such damage by the DIY owner is not really feasible, owing to the cost of the equipment and materials required for effecting such repairs. The basic technique involves making a groove along the line of the crack in the plastic, using a rotary burr in a power drill. The damaged part is then welded back together, using a hot-air gun to heat up and fuse a plastic filler rod into the groove. Any excess plastic is then removed and the area rubbed down to a smooth finish. It is important that a filler rod of the correct plastic is used, as body components can be made of a variety of different types (eg polycarbonate, ABS, polypropylene).

Damage of a less serious nature (abrasions, minor cracks etc) can be repaired by the DIY owner using a two-part epoxy filler repair material. Once mixed in equal proportions, this is used in similar fashion to the bodywork filler used on metal panels. The filler is usually cured in twenty to thirty minutes, ready for sanding and painting.

If the owner is renewing a complete component himself, or if he has repaired it with epoxy filler, he will be left with the problem of finding a suitable paint for finishing which is compatible with the type of plastic used. At one time, the use of a universal paint was not possible, owing to the complex range of plastics encountered in body component applications. Standard paints, generally speaking, will not bond to plastic or rubber satisfactorily. However, it is now possible to obtain a plastic body parts finishing kit which consists of a pre-primer treatment, a primer and coloured top coat. Full instructions are normally supplied with a kit, but basically, the method of use is to first apply the pre-primer to the component concerned and allow it to dry for up to 30 minutes. Then the primer is applied and left to dry for about an hour before finally applying the special-coloured top coat. The result is a correctly-coloured component, where the paint will flex with the plastic or rubber, a property that standard paint does not normally possess.

5 Major body damage - repair

Where serious damage has occurred, or large areas need renewal due to neglect, it means that complete new panels will need welding-in and this is best left to professionals. If the damage is due to impact, it will also be necessary to check completely the alignment of the bodyshell and this can only be carried out accurately by a Peugeot dealer, using special jigs. If the body is left misaligned, it is primarily dangerous, as the car will not handle properly; secondly, uneven stresses will be imposed on the steering, suspension and possibly transmission, causing abnormal wear, or complete failure, particularly to such items as the tyres.

11

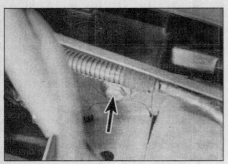

6.4 Front bumper securing bolt (arrowed) - viewed with headlight removed

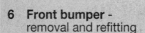

6 Front bumper -
removal and refitting

Removal

Pre-July 1996 models

1 Disconnect the battery negative terminal (refer to *"Disconnecting the battery"* in the Reference Section of this manual).
2 Remove both headlights as described in Chapter 12.
3 Working in the engine compartment, unscrew the filler neck from the washer fluid reservoir.
4 Reach down through the headlight apertures and unscrew the two front bumper securing bolts **(see illustration)**.
5 Chock the rear wheels then jack up the

6.6 Removing a wheel arch liner-to-front bumper securing screw

front of the vehicle and support it on axle stands (see *"Jacking and Vehicle Support"*). Remove the front roadwheels.
6 Remove the screws securing the wheel arch liners to the bumper **(see illustration)**, then release the securing clips (which are a push-fit) and remove the front wheel arch liners.
7 Unscrew the three lower bumper securing screws from the bottom edge of the bumper **(see illustration)**.
8 Working under the wheel arch, unscrew the left-hand bumper securing bolt. On models with headlight washers, if necessary, release the fluid reservoir securing strap and move the reservoir for access to the bolt - take care not to strain the wiring or the fluid hoses.
9 Working under the right-hand wheel arch, release the securing strap, then move the washer fluid reservoir to one side (take care not to strain the wiring or the fluid hoses). This

6.7 Front bumper lower securing screw

will provide access to the two right-hand bumper securing bolts (note that the outer bolt can be reached with the reservoir in place). Unscrew the bolts **(see illustrations)**.
10 Lift the bumper from the front of the vehicle **(see illustration)**. Where applicable, disconnect the wiring plugs from the front fog/driving lights; note the routing of the wiring to aid refitting. Similarly, where applicable, disconnect the headlight washer fluid hose.

July 1996 models onward

11 For improved access, apply the handbrake, then jack up the front of the vehicle and support securely on axle stands (see *"Jacking and Vehicle Support"*).
12 Undo the bolts securing the bumper lower mountings to the front panel **(see illustration)**.
13 Working at each side of the bumper, remove the screws, clips and where applicable drill out the rivets securing the splash shields and/or the wheelarch liners to the sides of the bumper.
14 Remove the washer fluid reservoir for access to the bumper right-hand attachments.
15 On models with foglights, disconnect the battery negative terminal (refer to *"Disconnecting the battery"* in the Reference Section of this manual), then disconnect the foglight wiring connectors.
16 Again working under the bumper, unscrew the bolts securing the bumper to the front body panel **(see illustration)**. Reach up behind the bumper for access to the bolts.

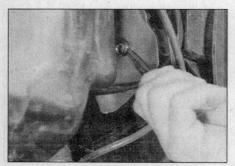

6.9a Unscrewing the outer . . .

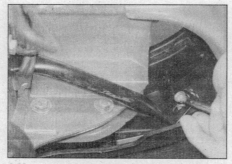

6.9b . . . and inner right-hand front bumper securing bolts

6.10 Lifting the front bumper from the vehicle

6.12 Left-hand front bumper lower mounting (arrowed) - later models

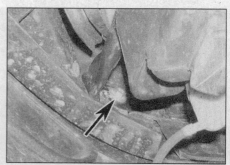

6.16 Right-hand front bumper-to-body panel bolt (arrowed) - later models

6.17 Withdraw the bumper forwards to release the side locating plates - later models

17 Carefully withdraw the bumper forwards to release the side locating plates then remove the bumper from the vehicle **(see illustration)**.

Refitting

18 Refitting is a reversal of removal. Ensure that the washer fluid reservoir securing strap(s) is/are correctly refitted and (where applicable) make sure that the fog/driving light wiring is correctly routed.

---

7 Rear bumper - removal and refitting

Removal

1 Disconnect the battery negative terminal

7.3 Prising the plastic cover from the left-hand rear light unit

(refer to *"Disconnecting the battery"* in the Reference Section of this manual).
2 Open the tailgate.
3 Prise the plastic cover from the left-hand rear light unit **(see illustration)**.
4 Remove the securing screw and unclip the air extraction grille from the side of the luggage compartment **(see illustration)**.
5 Reach up through the aperture behind the air extraction grille and separate the two halves of the rear number plate light wiring connector.
6 Working under the rear wheel arches, unscrew the side bumper securing bolts (one under each wheel arch) **(see illustration)**.
7 Working under the bumper, at each side, prise out the clips securing the bottom of the bumper to the wheel arch liners (one clip on each side) **(see illustration)**.
8 Working at the rear of the luggage compartment, prise out the rubber grommets

7.4 Removing the air extraction grille securing screw

to reveal the two bumper securing bolts and the central nut **(see illustration)**. Unscrew the bolts and the nut.
9 Again working in the luggage compartment, unscrew the two lower bumper securing bolts **(see illustration)**.
10 Carefully lift the bumper from the body and pull the number plate wiring grommet from the aperture in the body **(see illustrations)**. Feed the wiring through the body aperture and withdraw the bumper from the vehicle.

Refitting

11 Refitting is a reversal of removal, but make sure that the number plate wiring is correctly routed through the body and that the wiring grommet is securely located in the body aperture. Also make sure that the clips securing the bumper to the wheel arch liners are correctly refitted.

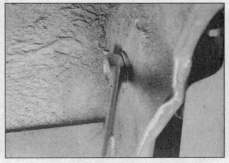

7.6 Unscrewing a rear bumper side securing bolt

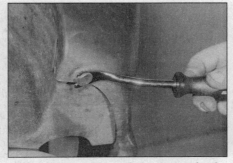

7.7 Prising out a rear bumper-to-wheel arch liner clip

7.8 Rear bumper central securing nut (arrowed)

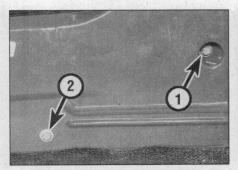

7.9 Rear bumper upper (1) and lower (2) securing bolts (one side shown)

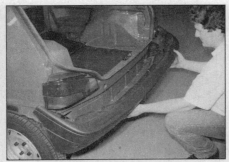

7.10a Lift the bumper from the body . . .

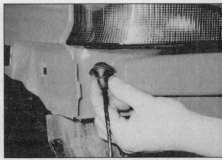

7.10b . . . and pull the number plate wiring grommet from the body

11

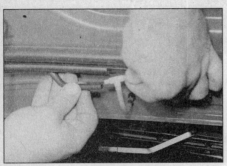

8.2 Disconnecting the windscreen washer supply pipe

8 Bonnet and support struts - removal, refitting and adjustment

Bonnet

Removal

1 Open the bonnet and have an assistant support it. Using a pencil or felt tip pen, mark the outline of each bonnet hinge relative to the bonnet, to use as a guide on refitting. On later models, release the spring clips using a screwdriver and pull the bonnet support struts from the balljoints on the bonnet.
2 Disconnect the windscreen washer supply pipe from its non-return valve on the right-hand side **(see illustration)**. Withdraw the hose from the bonnet, noting its routing.
3 Unscrew the bonnet retaining bolts and recover the washers. With the help of an assistant, carefully lift the bonnet clear **(see illustration)**. Store the bonnet out of the way in a safe place.
4 Inspect the bonnet hinges for signs of wear and free play at the pivots and if necessary, renew them. Each hinge is secured to the body by two bolts.

Refitting

5 With the aid of an assistant, offer up the bonnet and loosely fit the retaining bolts and washers. Align the hinges with the marks made on removal, then tighten the retaining bolts securely. Reconnect the windscreen washer supply pipe, ensuring that it is routed

as noted before removal. On later models, reconnect the support struts and secure with the spring clips.
6 Adjust the alignment of the bonnet as follows.

Adjustment

7 Close the bonnet and check for alignment with the adjacent panels. If necessary, slacken the hinge bolts and re-align the bonnet to suit. Once the bonnet is correctly aligned, tighten the hinge bolts securely.
8 If the lock striker has been removed from the bonnet, ensure that the washer is in place between the bonnet and the striker when refitting.
9 Once the bonnet is correctly aligned, check that the bonnet fastens and releases in a satisfactory manner. If adjustment is necessary, slacken the bonnet lock retaining bolts and adjust the position of the lock to suit. Once the lock is operating correctly, securely tighten its retaining bolts.

Support struts

10 On later models fitted with bonnet support struts, proceed as described for the tailgate support struts on Hatchback models in Section 15.

9 Bonnet release cable - removal and refitting

Removal

1 Working in the engine compartment, unhook the end of the bonnet release cable from the lock lever. If necessary, unbolt the lock and move it to one side to facilitate this.
2 Where applicable, unscrew the cable securing clip from the front body panel **(see illustration)**.
3 Working inside the vehicle, remove the securing bolt and withdraw the bonnet release lever from under the facia **(see illustration)**.
4 Note the routing of the cable and release it from any clips in the engine compartment, then feed the cable through the bulkhead grommet into the vehicle interior. Note that the cable is integral with the release lever and cannot be renewed separately.

8.3 Removing the bonnet

Refitting

5 Refitting is a reversal of removal, but ensure that the bulkhead grommet is securely located and make sure that the cable is routed as noted before removal.

10 Bonnet lock - removal and refitting

Removal

1 Open the bonnet.
2 Unscrew the two securing bolts and remove the lock assembly from the body panel **(see illustration)**.
3 Unhook the end of the bonnet release cable from the lock lever and withdraw the assembly from the vehicle.

Refitting

4 Refitting is a reversal of removal. If necessary, adjust the position of the striker on the bonnet, as described in Section 8.

11 Door - removal, refitting and adjustment

Front door

Removal

1 Open the door and, where applicable, disconnect the battery negative terminal (refer

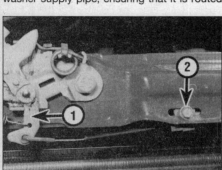

9.2 Bonnet release cable end fitting (1) and cable securing clip (2)

9.3 Withdrawing the bonnet release lever

10.2 Bonnet lock securing bolts (arrowed)

11.1 Disconnect the door wiring plug

11.2 Removing a door check strap securing bolt

11.4a Using a suitable Torx bit or key . . .

to *"Disconnecting the battery"* in the Reference Section of this manual), before disconnecting the door wiring plug. Twist the locking collar to release the wiring plug **(see illustration)**.

2 Unscrew the two bolts securing the door check strap to the body pillar **(see illustration)**.

3 Support the door either with the aid of an assistant, or using a trolley jack and a block of wood.

4 Using a suitable Torx key or bit, unscrew the door lower hinge pin, then the upper hinge pin **(see illustrations)**. Lift the door from the vehicle.

Refitting

5 Refitting is a reversal of removal, but lightly grease the hinge pins before refitting.

Adjustment

6 No adjustment of the door is possible.

Rear door

7 The procedure is as described previously for the front door, but note that on certain models, it will be necessary to remove the door inner trim panel (see Section 12) in order to disconnect the wiring from the components inside the door (no door wiring connector is used). Note the routing of the wiring, release it from any clips inside the door, then feed the wiring harness through the grommet in the front edge of the door.

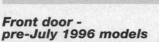

12 Door inner trim panels - removal and refitting

Front door - pre-July 1996 models

Note: *If the plastic sealing sheet is removed*

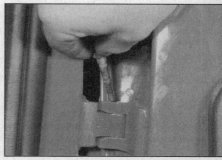

11.4b . . . unscrew the door hinge pins

from the inside of the door, a new sealing sheet will be required on refitting.

Removal

1 Where applicable, pull the window regulator handle from its spindle **(see illustration)**. Recover the trim disc.

2 Pull off the interior handle trim panel **(see illustration)**.

3 Remove the two securing screws and withdraw the armrest **(see illustration)**. Note the bushes, which may be loose in the armrest once the screws have been removed.

4 Where applicable, remove the securing screws and remove the door pocket from the lower edge of the door.

5 Release the securing clips and pull the trim panel from the door **(see illustration)**.

6 If desired (if the door internal components are to be worked on), pull the plastic sealing sheet from the door **(see illustration)**. Note

12.1 Pull off the window regulator handle . . .

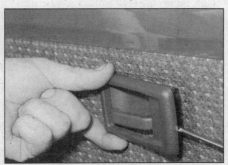

12.2 . . . then pull off the interior handle trim panel . . .

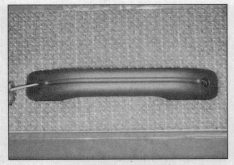

12.3 . . . remove the two securing screws and withdraw the armrest . . .

12.5 . . . then pull the trim panel from the door

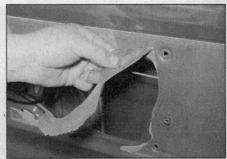

12.6 Pulling the plastic sealing sheet from the door

11

12.7 Fitting a new front door plastic sealing sheet

that the sheet will probably be destroyed during removal. Carefully scrape the remains of the sealing sheet from the inside of the door.

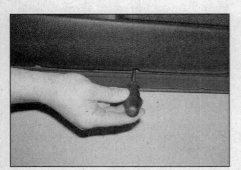

12.10a Undo the screws along the door pocket lower edge . . .

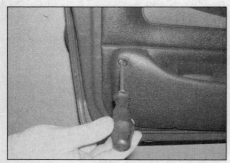

12.10b . . . and at the sides, and remove the pocket

12.13a Undo the remaining screws, located in the centre of the panel . . .

12.8 On later models pull off the interior handle trim panel . . .

 Use a hair dryer to heat the edge of the sealing sheet to ease removal.

Refitting

7 Refitting is a reversal of removal. Where applicable, use a new plastic sealing sheet and ensure that the bushes are in position in the armrest **(see illustration)**. Note that it may be necessary to cut suitable holes in the sealing sheet for the trim panel securing clips, etc.

Front door – July 1996 models onward

Note: *If the plastic sealing sheet is removed from the inside of the door, a new sealing sheet will be required on refitting.*

Removal

8 Pull off the interior handle trim panel **(see illustration)**.

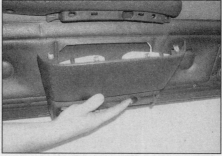

12.11 Unclip and remove the padded trim panel

12.13b . . . and around the speaker grille . . .

12.9 . . . then remove the regulator handle and trim disc

9 Where applicable, pull the window regulator handle from its spindle **(see illustration)**. Recover the trim disc.
10 Undo the screws along the lower edge and at the sides and remove the door pocket from the base of the door **(see illustrations)**.
11 Unclip and remove the padded trim from below the armrest **(see illustration)**.
12 Undo the screws and withdraw the armrest **(see illustration)**.
13 Undo the remaining trim panel screws located in the centre of the panel and around the speaker grille. Release the securing clips and pull the trim panel from the door **(see illustrations)**.
14 If desired (if the door internal components are to be worked on), pull the plastic sealing sheet from the door. Note that the sheet will probably be destroyed during removal. Carefully scrape the remains of the sealing sheet from the inside of the door.

12.12 Undo the screws and remove the armrest

12.13c . . . then release the clips and lift off the panel

Refitting

15 Refitting is a reversal of removal. Where applicable, use a new plastic sealing sheet, noting that it may be necessary to cut suitable holes in the sealing sheet for the trim panel securing clips, etc.

Rear door - all models

16 The procedure is as described previously for the front door trim panel. Where applicable, the ashtray must be pulled from the door before the door pocket can be removed **(see illustrations)**.

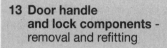

13 Door handle and lock components - removal and refitting

Interior door handle

Removal

1 Remove the door inner trim panel, as described in Section 12.
2 Slide the handle assembly towards the rear of the door, then pull the assembly from the door aperture and disconnect the link rod (if necessary, release the link rod from the clips on the door) **(see illustration)**.

Refitting

3 Refitting is a reversal of removal, but ensure that the link rod is correctly reconnected and refit the inner trim panel with reference to Section 12.

13.2 Removing a front door interior handle

12.16a Remove the securing screws . . .

12.16c . . . before removing the rear door inner trim panel . . .

Exterior door handle - 3-door models

Removal

4 Open the door.
5 Remove the door inner trim panel and the plastic sealing sheet as described in Section 12.
6 Reach in through the aperture in the door and unclip the plastic shield from the rear of the door lock **(see illustration)**.
7 Using a large flat-bladed screwdriver, turn the handle to release it from the door **(see illustration)**.
8 Working through the door aperture, detach the link rod from the rear of the handle and withdraw the handle assembly. Recover the trim plate from the outer door edge **(see illustration)**.

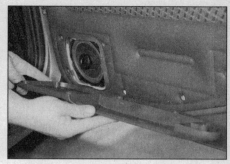

12.16b . . . and withdraw the door pocket . . .

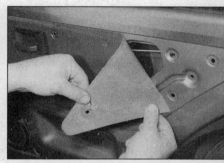

12.16d . . . and the plastic sealing sheet

Refitting

9 Refitting is a reversal of removal, but use a new plastic sealing sheet and refit the inner trim panel with reference to Section 12.

Exterior door handle - 5-door models

Note: *New rivets will be required when refitting the handle.*

Removal

10 Working outside the door, stick masking tape around the area surrounding the handle, to protect the paintwork.
11 Lift the handle for access to the securing rivets **(see illustration)**. Have an assistant hold the handle in the raised position, or wedge the handle in position.

13.6 Unclip the plastic shield from the door lock

13.7 Release the handle . . .

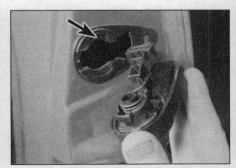

13.8 . . . and release it from the door. Note trim plate (arrowed)

11

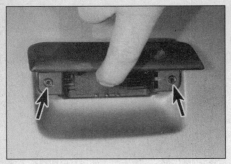

13.11 Door exterior handle securing rivets (arrowed) - 5-door model

12 Using a 4.0 mm drill bit, drill out the two securing rivets, then pull the handle assembly from the door and disconnect the link rods.

Refitting

13 Refitting is a reversal of removal, but make sure that the link rods are correctly reconnected to the handle and secure the assembly using new rivets.

Front door lock cylinder

14 The lock cylinder can be removed as follows, without the need to remove the door inner trim panel:

  a) Make up a suitable tool as shown in the accompanying illustration, using a medium-size self-tapping screw brazed to a length of rod, bent at a right-angle.

  b) Open the door and prise the cover plate from the rear edge of the door **(see illustration)**.

  c) Insert the tool through the aperture in the

13.17a Pull off the securing clip . . .

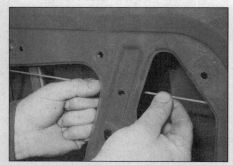

13.21 Unclip the link rod from the door panel

13.14a Prise the cover plate from the edge of the door . . .

  edge of the door **(see illustration)** and screw the self-tapping screw into the lock securing clip to the end of the thread on the screw.

  d) Push the tool to release the securing clip and withdraw the lock cylinder from outside the door. Leave the tool engaged with the clip.

  e) Refit the lock and use the tool to pull the securing clip into position.

  f) Ensure that the clip is securely engaged with the lock cylinder, then unscrew the tool from the clip and refit the cover plate.

Removal

15 Remove the door inner trim panel and the plastic sealing sheet, as described in Section 12.
16 Reach in through the aperture in the door and unclip the plastic shield from the rear of the door lock.
17 Working inside the door, pull the securing clip from the rear of the lock cylinder, then

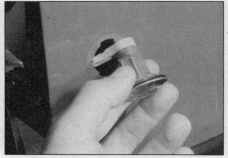

13.17b . . . and remove the lock cylinder

13.22 Unclip the plastic shield from the rear of the lock

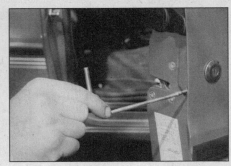

13.14b . . . and screw the tool into the lock securing clip

remove the lock cylinder from the outside of the door **(see illustrations)**.

Refitting

18 Refitting is a reversal of removal, but ensure that the lock cylinder securing clip is securely refitted and use a new plastic sealing sheet. Refit the door inner trim panel with reference to Section 12

Front door lock

Removal

19 Remove the door inner trim panel and the plastic sealing sheet, as described in Section 12.
20 Remove the interior handle by pulling it towards the front of the door to release it and unclip the link rod from the handle.
21 Unclip the link rod from the door panel **(see illustration)**.
22 Reach in through the door aperture behind the lock and unclip the plastic shield from the rear of the lock **(see illustration)**. Where applicable, also disconnect the wiring from the central locking motor. Disconnect the battery negative lead first; refer to *"Disconnecting the battery"* in the Reference Section of this manual.
23 Remove the three securing screws from the rear edge of the door, then withdraw the lock assembly, complete with the rods, through the aperture in the inner door skin **(see illustrations)**. As the lock is withdrawn, feed the lock button operating rod down through the hole in the top of the door. Note the routing of the lock rods to ensure correct refitting. Where applicable, disconnect the wiring plug from the lock assembly as it is withdrawn.

13.23a Remove the securing screws . . .

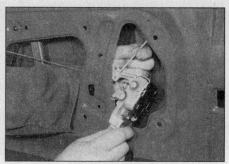

13.23b ... and withdraw the front door lock assembly

13.27 Removing the rear door interior handle

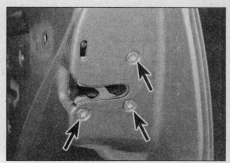

13.29 Rear door lock securing screws (arrowed)

Refitting

24 Refitting is a reversal of removal, bearing in mind the following points:
a) *Ensure that the lock rods are correctly reconnected and routed. Note that the link rod must pass in front of the window regulator operating cable.*
b) *Check the operation of the lock before fitting the plastic sealing sheet.*
c) *Use a new plastic sealing sheet and refit the door inner trim panel with reference to Section 12.*

Rear door lock

Removal

25 Remove the door inner trim panel and the plastic sealing sheet, as described in Section 12.
26 Remove the door exterior handle as described previously in this Section.
27 Slide the door interior handle assembly towards the rear of the door, then pull the

14.3 Removing the weatherstrip from the lower edge of the front door window aperture ...

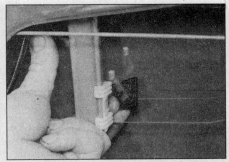

14.6 Remove the clip securing the glass panel to the regulator mechanism

assembly from the door aperture and disconnect the link rod **(see illustration)**. Release the link rod from the clips on the door.
28 Reach in through the door aperture, then release the securing clip and disconnect the lock button operating rod from the rear of the lock. Where applicable, also disconnect the wiring plug from the central locking motor. Disconnect the battery negative lead first; refer to *"Disconnecting the battery"* in the Reference Section of this manual.
29 Unscrew the three lock securing screws **(see illustration)**, then withdraw the lock, complete with the operating rod, through the aperture.

Refitting

30 Refitting is a reversal of removal, bearing in mind the following points:
a) *Ensure that the lock rods are correctly reconnected and routed.*
b) *Refit the door exterior handle, using new rivets.*

14.4 ... and from the remainder of the window aperture

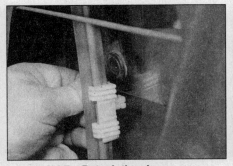

14.7a Detach the glass ...

c) *Check the operation of the lock before fitting the plastic sealing sheet.*
d) *Use a new plastic sealing sheet and refit the door inner trim panel with reference to Section 12.*

14 Door window glass and regulator - removal and refitting

Front door window glass

Removal

1 Remove the door inner trim panel and the plastic sealing sheet, as described in Section 12.
2 If not already done, remove the securing screws and remove the door pocket (where applicable, disconnect the speaker wiring).
3 Prise off the mirror trim panel, then carefully prise the weatherstrip from the inside lower edge of the window aperture **(see illustration)**.
4 Similarly, prise the weatherstrip from the remainder of the window aperture **(see illustration)**.
5 Temporarily refit the window regulator handle, or reconnect the switch (and reconnect the battery), as applicable and lower the window to its mid-position.
6 Working at the back of the glass, twist and remove the clip securing the glass panel to the regulator mechanism **(see illustration)**.
7 Support the glass panel, then detach it from the regulator mechanism. Lift the panel and manipulate it out through the window aperture, taking care not to scratch the paint on the door edge **(see illustrations)**.

14.7b ... and lift it through the window aperture

11

14.10 Drill out the rivets securing the front door window regulator mechanism

14.11 Remove the two window lift rail securing nuts (arrowed)

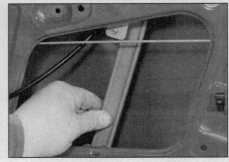

14.13 Removing the window regulator mechanism

Refitting

8 Refitting is a reversal of removal, bearing in mind the following points:
  a) *To ease refitting, coat the weatherstrips with soapy water (washing-up liquid is ideal).*
  b) *Before fitting the plastic sealing sheet, check the operation of the window regulator mechanism.*
  c) *Use a new plastic sealing sheet.*
  d) *Refit the door inner trim panel with reference to Section 12.*

Front door regulator

Note: *New rivets will be required when refitting the regulator mechanism.*

Removal

9 Remove the window glass as described previously.

14.18a Pull the outer . . .

10 Using a 6.0 mm drill, drill out the rivets securing the regulator mechanism to the door **(see illustration)**.
11 Where applicable, remove the two nuts securing the window lift rail **(see illustration)**.
12 Where applicable, disconnect the wiring plug(s) from the window lift motor.
13 Carefully tilt the assembly and lift it out through the aperture in the door **(see illustration)**.

Refitting

14 Refitting is a reversal of removal, but refit the regulator mechanism using new rivets and refit the window glass as described previously in this Section.

Rear door sliding window glass

Removal

15 Fully lower the sliding window glass.
16 Remove the door inner trim panel and the plastic sealing sheet, as described in Section 12.
17 Where applicable, pull the ashtray from the door panel, then remove the securing screws and withdraw the door pocket.
18 Carefully pull the weatherstrips from the lower edge of the sliding window aperture **(see illustrations)**.
19 Unclip the weatherstrip from the rear glass channel **(see illustration)**.
20 Temporarily refit the window regulator handle and raise the sliding glass to its mid-position.
21 Working at the back of the glass, twist

and remove the clip securing the glass panel to the regulator mechanism **(see illustration)**.
22 Support the glass panel, then detach it from the regulator mechanism and lower the panel to the bottom of the door.
23 Remove the upper and lower screws securing the rear glass channel to the door and withdraw the channel.
24 Lift the glass panel and manipulate it out through the window aperture, taking care not to scratch the paint on the door edge.

Refitting

25 Refitting is a reversal of removal, bearing in mind the following points:
  a) *To ease refitting, coat the weatherstrips with soapy water (washing-up liquid is ideal).*
  b) *Before fitting the plastic sealing sheet, check the operation of the window regulator mechanism.*
  c) *Use a new plastic sealing sheet.*
  d) *Refit the door inner trim panel with reference to Section 12.*

Rear door fixed window glass

Removal

26 Proceed as described in paragraphs 15 to 23 inclusive.
27 Carefully pull the fixed glass panel towards the front of the door and withdraw it.

Refitting

28 Refer to paragraph 25.

14.18b . . . and inner weatherstrips from the door

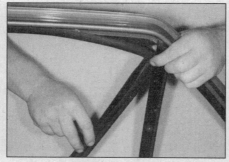

14.19 Unclip the weatherstrip from the rear glass channel

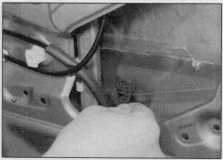

14.21 Remove the clip securing the glass panel to the regulator mechanism

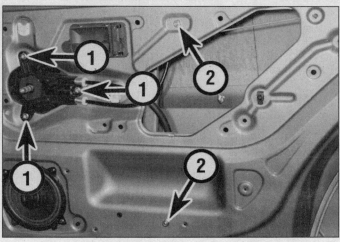

14.29 Rear door window regulator securing rivets (1) and nuts (2)

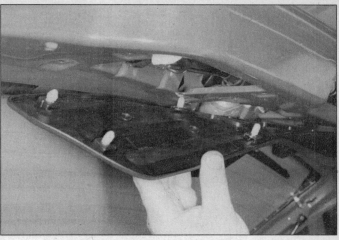

15.2 Removing the tailgate trim panel

Rear door regulator

29 The procedure is as described previously in this Section for the front door regulator. Note that there is no need to remove the fixed window glass **(see illustration)**.

---

15 Tailgate and support struts - removal, refitting and adjustment

Tailgate

Removal

1 Disconnect the battery negative terminal (refer to *"Disconnecting the battery"* in the Reference Section of this manual).
2 Remove the two screws securing the tailgate trim panel, then release the securing clips and withdraw the panel from the tailgate **(see illustration)**.
3 Working through the aperture in the left-hand side of the tailgate, disconnect the heated rear window wiring plug **(see illustration)**.
4 Where applicable, working through the aperture in the tailgate, disconnect the tailgate wiper motor and the central locking motor wiring plugs.
5 Pull the wiring grommets from the front corners of the tailgate **(see illustration)**.
6 If the original tailgate is to be refitted, tie string to the ends of all the relevant wiring, then feed the wiring through the top of the tailgate. Untie the string, leaving it in position in the tailgate to assist refitting.
7 Where applicable, prise the washer nozzle from the tailgate and disconnect the fluid hose from the nozzle. Tie a length of string to the hose, then pull the hose through the tailgate. Leave the string in position to aid refitting, as for the wiring.
8 Support the tailgate, then prise out the support strut spring clips and pull the struts from the balljoints on the tailgate.

9 Pull the weatherstrip from the upper edge of the tailgate aperture **(see illustration)** and carefully pull down the headlining to expose the tailgate hinge securing nuts.
10 Unscrew the hinge securing nuts **(see illustration)** and carefully lift the tailgate from the vehicle.

Refitting

11 If a new tailgate is to be fitted, transfer all serviceable components (rubber buffers, lock mechanism, etc) to it.
12 Refitting is a reversal of removal, bearing in mind the following points:
 a) *If the original tailgate is being refitted,*

draw the wiring and washer fluid hose (where applicable) through the tailgate using the string.
 b) *If necessary, adjust the rubber buffers to obtain a good fit when the tailgate is shut.*
 c) *If necessary, adjust the operation of the lock striker on the body, to achieve satisfactory lock operation.*

Adjustment

13 It is not possible to adjust the position of the tailgate on the hinges. If necessary, the rubber buffers at the lower corners of the tailgate can be adjusted to obtain a good fit when the tailgate is shut **(see illustration)**.

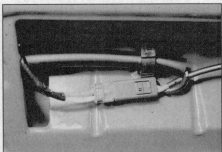
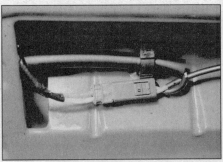

15.3 Heated rear window wiring plug

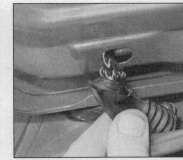

15.5 Pulling a wiring grommet from the front of the tailgate

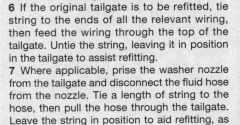

15.9 Pulling the weatherstrip from the tailgate aperture . . .

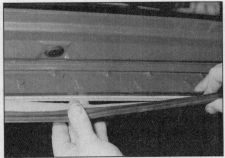
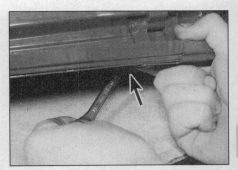

15.10 . . . for access to the tailgate hinge securing nuts

11

15.13 Adjust the rubber buffers to obtain a good fit when the tailgate is shut

The tailgate lock operation can be adjusted as described in Section 16.

Support struts

Removal

14 Support the tailgate in the open position, with the help of an assistant, or using a stout piece of wood.
15 Using a suitable flat-bladed screwdriver, release the spring clip and pull the support strut from its balljoint on the tailgate **(see illustration)**.
16 Similarly, release the strut from the balljoint on the body and withdraw the strut from the vehicle.

Refitting

17 Refitting is a reversal of removal, but ensure that the spring clips are correctly engaged.

16.6 Removing the tailgate lock cylinder assembly securing screw

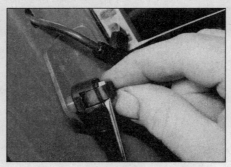

15.15 Releasing tailgate support strut balljoint spring clip

16 Tailgate lock components - removal and refitting

Tailgate lock

Removal

1 Open the tailgate, then remove the two securing screws and withdraw the lock from the tailgate, disengaging the lock lever as the lock is withdrawn **(see illustration)**.

Refitting

2 Refitting is a reversal of removal, but ensure that the lock lever engages correctly as the lock is positioned in the tailgate.

Tailgate lock cylinder

Removal

3 Open the tailgate.
4 Remove the two screws securing the tailgate trim panel, then release the securing clips and withdraw the panel from the tailgate.
5 Where applicable, remove the tailgate wiper motor as described in Chapter 12.
6 Remove the lock cylinder assembly securing screw **(see illustration)**.
7 Prise out the lock cylinder securing clip **(see illustrations)**.
8 Withdraw the lock cylinder assembly from the tailgate, disengaging the lock lever from the lock as it is removed **(see illustration)**.

Refitting

9 Refitting is a reversal of removal. Ensure

16.1 Removing the tailgate lock

that the lock lever engages correctly as the lock cylinder is refitted and refit the wiper motor with reference to Chapter 12.

Tailgate lock striker

Removal

10 Mark the position of the striker on the body, for use when refitting. Unscrew the two securing bolts and remove the striker from the body.

Refitting

11 Refitting is a reversal of removal. Before tightening the securing bolts, the position of the striker should be altered (the securing bolt holes are elongated) until satisfactory lock operation is obtained. Use the marks made prior to removal, if appropriate.

17 Central locking components - removal and refitting

Note: *Before attempting work on any of the central locking system components, disconnect the battery negative terminal (refer to "Disconnecting the battery" in the Reference Section of this manual). Reconnect the lead on completion of work.*

Electronic control unit

1 At the time of writing, no information was available for the electronic control unit.

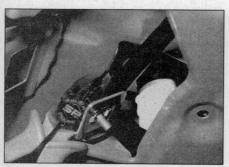

16.7a Using a pair of pliers . . .

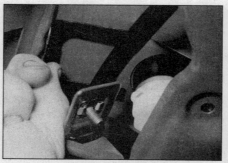

16.7b . . . prise out the lock cylinder securing clip . . .

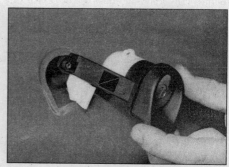

16.8 . . . and withdraw the lock assembly

19.2a Prise the mirror trim plate from the edge of the door . . .

19.2b . . . then remove the adjuster knob securing screw

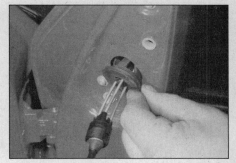

19.2c Pull the adjuster grommet from the door

Door lock actuator

2 The actuator is attached to the door lock assembly and can be detached from the lock after removing the lock assembly as described in Section 13.

Tailgate lock actuator

Removal

3 Open the tailgate.
4 Remove the two screws securing the tailgate trim panel, then release the securing clips and withdraw the panel from the tailgate.
5 If necessary, to improve access, remove the lock cylinder as described in Section 16.
6 Disconnect the actuator wiring connector.
7 Remove the securing screws and withdraw the actuator, disconnecting the operating rod as the actuator is withdrawn.

Refitting

8 Refitting is a reversal of removal.

Remote control receiver unit

Removal

9 Where applicable, remove the securing screw and withdraw the sunroof crank handle.
10 Remove the courtesy light and the map reading light, as applicable, as described in Chapter 12.
11 Remove the securing screws, then lower the roof console and disconnect the wiring connector(s).
12 Release the securing clips and remove the receiver unit from the top of the console.

Refitting

13 Refitting is a reversal of removal.

Remote control transmitter batteries - renewal

14 Using a small screwdriver, carefully prise the two halves of the transmitter apart and remove the two batteries, noting which way round they are fitted.
15 Fit the two new batteries, ensuring that they are fitted the correct way round; the battery and transmitter terminals are marked "+" and "-" to avoid confusion. Clip the transmitter back together.

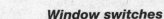
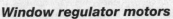

19.3a Remove the securing screws (arrowed) . . .

18 Electric window components
- removal and refitting

Window switches

1 Refer to Chapter 12.

Window regulator motors

2 The regulator motors are integral with the regulator assemblies and cannot be obtained separately.
3 Removal and refitting details for the regulator assemblies are given in Section 14.

19 Exterior mirror and associated components -
removal and refitting

Mirror assembly

Removal

1 On models with electric mirrors, disconnect the battery negative terminal (refer to *"Disconnecting the battery"* in the Reference Section of this manual).
2 Prise the mirror trim plate from the inner edge of the door. Where applicable, remove the screw securing the adjuster knob to the trim plate and withdraw the trim plate. Where applicable, pull the adjuster grommet from the door **(see illustrations)**.
3 Remove the three mirror securing screws, then where applicable, disconnect the wiring

19.3b . . . and withdraw the mirror assembly

plug(s) and withdraw the mirror assembly from the door, complete with the adjuster mechanism and grommet (where applicable) **(see illustrations)**.

Refitting

4 Refitting is a reversal of removal. Where applicable, ensure that the adjuster knob is securely fastened to the trim plate by the securing screw.

Mirror glass

Removal

5 Working at the bottom edge of the mirror glass, locate the ends of the spring clip which secures the glass **(see illustration)**.
6 Using a suitable screwdriver, prise the ends of the clip apart to release the glass **(see illustration)**.
7 Withdraw the glass and recover the spring clip if it is loose.

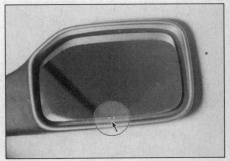

19.5 Locate the ends of the glass securing spring clip (arrowed) . . .

11

19.6 . . . then prise the ends of the clip apart to release the glass

Refitting

8 Fit the spring clip to the rear of the mirror glass, ensuring that the clip is correctly located in the slots in the rear of the mirror glass.

9 Push the mirror glass into the mirror until the spring clip locks into position in the mirror adjuster groove.

Lightly grease the plastic ring on the adjuster to aid refitting of the spring clip.

Manual adjustment mechanism

Removal

10 Prise the mirror trim plate from the inner edge of the door. Remove the screw securing the adjuster knob to the trim plate and withdraw the trim plate.

11 Remove the mirror glass as described previously in this Section.

12 Working inside the mirror housing, remove the three adjuster mechanism securing screws.

13 Pull the mechanism from the mirror housing and feed the adjuster cables and grommet through the door.

Refitting

14 Refitting is a reversal of removal. Make sure that the adjuster cables are free to move and not twisted. Refit the mirror glass as described previously in this Section.

Electric mirrors - general

15 No spare parts are available for the electric adjustment mechanism and if faulty, the complete mirror assembly must be renewed. The mirror glass can be renewed as described previously in this Section. Removal and refitting of the switch is described in Chapter 12.

20 Windscreen, tailgate and fixed windows - general information

These areas of glass are secured by the tight fit of the weatherstrip in the body aperture and are bonded in position with a special adhesive. Renewal of such fixed glass is a difficult, messy and time-consuming task, which is considered beyond the scope of the home mechanic. It is difficult, unless one has plenty of practice, to obtain a secure, waterproof fit. Furthermore, the task carries a high risk of breakage; this applies especially to the laminated glass windscreen. In view of this, owners are strongly advised to have this sort of work carried out by one of the many specialist windscreen fitters.

21 Opening rear quarter windows - removal and refitting

Removal

1 Open the window.

2 Support the glass, then working inside the vehicle, remove the screws securing the glass panel to the hinges and the handle. Withdraw the panel, taking care not to damage the surrounding paintwork. Where applicable, recover the plastic nuts and the trim from the panel.

3 To remove the handle, drill out the rivets securing the assembly to the body.

Refitting

4 Refitting is a reversal of removal. Where applicable, use new rivets to secure the handle to the body. Take care not to overtighten the glass panel securing screws (it is easy to strip the threads of the plastic nuts).

22 Sunroof - general information

Two different types of sunroof may be fitted, depending on model. A simple tilt sunroof is fitted to some models, whilst a more complicated tilt/slide sunroof is fitted to higher-specification models.

Removal of the sunroof glass on models with a tilt roof is straightforward. Remove the trim from the securing screws, then remove the screws securing the glass panel to the hinges and the handle **(see illustrations)**. Refitting is a reversal of removal, ensuring that the trim plates are correctly refitted to the panel and the securing screws.

On models with a tilt/slide sunroof, due to the complexity of the sunroof mechanism, considerable expertise is required to repair, replace or adjust the sunroof components successfully. Removal of the roof first requires the headlining to be removed, which is a tedious operation and not a task to be undertaken lightly (see Section 26). Therefore, any problems with this type of sunroof should be referred to a Peugeot dealer.

23 Body exterior fittings - removal and refitting

Wheel arch liners

1 The wheel arch liners are secured by a combination of self-tapping screws and push-fit clips. Removal is self-evident and normally the clips can be released by pulling the liner away from the wheel arch.

Body trim strips and badges

2 The various body trim strips and badges are held in position with a special adhesive tape. Removal requires the trim/badge to be heated, to soften the adhesive and then cut away from the surface. Due to the high risk of damage to the vehicle paintwork during this operation, it is recommended that this task should be entrusted to a Peugeot dealer.

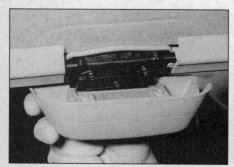

22.2a Remove the sunroof handle trim panel . . .

22.2b . . . then unscrew the glass panel-to-handle securing screws (arrowed) - tilt roof

22.2c Remove the plastic covers to expose the glass panel-to-hinge securing screws - tilt roof

24.6 Recover the washers from the seat bolts

24.7a Tighten the outer seat rail securing bolts (outer rear bolt shown) . . .

24.7b . . . before the inner seat rail securing bolts (inner rear bolt shown)

24 Seats - removal and refitting

Front seat

⚠ **Warning: On models with seat belt pre-tensioners, observe the following precautions before attempting to remove the seat:**

a) *Remove the ignition key.*
b) *Disconnect the battery negative terminal (refer to "Disconnecting the battery" in the Reference Section of this manual) and wait for two minutes before carrying out any further work.*
c) *Disconnect the pre-tensioner wiring plug from the tensioner unit.*

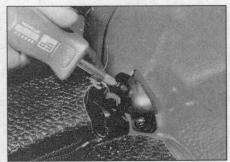

24.10 Remove a rear seat back hinge locking bracket securing screw

Removal

1 Move the seat fully forwards.
2 Tilt the seat backrest forwards.
3 Remove the bolts (one bolt on each side) securing the rear of the seat rails to the floor.
4 Move the seat fully rearwards.
5 Remove the bolts (one bolt on each side) securing the front of the seat rails to the floor.
6 Recover the washers, where applicable, then lift the seat from the vehicle **(see illustration)**.

⚠ **Warning: Do not tamper with the pre-tensioner unit in any way and do not attempt to test the unit.** Note that the unit is triggered if the mechanism is supplied with an electrical current (including via an ohmmeter), or if the assembly is subjected to a temperature of greater than 100°C.

Refitting

7 Refitting is a reversal of removal, but it is essential to tighten the outer seat rail securing bolts (nearest the door) **before** tightening the inner seat rail securing bolts (nearest the handbrake lever) to the specified torque setting **(see illustrations)**.

Rear seat back

Removal

8 Tilt the seat cushion forwards against the front seats.
9 Release the upper securing catch(es) and

fold the seat back forwards until the top of the seat back is level with the bottom of the rear window glass. Take care not to trap the seat belts.
10 Working at the outer edge of the seat back on models with split rear seat backs, or at both ends of the seat back on models with a one-piece seat back, remove the securing screws and withdraw the hinge locking bracket(s) **(see illustration)**.
11 On models with split rear seat backs, where applicable, working at the inner edge of the seat backs, remove the securing screw and pull the centre hinge locking bracket from the hinge assembly. Tilt the locking bracket upwards and push forwards to release it **(see illustrations)**.
12 Pull the seat back upwards to release the hinge pins and withdraw the seat back from the vehicle **(see illustration)**.

Refitting

13 Refitting is a reversal of removal.

Rear seat cushion

Removal

14 Tilt the cushion forwards against the front seats.
15 Pull the cushion upwards to release the hooks from the brackets in the floor.

Refitting

16 Refitting is a reversal of removal.

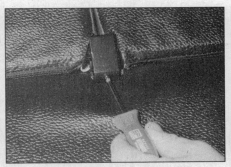

24.11a Remove the securing screw . . .

24.11b . . . and tilt the centre hinge locking bracket upwards - model with split rear seat backs

24.12 Pull the seat back upwards to release the hinge pins

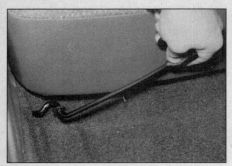

25.2 Freeing the seat belt from the lower anchorage bar - 3-door model

25.3 Remove the trim cap from the upper seat belt mounting bolt

25.5 Front seat belt inertia reel securing bolt (arrowed)

25 Seat belt components - removal and refitting

Front seat belt - 3-door models

Removal

1 Remove the rear passenger compartment side trim panel, as described in Section 26.

2 Prise off the trim cap from the lower belt anchorage bolt. Remove the bolt and washers, then pull out the anchorage bar and free the seat belt from the bar **(see illustration)**.

3 Prise the trim cap from the upper seat belt mounting bolt **(see illustration)**, then unscrew the bolt and release the seat belt mounting plate. Note the locations of any washers and spacers.

25.9a Remove the two securing screws (arrowed) . . .

4 Feed the seat belt and the upper mounting plate through the aperture in the trim panel.

5 Remove the inertia reel securing bolt **(see illustration)** and withdraw the seat belt from the vehicle.

Refitting

6 Refitting is a reversal of removal. Ensure that all washers and/or spacers are positioned as noted before removal and tighten all mounting bolts to the specified torque.

Front seat belt - 5-door models

Removal

7 Prise off the trim cap, then remove the lower belt anchorage bolt and recover the washer.

8 Similarly, remove the upper anchor bolt.

9 Remove the two securing screws, then unclip the centre pillar trim panel from the body **(see illustrations)**.

10 Remove the inertia reel securing bolt **(see illustration)**, then withdraw the seat belt assembly from the vehicle.

Refitting

11 Refitting is a reversal of removal. Tighten the mounting bolts to the specified torque.

Front seat belt stalk

⚠️ **Warning: On models with seat belt pre-tensioners, do not attempt to remove the seat belt stalk assembly, which incorporates the pre-tensioner assembly. Refer the operation to a Peugeot dealer.**

Removal

12 Each stalk is secured to the front seat frame by a bolt and washer.

Refitting

13 Tighten the securing bolt to the specified torque.

Rear side seat belt

Removal

14 Remove the parcel shelf support panel as described in Section 26.

15 Fold the rear seat cushion forwards to expose the lower seat belt anchorage.

16 Unbolt the lower seat belt mounting plate from the floor panel. Note the locations of any washers and spacers on the bolt.

17 Prise off the trim cap and unbolt the upper seat belt anchorage from the body. Again, note the locations of any washers and spacers.

18 Remove the bolt securing the inertia reel assembly to the body and withdraw the seat belt assembly from the vehicle **(see illustration)**.

Refitting

19 Refitting is a reversal of removal. Ensure that all washers and/or spacers are positioned as noted before removal and tighten all mounting bolts to the specified torque.

Rear centre belt and buckles

Removal

20 The assemblies can simply be unbolted

25.10 . . . for access to the inertia reel securing bolt (arrowed)

25.18 Rear side seat belt inertia reel securing bolt (arrowed) - 3-door model

25.9b . . . and withdraw the centre pillar trim panel . . .

from the floor panel, after folding the rear seat cushion forwards **(see illustration)**. Note the locations of any washers and spacers, to ensure correct refitting.

Refitting

21 Refitting is a reversal of removal. Ensure that all washers and/or spacers are positioned as noted before removal and tighten all mounting bolts to the specified torque.

26 Interior trim panels - removal and refitting

Door trim panels

1 Refer to Section 12.

Rear passenger compartment side trim panel - 3-door models

Removal

2 Remove the rear parcel shelf support panel, as described later in this Section.

3 Remove the rear seat cushion, with reference to Section 24 and fold the seat back fully forwards.

4 Carefully pull the panel from the body to release the securing clips **(see illustration)**. Where applicable, disconnect the wiring from the speaker.

5 Unbolt the seat belt upper and lower anchor brackets, with reference to Section 25 and feed the seat belt and anchor brackets through the aperture in the trim panel. Withdraw the trim panel from the vehicle.

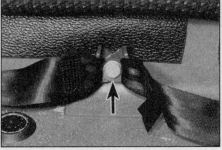

25.20 Rear seat belt buckle mounting bolt (arrowed)

Refitting

6 Refitting is a reversal of removal, bearing in mind the following points:
a) *Tighten the seat belt mountings to the specified torque.*
b) *Refit the rear parcel shelf support panel as described below.*

Rear parcel shelf support panel

Removal

7 Open the tailgate, remove the rear parcel shelf and fold the rear seat back forwards.

8 Pull the knob from the seat back locking lever and pull the weatherstrip from the rear edge of the panel **(see illustrations)**.

9 Remove the two securing screws, then pull the panel away from the body to release the securing clips and withdraw the panel. Note that the rear clip should be released last **(see illustration)**.

10 Where applicable, disconnect the battery negative terminal (refer to *"Disconnecting the battery"* in the Reference Section of this manual) and prise the luggage compartment light and the switch from the trim panel.

Refitting

11 Refitting is a reversal of removal, but ensure that the seat belt webbing is routed over the top of the panel and is not trapped behind the panel.

Windscreen pillar trim panel

Removal

12 Carefully prise the weatherstrip from the edge of the trim panel.

13 Starting at the top, pull the panel away from the pillar to release the securing clips and withdraw the panel.

Refitting

14 Refitting is a reversal of removal.

Centre pillar trim panel

15 The panel is in two halves.

16 To remove the lower panel, remove the two securing screws, then unclip the panel.

17 To remove the upper panel, first remove the lower panel, then remove the securing screw from the bottom of the upper panel. Prise off the trim cap and unscrew the seat belt upper anchor bolt (recover the washer, where applicable), then withdraw the panel.

18 Refitting is a reversal of removal. Where applicable, tighten the seat belt anchor bolt to the specified torque.

26.4 Pulling the rear passenger compartment side trim panel from the body - 3-door model

26.8a Pull the knob from the seat back locking lever . . .

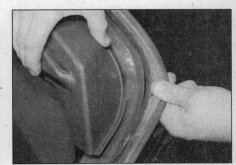

26.8b . . . and pull the weatherstrip from the rear edge of the panel

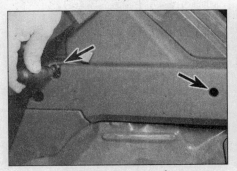

26.9a Remove the two securing screws (arrowed) . . .

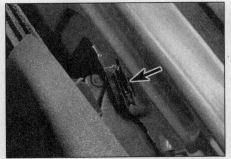

26.9b . . . release the rear clip (arrowed) last . . .

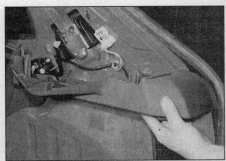

26.9c . . . then pull the panel away from the body

11

27.2 Removing a centre console securing screw - short console

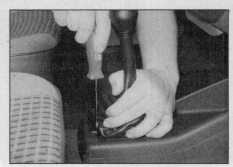

27.4a Remove the securing screws . . .

27.4b . . . and remove the full-length centre console

Rear pillar trim panel

19 Remove the rear parcel shelf support panel as described previously in this Section.
20 Prise off the trim cap and unscrew the seat belt upper anchor bolt (recover the washer, where applicable), then unclip the panel from the body. It may be necessary to prise the weatherstrip from the edge of the panel, where applicable.

Rear wheel arch trim panel - 5-door models

21 Open the rear door and prise the weatherstrip from the edge of the panel.
22 Release the panel from the securing clips, then release the panel from the rear parcel shelf support panel and withdraw the wheel arch trim panel.

Carpets

23 The passenger compartment floor carpet is in one piece and is secured at its edges by screws or various types of clips.
24 Carpet removal and refitting is reasonably straightforward, but time-consuming, due to the fact that all adjoining trim panels must be removed first, as must components such as the seats and centre console.

Headlining

25 The headlining is clipped to the roof and can be withdrawn only once all fittings such as the grab handles, sun visors, sunroof (if fitted), windscreen, centre and rear pillar trim panels and associated panels have been removed. The door, tailgate and sunroof

aperture weatherstrips will also have to be prised clear.
26 Note that headlining removal requires considerable skill and experience if it is to be carried out without damage and is therefore best entrusted to an expert.

27 Centre console - removal and refitting

Short console

Removal

1 On manual transmission models, carefully prise the gear lever gaiter from the centre console and move it up the lever. On automatic transmission models, remove the selector lever knob as described in Chapter 7B.
2 Unscrew the two securing screws (one screw at each side of the console) and slide the console over the gear lever and gaiter assembly **(see illustration)**.

Refitting

3 Refitting is a reversal of removal.

Full-length console

4 Proceed as described for the short console, noting the following points:
a) *The two securing screws are located under the gear lever gaiter (see illustration) and access can be gained once the gaiter has been pulled free.*
b) *If necessary, move the gear lever fully*

rearwards (2nd or 4th gear) to allow the console to slide rearwards from the facia to disengage the securing clip **(see illustration)**.
c) *When refitting, push the console forwards to engage the clip before refitting the securing screws*

28 Facia assembly - removal and refitting

Removal

⚠ *Warning: On models fitted with a passenger's air bag, seek the advice of a Peugeot dealer before proceeding. At the time of writing, no information was available concerning the passenger's air bag attachments or connections in the facia.*

1 Disconnect the battery negative terminal (refer to *"Disconnecting the battery"* in the Reference Section of this manual).
2 Carefully pull off the blower motor control knob. If necessary, use a pair of pliers, with thin card wrapped round the jaws to protect the switch **(see illustration)**.
3 Similarly, remove the heater/ventilation control levers **(see illustration)**.
4 Unscrew the heater control panel securing screw **(see illustration)**.
5 Withdraw the heater control panel and pull the illumination bulbholder from the rear of the panel **(see illustration)**.

28.2 Pull off the blower motor control knob . . .

28.3 . . . and the control levers

28.4 Unscrew the heater control panel securing screw . . .

28.5 . . . then withdraw the panel and pull out the bulbholder

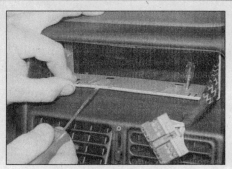

28.7 Releasing a radio/cassette player housing retaining lug

28.8 Unscrewing a ventilation nozzle/switch trim panel securing screw

6 Where applicable, remove the radio/cassette player as described in Chapter 12. If no radio is fitted, unclip the blanking plate from the facia.

28.9a Withdraw the ventilation nozzle/switch trim panel (securing nut studs arrowed) . . .

7 Depress the retaining lugs at the top and bottom of the radio/cassette player housing, then withdraw the housing from the facia (see illustration).

8 Remove the two ventilation nozzle/switch trim panel securing screws from the heater control panel aperture (see illustration). Where applicable, prise the switch blanking plug from the nozzle/switch trim panel.

9 Working through the radio/cassette player housing aperture, unscrew the two ventilation nozzle/switch trim panel securing nuts, then withdraw the panel. Disconnect the wiring plug from the heater blower motor switch (see illustrations).

10 Pull the ashtray liner and the ashtray from the facia (see illustrations).

11 Open the glovebox, then remove the two securing screws (located under the glovebox) and withdraw the glovebox (see illustration).

12 Remove the steering column, as described in Chapter 10.

13 On models with a full-length centre console, remove the console as described in Section 27.

14 Working under the centre of the facia, unclip the wiring connector cover, then unclip the wiring connectors from the panel on the bottom of the facia and separate the connectors (see illustrations).

15 Reach up behind the facia and disconnect the heater ducts from each side of the heater assembly (see illustration).

16 Where applicable, remove the heater duct securing screw(s), then remove the heater ducts.

17 Working through the ashtray aperture, remove the heater unit lower securing screw ("24" in illustration 28.15) (see illustration).

18 Working under the facia, remove the

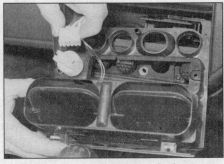

28.9b . . . and disconnect the heater blower motor switch wiring plug

28.10a Pull out the ashtray liner . . .

28.10b . . . and the ashtray

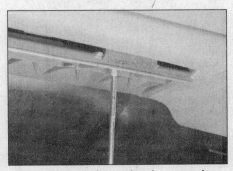

28.11 Unscrewing a glovebox securing screw

28.14a Unclip the cover . . .

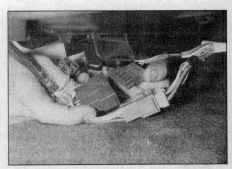

28.14b . . . and disconnect the wiring connectors under the centre of the facia

11

21 Heater duct
22 Heater duct
23 Heater duct securing screw
24 Heater lower securing screw
25 Heater upper securing screws (LHS only on models with air conditioning)
26 Heater lower securing screw
27 Facia securing nuts
28 Windscreen cowl panel
29 Facia side securing screws
30 Wiring connectors
31 Wiring connector
32 Earth lead
33 Radio aerial lead connector
34 Wiring connector
35 Facia central locating lug
36 Heater upper securing screws (models with air conditioning only)

remaining heater unit lower securing screw and the two upper securing screws ("25" and "26" in illustration 28.15) **(see illustrations)**. Access to the upper screws is difficult and a long-handled Torx screwdriver will be required. Note that on models with air conditioning, there is only one upper screw on the left-hand side.

19 On models with air conditioning, remove the two additional heater unit upper securing screws ("36" in illustration 28.15 - access can be gained through the glovebox aperture).

20 Reach up behind the facia and disconnect the speedometer cable from the instrument panel by pulling sharply on the top of the cable.

21 Where applicable, remove the choke cable as described in Chapter 4A.

22 Working in the footwells, carefully prise back the carpet panel from the sides of the facia, to expose the facia side securing screws (one on each side of the facia). Remove the screws. Note that the left-hand screw also secures the bonnet release lever **(see illustration)**.

23 Disconnect the wiring connectors, located at the sides of the facia (two connectors on the left-hand side, clipped to the facia and one on the right-hand side) **(see illustrations)**. Similarly disconnect the radio aerial lead connector at the right-hand side of the facia.

28.17 Heater unit lower securing screw (arrowed) is reached through ashtray aperture

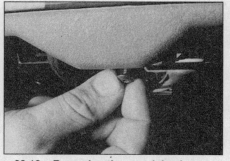

28.18a Removing the remaining heater unit lower securing screw

28.18b View through windscreen with facia removed, showing heater upper securing screw locations (arrowed)

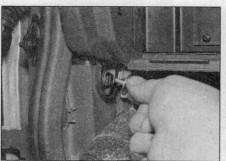

28.22 Removing the facia left-hand side securing screw

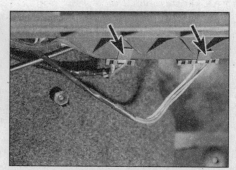

28.23a Unclip the wiring connectors from the left-hand end of the facia . . .

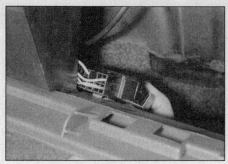

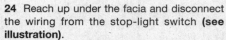

28.23b . . . and disconnect them

28.24 Stop-light switch wiring connector (arrowed)

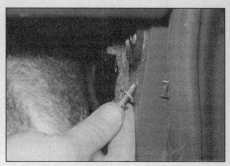

28.25 Remove the screw securing the earth lead

24 Reach up under the facia and disconnect the wiring from the stop-light switch **(see illustration)**.
25 Working in the right-hand footwell, remove the securing screw and washer securing the earth lead to the body **(see illustration)**.
26 Remove the windscreen wiper arms as described in Chapter 12.
27 Open the bonnet.
28 Remove the securing screw and the two nuts and withdraw the windscreen cowl panel from the scuttle. Note that the panel is clipped around the edge of the windscreen and the front wings.
29 Where fitted, remove the securing nuts and unclip the plastic cover panel from the left- or right-hand side of the scuttle (as applicable).
30 Working in the scuttle, unscrew the three

facia securing nuts **(see illustration)**.
31 Working inside the vehicle, carefully pull the facia assembly back from the bulkhead to disengage the central lug from the scuttle **(see illustration)**.
32 Support the facia, then working at the left-hand side of the passenger compartment, remove the securing nut and separate the two halves of the multi-pin wiring connector **(see illustrations)**.
33 Make a final check to ensure that all relevant wiring has been disconnected and moved clear to facilitate facia removal.
34 Once the assembly is free from the bulkhead, slide it out through one of the door apertures **(see illustration)**.

Refitting

35 Refitting is a reversal of removal, bearing in mind the following points:
 a) *Before pushing the facia into position,*

reconnect the two halves of the multi-pin wiring connector and refit the securing nut. Also, feed the speedometer cable through its hole in the top of the facia.
 b) *Make sure that the windscreen cowl panel is correctly refitted and refit the windscreen wiper arms as described in Chapter 12.*
 c) *Make sure that all wiring connectors are correctly reconnected and positioned.*
 d) *Where applicable, refit the choke cable as described in Chapter 4A.*
 e) *Ensure that the speedometer cable is correctly reconnected.*
 f) *Make sure that the heater ducts are securely reconnected.*
 g) *Refit the steering column as described in Chapter 10.*
 h) *Refit the radio/cassette player as described in Chapter 12.*

28.30 Unscrewing a facia securing nut

28.31 Facia central locating lug (arrowed) - viewed through windscreen

28.32a Remove the securing nut . . .

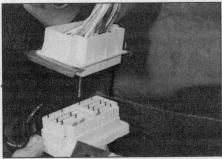

28.32b . . . and disconnect the multi-pin wiring connector

28.34 Removing the facia

11

Chapter 12
Body electrical system

Contents

Degrees of difficulty

Easy, suitable for novice with little experience	Fairly easy, suitable for beginner with some experience	Fairly difficult, suitable for competent DIY mechanic	Difficult, suitable for experienced DIY mechanic	Very difficult, suitable for expert DIY or professional

Specifications

Bulbs	Wattage	
Headlight (H4 type bulb)	60/55	
Front sidelight	5	
Front driving/foglight (H3 or H1 type bulb)	55	
Front direction indicator light	21	
Direction indicator side repeater light	5	
Stop light/tail light	21/5	
Tail light	5	
Direction indicator light	21	
Rear foglight	21	
Reversing light	21	
Rear number plate light	5	
High-level stoplight	5	
Torque wrench setting	**Nm**	**lbf ft**
Air bag unit securing screws	8	6

12

1 General information and precautions

⚠️ **Warning: Before carrying out any work on the electrical system, read through the precautions given in "Safety first!" at the beginning of this manual and in the relevant Part of Chapter 5.**

The electrical system is of 12-volt negative earth type. Power for the lights and all electrical accessories is supplied by a lead/acid type battery, which is charged by the alternator.

This Chapter covers repair and service procedures for the various electrical components not associated with the engine. Information on the battery, alternator and starter motor can be found in Chapter 5A.

It should be noted that, prior to working on any component in the electrical system, the battery negative terminal should first be disconnected, to prevent the possibility of electrical short-circuits and/or fires.

Caution: Before proceeding, refer to "Disconnecting the battery" in the Reference Section of this manual for further information.

2 Electrical fault-finding - general information

Note: Refer to the precautions given in "Safety first!" and in Section 1 of this Chapter before starting work. The following tests relate to testing of the main electrical circuits and should not be used to test delicate electronic circuits (such as anti-lock braking systems), especially not those where an electronic control unit is used.

General

A typical electrical circuit consists of an electrical component, any switches, relays, motors, fuses, fusible links or circuit breakers related to that component and the wiring and connectors which link the component to both the battery and the chassis. To help to pinpoint a problem in an electrical circuit, wiring diagrams are included at the end of this Chapter

Before attempting to diagnose an electrical fault, first study the appropriate wiring diagram, to obtain a more complete understanding of the components included in the particular circuit concerned. The possible sources of a fault can be narrowed down by noting whether other components related to the circuit are operating properly. If several components or circuits fail at one time, the problem is likely to be related to a shared fuse or earth connection.

Electrical problems usually stem from simple causes, such as loose or corroded connections, a faulty earth connection, a blown fuse, a melted fusible link, or a faulty

relay (refer to Section 3 for details of testing relays). Visually inspect the condition of all fuses, wires and connections in a problem circuit before testing the components. Use the wiring diagrams at the end of this Chapter to determine which terminal connections will need to be checked, in order to pinpoint the trouble-spot.

The basic tools required for electrical fault-finding include a circuit tester or voltmeter (a 12-volt bulb with a set of test leads can also be used for certain tests); a self-powered test light (sometimes known as a continuity tester); an ohmmeter (to measure resistance); a battery and set of test leads; and a jumper wire, preferably with a circuit breaker or fuse incorporated, which can be used to bypass suspect wires or electrical components. Before attempting to locate a problem with test instruments, use the wiring diagram to determine where to make the connections.

To find the source of an intermittent wiring fault (usually due to a poor or dirty connection, or damaged wiring insulation), a "wiggle" test can be performed on the wiring. This involves wiggling the wiring by hand, to see if the fault occurs as the wiring is moved. It should be possible to narrow down the source of the fault to a particular section of wiring. This method of testing can be used in conjunction with any of the tests described in the following sub-Sections.

Apart from problems due to poor connections, two basic types of fault can occur in an electrical circuit - open-circuit, or short-circuit.

Open-circuit faults are caused by a break somewhere in the circuit, which prevents current from flowing. An open-circuit fault will prevent a component from working, but will not cause the relevant circuit fuse to blow.

Short-circuit faults are caused by a "short" somewhere in the circuit, which allows the current flowing in the circuit to "escape" along an alternative route, usually to earth. Short-circuit faults are normally caused by a breakdown in wiring insulation, which allows a feed wire to touch either another wire, or an earthed component such as the bodyshell. A short-circuit fault will normally cause the relevant circuit fuse to blow.

Finding an open-circuit

To check for an open-circuit, connect one lead of a circuit tester or voltmeter to either the negative battery terminal or a known good earth.

Connect the other lead to a connector in the circuit being tested, preferably nearest to the battery or fuse.

Switch on the circuit, bearing in mind that some circuits are live only when the ignition switch is moved to a particular position.

If voltage is present (indicated either by the tester bulb lighting or a voltmeter reading, as applicable), this means that the section of the circuit between the relevant connector and the battery is problem-free.

Continue to check the remainder of the circuit in the same fashion.

When a point is reached at which no voltage is present, the problem must lie between that point and the previous test point with voltage. Most problems can be traced to a broken, corroded or loose connection.

Finding a short-circuit

To check for a short-circuit, first disconnect the load(s) from the circuit (loads are the components which draw current from a circuit, such as bulbs, motors, heating elements, etc).

Remove the relevant fuse from the circuit and connect a circuit tester or voltmeter to the fuse connections.

Switch on the circuit, bearing in mind that some circuits are live only when the ignition switch is moved to a particular position.

If voltage is present (indicated either by the tester bulb lighting or a voltmeter reading, as applicable), this means that there is a short-circuit.

If no voltage is present, but the fuse still blows with the load(s) connected, this indicates an internal fault in the load(s).

Finding an earth fault

The battery negative terminal is connected to "earth" - the metal of the engine /transmission unit and the car body - and most systems are wired so that they only receive a positive feed, the current returning via the metal of the car body. This means that the component mounting and the body form part of that circuit. Loose or corroded mountings can therefore cause a range of electrical faults, ranging from total failure of a circuit, to a puzzling partial fault. In particular, lights may shine dimly (especially when another circuit sharing the same earth point is in operation), motors (eg wiper motors or the radiator cooling fan motor) may run slowly and the operation of one circuit may have an apparently-unrelated effect on another. Note that on many vehicles, earth straps are used between certain components, such as the engine/transmission and the body, usually where there is no metal-to-metal contact between components, due to flexible rubber mountings, etc.

To check whether a component is properly earthed, disconnect the battery and connect one lead of an ohmmeter to a known good earth point. Connect the other lead to the wire or earth connection being tested. The resistance reading should be zero; if not, check the connection as follows.

If an earth connection is thought to be faulty, dismantle the connection and clean back to bare metal both the bodyshell and the wire terminal or the component earth connection mating surface. Be careful to remove all traces of dirt and corrosion, then use a knife to trim away any paint, so that a clean metal-to-metal joint is made. On reassembly, tighten the joint fasteners securely; if a wire terminal is being refitted,

3.7 Removing a fuse using the plastic tool

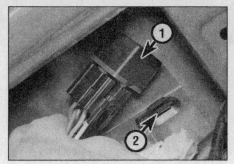

3.13a Rear wiper motor relay (1) and securing clip (2)

3.13b Relays located in auxiliary fusebox - diesel model shown

use serrated washers between the terminal and the bodyshell, to ensure a clean and secure connection. When the connection is remade, prevent the onset of corrosion in the future by applying a coat of petroleum jelly or silicone-based grease, or by spraying on (at regular intervals) a proprietary ignition sealer.

3 Fuses and relays - general information

Fuses

1 Fuses are designed to break a circuit when a predetermined current is reached, in order to protect the components and wiring which could be damaged by excessive current flow. Any excessive current flow will be due to a fault in the circuit, usually a short-circuit (see Section 2).

2 The main fuses are located in the fusebox behind the glovebox on right-hand drive models, or behind a panel in the driver's side facia on left-hand drive models.

3 For access to the fuses, on right-hand drive models, open the glovebox; on left-hand drive models, prise the fusebox cover panel from the facia.

4 On certain models, additional fuses may be located in the auxiliary fuseboxes in the engine compartment. According to model, these auxiliary fuseboxes are either attached to a bracket on the left-hand suspension turret, or situated alongside the battery.

5 A blown fuse can be recognised from its melted or broken wire.

6 To remove a fuse, first ensure that the relevant circuit is switched off.

7 Using the plastic tool provided in the fusebox, pull the fuse from its location **(see illustration)**.

8 Spare fuses are provided in the blank terminal positions in the fusebox.

9 Before renewing a blown fuse, trace and rectify the cause and always use a fuse of the correct rating. Never substitute a fuse of a higher rating, or make temporary repairs using wire or metal foil; more serious damage, or even fire, could result.

10 Note that the fuses are colour-coded as follows. Refer to the wiring diagrams for details of the fuse ratings and the circuits protected:

Colour	Rating
Orange	5A
Red	10A
Blue	15A
Yellow	20A
Clear or White	25A
Green	30A

11 The radio/cassette player has an in-line fuse located in the wiring behind the unit.

Relays

12 A relay is an electrically-operated switch, which is used for the following reasons:

a) *A relay can switch a heavy current remotely from the circuit in which the current is flowing, allowing the use of lighter-gauge wiring and switch contacts.*

b) *A relay can receive more than one control input, unlike a mechanical switch.*

c) *A relay can have a timer function - for example, the intermittent wiper relay.*

13 Most of the relays are located at the rear of the main fusebox (remove the securing screws and pull the fusebox forwards to improve access). The rear wiper motor relay is located in the tailgate, behind the tailgate trim panel. On some models, additional engine-related relays are located in an auxiliary fusebox mounted on the left-hand side of the engine compartment **(see illustrations)**.

14 If a circuit or system controlled by a relay develops a fault and the relay is suspect, operate the system. If the relay is functioning, it should be possible to hear it "click" as it is energised. If this is the case, the fault lies with the components or wiring of the system. If the relay is not being energised, then either the relay is not receiving a main supply or a switching voltage, or the relay itself is faulty. Testing is by the substitution of a known good unit, but be careful - while some relays are identical in appearance and in operation, others look similar but perform different functions.

15 To remove a relay, first ensure that the relevant circuit is switched off. The relay can then simply be pulled out from the socket and pushed back into position.

4 Switches - removal and refitting

Note: *Disconnect the battery negative terminal before removing any switch and reconnect the terminal after refitting the switch. Refer to "Disconnecting the battery" in the Reference Section of this manual.*

Ignition switch/ steering column lock

1 Refer to Chapter 10.

Steering column combination switches

2 Working under the steering column, remove the three steering column shroud securing screws. Unclip and lift off the upper shroud, then withdraw the lower shroud. Note that the lower shroud clips over a metal bracket on the steering column and the shroud must be slid from the bracket before it can be removed. On some models, it may be necessary to remove the steering wheel as described in Chapter 10 in order to allow the steering column shrouds to be removed.

3 Remove the two securing screws **(see illustration)** and withdraw the relevant switch from the housing on the steering column. Where applicable, note the location of the insulating foam around the switch body.

4.3 Remove the securing screws (arrowed) . . .

4.4 . . . then withdraw the combination switch and disconnect the wiring plug

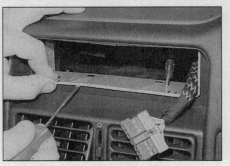

4.11a Depress the retaining lugs . . .

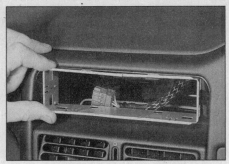

4.11b . . . then withdraw the radio/cassette player housing

4 Disconnect the wiring plug(s) from the rear of the switch **(see illustration)**.
5 Refitting is a reversal of removal, ensuring that, where applicable, the insulating foam is positioned around the switch as noted before removal.

Facia-mounted pushbutton switches

6 Carefully pull off the blower motor control knob. If necessary, use a pair of pliers, with thin card wrapped round the jaws to protect the switch.
7 Similarly, remove the heater/ventilation control levers.
8 Unscrew the heater control panel securing screw.
9 Withdraw the heater control panel and pull the illumination bulbholder from the rear of the panel.

10 Where applicable, remove the radio/cassette player as described in Section 20. If no radio is fitted, unclip the blanking plate from the facia.
11 Depress the retaining lugs at the top and bottom of the radio/cassette player housing, then withdraw the housing from the facia **(see illustrations)**.
12 Where applicable, prise out the switch blanking plug **(see illustration)**.
13 Remove the two ventilation nozzle/switch trim panel securing screws from the heater control panel aperture **(see illustration)**.
14 Working through the radio/cassette player housing aperture, unscrew the two ventilation nozzle/switch trim panel securing nuts. Withdraw the panel and disconnect the wiring plug from the heater blower motor switch **(see illustration)**.
15 Carefully prise the relevant switch out

through the front of the facia and disconnect the wiring plug **(see illustrations)**.
16 Refitting is a reversal of removal.

Heater blower motor switch

17 Remove the ventilation nozzle/switch trim panel, as described in paragraphs 6 to 14 inclusive.
18 The switch can be removed from the rear of the panel, after depressing the retaining lugs **(see illustrations)**.
19 Refitting is a reversal of removal.

Headlight adjustment and instrument light dimmer switches

20 Using a suitable flat-bladed screwdriver, carefully prise the relevant switch out of the facia, taking great care not to mark either the panel or the facia. Tilt the switch forward to remove it and disconnect the wiring connector.

4.12 Removing a switch blanking plug

4.13 Remove the ventilation nozzle/switch trim panel securing screws (arrowed)

4.14 Withdrawing the ventilation nozzle/switch trim panel. Securing nut studs arrowed

4.15a Prise out the relevant switch . . .

4.15b . . . and disconnect the wiring plug

4.18a Depress the retaining lugs . . .

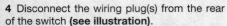

4.18b . . . and remove the heater blower motor switch from the ventilation nozzle/switch trim panel

21 Refitting is a reversal of removal.

Courtesy light switches

22 Open the door, then prise the rubber gaiter from the switch **(see illustration)**.
23 Remove the securing screw, then withdraw the switch from the door pillar. Disconnect the wiring connector as it becomes accessible.

 HAYNES HINT *Tape the wiring to the door pillar, to prevent it falling back into the door pillar. Alternatively, tie a piece of string to the wiring, to retrieve it.*

24 Refitting is a reversal of removal, but ensure that the rubber gaiter is correctly seated on the switch.

Glovebox and luggage compartment light switches

25 Open the glovebox, or the tailgate, as applicable, then carefully prise the switch from its location and disconnect the wiring connector **(see illustration)**.
26 Refitting is a reversal of removal.

Centre console-mounted switches

27 Using a suitable flat-bladed screwdriver, carefully prise the switch panel from the centre console **(see illustration)**.
28 Disconnect the switch wiring connectors.
29 Release the securing clips and withdraw the switch from the panel **(see illustration)**.

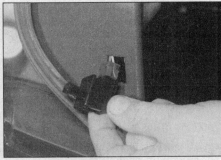

4.25 Removing the luggage compartment light switch

4.22 Prise the rubber gaiter from the courtesy light switch to expose the securing screw (arrowed)

30 Refitting is a reversal of removal.

Electric window switches

31 The electric window switches are located in the door pockets on early models, or in the centre console on later models.
32 Carefully prise the switch panel from its location. If necessary, remove the securing screws and withdraw the door pocket first to improve access.
33 Carefully prise the relevant switch from the switch panel and disconnect the wiring plug. Note that on some models, the switch wiring connector may be located inside the door, in which case it will be necessary to remove the inner trim panel and the plastic sealing sheet for access, as described in Chapter 11.
34 Refitting is a reversal of removal. Where applicable, refit the door inner trim panel with reference to Chapter 11 and use a new sealing sheet.

Electric door mirror adjustment switch

35 Carefully prise the switch from the interior door handle trim panel and disconnect he wiring plug. If necessary, prise the interior door handle trim panel from the door first to improve access. Note that on some models,

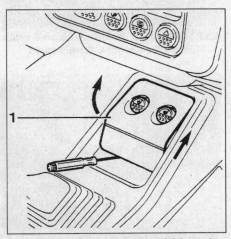

4.27 Prising the switch panel (1) from the centre console

the switch wiring connector may be located inside the door, in which case it will be necessary to remove the inner trim panel and the plastic sealing sheet for access, as described in Chapter 11.
36 Refitting is a reversal of removal. Where applicable, refit the door inner trim panel with reference to Chapter 11 and use a new sealing sheet.

5 Bulbs (exterior lights) - renewal

General

1 Whenever a bulb is renewed, note the following points:
a) *Disconnect the battery negative terminal before starting work. Refer to "Disconnecting the battery" in the Reference Section of this manual.*
b) *Remember that, if the light has just been in use, the bulb (and its holder) may be extremely hot.*
c) *Always check the bulb contacts and holder, ensuring that there is clean metal-to-metal contact between the bulb and its live contact(s) and earth. Clean off any corrosion or dirt before fitting a new bulb.*
d) *Wherever bayonet-type bulbs are fitted, ensure that the live contact(s) bear firmly against the bulb contact.*
e) *Always ensure that the new bulb is of the correct rating and that it is completely clean before fitting it; this applies particularly to headlight/foglight bulbs (see following paragraphs).*

Headlight

2 Open the bonnet, then working at the rear of the headlight assembly, release the securing clip and lift up the headlight rear cover **(see illustration)**. On later models, twist the headlight rear cover anti-clockwise to remove it from the headlight.

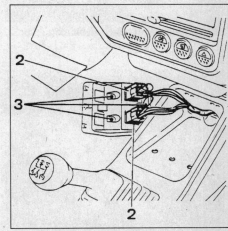

4.29 Centre console-mounted switches (2) and securing clips (3)

5.2 Lift up or twist off the headlight rear cover . . .

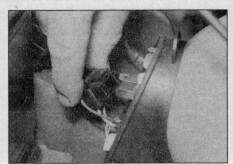

5.3 . . . pull the wiring plug from the bulb . . .

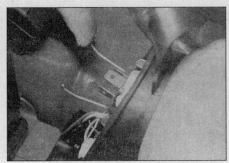

5.4 . . . release the retaining clip . . .

3 Pull the wiring plug from the rear of the bulb (see illustration).

4 Press together the ends of the bulb retaining clip and release it from the rear of the light (see illustration).

5 Withdraw the bulb (see illustration).

6 When handling the new bulb, use a tissue or clean cloth, to avoid touching the glass with the fingers; moisture and grease from the skin can cause blackening and rapid failure of this type of bulb.

HAYNES HINT *If the headlight glass is accidentally touched, wipe it clean using methylated spirit.*

7 Install the new bulb, ensuring that its locating tabs are correctly located in the light unit cut-outs. Secure the bulb in position with the retaining clip and reconnect the wiring connector plug.

8 Refit the headlight rear cover, ensuring that it is correctly seated on the rear of the light unit.

Front sidelight

9 Proceed as described in paragraphs 2 and 3.

10 Twist the bulbholder through quarter of a turn and withdraw it from the headlight housing.

11 Pull the push-fit bulb from the bulbholder (see illustration).

12 Fit the new bulb using a reversal of the removal procedure, ensuring that the bulbholder sealing ring is in good condition.

Front direction indicator - pre-July 1996 models

13 Open the bonnet and working at the front wing behind the direction indicator light, release the light unit retaining spring from the hole in the body panel (see illustration).

14 Withdraw the light unit forwards from the front wing (see illustration).

15 Twist the bulbholder anti-clockwise to release it from the rear of the light unit (see illustration).

16 The bulb is a bayonet fit in the bulbholder and can be removed by pressing it and twisting in an anti-clockwise direction (see illustration).

17 Refitting is a reversal of removal, bearing in mind the following points:

a) Ensure that the bulbholder sealing ring is in good condition.

b) When refitting the light unit, ensure that the lugs on the rear of the unit engage with the corresponding holes in the body panel.

c) Ensure that the light unit retaining spring is correctly located in the hole in the body panel.

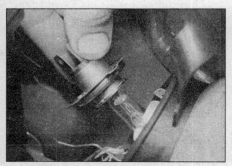

5.5 . . . and withdraw the bulb

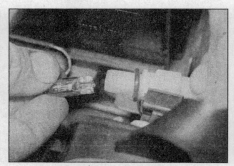

5.11 Removing a sidelight bulb

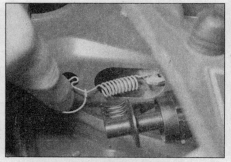

5.13 Release the front direction indicator light unit retaining spring . . .

5.14 . . . withdraw the light unit . . .

5.15 . . . remove the bulbholder . . .

5.16 . . . then withdraw the bulb

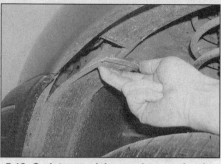

5.19 On later models, reach up under the wheel arch and open the access flap . . .

5.20 . . . remove the bulbholder . . .

5.21 . . . then withdraw the bulb

Front direction indicator - July 1996 models onward

18 Access to the bulbs is from under the front wheel arch. To change the left-hand bulb, turn the steering onto full right lock and to full left lock for the right-hand bulb.

19 Reach up under the wheel arch and open the access flap (see illustration).

20 Working through the aperture in the wheel arch liner, twist the bulbholder anti-clockwise to release it from the rear of the light unit (see illustration).

21 The bulb is a bayonet fit in the bulbholder and can be removed by pressing it and twisting in an anti-clockwise direction (see illustration).

22 Refitting is a reversal of removal, ensuring that the bulbholder sealing ring is in good condition and the access flap is securely closed.

Front direction indicator side repeater - pre-July 1996 models

23 Remove the light unit, as described in Section 7.

24 Pull the bulbholder from the rear of the light unit. The bulb is a push fit in the bulbholder (see illustrations).

Front direction indicator side repeater - July 1996 models onward

25 Pull the rear part of the transparent cover to release the assembly.

26 Support the connector, turn the transparent cover anti-clockwise then pull the bulb out of its holder (the bulb is a push-fit).

27 Refitting is a reversal of the removal procedure.

Front driving lights/foglights - pre-July 1996 models

28 Working at the front of the light unit, remove the two securing screws and withdraw the glass, surround and reflector assembly.

29 Disconnect the bulb wiring connector.

30 Release the spring clip and remove the bulb from the rear of the light unit.

31 When handling the new bulb, use a tissue or clean cloth, to avoid touching the glass with the fingers; moisture and grease from the skin can cause blackening and rapid failure of this type of bulb. If the glass is accidentally touched, wipe it clean using methylated spirit.

32 Install the new bulb, ensuring that its locating tabs are correctly located in the light

unit cut-outs. Secure the bulb in position with the retaining clip and reconnect the wiring connector.

33 Refit the glass, surround and reflector assembly and tighten the securing screws.

Front driving lights/foglights - July 1996 models onward

34 Working under the front bumper twist the bulbholder anti-clockwise to release it from the rear of the light unit, then remove the bulb from the holder.

35 When handling the new bulb, use a tissue or clean cloth, to avoid touching the glass with the fingers; moisture and grease from the skin can cause blackening and rapid failure of this type of bulb. If the glass is accidentally touched, wipe it clean using methylated spirit.

36 Install the new bulb, then refit the bulbholder to the light unit.

Rear light cluster - pre-July 1996 models

37 Remove the light unit as described in Section 7.

38 Remove the two securing screws from the lens (see illustration).

39 Slightly lift the top of the lens from the light unit, then release the clips at the lower edge of the lens (see illustration). Withdraw the lens from the light unit.

40 The bulbs are a bayonet fit in the bulbholder unit and can be removed by pressing and twisting in an anti-clockwise direction (see illustration). Note that the stop/tail light has offset pins, to ensure correct installation.

5.24a Pull the bulbholder from the direction indicator side repeater light . . .

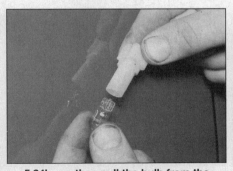

5.24b . . . then pull the bulb from the bulbholder

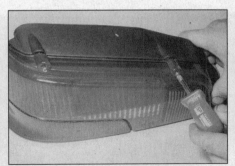

5.38 Remove the two securing screws . . .

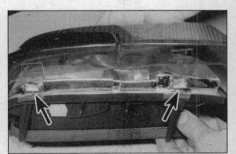

5.39 . . . then release the securing clips (arrowed) and withdraw the lens from the rear light cluster

12

5.40 Removing a bulb from the rear light cluster

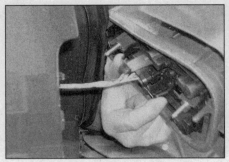

5.43 On later models, release the bulbholder by squeezing the tabs . . .

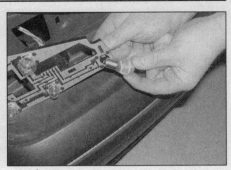

5.44 . . . then withdraw the bulb

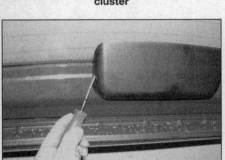

5.46 Depress the retaining tags and remove the high-level stoplight cover

41 Refitting is a reversal of removal, ensuring that the lens is located correctly in the seal. Refit the light unit with reference to Section 7.

5.47 Squeeze the retaining tabs to remove the bulbholder . . .

Rear light cluster - July 1996 models onward

42 Remove the light unit as described in Section 7.
43 Release the bulbholder from the light unit by squeezing the retaining tabs **(see illustration)**.
44 The bulbs are a bayonet fit in the bulbholder **(see illustration)**.
45 Refitting is a reversal of the removal procedure. Refit the light unit with reference to Section 7.

High-level stoplight

46 Using a small screwdriver, depress the retaining tags on the side of the light unit cover and remove the cover **(see illustration)**.
47 Release the bulbholder from the light unit by squeezing the retaining tabs **(see illustration)**.

48 The bulbs are a push-fit in the bulbholder **(see illustration)**.
49 Refitting is a reversal of the removal procedure.

Rear number plate light

50 Using a small flat-bladed screwdriver, carefully prise out the light lens to gain access to the bulb.
51 The bulb is a push fit in the light unit **(see illustration)**.
52 Refitting is a reversal of removal.

6 Bulbs (interior lights) - renewal

General

1 Refer to Section 5, paragraph 1.

Courtesy light

2 Carefully prise the light unit from its location in the roof console, then twist the bulbholder anti-clockwise and pull the bulb from the bulbholder **(see illustrations)**.
3 Refitting is a reversal of removal.

Glovebox and luggage compartment lights

4 Carefully prise the light unit from its location, then twist the bulbholder to remove it from the rear of the light unit **(see illustration)**.
5 The bulb is a push fit in the bulbholder.
6 Refitting is a reversal of removal.

5.48 . . . then remove the push-fit bulbs from the holder

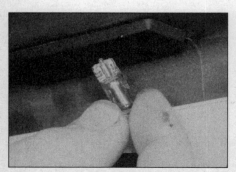

5.51 Removing a rear number plate light bulb

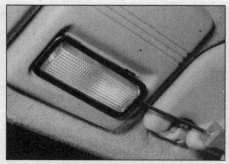

6.2a Prising the courtesy light from the roof console

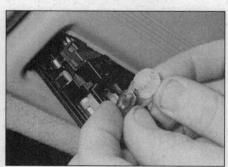

6.2b The bulb is a push fit in the bulbholder

6.4 Removing the luggage compartment light bulbholder

6.7 Prise the map reading light from the roof console . . .

6.8 . . . and remove the bulb

Map reading light

7 Carefully prise the light unit from its location in the roof console **(see illustration)**.
8 Twist the bulb anti-clockwise to remove it from the light unit **(see illustration)**.
9 The bulb is integral with bulbholder.
10 Refitting is a reversal of removal.

Instrument panel lights

11 Remove the instrument panel as described in Section 9.
12 Twist the relevant bulbholder anti-clockwise and withdraw it from the rear of the panel **(see illustration)**.
13 All bulbs are integral with their holders.
14 Refit the bulbholder to the rear of the instrument panel, then refit the instrument panel as described in Section 9.

Heater control panel illumination bulb

15 Carefully pull off the blower motor control knob. If necessary, use a pair of pliers, with thin card wrapped round the jaws to protect the switch.
16 Similarly, remove the heater/ventilation control levers.
17 Unscrew the heater control panel securing screw.
18 Withdraw the heater control panel and pull the illumination bulbholder from the rear of the panel.
19 The illumination bulb is a push fit in the bulbholder **(see illustration)**.
20 Fit the new bulb using a reversal of the removal procedure.

6.12 Removing an instrument panel light bulb

Switch illumination bulbs

21 All of the switches are fitted with illuminating bulbs and some are also fitted with a bulb to show when the circuit concerned is operating. The bulbs are an integral part of the switch assembly and cannot be obtained separately. Bulb renewal will therefore require renewal of the complete switch assembly.

7 Exterior light units - removal and refitting

Note: *Disconnect the battery negative terminal before removing any light unit and reconnect the terminal after refitting the unit. Refer to "Disconnecting the battery" in the Reference Section of this manual.*

6.19 Removing the heater control panel illumination bulb

Headlight - pre-July 1996 models

Removal

1 Remove the front direction indicator light as described in Section 5, paragraphs 13 and 14.
2 Working at the rear of the headlight assembly, release the securing clip and lift up the headlight rear cover.
3 Pull the wiring plugs from the rear of the bulbs in the headlight unit.
4 Carefully pull the corners of the headlight unit forwards to release the three balljoints and withdraw the headlight **(see illustrations)**.
5 Note that if desired, the balljoint and adjuster units (and the electric adjuster motor, where applicable) can be removed from the body after twisting the unit itself (or the locking collar, as applicable) to release the unit from the aperture in the body **(see illustration)**.

7.4a Pull the corners of the headlight unit from the balljoints (arrowed) . . .

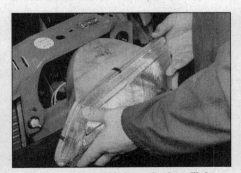

7.4b . . . then withdraw the headlight

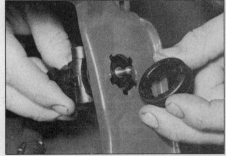

7.5 The headlight adjuster unit can be removed after twisting the locking collar

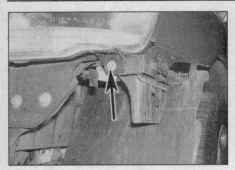

7.11a Later type headlight unit lower outer . . .

7.11b . . . lower inner . . .

7.11c . . . and upper retaining bolts (arrowed)

Refitting

6 Refitting is a reversal of removal, ensuring that the headlight balljoints are correctly engaged. Refit the direction indicator light as described in Section 5.

Headlight - July 1996 models onward

Removal

7 Remove the front bumper as described in Chapter 11.

8 Working at the rear of the headlight assembly, twist the headlight rear cover anti-clockwise to remove it from the headlight.

9 Pull the wiring plug from the rear of the headlight bulb.

10 Twist the sidelight bulbholder through quarter of a turn and withdraw it from the headlight unit.

11 Undo the three bolts securing the light unit to the front body panel **(see illustrations)**.

12 Withdraw the headlight unit from its location **(see illustration)**. When sufficient clearance exists, twist the direction indicator bulbholder anti-clockwise to release it from the rear of the light unit. Where applicable, disconnect the wiring plug for the headlight adjuster motor.

13 Note that if desired, the balljoint and adjuster units (and the electric adjuster motor, where applicable) can be removed from the light unit after twisting the adjuster itself (or the locking collar, as applicable) to release the adjuster from the aperture in the light unit.

Refitting

14 Refitting is a reversal of removal.

Front direction indicator light

15 On pre-July 1996 models, removal and refitting of the direction indicator light is described in Section 5, paragraphs 13 to 17. On later models the direction indicator and headlight unit are all one assembly. Refer to paragraphs 7 to 14 for headlight unit removal and refitting.

Front direction indicator side repeater light - pre-July 1996 models

Removal

16 Push the light unit towards the rear of the vehicle, to disengage it from the wing panel.

17 Withdraw the light unit from the wing panel and disconnect the wiring plug **(see illustration)**. Tape the wiring to the wing panel, to prevent it falling back into the hole.

Refitting

18 Refitting is a reversal of removal. Push the light unit towards the front of the vehicle until it locks into position.

Front direction indicator side repeater light - July 1996 models onward

19 The procedure is described as part of the bulb renewal procedure in Section 5.

Front driving light/foglight

Removal

20 On early models, trace the wiring back from the light unit and disconnect the wiring connector (usually located in the engine compartment, behind the headlight unit). Note the routing of the wiring, to aid refitting. On later models, twist the bulbholder anti-clockwise to release it from the rear of the light unit.

21 On early models, working up behind the front bumper, unscrew the nut and recover the washer from the light mounting stud. Note that the light will be free to pivot once the nut has been loosened. On later models, release the light unit mountings or plastic clips.

22 Withdraw the light unit from the bumper.

Refitting

23 Refitting is a reversal of removal. Ensure that the wiring is routed as noted before removal and check the aim of the light before finally tightening the securing nut (where applicable).

Rear light cluster - pre-July 1996 models

Removal

24 Open the tailgate.

25 Prise the plastic cover from the rear of the light unit **(see illustration)**.

26 Remove the securing screw and unclip the air extraction grille from the side of the luggage compartment **(see illustrations)**.

7.12 Withdrawing the later type headlight unit

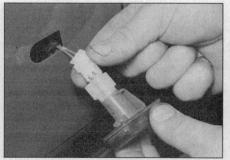

7.17 Removing a front direction indicator side repeater light

7.25 Prise the cover from the rear light unit

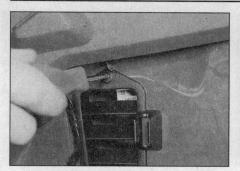

7.26a Remove the securing screw . . .

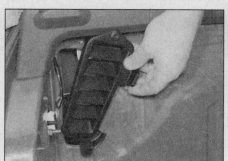

7.26b . . . then unclip the air extraction grille

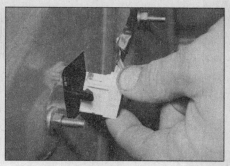

7.27 Pull the wiring plug from the rear of the light

27 Pull the wiring plug(s) from the rear of the light unit **(see illustration)**.
28 Unscrew the two securing nuts and withdraw the light unit from the vehicle **(see illustrations)**.

Refitting

29 Refitting is a reversal of removal, but check the condition of the seals on the rear of the light assembly.

Rear light cluster - July 1996 models onward

Removal

30 Open the tailgate.
31 Prise the plastic cover from the rear of the light unit **(see illustration 7.25)**.
32 Remove the securing screw and unclip the air extraction grille from the side of the luggage compartment **(see illustrations 7.26a**

and **7.26b)**.
33 Unscrew the two plastic wing nuts and withdraw the light unit for access to the bulbholder **(see illustration)**.
34 Release the bulbholder from the light unit by squeezing the retaining tabs, then remove the light unit **(see illustration)**.

Refitting

35 Refitting is a reversal of removal.

High-level stoplight

Removal

36 Using a small screwdriver, depress the retaining tags on the side of the light unit cover and remove the cover.
37 Undo the two screws and withdraw the light unit.
38 Disconnect the wiring connections and remove the unit.

Refitting

39 Refitting is a reversal of the removal procedure.

Rear number plate light

Removal

40 Using a suitable screwdriver, carefully prise the number plate light from the bumper **(see illustration)**.
41 Pull the wiring (and its protective rubber boot) from the bumper and pull the rubber boot from the wiring plug.
42 Pull the wiring plug from the rear of the light unit and withdraw the light unit **(see illustration)**.

Refitting

43 Refitting is a reversal of removal. Make sure that the rubber boot is located correctly over the wiring plug.

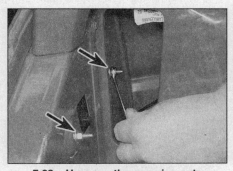

7.28a Unscrew the securing nuts (arrowed) . . .

7.28b . . . then withdraw the light unit

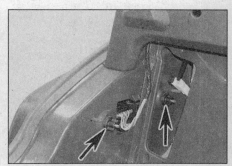

7.33 Unscrew the light unit plastic wing nuts (arrowed)

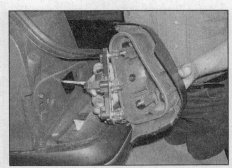

7.34 Release the bulbholder and remove the light unit

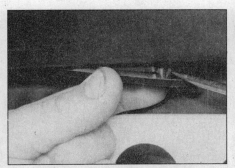

7.40 Prise the rear number plate light from the bumper . . .

7.42 . . . then pull off the boot and disconnect the wiring plug

12

9.5a Remove the lower . . .

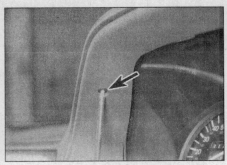

9.5b . . . and upper instrument panel shroud securing screws (arrowed)

9.6 Removing the instrument panel shroud

8 Headlight beam alignment - general information

Accurate adjustment of the headlight beam is only possible using optical beam-setting equipment and this work should therefore be carried out by a Peugeot dealer or suitably-equipped workshop.

All models are equipped with a headlight beam adjustment switch, which allows the aim of the headlights to be adjusted to compensate for the varying loads carried in the vehicle. Certain models have a switch on the facia, which enables beam adjustment via electric adjuster motors located in the in the rear of the headlight assemblies. Models not equipped with electric headlight adjusters have levers located on the rear of the

9.7a Remove the lower . . .

9.7b . . . and upper instrument panel securing screws (arrowed)

headlight units (in the outer top corner) in the engine compartment. The switch or levers, as applicable, should be positioned as follows according to the load being carried in the vehicle:

Position 0   Front seats occupied
Position 1   Front and rear seats occupied
Position 2   Front and rear seats occupied and luggage compartment full
Position 3   Driver's seat occupied and luggage compartment full

9 Instrument panel - removal and refitting

Removal

1 Disconnect the battery negative terminal (refer to *"Disconnecting the battery"* in the Reference Section of this manual).
2 Unclip the front edge of the under-facia trim panel from the facia and lower the panel. Unscrew the two nuts securing the trim panel to the studs in the footwell, then withdraw the panel from the footwell.
3 Working under the steering column, remove the three steering column shroud securing screws. Unclip and lift off the upper shroud, then withdraw the lower shroud. Note that the lower shroud clips over a metal bracket on the steering column and the shroud must be slid from the bracket before it can be removed.
4 Working under the steering column,

unscrew the two steering column securing nuts, then gently lower the steering column, taking care not to strain any of the wiring connected to the switches on the column assembly.
5 Remove the two securing screws from the lower edge of the instrument panel shroud, then remove the two upper shroud securing screws **(see illustrations)**.
6 Carefully prise the instrument panel shroud from the facia **(see illustration)**. Note that it will be necessary to bend the upper facia panel slightly by hand in order to release the shroud securing lugs.
7 Remove the two securing screws from the lower edge of the instrument panel and where applicable, the single upper securing screw **(see illustrations)**.
8 Pull the instrument panel forwards sufficiently to disconnect the wiring plugs and the speedometer cable (pull sharply on the cable) from the rear of the panel, then carefully withdraw the panel from the facia **(see illustrations)**.

Refitting

9 Refitting is a reversal of removal, bearing in mind the following points:
a) *Ensure that the speedometer cable is securely reconnected.*
b) *Ensure that the instrument panel shroud upper securing lugs engage with the facia.*
c) *Tighten the steering column securing nuts to the specified torque (see Chapter 10).*

9.8a Disconnect the wiring plugs . . .

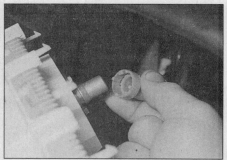

9.8b . . . and the speedometer cable from the instrument panel

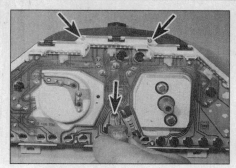

10.2 Remove the securing screws (arrowed) . . .

10.3a . . . then release the securing clips . . .

10.3b . . . and withdraw the lens assembly

10 Instrument panel components - removal and refitting

General

1 Remove the instrument panel as described in Section 9, then proceed as described under the relevant sub-heading.

Speedometer

2 Working at the rear of the instrument panel, remove the three screws securing the lens assembly (see illustration).
3 Using a flat-bladed screwdriver, carefully release the lens assembly securing clips, then withdraw the lens assembly (see illustrations).
4 Working at the front of the speedometer, unscrew the two securing screws (see illustration).
5 Remove the two securing screws from the rear of the speedometer and recover the bushes, then withdraw the speedometer from the instrument panel (see illustrations).
6 Refitting is a reversal of removal.

Tachometer

7 Proceed as described in paragraphs 1 to 3.
8 Working at the front of the tachometer, unscrew the three securing screws.
9 Working at the rear of the tachometer, remove the securing nuts.
10 Where applicable, pull the adjustment knob from the digital clock button, then withdraw the tachometer.
11 Refitting is a reversal of removal.

Analogue clock

12 Proceed as described in paragraphs 1 to 3.

13 Working at the front of the clock, unscrew the three securing screws (see illustration).
14 Working at the rear of the clock, remove the securing nuts (see illustration), then withdraw the clock.

Digital clock

15 Remove the tachometer as described previously in this Section.
16 Carefully unclip the clock from the instrument panel.
17 Refitting is a reversal of removal.

Fuel gauge, temperature gauge and oil pressure gauge

18 Proceed as described in paragraphs 1 to 3.
19 Working at the front of the gauge, remove the securing screw(s).
20 Working at the rear of the gauge, remove the securing nut(s), then withdraw the gauge from the instrument panel.

10.4 Removing a speedometer front securing screw

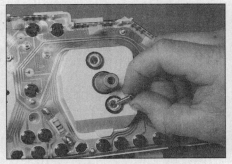

10.5a Remove the speedometer rear securing screws . . .

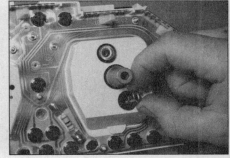

10.5b . . . and recover the bushes . . .

10.5c . . . then withdraw the speedometer

10.13 Clock front securing screws (arrowed)

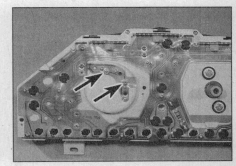

10.14 Clock rear securing nuts (arrowed)

12

Printed circuit

21 Remove all the instruments as described previously in this Section.

22 Remove all the bulbholders from the rear of the instrument panel, by twisting them in an anti-clockwise direction. Slacken and remove all the circuit securing screws, then release the printed circuit from the retaining pins and remove it from the rear of the instrument panel.

23 Refitting is a reversal of removal, ensuring that the circuit tracks are not damaged and that the circuit is correctly located on all the retaining pins.

11 "Lights on" warning system - general information

Most vehicles covered by this manual are fitted with a "lights-on" warning system. The purpose of this system is to inform the driver that the lights have been left switched on, once the ignition switch has been turned off - the buzzer will sound when a door is opened. The system consists simply of a buzzer unit which is connected to the door courtesy light switches.

The buzzer unit is located with the relays behind the fusebox (see Section 3).

14.4 Speedometer cable clip (arrowed) on the rear of the heater assembly

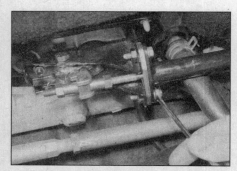

14.8 Loosen the brake pedal-to-servo linkage crosstube bolts

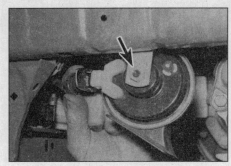

13.6 Disconnecting the horn wiring plug. Horn securing nut arrowed

12 Cigarette lighter - removal and refitting

At the time of writing, no information was available for removal and refitting of the cigarette lighter housing.

13 Horn - removal and refitting

Removal

1 The horn(s) is/are located at the lower left-hand or right-hand front corner of the engine compartment, depending on model.

2 Disconnect the battery negative terminal (refer to *"Disconnecting the battery"* in the Reference Section of this manual).

3 Access to the horn(s) is most easily obtained from under the relevant front wheel arch.

4 If desired to improve access, chock the rear wheels then jack up the front of the vehicle and support it on axle stands (see *"Jacking and Vehicle Support"*).

5 To further improve access, release the clip securing the front of the wheel arch liner and move the wheel arch liner to expose the horn.

6 Disconnect the horn wiring plug **(see illustration)**.

7 Unscrew the horn securing nut and withdraw the horn from the vehicle.

14.9 Pull the brake servo assembly forwards for access to the speedometer cable grommet (arrowed)

Refitting

8 Refitting is a reversal of removal.

14 Speedometer drive cable - removal and refitting

Right-hand drive models

Removal

1 Remove the instrument panel as described in Section 9.

2 Open the glovebox, then remove the two securing screws (underneath the glovebox) and withdraw the glovebox from the facia.

3 Tie a length of string to the cable at the speedometer end.

4 Reach up through the glovebox aperture and unclip the cable from the heater assembly **(see illustration)**.

5 Identify the speedometer grommet in the bulkhead, then pull the cable down through the facia and pass it out through the glovebox aperture.

6 Untie the string from the end of the cable and leave the string in position in the facia, to aid refitting.

7 Working in the engine compartment, remove the two bolts securing the left-hand end of the brake pedal-to-servo linkage crosstube to the brake servo bracket.

8 Similarly, remove the plastic cover and loosen the two bolts securing the right-hand end of the crosstube **(see illustration)**.

9 Unscrew the four bolts securing the brake servo bracket to the studs on the bulkhead, then carefully pull the servo assembly forwards sufficiently to gain access to the speedometer cable grommet in the bulkhead **(see illustration)**. Take care not to strain the master cylinder brake pipes.

10 Unscrew the securing collar (or pull out the rubber pin, as applicable) and withdraw the speedometer cable end from the gearbox **(see illustration)**.

11 Carefully push the cable grommet through the bulkhead into the passenger compartment and withdraw the complete assembly from the vehicle.

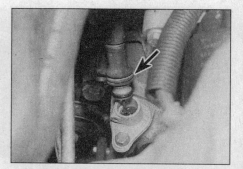

14.10 Disconnecting the speedometer cable end (arrowed) from the gearbox

14.28 Speedometer cable grommet (arrowed) - left-hand drive model

Refitting

12 If a new cable is being fitted and a new grommet and cable ball-fitting are not supplied, note the fitted position of the ball-fitting and grommet on the old cable and then transfer them to the new cable.

13 The aid of an assistant will now be required.

14 Working in the engine compartment, feed the end of the cable through the bulkhead into the passenger compartment.

15 Push the grommet through the bulkhead, with the assistant working in the passenger compartment helping to draw the grommet through. Work the grommet through the bulkhead until the circular section seats correctly on the sound insulation inside the vehicle.

16 Working in the engine compartment, grip the lugs on the grommet and pull gently until the grommet lip locks into position in the bulkhead aperture.

17 Make a final check to ensure that the grommet is correctly located.

18 Reconnect the end of the cable to the gearbox.

19 Carefully push the servo assembly back into position and tighten the bracket securing nuts.

20 Refit and tighten the brake pedal-to-servo linkage crosstube securing bolts.

21 Working through the glovebox aperture, tie the end of the string to the cable and pull on the free end of the string, guiding the cable up behind the facia. Some manipulation will be required. Take care not to kink the cable.

22 With the cable in position and correctly routed, untie the string, then clip the cable into position on the rear of the heater assembly.

23 Refit the glovebox.

24 Refit the instrument panel with reference to Section 9.

Left-hand drive models

Removal

25 Remove the instrument panel as described in Section 9.

26 Reach up under the facia and locate the speedometer grommet in the bulkhead, then pull the cable down through the facia.

27 Working in the engine compartment, unscrew the securing collar (or pull out the rubber pin, as applicable) and withdraw the speedometer cable end from the gearbox.

28 Carefully push the cable grommet through the bulkhead into the passenger compartment and withdraw the complete assembly from the vehicle **(see illustration)**.

Refitting

29 Proceed as described in paragraphs 12 to 18 inclusive.

30 Refit the instrument panel as described in Section 9.

15 Wiper arms - removal and refitting

Removal

1 Operate the wiper motor, then switch it off so that the wiper arm(s) return to the at-rest ("parked") position.

2 Stick a piece of tape along the edge of the wiper blade(s), to use as an alignment aid when refitting. If both windscreen wiper arms are removed, note their locations, as different arms are fitted to the driver's and passenger's sides.

3 Where applicable, lift up the wiper arm spindle nut cover, then slacken and remove the spindle nut **(see illustration)**. Lift the blade off the glass and pull the wiper arm off its spindle. If necessary, the arm can be levered off the spindle using a suitable flat-bladed screwdriver.

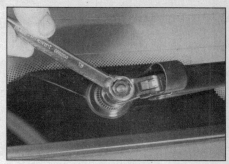

15.3 Unscrewing a tailgate wiper arm spindle nut

Refitting

4 Ensure that the wiper arm and spindle splines are clean and dry, then refit the arm to the spindle, aligning the wiper blade with the tape fitted before removal. If both windscreen wiper arms have been removed, ensure that the arms are refitted to their correct positions as noted before removal.

5 Refit the spindle nut, tighten it securely and where applicable, clip the cover back into position.

16 Windscreen wiper motor and linkage - removal and refitting

Removal

1 Disconnect the battery negative terminal (refer to *"Disconnecting the battery"* in the Reference Section of this manual).

2 On left-hand drive models, operate the wipers and switch off the ignition when the wiper arms are near the top of their arc of movement. This is necessary to position the wiper linkage to enable the motor/linkage assembly to pass out of the scuttle.

3 Remove the windscreen wiper arms as described in Section 15.

4 Open the bonnet.

5 Remove the securing screw and the two nuts and withdraw the windscreen cowl panel from the scuttle. Note that the panel is clipped around the edge of the windscreen and the front wings **(see illustrations)**.

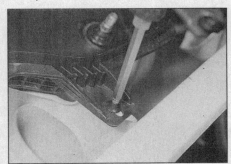

16.5a Removing the windscreen cowl panel securing screw - left-hand drive model shown

16.5b Windscreen cowl panel securing nut (arrowed)

16.5c Withdrawing the windscreen cowl panel - left-hand drive model shown

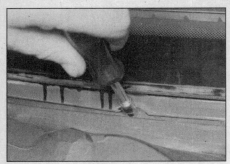

16.6a Remove the securing nuts . . .

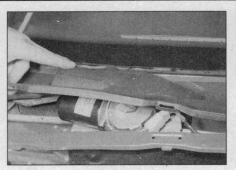

16.6b . . . and unclip the plastic cover panel to expose the wiper motor - right-hand drive model

16.7 Removing the plastic cover from the wiper motor - left-hand drive model shown

6 On right-hand drive models, remove the securing nuts (where applicable) and unclip the plastic cover panel from the scuttle to

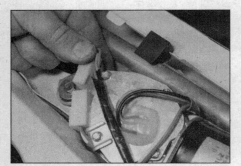

16.8 Disconnecting the wiper motor wiring plug - left-hand drive model shown

expose the wiper motor assembly (see illustrations).

7 Where applicable, pull the plastic cover from the wiper motor assembly (see illustration).

8 Disconnect the wiring plug from the motor (see illustration).

9 Where applicable, pull out the rubber spacer block which fits between the scuttle and the wiper linkage (see illustration). Note the location of the block, to ensure correct refitting.

10 Unscrew the six mounting bolts (recover the washers, where applicable) and withdraw the wiper motor and linkage assembly from the scuttle (see illustrations).

11 To separate the motor from the linkage, unscrew the nut securing the crank arm to the motor shaft, then unscrew the three motor

securing bolts and withdraw the motor from the linkage (see illustration).

12 If desired, the assembly mounting rubbers can be renewed. To renew a mounting rubber, pull the mounting sleeve (and the washer, where applicable) from the rubber, then prise the rubber from the mounting bracket (see illustration). Fit the new rubber using a reversal of removal procedure.

Refitting

13 Refitting is a reversal of removal, bearing in mind the following points:

a) On left-hand drive models, ensure that the wiper linkage is positioned as during removal - see paragraph 2.

b) Ensure that the spacer block is correctly positioned between the scuttle and wiper linkage, as noted before removal.

16.9 Pull the rubber block from the scuttle - left-hand drive model shown

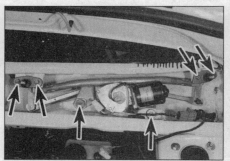

16.10a Unscrew the wiper motor and linkage assembly securing bolts (arrowed) . . .

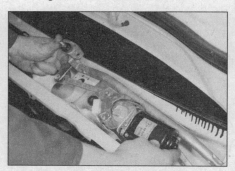

16.10b . . . and lift the assembly from the scuttle - left-hand drive model

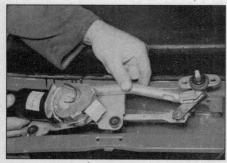

16.10c Lifting the wiper motor and linkage assembly from the scuttle - right-hand drive model

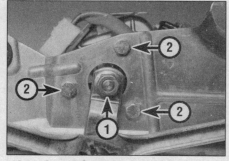

16.11 Crank arm-to-motor shaft securing nut (1) and motor securing bolts (2)

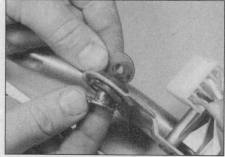

16.12 Remove the mounting sleeve and washer to enable renewal of the mounting rubber

17.3a Recover the spindle dust cover . . .

17.3b . . . then unscrew the trim disc . . .

17.3c . . . and lift off the grommet cover

c) On right-hand drive models, ensure that the plastic cover panel is correctly positioned on the scuttle.
d) Ensure that the windscreen cowl panel is

correctly engaged with the windscreen and the wing panels. Where applicable, ensure that the wiper spindle grommet is correctly located in the panel.
e) Refit the windscreen wiper arms as described in Section 15.

17 Tailgate wiper motor - removal and refitting

Removal

1 Disconnect the battery negative terminal (refer to *"Disconnecting the battery"* in the Reference Section of this manual).
2 Remove the tailgate wiper arm, as described in Section 15.
3 Recover the spindle dust cover, then

unscrew the trim disc and lift off the grommet cover **(see illustrations)**.
4 Open the tailgate.
5 Remove the two screws securing the tailgate trim panel, then release the securing clips and withdraw the panel from the tailgate **(see illustrations)**.
6 Unclip the wiper motor relay from the tailgate, then disconnect the wiring connectors and feed the wiring and the relay through the aperture in the tailgate **(see illustration)**. Note the routing of the wiring, to aid refitting.
7 Unscrew the three motor securing nuts and withdraw the assembly, complete with the wiring and relay **(see illustrations)**.

Refitting

8 Refitting is a reversal of removal, bearing in mind the following points:

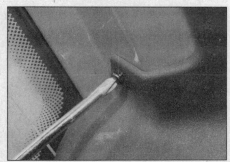

17.5a Remove the screws . . .

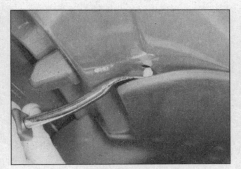

17.5b . . . then release the securing clips . . .

17.5c . . . and withdraw the trim panel

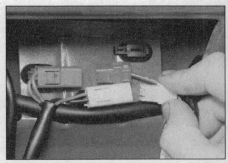

17.6 Disconnect the tailgate wiper motor wiring connectors

17.7a Unscrew the three motor securing nuts . . .

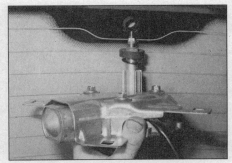

17.7b . . . then withdraw the assembly . . .

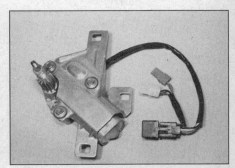

17.7c . . . complete with the wiring and the relay

12

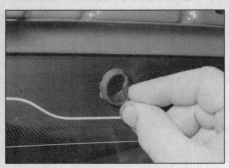

17.8 Renew the tailgate wiper motor spindle grommet if necessary

18.2 Unscrew the filler neck from the washer fluid reservoir

18.4a Release the securing clips . . .

a) *Before refitting the assembly, check the condition of the wiper spindle grommet in the tailgate* **(see illustration)** *and renew if necessary.*

b) *Ensure that the wiring is correctly routed, as noted before removal.*

c) *Refit the wiper arm with reference to Section 15.*

18 Windscreen/tailgate washer system components - removal and refitting

Washer fluid reservoir

Removal

1 Disconnect the battery negative terminal (refer to *"Disconnecting the battery"* in the Reference Section of this manual).

18.5 Release the securing strap (arrowed) . . .

2 Working in the engine compartment, unscrew the filler neck from the top of the reservoir **(see illustration)**.

3 Chock the rear wheels then jack up the front of the vehicle and support it on axle stands (see *"Jacking and Vehicle Support"*). Remove the right-hand front roadwheel.

4 Remove the screw securing the front of the wheel arch liner to the bumper, then release the securing clips (which are a push fit) and withdraw the liner from under the wheel arch **(see illustrations)**.

5 Release the securing strap from the reservoir, then lower the reservoir from the wheel arch **(see illustration)**.

6 Disconnect the washer pump wiring plug(s) **(see illustration)**. Disconnect the fluid hose(s) from the pump(s) - be prepared for fluid spillage - then withdraw the reservoir.

Refitting

7 Refitting is a reversal of removal.

Washer pump(s)

Removal

8 Remove the fluid reservoir as described previously in this Section.

9 The washer pump(s) is/are a push fit in the reservoir **(see illustration)**.

Refitting

10 Refitting is a reversal of removal, but check the condition of the mounting grommet in the reservoir and renew if necessary.

18.4b . . . and withdraw the wheel arch liner

Windscreen washer jet

11 Carefully prise the washer nozzle from the bonnet (take care not to damage the paintwork) and disconnect the fluid hose.

12 Refitting is a reversal of removal.

Tailgate washer jet

13 Carefully prise the washer jet from the tailgate (take care not to damage the paintwork) and disconnect the fluid hose **(see illustration)**.

14 Take care not to allow the hose to drop back into the tailgate - tape it to the tailgate if necessary.

15 Refitting is a reversal of removal.

18.6 . . . then disconnect the wiring plug(s) and the hose(s)

18.9 Removing a washer fluid pump

18.13 Removing the tailgate washer jet

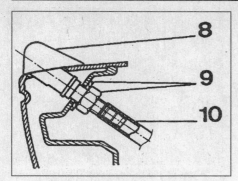

19.7 Headlight washer nozzle fixings in bumper

8 Washer nozzle   10 Fluid hose
9 Nut and washer

19 Headlight washer system components -
removal and refitting

Washer fluid reservoir

1 Proceed as described previously in Section 18 for the windscreen/tailgate washer fluid reservoir, but note that on early models, the headlight washer fluid reservoir is located on the left-hand side of the engine compartment and is secured by a wire strap.

Washer pump

2 Remove the fluid reservoir with reference to paragraph 1.
3 The washer pump is a push fit in the reservoir.

20.3 Slide the tools into position . . .

20.4 . . . and release the radio/cassette player securing clips (arrowed)

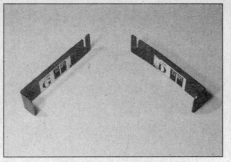

20.2a Make up two suitable tools . . .

4 Refitting is a reversal of removal.

Washer jets

5 Remove the bumper as described in Chapter 11.
6 Working behind the bumper, disconnect the fluid hose from the rear of the washer jet.
7 Prise off the securing clip (or unscrew the securing nut and washer, as applicable), then withdraw the washer jet from the top of the bumper **(see illustration).**
8 Refitting is a reversal of removal. Refit the bumper as described in Chapter 11.

20 Radio/cassette player -
removal and refitting

Note: *Once the battery has been disconnected, the radio/cassette unit cannot be re-activated until the appropriate security code has been entered. Do not remove the unit unless the appropriate code is known.*

Removal

1 Disconnect the battery negative terminal (refer to *"Disconnecting the battery"* in the Reference Section of this manual).
2 Using strips of thin metal, make up two suitable tools to the dimensions shown **(see illustrations). Note:** *These tools can be obtained from your Peugeot dealer, if preferred.*
3 Slide the tools between the sides of the radio/cassette player and the facia panel, until the slots in the tools are felt to engage with

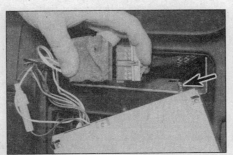

20.5 Disconnect the wiring plug and aerial lead (arrowed) and withdraw the radio/cassette player

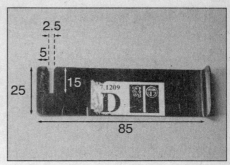

20.2b . . . from 1 mm thick metal plate, to the dimensions shown (in mm)

the radio/cassette player securing clips **(see illustration).**
4 Push the tools forwards to release the clips, then use the tools to pull the unit from the facia **(see illustration).**
5 Disconnect the wiring plug(s) and the aerial lead and withdraw the unit **(see illustration).**

Refitting

6 Reconnect the wiring and the aerial lead to the rear of the unit, then push the wiring into position at the rear of the radio/cassette player aperture. Ensure that the wiring is positioned correctly behind the radio/cassette player, to allow space for the unit to be pushed into position.
7 With the tools engaged with the securing clips, push the unit into position, then pull the tools forwards until the securing clips lock into position.

21 Speakers -
removal and refitting

Front door-mounted speakers

1 Disconnect the battery negative terminal (refer to *"Disconnecting the battery"* in the Reference Section of this manual).
2 Remove the securing screws (prise out the trim plate for access to the top screw) and withdraw the door pocket assembly **(see illustrations).** Where applicable, disconnect the wiring plug(s) from the switch(es) in the door pocket.

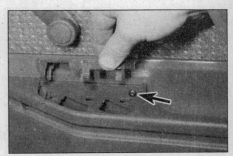

21.2a Prise out the door pocket trim plate for access to the top securing screw (arrowed) . . .

12

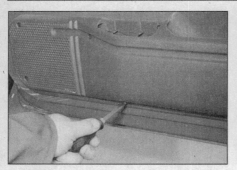

21.2b ... then remove the securing screws ...

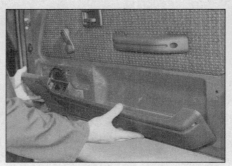

21.2c ... and withdraw the door pocket

21.3 Withdraw the speaker and disconnect the wiring plug

3 Remove the securing screws, then withdraw the speaker from the door and disconnect the wiring plug **(see illustration)**.

4 Refitting is a reversal of removal, but note the locating lug on the edge of the speaker which engages with the corresponding hole in the door **(see illustration)**.

Rear speakers - 3-door models

5 Disconnect the battery negative terminal (refer to *"Disconnecting the battery"* in the Reference Section of this manual).

6 Remove the relevant rear passenger compartment side trim panel, as described in Chapter 11.

7 Remove the securing screws and withdraw the speaker from the rear of the trim panel.

8 Refitting is a reversal of removal, but note that the speaker should be fitted with the wiring terminals pointing towards the rear of the trim panel. Refit the trim panel with reference to Chapter 11.

Rear-door-mounted speakers

9 Disconnect the battery negative terminal (refer to *"Disconnecting the battery"* in the Reference Section of this manual).

10 Where applicable, pull the ashtray from the door panel.

11 Remove the securing screws and withdraw the door pocket/armrest assembly from the door.

12 Carefully release the securing clips and pull the lower corner of the door inner trim panel away from the edge of the speaker.

13 Remove the four securing screws and

manipulate the speaker from its location in the door.

14 Disconnect the wiring plug and withdraw the speaker **(see illustration)**.

15 Refitting is a reversal of removal.

---

22 Radio aerial -
removal and refitting

Aerial mast

1 Note that the aerial mast can be unscrewed from the mounting on the roof and is available as a separate component. To remove the complete assembly, proceed as follows.

2 Carefully prise the courtesy light from the roof panel and disconnect the wiring plug.

3 Pull the suppressor can from the bottom of the aerial **(see illustration)**.

4 Unscrew the aerial securing nut, then disconnect the aerial lead from the stud and pull the aerial from the roof.

5 Refitting is a reversal of removal.

Upper aerial lead

6 Disconnect the lead from the aerial mast as described in paragraphs 2 to 4.

7 Carefully pull the front pillar trim panel from the pillar to expose the aerial lead. Take care not to break the trim panel securing clips.

8 Where applicable, unscrew the securing nuts and unclip the trim panel from under the facia.

9 Pull the carpet panel from the edge of the footwell (if necessary, prise the weatherstrip

from the front edge of the door aperture), to expose the lower aerial connector. Where applicable, pull the insulation from the connector.

10 Separate the two halves of the connector, then tie a length of string to the top of the aerial lead.

11 Release the lead from the clips on the body pillar, then carefully pull the lead down through the roof lining, pillar and facia. Untie the string from the end of the lead and leave it in place to aid refitting.

12 Refitting is a reversal of removal, bearing in mind the following points:

a) *Use the string to pull the lead up through the facia, body pillar and roof panel.*

b) *Make sure that the lead is securely clipped to the body pillar.*

Lower aerial lead

13 Remove the radio/cassette player as described in Section 20.

14 Separate the two halves of the aerial connector as described in paragraphs 8 to 10.

15 Tie a length of string to the upper end of the lead, then pull the lead down into the footwell. Untie the string and leave it in place in the facia to aid refitting.

16 Commence refitting by using the string to pull the lead back into position. With the lead correctly routed, untie the string.

17 Reconnect the lead connector, then refit the carpet panel and, where applicable, the trim panel.

18 Refit the radio/cassette player as described in Section 20.

21.4 Ensure that the locating lug (arrowed) engages with the hole in the door

21.14 Removing a rear door-mounted loudspeaker

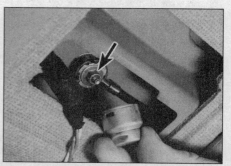

22.3 Pull the suppressor can from the aerial for access to the securing nut (arrowed)

23 Anti-theft alarm system and engine immobiliser - general information

Note: *This information is applicable only to the anti-theft alarm system fitted by Peugeot as standard equipment.*

General

Some models in the range are fitted with an anti-theft alarm system as standard equipment. The alarm is automatically armed and disarmed using the remote central locking transmitter (where applicable). When the system is activated, the alarm indicator light, located on the facia, will flash continuously. In addition to the alarm function, the system also incorporates an engine immobiliser.

Additionally, certain models are fitted with a coded engine immobiliser device, operated by a key pad in the centre console, or an electronic immobiliser activated by a transponder in the ignition key.

Anti-theft alarm system

Note that if the doors are operated using the key, the alarm will not be armed or disarmed (as applicable). If for some reason the remote central locking transmitter fails whilst the alarm is armed, the alarm can be disarmed using the key. To do this, open the door with the key, then enter the vehicle, noting that the alarm will sound as the door is opened and switch on the ignition switch whilst depressing the small alarm button, mounted on the right of the steering column. Note that the ignition switch must be turned on and the button depressed within 10 seconds of opening the door.

The alarm system has switches on the bonnet, tailgate and each of the doors. It also has ultrasonic sensing, which detects movement inside the vehicle, via sensors mounted on either side of the vehicle interior. If required, the ultrasonic sensing facility can be switched off, whilst retaining the switched side of the system. To switch off the ultrasonic sensing, with the ignition switched off, depress the alarm switch (mounted on the right of the steering column) until the alarm indicator light on the facia is continuously lit. Now, when the doors are locked using the remote central locking transmitter and the alarm is armed, only the switched side of the alarm system is operational (and the alarm indicator light will revert to its flashing mode). This facility is useful, as it allows you to leave the windows/sunroof open and still arm the alarm. If the windows/sunroof are left open with the ultrasonic sensing not switched off, the alarm may be falsely triggered by a gust of wind.

To de-activate the complete alarm system, a master switch is provided in the engine compartment, behind the right-hand headlight. The switch is operated by a dedicated key and is protected by a plastic cover.

Should the alarm system become faulty, the vehicle should be taken to a Peugeot dealer for examination.

Coded engine immobiliser

Caution: Do not forget the immobiliser code - if the correct code cannot be entered, the engine management electronic control unit must be renewed.

This device cuts out the engine management system and prevents the engine from being started unless a confidential code is keyed into the pad located in the centre console.

The code can be chosen by the owner and full details are given in the vehicle handbook.

When the ignition is turned on, if the green light on the key pad is illuminated, the system is not working and the engine can be started normally. If the red light is illuminated, the system is working (the engine cannot be started and the alarm will sound if starting is attempted).

To de-activate the system, enter the correct code, which should be confirmed by four flashes from the green light and four beeps. The red light should go out and the engine can then be started.

If the wrong code is entered, the red light will stay on and the engine cannot be started.

Electronic immobiliser

On later models, the coded engine immobiliser is replaced by an electronic immobiliser. The electronic immobiliser consists of a transponder fitted to the ignition key, an analogue module fitted around the ignition switch and a control module located in the facia.

When the ignition key is inserted in the switch and turned to the ignition on position, the control module sends a pre-programmed recognition code signal to the analogue module on the ignition switch. If the recognition code signal matches that of the transponder on the ignition key, an unlocking request signal is sent to the engine management ECU allowing the engine to be started. If the ignition key signal is not recognised, the engine management system remains immobilised.

When the ignition is switched off, a locking signal is sent to the ECU and the engine is immobilised until the unlocking request signal is again received.

The recognition code is programmed into the system during manufacture and is contained on a confidential card supplied with the vehicle. The card should be kept in a safe place - never in the vehicle. The confidential card will be required if any work is to be carried out on the system by a Peugeot dealer, or if replacement keys are required.

Disconnecting the vehicle battery

Refer to *"Disconnecting the battery"* in the Reference Section of this manual.

24 Heated front seat components - general information

Certain models may be equipped with heated front seats. The seats are heated by electrical elements built into the seat cushions.

For access to the heating elements, the seats must be dismantled; this work should be entrusted to a Peugeot dealer.

The heated seat switches are mounted in the centre console. Removal and refitting details are given in Section 4.

25 Air bag system - precautions and system de-activation

A driver's air bag is fitted as standard equipment on certain models and is an option on all other models. The air bag is fitted in the steering wheel centre pad. Additionally, on later models, a passenger's air bag located in the facia is also optionally available.

The system is armed only when the ignition is switched on, however, a reserve power source maintains a power supply to the system in the event of a break in the main electrical supply. The air bags are activated by a "g" sensor (deceleration sensor) and controlled by an electronic control unit which is integral with the steering wheel.

The air bags are inflated by a gas generator, which forces the bag out from its location in the steering wheel or facia.

Precautions

⚠️ *Warning: The following precautions must be observed when working on vehicles equipped with an air bag system, to prevent the possibility of personal injury.*

General precautions

The following precautions **must** be observed when carrying out work on a vehicle equipped with an air bag:

a) *Do not disconnect the battery with the engine running.*

b) *Before carrying out any work in the vicinity of the air bag, removal of any of the air bag components, or any welding work on the vehicle, de-activate the system as described in the following sub-Section.*

c) *Do not attempt to test any of the air bag system circuits using test meters or any other test equipment.*

d) *If the air bag warning light comes on, or any fault in the system is suspected, consult a Peugeot dealer without delay. Do not attempt to carry out fault diagnosis, or any dismantling of the components.*

12

Precautions to be taken when handling an air bag

a) Transport the air bag by itself, bag upward.

b) Do not put your arms around the air bag.

c) Carry the air bag close to the body, bag outward.

d) Do not drop the air bag or expose it to impacts.

e) Do not attempt to dismantle the air bag unit.

f) Do not connect any form of electrical equipment to any part of the air bag circuit.

Precautions to be taken when storing an air bag unit

a) Store the unit in a cupboard with the air bag upward.

b) Do not expose the air bag to temperatures above 80°C.

c) Do not expose the air bag to flames.

d) Do not attempt to dispose of the air bag - consult a Peugeot dealer.

e) Never refit an air bag which is known to be faulty or damaged.

De-activation of air bag system

The system must be de-activated before carrying out any work on the air bag components or surrounding area:

a) Switch off the ignition.

b) Remove the ignition key.

c) Switch off all electrical equipment.

d) Disconnect the battery negative terminal (refer to "Disconnecting the battery" in the Reference Section of this manual).

e) Insulate the battery negative terminal and the end of the battery negative lead to prevent any possibility of contact.

f) Wait for at least ten minutes before carrying out any further work.

Activation of air bag system

To activate the system on completion of any work, proceed as follows:

a) Ensure that there are no occupants in the vehicle and that there are no loose objects around the vicinity of the steering wheel. Close the vehicle doors and windows.

b) Insert the ignition key and switch on the ignition.

c) Reconnect the battery negative terminal.

d) Switch off the ignition.

e) Switch on the ignition once more and check that the air bag warning light illuminates for approximately 3 seconds and then extinguishes.

f) Switch off the ignition.

g) If the air bag warning light does not operate as described in paragraph e), consult a Peugeot dealer before driving the vehicle.

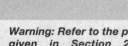

26 Air bag system components - removal and refitting

⚠️ Warning: Refer to the precautions given in Section 25 before attempting to carry out work on any of the air bag components.
Caution: The following information is applicable to vehicles fitted with a driver's air bag in the steering wheel. At the time of writing, no information was available concerning the passenger's air bag in the facia. On vehicles equipped with a passenger's air bag, consult a Peugeot dealer before carrying out any work in the vicinity of the air bag components.

General

1 The air bag sensors are integral with the electronic control unit, which is itself integral with the steering wheel.

2 Any suspected faults with the air bag system should be referred to a Peugeot dealer - under no circumstances attempt to carry out any work other than removal and refitting of the air bag unit and/or the rotary connector, as described in the following paragraphs.

Air bag electronic control unit

3 The unit is integral with the steering wheel and cannot be removed independently. Refer to Chapter 10 for details of steering wheel removal.

Air bag unit

Removal

4 The air bag unit is an integral part of the steering wheel centre boss.

5 De-activate the air bag system as described in Section 25.

6 Move the steering wheel as necessary for access to the two air bag unit securing screws. The screws are located at the rear of the steering wheel boss.

7 Remove the two air bag unit securing screws.

8 Gently pull the air bag unit from the centre of the steering wheel.

9 Carefully unclip the wiring connector from the air bag unit (use the fingers only and pull the connector upward from the air bag unit).

10 If the air bag unit is to be stored for any length of time, refer to the storage precautions given in Section 25.

Refitting

11 Refitting is a reversal of removal, bearing in mind the following points:

a) Do not strike the air bag unit, or expose it to impacts during refitting.

b) Tighten the air bag unit securing screws to the specified torque.

c) On completion of refitting, activate the air bag system as described in Section 25.

Air bag rotary connector

Removal

12 Remove the air bag unit, as described previously in this Section.

13 Remove the steering wheel as described in Chapter 10.

14 Remove the three steering column shroud securing screws. Unclip and lift off the upper shroud, then withdraw the lower shroud.

15 Carefully unclip the red rotary connector wiring plug from its bracket using a thin screwdriver blade inserted between the bracket and the connector.

16 Release the securing clip and separate the two halves of the plug.

17 Remove the two screws securing the left-hand steering column stalk switch, then slide the switch from its bracket so that the end of the switch clears the indicator cancelling finger.

18 Unscrew the three securing screws and withdraw the rotary connector from the steering column, feeding the wiring harness through the stalk switch bracket. Note the routing of the wiring harness.

Refitting

19 Refitting is a reversal of removal, bearing in mind the following points:

a) Before refitting the steering column shrouds, ensure that the rotary connector wiring harness is correctly routed as noted before removal. Ensure that the wiring plug securing clip (securing the two halves of the plug together) is securely engaged.

b) Refit the steering wheel as described in Chapter 10 and refit the air bag unit as described previously in this Section.

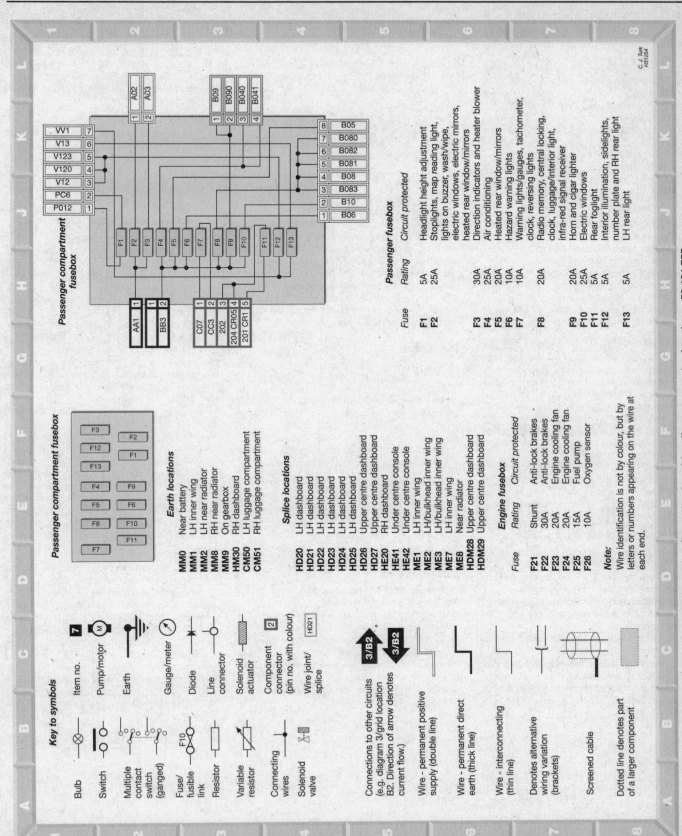

C. J. Turk
H31254

Passenger compartment fusebox

Passenger fusebox

Fuse	Rating	Circuit protected
F1	5A	Headlight height adjustment
F2	25A	Stoplights, map reading light, lights on buzzer, wash/wipe, electric windows, electric mirrors, heated rear window/mirrors
F3	30A	Direction indicators and heater blower
F4	25A	Air conditioning
F5	20A	Heated rear window/mirrors
F6	10A	Hazard warning lights
F7	10A	Warning lights/gauges, tachometer, clock, reversing lights
F8	20A	Radio memory, central locking, clock, luggage/interior light, infra-red signal receiver
F9	20A	Horn and cigar lighter
F10	25A	Electric windows
F11	5A	Rear foglight
F12	5A	Interior illumination, sidelights, number plate and RH rear light
F13	5A	LH rear light

Passenger compartment fusebox

F3	F2
F12	F1
F13	
F4	F9
F5	F6
F8	F10
F7	F11

Earth locations

MM0 Near battery
MM1 LH inner wing
MM2 RH near radiator
MM8 RH near radiator
MM9 On gearbox
HM30 RH dashboard
CM50 LH luggage compartment
CM51 RH luggage compartment

Splice locations

HD20 LH dashboard
HD21 LH dashboard
HD22 LH dashboard
HD23 LH dashboard
HD24 LH dashboard
HD25 LH dashboard
HD26 Upper centre dashboard
HD27 Upper centre dashboard
HE20 RH dashboard
HE41 Under centre console
HE42 Under centre console
ME1 LH inner wing
ME2 LH/bulkhead inner wing
ME3 LH/bulkhead inner wing
ME7 LH inner wing
ME8 Near radiator
HDM28 Upper centre dashboard
HDM29 Upper centre dashboard

Engine fusebox

Fuse	Rating	Circuit protected
F21	Shunt	Anti-lock brakes
F22	30A	Anti-lock brakes
F23	20A	Engine cooling fan
F24	20A	Engine cooling fan
F25	15A	Fuel pump
F26	10A	Oxygen sensor

Note:
Wire identification is not by colour, but by letters or numbers appearing on the wire at each end.

Key to symbols

Bulb	
Switch	
Multiple contact switch (ganged)	
Fuse/ fusible link	
Resistor	
Variable resistor	
Connecting wires	
Solenoid valve	
Item no.	
Pump/motor	
Earth	
Gauge/meter	
Diode	
Line connector	
Solenoid actuator	
Component connector (pin no. with colour)	
Wire joint/ splice	

Connections to other circuits
(e.g. diagram 3/grid location
B2. Direction of arrow denotes
current flow.)

Wire - permanent positive
supply (double line)

Wire - permanent direct
earth (thick line)

Wire - interconnecting
(thin line)

Denotes alternative
wiring variation
(brackets)

Screened cable

Dotted line denotes part
of a larger component

Diagram 1 : Information for wiring diagrams - up to chassis no. 50 191 755

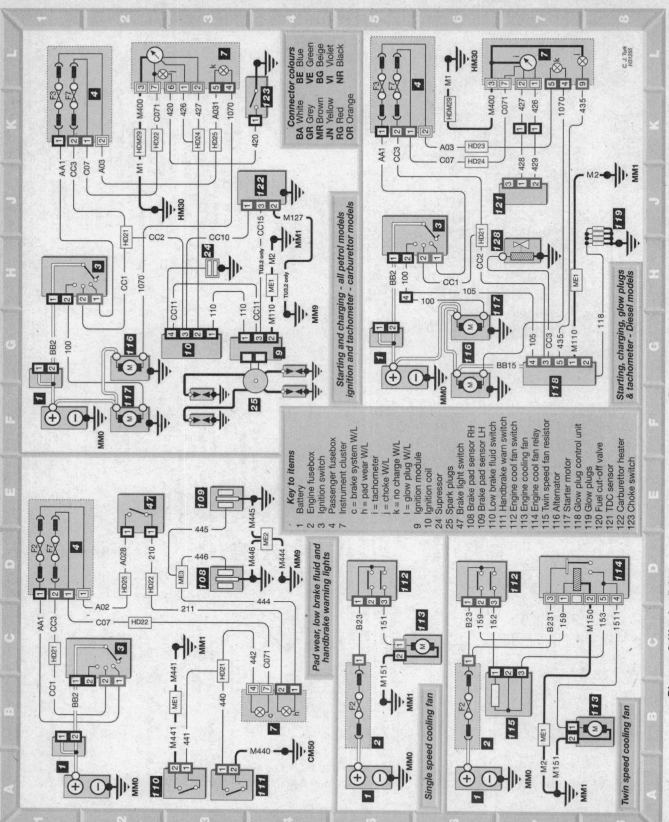

Diagram 2: Warning lights, starting, charging, ignition, glow plugs and tachometer - up to chassis no. 50 191 755

C.J. Turk
H31255

Connector colours

BA White
GR Grey
MR Brown
JN Yellow
OR Orange
BE Blue
VE Green
BG Beige
VI Violet
NR Black

Key to items

1 Battery
2 Engine fusebox
3 Ignition switch
4 Passenger fusebox
7 Instrument cluster
   c = brake system W/L
   h = pad wear W/L
   i = tachometer
   j = choke W/L
   k = no charge W/L
   l = glow plug W/L
9 Ignition module
10 Ignition coil
24 Supressor
25 Spark plugs
47 Brake light switch
108 Brake pad sensor RH
109 Brake pad sensor LH
110 Low brake fluid switch
111 Handbrake warn switch
112 Engine cool fan switch
113 Engine cooling fan
114 Engine cool fan relay
115 Twin speed fan resistor
116 Starter motor
117 Alternator
118 Glow plug control unit
119 Glow plugs
120 Fuel cut-off valve
121 TDC sensor
122 Carburettor heater
123 Choke switch

Starting and charging - all petrol models ignition and tachometer - carburettor models

Starting, charging, glow plugs & tachometer - Diesel models

Pad wear, low brake fluid and handbrake warning lights

Single speed cooling fan

Twin speed cooling fan

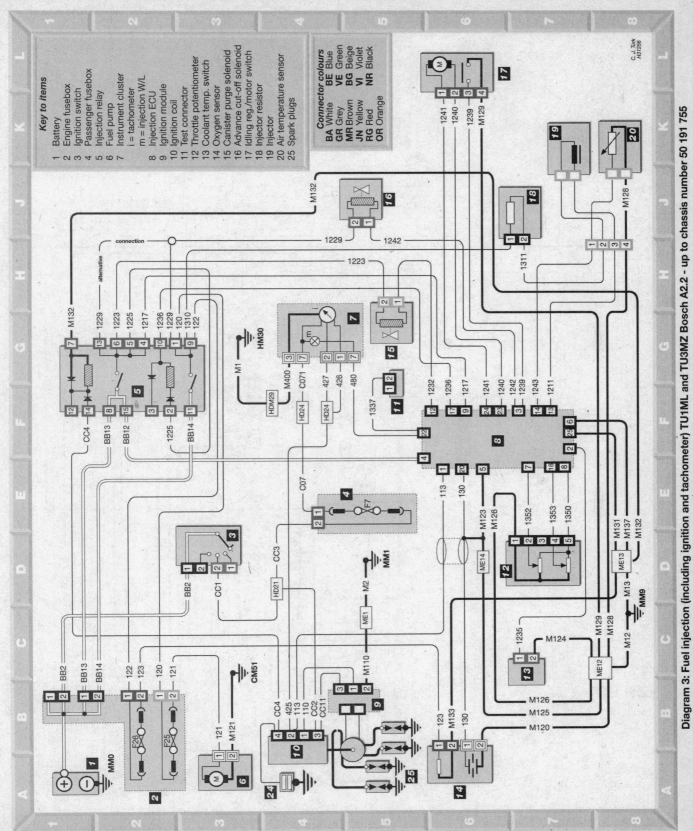

Diagram 3: Fuel injection (including ignition and tachometer) TU1ML and TU3MZ Bosch A2.2 - up to chassis number 50 191 755

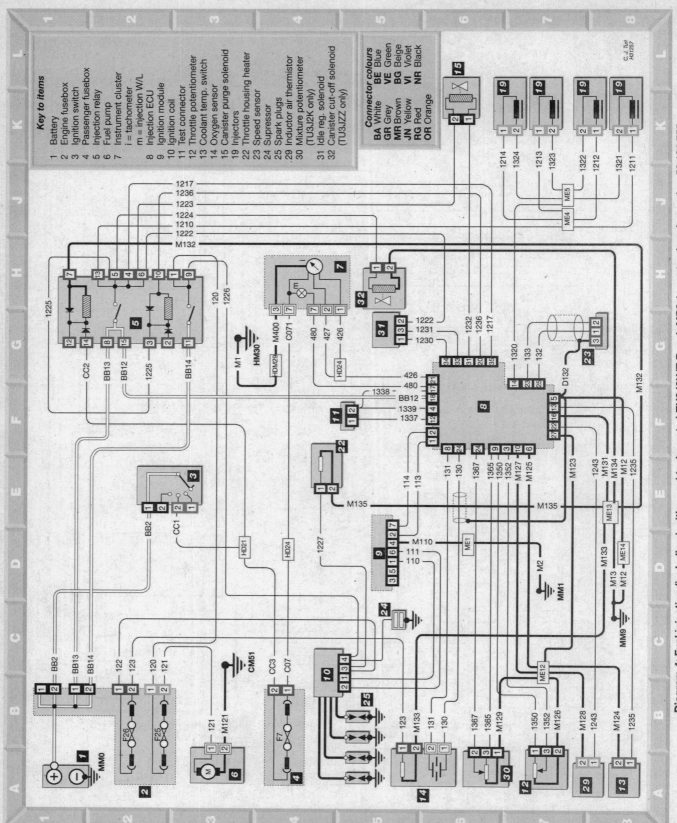

Key to items

1 Battery
2 Engine fusebox
3 Ignition switch
4 Passenger fusebox
5 Injection relay
6 Fuel pump
7 Instrument cluster
  i = tachometer
  m = injection W/L
8 Injection ECU
9 Ignition module
10 Ignition coil
11 Test connector
12 Throttle potentiometer
13 Coolant temp. switch
14 Oxygen sensor
15 Canister purge solenoid
19 Injectors
22 Throttle housing heater
23 Speed sensor
24 Supressor
25 Spark plugs
29 Inductor air thermistor
30 Mixture potentiometer
   (TU3J2K only)
31 Idle reg. solenoid
32 Canister cut-off solenoid
   (TU3JZZ only)

Connector colours

BA White	**BE** Blue		
GR Grey	**VE** Green		
MR Brown	**BG** Beige		
JN Yellow	**VI** Violet		
RG Red	**NR** Black		
OR Orange			

C. J. Turl
H31257

Diagram 4: Fuel injection (including ignition and tachometer) TU3J2K/Z Bosch MP3.1 – up to chassis number 50 191 755

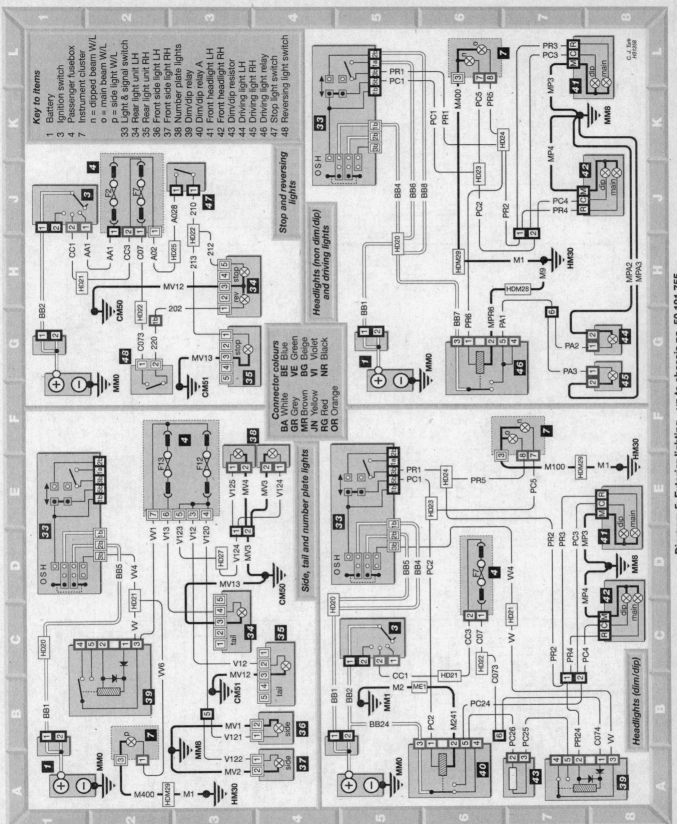

Diagram 5: Exterior lighting - up to chassis no. 50 191 755

Key to items
1 Battery
3 Ignition switch
4 Passenger fusebox
7 Instrument cluster
 n = dipped beam W/L
 o = main beam W/L
 p = side light W/L
33 Light & signal switch
34 Rear light unit LH
35 Rear light unit RH
36 Front side light LH
37 Front side light RH
38 Number plate lights
39 Dim/dip relay
40 Dim/dip relay A
41 Front headlight LH
42 Front headlight RH
43 Dim/dip resistor
44 Driving light LH
45 Driving light RH
46 Driving light relay
47 Stop light switch
48 Reversing light switch

Connector colours
BA White   BE Blue
GR Grey   VE Green
MR Brown   BG Beige
JN Yellow   VI Violet
RG Red   NR Black
OR Orange

Stop and reversing lights

Headlights (non dim/dip) and driving lights

Side, tail and number plate lights

Headlights (dim/dip)

12

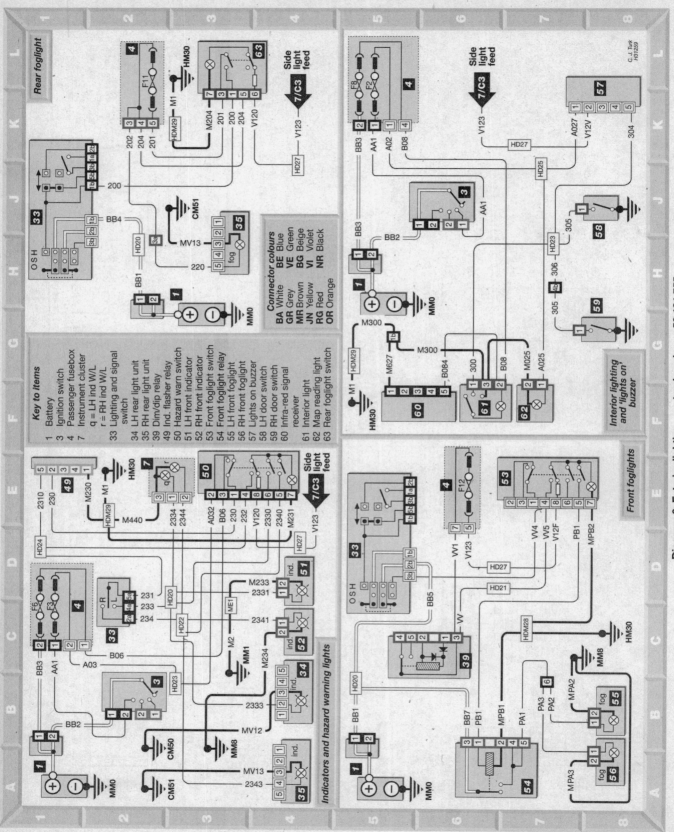

Rear foglight

Side light feed 7/C3

Side light feed 7/C3

Connector colours
BA White BE Blue
GR Grey VE Green
MR Brown BG Beige
JN Yellow VI Violet
RG Red NR Black
OR Orange

Key to items
1 Battery
3 Ignition switch
4 Passenger fusebox
7 Instrument cluster
  q = LH ind W/L
  r = RH ind W/L
33 Lighting and signal
   switch
34 LH rear light unit
35 RH rear light unit
39 Dim/dip relay
49 Ind. flasher relay
50 Hazard warn switch
51 LH front indicator
52 RH front indicator
53 Front foglight switch
54 Front foglight relay
55 LH front foglight
56 RH front foglight
57 Lights on buzzer
58 LH door switch
59 RH door switch
60 Infra-red signal
   receiver
61 Interior light
62 Map reading light
63 Rear foglight switch

Interior lighting and 'lights on' buzzer

Front foglights

Indicators and hazard warning lights

Side light feed 7/C3

Diagram 6: Exterior lighting - up to chassis no. 50 191 755

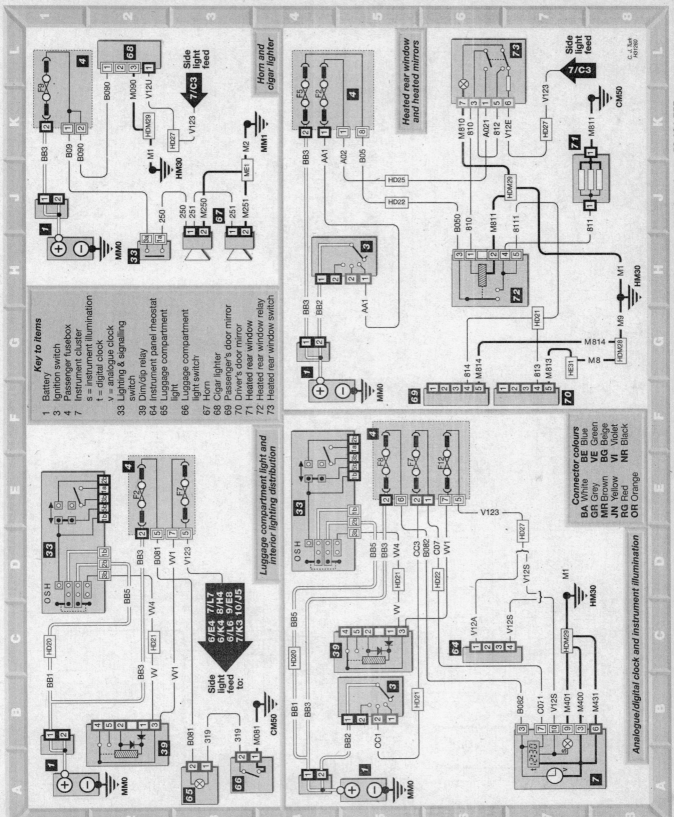

Diagram 7: Interior illumination, clock, horn, cigar lighter, heated rear window and heated mirrors - up to chassis no. 50 191 755

Key to items

1 Battery
3 Ignition switch
4 Passenger fusebox
7 Instrument cluster
   s = instrument illumination
   t = digital clock
   v = analogue clock
33 Lighting & signalling switch
39 Dim/dip relay
64 Instrument panel rheostat
65 Luggage compartment light
66 Luggage compartment light switch
67 Horn
68 Cigar lighter
69 Passenger's door mirror
70 Driver's door mirror
71 Heated rear window
72 Heated rear window relay
73 Heated rear window switch

Connector colours
BA White   BE Blue
GR Grey   VE Green
MR Brown   BG Beige
JN Yellow   VI Violet
RG Red   NR Black
OR Orange

Horn and cigar lighter

Heated rear window and heated mirrors

Luggage compartment light and interior lighting distribution

Analogue/digital clock and instrument illumination

C. J. Turk H31260

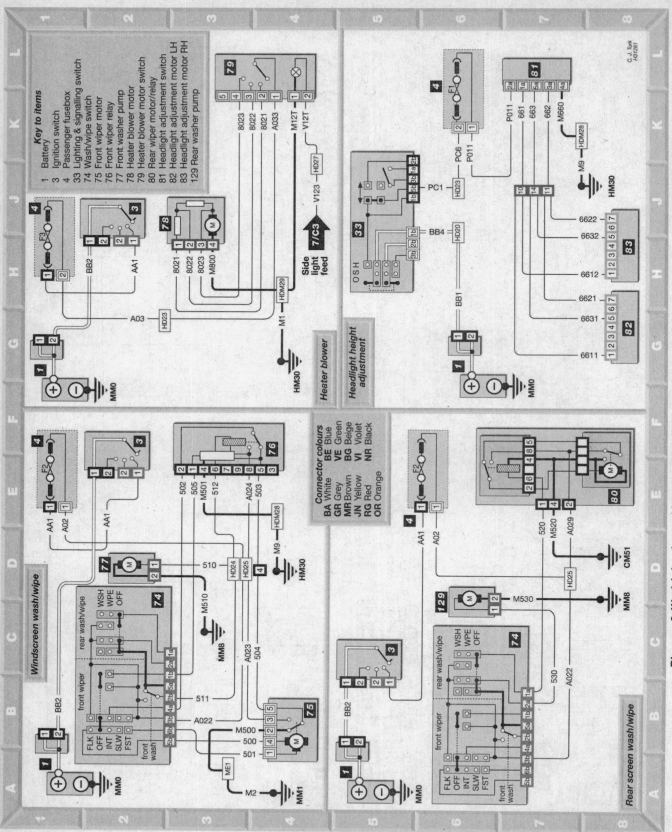

Key to items
1 Battery
3 Ignition switch
4 Passenger fusebox
33 Lighting & signalling switch
74 Wash/wipe switch
75 Front wiper motor
76 Front wiper relay
77 Front washer pump
78 Heater blower motor
79 Heater blower motor switch
80 Rear wiper motor/relay
81 Headlight adjustment switch
82 Headlight adjustment motor LH
83 Headlight adjustment motor RH
129 Rear washer pump

Connector colours
BA White   BE Blue
GR Grey   VE Green
MR Brown   BG Beige
JN Yellow   VI Violet
RG Red   NR Black
OR Orange

Side light feed

Heater blower

Headlight height adjustment

Windscreen wash/wipe

Rear screen wash/wipe

Diagram 8: Wash/wipe, heater blower and headlight height adjustment - up to chassis no. 50 191 755

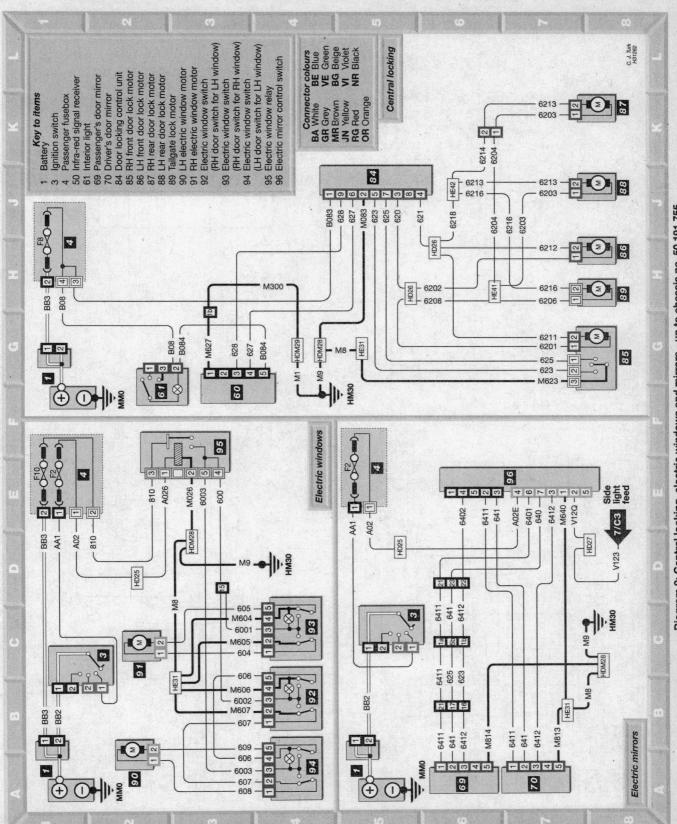

Key to items

1 Battery
3 Ignition switch
4 Passenger fusebox
50 Infra-red signal receiver
61 Interior light
69 Passenger's door mirror
70 Driver's door mirror
84 Door locking control unit
85 RH front door lock motor
86 LH front door lock motor
87 RH rear door lock motor
88 LH rear door lock motor
89 Tailgate lock motor
90 LH electric window motor
91 RH electric window motor
92 Electric window switch
    (RH door switch for LH window)
93 Electric window switch
    (RH door switch for RH window)
94 Electric window switch
    (LH door switch for LH window)
95 Electric window relay
96 Electric mirror control switch

Connector colours

BA	White	BE	Blue
GR	Grey	VE	Green
MR	Brown	BG	Beige
JN	Yellow	VI	Violet
RG	Red	NR	Black
OR	Orange		

Central locking

Electric windows

Electric mirrors

C. J. Turk
H31262

Side light feed

12

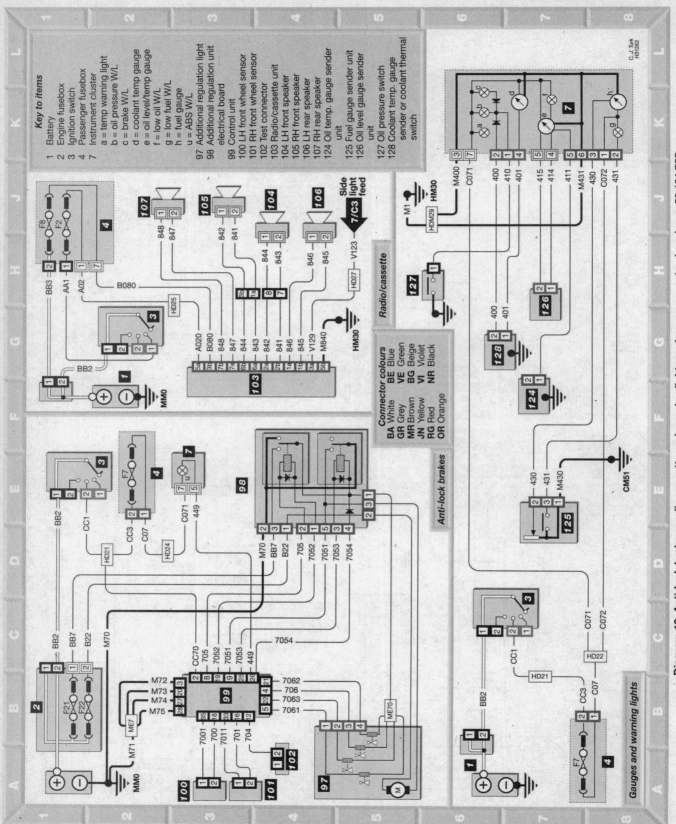

C.J. Turk
H31263

Key to items

1 Battery
2 Engine fusebox
3 Ignition switch
4 Passenger fusebox
7 Instrument cluster
 a = temp warning light
 b = oil pressure W/L
 c = brake W/L
 d = coolant temp gauge
 e = oil level/temp gauge
 f = low oil W/L
 g = low fuel W/L
 h = fuel gauge
 u = ABS W/L
97 Additional regulation light
98 Additional regulation unit
 electrical board
99 Control unit
100 LH front wheel sensor
101 RH front wheel sensor
102 Test connector
103 Radio/cassette unit
104 LH front speaker
105 RH front speaker
106 LH rear speaker
107 RH rear speaker
124 Oil temp. gauge sender unit
125 Fuel gauge sender unit
126 Oil level gauge sender unit
127 Oil pressure switch
128 Coolant temp. gauge sender or coolant thermal switch

Radio/cassette

Connector colours

BA White   BE Blue
GR Grey   VE Green
MR Brown   BG Beige
JN Yellow   VI Violet
RG Red   NR Black
OR Orange

Anti-lock brakes

Gauges and warning lights

Diagram 10: Anti-lock brakes, radio cassette and warning lights and gauges - up to chassis no. 50 191 755

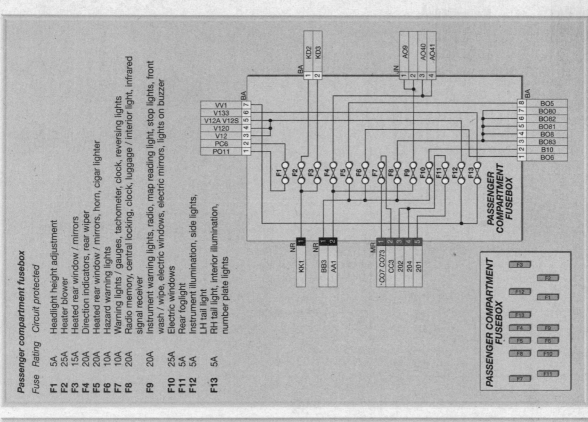

Passenger compartment fusebox

Fuse	Rating	Circuit protected
F1	5A	Headlight height adjustment
F2	25A	Heater blower
F3	15A	Heated rear window / mirrors
F4	20A	Direction indicators, rear wiper
F5	20A	Heated rear window / mirrors, horn, cigar lighter
F6	10A	Hazard warning lights
F7	10A	Warning lights / gauges, tachometer, clock, reversing lights
F8	20A	Radio memory, central locking, clock, luggage / interior light, infrared signal receiver
F9	20A	Instrument warning lights, radio, map reading light, stop lights, front wash / wipe, electric windows, electric mirrors, lights on buzzer
F10	25A	Electric windows
F11	5A	Rear foglight
F12	5A	Instrument illumination, side lights, LH tail light
F13	5A	RH tail light, interior illumination, number plate lights

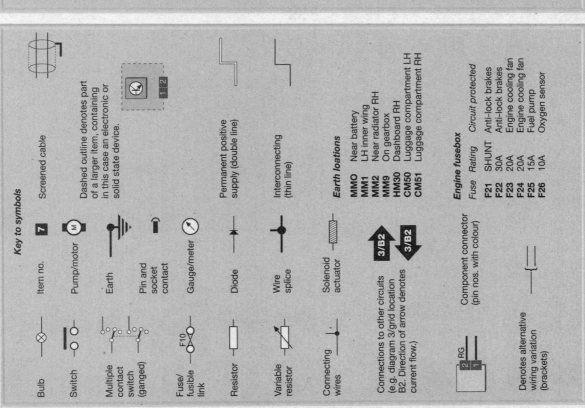

Key to symbols

Bulb
Switch
Multiple contact switch (ganged)
Fuse/ fusible link
Resistor
Variable resistor
Connecting wires
Connections to other circuits (e.g. diagram 3/grid location B2. Direction of arrow denotes current flow.)
Denotes alternative wiring variation (brackets)

Item no.
Pump/motor
Earth
Pin and socket contact
Gauge/meter
Diode
Wire splice
Solenoid actuator
Component connector (pin nos. with colour)

Screened cable
Dashed outline denotes part of a larger item, containing in this case an electronic or solid state device.
Permanent positive supply (double line)
Interconnecting (thin line)

Earth loations

MMO	Near battery
MM1	LH inner wing
MM2	Near radiator RH
MM9	On gearbox
HM30	Dashboard RH
CM50	Luggage compartment LH
CM51	Luggage compartment RH

Engine fusebox

Fuse	Rating	Circuit protected
F21	SHUNT	Anti-lock brakes
F22	30A	Anti-lock brakes
F23	20A	Engine cooling fan
F24	20A	Engine cooling fan
F25	15A	Fuel pump
F26	10A	Oxygen sensor

Diagram 11 : Notes, fuses, locations, key to symbols - from chassis no. 50 191 756

12

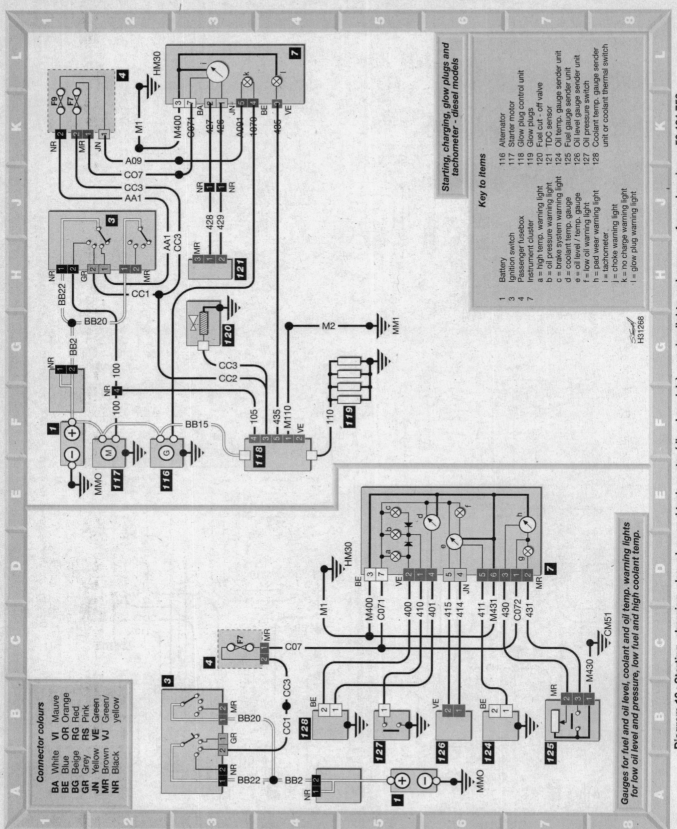

Key to items

1	Battery
3	Ignition switch
4	Passenger fusebox
7	Instrument cluster
	a = high temp. warning light
	b = oil pressure warning light
	c = brake system warning light
	d = coolant temp. gauge
	e = oil level / temp. gauge
	f = low oil warning light
	h = pad wear warning light
	i = tachometer
	j = choke warning light
	k = no charge warning light
	l = glow plug warning light

116	Alternator
117	Starter motor
118	Glow plug control unit
119	Glow plugs
120	Fuel cut - off valve
121	TDC sensor
124	Oil temp. gauge sender unit
125	Fuel gauge sender unit
126	Oil level gauge sender unit
127	Oil pressure switch
128	Coolant temp. gauge sender unit or coolant thermal switch

Starting, charging, glow plugs and tachometer - diesel models

H31268

Gauges for fuel and oil level, coolant and oil temp, warning lights for low oil level and pressure, low fuel and high coolant temp.

Connector colours

BA	White	VI	Mauve
BE	Blue	OR	Orange
BG	Beige	RG	Red
GR	Grey	RS	Pink
JN	Yellow	VE	Green
MR	Brown	VJ	Green/ yellow
NR	Black		

Diagram 12 : Starting, charging, glow plugs and tachometer (diesel models), warning lights and gauges - from chassis no. 50 191 756

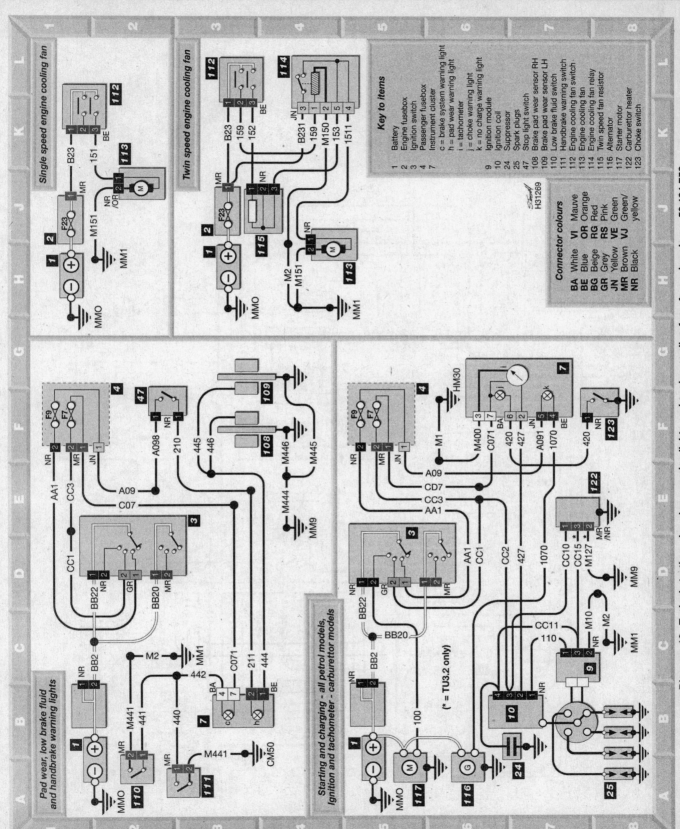

Single speed engine cooling fan

Twin speed engine cooling fan

Key to items

1 Battery
2 Engine fusebox
3 Ignition switch
4 Passenger fusebox
7 Instrument cluster
  c = brake system warning light
  h = pad wear warning light
  i = tachometer
  j = choke warning light
  k = no charge warning light
9 Ignition module
10 Ignition coil
24 Suppressor
25 Spark plugs
47 Stop light switch
108 Brake pad wear sensor RH
109 Brake pad wear sensor LH
110 Low brake fluid switch
111 Handbrake warning switch
112 Engine cooling fan switch
113 Engine cooling fan
114 Engine cooling fan relay
115 Twin speed fan resistor
116 Alternator
117 Starter motor
122 Carburettor heater
123 Choke switch

S.Fendt
H31269

Connector colours

BA	White	VI	Mauve
BE	Blue	OR	Orange
BG	Beige	RG	Red
GR	Grey	RS	Pink
JN	Yellow	VE	Green
MR	Brown	VJ	Green/yellow
NR	Black		

Pad wear, low brake fluid and handbrake warning lights

Starting and charging - all petrol models, Ignition and tachometer - carburettor models

(* = TU3.2 only)

Diagram 13 : Typical starting, charging, warning lights and engine cooling fan - from chassis no. 50 191 756

12

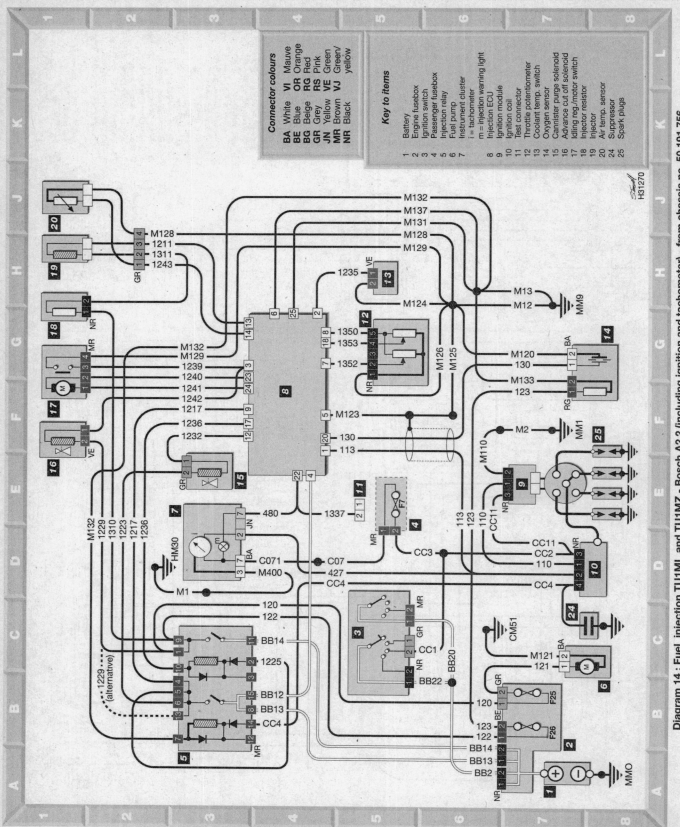

Connector colours

BA White	**VI** Mauve		
BE Blue	**OR** Orange		
BG Beige	**RG** Red		
GR Grey	**RS** Pink		
JN Yellow	**VE** Green		
MR Brown	**VJ** Green/		
NR Black	yellow		

Key to items

1 Battery
2 Engine fusebox
3 Ignition switch
4 Passenger fusebox
5 Injection relay
6 Fuel pump
7 Instrument cluster
    m = injection warning light
    i = tachometer
8 Injection ECU
9 Ignition module
10 Ignition coil
11 Test connector
12 Throttle potentiometer
13 Coolant temp. switch
14 Oxygen sensor
15 Cannister purge solenoid
16 Advance cut off solenoid
17 Idling reg./motor switch
18 Injector resistor
19 Injector
20 Air temp. sensor
24 Suppressor
25 Spark plugs

H31270

Diagram 14 : Fuel injection TU1ML and TU1MZ - Bosch A2.2 (including ignition and tachometer) - from chassis no. 50 191 756

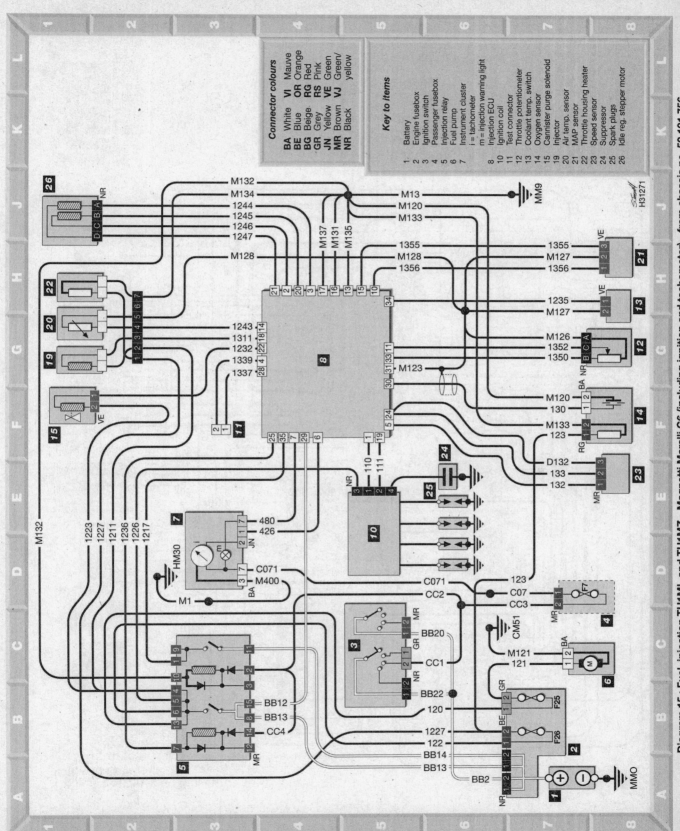

Connector colours

BA White **VI** Mauve
BE Blue **OR** Orange
BG Beige **RG** Red
GR Grey **RS** Pink
JN Yellow **VE** Green
MR Brown **VJ** Green/
NR Black yellow

Key to items

1 Battery
2 Engine fusebox
3 Ignition switch
4 Passenger fusebox
5 Injection relay
6 Fuel pump
7 Instrument cluster
i = tachometer
8 Injection ECU
10 Ignition coil
11 Test connector
12 Throttle potentiometer
13 Coolant temp. switch
14 Oxygen sensor
15 Cannister purge solenoid
19 Injector
20 Air temp. sensor
21 MAP sensor
22 Throttle housing heater
23 Speed sensor
24 Suppressor
25 Spark plugs
26 Idle reg. stepper motor

Diagram 15 : Fuel injection TU1ML and TU1MZ - Magnetti Marelli G6 (including ignition and tachometer) - from chassis no. 50 191 756

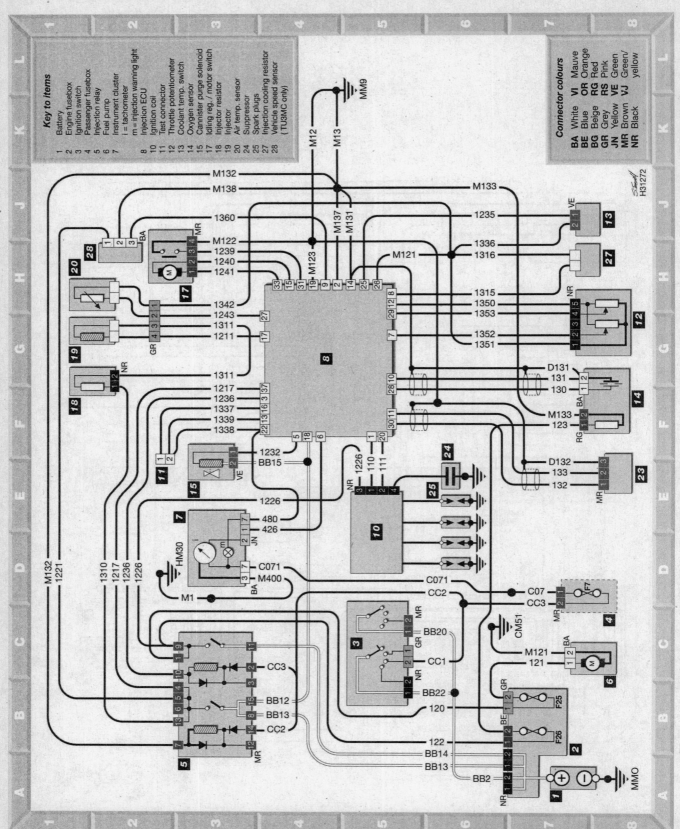

Diagram 16 : Fuel injection TU9ML/Z and TU3MCL/Z - Bosch MA3.0 (including ignition and tachometer) - from chassis no. 50 191 756

Key to items

1 Battery
2 Engine fusebox
3 Ignition switch
4 Passenger fusebox
5 Injection relay
6 Fuel pump
7 Instrument cluster
  m = injection warning light
  i = tachometer
8 Injection ECU
10 Ignition coil
11 Test connector
12 Throttle potentiometer
13 Coolant temp. switch
14 Oxygen sensor
15 Cannister purge solenoid
17 Idling reg. / motor switch
18 Injector resistor
19 Injector
20 Air temp. sensor
24 Suppressor
25 Spark plugs
27 Injection cooling resistor
28 Vehicle speed sensor
   (TU3MC only)

Connector colours

BA White   VI Mauve
BE Blue   OR Orange
BG Beige   RG Red
GR Grey   RS Pink
JN Yellow   VE Green
MR Brown   VJ Green/
NR Black   yellow

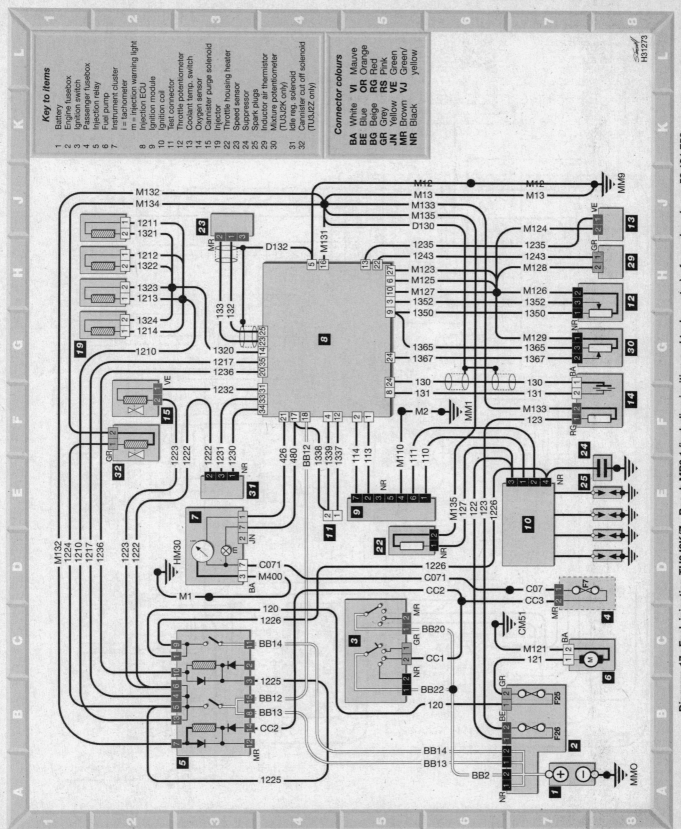

Key to items

1 Battery
2 Engine fusebox
3 Ignition switch
4 Passenger fusebox
5 Injection relay
6 Fuel pump
7 Instrument cluster
    i = tachometer
    m = injection warning light
8 Injection ECU
9 Ignition module
10 Ignition coil
11 Test connector
12 Throttle potentiometer
13 Coolant temp. switch
14 Oxygen sensor
15 Canister purge solenoid
19 Injector
22 Throttle housing heater
23 Speed sensor
24 Suppressor
25 Spark plugs
29 Inductor air thermistor
30 Mixture potentiometer
    (TU3J2K only)
31 Idle reg. solenoid
32 Cannister cut off solenoid
    (TU3J2Z only)

Connector colours

BA	White	VI	Mauve
BE	Blue	OR	Orange
BG	Beige	RG	Red
GR	Grey	RS	Pink
JN	Yellow	VE	Green
MR	Brown	VJ	Green/yellow
NR	Black		

Diagram 17 : Fuel injection TU3J2K/Z - Bosch MP3.1 (including ignition and tachometer) - from chassis no. 50 191 756

12

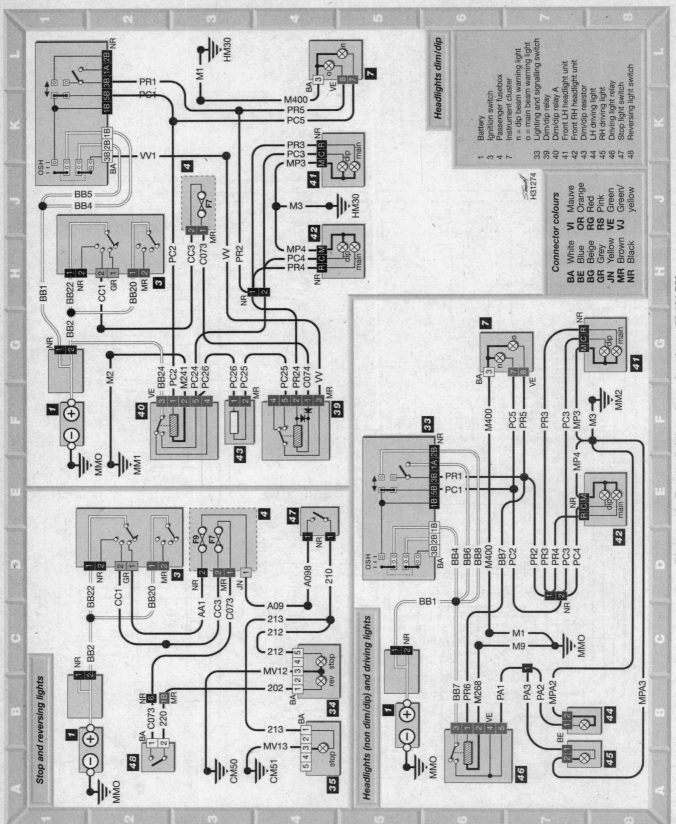

Diagram 18 : Exterior lighting - from chassis no. 50 191 756

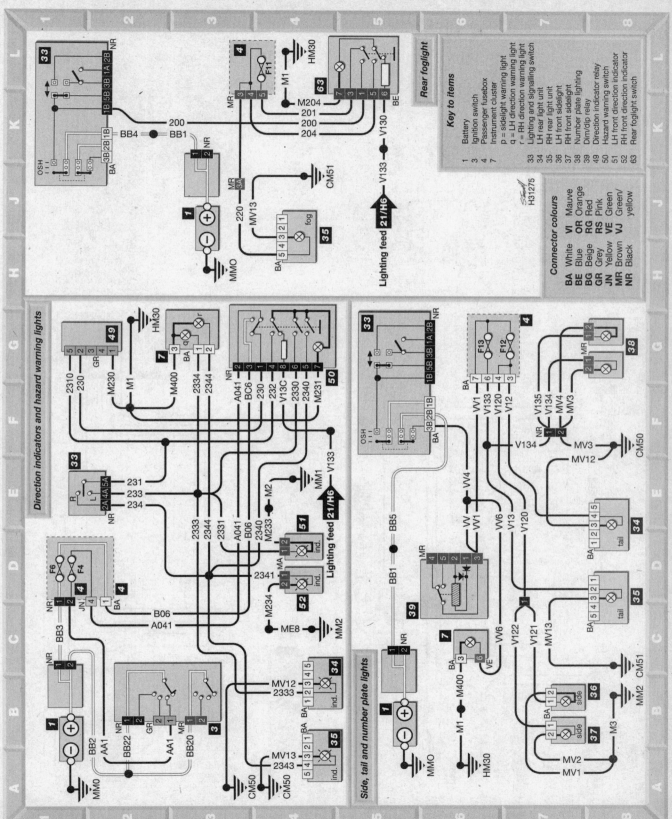

Rear foglight

Key to items

1 Battery
3 Ignition switch
4 Passenger fusebox
7 Instrument cluster
   p = sidelight warning light
   q = LH direction warning light
   r = RH direction warning light
   7 = Lighting and signalling switch
33 Lighting and signalling switch
34 LH rear light unit
35 RH rear light unit
36 LH front sidelight
37 RH front sidelight
38 Number plate lighting
39 Dim/dip relay
49 Direction indicator relay
50 Hazard warning switch
51 LH front direction indicator
52 RH front direction indicator
63 Rear foglight switch

Connector colours

BA	White	**VI**	Mauve
BE	Blue	**OR**	Orange
BG	Beige	**RG**	Red
GR	Grey	**RS**	Pink
JN	Yellow	**VE**	Green
MR	Brown	**VJ**	Green/yellow
NR	Black		

H31275

Direction indicators and hazard warning lights

Side, tail and number plate lights

Diagram 19 : Exterior and interior lighting - from chassis no. 50 191 756

12

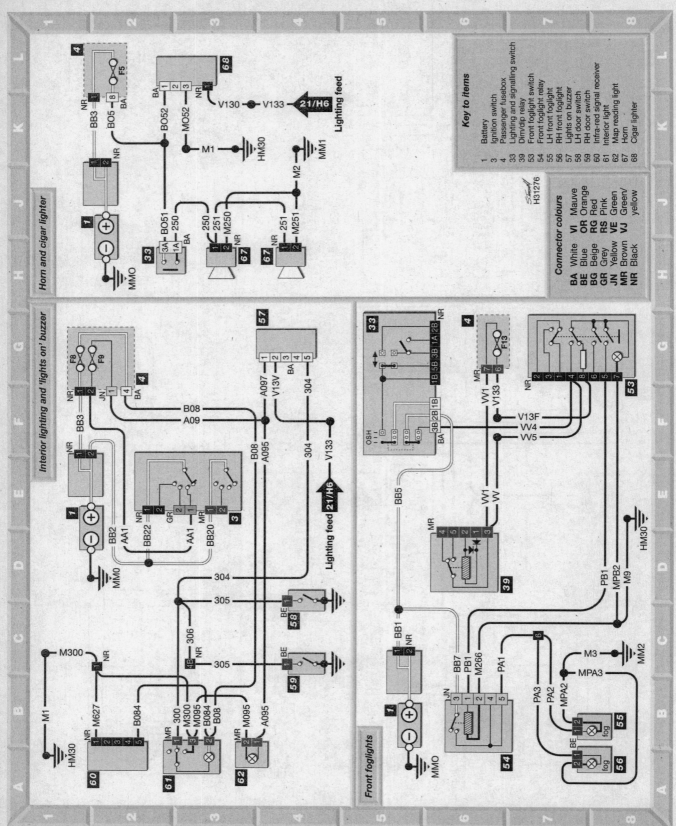

Diagram 20 : Exterior and interior lighting, horn and cigar lighter – from chassis no. 50 191 756

Key to items

1 Battery
3 Ignition switch
4 Passenger fusebox
33 Lighting and signalling switch
39 Dim/dip relay
53 Front foglight switch
54 Front foglight relay
55 LH front foglight
56 RH front foglight
57 Lights on buzzer
58 LH door switch
59 RH door switch
60 Infra-red signal receiver
61 Interior light
62 Map reading light
67 Horn
68 Cigar lighter

H31276

Connector colours

BA	White	VI	Mauve
BE	Blue	OR	Orange
BG	Beige	RG	Red
GR	Grey	RS	Pink
JN	Yellow	VE	Green
MR	Brown	VJ	Green/ yellow
NR	Black		

Horn and cigar lighter

Interior lighting and 'lights on' buzzer

Front foglights

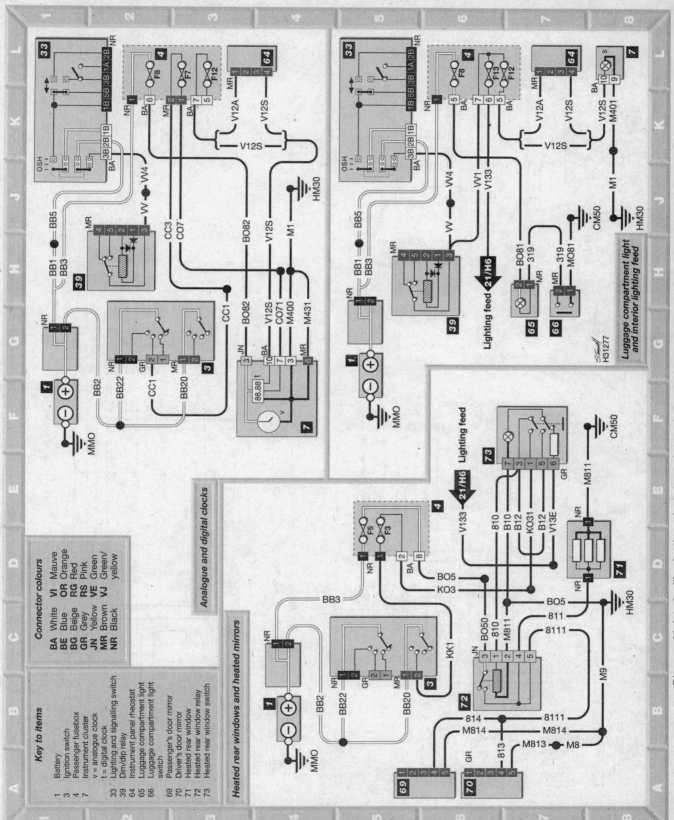

Diagram 21: Interior illumination, clock, heated rear window and heated mirrors - from chassis no. 50 191 756

Luggage compartment light and interior lighting feed

Analogue and digital clocks

Heated rear windows and heated mirrors

Connector colours

BA White	**VI** Mauve		
BE Blue	**OR** Orange		
BG Beige	**RG** Red		
GR Grey	**RS** Pink		
JN Yellow	**VE** Green		
MR Brown	**VJ** Green/		
NR Black	yellow		

Key to items

1 Battery
3 Ignition switch
4 Passenger fusebox
7 Instrument cluster
   v = analogue clock
   t = digital clock
33 Lighting and signalling switch
39 Dim/dip relay
64 Instrument panel rheostat
65 Luggage compartment light
66 Luggage compartment light switch
69 Passenger's door mirror
70 Driver's door mirror
71 Heated rear window
72 Heated rear window relay
73 Heated rear window switch

H31277

12

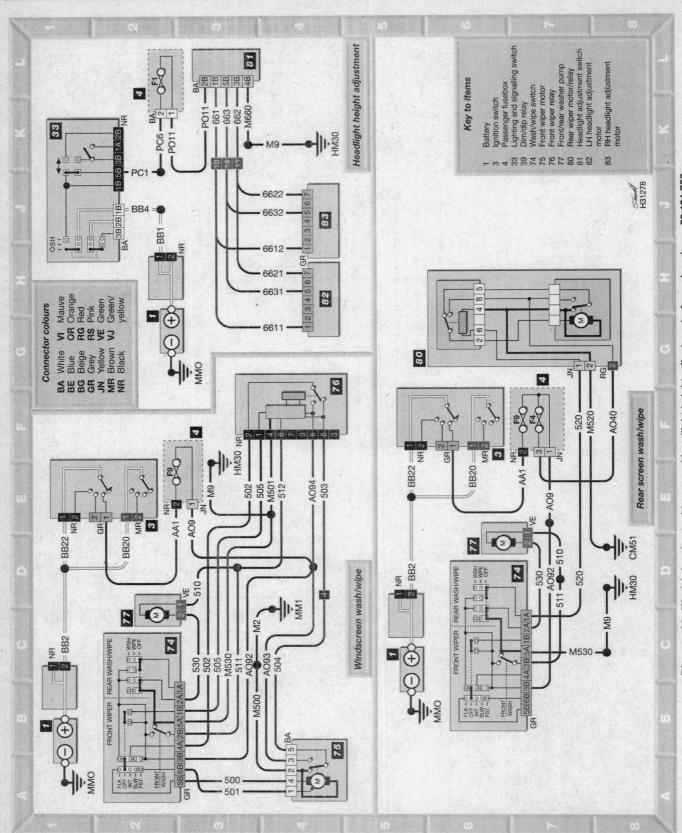

Headlight height adjustment

Windscreen wash/wipe

Rear screen wash/wipe

Key to items

1 Battery
3 Ignition switch
4 Passenger fusebox
33 Lighting and signalling switch
39 Dim/dip relay
74 Wash/wipe switch
75 Front wiper motor
76 Front wiper motor
77 Front/rear washer pump
80 Rear wiper motor/relay
81 Headlight adjustment switch
82 LH headlight adjustment motor
83 RH headlight adjustment motor

Connector colours

BA White   VI Mauve
BE Blue   OR Orange
BG Beige   RG Red
GR Grey   RS Pink
JN Yellow   VE Green
MR Brown   VJ Green/yellow
NR Black

H31278

Diagram 22 : Wash/wipe, heater blower and headlight height adjustment - from chassis no. 50 191 756

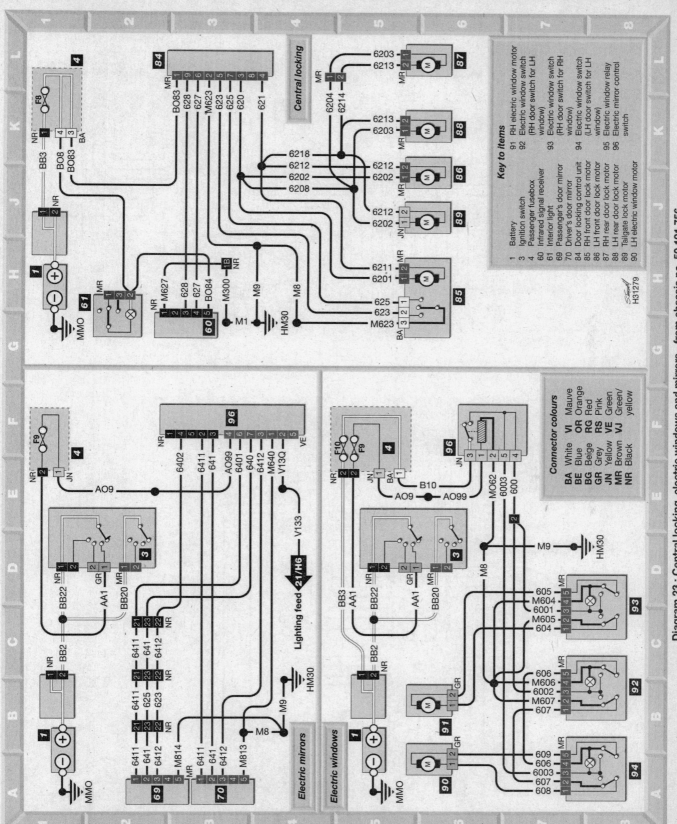

Diagram 23 : Central locking, electric windows and mirrors - from chassis no. 50 191 756

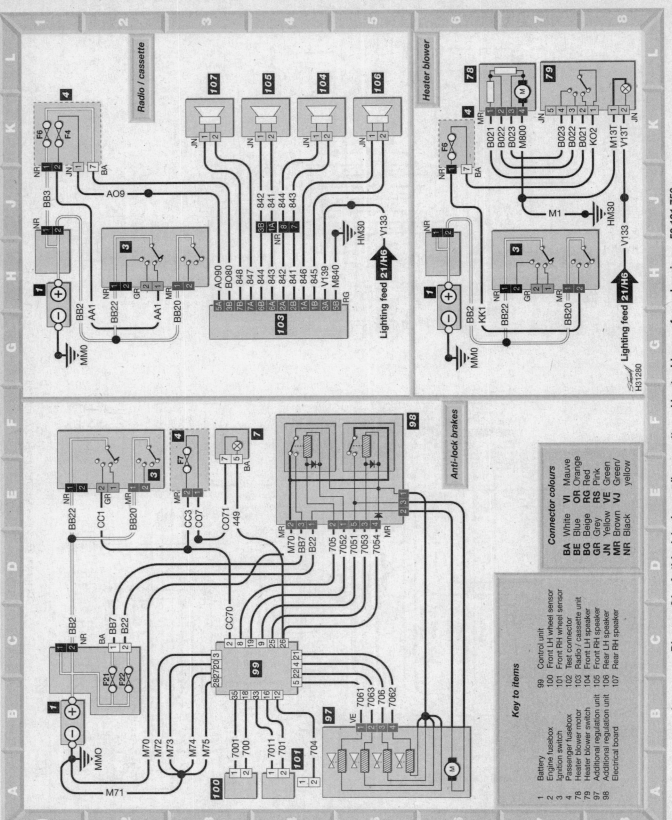

Diagram 24 : Anti-lock brakes, radio cassette and heater blower - from chassis no. 50 191 756

Connector colours

BA White VI Mauve
BE Blue OR Orange
BG Beige RG Red
GR Grey RS Pink
JN Yellow VE Green
MR Brown VJ Green/
NR Black yellow

Key to items

1 Battery
2 Engine fusebox
3 Ignition switch
4 Passenger fusebox
78 Heater blower motor
79 Heater blower switch
97 Additional regulation unit
98 Additional regulation unit
99 Control unit
100 Front LH wheel sensor
101 Front RH wheel sensor
102 Test connector
103 Radio / cassette unit
104 Front LH speaker
105 Front RH speaker
106 Rear LH speaker
107 Rear RH speaker
98 Electrical board

H31281

Engine fusebox

Fuse	Rating	Circuit protected
F1	10/15A	Injection or Diesel
F2	30A	Fan unit
F3	10/30A	ABS
F4	30A	Fan unit
F5	10/30A	ABS
F6	15/20A	Front fog lights, alarm
F7	15A	Daylight running lights
F8	30A	Headlight washer
F9	10A	Fuel pump
F10	15/20/30A	Automatic transmission
F11	5A	Oxygen sensor
F12	10A	LH main beam
F13	10A	RH main beam
F14	10A	LH dipped beam
F15	10A	RH dipped beam

F2 F1 F3

F4 F5

F6 F7

F8 F9

F10 F11

F12 F13

F14 F15

Earth locations

E1	LH inner wing near battery
E2	LH inner wing below battery
E3	On gearbox
E4	LH front footwell
E5	Base of RH 'C' pillar
E6	On transmission tunnel, under dash
E7	LH inner wing
E8	LH 'C' pillar
E9	Base of RH 'A' pillar
E10	Base of RH 'A' pillar
E11	RH 'C' pillar
E12	Base of LH 'A' pillar
E13	On transmission tunnel, under dash

Passenger fusebox

Fuse	Rating	Circuit protected
F1	5A	Headlight washer, headlight levelling
F2	25A	Heater blower
F3	15A	Heated screen/mirrors, air cond.
F4	15A	Map reading light, vanity mirror light, radio
F5	30A	Horn, cigar lighter, heated rear window
F6	10A	Hazard warning lights
F7	10A	Reversing lights, instrument panel, dim/dip
F8	20A	Luggage compartment and interior light, radio, clock, diagnostic socket, central locking
F9	30A	Front/rear wash/wipe, lights on buzzer, stop lights, glove box light, electric windows and mirrors
F10	30A	Electric windows
F11	5A	Rear fog lights, instrument panel illumination
F12	5A	Front side lights, LH tail light, instrument panel illumination
F13	5A	RH tail and number plate light, radio, lights on buzzer, electric mirrors

F6

F10 F5 F8

F3 F9 F4

F7 F2

F1

F12

F13

Maxi fusebox

Fuse	Rating	Circuit protected
MF1	20A	Batt +ve supply to lighting switch
MF2	80A	Batt +ve supply to pass. fusebox
MF3	40A	Theft protection supply
MF4	40A	Theft protection supply

MF4

MF3

MF2

MF1

Key to symbols

Bulb

Switch

Multiple contact switch (ganged)

Fuse/fusible link   F10

Resistor

Variable resistor

Connecting wires

Wire identifier   — M656

Connections to other circuits (e.g. diagram 3/grid location B2. Direction of arrow denotes current flow.)   3/B2

Denotes alternative wiring variation (brackets)

Screened cable

Dashed outline denotes part of a larger item, containing in this case an electronic or solid state device.

C2   — connector pin identification.

2VE   — 2 pin green connector.

Wire - permanent direct earth (thick line)

Wire - interconnecting (thin line)

Item no.   7

Pump/motor   M

Earth

Gauge/meter

Diode

Wire splice

Solenoid actuator

C2 C1   2VE

Diagram 25 : Information for wiring diagrams - from 1997 model year

12

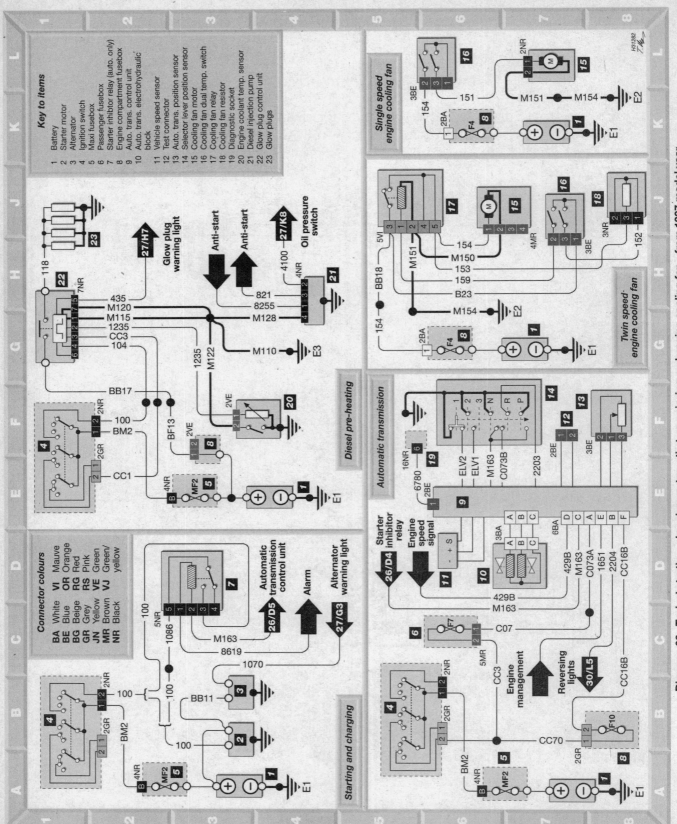

Key to items

1 Battery
2 Starter motor
3 Alternator
4 Ignition switch
5 Maxi fusebox
6 Passenger fusebox
7 Starter inhibitor relay (auto. only)
8 Engine compartment fusebox
9 Auto. trans. control unit
10 Auto. trans. electrohydraulic block
11 Vehicle speed sensor
12 Test connector
13 Auto. trans. position sensor
14 Selector lever position sensor
15 Cooling fan motor
16 Cooling fan dual temp. switch
17 Cooling fan relay
18 Cooling fan resistor
19 Diagnostic socket
20 Engine coolant temp. sensor
21 Diesel injection pump
22 Glow plug control unit
23 Glow plugs

Connector colours

BA	White	VI	Mauve
BE	Blue	OR	Orange
BG	Beige	RG	Red
GR	Grey	RS	Pink
JN	Yellow	VE	Green
MR	Brown	VJ	Green/yellow
NR	Black		

Diagram 26 : Typical starting, charging, automatic transmission and engine cooling fan – from 1997 model year

Single speed engine cooling fan

Twin speed engine cooling fan

Automatic transmission

Diesel pre-heating

Starting and charging

Glow plug warning light

Anti-start

Anti-start

Oil pressure switch

Automatic transmission control unit

Alarm

Alternator warning light

Starter inhibitor relay

Engine speed signal

Reversing lights

Engine management

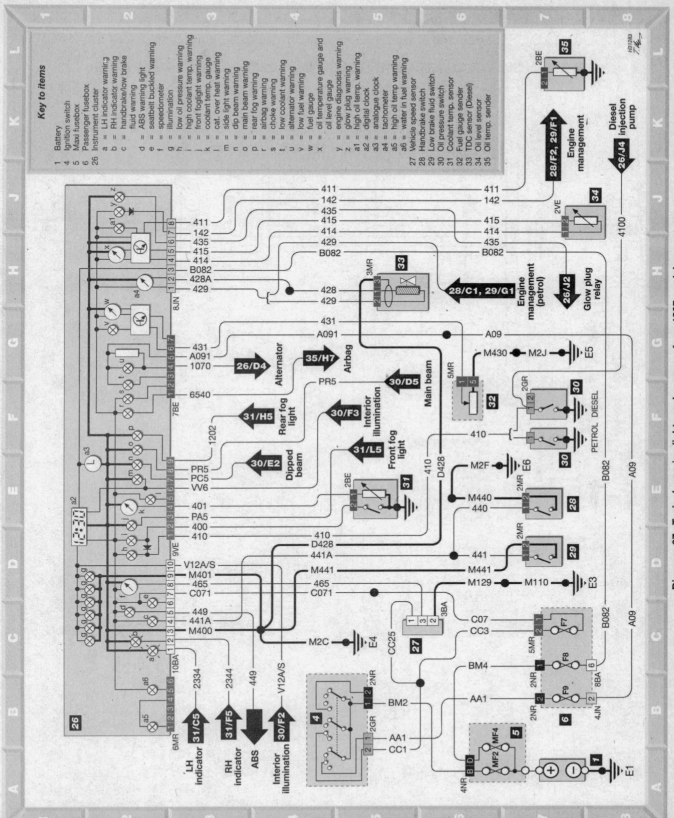

Diagram 27 : Typical warning lights and gauges - from 1997 model year

Key to items

1 Battery
4 Ignition switch
5 Maxi fusebox
6 Passenger fusebox
26 Instrument cluster
   a = LH indicator warning
   b = RH indicator warning
   c = handbrake/low brake fluid warning
   d = ABS warning light
   e = seatbelt buckled warning
   f = speedometer
   g = illumination
   h = low oil pressure warning
   i = high coolant temp. warning
   j = front foglight warning
   k = coolant temp. gauge
   l = cat. over heat warning
   m = side light warning
   n = dip beam warning
   o = main beam warning
   p = rear fog warning
   r = airbag warning
   s = choke warning
   t = low coolant warning
   u = alternator warning
   v = low fuel warning
   w = fuel gauge
   x = oil temperature gauge and oil level gauge
   y = engine diagnosis warning
   z = glow plug warning
   a1 = high oil temp. warning
   a2 = digital clock
   a3 = analogue clock
   a4 = tachometer
   a5 = high oil temp warning
   a6 = water in fuel warning
27 Vehicle speed sensor
28 Handbrake switch
29 Low brake fluid switch
30 Oil pressure switch
31 Coolant temp. sensor
32 Fuel gauge sender
33 TDC sensor (Diesel)
34 Oil level sensor
35 Oil temp. sender

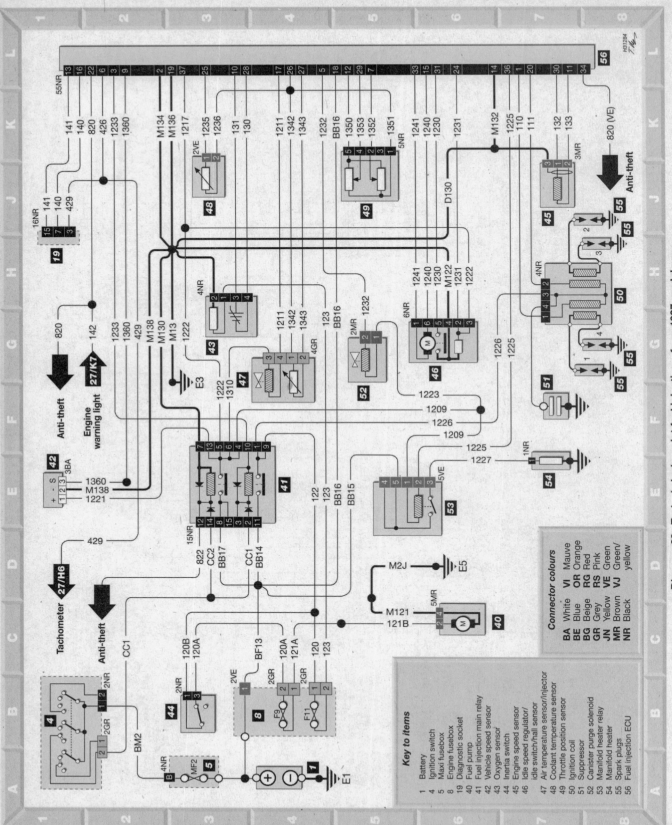

Diagram 28 : Typical single-point fuel injection – from 1997 model year

Connector colours

BA	White	VI	Mauve
BE	Blue	OR	Orange
BG	Beige	RG	Red
GR	Grey	RS	Pink
JN	Yellow	VE	Green
MR	Brown	VJ	Green/yellow
NR	Black		

Key to items

1 Battery
4 Ignition switch
5 Maxi fusebox
19 Engine fusebox
40 Diagnostic socket
41 Fuel injection main relay
42 Fuel pump
43 Vehicle speed sensor
44 Oxygen sensor
45 Inertia switch
46 Engine speed sensor
47 Idle speed regulator/
    Idle switch/hall sensor
48 Air temperature sensor/injector
49 Coolant temperature sensor
50 Throttle position sensor
51 Ignition coil
52 Canister purge solenoid
53 Manifold heater relay
54 Manifold heater
55 Spark plugs
56 Fuel injection ECU

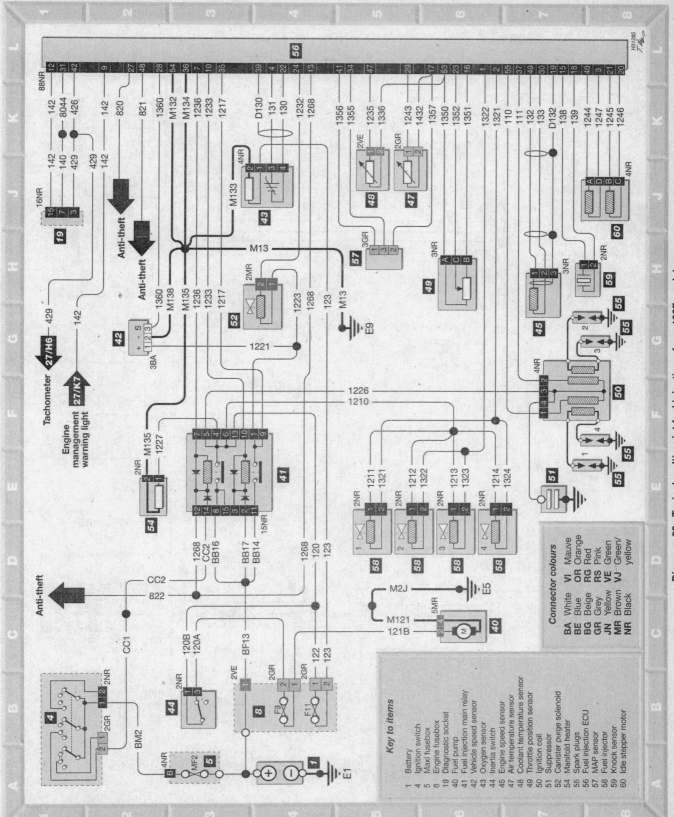

Diagram 29 : Typical multi-point fuel injection – from 1997 model year

Connector colours

BA	White	**VI**	Mauve
BE	Blue	**OR**	Orange
BG	Beige	**RG**	Red
GR	Grey	**RS**	Pink
JN	Yellow	**VE**	Green
MR	Brown	**VJ**	Green/ yellow
NR	Black		

Key to items

1 Battery
4 Ignition switch
5 Maxi fusebox
8 Engine fusebox
19 Diagnostic socket
40 Fuel pump
41 Fuel injection main relay
43 Vehicle speed sensor
44 Oxygen sensor
45 Inertia switch
46 Engine speed sensor
47 Air temperature sensor
48 Coolant temperature sensor
49 Throttle position sensor
50 Ignition coil
51 Suppressor
52 Canister purge solenoid
54 Fuel injection ECU
55 Manifold heater
56 Spark plugs
57 MAP sensor
58 Fuel injector
59 Knock sensor
60 Idle stepper motor

12

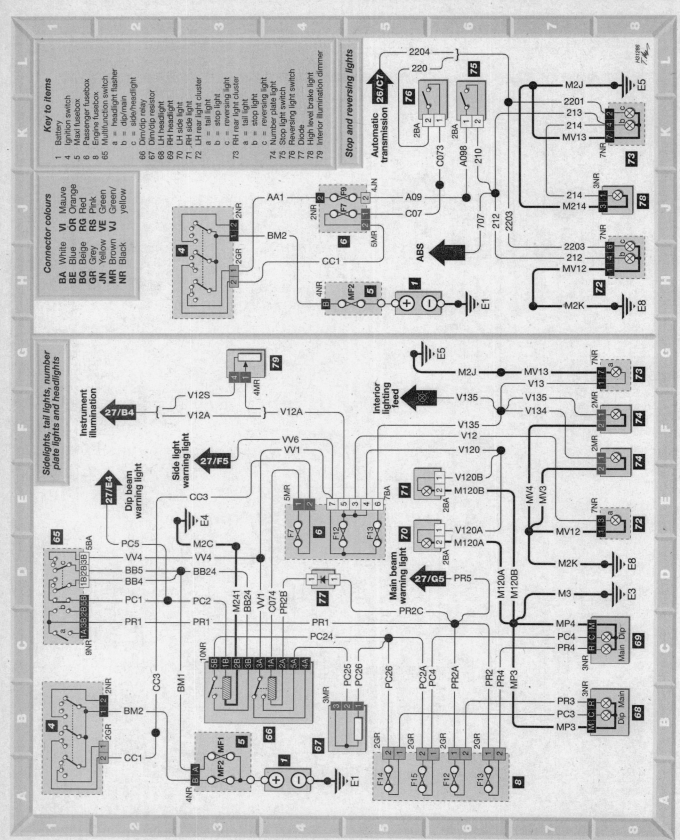

Key to items

1 Battery
4 Ignition switch
5 Maxi fusebox
6 Passenger fusebox
8 Engine fusebox
65 Multifunction switch
  a = headlight flasher
  b = dip/main
  c = side/headlight
66 Dim/dip relay
67 Dim/dip resistor
68 LH headlight
69 RH headlight
70 LH side light
71 RH side light
72 LH rear light cluster
  a = tail light
  b = stop light
  c = reversing light
73 RH rear light cluster
  a = tail light
  b = stop light
  c = reversing light
74 Number plate light
75 Stop light switch
76 Reversing light switch
77 Diode
78 High level brake light
79 Interior illumination dimmer

Connector colours

BA White   VI Mauve
BE Blue   OR Orange
BG Beige   RG Red
GR Grey   RS Pink
JN Yellow   VE Green
MR Brown   VJ Green/
NR Black   yellow

Diagram 30 : Typical exterior lighting - from 1997 model year

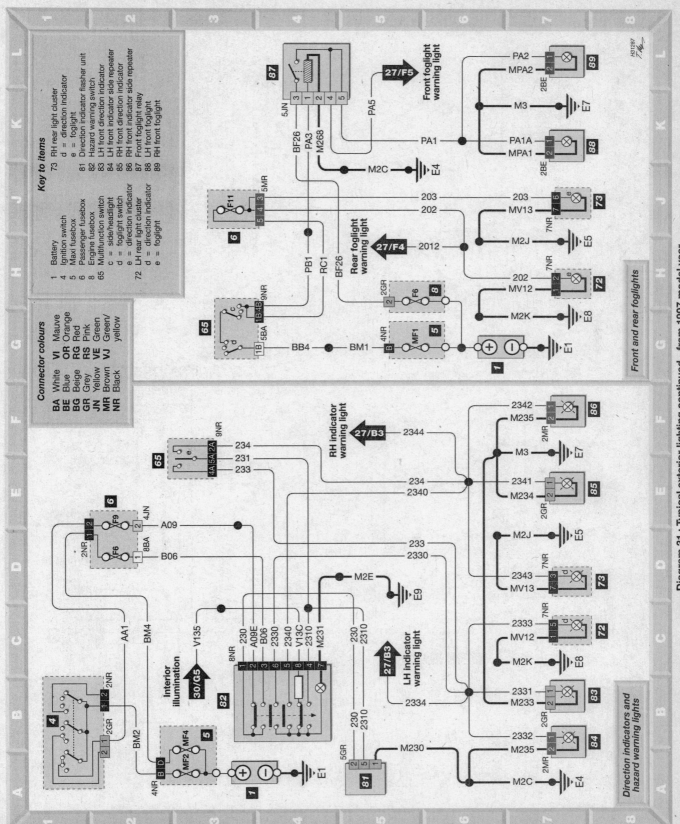

Key to items

73 RH rear light cluster
   d = direction indicator
   e = foglight
1 Battery
4 Ignition switch
5 Maxi fusebox
6 Passenger fusebox
8 Engine fusebox
65 Multifunction switch
   c = side/headlight
   d = foglight switch
   e = direction indicator
72 LH rear light cluster
   d = direction indicator
   e = foglight
81 Direction indicator flasher unit
82 Hazard warning switch
83 LH front direction indicator
84 LH front indicator side repeater
85 RH front direction indicator
86 RH front indicator side repeater
87 Front foglight relay
88 LH front foglight
89 RH front foglight

Connector colours

BA	White	VI	Mauve
BE	Blue	OR	Orange
BG	Beige	RG	Red
GR	Grey	RS	Pink
JN	Yellow	VE	Green
MR	Brown	VJ	Green/
NR	Black		yellow

Front and rear foglights

Direction indicators and hazard warning lights

Diagram 31 : Typical exterior lighting continued - from 1997 model year

12

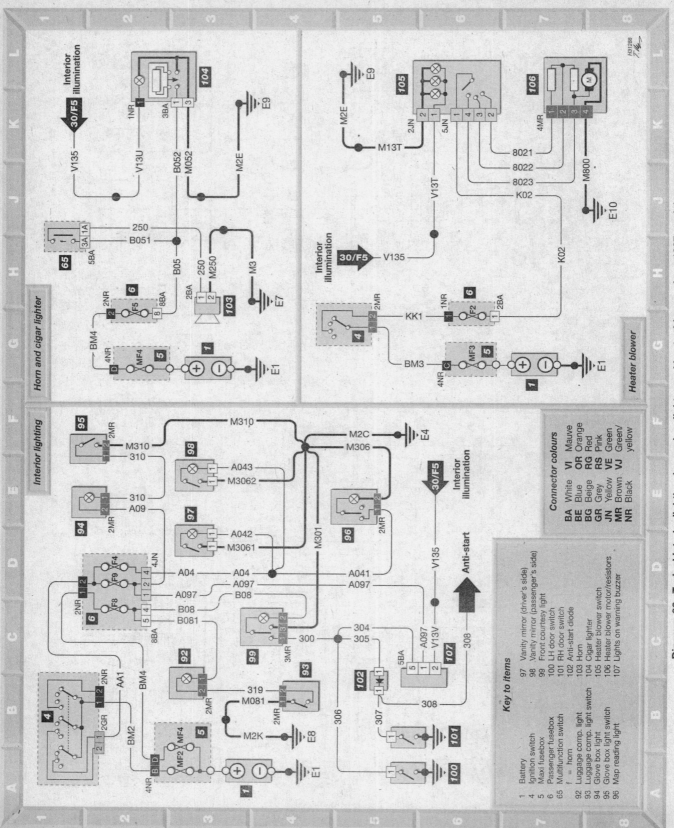

Diagram 32 : Typical interior lighting, horn, cigar lighter and heater blower - from 1997 model year

Connector colours

BA	White	VI	Mauve
BE	Blue	OR	Orange
BG	Beige	RG	Red
GR	Grey	RS	Pink
JN	Yellow	VE	Green
MR	Brown	VJ	Green/
NR	Black		yellow

Key to items

1	Battery	97	Vanity mirror (driver's side)
4	Ignition switch	98	Vanity mirror (passenger's side)
5	Maxi fusebox	99	Front courtesy light
6	Passenger fusebox	100	LH door switch
65	Multifunction switch	101	RH door switch
	f = horn	102	Anti-start diode
92	Luggage comp. light	103	Horn
93	Luggage comp. light switch	104	Cigar lighter
94	Glove box light	105	Heater blower switch
95	Glove box light switch	106	Heater blower motor/resistors
96	Map reading light	107	Lights on warning buzzer

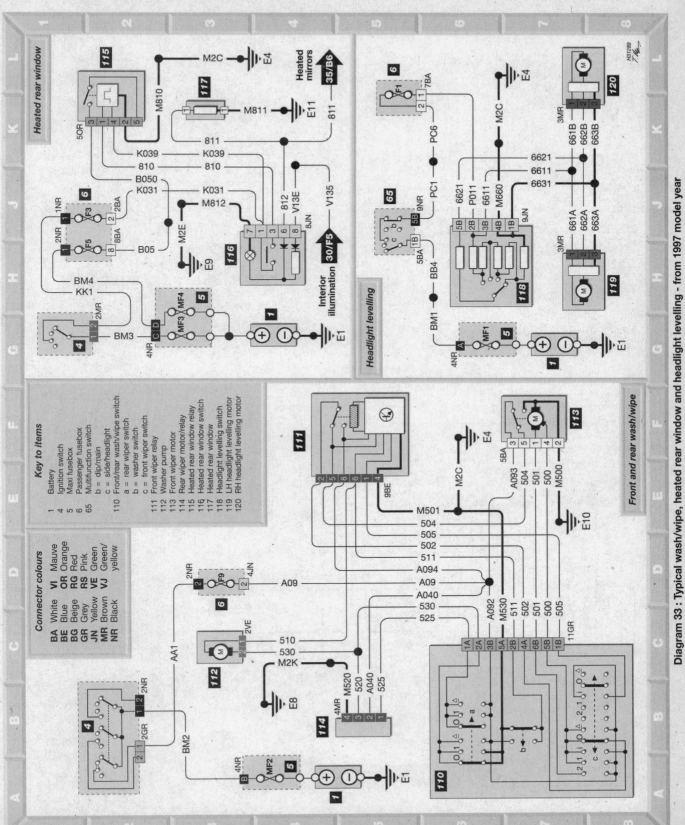

Heated rear window

Heated mirrors 35/B6

Headlight levelling

Interior illumination 30/F5

Front and rear wash/wipe

Key to items

1 Battery
4 Ignition switch
5 Maxi fusebox
6 Passenger fusebox
65 Multifunction switch
   b = dip/main
   c = side/headlight
110 Front/rear wash/wipe switch
   a = rear wiper switch
   b = washer switch
   c = front wiper switch
111 Front wiper relay
112 Washer pump
113 Front wiper motor
114 Rear wiper motor/relay
115 Heated rear window relay
116 Heated rear window switch
117 Heated rear window
118 Headlight levelling switch
119 LH headlight levelling motor
120 RH headlight levelling motor

Connector colours

BA	White	VI	Mauve
BE	Blue	OR	Orange
BG	Beige	RG	Red
GR	Grey	RS	Pink
JN	Yellow	VE	Green
MR	Brown	VJ	Green/
NR	Black		yellow

Diagram 33 : Typical wash/wipe, heated rear window and headlight levelling – from 1997 model year

12

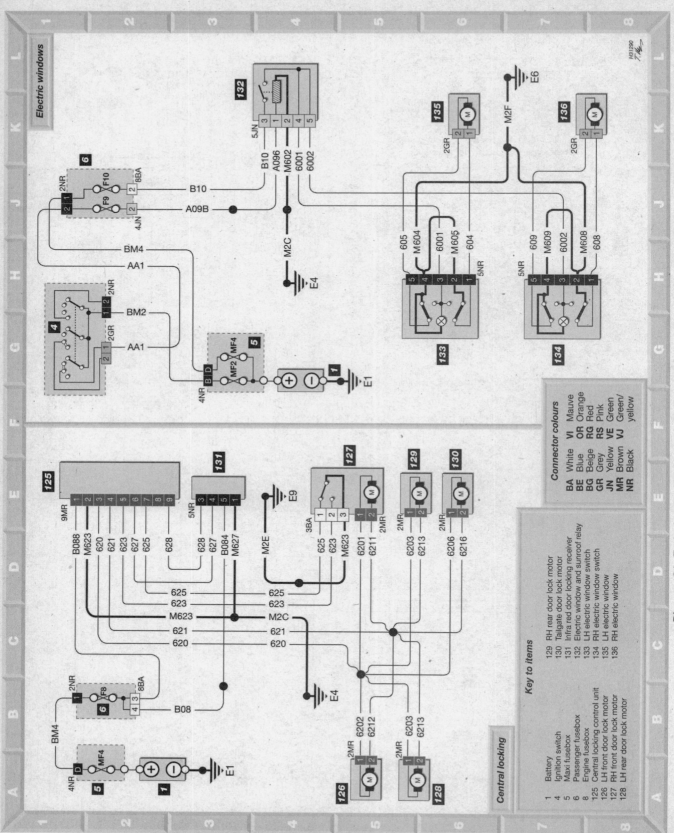

Diagram 34 : Typical central locking and electric windows - from 1997 model year

Electric windows

Central locking

Connector colours

BA	White	VI	Mauve
BE	Blue	OR	Orange
BG	Beige	RG	Red
GR	Grey	RS	Pink
JN	Yellow	VE	Green
MR	Brown	VJ	Green/ yellow
NR	Black		

Key to items

1	Battery
4	Ignition switch
5	Maxi fusebox
6	Passenger fusebox
8	Engine fusebox
125	Central locking control unit
126	LH front door lock motor
127	RH front door lock motor
128	LH rear door lock motor
129	RH rear door lock motor
130	Tailgate door lock motor
131	Infra red door locking receiver
132	Electric window and sunroof relay
133	LH electric window switch
134	RH electric window switch
135	LH electric window
136	RH electric window

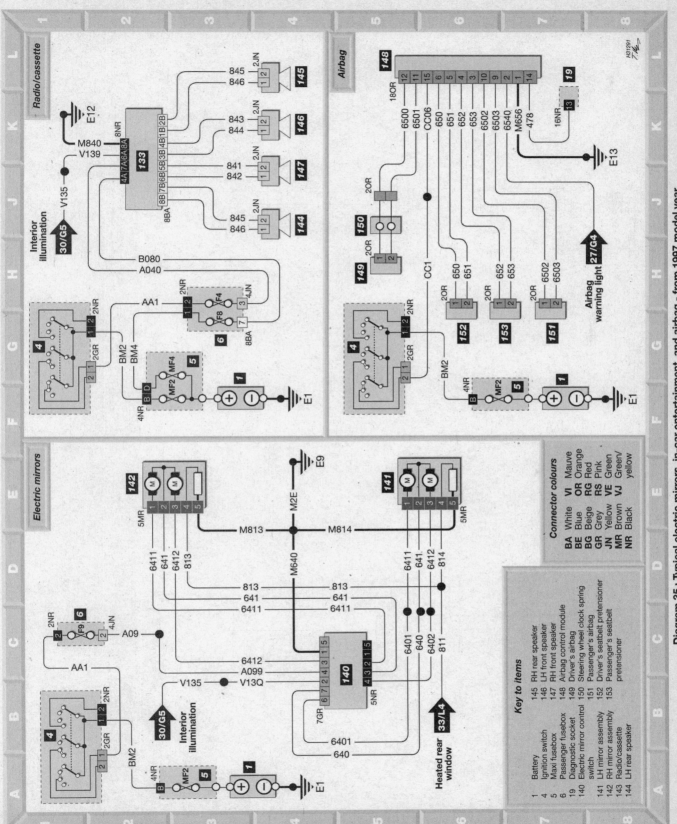

Diagram 35 : Typical electric mirrors, in-car entertainment and airbag - from 1997 model year

12

Dimensions and Weights

Note: *All figures are approximate and may vary according to model. Refer to manufacturer's data for exact figures.*

Dimensions

Overall length	3564 mm
Overall width	1590 mm
Overall height (unladen)	1369 mm
Wheelbase	2385 mm
Front track	1380 mm
Rear track	1300 mm

Weights

Kerb weight	760 to 860 kg*
Maximum gross vehicle weight**	1200 to 1300 kg*
Maximum roof rack load	40 kg
Maximum towing weight**:	
Braked trailer	500 to 700 kg*
Unbraked trailer	380 to 430 kg*
Maximum trailer nose weight	50 kg

Depending on model and specification.
**Refer to Peugeot dealer for exact recommendations.*

Conversion factors

Length (distance)

Inches (in)	x 25.4	= Millimetres (mm)	x 0.0394	= Inches (in)
Feet (ft)	x 0.305	= Metres (m)	x 3.281	= Feet (ft)
Miles	x 1.609	= Kilometres (km)	x 0.621	= Miles

Volume (capacity)

Cubic inches (cu in; in^3)	x 16.387	= Cubic centimetres (cc; cm^3)	x 0.061	= Cubic inches (cu in; in^3)
Imperial pints (Imp pt)	x 0.568	= Litres (l)	x 1.76	= Imperial pints (Imp pt)
Imperial quarts (Imp qt)	x 1.137	= Litres (l)	x 0.88	= Imperial quarts (Imp qt)
Imperial quarts (Imp qt)	x 1.201	= US quarts (US qt)	x 0.833	= Imperial quarts (Imp qt)
US quarts (US qt)	x 0.946	= Litres (l)	x 1.057	= US quarts (US qt)
Imperial gallons (Imp gal)	x 4.546	= Litres (l)	x 0.22	= Imperial gallons (Imp gal)
Imperial gallons (Imp gal)	x 1.201	= US gallons (US gal)	x 0.833	= Imperial gallons (Imp gal)
US gallons (US gal)	x 3.785	= Litres (l)	x 0.264	= US gallons (US gal)

Mass (weight)

Ounces (oz)	x 28.35	= Grams (g)	x 0.035	= Ounces (oz)
Pounds (lb)	x 0.454	= Kilograms (kg)	x 2.205	= Pounds (lb)

Force

Ounces-force (ozf; oz)	x 0.278	= Newtons (N)	x 3.6	= Ounces-force (ozf; oz)
Pounds-force (lbf; lb)	x 4.448	= Newtons (N)	x 0.225	= Pounds-force (lbf; lb)
Newtons (N)	x 0.1	= Kilograms-force (kgf; kg)	x 9.81	= Newtons (N)

Pressure

Pounds-force per square inch (psi; lbf/in^2; lb/in^2)	x 0.070	= Kilograms-force per square centimetre (kgf/cm^2; kg/cm^2)	x 14.223	= Pounds-force per square inch (psi; lbf/in^2; lb/in^2)
Pounds-force per square inch (psi; lbf/in^2; lb/in^2)	x 0.068	= Atmospheres (atm)	x 14.696	= Pounds-force per square inch (psi; lbf/in^2; lb/in^2)
Pounds-force per square inch (psi; lbf/in^2; lb/in^2)	x 0.069	= Bars	x 14.5	= Pounds-force per square inch (psi; lbf/in^2; lb/in^2)
Pounds-force per square inch (psi; lbf/in^2; lb/in^2)	x 6.895	= Kilopascals (kPa)	x 0.145	= Pounds-force per square inch (psi; lbf/in^2; lb/in^2)
Kilopascals (kPa)	x 0.01	= Kilograms-force per square centimetre (kgf/cm^2; kg/cm^2)	x 98.1	= Kilopascals (kPa)
Millibar (mbar)	x 100	= Pascals (Pa)	x 0.01	= Millibar (mbar)
Millibar (mbar)	x 0.0145	= Pounds-force per square inch (psi; lbf/in^2; lb/in^2)	x 68.947	= Millibar (mbar)
Millibar (mbar)	x 0.75	= Millimetres of mercury (mmHg)	x 1.333	= Millibar (mbar)
Millibar (mbar)	x 0.401	= Inches of water (inH$_2$O)	x 2.491	= Millibar (mbar)
Millimetres of mercury (mmHg)	x 0.535	= Inches of water (inH$_2$O)	x 1.868	= Millimetres of mercury (mmHg)
Inches of water (inH$_2$O)	x 0.036	= Pounds-force per square inch (psi; lbf/in^2; lb/in^2)	x 27.68	= Inches of water (inH$_2$O)

Torque (moment of force)

Pounds-force inches (lbf in; lb in)	x 1.152	= Kilograms-force centimetre (kgf cm; kg cm)	x 0.868	= Pounds-force inches (lbf in; lb in)
Pounds-force inches (lbf in; lb in)	x 0.113	= Newton metres (Nm)	x 8.85	= Pounds-force inches (lbf in; lb in)
Pounds-force inches (lbf in; lb in)	x 0.083	= Pounds-force feet (lbf ft; lb ft)	x 12	= Pounds-force inches (lbf in; lb in)
Pounds-force feet (lbf ft; lb ft)	x 0.138	= Kilograms-force metres (kgf m; kg m)	x 7.233	= Pounds-force feet (lbf ft; lb ft)
Pounds-force feet (lbf ft; lb ft)	x 1.356	= Newton metres (Nm)	x 0.738	= Pounds-force feet (lbf ft; lb ft)
Newton metres (Nm)	x 0.102	= Kilograms-force metres (kgf m; kg m)	x 9.804	= Newton metres (Nm)

Power

Horsepower (hp)	x 745.7	= Watts (W)	x 0.0013	= Horsepower (hp)

Velocity (speed)

Miles per hour (miles/hr; mph)	x 1.609	= Kilometres per hour (km/hr; kph)	x 0.621	= Miles per hour (miles/hr; mph)

Fuel consumption*

Miles per gallon, Imperial (mpg)	x 0.354	= Kilometres per litre (km/l)	x 2.825	= Miles per gallon, Imperial (mpg)
Miles per gallon, US (mpg)	x 0.425	= Kilometres per litre (km/l)	x 2.352	= Miles per gallon, US (mpg)

Temperature

Degrees Fahrenheit = (°C x 1.8) + 32   Degrees Celsius (Degrees Centigrade; °C) = (°F - 32) x 0.56

It is common practice to convert from miles per gallon (mpg) to litres/100 kilometres (l/100km), where mpg x l/100 km = 282

Spare parts are available from many sources, including maker's appointed garages, accessory shops, and motor factors. To be sure of obtaining the correct parts, it will sometimes be necessary to quote the vehicle identification number. If possible, it can also be useful to take the old parts along for positive identification. Items such as starter motors and alternators may be available under a service exchange scheme - any parts returned should always be clean.

Our advice regarding spare part sources is as follows.

Officially-appointed garages

This is the best source of parts which are peculiar to your car, and which are not otherwise generally available (eg badges, interior trim, certain body panels, etc). It is also the only place at which you should buy parts if the vehicle is still under warranty.

Accessory shops

These are very good places to buy materials and components needed for the maintenance of your car (oil, air and fuel filters, spark plugs, light bulbs, drivebelts, oils and greases, brake pads, touch-up paint, etc). Components of this nature sold by a reputable shop are of the same standard as those used by the car manufacturer.

Besides components, these shops also sell tools and general accessories, usually have convenient opening hours, charge lower prices, and can often be found not far from home. Some accessory shops have parts counters where the components needed for almost any repair job can be purchased or ordered.

Motor factors

Good factors will stock all the more important components which wear out comparatively quickly, and can sometimes supply individual components needed for the overhaul of a larger assembly (eg brake seals and hydraulic parts, bearing shells, pistons, valves, alternator brushes). They may also handle work such as cylinder block reboring, crankshaft regrinding and balancing, etc.

Tyre and exhaust specialists

These outlets may be independent, or members of a local or national chain. They frequently offer competitive prices when compared with a main dealer or local garage, but it will pay to obtain several quotes before making a decision. When researching prices, also ask what "extras" may be added - for instance, fitting a new valve and balancing the wheel are both commonly charged on top of the price of a new tyre.

Other sources

Beware of parts or materials obtained from market stalls, car boot sales or similar outlets. Such items are not invariably sub-standard, but there is little chance of compensation if they do prove unsatisfactory. In the case of safety-critical components such as brake pads, there is the risk not only of financial loss but also of an accident causing injury or death.

Second-hand components or assemblies obtained from a car breaker can be a good buy in some circumstances, but this sort of purchase is best made by the experienced DIY mechanic.

Vehicle identification

Modifications are a continuing and unpublicised process in vehicle manufacture, quite apart from major model changes. Spare parts manuals and lists are compiled upon a numerical basis, the individual vehicle identification numbers being essential to correct identification of the component concerned. When ordering spare parts, always give as much information as possible. Quote the car model, year of manufacture, body and engine numbers as appropriate.

The *Vehicle Identification Number (VIN)* plate is riveted to the top of the body front crossmember (just to the right of the bonnet lock) and can be viewed once the bonnet is open. The plate carries the VIN and vehicle weight information, as well as paint and trim colour codes. The plate situated to the left of the bonnet lock is the *homologation plate*. This plate gives details of the vehicle which are required by law for export to certain countries **(see illustration)**.

The *chassis number* is stamped into the body, along the top edge of the right-hand wing and can be viewed with the bonnet open **(see illustration)**. On some models, the chassis number may also be etched into the windscreen and window glass.

The *engine number* is situated on the left-hand end of the front face of the cylinder block. On models with an aluminium cylinder block, the number is stamped on a plate which is riveted to the block; on models with a cast-iron cylinder block, the number is stamped on a machined surface on the cylinder block, at the flywheel end **(see illustration)**. The first part of the engine number gives the engine code - eg "K9B".

The *paint code* is stamped onto the left-hand suspension turret **(see illustration)**.

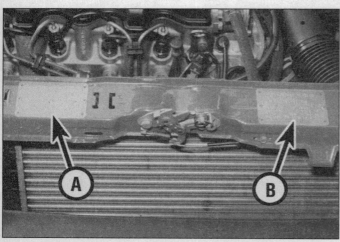

The VIN plate (A) is riveted to the body front crossmember. The plate on the left-hand side (B) is the homologation plate

The chassis number (arrowed) is stamped onto the right-hand wing

Engine number location - aluminium block engines. The first three letters of the plate indicate the engine code (K9B engine shown)

The paint code is stamped on the left-hand front suspension turret

Whenever servicing, repair or overhaul work is carried out on the car or its components, observe the following procedures and instructions. This will assist in carrying out the operation efficiently and to a professional standard of workmanship.

Joint mating faces and gaskets

When separating components at their mating faces, never insert screwdrivers or similar implements into the joint between the faces in order to prise them apart. This can cause severe damage which results in oil leaks, coolant leaks, etc upon reassembly. Separation is usually achieved by tapping along the joint with a soft-faced hammer in order to break the seal. However, note that this method may not be suitable where dowels are used for component location.

Where a gasket is used between the mating faces of two components, a new one must be fitted on reassembly; fit it dry unless otherwise stated in the repair procedure. Make sure that the mating faces are clean and dry, with all traces of old gasket removed. When cleaning a joint face, use a tool which is unlikely to score or damage the face, and remove any burrs or nicks with an oilstone or fine file.

Make sure that tapped holes are cleaned with a pipe cleaner, and keep them free of jointing compound, if this is being used, unless specifically instructed otherwise.

Ensure that all orifices, channels or pipes are clear, and blow through them, preferably using compressed air.

Oil seals

Oil seals can be removed by levering them out with a wide flat-bladed screwdriver or similar implement. Alternatively, a number of self-tapping screws may be screwed into the seal, and these used as a purchase for pliers or some similar device in order to pull the seal free.

Whenever an oil seal is removed from its working location, either individually or as part of an assembly, it should be renewed.

The very fine sealing lip of the seal is easily damaged, and will not seal if the surface it contacts is not completely clean and free from scratches, nicks or grooves. If the original sealing surface of the component cannot be restored, and the manufacturer has not made provision for slight relocation of the seal relative to the sealing surface, the component should be renewed.

Protect the lips of the seal from any surface which may damage them in the course of fitting. Use tape or a conical sleeve where possible. Lubricate the seal lips with oil before fitting and, on dual-lipped seals, fill the space between the lips with grease.

Unless otherwise stated, oil seals must be fitted with their sealing lips toward the lubricant to be sealed.

Use a tubular drift or block of wood of the appropriate size to install the seal and, if the seal housing is shouldered, drive the seal down to the shoulder. If the seal housing is unshouldered, the seal should be fitted with its face flush with the housing top face (unless otherwise instructed).

Screw threads and fastenings

Seized nuts, bolts and screws are quite a common occurrence where corrosion has set in, and the use of penetrating oil or releasing fluid will often overcome this problem if the offending item is soaked for a while before attempting to release it. The use of an impact driver may also provide a means of releasing such stubborn fastening devices, when used in conjunction with the appropriate screwdriver bit or socket. If none of these methods works, it may be necessary to resort to the careful application of heat, or the use of a hacksaw or nut splitter device.

Studs are usually removed by locking two nuts together on the threaded part, and then using a spanner on the lower nut to unscrew the stud. Studs or bolts which have broken off below the surface of the component in which they are mounted can sometimes be removed using a stud extractor. Always ensure that a blind tapped hole is completely free from oil, grease, water or other fluid before installing the bolt or stud. Failure to do this could cause the housing to crack due to the hydraulic action of the bolt or stud as it is screwed in.

When tightening a castellated nut to accept a split pin, tighten the nut to the specified torque, where applicable, and then tighten further to the next split pin hole. Never slacken the nut to align the split pin hole, unless stated in the repair procedure.

When checking or retightening a nut or bolt to a specified torque setting, slacken the nut or bolt by a quarter of a turn, and then retighten to the specified setting. However, this should not be attempted where angular tightening has been used.

For some screw fastenings, notably cylinder head bolts or nuts, torque wrench settings are no longer specified for the latter stages of tightening, "angle-tightening" being called up instead. Typically, a fairly low torque wrench setting will be applied to the bolts/nuts in the correct sequence, followed by one or more stages of tightening through specified angles.

Locknuts, locktabs and washers

Any fastening which will rotate against a component or housing during tightening should always have a washer between it and the relevant component or housing.

Spring or split washers should always be renewed when they are used to lock a critical component such as a big-end bearing retaining bolt or nut. Locktabs which are folded over to retain a nut or bolt should always be renewed.

Self-locking nuts can be re-used in non-critical areas, providing resistance can be felt when the locking portion passes over the bolt or stud thread. However, it should be noted that self-locking stiffnuts tend to lose their effectiveness after long periods of use, and should then be renewed as a matter of course.

Split pins must always be replaced with new ones of the correct size for the hole.

When thread-locking compound is found on the threads of a fastener which is to be re-used, it should be cleaned off with a wire brush and solvent, and fresh compound applied on reassembly.

Special tools

Some repair procedures in this manual entail the use of special tools such as a press, two or three-legged pullers, spring compressors, etc. Wherever possible, suitable readily-available alternatives to the manufacturer's special tools are described, and are shown in use. In some instances, where no alternative is possible, it has been necessary to resort to the use of a manufacturer's tool, and this has been done for reasons of safety as well as the efficient completion of the repair operation. Unless you are highly-skilled and have a thorough understanding of the procedures described, never attempt to bypass the use of any special tool when the procedure described specifies its use. Not only is there a very great risk of personal injury, but expensive damage could be caused to the components involved.

Environmental considerations

When disposing of used engine oil, brake fluid, antifreeze, etc, give due consideration to any detrimental environmental effects. Do not, for instance, pour any of the above liquids down drains into the general sewage system, or onto the ground to soak away. Many local council refuse tips provide a facility for waste oil disposal, as do some garages. If none of these facilities are available, consult your local Environmental Health Department, or the National Rivers Authority, for further advice.

With the universal tightening-up of legislation regarding the emission of environmentally-harmful substances from motor vehicles, most vehicles have tamperproof devices fitted to the main adjustment points of the fuel system. These devices are primarily designed to prevent unqualified persons from adjusting the fuel/air mixture, with the chance of a consequent increase in toxic emissions. If such devices are found during servicing or overhaul, they should, wherever possible, be renewed or refitted in accordance with the manufacturer's requirements or current legislation.

OIL CARE FOLLOW THE CODE

OIL BANK LINE
0800 66 33 66
www.oilbankline.org.uk

Note: It is antisocial and illegal to dump oil down the drain. To find the location of your local oil recycling bank, call this number free.

The jack supplied with the vehicle tool kit should only be used for changing the roadwheels - see *"Wheel changing"* at the beginning of this manual. When carrying out any other kind of work, raise the vehicle using a hydraulic (or "trolley") jack and always supplement the jack with axle stands positioned under the vehicle jacking points **(see illustration)**.

When using a hydraulic jack or axle stands, always position the jack head or axle stand head under one of the relevant jacking points.

To raise the front of the vehicle, position the jack with an interposed block of wood underneath the suspension lower arm mounting bracket **(see illustration)**. **Do not** jack the vehicle under the sump, or any of the steering or suspension components.

To raise the rear of the vehicle, remove the spare wheel then position the jack head underneath the rear crossmember **(see illustration)**. **Do not** attempt to raise the vehicle with the jack positioned underneath the spare wheel, as the vehicle floor will almost certainly be damaged.

The jack supplied with the vehicle locates in the jacking points in the ridge on the underside of the sill. Ensure that the jack head is correctly engaged before attempting to raise the vehicle.

Never work under, around, or near a raised vehicle, unless it is adequately supported in at least two places.

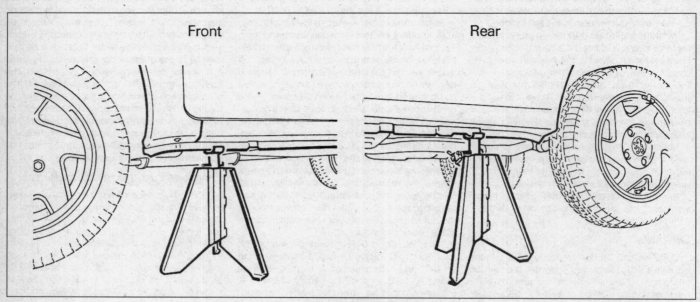

Front   Rear

Location points for axle stands

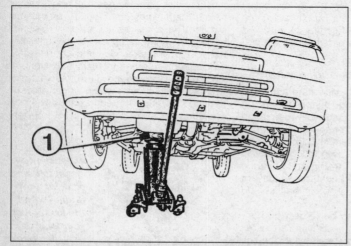

When raising the front of the vehicle, locate the jack underneath the suspension lower arm mounting bracket (1)

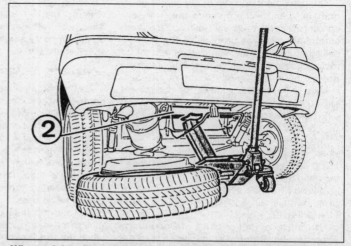

When raising the rear of the vehicle, remove the spare wheel and position the jack head underneath the rear crossmember (2)

Several systems fitted to the vehicle require battery power to be available at all times, either to ensure their continued operation (such as the clock) or to maintain control unit memories which would be wiped if the battery were to be disconnected. Whenever the battery is to be disconnected therefore, first note the following, to ensure that there are no unforeseen consequences of this action:

a) First, on any vehicle with central locking, it is a wise precaution to remove the key from the ignition and to keep it with you, so that it does not get locked in if the central locking should engage accidentally when the battery is reconnected.

b) If the vehicle is equipped with a Peugeot factory option anti-theft alarm system, the system should be de-activated before disconnecting the battery. To de-activate the system on early models, a master switch is provided in the engine compartment, behind the right-hand headlight. The switch is operated by a dedicated key and is protected by a plastic cover. Lift up the cover and turn off the switch using the dedicated key. When reconnecting the battery, as soon as the battery is connected, the alarm is automatically activated. Use the remote transmitter to turn off the alarm, then activate the alarm siren using the dedicated key. To de-activate the system on later models, switch on the ignition switch and then within ten seconds, depress the alarm switch on the side of the steering column shroud and hold for approximately two seconds. The alarm indicator light should then flash rapidly for three seconds indicating the alarm is de-activated. To re-activate the system once the battery is reconnected, lock then unlock the vehicle using the remote transmitter; the alarm will be functional again the next time the vehicle is locked with the remote transmitter.

c) If a security-coded audio unit is fitted and the unit and/or the battery is disconnected, the unit will not function again on reconnection until the correct security code is entered. Details of this procedure, which varies according to the unit fitted, are given in the vehicle owner's handbook. Ensure you have the correct code before you disconnect the battery. If you do not have the code or details of the correct procedure, but can supply proof of ownership and a legitimate reason for wanting this information, a Peugeot dealer may be able to help.

d) On certain petrol injection engines, the electronic control unit is of the "self-learning" type, meaning that as it operates, it also monitors and stores the settings which give optimum engine performance under all operating conditions. When the battery is disconnected, these settings are lost and the ECU reverts to the base settings programmed into its memory at the factory. On restarting, this may lead to the engine running/idling roughly for a short while, until the ECU has re-learned the optimum settings. This process is best accomplished by taking the vehicle on a road test (for approximately 15 minutes), covering all engine speeds and loads, concentrating mainly in the 2,500 to 3,500 rpm region.

Devices known as 'memory-savers' (or 'code-savers') can be used to avoid some of the above problems. Precise details vary according to the device used. Typically, it is plugged into the cigarette lighter and is connected by its own wires to a spare battery; the vehicle's own battery is then disconnected from the electrical system, leaving the "memory-saver" to pass sufficient current to maintain audio unit security codes and any other memory values and also to run permanently-live circuits such as the clock.

⚠️ **Warning: Some of these devices allow a considerable amount of current to pass, which can mean that many of the vehicle's systems are still operational when the main battery is disconnected. If a "memory saver" is used, ensure that the circuit concerned is actually "dead" before carrying out any work on it!**

Introduction

A selection of good tools is a fundamental requirement for anyone contemplating the maintenance and repair of a motor vehicle. For the owner who does not possess any, their purchase will prove a considerable expense, offsetting some of the savings made by doing-it-yourself. However, provided that the tools purchased meet the relevant national safety standards and are of good quality, they will last for many years and prove an extremely worthwhile investment.

To help the average owner to decide which tools are needed to carry out the various tasks detailed in this manual, we have compiled three lists of tools under the following headings: *Maintenance and minor repair, Repair and overhaul,* and *Special.* Newcomers to practical mechanics should start off with the *Maintenance and minor repair* tool kit, and confine themselves to the simpler jobs around the vehicle. Then, as confidence and experience grow, more difficult tasks can be undertaken, with extra tools being purchased as, and when, they are needed. In this way, a *Maintenance and minor repair* tool kit can be built up into a *Repair and overhaul* tool kit over a considerable period of time, without any major cash outlays. The experienced do-it-yourselfer will have a tool kit good enough for most repair and overhaul procedures, and will add tools from the *Special* category when it is felt that the expense is justified by the amount of use to which these tools will be put.

Maintenance and minor repair tool kit

The tools given in this list should be considered as a minimum requirement if routine maintenance, servicing and minor repair operations are to be undertaken. We recommend the purchase of combination spanners (ring one end, open-ended the other); although more expensive than open-ended ones, they do give the advantages of both types of spanner.

☐ *Combination spanners:*
  Metric - 8 to 19 mm inclusive
☐ *Adjustable spanner - 35 mm jaw (approx.)*
☐ *Spark plug spanner (with rubber insert) - petrol models*
☐ *Spark plug gap adjustment tool - petrol models*
☐ *Set of feeler gauges*
☐ *Brake bleed nipple spanner*
☐ *Screwdrivers:*
  Flat blade - 100 mm long x 6 mm dia
  Cross blade - 100 mm long x 6 mm dia
  Torx - various sizes (not all vehicles)
☐ *Combination pliers*
☐ *Hacksaw (junior)*
☐ *Tyre pump*
☐ *Tyre pressure gauge*
☐ *Oil can*
☐ *Oil filter removal tool*
☐ *Fine emery cloth*
☐ *Wire brush (small)*
☐ *Funnel (medium size)*
☐ *Sump drain plug key (not all vehicles)*

Repair and overhaul tool kit

These tools are virtually essential for anyone undertaking any major repairs to a motor vehicle, and are additional to those given in the *Maintenance and minor repair* list. Included in this list is a comprehensive set of sockets. Although these are expensive, they will be found invaluable as they are so versatile - particularly if various drives are included in the set. We recommend the half-inch square-drive type, as this can be used with most proprietary torque wrenches.

The tools in this list will sometimes need to be supplemented by tools from the *Special* list:

☐ *Sockets (or box spanners) to cover range in previous list (including Torx sockets)*
☐ *Reversible ratchet drive (for use with sockets)*
☐ *Extension piece, 250 mm (for use with sockets)*
☐ *Universal joint (for use with sockets)*
☐ *Flexible handle or "breaker bar" (for use with sockets)*
☐ *Torque wrench (for use with sockets)*
☐ *Self-locking grips*
☐ *Ball pein hammer*
☐ *Soft-faced mallet (plastic or rubber)*
☐ *Screwdrivers:*
  Flat blade - long & sturdy, short (chubby), and narrow (electrician's) types
  Cross blade – long & sturdy, and short (chubby) types
☐ *Pliers:*
  Long-nosed
  Side cutters (electrician's)
  Circlip (internal and external)
☐ *Cold chisel - 25 mm*
☐ *Scriber*
☐ *Scraper*
☐ *Centre-punch*
☐ *Pin punch*
☐ *Hacksaw*
☐ *Brake hose clamp*
☐ *Brake/clutch bleeding kit*
☐ *Selection of twist drills*
☐ *Steel rule/straight-edge*
☐ *Allen keys (inc. splined/Torx type)*
☐ *Selection of files*
☐ *Wire brush*
☐ *Axle stands*
☐ *Jack (strong trolley or hydraulic type)*
☐ *Light with extension lead*
☐ *Universal electrical multi-meter*

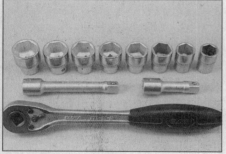

Sockets and reversible ratchet drive

Brake bleeding kit

Torx key, socket and bit

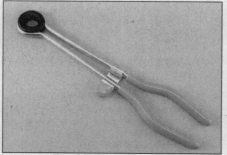

Hose clamp

Angular-tightening gauge

Special tools

The tools in this list are those which are not used regularly, are expensive to buy, or which need to be used in accordance with their manufacturers' instructions. Unless relatively difficult mechanical jobs are undertaken frequently, it will not be economic to buy many of these tools. Where this is the case, you could consider clubbing together with friends (or joining a motorists' club) to make a joint purchase, or borrowing the tools against a deposit from a local garage or tool hire specialist. It is worth noting that many of the larger DIY superstores now carry a large range of special tools for hire at modest rates.

The following list contains only those tools and instruments freely available to the public, and not those special tools produced by the vehicle manufacturer specifically for its dealer network. You will find occasional references to these manufacturers' special tools in the text of this manual. Generally, an alternative method of doing the job without the vehicle manufacturer's special tool is given. However, sometimes there is no alternative to using them. Where this is the case and the relevant tool cannot be bought or borrowed, you will have to entrust the work to a dealer.

- ☐ Angular-tightening gauge
- ☐ Valve spring compressor
- ☐ Valve grinding tool
- ☐ Piston ring compressor
- ☐ Piston ring removal/installation tool
- ☐ Cylinder bore hone
- ☐ Balljoint separator
- ☐ Coil spring compressors (where applicable)
- ☐ Two/three-legged hub and bearing puller
- ☐ Impact screwdriver
- ☐ Micrometer and/or vernier calipers
- ☐ Dial gauge
- ☐ Stroboscopic timing light
- ☐ Dwell angle meter/tachometer
- ☐ Fault code reader
- ☐ Cylinder compression gauge
- ☐ Hand-operated vacuum pump and gauge
- ☐ Clutch plate alignment set
- ☐ Brake shoe steady spring cup removal tool
- ☐ Bush and bearing removal/installation set
- ☐ Stud extractors
- ☐ Tap and die set
- ☐ Lifting tackle
- ☐ Trolley jack

Buying tools

Reputable motor accessory shops and superstores often offer excellent quality tools at discount prices, so it pays to shop around.

Remember, you don't have to buy the most expensive items on the shelf, but it is always advisable to steer clear of the very cheap tools. Beware of 'bargains' offered on market stalls or at car boot sales. There are plenty of good tools around at reasonable prices, but always aim to purchase items which meet the relevant national safety standards. If in doubt, ask the proprietor or manager of the shop for advice before making a purchase.

Care and maintenance of tools

Having purchased a reasonable tool kit, it is necessary to keep the tools in a clean and serviceable condition. After use, always wipe off any dirt, grease and metal particles using a clean, dry cloth, before putting the tools away. Never leave them lying around after they have been used. A simple tool rack on the garage or workshop wall for items such as screwdrivers and pliers is a good idea. Store all normal spanners and sockets in a metal box. Any measuring instruments, gauges, meters, etc, must be carefully stored where they cannot be damaged or become rusty.

Take a little care when tools are used. Hammer heads inevitably become marked, and screwdrivers lose the keen edge on their blades from time to time. A little timely attention with emery cloth or a file will soon restore items like this to a good finish.

Working facilities

Not to be forgotten when discussing tools is the workshop itself. If anything more than routine maintenance is to be carried out, a suitable working area becomes essential.

It is appreciated that many an owner-mechanic is forced by circumstances to remove an engine or similar item without the benefit of a garage or workshop. Having done this, any repairs should always be done under the cover of a roof.

Wherever possible, any dismantling should be done on a clean, flat workbench or table at a suitable working height.

Any workbench needs a vice; one with a jaw opening of 100 mm is suitable for most jobs. As mentioned previously, some clean dry storage space is also required for tools, as well as for any lubricants, cleaning fluids, touch-up paints etc, which become necessary.

Another item which may be required, and which has a much more general usage, is an electric drill with a chuck capacity of at least 8 mm. This, together with a good range of twist drills, is virtually essential for fitting accessories.

Last, but not least, always keep a supply of old newspapers and clean, lint-free rags available, and try to keep any working area as clean as possible.

Vernier calipers

Dial test indicator ("dial gauge")

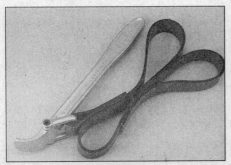

Strap wrench

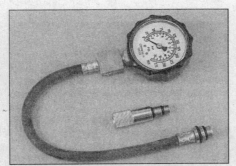

Compression tester

Fault code reader

This is a guide to getting your vehicle through the MOT test. Obviously it will not be possible to examine the vehicle to the same standard as the professional MOT tester. However, working through the following checks will enable you to identify any problem areas before submitting the vehicle for the test.

Where a testable component is in borderline condition, the tester has discretion in deciding whether to pass or fail it. The basis of such discretion is whether the tester would be happy for a close relative or friend to use the vehicle with the component in that condition. If the vehicle presented is clean and evidently well cared for, the tester may be more inclined to pass a borderline component than if the vehicle is scruffy and apparently neglected.

It has only been possible to summarise the test requirements here, based on the regulations in force at the time of printing. Test standards are becoming increasingly stringent, although there are some exemptions for older vehicles.

An assistant will be needed to help carry out some of these checks.

The checks have been sub-divided into four categories, as follows:

1 Checks carried out **FROM THE DRIVER'S SEAT**

2 Checks carried out **WITH THE VEHICLE ON THE GROUND**

3 Checks carried out **WITH THE VEHICLE RAISED AND THE WHEELS FREE TO TURN**

4 Checks carried out on **YOUR VEHICLE'S EXHAUST EMISSION SYSTEM**

---

1 Checks carried out **FROM THE DRIVER'S SEAT**

Handbrake

☐ Test the operation of the handbrake. Excessive travel (too many clicks) indicates incorrect brake or cable adjustment.

☐ Check that the handbrake cannot be released by tapping the lever sideways. Check the security of the lever mountings.

Footbrake

☐ Depress the brake pedal and check that it does not creep down to the floor, indicating a master cylinder fault. Release the pedal, wait a few seconds, then depress it again. If the pedal travels nearly to the floor before firm resistance is felt, brake adjustment or repair is necessary. If the pedal feels spongy, there is air in the hydraulic system which must be removed by bleeding.

☐ Check that the brake pedal is secure and in good condition. Check also for signs of fluid leaks on the pedal, floor or carpets, which would indicate failed seals in the brake master cylinder.

☐ Check the servo unit (when applicable) by operating the brake pedal several times, then keeping the pedal depressed and starting the engine. As the engine starts, the pedal will move down slightly. If not, the vacuum hose or the servo itself may be faulty.

Steering wheel and column

☐ Examine the steering wheel for fractures or looseness of the hub, spokes or rim.

☐ Move the steering wheel from side to side and then up and down. Check that the steering wheel is not loose on the column, indicating wear or a loose retaining nut. Continue moving the steering wheel as before, but also turn it slightly from left to right.

☐ Check that the steering wheel is not loose on the column, and that there is no abnormal

movement of the steering wheel, indicating wear in the column support bearings or couplings.

Windscreen, mirrors and sunvisor

☐ The windscreen must be free of cracks or other significant damage within the driver's field of view. (Small stone chips are acceptable.) Rear view mirrors must be secure, intact, and capable of being adjusted.

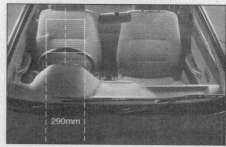

290mm

☐ The driver's sunvisor must be capable of being stored in the "up" position.

Seat belts and seats

Note: *The following checks are applicable to all seat belts, front and rear.*

☐ Examine the webbing of all the belts (including rear belts if fitted) for cuts, serious fraying or deterioration. Fasten and unfasten each belt to check the buckles. If applicable, check the retracting mechanism. Check the security of all seat belt mountings accessible from inside the vehicle.

☐ Seat belts with pre-tensioners, once activated, have a "flag" or similar showing on the seat belt stalk. This, in itself, is not a reason for test failure.

☐ The front seats themselves must be securely attached and the backrests must lock in the upright position.

Doors

☐ Both front doors must be able to be opened and closed from outside and inside, and must latch securely when closed.

2 Checks carried out WITH THE VEHICLE ON THE GROUND

Vehicle identification

☐ Number plates must be in good condition, secure and legible, with letters and numbers correctly spaced – spacing at (A) should be at least twice that at (B).

☐ The VIN plate and/or homologation plate must be legible.

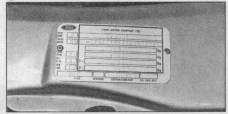

Electrical equipment

☐ Switch on the ignition and check the operation of the horn.

☐ Check the windscreen washers and wipers, examining the wiper blades; renew damaged or perished blades. Also check the operation of the stop-lights.

☐ Check the operation of the sidelights and number plate lights. The lenses and reflectors must be secure, clean and undamaged.

☐ Check the operation and alignment of the headlights. The headlight reflectors must not be tarnished and the lenses must be undamaged.

☐ Switch on the ignition and check the operation of the direction indicators (including the instrument panel tell-tale) and the hazard warning lights. Operation of the sidelights and stop-lights must not affect the indicators - if it does, the cause is usually a bad earth at the rear light cluster.

☐ Check the operation of the rear foglight(s), including the warning light on the instrument panel or in the switch.

☐ The ABS warning light must illuminate in accordance with the manufacturers' design. For most vehicles, the ABS warning light should illuminate when the ignition is switched on, and (if the system is operating properly) extinguish after a few seconds. Refer to the owner's handbook.

Footbrake

☐ Examine the master cylinder, brake pipes and servo unit for leaks, loose mountings, corrosion or other damage.

☐ The fluid reservoir must be secure and the fluid level must be between the upper (**A**) and lower (**B**) markings.

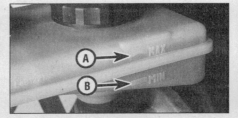

☐ Inspect both front brake flexible hoses for cracks or deterioration of the rubber. Turn the steering from lock to lock, and ensure that the hoses do not contact the wheel, tyre, or any part of the steering or suspension mechanism. With the brake pedal firmly depressed, check the hoses for bulges or leaks under pressure.

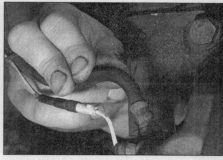

Steering and suspension

☐ Have your assistant turn the steering wheel from side to side slightly, up to the point where the steering gear just begins to transmit this movement to the roadwheels. Check for excessive free play between the steering wheel and the steering gear, indicating wear or insecurity of the steering column joints, the column-to-steering gear coupling, or the steering gear itself.

☐ Have your assistant turn the steering wheel more vigorously in each direction, so that the roadwheels just begin to turn. As this is done, examine all the steering joints, linkages, fittings and attachments. Renew any component that shows signs of wear or damage. On vehicles with power steering, check the security and condition of the steering pump, drivebelt and hoses.

☐ Check that the vehicle is standing level, and at approximately the correct ride height.

Shock absorbers

☐ Depress each corner of the vehicle in turn, then release it. The vehicle should rise and then settle in its normal position. If the vehicle continues to rise and fall, the shock absorber is defective. A shock absorber which has seized will also cause the vehicle to fail.

Exhaust system

☐ Start the engine. With your assistant holding a rag over the tailpipe, check the entire system for leaks. Repair or renew leaking sections.

3 Checks carried out **WITH THE VEHICLE RAISED AND THE WHEELS FREE TO TURN**

Jack up the front and rear of the vehicle, and securely support it on axle stands. Position the stands clear of the suspension assemblies. Ensure that the wheels are clear of the ground and that the steering can be turned from lock to lock.

Steering mechanism

☐ Have your assistant turn the steering from lock to lock. Check that the steering turns smoothly, and that no part of the steering mechanism, including a wheel or tyre, fouls any brake hose or pipe or any part of the body structure.
☐ Examine the steering rack rubber gaiters for damage or insecurity of the retaining clips. If power steering is fitted, check for signs of damage or leakage of the fluid hoses, pipes or connections. Also check for excessive stiffness or binding of the steering, a missing split pin or locking device, or severe corrosion of the body structure within 30 cm of any steering component attachment point.

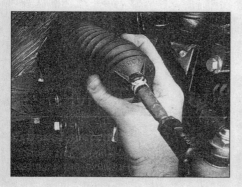

Front and rear suspension and wheel bearings

☐ Starting at the front right-hand side, grasp the roadwheel at the 3 o'clock and 9 o'clock positions and rock gently but firmly. Check for free play or insecurity at the wheel bearings, suspension balljoints, or suspension mountings, pivots and attachments.
☐ Now grasp the wheel at the 12 o'clock and 6 o'clock positions and repeat the previous inspection. Spin the wheel, and check for roughness or tightness of the front wheel bearing.

☐ If excess free play is suspected at a component pivot point, this can be confirmed by using a large screwdriver or similar tool and levering between the mounting and the component attachment. This will confirm whether the wear is in the pivot bush, its retaining bolt, or in the mounting itself (the bolt holes can often become elongated).

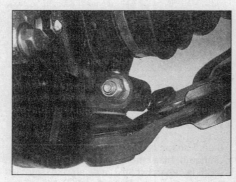

☐ Carry out all the above checks at the other front wheel, and then at both rear wheels.

Springs and shock absorbers

☐ Examine the suspension struts (when applicable) for serious fluid leakage, corrosion, or damage to the casing. Also check the security of the mounting points.
☐ If coil springs are fitted, check that the spring ends locate in their seats, and that the spring is not corroded, cracked or broken.
☐ If leaf springs are fitted, check that all leaves are intact, that the axle is securely attached to each spring, and that there is no deterioration of the spring eye mountings, bushes, and shackles.

☐ The same general checks apply to vehicles fitted with other suspension types, such as torsion bars, hydraulic displacer units, etc. Ensure that all mountings and attachments are secure, that there are no signs of excessive wear, corrosion or damage, and (on hydraulic types) that there are no fluid leaks or damaged pipes.
☐ Inspect the shock absorbers for signs of serious fluid leakage. Check for wear of the mounting bushes or attachments, or damage to the body of the unit.

Driveshafts (fwd vehicles only)

☐ Rotate each front wheel in turn and inspect the constant velocity joint gaiters for splits or damage. Also check that each driveshaft is straight and undamaged.

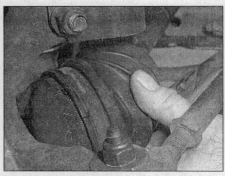

Braking system

☐ If possible without dismantling, check brake pad wear and disc condition. Ensure that the friction lining material has not worn excessively, (A) and that the discs are not fractured, pitted, scored or badly worn (B).

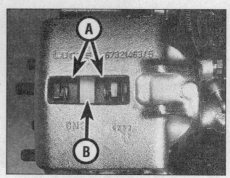

☐ Examine all the rigid brake pipes underneath the vehicle, and the flexible hose(s) at the rear. Look for corrosion, chafing or insecurity of the pipes, and for signs of bulging under pressure, chafing, splits or deterioration of the flexible hoses.
☐ Look for signs of fluid leaks at the brake calipers or on the brake backplates. Repair or renew leaking components.
☐ Slowly spin each wheel, while your assistant depresses and releases the footbrake. Ensure that each brake is operating and does not bind when the pedal is released.

□ Examine the handbrake mechanism, checking for frayed or broken cables, excessive corrosion, or wear or insecurity of the linkage. Check that the mechanism works on each relevant wheel, and releases fully, without binding.

□ It is not possible to test brake efficiency without special equipment, but a road test can be carried out later to check that the vehicle pulls up in a straight line.

Fuel and exhaust systems

□ Inspect the fuel tank (including the filler cap), fuel pipes, hoses and unions. All components must be secure and free from leaks.

□ Examine the exhaust system over its entire length, checking for any damaged, broken or missing mountings, security of the retaining clamps and rust or corrosion.

Wheels and tyres

□ Examine the sidewalls and tread area of each tyre in turn. Check for cuts, tears, lumps, bulges, separation of the tread, and exposure of the ply or cord due to wear or damage. Check that the tyre bead is correctly seated on the wheel rim, that the valve is sound and properly seated, and that the wheel is not distorted or damaged.

□ Check that the tyres are of the correct size for the vehicle, that they are of the same size and type on each axle, and that the pressures are correct.

□ Check the tyre tread depth. The legal minimum at the time of writing is 1.6 mm over at least three-quarters of the tread width. Abnormal tread wear may indicate incorrect front wheel alignment.

Body corrosion

□ Check the condition of the entire vehicle structure for signs of corrosion in load-bearing areas. (These include chassis box sections, side sills, cross-members, pillars, and all suspension, steering, braking system and seat belt mountings and anchorages.) Any corrosion which has seriously reduced the thickness of a load-bearing area is likely to cause the vehicle to fail. In this case professional repairs are likely to be needed.

□ Damage or corrosion which causes sharp or otherwise dangerous edges to be exposed will also cause the vehicle to fail.

4 Checks carried out on YOUR VEHICLE'S EXHAUST EMISSION SYSTEM

Petrol models

□ Have the engine at normal operating temperature, and make sure that it is in good tune (ignition system in good order, air filter element clean, etc).

□ Before any measurements are carried out, raise the engine speed to around 2500 rpm, and hold it at this speed for 20 seconds. Allow the engine speed to return to idle, and watch for smoke emissions from the exhaust tailpipe. If the idle speed is obviously much too high, or if dense blue or clearly-visible black smoke comes from the tailpipe for more than 5 seconds, the vehicle will fail. As a rule of thumb, blue smoke signifies oil being burnt (engine wear) while black smoke signifies unburnt fuel (dirty air cleaner element, or other carburettor or fuel system fault).

□ An exhaust gas analyser capable of measuring carbon monoxide (CO) and hydrocarbons (HC) is now needed. If such an instrument cannot be hired or borrowed, a local garage may agree to perform the check for a small fee.

CO emissions (mixture)

□ At the time of writing, for vehicles first used between 1st August 1975 and 31st July 1986 (P to C registration), the CO level must not exceed 4.5% by volume. For vehicles first used between 1st August 1986 and 31st July 1992 (D to J registration), the CO level must not exceed 3.5% by volume. Vehicles first

used after 1st August 1992 (K registration) must conform to the manufacturer's specification. The MOT tester has access to a DOT database or emissions handbook, which lists the CO and HC limits for each make and model of vehicle. The CO level is measured with the engine at idle speed, and at "fast idle". The following limits are given as a general guide:

> At idle speed -
> CO level no more than 0.5%
> At "fast idle" (2500 to 3000 rpm) -
> CO level no more than 0.3%
> (Minimum oil temperature 60°C)

□ If the CO level cannot be reduced far enough to pass the test (and the fuel and ignition systems are otherwise in good condition) then the carburettor is badly worn, or there is some problem in the fuel injection system or catalytic converter (as applicable).

HC emissions

□ With the CO within limits, HC emissions for vehicles first used between 1st August 1975 and 31st July 1992 (P to J registration) must not exceed 1200 ppm. Vehicles first used after 1st August 1992 (K registration) must conform to the manufacturer's specification. The MOT tester has access to a DOT database or emissions handbook, which lists the CO and HC limits for each make and model of vehicle. The HC level is measured with the engine at "fast idle". The following is given as a general guide:

> At "fast idle" (2500 to 3000 rpm) -
> HC level no more than 200 ppm
> (Minimum oil temperature 60°C)

□ Excessive HC emissions are caused by incomplete combustion, the causes of which can include oil being burnt, mechanical wear and ignition/fuel system malfunction.

Diesel models

□ The only emission test applicable to Diesel engines is the measuring of exhaust smoke density. The test involves accelerating the engine several times to its maximum unloaded speed.

Note: It is of the utmost importance that the engine timing belt is in good condition before the test is carried out.

□ The limits for Diesel engine exhaust smoke, introduced in September 1995 are:
Vehicles first used before 1st August 1979:
  Exempt from metered smoke testing, but must not emit "dense blue or clearly visible black smoke for a period of more than 5 seconds at idle" or "dense blue or clearly visible black smoke during acceleration which would obscure the view of other road users".
Non-turbocharged vehicles first used after 1st August 1979: 2.5m-1
Turbocharged vehicles first used after 1st August 1979: 3.0m-1

□ Excessive smoke can be caused by a dirty air cleaner element. Otherwise, professional advice may be needed to find the cause.

Engine   1

- ☐ Engine fails to rotate when attempting to start
- ☐ Engine rotates, but will not start
- ☐ Engine difficult to start when cold
- ☐ Engine difficult to start when hot
- ☐ Starter motor noisy or excessively-rough in engagement
- ☐ Engine starts, but stops immediately
- ☐ Engine idles erratically
- ☐ Engine misfires at idle speed
- ☐ Engine misfires throughout the driving speed range
- ☐ Engine hesitates on acceleration
- ☐ Engine stalls
- ☐ Engine lacks power
- ☐ Engine backfires
- ☐ Oil pressure warning light on with engine running
- ☐ Engine runs-on after switching off
- ☐ Engine noises

Cooling system   2

- ☐ Overheating
- ☐ Overcooling
- ☐ External coolant leakage
- ☐ Internal coolant leakage
- ☐ Corrosion

Fuel and exhaust systems   3

- ☐ Excessive fuel consumption
- ☐ Fuel leakage and/or fuel odour
- ☐ Excessive noise or fumes from exhaust system

Clutch   4

- ☐ Pedal travels to floor - no pressure or very little resistance
- ☐ Clutch fails to disengage (unable to select gears)
- ☐ Clutch slips (engine speed rises, with no increase in vehicle speed)
- ☐ Judder as clutch is engaged
- ☐ Noise when depressing or releasing clutch pedal

Manual transmission   5

- ☐ Noisy in neutral with engine running
- ☐ Noisy in one particular gear
- ☐ Difficulty engaging gears
- ☐ Jumps out of gear
- ☐ Vibration
- ☐ Lubricant leaks

Automatic transmission   6

- ☐ Fluid leakage
- ☐ Transmission fluid brown, or has burned smell
- ☐ General gear selection problems
- ☐ Transmission will not downshift (kickdown) at full throttle
- ☐ Engine won't start in any gear, or starts in gears other than Park or Neutral
- ☐ Transmission slips, shifts roughly, is noisy, or has no drive in forward or reverse gears

Driveshafts   7

- ☐ Clicking or knocking noise on turns (at slow speed on full-lock)
- ☐ Vibration when accelerating or decelerating

Braking system   8

- ☐ Vehicle pulls to one side under braking
- ☐ Noise (grinding or high-pitched squeal) when brakes applied
- ☐ Excessive brake pedal travel
- ☐ Brake pedal feels spongy when depressed
- ☐ Excessive brake pedal effort required to stop vehicle
- ☐ Judder felt through brake pedal or steering wheel when braking
- ☐ Brakes binding
- ☐ Rear wheels locking under normal braking

Suspension and steering systems   9

- ☐ Vehicle pulls to one side
- ☐ Wheel wobble and vibration
- ☐ Excessive pitching and/or rolling around corners, or during braking
- ☐ Wandering or general instability
- ☐ Excessively-stiff steering
- ☐ Excessive play in steering
- ☐ Lack of power assistance
- ☐ Tyre wear excessive

Electrical system   10

- ☐ Battery will not hold a charge for more than a few days
- ☐ Ignition/no-charge warning light stays on with engine running
- ☐ Ignition/no-charge warning light fails to come on
- ☐ Lights inoperative
- ☐ Instrument readings inaccurate or erratic
- ☐ Horn inoperative, or unsatisfactory in operation
- ☐ Windscreen/tailgate wipers failed, or unsatisfactory in operation
- ☐ Windscreen/tailgate washers failed, or unsatisfactory in operation
- ☐ Electric windows inoperative, or unsatisfactory in operation
- ☐ Central locking system inoperative, or unsatisfactory in operation

Introduction

The vehicle owner who does his or her own maintenance according to the recommended service schedules should not have to use this section of the manual very often. Modern component reliability is such that, provided those items subject to wear or deterioration are inspected or renewed at the specified intervals, sudden failure is comparatively rare. Faults do not usually just happen as a result of sudden failure, but develop over a period of time. Major mechanical failures in particular are usually preceded by characteristic symptoms over hundreds or even thousands of miles. Those components which do occasionally fail without warning are often small and easily carried in the vehicle.

With any fault-finding, the first step is to decide where to begin investigations. This may be obvious, but some detective work may be necessary. The owner who makes half a dozen haphazard adjustments or replacements may be successful in curing a fault (or its symptoms), but will be none the wiser if the fault recurs and ultimately may have spent more time and money than was necessary. A calm and logical approach will be found to be more satisfactory in the long run. Always take into account any warning signs that may have been noticed in the period preceding the fault - power loss, high or low gauge readings, unusual smells, etc - and remember - failure of components such as fuses or spark plugs may only be pointers to some underlying fault.

The pages which follow provide an easy-reference guide to the more common problems which may occur during the operation of the vehicle. These problems and their possible causes are grouped under headings denoting various components or systems, such as Engine, Cooling system, etc. The Chapter and/or Section which deals with the problem is also shown in brackets. Whatever the fault, certain basic principles apply. These are as follows:

Verify the fault. This is simply a matter of being sure that you know what the symptoms are before starting work. This is particularly important if you are investigating a fault for someone else, who may not have described it very accurately.

Don't overlook the obvious. For example, if the vehicle won't start, is there fuel in the tank? (Don't take anyone else's word on this particular point and don't trust the fuel gauge either!) If an electrical fault is indicated, look for loose or broken wires before digging out the test gear.

Cure the disease, not the symptom. Substituting a flat battery with a fully-charged one will get you off the hard shoulder, but if the underlying cause is not attended to, the new battery will go the same way. Similarly, changing oil-fouled spark plugs for a new set will get you moving again, but remember that the reason for the fouling (if it wasn't simply an incorrect grade of plug) will have to be established and corrected.

Don't take anything for granted. Particularly, don't forget that a "new" component may itself be defective (especially if it's been rattling around in the boot for months) and don't leave components out of a fault diagnosis sequence just because they are new or recently-fitted. When you do finally diagnose a difficult fault, you'll probably realise that all the evidence was there from the start.

1 Engine

Engine fails to rotate when attempting to start

- [ ] Battery terminal connections loose or corroded ("*Weekly Checks*").
- [ ] Battery discharged or faulty (Chapter 5A).
- [ ] Broken, loose or disconnected wiring in the starting circuit (Chapter 5A).
- [ ] Defective starter solenoid or switch (Chapter 5A).
- [ ] Defective starter motor (Chapter 5A).
- [ ] Starter pinion or flywheel ring gear teeth loose or broken (Chapters 2A, 2B and 5A).
- [ ] Engine earth strap broken or disconnected (Chapter 5A).

Engine rotates, but will not start

- [ ] Fuel tank empty.
- [ ] Battery discharged (engine rotates slowly) (Chapter 5A).
- [ ] Battery terminal connections loose or corroded ("*Weekly Checks*").
- [ ] Ignition components damp or damaged - petrol models (Chapters 1A and 5B).
- [ ] Broken, loose or disconnected wiring in the ignition circuit - petrol models (Chapters 1A and 5B).
- [ ] Worn, faulty or incorrectly-gapped spark plugs - petrol models (Chapter 1A).
- [ ] Preheating system faulty - diesel models (Chapter 5C).
- [ ] Choke mechanism incorrectly adjusted, worn or sticking - carburettor petrol models (Chapter 4A).
- [ ] Faulty fuel cut-off solenoid - carburettor petrol models (Chapter 4A).
- [ ] Fuel injection system fault - fuel-injected petrol models (Chapter 4B or 4C).
- [ ] Stop solenoid faulty - diesel models (Chapter 4D).
- [ ] Air in fuel system - diesel models (Chapter 4D).
- [ ] Major mechanical failure (eg camshaft drive) (Chapter 2A, 2B or 2C).

Engine difficult to start when cold

- [ ] Battery discharged (Chapter 5A).
- [ ] Battery terminal connections loose or corroded ("*Weekly Checks*").
- [ ] Worn, faulty or incorrectly-gapped spark plugs - petrol models (Chapter 1A).
- [ ] Preheating system faulty - diesel models (Chapter 5C).
- [ ] Choke mechanism incorrectly adjusted, worn or sticking - carburettor petrol models (Chapter 4A).
- [ ] Fuel injection system fault - fuel-injected petrol models (Chapter 4B or 4C).
- [ ] Other ignition system fault - petrol models (Chapters 1A and 5B).
- [ ] Fast idle valve incorrectly adjusted - diesel models (Chapter 4D).
- [ ] Low cylinder compressions (Chapter 2A or 2B).

Engine difficult to start when hot

- [ ] Air filter element dirty or clogged (Chapter 1A or 1B).
- [ ] Choke mechanism incorrectly adjusted, worn or sticking - carburettor petrol models (Chapter 4A).
- [ ] Fuel injection system fault - fuel-injected petrol models (Chapter 4B or 4C).
- [ ] Low cylinder compressions (Chapter 2A or 2B).

Starter motor noisy or excessively-rough in engagement

- [ ] Starter pinion or flywheel ring gear teeth loose or broken (Chapters 2A, 2B and 5A).
- [ ] Starter motor mounting bolts loose or missing (Chapter 5A).
- [ ] Starter motor internal components worn or damaged (Chapter 5A).

Engine starts, but stops immediately

- [ ] Loose or faulty electrical connections in the ignition circuit - petrol models (Chapters 1A and 5B).
- [ ] Vacuum leak at the carburettor/throttle body or inlet manifold - petrol models (Chapter 4A, 4B or 4C).
- [ ] Blocked carburettor jet(s) or internal passages - carburettor petrol models (Chapter 4A).
- [ ] Blocked injector/fuel injection system fault - fuel-injected petrol models (Chapter 4B or 4C).

Engine idles erratically

- [ ] Air filter element clogged (Chapter 1A or 1B).
- [ ] Vacuum leak at the carburettor/throttle body, inlet manifold or associated hoses - petrol models (Chapter 4A, 4B or 4C).
- [ ] Worn, faulty or incorrectly-gapped spark plugs - petrol models (Chapter 1A).
- [ ] Uneven or low cylinder compressions (Chapter 2A or 2B).
- [ ] Camshaft lobes worn (Chapter 2A or 2B).
- [ ] Timing belt incorrectly tensioned (Chapter 2A or 2B).
- [ ] Blocked carburettor jet(s) or internal passages - carburettor petrol models (Chapter 4A).
- [ ] Blocked injector/fuel injection system fault - fuel-injected petrol models (Chapter 4B or 4C).
- [ ] Faulty injector(s) - diesel models (Chapter 4D).

Engine misfires at idle speed

- [ ] Worn, faulty or incorrectly-gapped spark plugs - petrol models (Chapter 1A).
- [ ] Faulty spark plug HT leads - petrol models (Chapter 1A).
- [ ] Vacuum leak at the carburettor/throttle body, inlet manifold or associated hoses - petrol models (Chapter 4A, 4B or 4C).
- [ ] Blocked carburettor jet(s) or internal passages - carburettor petrol models (Chapter 4A).
- [ ] Blocked injector/fuel injection system fault - fuel-injected petrol models (Chapter 4B or 4C).
- [ ] Faulty injector(s) - diesel models (Chapter 4D).
- [ ] Distributor cap cracked or tracking internally - petrol models (where applicable) (Chapter 1A).
- [ ] Uneven or low cylinder compressions (Chapter 2A or 2B).
- [ ] Disconnected, leaking, or perished crankcase ventilation hoses (Chapter 4E).

Engine (continued)

Engine misfires throughout the driving speed range

- ☐ Fuel filter choked (Chapter 1A or 1B).
- ☐ Fuel pump faulty, or delivery pressure low (Chapter 4A, 4B or 4C).
- ☐ Fuel tank vent blocked, or fuel pipes restricted (Chapter 4A, 4B or 4C).
- ☐ Vacuum leak at the carburettor/throttle body, inlet manifold or associated hoses - petrol models (Chapter 4A, 4B or 4C).
- ☐ Worn, faulty or incorrectly-gapped spark plugs - petrol models (Chapter 1A).
- ☐ Faulty spark plug HT leads - petrol models (Chapter 1A).
- ☐ Faulty injector(s) - diesel models (Chapter 4D).
- ☐ Distributor cap cracked or tracking internally - petrol models (where applicable) (Chapter 1A).
- ☐ Faulty ignition coil - petrol models (Chapter 5B).
- ☐ Uneven or low cylinder compressions (Chapter 2A or 2B).
- ☐ Blocked carburettor jet(s) or internal passages - carburettor petrol models (Chapter 4A).
- ☐ Blocked injector/fuel injection system fault - fuel-injected petrol models (Chapter 4B or 4C).

Engine hesitates on acceleration

- ☐ Worn, faulty or incorrectly-gapped spark plugs - petrol models (Chapter 1A).
- ☐ Vacuum leak at the carburettor/throttle body, inlet manifold or associated hoses (Chapter 4A, 4B or 4C).
- ☐ Blocked carburettor jet(s) or internal passages - carburettor petrol models (Chapter 4A).
- ☐ Blocked injector/fuel injection system fault - fuel-injected petrol models (Chapter 4B or 4C).
- ☐ Faulty injector(s) - diesel models (Chapter 4D).

Engine stalls

- ☐ Vacuum leak at the carburettor/throttle body, inlet manifold or associated hoses - petrol models (Chapter 4A, 4B or 4C).
- ☐ Fuel filter choked (Chapter 1A or 1B).
- ☐ Fuel pump faulty, or delivery pressure low - petrol models (Chapter 4A, 4B or 4C).
- ☐ Fuel tank vent blocked, or fuel pipes restricted (Chapter 4A, 4B, 4C or 4D).
- ☐ Blocked carburettor jet(s) or internal passages - carburettor petrol models (Chapter 4A).
- ☐ Blocked injector/fuel injection system fault - fuel-injected petrol models (Chapter 4B or 4C).
- ☐ Faulty injector(s) - diesel models (Chapter 4D).

Engine lacks power

- ☐ Timing belt incorrectly fitted or tensioned (Chapter 2A or 2B).
- ☐ Fuel filter choked (Chapter 1A or 1B).
- ☐ Fuel pump faulty, or delivery pressure low (Chapter 4A, 4B, or 4C).
- ☐ Uneven or low cylinder compressions (Chapter 2A or 2B).
- ☐ Worn, faulty or incorrectly-gapped spark plugs - petrol models (Chapter 1A).
- ☐ Vacuum leak at the carburettor/throttle body, inlet manifold or associated hoses - petrol models (Chapter 4A, 4B or 4C).
- ☐ Blocked carburettor jet(s) or internal passages - carburettor petrol models (Chapter 4A).
- ☐ Blocked injector/fuel injection system fault - fuel-injected petrol models (Chapter 4B or 4C).
- ☐ Faulty injector(s) - diesel models (Chapter 4D).
- ☐ Injection pump timing incorrect - diesel models (Chapter 4D).
- ☐ Brakes binding (Chapters 1 and 9).
- ☐ Clutch slipping (Chapter 6).

Engine backfires

- ☐ Timing belt incorrectly fitted or tensioned (Chapter 2A).
- ☐ Vacuum leak at the carburettor/throttle body, inlet manifold or associated hoses - petrol models (Chapter 4A, 4B or 4C).
- ☐ Blocked carburettor jet(s) or internal passages - carburettor petrol models (Chapter 4A).
- ☐ Blocked injector/fuel injection system fault - fuel-injected petrol models (Chapter 4B or 4C).

Oil pressure warning light on with engine running

- ☐ Low oil level, or incorrect oil grade ("Weekly Checks").
- ☐ Faulty oil pressure warning light switch (Chapter 5A).
- ☐ Worn engine bearings and/or oil pump (Chapter 2C).
- ☐ High engine operating temperature (Chapter 3).
- ☐ Oil pressure relief valve defective (Chapter 2A or 2B).
- ☐ Oil pick-up strainer clogged (Chapter 2A or 2B).

Engine runs-on after switching off

- ☐ Excessive carbon build-up in engine (Chapter 2C).
- ☐ High engine operating temperature (Chapter 3).
- ☐ Faulty fuel cut-off solenoid - carburettor petrol models (Chapter 4A).
- ☐ Fuel injection system fault - fuel-injected petrol models (Chapter 4B or 4C).
- ☐ Faulty stop solenoid - diesel models (Chapter 4D).

Engine noises

Pre-ignition (pinking) or knocking during acceleration or under load

- ☐ Ignition timing incorrect/ignition system fault - petrol models (Chapters 1A and 5B).
- ☐ Incorrect grade of spark plug - petrol models (Chapter 1A).
- ☐ Incorrect grade of fuel (Chapter 4A, 4B, 4C or 4D).
- ☐ Vacuum leak at the carburettor/throttle body, inlet manifold or associated hoses - petrol models (Chapter 4A, 4B or 4C).
- ☐ Excessive carbon build-up in engine (Chapter 2C).
- ☐ Blocked carburettor jet(s) or internal passages - carburettor petrol models (Chapter 4A).
- ☐ Blocked injector/fuel injection system fault - fuel-injected petrol models (Chapter 4B or 4C).

Whistling or wheezing noises

- ☐ Leaking inlet manifold or carburettor/throttle body gasket - petrol models (Chapter 4A, 4B or 4C).
- ☐ Leaking exhaust manifold gasket or pipe-to-manifold joint (Chapter 4A, 4B, 4C or 4D).
- ☐ Leaking vacuum hose (Chapters 4A, 4B, 4C, 4D, 5B and 9).
- ☐ Blowing cylinder head gasket (Chapter 2A or 2B).

Tapping or rattling noises

- ☐ Worn valve gear or camshaft (Chapter 2A or 2B).
- ☐ Ancillary component fault (coolant pump, alternator, etc) (Chapters 3, 5A, etc).

Knocking or thumping noises

- ☐ Worn big-end bearings (regular heavy knocking, perhaps less under load) (Chapter 2C).
- ☐ Worn main bearings (rumbling and knocking, perhaps worsening under load) (Chapter 2C).
- ☐ Piston slap (most noticeable when cold) (Chapter 2C).
- ☐ Ancillary component fault (coolant pump, alternator, etc) (Chapters 3, 5A, etc).

2 Cooling system

Overheating

- ☐ Insufficient coolant in system ("*Weekly Checks*").
- ☐ Thermostat faulty (Chapter 3).
- ☐ Radiator core blocked, or grille restricted (Chapter 3).
- ☐ Electric cooling fan or thermoswitch faulty (Chapter 3).
- ☐ Pressure cap faulty (Chapter 3).
- ☐ Ignition timing incorrect/ignition system fault - petrol models (Chapters 1A and 5B).
- ☐ Inaccurate temperature gauge sender unit (Chapter 3).
- ☐ Airlock in cooling system (Chapter 1A or 1B).

Overcooling

- ☐ Thermostat faulty (Chapter 3).
- ☐ Inaccurate temperature gauge sender unit (Chapter 3).

External coolant leakage

- ☐ Deteriorated or damaged hoses or hose clips (Chapter 1A or 1B).
- ☐ Radiator core or heater matrix leaking (Chapter 3).
- ☐ Pressure cap faulty (Chapter 3).
- ☐ Water pump seal leaking (Chapter 3).
- ☐ Boiling due to overheating (Chapter 3).
- ☐ Core plug leaking (Chapter 2C).

Internal coolant leakage

- ☐ Leaking cylinder head gasket (Chapter 2A, 2B or 2C).
- ☐ Cracked cylinder head or cylinder bore (Chapter 2A, 2B or 2C).

Corrosion

- ☐ Infrequent draining and flushing (Chapter 1A or 1B).
- ☐ Incorrect coolant mixture or inappropriate coolant type ("*Weekly checks*").

3 Fuel and exhaust systems

Excessive fuel consumption

- ☐ Air filter element dirty or clogged (Chapter 1A or 1B).
- ☐ Choke cable incorrectly adjusted, or choke sticking - carburettor petrol models (Chapter 4A).
- ☐ Fuel injection system fault - fuel injected petrol models (Chapter 4B or 4C).
- ☐ Faulty injector(s) - diesel models (Chapter 4D).
- ☐ Ignition timing incorrect/ignition system fault - petrol models (Chapters 1 and 5B).
- ☐ Tyres under-inflated ("*Weekly Checks*").
- ☐ Brakes binding (Chapters 1 and 9).

Fuel leakage and/or fuel odour

- ☐ Damaged or corroded fuel tank, pipes or connections (Chapter 4A, 4B, 4C or 4D).
- ☐ Carburettor float chamber flooding (float height incorrect) - carburettor petrol models (Chapter 4A).

Excessive noise or fumes from exhaust system

- ☐ Leaking exhaust system or manifold joints (Chapters 1 and 4A, 4B, 4C or 4D).
- ☐ Leaking, corroded or damaged silencers or pipe (Chapters 1 and 4A, 4B, 4C or 4D).
- ☐ Broken mountings causing body or suspension contact (Chapter 1A or 1B).

4 Clutch

Pedal travels to floor - no pressure or very little resistance

- ☐ Broken clutch cable (Chapter 6).
- ☐ Incorrect clutch cable adjustment (Chapter 6).
- ☐ Broken clutch release bearing or fork (Chapter 6).
- ☐ Broken diaphragm spring in clutch pressure plate (Chapter 6).

Clutch fails to disengage (unable to select gears)

- ☐ Incorrect clutch cable adjustment (Chapter 6).
- ☐ Clutch disc sticking on gearbox input shaft splines (Chapter 6).
- ☐ Clutch disc sticking to flywheel or pressure plate (Chapter 6).
- ☐ Faulty pressure plate assembly (Chapter 6).
- ☐ Clutch release mechanism worn or incorrectly assembled (Chapter 6).

Clutch slips (engine speed rises, with no increase in vehicle speed)

- ☐ Incorrect clutch cable adjustment (Chapter 6).

- ☐ Clutch disc linings excessively worn (Chapter 6).
- ☐ Clutch disc linings contaminated with oil or grease (Chapter 6).
- ☐ Faulty pressure plate or weak diaphragm spring (Chapter 6).

Judder as clutch is engaged

- ☐ Clutch disc linings contaminated with oil or grease (Chapter 6).
- ☐ Clutch disc linings excessively worn (Chapter 6).
- ☐ Clutch cable sticking or frayed (Chapter 6).
- ☐ Faulty or distorted pressure plate or diaphragm spring (Chapter 6).
- ☐ Worn or loose engine or gearbox mountings (Chapter 2A or 2B).
- ☐ Clutch disc hub or gearbox input shaft splines worn (Chapter 6).

Noise when depressing or releasing clutch pedal

- ☐ Worn clutch release bearing (Chapter 6).
- ☐ Worn or dry clutch pedal bushes (Chapter 6).
- ☐ Faulty pressure plate assembly (Chapter 6).
- ☐ Pressure plate diaphragm spring broken (Chapter 6).
- ☐ Broken clutch disc cushioning springs (Chapter 6).

5 Manual transmission

Noisy in neutral with engine running

- ☐ Input shaft bearings worn (noise apparent with clutch pedal released, but not when depressed) (Chapter 7A).*
- ☐ Clutch release bearing worn (noise apparent with clutch pedal depressed, possibly less when released) (Chapter 6).

Noisy in one particular gear

- ☐ Worn, damaged or chipped gear teeth (Chapter 7A).*

Difficulty engaging gears

- ☐ Clutch fault (Chapter 6).
- ☐ Worn or damaged gear linkage (Chapter 7A).
- ☐ Incorrectly-adjusted gear linkage (Chapter 7A).
- ☐ Worn synchroniser units (Chapter 7A).*

Jumps out of gear

- ☐ Worn or damaged gear linkage (Chapter 7A).

- ☐ Incorrectly-adjusted gear linkage (Chapter 7A).
- ☐ Worn synchroniser units (Chapter 7A).*
- ☐ Worn selector forks (Chapter 7A).*

Vibration

- ☐ Lack of oil (Chapter 1A or 1B).
- ☐ Worn bearings (Chapter 7A).*

Lubricant leaks

- ☐ Leaking differential output oil seal (Chapter 7A).
- ☐ Leaking housing joint (Chapter 7A).*
- ☐ Leaking input shaft oil seal (Chapter 7A).*

Although the corrective action necessary to remedy the symptoms described is beyond the scope of the home mechanic, the above information should be helpful in isolating the cause of the condition, so that the owner can communicate clearly with a professional mechanic.

6 Automatic transmission

Note: *Due to the complexity of the automatic transmission, it is difficult for the home mechanic to properly diagnose and service this unit. For problems other than the following, the vehicle should be taken to a dealer service department or automatic transmission specialist. Don't be in a hurry to remove the transmission if a fault is suspected, as most testing is carried out with the unit still fitted.*

Fluid leakage

☐ Automatic transmission fluid is usually dark in colour. Fluid leaks should not be confused with engine oil, which can easily be blown onto the transmission by airflow.

☐ To determine the source of a leak, first remove all built-up dirt and grime from the transmission housing and surrounding areas using a degreasing agent, or by steam-cleaning. Drive the vehicle at low speed, so airflow will not blow the leak far from its source. Raise and support the vehicle and determine where the leak is coming from. The following are common areas of leakage:
  a) *Fluid pan or "sump" (Chapter 1 and 7B).*
  b) *Dipstick tube (Chapter 1 and 7B).*
  c) *Transmission-to-fluid cooler pipes/unions (Chapter 7B).*

Transmission fluid brown, or has burned smell

☐ Transmission fluid level low, or fluid in need of renewal (Chapter 1A).

General gear selection problems

☐ Chapter 7B deals with checking and adjusting the selector cable on automatic transmissions. The following are common problems which may be caused by a poorly-adjusted cable:
  a) *Engine starting in gears other than Park or Neutral.*
  b) *Indicator panel showing a gear other than that being used.*
  c) *Vehicle moves when in Park or Neutral.*
  d) *Poor gear shift quality or erratic gear changes.*
☐ Refer to Chapter 7B for the selector cable adjustment procedure.

Transmission will not downshift (kickdown) at full throttle

☐ Low transmission fluid level (Chapter 1A).
☐ Incorrect selector cable adjustment (Chapter 7B).

Engine won't start in any gear, or starts in gears other than Park or Neutral

☐ Incorrect starter/inhibitor switch adjustment (Chapter 7B).
☐ Incorrect selector cable adjustment (Chapter 7B).

Transmission slips, shifts roughly, is noisy, or has no drive in forward or reverse gears

☐ There are many probable causes for the above problems, but the home mechanic should be concerned with only one possibility - fluid level. Before taking the vehicle to a dealer or transmission specialist, check the fluid level and condition of the fluid as described in Chapter 1A. Correct the fluid level as necessary, or change the fluid and filter. If the problem persists, professional help will be necessary.

7 Driveshafts

Clicking or knocking noise on turns (at slow speed on full-lock)

☐ Lack of constant velocity joint lubricant, possibly due to damaged gaiter (Chapter 8).
☐ Worn outer constant velocity joint (Chapter 8).

Vibration when accelerating or decelerating

☐ Worn inner constant velocity joint (Chapter 8).
☐ Bent or distorted driveshaft (Chapter 8).

8 Braking system

Note: *Before assuming that a brake problem exists, make sure that the tyres are in good condition and correctly inflated, that the front wheel alignment is correct and that the vehicle is not loaded with weight in an unequal manner. Apart from checking the condition of all pipe and hose connections, any faults occurring on the anti-lock braking system should be referred to a Peugeot dealer for diagnosis.*

Vehicle pulls to one side under braking

- ☐ Worn, defective, damaged or contaminated brake pads/shoes on one side (Chapters 1 and 9).
- ☐ Seized or partially-seized front brake caliper/wheel cylinder piston (Chapters 1 and 9).
- ☐ A mixture of brake pad/shoe lining materials fitted between sides (Chapters 1 and 9).
- ☐ Brake caliper or backplate mounting bolts loose (Chapter 9).
- ☐ Worn or damaged steering or suspension components (Chapters 1 and 10).

Noise (grinding or high-pitched squeal) when brakes applied

- ☐ Brake pad or shoe friction lining material worn down to metal backing (Chapters 1 and 9).
- ☐ Excessive corrosion of brake disc or drum. May be apparent after the vehicle has been standing for some time (Chapters 1 and 9).
- ☐ Foreign object (stone chipping, etc) trapped between brake disc and shield (Chapters 1 and 9).

Excessive brake pedal travel

- ☐ Inoperative rear brake self-adjust mechanism - drum brakes (Chapters 1 and 9).
- ☐ Faulty master cylinder (Chapter 9).
- ☐ Air in hydraulic system (Chapters 1 and 9).
- ☐ Faulty vacuum servo unit (Chapter 9).

Brake pedal feels spongy when depressed

- ☐ Air in hydraulic system (Chapters 1 and 9).
- ☐ Deteriorated flexible rubber brake hoses (Chapters 1 and 9).
- ☐ Master cylinder mounting nuts loose (Chapter 9).
- ☐ Faulty master cylinder (Chapter 9).

Excessive brake pedal effort required to stop vehicle

- ☐ Faulty vacuum servo unit (Chapter 9).
- ☐ Disconnected, damaged or insecure brake servo vacuum hose (Chapter 9).
- ☐ Primary or secondary hydraulic circuit failure (Chapter 9).
- ☐ Seized brake caliper or wheel cylinder piston(s) (Chapter 9).
- ☐ Brake pads or brake shoes incorrectly fitted (Chapters 1 and 9).
- ☐ Incorrect grade of brake pads or brake shoes fitted (Chapters 1 and 9).
- ☐ Brake pads or brake shoe linings contaminated (Chapters 1 and 9).

Judder felt through brake pedal or steering wheel when braking

- ☐ Excessive run-out or distortion of discs/drums (Chapters 1 and 9).
- ☐ Brake pad or brake shoe linings worn (Chapters 1 and 9).
- ☐ Brake caliper or brake backplate mounting bolts loose (Chapter 9).
- ☐ Wear in suspension or steering components or mountings (Chapters 1 and 10).

Brakes binding

- ☐ Seized brake caliper or wheel cylinder piston(s) (Chapter 9).
- ☐ Incorrectly-adjusted handbrake mechanism (Chapter 9).
- ☐ Faulty master cylinder (Chapter 9).

Rear wheels locking under normal braking

- ☐ Rear brake shoe linings contaminated (Chapters 1 and 9).
- ☐ Faulty brake pressure regulator (Chapter 9).

9 Suspension and steering systems

Note: *Before diagnosing suspension or steering faults, be sure that the trouble is not due to incorrect tyre pressures, mixtures of tyre types or binding brakes.*

Vehicle pulls to one side

- [ ] Defective tyre ("*Weekly Checks*").
- [ ] Excessive wear in suspension or steering components (Chapters 1 and 10).
- [ ] Incorrect front wheel alignment (Chapter 10).
- [ ] Damage to steering or suspension components (Chapter 1A or 1B).

Wheel wobble and vibration

- [ ] Front roadwheels out of balance (vibration felt mainly through the steering wheel) (Chapters 1 and 10).
- [ ] Rear roadwheels out of balance (vibration felt throughout the vehicle) (Chapters 1 and 10).
- [ ] Roadwheels damaged or distorted (Chapters 1 and 10).
- [ ] Faulty or damaged tyre ("*Weekly Checks*").
- [ ] Worn steering or suspension joints, bushes or components (Chapters 1 and 10).
- [ ] Wheel bolts loose.

Excessive pitching and/or rolling around corners, or during braking

- [ ] Defective shock absorbers (Chapters 1 and 10).
- [ ] Broken or weak spring and/or suspension part (Chapters 1 and 10).
- [ ] Worn or damaged anti-roll bar or mountings (Chapter 10).

Wandering or general instability

- [ ] Incorrect front wheel alignment (Chapter 10).
- [ ] Worn steering or suspension joints, bushes or components (Chapters 1 and 10).
- [ ] Roadwheels out of balance.
- [ ] Faulty or damaged tyre ("*Weekly Checks*").
- [ ] Wheel bolts loose.
- [ ] Defective shock absorbers (Chapters 1 and 10).

Excessively-stiff steering

- [ ] Lack of steering gear lubricant (Chapter 10).
- [ ] Seized track rod end balljoint or suspension balljoint (Chapters 1 and 10).
- [ ] Broken or incorrectly-adjusted auxiliary drivebelt - power steering (Chapter 1A or 1B).
- [ ] Incorrect front wheel alignment (Chapter 10).
- [ ] Steering rack or column bent or damaged (Chapter 10).

Excessive play in steering

- [ ] Worn steering column intermediate shaft universal joint (Chapter 10).
- [ ] Worn steering track rod end balljoints (Chapters 1 and 10).
- [ ] Worn rack-and-pinion steering gear (Chapter 10).
- [ ] Worn steering or suspension joints, bushes or components (Chapters 1 and 10).

Lack of power assistance

- [ ] Broken or incorrectly-adjusted auxiliary drivebelt (Chapter 1A or 1B).
- [ ] Incorrect power steering fluid level ("*Weekly Checks*").
- [ ] Restriction in power steering fluid hoses (Chapter 1A or 1B).
- [ ] Faulty power steering pump (Chapter 10).
- [ ] Faulty rack-and-pinion steering gear (Chapter 10).

Tyre wear excessive

Tyre treads exhibit feathered edges

- [ ] Incorrect toe setting (Chapter 10).

Tyres worn in centre of tread

- [ ] Tyres over-inflated ("*Weekly Checks*").

Tyres worn on inside and outside edges

- [ ] Tyres under-inflated ("*Weekly Checks*").

Tyres worn on inside or outside edges

- [ ] Incorrect camber/castor angles (wear on one edge only) (Chapter 10).
- [ ] Worn steering or suspension joints, bushes or components (Chapters 1 and 10).
- [ ] Excessively-hard cornering.
- [ ] Accident damage.

Tyres worn unevenly

- [ ] Tyres/wheels out of balance ("*Weekly Checks*").
- [ ] Excessive wheel or tyre run-out ("*Weekly Checks*").
- [ ] Worn shock absorbers (Chapters 1 and 10).
- [ ] Faulty tyre ("*Weekly Checks*").

10 Electrical system

Note: *For problems associated with the starting system, refer to the faults listed under "Engine" earlier in this Section.*

Battery will not hold a charge for more than a few days

☐ Battery defective internally (Chapter 5A).
☐ Battery terminal connections loose or corroded ("*Weekly Checks*").
☐ Auxiliary drivebelt worn or incorrectly adjusted (Chapter 1A or 1B).
☐ Alternator not charging at correct output (Chapter 5A).
☐ Alternator or voltage regulator faulty (Chapter 5A).
☐ Short-circuit causing continual battery drain (Chapters 5A and 12).

Ignition/no-charge warning light stays on with engine running

☐ Auxiliary drivebelt broken, worn, or incorrectly adjusted (Chapter 1A or 1B).
☐ Alternator brushes worn, sticking, or dirty (Chapter 5A).
☐ Alternator brush springs weak or broken (Chapter 5A).
☐ Internal fault in alternator or voltage regulator (Chapter 5A).
☐ Broken, disconnected, or loose wiring in charging circuit (Chapter 5A).

Ignition/no-charge warning light fails to come on

☐ Warning light bulb blown (Chapter 12).
☐ Broken, disconnected, or loose wiring in warning light circuit (Chapter 12).
☐ Alternator faulty (Chapter 5A).

Lights inoperative

☐ Bulb blown (Chapter 12).
☐ Corrosion of bulb or bulbholder contacts (Chapter 12).
☐ Blown fuse (Chapter 12).
☐ Faulty relay (Chapter 12).
☐ Broken, loose, or disconnected wiring (Chapter 12).
☐ Faulty switch (Chapter 12).

Instrument readings inaccurate or erratic

Instrument readings increase with engine speed

☐ Faulty voltage regulator (Chapter 12).

Fuel or temperature gauges give no reading

☐ Faulty gauge sender unit (Chapters 3 and 4A, 4B, 4C or 4D).
☐ Wiring open-circuit (Chapter 12).
☐ Faulty gauge (Chapter 12).

Fuel or temperature gauges give continuous maximum reading

☐ Faulty gauge sender unit (Chapters 3 and 4A, 4B, 4C and 4D).
☐ Wiring short-circuit (Chapter 12).
☐ Faulty gauge (Chapter 12).

Horn inoperative, or unsatisfactory in operation

Horn operates all the time

☐ Horn push either earthed or stuck down (Chapter 12).
☐ Horn cable-to-horn push earthed (Chapter 12).

Horn fails to operate

☐ Blown fuse (Chapter 12).
☐ Cable or cable connections loose, broken or disconnected (Chapter 12).
☐ Faulty horn (Chapter 12).

Horn emits intermittent or unsatisfactory sound

☐ Cable connections loose (Chapter 12).
☐ Horn mountings loose (Chapter 12).
☐ Faulty horn (Chapter 12).

Windscreen/tailgate wipers failed, or unsatisfactory in operation

Wipers fail to operate, or operate very slowly

☐ Wiper blades stuck to screen, or linkage seized or binding (Chapter 12).
☐ Blown fuse (Chapter 12).
☐ Cable or cable connections loose, broken or disconnected (Chapter 12).
☐ Faulty relay (Chapter 12).
☐ Faulty wiper motor (Chapter 12).

Wiper blades sweep over too large or too small an area of the glass

☐ Wiper arms incorrectly positioned on spindles.
☐ Excessive wear of wiper linkage (Chapter 12).
☐ Wiper motor or linkage mountings loose or insecure (Chapter 12).

Wiper blades fail to clean the glass effectively

☐ Wiper blade rubbers worn or perished ("*Weekly Checks*").
☐ Wiper arm tension springs broken, or arm pivots seized (Chapter 12).
☐ Insufficient windscreen washer additive to adequately remove road film ("*Weekly Checks*").

Electrical system (continued)

Windscreen/tailgate washers failed, or unsatisfactory in operation

One or more washer jets inoperative

☐ Blocked washer jet.
☐ Disconnected, kinked or restricted fluid hose (Chapter 12).
☐ Insufficient fluid in washer reservoir ("*Weekly Checks*").

Washer pump fails to operate

☐ Broken or disconnected wiring or connections (Chapter 12).
☐ Blown fuse (Chapter 12).
☐ Faulty washer switch (Chapter 12).
☐ Faulty washer pump (Chapter 12).

Washer pump runs for some time before fluid is emitted from jets

☐ Faulty one-way valve in fluid supply hose (Chapter 12).

Electric windows inoperative, or unsatisfactory in operation

Window glass will only move in one direction

☐ Faulty switch (Chapter 12).

Window glass slow to move

☐ Regulator seized or damaged, or in need of lubricant (Chapter 11).
☐ Door internal components or trim fouling regulator (Chapter 11).
☐ Faulty motor (Chapter 11).

Window glass fails to move

☐ Blown fuse (Chapter 12).
☐ Faulty relay (Chapter 12).
☐ Broken or disconnected wiring or connections (Chapter 12).
☐ Faulty motor (Chapter 11).

Central locking system inoperative, or unsatisfactory in operation

Complete system failure

☐ Blown fuse (Chapter 12).
☐ Faulty relay (Chapter 12).
☐ Broken or disconnected wiring or connections (Chapter 12).
☐ Faulty control unit (Chapter 11).

Latch locks but will not unlock, or unlocks but will not lock

☐ Faulty master switch (Chapter 12).
☐ Broken or disconnected latch operating rods or levers (Chapter 11).
☐ Faulty relay (Chapter 12).
☐ Faulty control unit (Chapter 11).

One solenoid/motor fails to operate

☐ Broken or disconnected wiring or connections (Chapter 12).
☐ Faulty solenoid/motor (Chapter 11).
☐ Broken, binding or disconnected latch operating rods or levers (Chapter 11).
☐ Fault in door latch (Chapter 11).

A

ABS (Anti-lock brake system) A system, usually electronically controlled, that senses incipient wheel lockup during braking and relieves hydraulic pressure at wheels that are about to skid.

Air bag An inflatable bag hidden in the steering wheel (driver's side) or the dash or glovebox (passenger side). In a head-on collision, the bags inflate, preventing the driver and front passenger from being thrown forward into the steering wheel or windscreen.

Air cleaner A metal or plastic housing, containing a filter element, which removes dust and dirt from the air being drawn into the engine.

Air filter element The actual filter in an air cleaner system, usually manufactured from pleated paper and requiring renewal at regular intervals.

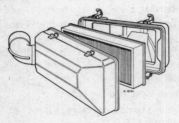

Air filter

Allen key A hexagonal wrench which fits into a recessed hexagonal hole.

Alligator clip A long-nosed spring-loaded metal clip with meshing teeth. Used to make temporary electrical connections.

Alternator A component in the electrical system which converts mechanical energy from a drivebelt into electrical energy to charge the battery and to operate the starting system, ignition system and electrical accessories.

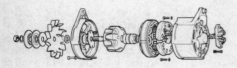

Alternator (exploded view)

Ampere (amp) A unit of measurement for the flow of electric current. One amp is the amount of current produced by one volt acting through a resistance of one ohm.

Anaerobic sealer A substance used to prevent bolts and screws from loosening. Anaerobic means that it does not require oxygen for activation. The Loctite brand is widely used.

Antifreeze A substance (usually ethylene glycol) mixed with water, and added to a vehicle's cooling system, to prevent freezing of the coolant in winter. Antifreeze also contains chemicals to inhibit corrosion and the formation of rust and other deposits that would tend to clog the radiator and coolant passages and reduce cooling efficiency.

Anti-seize compound A coating that reduces the risk of seizing on fasteners that are subjected to high temperatures, such as exhaust manifold bolts and nuts.

Anti-seize compound

Asbestos A natural fibrous mineral with great heat resistance, commonly used in the composition of brake friction materials. Asbestos is a health hazard and the dust created by brake systems should never be inhaled or ingested.

Axle A shaft on which a wheel revolves, or which revolves with a wheel. Also, a solid beam that connects the two wheels at one end of the vehicle. An axle which also transmits power to the wheels is known as a live axle.

Axle assembly

Axleshaft A single rotating shaft, on either side of the differential, which delivers power from the final drive assembly to the drive wheels. Also called a driveshaft or a halfshaft.

B

Ball bearing An anti-friction bearing consisting of a hardened inner and outer race with hardened steel balls between two races.

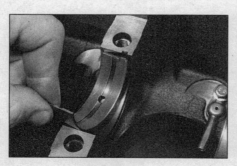

Bearing

Bearing The curved surface on a shaft or in a bore, or the part assembled into either, that permits relative motion between them with minimum wear and friction.

Big-end bearing The bearing in the end of the connecting rod that's attached to the crankshaft.

Bleed nipple A valve on a brake wheel cylinder, caliper or other hydraulic component that is opened to purge the hydraulic system of air. Also called a bleed screw.

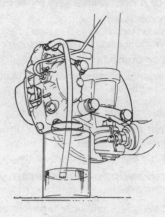

Brake bleeding

Brake bleeding Procedure for removing air from lines of a hydraulic brake system.

Brake disc The component of a disc brake that rotates with the wheels.

Brake drum The component of a drum brake that rotates with the wheels.

Brake linings The friction material which contacts the brake disc or drum to retard the vehicle's speed. The linings are bonded or riveted to the brake pads or shoes.

Brake pads The replaceable friction pads that pinch the brake disc when the brakes are applied. Brake pads consist of a friction material bonded or riveted to a rigid backing plate.

Brake shoe The crescent-shaped carrier to which the brake linings are mounted and which forces the lining against the rotating drum during braking.

Braking systems For more information on braking systems, consult the *Haynes Automotive Brake Manual*.

Breaker bar A long socket wrench handle providing greater leverage.

Bulkhead The insulated partition between the engine and the passenger compartment.

C

Caliper The non-rotating part of a disc-brake assembly that straddles the disc and carries the brake pads. The caliper also contains the hydraulic components that cause the pads to pinch the disc when the brakes are applied. A caliper is also a measuring tool that can be set to measure inside or outside dimensions of an object.

Camshaft A rotating shaft on which a series of cam lobes operate the valve mechanisms. The camshaft may be driven by gears, by sprockets and chain or by sprockets and a belt.

Canister A container in an evaporative emission control system; contains activated charcoal granules to trap vapours from the fuel system.

Canister

Carburettor A device which mixes fuel with air in the proper proportions to provide a desired power output from a spark ignition internal combustion engine.

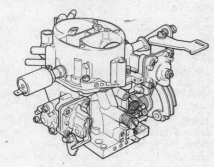

Carburettor

Castellated Resembling the parapets along the top of a castle wall. For example, a castellated balljoint stud nut.

Castellated nut

Castor In wheel alignment, the backward or forward tilt of the steering axis. Castor is positive when the steering axis is inclined rearward at the top.

Catalytic converter A silencer-like device in the exhaust system which converts certain pollutants in the exhaust gases into less harmful substances.

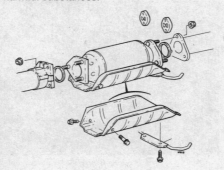

Catalytic converter

Circlip A ring-shaped clip used to prevent endwise movement of cylindrical parts and shafts. An internal circlip is installed in a groove in a housing; an external circlip fits into a groove on the outside of a cylindrical piece such as a shaft.

Clearance The amount of space between two parts. For example, between a piston and a cylinder, between a bearing and a journal, etc.

Coil spring A spiral of elastic steel found in various sizes throughout a vehicle, for example as a springing medium in the suspension and in the valve train.

Compression Reduction in volume, and increase in pressure and temperature, of a gas, caused by squeezing it into a smaller space.

Compression ratio The relationship between cylinder volume when the piston is at top dead centre and cylinder volume when the piston is at bottom dead centre.

Constant velocity (CV) joint A type of universal joint that cancels out vibrations caused by driving power being transmitted through an angle.

Core plug A disc or cup-shaped metal device inserted in a hole in a casting through which core was removed when the casting was formed. Also known as a freeze plug or expansion plug.

Crankcase The lower part of the engine block in which the crankshaft rotates.

Crankshaft The main rotating member, or shaft, running the length of the crankcase, with offset "throws" to which the connecting rods are attached.

Crankshaft assembly

Crocodile clip See Alligator clip

D

Diagnostic code Code numbers obtained by accessing the diagnostic mode of an engine management computer. This code can be used to determine the area in the system where a malfunction may be located.

Disc brake A brake design incorporating a rotating disc onto which brake pads are squeezed. The resulting friction converts the energy of a moving vehicle into heat.

Double-overhead cam (DOHC) An engine that uses two overhead camshafts, usually one for the intake valves and one for the exhaust valves.

Drivebelt(s) The belt(s) used to drive accessories such as the alternator, water pump, power steering pump, air conditioning compressor, etc. off the crankshaft pulley.

Accessory drivebelts

Driveshaft Any shaft used to transmit motion. Commonly used when referring to the axleshafts on a front wheel drive vehicle.

Driveshaft

Drum brake A type of brake using a drum-shaped metal cylinder attached to the inner surface of the wheel. When the brake pedal is pressed, curved brake shoes with friction linings press against the inside of the drum to slow or stop the vehicle.

Drum brake assembly

E

EGR valve A valve used to introduce exhaust gases into the intake air stream.

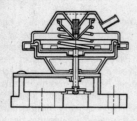

EGR valve

Electronic control unit (ECU) A computer which controls (for instance) ignition and fuel injection systems, or an anti-lock braking system. For more information refer to the *Haynes Automotive Electrical and Electronic Systems Manual.*

Electronic Fuel Injection (EFI) A computer controlled fuel system that distributes fuel through an injector located in each intake port of the engine.

Emergency brake A braking system, independent of the main hydraulic system, that can be used to slow or stop the vehicle if the primary brakes fail, or to hold the vehicle stationary even though the brake pedal isn't depressed. It usually consists of a hand lever that actuates either front or rear brakes mechanically through a series of cables and linkages. Also known as a handbrake or parking brake.

Endfloat The amount of lengthwise movement between two parts. As applied to a crankshaft, the distance that the crankshaft can move forward and back in the cylinder block.

Engine management system (EMS) A computer controlled system which manages the fuel injection and the ignition systems in an integrated fashion.

Exhaust manifold A part with several passages through which exhaust gases leave the engine combustion chambers and enter the exhaust pipe.

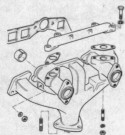

Exhaust manifold

F

Fan clutch A viscous (fluid) drive coupling device which permits variable engine fan speeds in relation to engine speeds.

Feeler blade A thin strip or blade of hardened steel, ground to an exact thickness, used to check or measure clearances between parts.

Feeler blade

Firing order The order in which the engine cylinders fire, or deliver their power strokes, beginning with the number one cylinder.

Flywheel A heavy spinning wheel in which energy is absorbed and stored by means of momentum. On cars, the flywheel is attached to the crankshaft to smooth out firing impulses.

Free play The amount of travel before any action takes place. The "looseness" in a linkage, or an assembly of parts, between the initial application of force and actual movement. For example, the distance the brake pedal moves before the pistons in the master cylinder are actuated.

Fuse An electrical device which protects a circuit against accidental overload. The typical fuse contains a soft piece of metal which is calibrated to melt at a predetermined current flow (expressed as amps) and break the circuit.

Fusible link A circuit protection device consisting of a conductor surrounded by heat-resistant insulation. The conductor is smaller than the wire it protects, so it acts as the weakest link in the circuit. Unlike a blown fuse, a failed fusible link must frequently be cut from the wire for replacement.

G

Gap The distance the spark must travel in jumping from the centre electrode to the side

Adjusting spark plug gap

electrode in a spark plug. Also refers to the spacing between the points in a contact breaker assembly in a conventional points-type ignition, or to the distance between the reluctor or rotor and the pickup coil in an electronic ignition.

Gasket Any thin, soft material - usually cork, cardboard, asbestos or soft metal - installed between two metal surfaces to ensure a good seal. For instance, the cylinder head gasket seals the joint between the block and the cylinder head.

Gasket

Gauge An instrument panel display used to monitor engine conditions. A gauge with a movable pointer on a dial or a fixed scale is an analogue gauge. A gauge with a numerical readout is called a digital gauge.

H

Halfshaft A rotating shaft that transmits power from the final drive unit to a drive wheel, usually when referring to a live rear axle.

Harmonic balancer A device designed to reduce torsion or twisting vibration in the crankshaft. May be incorporated in the crankshaft pulley. Also known as a vibration damper.

Hone An abrasive tool for correcting small irregularities or differences in diameter in an engine cylinder, brake cylinder, etc.

Hydraulic tappet A tappet that utilises hydraulic pressure from the engine's lubrication system to maintain zero clearance (constant contact with both camshaft and valve stem). Automatically adjusts to variation in valve stem length. Hydraulic tappets also reduce valve noise.

I

Ignition timing The moment at which the spark plug fires, usually expressed in the number of crankshaft degrees before the piston reaches the top of its stroke.

Inlet manifold A tube or housing with passages through which flows the air-fuel mixture (carburettor vehicles and vehicles with throttle body injection) or air only (port fuel-injected vehicles) to the port openings in the cylinder head.

J

Jump start Starting the engine of a vehicle with a discharged or weak battery by attaching jump leads from the weak battery to a charged or helper battery.

L

Load Sensing Proportioning Valve (LSPV) A brake hydraulic system control valve that works like a proportioning valve, but also takes into consideration the amount of weight carried by the rear axle.

Locknut A nut used to lock an adjustment nut, or other threaded component, in place. For example, a locknut is employed to keep the adjusting nut on the rocker arm in position.

Lockwasher A form of washer designed to prevent an attaching nut from working loose.

M

MacPherson strut A type of front suspension system devised by Earle MacPherson at Ford of England. In its original form, a simple lateral link with the anti-roll bar creates the lower control arm. A long strut - an integral coil spring and shock absorber - is mounted between the body and the steering knuckle. Many modern so-called MacPherson strut systems use a conventional lower A-arm and don't rely on the anti-roll bar for location.

Multimeter An electrical test instrument with the capability to measure voltage, current and resistance.

N

NOx Oxides of Nitrogen. A common toxic pollutant emitted by petrol and diesel engines at higher temperatures.

O

Ohm The unit of electrical resistance. One volt applied to a resistance of one ohm will produce a current of one amp.

Ohmmeter An instrument for measuring electrical resistance.

O-ring A type of sealing ring made of a special rubber-like material; in use, the O-ring is compressed into a groove to provide the sealing action.

O-ring

Overhead cam (ohc) engine An engine with the camshaft(s) located on top of the cylinder head(s).

Overhead valve (ohv) engine An engine with the valves located in the cylinder head, but with the camshaft located in the engine block.

Oxygen sensor A device installed in the engine exhaust manifold, which senses the oxygen content in the exhaust and converts this information into an electric current. Also called a Lambda sensor.

P

Phillips screw A type of screw head having a cross instead of a slot for a corresponding type of screwdriver.

Plastigage A thin strip of plastic thread, available in different sizes, used for measuring clearances. For example, a strip of Plastigage is laid across a bearing journal. The parts are assembled and dismantled; the width of the crushed strip indicates the clearance between journal and bearing.

Plastigage

Propeller shaft The long hollow tube with universal joints at both ends that carries power from the transmission to the differential on front-engined rear wheel drive vehicles.

Proportioning valve A hydraulic control valve which limits the amount of pressure to the rear brakes during panic stops to prevent wheel lock-up.

R

Rack-and-pinion steering A steering system with a pinion gear on the end of the steering shaft that mates with a rack (think of a geared wheel opened up and laid flat). When the steering wheel is turned, the pinion turns, moving the rack to the left or right. This movement is transmitted through the track rods to the steering arms at the wheels.

Radiator A liquid-to-air heat transfer device designed to reduce the temperature of the coolant in an internal combustion engine cooling system.

Refrigerant Any substance used as a heat transfer agent in an air-conditioning system. R-12 has been the principle refrigerant for many years; recently, however, manufacturers have begun using R-134a, a non-CFC substance that is considered less harmful to the ozone in the upper atmosphere.

Rocker arm A lever arm that rocks on a shaft or pivots on a stud. In an overhead valve engine, the rocker arm converts the upward movement of the pushrod into a downward movement to open a valve.

Rotor In a distributor, the rotating device inside the cap that connects the centre electrode and the outer terminals as it turns, distributing the high voltage from the coil secondary winding to the proper spark plug. Also, that part of an alternator which rotates inside the stator. Also, the rotating assembly of a turbocharger, including the compressor wheel, shaft and turbine wheel.

Runout The amount of wobble (in-and-out movement) of a gear or wheel as it's rotated. The amount a shaft rotates "out-of-true." The out-of-round condition of a rotating part.

S

Sealant A liquid or paste used to prevent leakage at a joint. Sometimes used in conjunction with a gasket.

Sealed beam lamp An older headlight design which integrates the reflector, lens and filaments into a hermetically-sealed one-piece unit. When a filament burns out or the lens cracks, the entire unit is simply replaced.

Serpentine drivebelt A single, long, wide accessory drivebelt that's used on some newer vehicles to drive all the accessories, instead of a series of smaller, shorter belts. Serpentine drivebelts are usually tensioned by an automatic tensioner.

Serpentine drivebelt

Shim Thin spacer, commonly used to adjust the clearance or relative positions between two parts. For example, shims inserted into or under bucket tappets control valve clearances. Clearance is adjusted by changing the thickness of the shim.

Slide hammer A special puller that screws into or hooks onto a component such as a shaft or bearing; a heavy sliding handle on the shaft bottoms against the end of the shaft to knock the component free.

Sprocket A tooth or projection on the periphery of a wheel, shaped to engage with a chain or drivebelt. Commonly used to refer to the sprocket wheel itself.

Starter inhibitor switch On vehicles with an automatic transmission, a switch that prevents starting if the vehicle is not in Neutral or Park.

Strut See MacPherson strut.

T

Tappet A cylindrical component which transmits motion from the cam to the valve stem, either directly or via a pushrod and rocker arm. Also called a cam follower.

Thermostat A heat-controlled valve that regulates the flow of coolant between the cylinder block and the radiator, so maintaining optimum engine operating temperature. A thermostat is also used in some air cleaners in which the temperature is regulated.

Thrust bearing The bearing in the clutch assembly that is moved in to the release levers by clutch pedal action to disengage the clutch. Also referred to as a release bearing.

Timing belt A toothed belt which drives the camshaft. Serious engine damage may result if it breaks in service.

Timing chain A chain which drives the camshaft.

Toe-in The amount the front wheels are closer together at the front than at the rear. On rear wheel drive vehicles, a slight amount of toe-in is usually specified to keep the front wheels running parallel on the road by offsetting other forces that tend to spread the wheels apart.

Toe-out The amount the front wheels are closer together at the rear than at the front. On front wheel drive vehicles, a slight amount of toe-out is usually specified.

Tools For full information on choosing and using tools, refer to the *Haynes Automotive Tools Manual.*

Tracer A stripe of a second colour applied to a wire insulator to distinguish that wire from another one with the same colour insulator.

Tune-up A process of accurate and careful adjustments and parts replacement to obtain the best possible engine performance.

Turbocharger A centrifugal device, driven by exhaust gases, that pressurises the intake air. Normally used to increase the power output from a given engine displacement, but can also be used primarily to reduce exhaust emissions (as on VW's "Umwelt" Diesel engine).

U

Universal joint or U-joint A double-pivoted connection for transmitting power from a driving to a driven shaft through an angle. A U-joint consists of two Y-shaped yokes and a cross-shaped member called the spider.

V

Valve A device through which the flow of liquid, gas, vacuum, or loose material in bulk may be started, stopped, or regulated by a movable part that opens, shuts, or partially obstructs one or more ports or passageways. A valve is also the movable part of such a device.

Valve clearance The clearance between the valve tip (the end of the valve stem) and the rocker arm or tappet. The valve clearance is measured when the valve is closed.

Vernier caliper A precision measuring instrument that measures inside and outside dimensions. Not quite as accurate as a micrometer, but more convenient.

Viscosity The thickness of a liquid or its resistance to flow.

Volt A unit for expressing electrical "pressure" in a circuit. One volt that will produce a current of one ampere through a resistance of one ohm.

W

Welding Various processes used to join metal items by heating the areas to be joined to a molten state and fusing them together. For more information refer to the *Haynes Automotive Welding Manual.*

Wiring diagram A drawing portraying the components and wires in a vehicle's electrical system, using standardised symbols. For more information refer to the *Haynes Automotive Electrical and Electronic Systems Manual.*

Note: *References through-out this index are in the form "Chapter number" • "Page number"*

Haynes Manuals – The Complete List

Title	Book No.
ALFA ROMEO	
Alfa Romeo Alfasud/Sprint (74 - 88) up to F	0292
Alfa Romeo Alfetta (73 - 87) up to E	0531
AUDI	
Audi 80 (72 - Feb 79) up to T	0207
Audi 80, 90 (79 - Oct 86) up to D & Coupe (81 - Nov 88) up to F	0605
Audi 80, 90 (Oct 86 - 90) D to H & Coupe (Nov 88 - 90) F to H	1491
Audi 100 (Oct 82 - 90) up to H & 200 (Feb 84 - Oct 89) A to G	0907
Audi 100 & A6 Petrol & Diesel (May 91 - May 97) H to P	3504
Audi A4 (95 - Feb 00) M to V	3575
AUSTIN	
Austin A35 & A40 (56 - 67) *	0118
Austin Allegro 1100, 1300, 1.0, 1.1 & 1.3 (73 - 82)*	0164
Austin Healey 100/6 & 3000 (56 - 68) *	0049
Austin/MG/Rover Maestro 1.3 & 1.6 (83 - May 95) up to M	0922
Austin/MG Metro (80 - May 90) up to G	0718
Austin/Rover Montego 1.3 & 1.6 (84 - 94) A to L	1066
Austin/MG/Rover Montego 2.0 (84 - 95) A to M	1067
Mini (59 - 69) up to H	0527
Mini (69 - Oct 96) up to P	0646
Austin/Rover 2.0 litre Diesel Engine (86 - 93) C to L	1857
BEDFORD	
Bedford CF (69 - 87) up to E	0163
Bedford/Vauxhall Rascal & Suzuki Supercarry (86 - Oct 94) C to M	3015
BMW	
BMW 1500, 1502, 1600, 1602, 2000 & 2002 (59 - 77)*	0240
BMW 316, 320 & 320i (4-cyl) (75 - Feb 83) up to Y	0276
BMW 320, 320i, 323i & 325i (6-cyl) (Oct 77 - Sept 87) up to E	0815
BMW 3-Series (Apr 91 - 96) H to N	3210
BMW 3- & 5-Series (sohc) (81 - 91) up to J	1948
BMW 520i & 525e (Oct 81 - June 88) up to E	1560
BMW 525, 528 & 528i (73 - Sept 81) up to X	0632
CITROËN	
Citroën 2CV, Ami & Dyane (67 - 90) up to H	0196
Citroën AX Petrol & Diesel (87 - 97) D to P	3014
Citroën BX (83 - 94) A to L	0908
Citroën C15 Van Petrol & Diesel (89 - Oct 98) F to S	3509
Citroën CX (75 - 88) up to F	0528
Citroën Saxo Petrol & Diesel (96 - 01) N to X	3506
Citroën Visa (79 - 88) up to F	0620
Citroën Xantia Petrol & Diesel (93 - 98) K to S	3082
Citroën XM Petrol & Diesel (89 - 00) G to X	3451
Citroën Xsara Petrol & Diesel (97 - Sept 00) R to W	3751
Citroën ZX Diesel (91 - 98) J to S	1922
Citroën ZX Petrol (91 - 98) H to S	1881
Citroën 1.7 & 1.9 litre Diesel Engine (84 - 96) A to N	1379
FIAT	
Fiat 126 (73 - 87) *	0305
Fiat 500 (57 - 73) up to M	0090
Fiat Bravo & Brava (95 - 00) N to W	3572
Fiat Cinquecento (93 - 98) K to R	3501
Fiat Panda (81 - 95) up to M	0793
Fiat Punto Petrol & Diesel (94 - Oct 99) L to V	3251
Fiat Regata (84 - 88) A to F	1167
Fiat Tipo (88 - 91) E to J	1625
Fiat Uno (83 - 95) up to M	0923
Fiat X1/9 (74 - 89) up to G	0273
FORD	
Ford Anglia (59 - 68) *	0001
Ford Capri II (& III) 1.6 & 2.0 (74 - 87) up to E	0283

Title	Book No.
Ford Capri II (& III) 2.8 & 3.0 (74 - 87) up to E	1309
Ford Cortina Mk III 1300 & 1600 (70 - 76) *	0070
Ford Cortina Mk IV (& V) 1.6 & 2.0 (76 - 83) *	0343
Ford Cortina Mk IV (& V) 2.3 V6 (77 - 83) *	0426
Ford Escort Mk I 1100 & 1300 (68 - 74) *	0171
Ford Escort Mk I Mexico, RS 1600 & RS 2000 (70 - 74)*	0139
Ford Escort Mk II Mexico, RS 1800 & RS 2000 (75 - 80)*	0735
Ford Escort (75 - Aug 80) *	0280
Ford Escort (Sept 80 - Sept 90) up to H	0686
Ford Escort & Orion (Sept 90 - 00) H to X	1737
Ford Fiesta (76 - Aug 83) up to Y	0334
Ford Fiesta (Aug 83 - Feb 89) A to F	1030
Ford Fiesta (Feb 89 - Oct 95) F to N	1595
Ford Fiesta (Oct 95 - 01) N-reg. onwards	3397
Ford Focus (98 - 01) S to Y	3759
Ford Granada (Sept 77 - Feb 85) up to B	0481
Ford Granada & Scorpio (Mar 85 - 94) B to M	1245
Ford Ka (96 - 02) P-reg. onwards	3570
Ford Mondeo Petrol (93 - 99) K to T	1923
Ford Mondeo Diesel (93 - 96) L to N	3465
Ford Orion (83 - Sept 90) up to H	1009
Ford Sierra 4 cyl. (82 - 93) up to K	0903
Ford Sierra V6 (82 - 91) up to J	0904
Ford Transit Petrol (Mk 2) (78 - Jan 86) up to C	0719
Ford Transit Petrol (Mk 3) (Feb 86 - 89) C to G	1468
Ford Transit Diesel (Feb 86 - 99) C to T	3019
Ford 1.6 & 1.8 litre Diesel Engine (84 - 96) A to N	1172
Ford 2.1, 2.3 & 2.5 litre Diesel Engine (77 - 90) up to H	1606
FREIGHT ROVER	
Freight Rover Sherpa (74 - 87) up to E	0463
HILLMAN	
Hillman Avenger (70 - 82) up to Y	0037
Hillman Imp (63 - 76) *	0022
HONDA	
Honda Accord (76 - Feb 84) up to A	0351
Honda Civic (Feb 84 - Oct 87) A to E	1226
Honda Civic (Nov 91 - 96) J to N	3199
HYUNDAI	
Hyundai Pony (85 - 94) C to M	3398
JAGUAR	
Jaguar E Type (61 - 72) up to L	0140
Jaguar MkI & II, 240 & 340 (55 - 69) *	0098
Jaguar XJ6, XJ & Sovereign; Daimler Sovereign (68 - Oct 86) up to D	0242
Jaguar XJ6 & Sovereign (Oct 86 - Sept 94) D to M	3261
Jaguar XJ12, XJS & Sovereign; Daimler Double Six (72 - 88) up to F	0478
JEEP	
Jeep Cherokee Petrol (93 - 96) K to N	1943
LADA	
Lada 1200, 1300, 1500 & 1600 (74 - 91) up to J	0413
Lada Samara (87 - 91) D to J	1610
LAND ROVER	
Land Rover 90, 110 & Defender Diesel (83 - 95) up to N	3017
Land Rover Discovery Petrol & Diesel (89 - 98) G to S	3016
Land Rover Series IIA & III Diesel (58 - 85) up to C	0529
Land Rover Series II, IIA & III Petrol (58 - 85) up to C	0314
MAZDA	
Mazda 323 (Mar 81 - Oct 89) up to G	1608
Mazda 323 (Oct 89 - 98) G to R	3455
Mazda 626 (May 83 - Sept 87) up to E	0929
Mazda B-1600, B-1800 & B-2000 Pick-up (72 - 88) up to F	0267
Mazda RX-7 (79 - 85) *	0460

Title	Book No.
MERCEDES-BENZ	
Mercedes-Benz 190, 190E & 190D Petrol & Diesel (83 - 93) A to L	3450
Mercedes-Benz 200, 240, 300 Diesel (Oct 76 - 85) up to C	1114
Mercedes-Benz 250 & 280 (68 - 72) up to L	0346
Mercedes-Benz 250 & 280 (123 Series) (Oct 76 - 84) up to B	0677
Mercedes-Benz 124 Series (85 - Aug 93) C to K	3253
Mercedes-Benz C-Class Petrol & Diesel (93 - Aug 00) L to W	3511
MG	
MGA (55 - 62) *	0475
MGB (62 - 80) up to W	0111
MG Midget & AH Sprite (58 - 80) up to W	0265
MITSUBISHI	
Mitsubishi Shogun & L200 Pick-Ups (83 - 94) up to M	1944
MORRIS	
Morris Ital 1.3 (80 - 84) up to B	0705
Morris Minor 1000 (56 - 71) up to K	0024
NISSAN	
Nissan Bluebird (May 84 - Mar 86) A to C	1223
Nissan Bluebird (Mar 86 - 90) C to H	1473
Nissan Cherry (Sept 82 - 86) up to D	1031
Nissan Micra (83 - Jan 93) up to K	0931
Nissan Micra (93 - 99) K to T	3254
Nissan Primera (90 - Aug 99) H to T	1851
Nissan Stanza (82 - 86) up to D	0824
Nissan Sunny (May 82 - Oct 86) up to D	0895
Nissan Sunny (Oct 86 - Mar 91) D to H	1378
Nissan Sunny (Apr 91 - 95) H to N	3219
OPEL	
Opel Ascona & Manta (B Series) (Sept 75 - 88) up to F	0316
Opel Ascona (81 - 88) (Not available in UK see Vauxhall Cavalier 0812)	3215
Opel Astra (Oct 91 - Feb 98) (Not available in UK see Vauxhall Astra 1832)	3156
Opel Astra & Zafira Diesel (Feb 98 - Sept 00) (See Astra & Zafira Diesel Book No. 3797)	
Opel Astra & Zafira Petrol (Feb 98 - Sept 00) (See Vauxhall/Opel Astra & Zafira Petrol Book No. 3758)	
Opel Calibra (90 - 98) (See Vauxhall/Opel Calibra Book No. 3502)	
Opel Corsa (83 - Mar 93) (Not available in UK see Vauxhall Nova 0909)	3160
Opel Corsa (Mar 93 - 97) (Not available in UK see Vauxhall Corsa 1985)	3159
Opel Frontera Petrol & Diesel (91 - 98) (See Vauxhall/Opel Frontera Book No. 3454)	
Opel Kadett (Nov 79 - Oct 84) up to B	0634
Opel Kadett (Oct 84 - Oct 91) (Not available in UK see Vauxhall Astra & Belmont 1136)	3196
Opel Omega & Senator (86 - 94) (Not available in UK see Vauxhall Carlton & Senator 1469)	3157
Opel Omega (94 - 99) (See Vauxhall/Opel Omega Book No. 3510)	
Opel Rekord (Feb 78 - Oct 86) up to D	0543
Opel Vectra (Oct 88 - Oct 95) (Not available in UK see Vauxhall Cavalier 1570)	3158
Opel Vectra Petrol & Diesel (95 - 98) (Not available in UK see Vauxhall Vectra 3396)	3523
PEUGEOT	
Peugeot 106 Petrol & Diesel (91 - 01) J to X	1882
Peugeot 205 Petrol (83 - 97) A to P	0932
Peugeot 206 Petrol and Diesel (98 - 01) S to X	3757
Peugeot 305 (78 - 89) up to G	0538

* Classic reprint

Title	Book No.
Peugeot 306 Petrol & Diesel (93 - 99) K to T	3073
Peugeot 309 (86 - 93) C to K	1266
Peugeot 405 Petrol (88 - 97) E to P	1559
Peugeot 405 Diesel (88 - 97) E to P	3198
Peugeot 406 Petrol & Diesel (96 - 97) N to R	3394
Peugeot 505 (79 - 89) up to G	0762
Peugeot 1.7/1.8 & 1.9 litre Diesel Engine (82 - 96) up to N	0950
Peugeot 2.0, 2.1, 2.3 & 2.5 litre Diesel Engines (74 - 90) up to H	1607

PORSCHE
Title	Book No.
Porsche 911 (65 - 85) up to C	0264
Porsche 924 & 924 Turbo (76 - 85) up to C	0397

PROTON
Title	Book No.
Proton (89 - 97) F to P	3255

RANGE ROVER
Title	Book No.
Range Rover V8 (70 - Oct 92) up to K	0606

RELIANT
Title	Book No.
Reliant Robin & Kitten (73 - 83) up to A	0436

RENAULT
Title	Book No.
Renault 4 (61 - 86) *	0072
Renault 5 (Feb 85 - 96) B to N	1219
Renault 9 & 11 (82 - 89) up to F	0822
Renault 18 (79 - 86) up to D	0598
Renault 19 Petrol (89 - 94) F to M	1646
Renault 19 Diesel (89 - 96) F to N	1946
Renault 21 (86 - 94) C to M	1397
Renault 25 (84 - 92) B to K	1228
Renault Clio Petrol (91 - May 98) H to R	1853
Renault Clio Diesel (91 - June 96) H to N	3031
Renault Clio Petrol & Diesel (May 98 - May 01) R to Y	3906
Renault Espace Petrol & Diesel (85 - 96) C to N	3197
Renault Fuego (80 - 86) *	0764
Renault Laguna Petrol & Diesel (94 - 00) L to W	3252
Renault Mégane & Scénic Petrol & Diesel (96 - 98) N to R	3395
Renault Mégane & Scénic (Apr 99 - 02) T-reg onwards	3916

ROVER
Title	Book No.
Rover 213 & 216 (84 - 89) A to G	1116
Rover 214 & 414 (89 - 96) G to N	1689
Rover 216 & 416 (89 - 96) G to N	1830
Rover 211, 214, 216, 218 & 220 Petrol & Diesel (Dec 95 - 98) N to R	3399
Rover 414, 416 & 420 Petrol & Diesel (May 95 - 98) M to R	3453
Rover 618, 620 & 623 (93 - 97) K to P	3257
Rover 820, 825 & 827 (86 - 95) D to N	1380
Rover 3500 (76 - 87) up to E	0365
Rover Metro, 111 & 114 (May 90 - 98) G to S	1711

SAAB
Title	Book No.
Saab 90, 99 & 900 (79 - Oct 93) up to L	0765
Saab 95 & 96 (66 - 76) *	0198
Saab 99 (69 - 79) *	0247
Saab 900 (Oct 93 - 98) L to R	3512
Saab 9000 (4-cyl) (85 - 98) C to S	1686

SEAT
Title	Book No.
Seat Ibiza & Cordoba Petrol & Diesel (Oct 93 - Oct 99) L to V	3571
Seat Ibiza & Malaga (85 - 92) B to K	1609

SKODA
Title	Book No.
Skoda Estelle (77 - 89) up to G	0604
Skoda Favorit (89 - 96) F to N	1801
Skoda Felicia Petrol & Diesel (95 - 01) M to X	3505

SUBARU
Title	Book No.
Subaru 1600 & 1800 (Nov 79 - 90) up to H	0995

SUNBEAM
Title	Book No.
Sunbeam Alpine, Rapier & H120 (67 - 76) *	0051

SUZUKI
Title	Book No.
Suzuki SJ Series, Samurai & Vitara (4-cyl) (82 - 97) up to P	1942
Suzuki Supercarry & Bedford/Vauxhall Rascal (86 - Oct 94) C to M	3015

TALBOT
Title	Book No.
Talbot Alpine, Solara, Minx & Rapier (75 - 86) up to D	0337
Talbot Horizon (78 - 86) up to D	0473
Talbot Samba (82 - 86) up to D	0823

TOYOTA
Title	Book No.
Toyota Carina E (May 92 - 97) J to P	3256
Toyota Corolla (Sept 83 - Sept 87) A to E	1024
Toyota Corolla (80 - 85) up to C	0683
Toyota Corolla (Sept 87 - Aug 92) E to K	1683
Toyota Corolla (Aug 92 - 97) K to P	3259
Toyota Hi-Ace & Hi-Lux (69 - Oct 83) up to A	0304

TRIUMPH
Title	Book No.
Triumph Acclaim (81 - 84) *	0792
Triumph GT6 & Vitesse (62 - 74) *	0112
Triumph Herald (59 - 71) *	0010
Triumph Spitfire (62 - 81) up to X	0113
Triumph Stag (70 - 78) up to T	0441
Triumph TR2, TR3, TR3A, TR4 & TR4A (52 - 67) *	0028
Triumph TR5 & 6 (67 - 75) *	0031
Triumph TR7 (75 - 82) *	0322

VAUXHALL
Title	Book No.
Vauxhall Astra (80 - Oct 84) up to B	0635
Vauxhall Astra & Belmont (Oct 84 - Oct 91) B to J	1136
Vauxhall Astra (Oct 91 - Feb 98) J to R	1832
Vauxhall/Opel Astra & Zafira Diesel (Feb 98 - Sept 00) R to W	3797
Vauxhall/Opel Astra & Zafira Petrol (Feb 98 - Sept 00) R to W	3758
Vauxhall/Opel Calibra (90 - 98) G to S	3502
Vauxhall Carlton (Oct 78 - Oct 86) up to D	0480
Vauxhall Carlton & Senator (Nov 86 - 94) D to L	1469
Vauxhall Cavalier 1300 (77 - July 81) *	0461
Vauxhall Cavalier 1600, 1900 & 2000 (75 - July 81) up to W	0315
Vauxhall Cavalier (81 - Oct 88) up to F	0812
Vauxhall Cavalier (Oct 88 - 95) F to N	1570
Vauxhall Chevette (75 - 84) up to B	0285
Vauxhall Corsa (Mar 93 - 97) K to R	1985
Vauxhall/Opel Corsa (Apr 97 - Oct 00) P to X	3921
Vauxhall/Opel Frontera Petrol & Diesel (91 - Sept 98) J to S	3454
Vauxhall Nova (83 - 93) up to K	0909
Vauxhall/Opel Omega (94 - 99) L to T	3510
Vauxhall Vectra Petrol & Diesel (95 - 98) N to R	3396
Vauxhall/Opel 1.5, 1.6 & 1.7 litre Diesel Engine (82 - 96) up to N	1222

VOLKSWAGEN
Title	Book No.
Volkswagen 411 & 412 (68 - 75) *	0091
Volkswagen Beetle 1200 (54 - 77) up to S	0036
Volkswagen Beetle 1300 & 1500 (65 - 75) up to P	0039
Volkswagen Beetle 1302 & 1302S (70 - 72) up to L	0110
Volkswagen Beetle 1303, 1303S & GT (72 - 75) up to P	0159
Volkswagen Beetle Petrol & Diesel (Apr 99 - 01) T reg onwards	3798
Volkswagen Golf & Bora Petrol & Diesel (April 98 - 00) R to X	3727
Volkswagen Golf & Jetta Mk 1 1.1 & 1.3 (74 - 84) up to A	0716
Volkswagen Golf, Jetta & Scirocco Mk 1 1.5, 1.6 & 1.8 (74 - 84) up to A	0726
Volkswagen Golf & Jetta Mk 1 Diesel (78 - 84) up to A	0451
Volkswagen Golf & Jetta Mk 2 (Mar 84 - Feb 92) A to J	1081
Volkswagen Golf & Vento Petrol & Diesel (Feb 92 - 96) J to N	3097
Volkswagen LT vans & light trucks (76 - 87) up to E	0637
Volkswagen Passat & Santana (Sept 81 - May 88) up to E	0814
Volkswagen Passat Petrol & Diesel (May 88 - 96) E to P	3498
Volkswagen Passat 4-cyl Petrol & Diesel (Dec 96 - Nov 00) P to X	3917
Volkswagen Polo & Derby (76 - Jan 82) up to X	0335
Volkswagen Polo (82 - Oct 90) up to H	0813
Volkswagen Polo (Nov 90 - Aug 94) H to L	3245
Volkswagen Polo Hatchback Petrol & Diesel (94 - 99) M to S	3500
Volkswagen Scirocco (82 - 90) up to H	1224
Volkswagen Transporter 1600 (68 - 79) up to V	0082
Volkswagen Transporter 1700, 1800 & 2000 (72 - 79) up to V	0226
Volkswagen Transporter (air-cooled) (79 - 82) up to Y	0638
Volkswagen Transporter (water-cooled) (82 - 90) up to H	3452
Volkswagen Type 3 (63 - 73) *	0084

VOLVO
Title	Book No.
Volvo 120 & 130 Series (& P1800) (61 - 73) *	0203
Volvo 142, 144 & 145 (66 - 74) up to N	0129
Volvo 240 Series (74 - 93) up to K	0270
Volvo 262, 264 & 260/265 (75 - 85) *	0400
Volvo 340, 343, 345 & 360 (76 - 91) up to J	0715
Volvo 440, 460 & 480 (87 - 97) D to P	1691
Volvo 740 & 760 (82 - 91) up to J	1258
Volvo 850 (92 - 96) J to P	3260
Volvo 940 (90 - 96) H to N	3249
Volvo S40 & V40 (96 - 99) N to V	3569
Volvo S70, V70 & C70 (96 - 99) P to V	3573

AUTOMOTIVE TECHBOOKS
Title	Book No.
Automotive Air Conditioning Systems	3740
Automotive Brake Manual	3050
Automotive Carburettor Manual	3288
Automotive Diagnostic Fault Codes Manual	3472
Automotive Diesel Engine Service Guide	3286
Automotive Electrical and Electronic Systems Manual	3049
Automotive Engine Management and Fuel Injection Systems Manual	3344
Automotive Gearbox Overhaul Manual	3473
Automotive Service Summaries Manual	3475
Automotive Timing Belts Manual – Austin/Rover	3549
Automotive Timing Belts Manual – Ford	3474
Automotive Timing Belts Manual – Peugeot/Citroën	3568
Automotive Timing Belts Manual – Vauxhall/Opel	3577
Automotive Welding Manual	3053
In-Car Entertainment Manual (3rd Edition)	3363

* Classic reprint

CL13.4/02

All the products featured on this page are available through most motor accessory shops, cycle shops and book stores. Our policy of continuous updating and development means that titles are being constantly added to the range. For up-to-date information on our complete list of titles, please telephone: (UK) **+44 1963 442030** • (USA) **+1 805 498 6703** • (France) **+33 1 47 78 50 50** • (Sweden) **+46 18 124016** • (Australia) **+61 3 9763 8100**

Preserving Our Motoring Heritage

< The Model J Duesenberg Derham Tourster. Only eight of these magnificent cars were ever built – this is the only example to be found outside the United States of America

Almost every car you've ever loved, loathed or desired is gathered under one roof at the Haynes Motor Museum. Over 300 immaculately presented cars and motorbikes represent every aspect of our motoring heritage, from elegant reminders of bygone days, such as the superb Model J Duesenberg to curiosities like the bug-eyed BMW Isetta. There are also many old friends and flames. Perhaps you remember the 1959 Ford Popular that you did your courting in? The magnificent 'Red Collection' is a spectacle of classic sports cars including AC, Alfa Romeo, Austin Healey, Ferrari, Lamborghini, Maserati, MG, Riley, Porsche and Triumph.

A Perfect Day Out

Each and every vehicle at the Haynes Motor Museum has played its part in the history and culture of Motoring. Today, they make a wonderful spectacle and a great day out for all the family. Bring the kids, bring Mum and Dad, but above all bring your camera to capture those golden memories for ever. You will also find an impressive array of motoring memorabilia, a comfortable 70 seat video cinema and one of the most extensive transport book shops in Britain. The Pit Stop Cafe serves everything from a cup of tea to wholesome, home-made meals or, if you prefer, you can enjoy the large picnic area nestled in the beautiful rural surroundings of Somerset.

John Haynes O.B.E., Founder and Chairman of the museum at the wheel of a Haynes Light 12. >

< Graham Hill's Lola Cosworth Formula 1 car next to a 1934 Riley Sports.

The Museum is situated on the A359 Yeovil to Frome road at Sparkford, just off the A303 in Somerset. It is about 40 miles south of Bristol, and 25 minutes drive from the M5 intersection at Taunton.
Open 9.30am - 5.30pm (10.00am - 4.00pm Winter) 7 days a week, *except Christmas Day, Boxing Day and New Years Day*
Special rates available for schools, coach parties and outings Charitable Trust No. 292048